THE FRACTURED
HIMALAYA

ADVANCE PRAISE

'*The Fractured Himalaya* is a deeply researched, critical and lucid discussion of the complex diplomatic processes that led to the Sino-Indian war of 1962, identifying much that has been overlooked or misread. More importantly, it requires us to engage with the multiple perspectives that shaped the decisions and calculations of policy-makers on all sides at the time. This leads it to be not just a highly readable historical analysis, but also a detailed demonstration of the intellectual rigour and breadth that are needed if policy practitioners and analysts are ever to resolve major conflicts or balance competing national interests. With its emphasis on the necessity of maintaining highly informed but flexible approaches in policy-making, alongside its attention to borders as zones of connection rather than as dividing lines, it should be required reading for all interested in the study or practice of diplomacy and international negotiation'

—**Robert Barnett,**
Scholar of Tibet, Author, Professorial Research Associate,
School of Oriental and African Studies, University of London

'Combining deep research with an engaging literary style, this book is a must read for anyone interested in India's foreign and defence policies'

—**Chandrashekhar Dasgupta**,
Author and former Ambassador of India to China

'Nirupama Rao, uniquely combining stellar diplomatic experience and deep scholarship, provides profound insights into why the initially-friendly relations between Communist China and Democratic India gave way to the Chinese invasion of 1962. With the two giants confronting each other anew, this fabulous book is indispensable reading'

—**Padma Desai**
Gladys and Roland Harriman Professor
of Comparative Economic Systems Emerita, Columbia University, New York

'In *The Fractured Himalaya*, Nirupama Rao has written a compelling, insightful, detailed history of how India and newly-Communist China dealt with one another in their earliest years, from the friendship of the early 1950s to the 1962 war. Her account is full of insights about the leading figures, from Nehru to Sardar Patel in India to Mao Zedong and Zhou Enlai to, above all, the current Dalai Lama, whom the author interviewed at length about Tibet in the 1950's and the sequence of events leading up to his flight from Lhasa. This is both an authoritative history and a smooth-reading narrative'

—**James Mann,**
Former China correspondent for the *Los Angeles Times*,
author of three books about the United States and China

'A rare gem of a book that combines deep scholarship with felicitous writing. Nirupama Rao's unique knowledge and experience brings to life and makes accessible the important triangular interplay between India, Tibet and China which had such significant effects on all three polities and peoples, and on Asia as a whole, which still resonate to this day. As relations between the three polities are being recast and contested again, there is no better guide than Nirupama Rao to show us how the past illuminates the future. Her book is essential reading for an understanding of this part of the world'

—**Shivshankar Menon,**
Former National Security Adviser of India, Foreign Secretary, and author

'In her book *The Fractured Himalaya*, Ambassador Nirupama Rao draws on an unprecedented diversity of sources, primary and secondary, to provide amazing breadth of analysis and insight on the history of India's relations with China covering the period from 1947 to 1962. Rao is erudite, multi-textured and highly nuanced. Her sensitive and balanced portrayal of the complex relationships between various key actors during this complicated period of Asia's early postcolonial history is truly impressive. A definitive work'

—**Vijay Nambiar,**
Former Indian Ambassador to China,
Chef de Cabinet to the U.N. Secretary-General, Ban Ki Moon

'With elegance, authority and a prodigious amount of research, Rao tells us how a mountainous wasteland in the Himalayas once viewed as just a 'blank place on the map' became a field of combat between India and China in 1962. As the two nations find themselves again in conflict, hers is a cautionary tale worth heeding'

—**Orville Schell,**
Arthur Ross Director, Center on
US-China Relations, The Asia Society, New York

'An extraordinary work of historical scholarship, Rao's expose is elegantly written and offers nuanced texture to the origins of Sino-Indian frictions during the 1950s-1960s that still resonate today. Not only are the territorial, border, diplomatic, and security dimensions carefully dealt with, but she reveals the centrality of the Tibet issue (which is not well understood). A signal accomplishment that should be carefully read by all concerned'

—**Professor David Shambaugh,**
George Washington University, and
author of *China›s Leaders: From Mao to Now*

'Nirupama Rao has written a fascinating and deeply researched history of the interactions among India, Tibet and China during the short thirteen years between the founding of the PRC (1949) and the India-China War (1962), as their initial desire for "brotherly friendship" deteriorated into military confrontation.

Rao utilizes her unique perspective as a historian-diplomat with years of experience dealing with China to explain the logic behind the decisions of the key players in the drama, especially the tragic hero of the story, Jawaharlal Nehru. The book provides crucial lessons from history to guide contemporary efforts to preserve peace between these two rising Asian powers'

—**Susan Shirk,**
Chair, Twenty-First Century China Center,
School of Global Policy and Strategy, UC San Diego

'This elegantly written book illuminates the dark corners of the India-China relationship in its foundational period – from the birth of a Communist China to a war that inflicted defeat on India. It is especially relevant today, as tensions and clashes on the border have returned. Why were the two Asian giants, both emerging from the shadow of imperialist control, unable to solve their border dispute? We learn that Mao craftily combined anti-imperialism with nationalism, as Nehru sought to turn his anti-imperialism into an attempt at post-imperial, anti-war high-mindedness, an attempt that eventually failed. Combining meticulous archival research with the subtle gaze of a professional diplomat, Nirupama Rao has produced a historical account that compels reflection and deserves wide readership'

—**Ashutosh Varshney**,
Sol Goldman Professor of International Studies
and the Social Sciences, Brown University

The Fractured Himalaya

India Tibet China

1949 to 1962

Nirupama Rao

PENGUIN
VIKING

An imprint of Penguin Random House

VIKING

USA | Canada | UK | Ireland | Australia
New Zealand | India | South Africa | China

Viking is part of the Penguin Random House group of companies
whose addresses can be found at global.penguinrandomhouse.com

Published by Penguin Random House India Pvt. Ltd
4th Floor, Capital Tower 1, MG Road,
Gurugram 122 002, Haryana, India

Penguin
Random House
India

First published in Viking by Penguin Random House India 2021

Copyright © Nirupama Rao 2021

All sketches in the book are the perception of the author specifically created for
explaining her views in this book, and the use thereof shall remain limited to
interpreting/inferring the author's views in this book.

10 9 8 7 6 5 4 3 2

The views and opinions expressed in this book are the author's own and the
facts are as reported by her which have been verified to the extent possible,
and the publishers are not in any way liable for the same.

ISBN 9780670088294

Typeset in Minion Pro by Manipal Technologies Limited, Manipal
Printed at Thomson Press India Ltd, New Delhi

www.penguin.co.in

For my parents
Narayani and Narayana Menon,
who belonged to a generation, who witnessed
the period covered in this history, at first hand.

'Upon the mountains reverberate the drums and kettle-drums ... Suddenly there begins to thunder forth the dance, with its flame and fireworks.' – Nicholas Roerich, Himalaya, 1926

Contents

Abbreviations

Border Roads Organisation	BRO
Chinese Communist Party	CCP
Commonwealth Relations Office, London	CRO
Indian Frontier Administrative Service	IFAS
Indian National Congress	INC
Intelligence Bureau	IB
National Archives Record Administration	NARA
National Archives of India, New Delhi	NAI
Nehru Memorial Museum and Library, New Delhi	NMML
Neutral Nations Repatriation Commission	NNRC
North East Frontier Agency	NEFA
People's Liberation Army	PLA
People's Republic of China	PRC
The National Archives of the U.K., Kew	TNA
UK High Commissioner in Delhi	UKHC

Major Dramatis Personae

(In alphabetical order)

Bajpai, Sir Girija Shankar (1891–1954): civil servant, diplomat, Secretary-General, Ministry of External Affairs

Caroe, Olaf Kirkpatrick (1892–1981): British civil servant and key influencer of frontier policy in pre-independent India

Chen Yi, Marshal (1901–1972): military commander, Foreign Minister of China

Chiang, Kai-shek (Jiang Jieshi) (1887–1975): Chinese Nationalist (Guomindang) Party leader

Dalai Lama, The 14th (1935–): Tenzin Gyatso, spiritual leader of Tibet

Dayal, Harishwar (1915-1964): civil servant, Political Officer in Sikkim, later Ambassador to Nepal

Dutt, Subimal (1903–1992): civil servant, diplomat, Ambassador, and Foreign Secretary, Ministry of External Affairs

Hopkinson, Arthur J. (1894-1953): Political Officer, Sikkim, 1944 to 1948

Jangpangi, Laxman Singh (1905–1976): Trade Agent, Gartok, who sent the first reports on the building of the Aksai Chin highway by the Chinese

Jigme, Ngapoi Ngawang (1910–2009): Tibetan aristocrat, who pledged allegiance to the People's Republic of China post-1951 and was a signatory of the 17-Point Agreement between Tibet and China, 1951

Kaul, Triloki Nath (1913–2000): diplomat involved in negotiations for the 1954 Agreement on Tibet, later Foreign Secretary, Ministry of External Affairs

Kaul, Brij Mohan (1912–1972): Lieutenant-General in the Indian Army, seen as having played a controversial role in the 1962 operations

Khan, Zafrulla (1893–1985): civil servant, agent-general for India in Chongqing, later Foreign Minister of Pakistan

(Major) Khathing, Ralengnao 'Bob' (1912–1990): soldier, civil servant, and diplomat; the liberator of Tawang in 1951

(Doctor) Kotnis, Dwarkanath (1910–1942): Indian physician, member of the Medical Mission sent to China in 1939, and regarded as a Communist Party hero in China

(Major) Johorey, Krishna Chandra (1927–2021): Indian civil servant and diplomat, member of the Indian Frontier Administrative Service. He served in various locations in the erstwhile North-East Frontier Agency, now Arunachal Pradesh. Was also Trade Agent in Yadong

Luthra, Pran Nath (1917–2000): Indian Frontier Administrative Service, Special Officer, Border Areas

Mao, Zedong (1893–1976): Chinese Communist Party leader, revolutionary; and 'helmsman'

Mehta, Jagat Singh (1922–2014): diplomat, leader of Indian delegation at Officials' Talks with China, 1960; later Foreign Secretary, Ministry of External Affairs

Menon, Kumara Padmanabha Sivasankara (K.P.S) (1898–1982): civil servant, diplomat, Foreign Secretary, Ministry of External Affairs

Menon, Parappil Narayana (P.N.) (1920–1975): diplomat, Consul-General in Lhasa

Menon, Vengalil Krishnan Krishna (V.K. Krishna) (1896–1974): confidant of Prime Minister Jawaharlal Nehru, and Defence Minister

Mullik, Bhola Nath (B.N.) (1905–1984): Director of the Intelligence Bureau of India (1950–1964)

Nehru, Jawaharlal (1889-1964): independent India's first prime minister and sculptor of China policy

Nehru, Ratan Kumar (R.K.) (1902–1981): civil servant, Foreign Secretary and Secretary-General, Ministry of External Affairs; and Ambassador to China

Pandit, Vijaya Lakshmi (1900–1990): sister of Prime Minister Nehru, Ambassador to the Soviet Union, the United States, and the United Kingdom; and first woman president of the United Nations General Assembly

Panchen Lama, the 10th (Lobsang Trinley Lhundrub Chokyi Gyaltsen) (1938–1989): accompanied the Dalai Lama to India in 1956

Panikkar, Kavalam Madhava (K.M.) (1895–1963): historian, diplomat, India's first Ambassador to the People's Republic of China

Pant, Apa Balasaheb (1912–1992): freedom fighter, diplomat, Political Officer in Sikkim

Paranjpe, Vasant Vasudeo (1921–2010): diplomat, China and Chinese-language expert, interpreter for Prime Minister Nehru in his talks with Premier Zhou Enlai

Parthasarathy, Gopalaswami (1912–1995): Ambassador to China, 1958–1962

Patel, Sardar Vallabhbhai (1875–1950): Deputy Prime Minister of India, primary architect of a united and integrated India, post-1947

Pillai, Narayanan Raghavan (N.R.) (1898–1992): civil servant, Secretary-General, Ministry of External Affairs

Radhakrishnan, Sarvepalli (1888–1975): writer and philosopher, Vice-President and later President of India

Raghavan, Nedyam (1900–1977): associate of Subhas Chandra Bose, member of the Indian National Army (INA); succeeded K.M. Panikkar as Ambassador in Beijing

Richardson, Hugh (1905–2000): British civil servant, Tibetologist, Political Officer in Lhasa

Rustomji, Nari K. (1919-): civil servant, was Dewan to the Chogyal of Sikkim, with years of distinguished service in the Northeast

Sarvepalli, Gopal (1923–2002): historian, key member of Indian team at Officials Talks with China, 1960, and biographer of Jawaharlal Nehru

Sathe, Ram Chandra Dattatraya (R.D.) (1923–2008): last Indian Consul-General in Kashgar, later Ambassador to China and Foreign Secretary of India, Ministry of External Affairs

Singh, Har Mander (1926–2020): Indian Frontier Administrative Service, Political Officer, Kameng Frontier Division

Sinha, Sumul (1920–1983): Political Officer in Lhasa, later Consul-General, Indian diplomat

Soong, Ching-l'ing (Song Qingling) (1893–1981): widow of Sun Yat-sen (Sun Zhongshan), leading figure in the Chinese Communist Party, Honorary President of the People's Republic of China

Tagore, Rabindranath (1861–1941): poet, writer, Nobel Laureate

Tan, Yun-Shan (1898–1983): leading scholar and founder of Cheena Bhavana, Santiniketan (West Bengal)

Thondup, Gyalo (1927–): elder brother of the 14th Dalai Lama

Yang, Gongsu (1910–2015): Chinese Communist Party cadre sent to Tibet in 1951, later Ambassador to Nepal

Zhang, Hanfu (1905–1972): Chinese diplomat and Vice-Minister, signatory to the 1954 Agreement on Tibet with India which inscribed the Panchsheel or the Five Principles of Peaceful Coexistence

Zhang, Jingwu (1906–1971): Lieutenant-General in the People's Liberation Army; Party Secretary in Tibet 1952–1965, purged during the Cultural Revolution, died in prison.

Zhang, Wenjin (1914–1991): Chinese diplomat, leader of Chinese delegation to Officials' Talks with India, 1960; later Ambassador to the United States

Zhou, Enlai (1898–1976): Chinese Premier and Nehru's key interlocutor

Introduction

When the past no longer illuminates the future, the spirit walks in darkness.

—Alexis de Tocqueville

Not far away and not long ago, in the mid-twentieth century and in the brave new dawn of their existence as independent nations, India and China began to craft a diplomatic relationship that aimed at peaceful coexistence between two very different political systems—one a constitutional democracy built on the principles of pluralism and respect for diversity, and the other Marxist-Leninist and authoritarian. The relationship of so-called brotherly friendship they built in that pioneering phase was short-lived. It foundered on the rocks of a boundary dispute that exposed the relationship's critical flaws and its brittleness—both of political vision and policymaking—and the differences between their top leaderships in character, personality and experience.

This is a history retold about India and China in mid-century from 1949 to 1962, a formative and yet self-destructive phase in a troubled relationship. Although this history has been copiously rendered previously by many scholars and historians over the decades, this interpretation is the viewpoint of a diplomat-practitioner, whose immersion in the subject in both India and China, studying it from a unique vantage point at close quarters, has spurred an attempt at understanding both the human factors and policy decisions involved in its unfolding. It is founded on a practitioner's assessment of facets, policies, personalities: a panorama intended to provide perspective, an account that stems from personal 'border crossings'—crossings between the practitioner's world and that of the historian's—a cross-fertilization of experiences from both these worlds. Its purpose is to provide a rational understanding of a complex subject for a lay audience, and to understand as Martin Luther King said, that wars are imperfect chisels to carve out peaceful tomorrows.[1]

All this happened in a short time-frame of thirteen years between 1949 and 1962. Today, as differences and tensions have resurfaced between India and China—particularly after the tragic events in the Galwan Valley of India's Ladakh—a wide-angle perspective of the early history of India-China ties and how those fateful years influence thinking on the disputes that complicate the relationship to this day, is a felt need. A more textured understanding of the complex past in India-China relations can also prepare us for the challenges that confront the Indo-Pacific region today, consonant with China's rise, and enable more creative statecraft.

India's bitter memories of the conflict with China of 1962 are often the sole touchstone for the nation's flashback to the history of this period. Blame for India's defeat by China is easily apportioned, with Jawaharlal Nehru, independent India's first Prime Minister, being the chief accused. But history should be envisioned with the aim of understanding the complex warp and weft of its fabric, and not through simplistic deduction if it is to be of value to the course of negotiation of outstanding issues in relations with China. It should be, as Edmund Burke famously said, 'an exercise to strengthen the mind', a source of value in our understanding of the present. Why did India and China stumble into war in 1962? The so-called follies of Jawaharlal Nehru, a lead actor in our story, cannot be the simple or default answer, our textbook gospel. The answers are complex and the reasons are many. History should not burden policy but should provide it with ballast. Without a grasp of its inherent complexities, it is often confining and narrowly circumscribed.

The India-China relationship in its mid-20th century phase was a history of politics, of ideologies, of the disposition of leaders, and a history of diplomacy and war. An investigation into 'the nature of being human'2, this study focuses on the human quotient of the history of relations between these two Asian nations; two civilizations and their leaders coming face-to-face with the geopolitics of their time. The attempt is to write a history with human characteristics, an encapsulated set of moving pictures that should interest the lay reader in particular, that aspires to be colourful and evanescent to borrow a phrase from Isaiah Berlin, and not dry as dust, the aim being to etch this history onto the surface of the reader's mind. A young demographic, it is hoped, will base their understanding of it both on reason—by drawing inferences about major events from a grasp of the facts; and also through a kindling of the imagination, recreating in the mind's eye, the events that marked a formative period of the contemporary history of two nations, binding together diplomacy and war. It is populated with not only politicians but also bureaucrats—mainly Indian diplomats and some Chinese ones—and a few military commanders. No doubt, it is dominated on the Indian side by Jawaharlal Nehru, whose mind was inspired by those pioneering voyagers in millennia past, both Indian and Chinese, who reached out across deserts to build a partnership of civilizations; a Caesar who was neither Bismarck nor Kissinger, but more philosopher and historian.

What propelled Nehru's vision of China? He saw China as this emergent nation ready to shake off the clutter of backwardness and foreign subjugation and the shackles of the past; a potential best friend and a geo-civilizational 'equal' to India. For Nehru, India and China could together be that mid-twentieth century definition of an independent force in world politics, unhitched to east or west. India, Nehru held, would bring China to the global stage so that it would become a responsible stakeholder in world politics. It was a lofty aspiration, and India would feel betrayed when she saw her goodwill as inadequately reciprocated—even spurned—by China, as the relationship unravelled.

There were weaknesses, oversights born of haphazard, ad hoc and careless policymaking during the period covered in this history. There is no intention to apportion blame for such shortcomings because the exercise of critiquing India's China policy in those early years and the role of Prime Minister Nehru, particularly, has persisted for years now. It is considered *de rigueur* to fault Nehru for all his 'wrong' decisions on China policy, overlooking that hindsight is never 20/20 and that it is essential to better understand the circumstances in which he made those decisions for which we fault him today. Decisions by leaders are made in real time, and not by scholars in retrospect as the historian Srinath Raghavan notes.[3] One must visualize the circumstances in which Nehru was placed. The luxury of simplified hindsight, as we often use it, blinds us. The lessons of history are useful only if they help us overcome that visual incapacity and understand not only those aspects on which a blinding bright light tends to shine typically but also the rest of the picture that exists in the shadows.[4]

India's collective memory coheres around imaging of the conflict with China as a betrayal by the country's largest neighbour, the failure and misplaced trust in China of Jawaharlal Nehru, the role of his Defence Minister in the military debacle surrounding the conflict, the gallantry of the men who fought the Chinese as well as the hubris and strategic errors in what post-mortems of the conflict of 1962 called 'the higher direction of war' by senior Indian military commanders.

Where national honour is at stake, emotions run high. The national humiliation resulting from the 1962 conflict with China haunts the national consciousness. China continues to be the adversary (a term that is synonymous with enemy, after the Galwan Valley killings of June 2020) whose alignment with Pakistan and whose now-established economic and military resurgence are seen as posing a clear and present danger to India's national security and sovereignty.

Stories cut across maps and this story is no exception. Map lines are complex and convoluted because they involve contested domains and histories, competitive statecraft and token expressions of coexistence. The events post-1950 in Tibet had profound implications for the Himalayan frontier zones of India. The moves that the Indian government would make in the determination of frontier and foreign policy towards China were a complex fusion of lofty aspirations about lasting concord between two Asian giants and, at a granular level, an entrenched determination to safeguard borders and territories that were non-negotiable and not open to barter. In those early years of these first encounters between two newly-minted independent nations, the border zones along their shared frontiers were still the scenes of many crossings, seasonal migrations and were braided together by closely-linked trading communities. India's connections with Xinjiang and Tibet were still a living bond, though soon to be weakened and slowly severed by the entry of Communist China into both regions.

Nehru worried about Chinese expansionism but it was a suspicion that did not speak its name. He was no strategist but more like Isaiah Berlin's 'fox'—the one 'who knows many things' but finds it difficult to deduce the core meaning of any one of them, fully. In recalling Nehru, one is reminded of Lloyd George: 'He thought he knew more history than they (the experts) knew. He decides by inspiration.' [5] For their part, the bureaucrats who assisted him did not seek to influence his thinking—perhaps this is a failing that can be attributed to many in the bureaucratic tribe, the tradition of not contradicting their Caesar.

Given the sense of unease that always lurked beneath the surface in New Delhi (and even in Nehru's mind) about China's predilection for expansionism, should Nehru's policy toward India's northern neighbour have been calibrated differently? As proof of this unease, he told an Indian delegation to China in 1952 that 'we must not let China have the upper hand. Else we start on the slippery path', adding that 'the basic challenge in Southeast Asia is between India and China. That challenge runs across the spine of Asia.'[6] Should he have trusted this basic instinct and de-emphasized an extravagance of friendship and amity, focusing more on the linkage of the Tibetan question with India's northern boundaries and the securitization of frontiers? Should his policy have concentrated on improving infrastructure, enhancing intelligence-gathering, and improving ties with democracies like the United States? The answer to all these is a qualified yes. One day China would mock Nehru's dreams. But partial hindsight, like nationalism, is an unsafe historian. Every decision is born of a context, a surrounding set of circumstances, often complex. Simplification is not an answer.

For countries like China, the 'cartography of national humiliation'[7] signifies borders imposed by foreign interference and machinations seen as taking away the Chinese people's birth right. Similarly, in India, events like the Partition took away from the country's sacred 'geo body' and to contemplate a similar loss of territory through boundary settlements with neighbouring countries in an electoral democracy bound by nationalistic public opinion, is anathema. Both countries are seen also as affected by a sense of 'victimhood', saying that they are victims of imperialism and that they are claiming boundaries that have always been sacrosanct parts of their nations, historically.[8] There is what some scholars have called the 'reputational imperative'[9] that compelled leaders like Nehru to safeguard their position in the nation's body politic and its history by never succumbing to larger powers and compromising their country's sovereignty and territorial integrity. It is a fact that Nehru could not pursue a pragmatic, negotiated settlement of the boundary problem once political and public opinion in India had hardened against China. In the end, his purgatorial dark night of the soul left him torn between what he was convinced was the correctness of India's case and the contrasting imperative of seeking a negotiated settlement involving give-and-take, which could have witnessed the writing of a different history.

There was a huge chasm between each country's approach to the problem. The Chinese case was that a boundary line had no validity if it was not jointly surveyed, described, or negotiated – in other words, formally delimited; whereas for India, the traditional limits were absolutely clear and unambiguous, and publicly affirmed on an official map. There were also constitutional obstacles in India's democratic framework that disallowed any modification of such boundaries. When officials of the two countries met on the direction of their Prime Ministers in 1960 to exchange documentary evidence on their respective cases on the boundary dispute, it was clear that differences could not be bridged at all. Writing in 1961, Olaf Caroe once the Foreign Secretary of India before independence, noted the lack of common ground in the reports of the officials of the two sides after their talks, rendering the complex task of creating a forward pathway to an eventual settlement even more complex and complicated, 'piling Pelion on Ossa and Ossa on Olympus'[10] as he termed it.

A settlement of the 'outstanding boundary question' which is the terminology used by Indian diplomats over the years, and is the 'area of darkness' in the relationship, eludes both countries. The border discussions have stretched on for close to four decades now, excluding the primary iteration before the 1962 conflict. One recalls the words of the Indian editor and commentator Frank Moraes, who said, 'Some caustic observers say that like (King) Charles the Second the Sino-Indian talks take a long time dying.

It is the old story of the immovable object meeting an irresistible force. Which is Communist China and which India, is anybody's guess.'[11] There is a stalemate and no solution based on mutual adjustment or compromise is really in sight.

India's closeness to Tibet, dictated not only by geography but ties of religion, pilgrimage, trade and cultural osmosis, makes the India-China relationship a three-body problem. In many ways, if a subaltern history of India-China ties is to be written in the future, it should center on a significant minority—the Tibetan people and their lost voices. The willful and deliberate dissociation of the subject of Tibet, and her status, from the issue of India's frontiers with Xinjiang and Tibet by the policy makers in Delhi, once China entered Tibet in 1950-51, was an ill-conceived move and the wages paid for that dissociation have yielded little benefit for India. It is for this reason that this history makes an attempt to present the *dramatis personae* from India, China and Tibet involved in the events that created this history so that the reader is acquainted with the promenade of especially the Indian personalities populating this canvas, all functioning in a difficult situation which India as a country was placed during the years following Partition, in times of a global Cold War and a period of national consolidation in the face of numerous economic and developmental challenges. Today, the impending issue of the succession to the 14th Dalai Lama (who received asylum in India in 1959 and has lived there since then) gives the Tibetan factor in India's relations with China a continued saliency, as does the presence of a large community of Tibetan refugees in India, and the presence of the Central Tibetan Administration—often seen as a government-in-exile— in Dharamshala in Northern India. As relations with China deteriorate, democracies like India and the United States (which also hosts a number of Tibetan refugees) will need to focus on how the identity of the Tibetan people as a distinct religious and cultural community, struggling to keep this identity alive, can be safeguarded and fostered as the current Dalai Lama advances in years and China increasingly asserts her 'right' to name a suppliant successor while clamping down further on the human rights of Tibetans and their communication links with the outside world.

Taking up the skein of our narrative further, Jawaharlal Nehru emerges from this story as flawed, but flawed in a heroic sense: faltering, eclipsed and stooped at the end of our story, wrestling with his own internal demons as the relationship with China disintegrated in full sight, with damage done to the national interest and prestige. History has not been kind to Nehru but a detailed telling of the story of India and China and their relationship from 1949 to 1962 reveals a leader whose patriotism cannot be doubted, whose vision for India was defined by the big picture of his country's place in the world, and who grasped at the end of this story his own failings and missteps on dealing with China and in the sculpting of his frontier and foreign policies. Nehru blamed no one in India for this debacle. The unravelling of his China policy was personally devastating, and as he grappled with the torment it unleashed, he saw the beginning of his end.

The nineteen-fifties were a period of newly emergent, independent and aspirational nations in Asia, all belonging as Carlos Romulo of the Philippines said at the Afro-Asian Conference of Bandung in 1955, to a 'community of hurt, heartbreak, and deferred hopes' that the past had bequeathed to them.[12] Given that they looked to the future with a new-found, exhilarating sense of liberation, and the realization of that deferred hope, leaders like Nehru cannot be faulted for the dreams and the idealism that they brought to the exercise of their statecraft. They are an inescapable part of India's history, and their legacy is an Indian inheritance, never to discard.

The world of the 'Indo-Pacific' is no doubt very different from the universe of the nineteen fifties. The 'China factor' was less a determinant of the geopolitics of that time than it is today. China was poor, emerging from civil war, undergoing inner chaos and social churn, and isolated in the world although her own sense of self and 'manifest destiny', as a nation destined to lead, was clearly enunciated even in the early years of the history of the People's Republic. The 'lessons' learnt about China by the United States in the last decade, the deterioration in U.S.-China relations, and their increasingly adversarial cast, after a long period of engagement and belief that this engagement would induce a change in the intrinsic nature of Chinese politics, systems and statecraft, recall the experiences of Nehruvian India and the failures of policy founded on best intentions. Great power competition and a complex Indo-Pacific equilibrium are the order of the day. Today, as India and the United States forge a partnership much closer and developed than at any period in their history, a deeper understanding of India's troubled history of bilateral relations with China, and why what one may call the oldest territorial dispute in modern history has persisted across a land border close to four thousand kilometres in length, is necessary. Necessary, because such problems present no easy solutions, and make both the land and maritime environments of the Indo-Pacific extremely unstable and riven with fault-lines. The choices for countries like India are stark. In 1962, at the end of the short conflict that shook the country at the foundations, Nehru declared that there could be no nonalignment vis-à-vis China. The close alignment between the United States and India today has the implied acceptance, even if it is unsaid, of the need to build a coalition that is better prepared to withstand the threat posed by China in an Asia whose environment is a disturbed one; of the need to build an equilibrium that provides reassurance to the smaller nations of Asia, that it will not be smooth sailing for the Chinese as they push their well-resourced and well-endowed plans for a Sino-centric world order. By this reasoning, a many-faceted awareness of history is an essential requirement, because India's own place in the world, her democratic systems, her economic strengths and her strategic position in the Indo-Pacific world, dictate the need for such an understanding as we set our compass towards the future.

1

Freedom, Liberation and Nationhood

My own rather cynical view is that in us, China sees the only potential rival to political and economic equality in Asia and, therefore, jealousy rather than love is likely to be the real sentiment of China toward us. While we should do our best to cultivate her friendship, we must not be led away by false sentiment or illusion.

—Girija Shankar Bajpai, Secretary-General, Ministry of External Affairs, New Delhi to Ambassador Vijaya Lakshmi Pandit, 21 August 1950[1]

For India's first Prime Minister, Jawaharlal Nehru, China was an affair of both head and heart. This attraction to China was not the product of a clear or profound understanding. It was rather a sense of the need to bind together two Asian giants, a newly independent India and a newly 'liberated' China, in a modus vivendi. The birth of New China and the independence of India took place in a troubled post–World War II era. China had emerged from Japanese occupation and from a bitterly fought civil war. The vanquished

Guomindang forces led by Chiang Kai-shek had fled to Taiwan. The pledge of American allegiance and support for the nationalist Chinese forces and non-recognition of the new Communist regime constituted one of the core chapters in the saga of the early Cold War. The conflict in the Korean Peninsula from 1950 onwards and the military combat between U.S-led forces and the Chinese 'People's Volunteer Forces led many in Asia to believe that a Third World War was imminent. In India, on the other hand, the bloody history of Partition and creation of Pakistan, the struggle over Kashmir, and the epic consolidation of nationhood within the new Union of States, were all manifestations of turbulent times for the newly independent country.

In fact, India's contemporary relationship with China had begun in the early twentieth century even before the momentous developments referred to. India's Nobel-laureate poet Rabindranath Tagore—long an advocate of a regional vision for Asia that moved beyond narrow nationalisms, towards civilizational dialogue based on rationalism and universality[2]— visited China in 1924. Arriving in Beijing, he told his Chinese audience that India felt a 'very great kinship with China', *sraddha*, as he called it. The fact that Tagore was an early champion of the rights of the Chinese people against foreign exploitation won him many Chinese admirers, including the first Premier of the People's Republic of China, Zhou Enlai. Speaking in 1956 at Santiniketan (the university established by Tagore), Zhou remarked that the former's warm affection for China would not be forgotten as also his support for the Chinese people's struggle for national independence.

In his interactions with Chinese intellectuals, Tagore was thinking about China's future place in the world. Speaking to such a group in Tokyo in the late 1920s, he said:

'With all their strength and determination and power of self-sacrifice, let your people effectively decide to have a long period of settled government even if it is not the best government possible. Let it only give you sufficient time completely to irrigate the mind of your people, to develop its potential wealth and thus enable your nation to realize the majesty of its humanity.'[3]

One can only speculate that this line of thinking is what sustains the Chinese people as they lead lives under the shadow of an authoritarian, centrist form of government, in a country that is today seen as a front-ranking economic and military superpower.

Nehru's first contact with China and the Chinese came at the Anti-Imperialist Conference in Brussels in 1927[4], after which he expressed his envy of the energy and forward-looking nature of the Chinese—wishing India could imbibe some of that energy[5]. Efforts to cement cooperation between the Chinese Guomindang (Nationalist) Party and the Indian National Congress (INC) did not progress then, due to British hostility that was firmly opposed to any fraternizing between the representatives of two subjugated countries.[6] Later, the INC, inspired by Nehru and Subhas Chandra Bose, organized rallies in India in support of China's liberation from Japanese aggression.[7]

In 1938, during China's struggle against Japanese occupation, the INC—then fully engaged in the struggle for Indian independence—dispatched a medical mission to China to help the Chinese people. The London Representative of the 'Congress China Medical Aid Committee' issued a poster seeking donations. It began by saying, 'Jawaharlal Nehru asks you to help the China Committee formed by the Congress in India.' Nehru wished to make the medical unit thus sent 'worthy of the Congress and of India'. It was mentioned that several Indian doctors had volunteered to 'place their time and skill at the service of the Chinese people.' The appeal was signed, among others, by S. Radhakrishnan (later to become the President of India), V.K. Krishna Menon (later India's Defence Minister), S.A. Wickremesinghe (Sri Lanka),

Indira Nehru (later Indira Gandhi) and Feroze Gandhi (the future husband of Indira Nehru).[8] Ironically, even though the official response welcoming the decision to send the Mission came from the Nationalist/Guomindang government[9], many prominent members of the Unit, including its leader Dr Atal and Dr Dwarkanath Kotnis, a young physician from Maharashtra, developed close ties with the Communist Eighth Route Army[10]. Dr Kotnis continues to be revered as a hero of their liberation struggle by the Chinese until this day.

A China Relief Fund was, meanwhile, set up in India and a number of China Days, including a boycott of Japanese goods, were observed to drum up support for China in its struggle against foreign invasion. Mahatma Gandhi spoke of the real friendship between India and China being based not on economics and politics but on 'irresistible attraction'. Only this, he felt, could lead to the 'real brotherhood of man'.[11] In Gandhi's view, India's freedom could not be gained at the expense of China's freedom.

Nehru came to China in August 1939, flying to Chongqing (the wartime capital) and was greeted on arrival by a rendition of 'Vande Mataram', performed by Dhiresh Mukerji of the Congress Medical Unit[12]. Nehru's route from Allahabad, traversed Calcutta, Akyab, Bangkok, Saigon, Hanoi and Kunming. In a radio broadcast[13] to the Chinese people on 31 August 1939 he said: 'a dream I had cherished for long years past was realized, and a strange excitement filled me as I looked at this mighty land and the great people who inhabit it.' He saw himself as 'one of the long succession of pilgrims who had travelled to and from, between India and China from dim ages past.' In the same tone he added, 'Perhaps, I thought, that even I, small as I am, a soldier in India's cause, might be an agent of historic destiny' in assisting both countries to 'pledge their comradeship in the great tasks of today and tomorrow.' He was critical about the Japanese and their 'brutal aggression and barbarous destruction in China'. But the Chinese people would overcome their difficulties, because they had 'the strength of ages in them'. He concluded on the note that China and India 'have been countries of yesterday, but the future beckons to them, and tomorrow is theirs.'

What then was Nehru's mission, on this first trip to China? A letter from the British Consulate General in Saigon to the Secretary to the Government of India, External Affairs Department in Simla, dated 25 August 1939[14] spoke of Nehru being welcomed by the expatriate Chettiar business community in Saigon. Nehru, apparently, was 'most guarded' in his remarks saying he was going to China to express India's sympathy for China. But French officials who were in touch with the British consulate had another version to relate; according to them a 'trustworthy' source had informed them that Nehru had made the following statement in private conversation with some local Indian residents:

> I have been sent by my party on a mission to settle certain questions dividing China and Japan. I am an intermediary between them and my task is to effect an agreement. Before war breaks out, as it will soon, in Europe, the peoples of Asia should not destroy each other but should unite so that with one accord they can join forces and victoriously wage war against England our mortal enemy.[15]

Nehru, according to the same source, was convinced that 'I will be assured of the help of Japan and we will profit from the existing tension to demand from England the independence of India. In case this is refused by England, not only will no Hindu soldier fight in the ranks, but it will be with the help of Japanese arms and ammunition that we shall free ourselves from England's rule.'[16] The British in Saigon were however inclined to dismiss this report saying even the French agreed that it was more attributable to the 'lively imagination' of their Indian source than to what Nehru had actually said.

There is no record to suggest that Nehru went to China on a mission to promote understanding between the Chinese and the Japanese as in any case this would have not succeeded given the nature of the ongoing life-and-death struggle being waged by the Chinese people against the imperialist Japanese occupation forces. It is more likely that Nehru was going to Chongqing with a view to gaining greater clarity of the ground situation through his discussions with the Nationalist Chinese leadership. It was also to cement solidarity with the latter in their struggle against foreign aggression in order to win reciprocal support for the Congress Party's struggle against the British. Although an early admirer of Japan, Nehru's attitude had shifted to criticism of Japanese aggression in China, and his sympathies were clearly with the Chinese as victims of such aggression.

While Nehru did have discussions with the 'Generalissimo', Chiang Kai-shek in Chongqing[17], his trip had to be cut short before a planned meeting with Mao Zedong in Yenan because of the outbreak of the Second World War in September 1939. Before his departure, however, he did meet Marshal Ye Jianying[18] of the Communist Eighth Route Army who called on him in Chongqing.[19] It is one of the 'what ifs' of the history of the India-China relationship as to what the trajectory of subsequent events might have been if Nehru had met Mao at that stage. He had already professed great admiration for the feats of the Eighth Route Army as far back as 1937.[20] Be that as it may, Indian interest in China was growing significantly. Edgar Snow, writing in 1942[21], spoke of the 'broadening' of the foundations of Indian nationalism, with increasing admiration and esteem being expressed by Indians for the Chinese people in their struggle against Japanese invasion. The Burma-Assam-China frontier, 'so long a barrier to intercourse', had 'become a gateway, a center of struggle', with Indians now feeling politically and spiritually wedded to China and being aware of 'the mutual interdependence of their destiny'. It is also significant that Nehru's trip to Chongqing was his first to the Far East. Mahatma Gandhi said of this new phenomenon of Indian interest in China, 'Jawaharlal Nehru, whose love of China is only excelled, if at all, by his love of his own country, has kept us in intimate touch with the developments of the Chinese struggle.' Edgar Snow believed that 'China has no more devoted friend alive—and hence neither has the cause of world freedom and brotherhood.'[22]

Was this a tale of unrequited love? The Chinese leadership had aspirations that were much larger in their sweep and ambition than those in Nehru's mind. The Agent-General of India in Chongqing, Mohammad Zafrulla Khan, had sized up the Chinese approach with considerable prescience. The External Affairs Department in Delhi reported thus on a conversation with him: 'Zafrulla(h) said that his stay in China, coupled with all his experience of Chinese activities in India, left him in no doubt as to Chinese aspirations and intentions. Chiang Kai-shek was thinking very big. His aim was that after the war China would occupy the position Japan had mapped out for herself in Asia. The Marshal aimed, not only at acquiring all territory that had been Chinese, but of assuming a predominant position in Asia.'[23] Khan was of the further opinion that one reason why the Marshal (Chiang Kai-shek) wanted a Congress government (in India) was that it would be weak and amenable to 'his pressure'.[24]

On the surface it seemed that Chinese opinion supported the Congress efforts for Indian independence. The 'conservative cosmopolitanism' of the Guomindang[25] stressed civilizational affinities with the Indian nationalist movement. The Chinese press spoke 'as if the Congress Party represented the United voice of India against Britain.'[26] The British were not amused, claiming that India was made up of many races and religions, 'whose lack of compromise to each other is perhaps incomprehensible to more philosophic and traditionally tolerant Chinese minds.'[27] In their view, the Congress aim was to put forward a 'totalitarian claim to be the sole party' and it was doubtful if a 'Congress-controlled government would resist Japan, other than by non-violence.' Gandhi's opposition to militarism was cited as another reason why the Chinese should not take the Congress Party seriously. 'Gandhi's idea of assistance to China is a personal visit to Tokyo.'[28]

The British ambassador in wartime China, Horace Seymour, was meanwhile working hard at convincing the Generalissimo that any sympathy for the Indian 'cause' was unwarranted. The latter, however, claimed that he had no personal feelings for the Indians and that he was not bound by any close relationship with them. His desire to win the confidence of Indian leaders, he said was so that 'I may have greater chance for the attainment of the object which I have had in mind, namely, a peaceful settlement of the Indian problem in the interest of the allied cause' and that 'we must do everything within our power to prevent Japan's use of India as her tool.'[29] Even mediation by America between the Indians and the British should not be ruled out, Chiang felt.

An editorial in the Chinese *Central Daily News* of 29 July 1942 talked of the need to relieve the tension between the British and the Indians and iterated that this advice was offered in a spirit of sincerity. Especially to the people of India, the paper said, 'we wish to say that in the course of their fight for freedom, they will not forget the sacred duty to participate in the anti-aggression war and to strive for the freedom of mankind.'[30] A note from Ambassador Seymour to Foreign Secretary Olaf Caroe in September 1942 spoke of the Chinese estimation that a Congress-ruled India would prove to be the neighbour that was not powerful enough 'to intervene in Chinese affairs and perhaps even weak enough to have to countenance a certain amount of expansion on the part of China itself.' Therefore, China, it was said, would be glad to see India free of British control. Seymour lamented that the 'legitimacy' of British rule was of no interest to the Chinese who basically wanted 'liberation' from powerful neighbours, 'whoever they may be'.[31]

The Chinese Nationalist leadership assumed that they could be mediators between the British and the Indian Congress Party as the latter led the struggle for Indian independence. For the Chinese, this was in a manner, fulfilment of a basic trait in Chinese character as Ambassador Seymour referred to it: 'Compromise is the guiding principle of Chinese life—social and political—and the mediator's role is not only deeply honoured as such, but has been shown to be the traditional path to consideration, wealth and power. The attraction of trying to mediate between the Congress and ourselves would probably have proved irresistible whether we had encouraged mediation or not.'[32] Meanwhile, the British were sparing no effort to tell the Chinese that Nehru and the Congress 'were only interested in their own predominance in India and were in fact China's worst enemies.'[33] The Viceroy himself stopped transmission of Chiang's messages to Nehru and Gandhi.

Nehru's fascination for China through all this showed no abatement. The Indian envoy to the Chinese Nationalists in Nanjing, veteran diplomat, K.P.S. Menon told the historian B.R. Nanda[34] of a meeting with Nehru in 1946 when Menon was proceeding to China:

He had so many questions to ask about the Chiang Kai-shek regime ... He knew Chiang Kai-shek ... All the same, Panditji[35] did realize that the Kuomintang regime was a corrupt regime, and worse than corrupt and it did not live up to the ideals of Dr. Sun Yat-sen ... I must say, I was amazed at Panditji's intuition, and knowledge as to what was happening in China. In fact, he made a rather strange suggestion to me. He said that if I got a chance, I should get in touch with Mao Tse-tung or Chou En-lai or this group in Yenan.[36]

In 1947, on the eve of Indian Independence, an Inter-Asian Relations Conference was convened in Delhi. Inspired by Nehru's vision of Asian unity being forged on the anvil of anti-imperialism and anti-colonialism, here again the call for unity with China was sounded. Speaking from the Mughal-era Purana Qila (Old Fort) at the inaugural session of the Conference, Nehru said, 'China, that mighty country with a mighty past, our neighbour, has been our friend throughout the ages, and that friendship will endure and grow'[37]. Delegates from China were welcomed as being from 'that great country to which Asia owes so much and from whom so much is expected.'[38] It was observed, however, that India's aim at the Conference was to secure 'recognition of her cultural leadership in the new Asia' to which China was 'evidently opposed.'[39] The Chinese spared no opportunity to stress that all nations in Asia were equal, 'that there was no question of leadership.' It was the Chinese view that prevailed, according to this assessment.[40]

Nehru's expressed hope for an enduring and growing friendship with China encountered obstacles. That a separate delegation from Tibet attended the Conference in addition to the delegation from Nanjing (the seat of the Nationalist government) caused some turbulence in the proceedings. Senior members of the Chinese establishment like Dai Jitao—a long-time friend of Nehru who had been closely involved in the setting up of the Sino–Indian Cultural Society and Tagore's Cheena Bhavana[41]—declined to attend. He and his cohorts saw some ulterior motive in the Indian invitation to the Tibetans and a questioning of China's territorial integrity. The official Chinese delegation on its way to Delhi met the Tibetan delegation on board the aircraft in which both were travelling. This led to the Chinese protesting the issue of Tibetan participation with the conference organizers as a result of which 'Tibet was not listed at the conference as an independent country.'[42] That was not all. The world map displayed at the conference showed Tibet outside Chinese national boundaries. The situation was retrieved, according to the memoirs of Zheng Yanfen[43] (leader of the Chinese delegation), when the Chinese diplomat George Yeh—a calligrapher and painter—amended the map by 'painting the Tibetan region in the same colour as that used for China.' This was the first and last time that there was a controversy involving a separate Tibetan delegation in an official conference held in India with Chinese participation. The situation was not repeated. But the single instance was enough to kindle Chinese suspicions about a core ambivalence regarding Tibet in the crucible of Indian political and public opinion.

Around this time, close to the dawn of Indian Independence, Luo Jialun (1897-1969), the Guomindang Ambassador to India, claims to have made a contribution to the creation of the National Flag of India.[44] Luo was an interesting personality, an educator, historian, a former president of Tsing Hua (Qinghua) University, and a political activist of the May Fourth Movement in 1919. He served as the Republic of China's first and only Ambassador to India from May 1947 to late 1949. Luo was an appointee of Chiang Kai-shek who chose him for the post because of his expertise in 'frontier affairs', especially on Xinjiang and Tibet, telling him before his departure for India that apart from 'China's own interest, India's interest is the most important one to China'[45]. Luo's arrival in India came after Guomindang China had emerged as one of the victors of the Second World War and had become a permanent member of the UN Security Council. India was to become independent a few months thereafter. The anecdote about India's national flag concerns a dinner hosted by Luo for Nehru, Vijaya Lakshmi Pandit, Indira Gandhi and K.M. Panikkar on 30 July 1947—before Mrs Pandit's departure for Moscow as India's Ambassador. The design of the new flag came up for discussion during the dinner.

'The design was a little different from the tricolour adopted by the Indian National Congress in 1931. While the tricolour design remained the same, the Dharma Chakra of Emperor

Asoka was adopted in place of Mahatma Gandhi's spinning wheel at the centre of the flag. While few know the reason for the change, part of the credit, according to Luo and some Chinese sources, should go to Luo also. Luo himself recounted that he had hosted a dinner for Nehru, Vijaylakshmi Pandit, Indira Gandhi, K.M. Panikkar and several other guests on 30 July 1947. On that occasion, Nehru told Luo that there had been a debate on the new national flag of India, and that the Constituent Assembly was not able to reach a consensus about the form. Luo was then requested to offer suggestions on the issue. Luo told Nehru and other Indian guests that for a newly independent country, the national flag should be easy to draw in order to popularise it. Compared to the spinning wheel, the Dharma Chakra of Emperor Asoka seemed to be much easier to be represented. In addition, Emperor Asoka had unified the Indian subcontinent. This bore some significance at a time when the partition between India and Pakistan was imminent.'[46]

The Constituent Assembly of India had adopted the design of the Indian national flag on 22 July 1947, before the date of the Ambassador's dinner.[47] Nehru probably raised the issue with Luo as a conversation point and to elicit a response. Luo then 'provided a reasonable argument to endorse the wheel of Asoka in place of the spinning wheel.'[48]

This account remains uncorroborated by other sources, but its intriguing nature merits mention.[49] From this author's experience in China, older generations of Chinese have long held the historical accounts of the Emperor Ashoka in high regard. Ambassador Luo Jialun's interpretation of this extraordinary story about the 'genesis' of India's national emblem, apocryphal as it may seem, is an interesting historical footnote. It is also indicative of the relatively intertwined quality of the intellectual discourse between the elites of the two countries at a time of fundamental historical shifts in national destinies.

Both countries were at this stage grappling with momentous changes in their situation, their own trysts with destiny. Indian independence in August 1947—accompanied by the horrors of the Partition—and the dawn of a new India under the Indian National Congress leadership, were co-synchronous with the rapid unfolding of events in China leading to the end of the Civil War between the Guomindang and the Communists, and the flight of Chiang Kai-shek to Taiwan. Nehru was of the view that 'the Chiang Kai-sheks and their group have singularly failed in China, failed not because of military reasons, but essentially because of their other policies. There is not a ghost of a chance of their succeeding now. Hardly anybody who counts in China thinks so.'[50] He told Mrs Pandit—his sister and then Ambassador to the United States—that he was considering the barometer of public opinion in India on the Guomindang and the general disillusionment with the latter's record of corruption and national mismanagement. 'There are in India today very few people who have a good word for the Guomindang. Our newspapers are nearly all against it. Therefore, even if I wanted to, I just could not adopt a policy which was completely against public opinion.'[51]

For Nehru, there was no reason, or logic, or 'idealism' as he put it, in adopting a policy to the contrary.

> It is absurd to think that Chiang Kai-shek, with the remnants of the army, unaided by America, can now meet and defeat the Communist forces in China . . . The Communists have won in China not so much by their strength, but by the innumerable mistakes and errors of Chiang Kai-shek and the Guomindang . . . We have to take facts as they are and the biggest fact of this decade is this continuing Chinese revolution.[52]

Rivalries between the two countries were not absent even at this stage of historical tumult. The news of Nehru's first state visit to the United States in 1949 was not welcome to the Chiang

Kai-sheks and their coterie, even as their government was then in its death throes as the Civil War drew to its end. Writing to Prime Minister Nehru from the United Nations in New York, Vijaya Lakshmi Pandit noted:

> The Chinese Ambassador here and the delegation at Lake Success are very angry with India. Madame Chiang is still here and this group revolves around her and takes its lead from her. They are extremely bitter about your forthcoming visit and the reception that you are expected to receive. One of them said to me that the red carpet had been laid out before and the pattern that was unfolding itself for India was not a new one. They resent all references to you in the press and to the potential greatness of India.'[53]

The advent of the Communists in China did not appear to shake Nehru's fundamental belief in the continuity of Chinese civilization (he held the same belief about India) and in the country's shedding the weakness and lethargy of the ages. A united, oppressed Asia was reasserting itself against the imperial West, in this view, whichever party was sovereign in China.[54] Was this a view shared by the Chinese?

Years later, in a seminal essay, the China scholar Giri Deshingkar[55] referred to the glaring asymmetries in the way India and China looked at each other. Western-educated Indians tended to subscribe to an 'Orientalist' view of China essentially sourced in the West. Looking at the supposedly ancient ties between the two countries, including the Buddhist connection, many Indian scholars had a distorted picture of 'India's place in China's world-view'.[56] Peripheral encounters between the two societies in centuries gone by had been misinterpreted in India to mean strong contacts between two nations leading to the myth of India and China being 'sister-countries', a myth given currency by many, including Nehru. By way of contrast, India in Chinese perception, was 'the land from which soldiers of the British Indian Army came to loot and kill; it was from where opium came . . . They saw Indians as '*zou gou*' (running dogs) of the British . . . Chinese thinkers when debating the Western challenge to China cited India as a negative example.'[57] Nor did the Chinese subscribe to Nehru's view that India could be a bridge between the East and the West. Yet, as we shall see later, in the early years after the establishment of the People's Republic, Chinese leadership did use India as a channel of communication with the United States. But the perceived unilateralism of India's taking upon itself the role of mediator in Korea and Indo-China, did not appeal to the Chinese who saw themselves as leaders in their own right, as noted by Deshingkar.

Nehru was loath to take an ideological view of China. He saw the rise of the Communists in China more as an expression of a new nationalism in China[58]—a nationalism that the world needed to comprehend and come to terms with. As differences between the two countries over the border, which were to surface much later, would suggest, the Chinese saw Nehru's own nationalist convictions as concealing 'colonial' impulses towards Sikkim, Nepal and Bhutan. On the Indian side, however, especially in the early years after the establishment of the People's Republic, British diplomats saw such views about China as lacking 'realism and hard headedness' which 'cut no ice with the Chinese Communists who can (and apparently do) run rings around the Indians.'[59] Talk in India about admiration for the high qualities of the Chinese leadership was 'both absurd and dangerous' according to this interpretation. India was only likely to 'learn the hard way. Let us hope they do not learn too late.'[60]

In April 1948, K.M. Panikkar (historian and administrator with a long record of service to the Princely States in India before independence) arrived in Nanjing to take up his assignment as Indian Ambassador to China. By Panikkar's own description,[61] he came to China at a turning point in its history. Nationwide general elections had been held at the prodding of the Americans, and at his installation as President, Chiang Kai-shek pledged that he would eliminate all Communist opposition in three months. Panikkar felt that the Guomindang attitude to India, though friendly was a trifle patronizing. 'Independence of India was welcome, but of course it was understood that China as the recognized Great Power in the East after the war expected India to know her place.'[62]

Panikkar was witness to the fall of the Guomindang and left Nanjing soon after the proclamation of the Central Government of the People's Republic of China from Tiananmen Square on 1 October 1949. Soon thereafter, he received a communication from the Prime Minister and Foreign Minister of the Communist regime, 'General' Zhou Enlai inviting the establishment of diplomatic relations. Prime Minister Nehru's reply indicated that there would be, according to Panikkar's account, 'early recognition and exchange of representatives'.[63] Pending formal recognition, Panikkar left Nanjing for India, awaiting further instructions. Nehru intended to send him back to China, although this, reportedly, was opposed by senior officials in the Foreign Office who saw this as a violation of protocol since Panikkar had been Ambassador to the previous Chinese regime. Differences also surfaced about the timing of recognition of the new government, with leaders like C. Rajagopalachari and Sardar Vallabhbhai Patel (then the Home Minister) advocating that India go slow on this matter. Patel, as will be seen in a later chapter, took an active interest in the case of India's relations with China. As early as June 1949,[64] he wrote to Nehru advocating that 'we have to strengthen our position in Sikkim and Tibet. The farther we keep away from the Communist forces the better. I anticipate that as soon as the Communists have established themselves in the rest of China, they will try to destroy Tibet's autonomous existence. You have to consider carefully your policy towards Tibet in such circumstances and prepare from now for that eventuality.' The comment was sparked by a letter from Atlee to Nehru about the difficulties posed to Hong Kong by Mao's rise. Patel added: 'As regards Atlee's letter to you, if I may suggest, you might send the draft reply to me before dispatching it to London. It is possible I may be able to offer some useful suggestions . . . The problem is difficult. On the one side, we have undoubtedly Hong Kong's imperialistic history. On the other hand, we have to reckon with the growing Communist menace.' Nehru ignored this view.

Six months later, the two leaders differed on the timing of India's recognition of China's new government. Patel wrote to Nehru: 'My own feeling is that we do not stand to gain anything by being in the lead (by recognizing China ahead of most other countries). In case you feel we must recognize China ahead of others, I feel we must have a discussion in the Cabinet.'[65] Nehru's reply was that 'if we follow others, it would mean that we have no policy of our own.'

The Indian government's assessment of the emergent situation in China after the fall of the Guomindang was communicated in a letter dated 12 January 1949 from Foreign Secretary K.P.S. Menon to the British High Commissioner in India, Archibald Nye.[66] The assessment was that after the fall of Chiang Kai-shek, a coalition government was likely to emerge since the Communist Party, while possessing considerable military and political leadership, was lacking in administrative talent and experience. 'Compromise is likely to be keynote of Government's policy; and the Chinese have a special genius for it,' Menon noted. This heterogeneous Government though dominated by the Communists 'will not necessarily be dominated by Russia' since China was too 'vast, too different ethnically and culturally from the Slav Group and too tenacious of her own traditions to be absorbed by Russia, even in an ideological sense. Indeed, it may be that Communist China may be the first to provide a national counter-weight to the U.S.S.R.'[67] India, for its part, did not need to fear any serious danger from China since political consolidation and economic rehabilitation would take time. But any hostility towards a Communist-controlled China would only tend to throw it more in the Soviet orbit.

In November 1949, a telegram from the Ministry of External Affairs in New Delhi to the Indian mission to the United Nations in New York spoke of recognition of the new government in Beijing because India respected China's sovereignty and integrity and it was for the Chinese people to decide what government 'they shall have'.[68] Recognition, it was opined, did not involve approval of the policy of the new government; it was only a recognition of a political and historical fact, ignoring which 'is only to court embarrassment both in the present and the future.'[69] In early December 1949, in a communication addressed to the Chinese scholar Tan Yun-Shan in Santiniketan, Nehru said that while India was not in a hurry to recognize the new regime, the step to recognize had to be taken at the right time, 'neither too early nor too late. To do it late means that it had been taken under compulsion.' He had little doubt 'that the Chinese people will ultimately function in accordance with their genius. The whole of their history shows that.'[70]

Formal recognition of the new government in China was communicated via a diplomatic note dated 30 December 1949 in which Prime Minister Nehru conveyed to Zhou Enlai that the Government of India had decided to accord recognition to the People's Republic of China and to enter into diplomatic relations with it.[71] The Indian recognition of the new government came a day after the Burmese decision to do the same: Burma had specifically sought that its recognition should precede that of all other countries outside the Soviet bloc. The Chinese response to Burmese alacrity was to pour cold water on the latter's eager enthusiasm. Zhou Enlai said that his government would be 'pleased' to establish diplomatic relations with Burma once its government had 'severed relations with the remnants of the Guomindang reactionaries.'[72]

In correspondence with the Burmese Prime Minister, Thakin Nu, Nehru spoke of the close coordination between his government and the Burmese on the timing of recognition. His correspondence with the Burmese leader also referred to the reluctance of the United States to take a similar step because of the treatment of their consular officials by the new regime.[73] The attitude of the British government was non-committal—they had taken the decision to recognize the new regime but the date was to be decided. Krishna Menon, the Indian High Commissioner in London, wrote to Nehru that 'it is ill conceded that Bevin and the Foreign Office propose to include China in their Cold War strategy and attitude and that it has been decided to treat her as a satellite state with correctness perhaps but no more.'[74]

In a note prepared by the Prime Minister himself for Sir Girija Shankar Bajpai, the Secretary-General in the Ministry of External Affairs, for a meeting with the U.S. Ambassador Loy Henderson in February 1950,[75] Nehru argued in favour of why the world needed to pay attention to China and the developments there:

It is obvious that China is the most important question in Asia and the world today. India does not like much that has happened in China. But it feels that it would be very dangerous for the future to make China a professed enemy. We do not propose to submit to anything we consider wrong . . . We have, therefore, decided to be watchful and firm and at the same time friendly . . . We should try to follow what seems to us obviously the safer policy from the point of view of Asia and the world.

Speaking at a press conference in Colombo, (then) Ceylon, in January 1950,[76] Nehru advanced his views on why the Nationalists had lost the Civil War, attributing it to inflation, nepotism, corruption, and gross mismanagement leading to the cracking of the whole system. He then added, 'The fact emerges, therefore that China has got a strong centralized Communist-controlled government and that this government is not going to be swept away by either internal or external force short of some world upheaval.' He regarded China as 'too big and distinctive, with its own peculiar way of life, to function just in the Russian way. The manner in which the Communists in China have succeeded, that is through their own efforts, also makes them rather independent of the Soviets. How this Communist China will develop is a matter of great importance to the rest of Asia and the world.' For Nehru, the establishment of the People's Republic, was a 'world event of the first magnitude.'[77]

All this took place even as the Chinese media, particularly the Communist-supporting sections, were sharply critical of Nehru, especially after his visit to the United States in the autumn of 1949. The *New China Daily* in Nanjing in a dispatch on 22 October of that year said the U.S. wanted to make Nehru 'a thoroughly loyal servant of the U.S. imperialists' and, 'a leader of anti-Communist and anti-national liberation movement in Asia.'[78] The *Ta Kung Pao* of 26 October[79] had an article on the subject by Li Hsin captioned: 'The American running DOG—Nehru'. The *People's Daily* of 29 October carried a TASS dispatch from Moscow, the main theme of which was that the 'United States imperialists having failed in China, have fixed their eye on India's representative of nationalism within the capitalist class' wanting to make him 'into a blind tool of the United States'. And, on 2 November, the *New People's Daily* of Nanjing published a Hong Kong report of 15 October, saying that on 13 October, 'the Indian Government had taken a decision which was considered to be the first step towards recognizing the Chinese People's Republic . . . This news was published under the derisive heading 'Indian Government is turning RUDDER by the wind . . . She also wants to recognize the new China.'[80]

After the announcement of recognition in December 1949, K.M. Panikkar was sent back to China, this time as India's representative to the government of the People's Republic. He presented his letter of credentials on 20 May 1950 saying 'the People's Republic of China (PRC) and the Republic of India, representing the oldest communities in the world, are now in a position to cooperate effectively for mutual advantage and for the welfare of their people.' Mao Zedong, in his capacity as Chairman of the PRC, spoke of the 'profound understanding, sympathy and concerns' that existed between China and India, 'with our common boundary and prolonged and close relations in both history and culture'. He extended a warm welcome to the new Ambassador.[81] The acrimonious tone of media comments on Nehru and India in the previous months seemed to have been buried for the moment by the new government of the Chinese Communists.

The personality of India's Ambassador was the subject of some study among foreign governments, particularly the western ones, at the time. A biographical note (1950) by the Commonwealth Relations Office, London, prepared on the basis of 'confidential reports' from the British High Commission in Delhi[82] speaks of Mr. 'Panikkar as having 'a strong belief in Asia's destiny' and holding the view 'that India should hold the 'Ring Fence' against invasion from the North and that the Indian Navy should be built up as the police force for the whole Indian Ocean area.' Panikkar was assessed as having a 'strong admiration of the new Communist China, believing the communist seizure of power to have been inevitable and in the circumstances the only solution to China's immediate problems.' Panikkar did not lack in agility of mind or in the ability to generate a 'constant stream of ideas.' However,

experience based on personal contact suggests that with a scholar's ability Sardar Panikkar possesses also the defect to which the academic mind is liable, the formation of theories based on abstract speculation insufficiently related to practical reality, and it is significant that there is a school of thought in the Government of India which holds that he went to Peking with set ideas and is not reporting objectively but fitting the facts to his theories.[83]

In general, Panikkar's British counterparts saw him as a 'high pressure gentleman who plugs a line.'[84]

British observers contrasted the attitude of Nehru and some of his officials like Panikkar to Communist China's ascendance, with that of the Chinese towards the Indians. Their Foreign Office[85] had this to say in May 1950:

> [I]t is worth keeping in mind that the Chinese on the whole have a profound contempt for the Indians, and also a sense of very considerable superiority towards them . . . While an Indian on occasion may be sentimental, the Chinese is essentially a realist . . . on the personality side while the Indians are frequently superior, the present Chinese Communist leaders are physically and morally of an altogether tougher breed and fibre. Of the physical toughness of the Chinese Communist, the 'Long March' is the classic, heroic symbol . . . There is no doubt whatsoever that in the technique of political organization, hardheadedness and ruthless determination and above all in realism, the Chinese Communists win hands down . . .

Panikkar, while enjoying the confidence of the Prime Minister was not regarded in a strictly positive light by the Foreign Office mandarins in New Delhi. Secretary-General G.S. Bajpai, writing[86] to Vijaya Lakshmi Pandit in August 1950 regarded the Ambassador as being 'a little too responsive to the atmosphere, whether for our conviction or as a safe guide to our policy. His eulogy of the men who now rule China, their great reforms and their friendship for us, leave me somewhat skeptical, especially the last. My own rather cynical view is that in us, China sees the only potential rival to political and economic equality in Asia and, therefore, jealousy rather than love is likely to be the real sentiment of China towards us.' In yet another letter,[87] Bajpai would say, 'Panikkar's enthusiasm, genuine or feigned, causes me personally a good deal of difficulty at times. The P.M. is impressed with his reports and I have to work hard to control his enthusiasm when, in my own rather conservative judgement, caution seems to be necessary.'

The new Chinese Ambassador to India, Yuan Zhongxian, arrived in New Delhi in September 1950. The next day he met Prime Minister Nehru who wrote to his sister the same day regarding the meeting.[88] The Ambassador apparently had a much bigger welcome at the railway station than any other foreign ambassador had had. 'Indeed, it was a popular welcome and some hundreds of people gathered there, chiefly students,' according to Nehru. That was the way 'the wind blows here while Americans are taking up their uncompromising attitude towards the New China.'[89] Nehru described his talk with the Ambassador, who brought with him a gift of two 'huge' vases from Premier Zhou Enlai, as friendly. The Prime Minister sounded sanguine about the 'remarkable' change in relations between India and China which had begun 'slowly' after his visit to America in September 1949 when, in his estimation, the Chinese realized that he 'was not exactly anybody's stooge, as they had imagined.' India's championing China's cause (for membership) at the United Nations had also gone a 'long way' (in effecting a change in Chinese behavior towards India), Nehru felt. He was confident about Panikkar, saying he had done a good job, and 'gets on very well with the Chinese government.'

Panikkar, meanwhile, was setting himself up in Beijing. He had found a residence with 'numerous courtyards and reception rooms in Chinese style' just outside the Legation area of the Forbidden City, with 'up-to-date' fittings.[90] The historian and aesthete in him were happy that the 'pavilion attached to the garden had scenes from the *Dream of the Red Chamber*[91] painted on its sides.' Three days after his arrival in Beijing, he was received by Zhou Enlai. The latter, in his view, seemed to possess 'an extraordinary serenity of countenance' with fingers like 'tender onion shoots' that he used to gesticulate with great effect. Nehru, on the other hand, 'looks worried, except when he smiles or laughs in company,' according to Panikkar. In an hour-and-a-half meeting, Zhou peppered Panikkar with questions about India, about which his information seemed 'vague', and particularly stressed the importance of growing capacity in steel production and electric power generation for both countries. Panikkar came away from the meeting with the impression that Zhou was 'no doctrinaire, but a practical statesman' who, despite being a staunch Communist had his feet 'firmly planted on mother earth.'[92]

The tendency of the new regime was to hold meetings with foreign envoys late at night (a practice that is still employed, occasionally, in the Chinese Foreign Office), as the Ambassador's first meetings with Zhou and, then, with Mao would show. The presentation of credentials took place in the palace of the Fragrant Concubine, a relic from Manchu times, where after the ceremony, Mao and Panikkar held a meeting, with Mao saying at the outset that in China there was 'an old belief that if a man lived a good life, he would be reborn in India.'[93] To Panikkar, Mao appeared impressive—but not intimidating, of philosophical mind, with a sense of history, 'a little dreamy but absolutely sure of himself.' Panikkar's instinct was to compare Mao with Nehru—both in his view, were men of action, but with dreamy, idealistic temperaments.

Panikkar's arrival in Beijing and his ease of access to the top leadership certainly won the attention of opinion makers in the western capitals. Writing to her brother, Vijaya Lakshmi Pandit[94] referred to *Time* magazine having published (in their issue of 5 February 1951) a picture of Panikkar presenting his credentials to Mao under the title 'Contact man between Peking and New Delhi is Sardar K.M. Panikkar bowing low to Mao Tse-tung whom he greatly admires. Oxford-educated Panikkar loves to parade his nodding acquaintance with European history. He served under several maharajas, calls himself a 'reformed landlord', cultivates his resemblance to Lenin by wearing a Lenin-esque beard.'

'We do not propose to align ourselves with anybody in regard to China,' said Nehru in June 1949, responding to reports that the Indian government had promised to cooperate with the United States on China.[95] The Prime Minister was ready to brush aside opposition from a section of his Cabinet who felt that based on the assumption that the Soviet Union and China were close allies, India should draw closer to the United States. According to R.K. Nehru, who served as Ambassador to China and as Foreign Secretary and Secretary General in the Ministry of External Affairs, the Prime Minister's assessment of the situation was different: 'First of all, he did not regard China as a natural ally of the Soviet Union, and, secondly, he realized that any close alliance with the U.S. would have an adverse effect' in terms of China and the Soviet Union drawing closer together with a capacity 'to cause damage' to Indian interests. The U.S. would demand its 'price' for such closeness, and that 'price could be to urge India to yield more on Kashmir'. Finally, Nehru's main concern was 'to consolidate our independence', according to this account. It was deemed a 'sophisticated approach.'[96] In the words of Nehru's biographer S. Gopal, 'Without necessarily agreeing with or supporting China in everything, he refused to line up against her in any way.'[97] This was still a few years before China came to shake Nehru's confidence and mock his dreams.

2

Top of the World

When the blow fell on Tibet in 1950 there was no generally informed international knowledge of [its] status. . . . Only the British and Indian governments . . . could have made some positive statement but the situation was dominated by India's relations . . . friendly at that time . . . with China; and the opportunity to speak out before the United Nations was rejected . . .

—Hugh Richardson,
British civil servant and Tibetologist.[1]

In the autumn of 1972, His Holiness the Dalai Lama, then in the thirteenth year of his exile in India, gave an interview[2] to *Newsweek* magazine. Characteristically, he was realistic and his tone measured and low-key. He told Tony Clifton, his interviewer, that if Tibetans in Tibet accepted Chinese rule willingly, he would accept it too. It was not that he wanted to conduct a court in exile like some European king. [After all] Gautama, the Buddha, had given up a kingdom. Nationality was not important to him, the

26

Dalai Lama said. He was ready to be a solely religious leader, if asked. He knew that changes were needed in Tibet and had realized that even in 1950 when he was fifteen. But sounding a note of contradiction to these statements, he mused that if the Chinese invasion had not happened, he would, in time, have become a conservative old man.

Our story is intimately bound with the narrative of events in Tibet as played out in the early years of the relationship between India and China in the 1950s. The point of departure is October 1950 and the news of the advance of troops of the Chinese People's Liberation Army (PLA) into Tibet. The Chinese troops entered Tibet through four routes situated in provinces adjacent to Tibet—through Sichuan, Yunnan, Qinghai and Xinjiang.[3] Prior to 1950, Tibet had an eventful individual history, notwithstanding the Chinese claim of possession and (tenuous) historical domination of the area. In a conversation with this author in 2014, the Dalai Lama spoke of a period from the seventh to ninth centuries when Tibetan people settled across vast areas from Ngari in western Tibet to Amdo or Qinghai[4]. That was a time when Buddhism from India, together with the importation of the Devanagari (Sanskrit) alphabet, began to influence Tibetan culture and language. This spiritual 'imperialism' of India, as the Dalai Lama said jocularly in the same interview, was very different from Chinese overlordship.

The influence of India, as the Dalai Lama said, was immensely significant in the forging of Tibetan religious and cultural identity. Buddhism and the philosophical traditions of Nalanda (in today's Bihar state, where one of the world's most ancient universities had thrived) had reached Tibetans wherever they lived. Monks of the Nalanda tradition, had contributed significantly to the education of Tibetans in 'the Nalanda way', a tradition that had been kept intact for over a thousand years. The Tibetan influence, born of these traditions, had stretched into areas far beyond what was traditionally regarded as the area of Tibet—so the concept of a 'Greater Tibet', which the Chinese often accused the

Tibetan refugee community leaders of fostering, really meant the extensive area of such Tibetan influence stretching into adjoining Chinese provinces. At the 'deeper level', Tibetans could never feel Chinese, because of this distinct civilizational identity, he added. 'The Chinese Government has to deal with this,' he said.[5] In the years before the events of 1950–51 and the entry of Chinese troops into Tibet, during the period stretching from 1911 onwards, Tibet had practised what the Dalai Lama called 'de facto independence', free of Chinese interference.

When the Chinese PLA entered Tibet in 1950, there was a distinct sense of unease in India. The 'Chronology of Events in Tibet' prepared by the Political Officer in Gangtok, Sikkim[6]— when the proclaimed intention of the Chinese Communist Government to 'liberate' Tibet during 1950 became known— documents that strong protests were made by the Government of India to Beijing.[7] On 13 August 1950 the Government of India represented to the Government of China that they felt 'concerned at the possibility of unsettled conditions across the border and would therefore strongly urge that Sino-Tibetan relations should be adjusted through peaceful negotiations.' But these political concerns seemed to emanate more from the Indian establishment's concern about the impact that the Chinese entry into Tibet would have on the peace and security of India's frontiers with Tibet. The Indian officials led by Prime Minister Nehru were less concerned about Tibet's own status as distinct from China, than about the need to adjust relations in order to accommodate the resolution of 'unsettled conditions' in the border areas which would directly affect India.

The aspect that related to Tibet as imagined by Indian Hindus and Buddhists and which predominated in public opinion, was obscured. This was much more than the image of isolation and seclusion that Tibet signified for the rest of the world. For India, Tibet was the abode of the sacred, the spiritual, and everything sanctified by religion. The affairs of Tibet had traditionally exerted a deep impact on the spiritually inclined Indian. Tibet was the holy land for millions of devout Indian Hindus and Buddhists, the seat of pilgrimage to such places as Mount Kailash (Gang Rinpoche in Tibetan), considered the abode of the Hindu god Shiva, and Lake Manasarovar (Mapam Yumtso in Tibetan) in the Ngari Prefecture of western Tibet. Tibet, the land of high snow mountains, the source of great, sacred rivers like the Indus and the Brahmaputra, a lofty country of 'high peaks and pure earth'— this was the image enshrined in the Indian psyche.

Tibet exerted a huge religious and cultural influence on the Himalayan regions. The Tibetans had never regarded mountain ranges, passes, watersheds and river valleys as boundaries, and neither did the pilgrims from the Himalayan regions and various parts of India, who frequented sacred places of worship. To illustrate this point, there is a magnificent example of a traditional Tibetan map in the Department of Oriental Antiquities at the British Museum in London which originally belonged to Hugh Richardson who received it in 1944 from Tsarong Shape,[8] then a leading political figure in Tibet.[9] It is called the 'Pilgrimage map for Tsa-ri rong skor'. Working from the westward end, the map 'follows the course of a major trans-Himalayan river valley system comprising the Lo-ro chu, Bya-yul chu and upper reaches of the Subansiri River'. Painted on a long cotton scroll (thang-ka), it has outlines painted as fine black lines, and landscape features filled in with natural colour washes. Paths and travel routes stand out conspicuously, and monasteries, stupas, shrines, and domestic buildings are also shown. The western sections of the map depict the barren and rolling landscape of the Tibetan plateau, while the eastward sections show thatched huts of the sort used by tribals from Arunachal Pradesh in the upper Subansiri reaches. The scene here shows dramatic cliffs, waterfalls, and a variety of vegetation including bamboo, flowering herbs and different species of trees, reflecting a high-rainfall area. Notes on local monastic estates are also found, and data is provided for a number of places of geographical and cultural interest. The map shows a wealth of data covering both the northern and southern banks of the river valleys depicted, and is a rendition of a religious and cultural cosmology that had crossed the high Himalaya and descended to lower heights as far as climate and terrain suited—the 'upland tree-lowland tree' (trees found in the higher Himalayan altitudes and those that grow in the lower, warmer altitudes) line of pine tree and bamboo, as in the Sikkim and Bhutan Himalaya, for instance. The words of a veteran civil servant and administrator who served long years in these frontier areas sum it up: 'The cultural boundaries transcend the political boundaries, and always overflow, linguistically, culturally, no matter how much you divide them by McMahon and Durand Lines. On both sides, the people were almost the same and there was free flow of trade and ideas.'[10]

The cosmological mandala of Himalayan India abuts Tibet in a long border stretching from the Karakoram ranges in Kashmir to the mountains on the Burmese frontier of northeast India. Ladakh, the Himachal and Uttarakhand Himalaya, Sikkim and Arunachal Pradesh are all part of what Olaf Caroe called 'The Mongolian Fringe' in a January 1940 paper speaking of the 'defence of the Indian glacis' to prevent occupation by 'any Great Power'.[11] This was a frontier that for China, represented 'irredenta',[12] which made it necessary in Caroe's estimation, to 'fasten in the Indian orbit all that Mongolian Fringe from Nepal to the furthest tribal areas of Assam.' For Caroe, ensuring an Indian presence in Lhasa, the Tibetan capital, was essential. For one, this town, the centre of Tibetan authority, was closer to India than China or Russia, which made it necessary for India to take advantage of this geographical position, 'and to keep the window open'. Caroe, therefore, in 1940 was advocating the strengthening of an Indian military presence in Tibet (apart from platoons at Yadong and Gyantse in the Chumbi Valley adjacent to Sikkim and Bhutan, in place since the Younghusband expedition of

1904[13] when Tibetans, it is said, were 'shot down like partridges')
'to reinforce this line in order to prevent Lhasa falling into enemy
hands.' This 'imperialist' vision (in regard to Tibet) would not be
subscribed to by an independent India, post-1947. The vision that
Tibet should be maintained as an 'integral, inter-national unit'
would fade into the annals of history, although frontier policy in
the Nehru years would seek to establish what Caroe termed 'an
indissoluble union of interest' with India's 'Mongolian Fringe'—
that is, Nepal, Sikkim and Bhutan. The thinking behind this was
that the Mongolian Fringe's disintegration, or a takeover by China,
would only render India's own defences insecure and vulnerable.
On Tibet, India's primary concern was that her frontiers with
this region should be regarded as fixed and determined, and not
open to alteration. But, the implicit acknowledgement by India of
Chinese sovereignty over Tibet after 1950 without ensuring, as a
quid pro quo, that China would affirm and endorse the traditional
Indo-Tibetan frontier would have fateful repercussions.

Notwithstanding Chinese claims to Tibet, the latter had enjoyed
a de facto independence since 1911, entering for example, 'into
international obligations', as Algernon Rumbold—an ex-British
civil servant who served in the Foreign and Commonwealth Office
'in charge' of Tibet in the 1940s—put it in 1988.[14] Here, Rumbold
draws the distinction between 'suzerainty' and 'sovereignty',[15]
saying the British government had always 'been ready to recognize
China's suzerainty over Tibet, but only on the understanding that
China accepted the autonomy of Tibet.' Rumbold added that 'As
the Chinese government had not accepted Tibet's autonomy, our
readiness to recognize suzerainty remained a contingent offer.'
Tellingly, Rumbold wrote that the Tibetans had never accepted
'suzerainty' (or 'sovereignty') of China over Tibet as the 1914
Simla Conference between British India, China and Tibet (see
below) had never been accepted by China and because of this,
subsequently, the Tibetans 'never accepted suzerainty'. As for
the British, according to Rumbold, 'We ourselves regarded

'suzerainty' as merely a word without substance preferred as a sop for Chinese face.' And as for the Chinese, post-1951, when Tibet was occupied by the People's Republic, only a 'bogus' autonomy had been applied to Tibet. The Chinese attached to 'autonomy' or 'suzerainty', 'no more significance than we [the British] did before 1950 to suzerainty'[16].

From the heyday of its empire, the British view was that a hostile Tibet was capable of upsetting the peace of northern India. A process of a controlled escalation in British influence in Tibet was pursued from the early 1900s commencing with the Younghusband expedition, with mixed success in an on-again off-again manner. It was the British concern about China filling the Tibetan vacuum in the waning years of the Qing or Manchu empire with a series of forays into Tibet, that spurred the move to define India's eastern frontiers with Tibet. When Chinese power in Tibet collapsed following the Revolution of 1911 on the mainland, the right conditions were provided for Britain to exert pressure. China was not excluded from the process. This is what led to the Simla Conference of 1914 and the meeting of the British, Tibetan and Chinese Plenipotentiaries where discussions centered around the defining of zones of Tibetan paramountcy and Chinese influence. At that Conference, the British representative Sir Henry McMahon proposed the separation of Tibet into two zones called Outer and Inner Tibet: Outer Tibet signifying an area where Tibetan 'autonomy' would be paramount though Chinese 'suzerainty' would be acknowledged, and Inner Tibet, allowing for much more Chinese control although not specifically spelt out as such. Ostensibly over this alignment of the borders of Inner Tibet, the Chinese rejected the outcomes of the Conference. Their envoy, Ivan Chen's initialing of the draft Simla Convention of April 1914 was repudiated by his government, and the final Convention of July 1914 was signed only by McMahon and the Tibetan representative at the Conference, Lonchen Shatra Paljor Dorje.

Today, the Simla Conference of 1914 is remembered because it marks the genesis of what is called the McMahon Line (the marking of the Indo-Tibetan boundary in what was then the Assam Himalaya) on a small-scale map and defined in notes exchanged between McMahon and Lonchen Shatra. The Chinese were not party to these discussions which were held in Delhi, away from Simla, in March 1914. The Chinese repudiation of the Conference deliberations at Simla rested entirely on the demarcation of the zones of Outer and Inner Tibet, even though the red line marking the Indo-Tibetan boundary agreed upon in March 1914 was contained in the map attached to the draft of the Convention initialed (but not signed) by Ivan Chen, the Chinese Plenipotentiary, in April 1914.

The period after the Chinese Revolution of 1911 was marked by a state of de facto independence for Tibet. The Trade Regulations between Britain and Tibet of 1914 provided for the securing of British commercial interests in Tibet and implicitly recognized the right of the Tibetans to conduct trade with Britain and India entirely by themselves. The Regulations also provided for the retention of British military escorts[17] in Tibet, and control by the British of the Post and Telegraph installations and rest houses set up after the Younghusband Expedition of 1904.

The 13th Dalai Lama died in 1933.[18] A Regent was appointed by the Tibetan leadership in Lhasa. He was the incarnate Lama (Rinpoche) of Reting Monastery.[19] A Chinese mission came to Lhasa ostensibly to offer condolences on the death of the Dalai Lama and left behind two liaison officers with a wireless set—thus securing the first foothold in the Tibetan capital after twenty years. Chinese influence on leading members of the Tibetan clergy, including the Reting Rinpoche, was established. This was also the time when the 9th Panchen Lama—traditionally a rival pole of influence to the Dalai Lama in Tibet[20]—who had been in China because of differences with the 13th Dalai Lama, died in 1937 on a return journey to Tibet at Jyekundo near the Tibetan border with

China. This coincided with what was called the Gould Mission to Tibet led by Basil Gould (the British Political Officer in Sikkim and a veteran of the North-West Frontier), which was sent with the purpose of exploring the possibilities of some reconciliation between Lhasa and the Panchen Lama. While nothing was to come of this effort to intervene in the Panchen matter,[21] the mission resulted in the establishment of a form of permanent British representation in Lhasa. Gould left behind Hugh Richardson with a wireless officer. The Lhasa post was considered an extension of the office of the Political Officer in Gangtok. For the British, Lhasa was the only place in Tibet where it was possible to get accurate information, and the officer in Lhasa could remain in close touch with Tibetan affairs. In the words of Hugh Richardson,[22] with the passage of time, the Mission in Lhasa became, in Tibetan eyes, a familiar, accepted, 'and almost necessary institution.'

Writing in the nineteen nineties,[23] over a half century after he first visited Lhasa, Richardson was to speak about 'swift, protean memories' of the road from Gangtok to Lhasa, of rhododendrons, freezing streams, 'tiny, pink primulas and blue gentians,' battering, blinding curtains of snow, all leading to the little house of Dekyilingka (Grove of Happiness)[24] where the Political Officer in Lhasa lived and worked. Richardson, a pronounced Tibetophile, felt that those 'fortunate enough to live there (Tibet) in its days of freedom and independence knew the warm friendliness of a courteous, humorous people living a leisurely and generally peaceful life, dedicated to their religion but quite able to enjoy themselves too . . . before its devastation by a violent, sour and repressive communist regime.'

Gould's expedition was pitched in the language of the Raj: it was a cavalcade, four days of rest after it reached Gyantse, calls from local officials, and entertainments. 'There had never been anything like it, at least on a peaceful footing,' writes Richardson.[25] Besides Gould and Richardson, there were senior army officers, private secretaries, botanists, photographers, Sikkimese clerical staff, 'a host of personal servants, orderlies, camp followers and so on.'[26] Each officer had a comfortable tent with a small bathroom; two large mess tents, personal baggage, 'each man's wash basin with a leather cover,'[27] presents including cases of rifles, and even three spaniels. All these were carried by over two hundred mules, ponies, donkeys and an occasional bullock and many porters, men, women, girls and boys. And for this expedition, the moment of arrival in Lhasa, and the point from which the Potala Palace[28] could first be seen 'sailing above the plain in the clear air like a white ship gleaming with hints of gold and crimson,' the sense of wonder was 'mixed with a rather British sense of achievement. We had done it. We had got there.'[29]

But a clear determination of the status of Tibet—of independence, autonomy, suzerainty and sovereignty—continued to elude the British, and this lack of granularity was to contribute a great deal to the indecisiveness of the international community in responding to the crisis faced by Tibet when the PLA marched there in 1950–51. The inconclusive nature of the deliberations at Simla in 1914 also left the British attempting over the next few years, thereafter to seek Chinese endorsement of the outcomes of the Conference to little or no avail. Of note was the fact that in 1919, the Chinese government put forward written proposals for a settlement based on the 1914 deliberations. The course of negotiations at Beijing was affected adversely by a malicious press campaign inspired by the Japanese, by the opposition of Chinese militarists, and by the treatment of the Shandong[30] question at Versailles as an outcome of the First World War. It ended with the Chinese Foreign Minister confessing in a confused and unconvincing stream of bluster and explanation[31] that public opinion had turned against the negotiations, and was now in opposition to British 'interference' in Tibet.

Through these years, the governments of Britain and of British India differed on the need for establishing a permanent representation in Lhasa, with the latter arguing against such a presence, fearing that the resumption of negotiations with China would be jeopardized as a result. At this juncture in 1920, it was decided that Charles Bell, who had earlier served as Political Officer in Sikkim, should lead a special mission to Lhasa. The mission marked a turning point in British policy towards Tibet. Bell, who is known for the close friendship he developed with the 13ᵗʰ Dalai Lama, and is often called 'the father of the McMahon Line' by virtue of having closely advised Lonchen Shatra, the Tibetan delegate to the Simla Convention negotiations of 1914, was critical of the Indian government's aloofness to the Tibetans, saying that this would only make them draw closer to China[32]. The risk of Japan and China gaining power 'together' in Tibet was real, he felt, and this could jeopardize India's north east frontier. India had a vital interest in the problems surrounding Tibet and, in Bell's view, India's aims ought to have been to see Tibet 'enjoying internal autonomy under the lightest form of Chinese suzerainty, a barrier for the Northern Frontier of India, free to develop on her own lines.'[33]

Bell's proposals were followed by the Memorandum submitted to the Chinese government in August 1921, requesting the latter to reopen negotiations in London or Beijing on the finalization of the 1914 Agreement. It was conveyed that in the event of the non-resumption of these negotiations, the British government intended to recognize the status of Tibet 'as an autonomous state under the suzerainty of China and intend dealing with Tibet on future on this basis.' The British government did not consult the Tibetan government about the reference to Chinese suzerainty in this Memorandum, and the Tibetans were not informed about the decision to include this in the said document. At the same time, however, communication with the Tibetans was opened up on a much freer basis, the policy being defined as new and liberal, and designed to help Tibet to protect and develop itself. This included the limited supply of guns and ammunition; training of Tibetan forces to a limited extent; construction of a telegraph line from Gyantse to Lhasa; assistance, if required, in the manufacture of ammunitions; development of mineral resources; and the opening of a school at Gyantse or Lhasa. Tibet would no longer be a hermetic space, free of British presence. All this transpired as chauvinistic forces in China were gaining ascendance even as the prestige of the Central government in Beijing was at its lowest ebb. The recommendation of the British Embassy in Beijing was that the tripartite negotiations relating to Simla 1914 should not be reopened given the state of Chinese affairs; that the Tibetan government should be informed about there being little chance of coming to an agreement with China at that stage; and, finally, Britain should consolidate relations with Tibet independently of China. No further pressure was put on the Chinese government thereafter to agree to a tripartite settlement based on the Simla Conference.

The death of the 13th Dalai Lama saw the launch of the search for his incarnate successor. The Tibetan government had to pay 400,000 Chinese dollars to the Governor of Qinghai for the release of the young child who had been identified as the potential successor. Qinghai was the province from which the boy came. When the child was safely inside Tibetan territory, he was declared the true incarnation. He reached Lhasa on 8 October 1939. The Government of India was believed to have assisted the Tibetan government in the release of the ransom money. The Tibetan move enabled the journey of the child into Tibet without a formal Chinese escort; the Tibetans took care to declare him the chosen incarnation only after he was approaching Lhasa. The preoccupation of the Chinese government with the ongoing war with Japan helped, as did the greed of the Qinghai governor. The Chinese, making the best of a bad bargain, declared once the child had left Xining that he had been declared the Dalai Lama with the approval of the Chinese and Tibetan authorities. Their representative, Wu Zhongxin, was present in Lhasa (as also Basil Gould) during the installation ceremony of the new Dalai Lama, and claims were made in the Chinese press that the child had prostrated himself in the direction of Beijing and that he had been permitted to succeed to the title by the Chinese. In Richardson's description, 'These announcements are evidence of the Chinese addiction to make believe, and their tendency to treat events that have happened despite them as having happened through their agency.' The Chinese had the ear of the world and many of these claims therefore went uncontested since the Tibetans had no such outreach.

Richardson was in Lhasa at the time of arrival of the young boy who had been identified as the 14th Dalai Lama. The four-year old sat through the ceremony of entry into the city and of blessing 'without turning a hair, looking most solemn and self-possessed.' He was not afraid of the Oracle who 'met him in a wild trance'. The boy kept gazing in the direction of the British entourage. By the third day of these ceremonies, the child was obviously tired and began to throw the money offerings into the open space in front of him; when his attendants tried to stop him, he turned his back to them and started to cry. At this, the Tibetans, according to Richardson, were very upset, regarding it as a bad omen. But the boy, in his words[34] was 'really extraordinary and one can almost believe in re-incarnation', as he was presented before the crowds and he was thought to behave exactly like his predecessor, the 13th Dalai Lama.

During the Second World War, Tibet remained neutral, voicing aspirations for peace and offering prayers. The authorities in Lhasa continued to be cautious about admitting Chinese, although a representative had been left behind in Lhasa by the envoy, Wu. In 1942, a new Tibetan Office of Foreign Affairs was opened in Lhasa by the local government for contact, liaison and communication with foreign representatives. The move was not welcomed by the Chinese representative who refused to deal with the new office. At the same time, the Tibetans, particularly the National Assembly, refused to dilute their idea of the neutrality and independence of Tibet. Two United States envoys for President Franklin D. Roosevelt, Captain Ilia Tolstoy (grandson of the writer Leo Tolstoy) and Lieutenant Brooke Dolan came to Lhasa around this time, bearing a letter for the Dalai Lama from the President. The Dalai Lama, in this author's interview with him in 2014,[35] recalled his meeting with the two Americans in 1942 in the presence of the Regent (the Reting Rinpoche), although as a young child, by his own admission, he had 'no interest in the letter' but only in the watch sent as a present by the U.S. President. He was to see the letter again when he was shown a copy by President Barack Obama during a meeting at the White House; that letter spoke of America engaging in a war to protect western civilization, democracy, and freedom. Permission for the journey of the Americans to Tibet had been first sought through the Chinese government and was refused by the Tibetans; it was later obtained through the Government of India. The principal object of their mission was reportedly to examine the possibility of a road route from India to China, although the Tibetans were not told of this. The Tibetan reply[36] to President Roosevelt's letter was to refer, in carefully chosen words, to the American advocacy of the rights of small nations, and their own desire to remain independent.

Throughout the period from the Chinese Revolution of 1911 until the entry of the PLA into Tibet, the Tibetans were unwilling to accept either sovereignty or suzerainty of China over Tibet, acknowledging only a relationship between Lama and disciple. Any acceptance of Chinese suzerainty was made conditional only in exchange for a formal recognition of Tibetan autonomy and a fixed boundary, as the discussions and outcome of the 1914 Simla Conference had shown. Until 1919, the Chinese did show some willingness to accept such terms but disagreement on the frontier between Inner and Outer Tibet prevented a resolution of this problem. After 1919, nationalist opinion in China hardened and the Chinese stand was that Tibet was a part of China that had temporarily broken away. The British never contested Chinese suzerainty over Tibet, with Prime Minister Churchill telling the Chinese Foreign Minister, Dr T.V. Soong in 1943 exactly this.[37] But growing concerns about the Chinese attitude towards Tibet resulted in the British reviewing the situation and the adoption of a new position. In August 1943, a memorandum addressed by Antony Eden (then British Foreign Secretary) to Dr Soong conveyed that the British government was prepared to accord the recognition of Chinese suzerainty over Tibet only on the understanding that Tibet was regarded as autonomous.

The Eden memorandum[38] began by stating that since the Chinese Revolution of 1911—when Chinese forces were withdrawn from Tibet—the latter had enjoyed de facto independence, regarding itself in practice as completely autonomous. The principle which guided the attitude of the British government towards Tibet was based on the memorandum sent by Lord Curzon (the then Foreign Secretary) to the then Chinese Minister in London, Dr Wellington Koo, in 1921. The memorandum stated that the British government did not feel justified in withholding any longer their recognition of the status of Tibet as an autonomous State under the suzerainty of China. It emphasized that the British government had always been prepared to recognize Chinese suzerainty over Tibet but 'only on the understanding that Tibet is regarded as autonomous'. There were no British territorial ambitions about Tibet, it was averred, but there was interest in maintaining friendly relations with Tibet, and 'the preservation of peaceful conditions in an area which is coterminous with the North-East frontiers of India.' It concluded by stating that Britain would welcome 'any amicable arrangements' which the Chinese government 'might be disposed to make with Tibet whereby the latter recognized Chinese suzerainty in return for an agreed frontier and an undertaking to recognize Tibetan autonomy, and they would gladly offer any help desired by both parties to this end.'

While a strict interpretation of the concept of suzerainty might have deterred Britain from assuming that Tibet could conduct its foreign relations, the authorities in Delhi felt free to deal in Lhasa with the newly established 'foreign office'. Indian support for Tibetan autonomy, it was felt, would help protect India's land frontier against any eventuality, with Tibet being added to a succession of buffer states that included Persia, Afghanistan and Nepal. Furthermore, any disputes that arose on the Himalayan border—the Mongolian Fringe—could be more easily settled with Tibet, was the view, than with China which, once in control of Tibet, could make the settlement of these disputes more difficult and contingent on various concessions. Pragmatism overruled the precepts of international law in this regard, as far as the British were concerned. Suzerainty seemed an academic inconvenience. The real question was what to do if the Chinese were to send their armies to occupy Tibet.

Indeed, the Chinese interest in Tibet did not flag during the war years, whatever the actual circumstances on the ground were, including the compulsions of the Anti-Japanese War and the conflict between the Guomindang and the Communists. The new Chairman of the Mongolian and Tibetan Affairs Commission, Harvard- and Sorbonne-educated Shen Tsung-lien (Shen Zonglian) told Basil Gould in October 1944 that Chiang Kai-shek could not regard Tibet otherwise than as an integral part of China. An amicable solution on Tibet should not conflict with basic Chinese beliefs. Shen even suggested to Gould that there might be value in a strictly bilateral Anglo-Chinese Conference on the subject.[39] The Government of India did not regard this as such a good idea.

The Tibetan attempts to present themselves as independent of China continued during the period. Internal chaos within China acted as a spur to these efforts. Surkhang Dzasa, one of the chief architects of Tibetan foreign policy during the period, was zealous about propagating the idea of Tibetan independence. A Tibetan goodwill mission was dispatched to India and China after the end of the war and the Allied victory. It was thought that this would be a means of establishing Tibetan representation abroad. In Nanjing, seat of the Chinese government, they attended the National Assembly. This suited the Chinese, demonstrating as it did, an act of the Tibetans folding into the great coming together of China's various ethnic groups. The Tibetans tried to explain the matter by saying they had intended to hand over a letter to Chiang Kai-shek asking for the return of Tibetan territory, and were told that this letter could only be answered in the Assembly to which they were invited. A similar attempt to present themselves as sovereign, was seen in the presence of a separate Tibetan delegation at the Asian Relations Conference in Delhi in 1947. The Guomindang delegation's protest resulted in the Tibetans agreeing not to use their flag. The Indian organizers did not go out of their way to contradict the Chinese demand.

There were similar Tibetan attempts to question the McMahon Line that had been drawn following the Lonchen Shatra–McMahon discussions of 1914. Writing in February 1946, Richardson[40] counselled against surprise in Delhi at the methods of the Tibetan government. He stated: 'The Tibetan government are aware of our claims to the McMahon Line; but it is their typical modus operandi to ignore those claims for as long as possible and to continue to regard themselves as being entitled to collect taxes in our jurisdiction in the hope they we may eventually give in to their persistence.' In Richardson's view, 'the Tibetan government has standards far different from those of any Western power, and that Tibetan methods must be met by an equally bland persistence in stating and restating our position.' An 'over-dramatization of the situation' was to be avoided. The best would be to follow 'Horace's precepts and be astonished at nothing; and preserve an 'equal mind'.'

Britain's involvement in Tibetan affairs from 1904 onwards was steered mainly by the need to ensure the presence of a buffer first against Czarist Russia and then, increasingly, against Chinese domination of Tibet, primarily to ensure the security of India. Never during this period did Britain recognize the independence of Tibet or attempt to incorporate it into the line of strategic defence of its empire as it had done in the case of Bhutan, Sikkim, and Nepal. Its emphasis appears to have been to neutralize or outweigh the influence of China and not seek undue influence or interference in the affairs of the Tibetan state. Also, China's position in what had been defined as 'Outer Tibet' in the 1914 Simla Convention was relegated to more foreign-power than suzerain presence. That was the British preference and it played to the advantage of the Tibetan ruling class in Lhasa, who in any event, was not at all averse to playing the British against the Chinese to their own advantage.

What about China's relations with Tibet? Writing in 1948, before the establishment of the Chinese People's Republic, the Chinese scholar Shenchi Liu[41] spoke of the manner in which ordinary Chinese perceived border regions like Tibet as being tied to China in a special 'blood' relationship forged at the time of the marriage of a Tang dynasty princess to the Tibetan king Songsten Gampo in 642 C.E. A common religion, Buddhism, provided another bond even if the Chinese people were never ever as religious as the Tibetans. According to Liu, the Chinese people saw the Dalai Lama as a Pope of the Buddhist faith and Tibet as a holy land. Further, the 14th Dalai Lama being from 'a Chinese family in Xining', Qinghai province, made this link even stronger. The power and influence of the Dalai Lama inside Tibet, according to this view, had been consolidated with Chinese help—all Chinese intervention against the Mongols, the Nepalese, and to quell internal strife in Tibet—had been done to protect the interests of the Dalai Lama.

'To the average Chinese, British expansion into Tibet dating from the 1904 military expedition is just the chip off the old block of England's China policy of the nineteenth century beginning with the notorious Opium War.'[42] This nationalist view of the Chinese was not regime-specific. It has persisted into the present. The Chinese had realized, according to this school of thought, that they had

> been called to pay a heavy price for India's security. First in the year 1886, she had signed off Burma which up till then was one of her tributary states. Then in the year 1890, she had to sign off Sikkim, another of her tributaries. And from about the same year to the eve of the Chinese Revolution, her political relation with two more tributaries, Nepal and Bhutan, was gradually replaced by that of England and ultimately disconnected in 1911. Now again this Lhasa Convention of 1904 completely ignored her legitimate rights over Tibet.

The demands for India's security[43] 'seemed to be growing with an insatiable appetite, all at the expense of China.' Little seems to have changed in terms of this Sino-centric view of questions of territory and nationhood grafted on to a pervasive sense of injury and historic grievance; the twenty-first century Chinese world view echoes it.

Liu's comments were expressed as the British were leaving India and a newly independent nation was finding its place on the global stage. Would India now adopt a new approach to Tibet, was the question this Chinese commentary asked. Would India be a mere inheritor of the British policy of buffer states and spheres of influence? And what would the Chinese Republic do? It would not grant Tibet independence. The 'folly' of what had happened with Outer Mongolia would not be repeated.[44] Thus, the fate of Tibet as always was to be dictated by forces beyond her borders; in 1947, she stood at history's crossroads, with little sense of direction, assuming that a long-prevailing status quo would continue. And to the Chinese mind at least, Tibet was an anachronism—its ruling class, whether religious or secular, only interested in self-preservation to the exclusion of their compatriots outside the circle of privilege, modernization, progress and exposure to the outside world.

On 15 August 1947, the British Mission in Lhasa became the Indian Mission. The head of the Lhasa office, Hugh Richardson, was asked to stay on by the Indian Government, pending the nomination of a successor. Richardson noted the anxiety among the Tibetan ruling circles about what the new dispensation in free India would hold for Tibet in terms of policy. Typical of affairs in Tibet, however, when the new flag of India went up over the Lhasa Mission on Independence Day, the Tibetans, according to Richardson, 'did not seem to notice the change'.[45] All this took place against the backdrop of the Reting affair[46] or conspiracy in which the Reting Rinpoche was arrested and put to death for allegedly conspiring with the Guomindang to establish a special relationship between Tibet and China. In November 1947, in a move illustrating their seeming ignorance of the protocols and practices of diplomatic communication between states, the Foreign Bureau in Lhasa also sent an en clair (uncoded) message to the British High Commission in Delhi (through the Indian Government's wireless channel and its Cypher Bureau) asking for British support in negotiations regarding the return of disputed territory in Assam to Tibet.[47]

In 1947, it was unclear what the future would hold for Tibet. A mission was dispatched abroad by the Tibetan authorities in Lhasa to indicate that Tibet was fully independent. The mission travelled on Tibetan passports (obtaining visas on them from the U.S. Consulate in Hong Kong), called on the U.S. Secretary of State without a Chinese escort and also made a gold purchase from the U.S. government. But independent India, which had inherited Britain's treaty obligations with regard to Tibet, was not prepared to take an unambiguous stand on Tibetan autonomy under Chinese suzerainty.[48]

In March 1948, the Indian Mission in Lhasa, under Hugh Richardson, reported that the Tibetan government had

reiterated a demand they asserted had been made at the Asian
Relations Conference in 1947, when 'leading functionaries' of the
Government of India had been approached 'for return to Tibet of
Tibetan territories on Indo-Tibet frontier viz. ZAYUL, Walong,
PEMAKO, LONAK LOPA MON, Bhutan, Sikkim, Darjeeling,
etc. on this side of river Ganges and LOWO, Ladakh, etc., up
boundary of Yarkhim.'[49] The Indian Mission in Lhasa noted
that the main object of Tibetan attention was the McMahon
Line area of the frontier and they were taking advantage of
the transitional period in India post-independence to seek a
favourable consideration of their request from the Government
of India. In response, the Government of India instructed the
Political Officer in Lhasa, Richardson, to tell the Tibetans that
India had succeeded to the rights and obligations of the British
government with regard to Tibet and 'will continue to abide by
the existing treaties until either party should wish to enter into
fresh arrangements'. On the basis of the continuation of these
treaty relations, the Government of India would stand by the
pledge as stipulated under the Anglo-Tibetan Convention of
1914 not to annex Tibet 'or any part of it.'[50] The message added
that the Government of India stood by an earlier offer, made in
January 1946 to the Tibetan government by the Political Officer in
Sikkim, A.J. Hopkinson, 'regarding negotiation of an adjustment
of the Indo-Tibetan frontier, particularly in the Tawang area'.[51] In
January 1946, Hopkinson left an aide memoire with the Tibetan
government in Lhasa in which it was stated that while India would
not vacate any territory that belonged to her (referring to territory
south of the McMahon Line and posts already occupied), she
had 'no intention of touching Tibetan territory' and in fact had
expressed 'willingness to make certain adjustments for the benefit
of the Tibetans'. In particular, the British Indian government was
'willing to negotiate a change in frontier in area of Tawang, north
of Sela (the Sela Pass), which would have the effect of adding that
area to the territory of Tibet.'[52] A final settlement of the Tibetan

frontier with India would be of great advantage to both Tibet and India, it was added.

In a note on the McMahon Line recorded on 19 July 1945, G.V. Kitson of the China Department of the UK Foreign Office[53] gave some more context to the decisions behind the offer made to the Tibetans in January 1946. The note revealed differences of opinion between the India Office and the Foreign Office on the issue. The former was in favour of the extension of effective control and administration in the territory south of the McMahon Line so as to bring to an end Tibetan encroachments there rather than 'to run the risk of having at a later stage to choose between driving out Chinese encroachments, with all the friction this would entail, and acquiescing in an unsatisfactory frontier.' The Foreign Office did not concur, taking the view that 'forcible action against the Tibetans, particularly if it led to a clash, would provide the Chinese with welcome material to attack our championship of Tibetan autonomy against Chinese aggression; and the resulting damage to our case (e.g. in the United States of America) might be more than the object to be achieved was worth.' The risks involved, according to this view, 'were out of all proportion to the advantages to be gained.' A meeting between the India Office and the Foreign Office in April 1943 then resulted in instructions being sent to the Government of India to postpone active steps to 'occupy the disputed districts pending the outcome of representations' to Lhasa and that 'there was much to be said for avoiding extension of control at any rate at the first stage to Tawang (north of the Se La Pass) or any other area to which the Tibetan Government attached special importance, and which was not essential to a satisfactory frontier, in the hope that we might secure an eventual agreement with the Tibetan Government under which, in return for the retrocession of such areas, they would reaffirm the rest of the McMahon Line.' Sir Basil Gould, the Political Officer for Sikkim, Bhutan and Tibet had then discussed these matters with the Tibetans in Lhasa. He had told them that Britain would

not withdraw posts already established on a permanent basis in
the areas south of the McMahon Line, and were not prepared
to forego their Treaty rights with Tibet. At the same time, they
regarded it important to do everything possible to avoid action
'which would make difficulties for the Tibetans vis-à-vis China'
and therefore, were willing to 'be accommodating over the details
of the McMahon Line settlement', and would 'be willing to alter
the frontier so as to include Tawang on the Tibetan side'. These
overtures apparently did not work. The Tibetans were brazen in
their violations of the McMahon Line. They claimed in April 1945
that any action by India to send personnel into 'Tibetan areas'
could not be accepted and such action 'would look something
like a big insect eating a smaller one'. It was following this protest
that the Government of India, while staying firm on their resolve
not to vacate posts already established, said they were prepared to
'agree to an adjustment in Tibet's favour in the Tawang area'. It
was hoped that this would provide a solution to the dispute with
the worst possible outcome being that the Tibetan Government
'under the influence of the monasteries (who are themselves
under Chinese influence) and prompted by the Chinese, might
denounce the 1914 Convention, or declare it to have been
abortive, at the same time shifting their policy towards China.'[54]
This was the background to the Hopkinson offer made through
the aide-memoire handed over to the Tibetans in January 1946,
which they did not respond to.

The offer on Tawang expressed a fundamental British
inclination not to disturb the status quo along the Assam frontier
(administration had not been extended into Tawang although
the town was clearly south of the McMahon Line, and therefore
British Indian territory although Tibetan officials and clergy
continued to be present), to keep the Tibetans placated during a
time of upheaval within China, an unspoken acknowledgement
that the Agreement of 1914 had not been consummated by
bringing China on board, that the borders of Inner Tibet with

China had not been affirmed by China or true autonomy for Tibet guaranteed, and that it was essential to keep the Tibet as a buffer,[55] which would mean that Lhasa should not be distanced from Delhi. It was also an offer that Britain told the Tibetans, where they were willing to make an adjustment along the boundary 'to meet Tibetan wishes', that could not be extended indefinitely, it required a quick reply because the settlement of the Indo-Tibetan boundary was an urgent need, too much time had been lost by failing to act on the McMahon-Lonchen Shatra discussions of 1914 which had essentially resulted in an unstable situation of growing confrontation in these frontier areas between the Tibetan and British Indian officials. The premise was that this was not Tibetan territory but territory south of the McMahon Line and therefore British/Indian, where an adjustment of the frontier was being made to favour the Tibetans. The offer was also predicated on the assumption that Britain/India would deal only with the Tibetans, that Tibet would remain Tibetan without any spectre of Chinese ingress or takeover. Why the offer was reiterated in 1948 is difficult to explain, until the archives are fully accessible for scholars to understand the reasoning that prompted its repetition. In any event, once the Chinese PLA had begun its military push into Tibet from 1950 onwards, Delhi knew that the Tibetan buffer no longer foregrounded China for India, that the buffer concept had lost all meaning. The Northeast frontier had to be fully secured, and Tawang being south of the McMahon Line, was sovereign Indian territory and was legitimately included in this process of consolidation of Indian administration over territory deemed as fully Indian.

In October 1948, it was reported by the British Embassy in Nanjing that the Indian Ambassador there had received a note from the Chinese Foreign Office stating that 'the Chinese government wish to regulate their relations with India by a treaty of commerce and amity, which as drafted by the Chinese government, would contain a provision for redefinition of the boundaries of China and

India.'[56] It was reported by the Embassy that 'reference is made to Tibet with the implication that this is a question affecting Chinese trade'. The Indian Ambassador in Nanjing, K.M. Panikkar was reportedly not favourably disposed to this Chinese demand saying that any trade arrangements previously concluded by the British Indian government with Tibet could not be arbitrarily abrogated without consulting the Tibetans, 'the Indian government having accepted the obligation of H.M.G towards Tibet continued to recognize Tibetan autonomy and only the suzerainty as opposed to the sovereignty of China.' Meanwhile, the British in Nanjing were also reporting to London the interest in Tibet as expressed in the Chinese media. The leading vernacular *Ch'ien Hsien Jih Pao* in a front-page article was speaking of the 'very frightening things' going on in Tibet because of its proximity to India.[57] The British still had political agents in Lhasa it was alleged. The growth of a centrifugal tendency had been encouraged in Tibet. 'We feel extreme alarm about the future of Tibet,' it was stated.

A telegram[58] from the Government of India to the Commonwealth Relations Office (CRO) in London at the same time said that both the British and Indian governments had informed the Tibetan government that the (Indian) government 'has acquiesced in position that since 15 August 1947 rights and obligations arising from existing treaties with Tibet have devolved on the Government of India.' The position was further confirmed by the CRO to the UK High Commission in Delhi on the 29 October 1948, in a secret letter[59] that stated: 'We have always considered that the relations between ourselves and Tibet were governed by the 1914 Convention, despite China's refusal to ratify or to take any account of it, since by that time Tibet had established the autonomy and has maintained it ever since. We recognized China's suzerainty over Tibet but never accepted the Chinese claim that Tibet was a part of China.'

Contemporaneous with the Partition and the Independence of India, China had plunged into a full-scale civil war between the Nationalists and the Communists. India's ties with the Nationalist government in Nanjing started off as cordial and close, although these deteriorated with the withdrawal of the Nationalists from Nanjing in early 1949 and terminated with the recognition of the People's Republic on 30 December that year. Tibet was the only issue that caused friction between India and the Nationalist government (the case of the separate Tibetan delegation at the Asian Relations Conference in 1947 discussed earlier). The Tibetans in Lhasa were questioning the validity of the McMahon Line and claiming border areas south of the line—something Nehru also revealed in Parliament in September 1959. China's desire to review and terminate the 1908 Trade Regulations was disputed by India which stated that relations with Tibet were regulated by the 1914 Simla Convention. The close contacts between the Tibetan Trade delegation and Delhi, instead of Nanjing, and the expelling of the Chinese mission in Lhasa by the Tibetans in July 1949 (with all Chinese officials leaving via India) even as the British representative, Richardson remained there after independence to represent India, were other sources of friction.[60] To the Tibetan claim on border areas, the reply from Delhi was that the Government of India 'would be glad to have an assurance that it is the intention of the Tibetan Government to continue relations on the existing basis until new agreements are reached on matters that either party may wish to take up. This is the procedure adopted by all other countries with which India has inherited treaty relations from His Majesty's Government.'[61] The expulsion of the Chinese mission was interpreted as an assertion of Tibetan independence by the British media.[62] On the Chinese part, the retention of Richardson as head of the Indian mission in Lhasa was seen as symbolizing 'the continuity of the British forward Tibet policy' and as having 'incited and, perhaps prompted the new communist regime to mount the military occupation of Tibet in October 1950.'[63]

Richardson was to stay in Lhasa until the arrival of his Indian successor, Sumul Sinha; his diary in those last days before the Chinese army effectively displaced the old regime in Lhasa speaks nostalgically about Tibet before the fall. In his words,[64] to call Tibet anything but independent would have been blatantly untrue. These were a friendly, humourous people, totally devoted to their religion. The Tibetan world was self-governing, self-sufficient, apart in race, language, thinking and behaviour from the Chinese. But that world was not ever-lasting—1950 was a watershed year.

Some of the old Tibet hands like Richardson, Robert Ford[65] and Algernon Rumbold were still around in 1990 when late that year, a meeting—described as an 'extraordinary throwback to 1947–50'[66]—was held in the Foreign and Commonwealth Office in London to discuss Tibet. In a throwback to Empire, present at the meeting were Sinophiles who took their lead from Nanjing (China before 1949) and the British Foreign Office, as also 'Tibetophiles' who depended on (pre-Independence) Delhi for directions and the approach to Tibetan affairs. Differences of emphasis among British policy makers on Tibet were endemic, it was felt, going back to the 'forward' and 'masterly inactivity' dichotomy. When the question of Tibet and the imminent invasion by China came up before the United Nations in 1950, it was the China/Foreign Office line of the Sinophiles which prevailed (masterly inactivity). At the 1990 meeting, Richardson who was present, reiterated that the government in Lhasa prior to 1950 was 'beyond question in complete control of its own affairs, dealing directly with the Government of India in such matters as frontier disputes, trade questions, supply of arms and ammunition'. Despite threats from China, they had refused permission for the Chinese to send troops into Tibet to accompany the Panchen Lama and, also in the face of threats, they maintained their neutrality during the war by refusing to allow the transit of military supplies to China across Tibet. According to Richardson, in 1950, at the United Nations, the British—who were the only government to have treaty relations with the Tibetans—had sold them down the river. The view about independent Tibet was corroborated by Robert Ford who drew reference to the fact that he had been employed by the Tibetan government and had travelled in Tibet on Tibetan documents.

At the same meeting, Algernon Rumbold said that the most salient factor along the northern border of India was that Tibet was a totally separate and distinct area, racially different and with a distinct religion. What mattered was the situation and policies of 1911–50. The British had contained the military threat from China and outside powers up to 1947, 'something the Indians signally failed to maintain.' Rumbold brought up the issue of suzerainty and autonomy saying that these had never been accepted by the Chinese or Tibetans. The clearest statement of the British position had been given by Anthony Eden in 1943—it balanced suzerainty against autonomy for Tibet, implicitly acknowledging its right to enter into treaties and to send and receive diplomatic agents.

In 1993, the British government claimed in a communication to Hugh Richardson that there was no 'legally authoritative', or UN-approved definition of autonomy.[67] Interestingly, at the same time, it referred to most countries, including India, ostensibly recognizing Chinese sovereignty over Tibet and only Britain, alone, regarding the relationship of China to Tibet 'as one of suzerainty'. This position was to alter irrevocably in 2008[68] when Foreign Secretary David Miliband, in a written ministerial statement, described the concept of suzerainty as outdated and casting doubts that Britain was denying Chinese sovereignty over Tibet. Miliband went on record to further state that Britain regarded Tibet as part of the People's Republic of China and that it did not 'support Tibetan independence'. The statement while not specifically acknowledging Chinese sovereignty in Tibet spoke of 'meaningful autonomy' for Tibet 'within the framework of the Chinese constitution.' It was a move with significant implications, tearing up as it did, ninety-four years of British policy toward Tibet, dating back to the early twentieth century, in what smelt of a Faustian bargain aimed at placating China and its economic and political weight on the world stage. The change in policy was not subjected to public or parliamentary debate. The decision had wider implications, as some experts[69] noted: 'India's claim to a part of its northeast territories, for example, is largely based on the notes exchanged (between the British and Tibetan representatives) during the Simla convention of 1914, which set the boundary between India and Tibet—that the British appear to have just discarded. That may seem minor to London, but it was over those same documents that a major war between India and China was fought in 1962 . . .' *The Economist* magazine[70] called it 'an early twenty-first century solution to an early-twentieth century problem'. Britain had 'quietly junked' its long-standing position on Tibet—a position it had held even into the 1990s, as the letter to Richardson, quoted above, shows.

These developments recalled a past debate on the McMahon Line and Tibet's competence to sign international agreements. It took place after the conflict of 1962, and the Chinese operations south of the international border in the North East Frontier Agency (NEFA). A British Foreign Office note[71] of 20 November 1962 dealt with the question at some length. The British, with their involvement in the subject from pre-independence days, were of the view that the validity of the Simla Convention of 1914 and particularly the Anglo-Tibetan Exchange of Letters of March 1914, formalizing the Line, depended on 'whether at that time Tibet was competent to enter into them.' If Tibet did 'not have a sufficient degree of independence to do so, then those agreements have no effect'. If, however, Tibet was competent to do so, 'any subsequent loss of competence would not affect their validity'. The British, the note went on to say, had dealt with Tibet in 1914 'on the basis that she was competent' and it would be 'difficult for us to go back on that now'. Referring to the defining of India's frontiers in the arrangements made for the independence of India, it was stated that 'the general rule is that in the case of change of sovereignty agreements relating to frontiers pass to the Successor State, in other words, the frontiers of that State are those which were established before the change of sovereignty.' Similarly, on China extending her authority over Tibet, 'her frontier with India would be that established in 1914'.

Today, the question of Tibet's legal position appears to have been summarily consigned to the pages of history. As discussed earlier, the Chinese claim had been vested in the concept of suzerainty—the suzerain-vassal relationship. It was a system not unknown to other parts of the world as was the case with the vassal states of the Balkans which had been liberated from Turkish domination in the nineteenth century and entered the global comity of nations. Absorption by the suzerain was uncommon in the mid-twentieth century at a time when overlordship was disappearing internationally, and the world was seeing the end of imperial domination of colonial territories. The Chinese action in Tibet had gone against the grain and the trend established in this era. Writing on the subject in April 1954, C.H. Alexandrowicz, a Research Professor at the University of Madras,[72] termed suzerainty as lacking juristic precision being originally an institution of feudal law. With the disappearance of feudalism and dynastic politics, such suzerainty had also been erased. A different type of suzerainty that existed in modern international law was a kind of international guardianship. The vassal states of the nineteenth and twentieth centuries did not possess external sovereignty though they retained internal sovereignty, which the suzerain state is under duty to respect. However, as the instances of the Balkan states had shown, many of these vassal states had thrown off the suzerain's control and become independent. Thus, suzerainty 'became a *nominal* title ripe for elimination or conversion into a title more favourable to the subordinate state.' Alexandrowicz saw this latter development as of great importance in the consideration of the Tibetan case.

In the early twentieth century, Tibet had begun to enter the field of wider international intercourse with the advent of British influence and ingress in its territory and the collapse of the Manchu empire. At the end of empire in China and the emergence of the Chinese Republic in 1911, suzerainty over Tibet could, in Alexandrowicz's view, no longer operate under the concept of feudal law but in the wider orbit of international law. The Simla Conference of 1914 saw a greatly reduced role for China in Tibet. Furthermore, Tibet unlike in the normal vassal-suzerain relationship, did not participate in the military conflicts that China was engaged in as a belligerent during the First and Second World Wars. During the Second World War, Tibet—in emphasis of her neutrality—had opposed the opening of strategic communications and the transport of military goods through her territory. But the British persisted in using the concept of suzerainty, or at least the term, to define China's connection with Tibet, even though this had been reduced to a completely nominal state. Of course, China did not at any stage, give up its aspirations regarding Tibet. And with the Chinese invasion of 1950, Tibet's brief interlude of having moved from vassal to virtual independence, had ended forever. Attempts by Tibet to raise the issue before the United Nations did not succeed given the lack of support from India, since, as has been observed, 'it was clear that Indian policy was to 'sacrifice' Tibet in exchange for playing a role on the Korean Peninsula and on the world stage.'[73] Perhaps, Indian policy makers post-independence, and especially Prime Minister Nehru, should have read Foreign Secretary Caroe's advice in 1945 more carefully[74]. That advice stated firstly that the maintenance of the Tibetan buffer was a matter of the utmost importance for India (especially from the point of view of defence), secondly, that Tibet should enjoy internal autonomy and the right to conduct direct foreign relations, recognizing Chinese suzerainty as more or less ceremonial, thirdly, support for Tibetan autonomy should involve outspoken diplomatic pressure internationally, publicity for the 'realities of Tibet's position' since 1912, and the supply of munitions and equipment if sought by the Tibetan government. Lastly, Caroe opined that there could be advantage in bringing the position of Tibet before the United Nations. By 1950, it was too late for such advice to be a complete tool-kit for India on Tibet, but even the language of 'buffer' aside, India's public stance could have been more unequivocal about the preservation of meaningful autonomy for Tibet, speaking about Tibet's de-facto independence and conduct of foreign relations, providing arms and ammunition to the Tibetan government as needed, and supporting Tibet's position in the United Nations. In retrospect, India's approach can be faulted for its excessive circumspection, caution bordering on timidity, and the suspension of disbelief about Communist China and its policies on strategic peripheries like Tibet and Xinjiang. Strategically, India acquiesced in being short-changed and where she could have led a global initiative questioning China's Tibet policy, she preferred the path of renunciation and calculated indifference.

Submerged in this debate is the question of how the Chinese reconciled their vision of a Sinocentric world order in Westphalian terms, including the concepts of suzerainty or sovereignty regarding Tibet. New research in the Taiwanese archives has revealed some interesting insights. This indicates that the concept of 'Chinese suzerainty over Tibet' was a Western term the Chinese, during the Qing period, could not be coerced into accepting by the British. The Qing were 'quite skillful in diplomatic negotiations, deliberately forwarding a position of ambiguity on Tibet's status until it could ensure more favourable terms.'[75] The Qing had, by this account, offered Tibet 'patronage and protection in exchange for the spiritual guidance of Tibetan Buddhism'. At the same time, Tibet had control over its diplomatic ties with the Himalayan 'polities' especially, while at the same time pledging a form of allegiance to the Qing court. Terms like 'suzerain' and 'vassal' are essentially terms from European feudal law (although as the Japanese

scholar Okamoto Takashi[76] points out, *concepts like shangguo* or
zongzhuguo—upper state/suzerain state — and *shuguo*—dependent
state—existed historically, in East Asia between China and Korea
and China and Mongolia or China and Tibet). But suzerainty
'defies sameness' across the spectrum of its application—in some
cases, it is nominal, while in others it is substantive. In the early
twentieth century, Tibetans, Chinese and British officials each
tried their best to define Tibetan institutions and polity 'in forms
compatible with Western international order that would further
their own respective parochial interests.' The Chinese refused to
endorse the 1904 Anglo-Tibetan Convention on the grounds that it
violated Chinese *zhuquan* which can be considered commensurate
with the English word 'sovereignty'. The Qing had started to coin
Chinese neologisms to fit the construct of Western legal terms. The
British interpreted the term *zhuquan* to mean 'suzerainty'—all this
was not just a matter of semantics, but politics. Tang Shaoyi, the
Qing diplomat negotiating the terms of 'adhesion' by China to the
1904 Convention had served in Korea and was witness to Korea
being 'formally wrested from the Sinocentric world order with the
conclusion of the 1895 Shimonoseki Treaty'. Tang understood the
'centrality of language' to the transformation of the international
order. If China accepted 'suzerainty' in Tibet, it could devolve into
her having no political authority in Tibet. He skirted both terms—
sovereignty and suzerainty—and suggested that the British should
simply refer to 'the existing authority of China over Tibet.' This
was unacceptable to Lord Curzon, the British viceroy in India, who
saw China as seeking to extract a recognition of her sovereignty
over Tibet which the term 'existing authority' could always be
interpreted to imply at a later stage. Britain, said Curzon, was
doing a 'very handsome thing in recognizing Chinese suzerainty
at all.' The wrangle over suzerainty vs. sovereignty continued until
the Chinese occupation of Tibet in 1951. China had a weak hand
in Tibet until then but she played it adroitly, resisting pressure to
resolve Tibet's status until the terms were more favourable to her.

No country in the world questions Chinese sovereignty over Tibet, today. Concepts like suzerainty, sovereignty, autonomy and independence are terms from the Western political imaginary, as has been noted, denoting a scripting of Tibetan status in a manner that can only be described as 'strategic hypocrisy'.[77] And, the Chinese had the last word when they applied the most absolute term in the European 'terminological armory—sovereignty' to Tibet from 1951.'[78] Tibet, from being the 'Cinderella of the (British) Indian Foreign Office' (Hopkinson quoting Charles Bell)[79] moved on to being the geopolitical Cinderella of independent India's Foreign Office and then of the world community of nations. At no point did either Britain or India (or for that matter, the United States) make any serious commitment to Tibetan autonomy—the ambiguity of this term was eminently embraceable. In that sense, it is not misplaced to observe, that the West, 'through its imperial scripting of modern Tibet, has been an ally of China in the latter's appropriation of the modern vocabulary of sovereignty.'[80] The 2008 move by the British Foreign Office, finally negating their previous concept of Chinese suzerainty over Tibet—in an unambiguous endorsement of Chinese sovereignty—settled any debate that had previously existed on the issue. The United States, for its part, during those eventful days leading up to the entry of Chinese forces into Tibet, and the conclusion of the 17-Point Agreement, never took a final legal position relative to Tibet, leaving it open if 'developments warrant' for consideration to be given to 'recognition of Tibet as an independent state.' An aide-memoire from the State Department to the British Embassy in Washington D.C. of 6 January 1951, stated that 'the United States Government recognizes the de facto autonomy that Tibet has exercised since the fall of the Manchu Dynasty and particularly since the Simla Conference'. It added that if the Tibetan case be introduced into the United Nations, there would be 'ample basis for international concern regarding Chinese Communist intentions toward Tibet to justify under the U.N. Charter, a hearing of the case in either the

United Nations Security Council or the United Nations General Assembly'. It did not appear, however that the United States had 'ever taken an official public stand in respect to the legal position of Tibet' despite being one of the early supporters of the principle of self-determination of peoples. Events in Korea seemed to take precedence over Tibet. It appeared to seem that the Western powers had decided that it was India that had a 'primary interest' in Tibet and that India's reactions should guide the trajectory of the global response to events there[81].

In 1947 as the successor state to Britain, India inherited all the obligations with regard to agreements relating to frontiers, reached before the transfer of power. By that definition, India was entitled to maintain that her northeastern frontier was based on the McMahon Line as agreed between the UK and Tibet in 1914. The question was whether China could be regarded as a successor state in regard to Tibet's frontiers. The answer to that question was never given, for the Chinese Communist interlocutors of the young Indian Republic consistently maintained that the McMahon Line was illegal.[82]

In the wake of the Chinese invasion of Tibet in 1950, India gradually and voluntarily conceded her privileges in Tibet, signalling an acknowledgement of Chinese sovereignty. Even as Nehru and the Government of India were emphasizing the inviolability of India's mountain frontiers with China, the intrinsic linkage between this frontier in its northeastern section with the status of Tibet, was never made.

With the fate of Tibet thus sealed, the advice from Richardson in Lhasa in November 1949 seems prescient, almost foretelling the fateful events of the decade that followed. With the imminent danger of the new Communist government in Beijing entering Tibet, Richardson advocated[83] 'diplomatic negotiations on Tibet' after the recognition of the Communist regime. Tibet, he said, had served as an effective buffer for over forty years. Its commercial value to India was insignificant—but not its geopolitical value. The Government of India's relations with Tibet were governed by the 1914 Simla Convention which had replaced earlier agreements, and under this Convention, recognition of Chinese suzerainty was conditional on Chinese acceptance of Tibetan autonomy and of the China-Tibet boundary (i.e., the boundary between Inner and Outer Tibet). The Government of India had not acknowledged Chinese suzerainty over Tibet since it ended in 1911. They had, on the contrary, asserted and exercised their right to have direct dealings with Tibet and refused transit visas to Chinese travellers to Tibet whose entry was not agreed to by the Tibetan government. All the rights and obligations of the Government of India in Tibet were based on the 1914 Convention, 'and we cannot claim the one while repudiating the other'. Importantly, the boundary between India and Tibet was laid down in 1914 and if the Convention was disregarded, India would be exposed to 'renewed Chinese claims to the Assam tribal area'.

These words were to have little impact in Delhi. The Prime Minister himself, was sanguine that there would be practically 'no chance of any military danger in India arising from any possible change in Tibet'.[84] It was only after the divisions in the Cabinet began to surface, culminating in a letter to the Prime Minister from Sardar Patel in November 1950 (discussed in our next chapter), that the recognition of a new military threat facing India squarely on its once-Tibetan and now-Chinese frontier began to be acted upon from late 1950 onwards.

On the Chinese side, suspicions about the Indian position regarding Tibet were always rampant. The view was that India was emphasizing its interest in the Tibet issue, the border issue, and the 'Tibetan autonomy issue with an aim to prevent our (Chinese) liberation of Tibet under the disguise of the peaceful settlement of the Tibet issue.' The Chinese claimed that the Indians had been told on more than one occasion that China wished to settle the issue in a peaceful manner. According to the Chinese version of events[85], from October 1950 onwards, 'India publicly expressed its intention to interfere with our internal affairs with an aim to prevent our liberation of Tibet' and that China had emphasized that the Tibet issue was a 'domestic issue of China and no foreign interference is allowed.'[86]

The victory of the Communists in the civil war in China directly influenced the official Indian attitude on Tibet. In a Secret note[87] addressed to Secretary General G.S. Bajpai in the Ministry of External Affairs on 9 July 1949, Prime Minister Nehru conveyed directions that the Indian mission in Lhasa should be continued. Friendly relations with the Tibetan government should be maintained and India 'should give them such aid as we have been giving in the past.' At the same time, Nehru was emphatic in cautioning that no measures 'which might be considered a challenge to the Chinese Communist government or might mean an invasion of Tibetan sovereignty' should be taken.' Strangely enough, the Prime Minister appeared sanguine about any military threat from Tibet, discounting it altogether 'whatever may be the ultimate fate of Tibet in relation to China.' There was no necessity for the Defence Ministry to consider any possible military repercussions on the India-Tibetan frontier, Nehru concluded.

Prime Minister Nehru went on record[88] on the subject in November 1949 on the eve of the recognition of the People's Republic, at a press conference in New Delhi. Asked about Tibet, Mr. Nehru spoke in Hindi to say that for the last forty years, during British rule in India, 'a certain autonomy of Tibet' had been recognized. This had enabled 'direct relations' between India and Tibet, he said. At the same time, regarding China's position in Tibet, 'a vague kind of suzerainty was recognized.' These matters had never been clearly defined, and the 'matter remained vague', he added. In a 'vague sense we have accepted the fact of Chinese suzerainty' he told the media. 'How far it goes, one does not know.'

Secretary-General Bajpai told the UK High Commissioner that he had discussed the Tibet problem with the Prime Minister and that the 'Government of India were as anxious as any past Government of India to retain Tibet as a buffer between them and China and they certainly did not want to see any increase in Chinese and still less Chinese Communist influence there. On the other hand, the present regime in Tibet was completely out of date and they did not feel the Lamas could in the long run resist Chinese infiltration'. Sir Girija felt that India did not have the military resources to 'effectively defend' Tibet if the Chinese Communists intervened there. India would then only have to concentrate on defending her borders against Chinese military aggression and infiltration.[89]

The Foreign Secretary K.P.S. Menon spoke to the UK High Commissioner on the quandary confronting New Delhi on Tibet.[90] India was concerned about whether the Indian mission in Lhasa should be retained with the Foreign Secretary saying that the mission 'had in fact no right to be at Lhasa since the 1914 Treaty (the Simla Convention) which had not been accepted by China only provided for occasional visits.' The American Ambassador in Delhi, Loy Henderson reporting to the Secretary of State in January 1950 on a conversation with Menon, said that the latter told him India would give diplomatic support to Tibet to enable it to retain its autonomous status if the Chinese refused to recognize such autonomy. But he also emphasized that 'India wished to leave the matter alone and would not initiate any conversations with the Chinese regarding Tibet unless compelled to do so by Chinese actions.' Sounding a note of contradiction, Menon added that his government 'looks with disfavour on any attempt by Tibet to join the U.N. because it raises issue of Tibet's status and could not possibly succeed.' Several times Menon said during this conversation that India also wishes to avoid 'any provocative action' regarding Tibet.[91] Earlier, the British had reported their impression that Ambassador Panikkar seemed to be partly responsible for the Indian Government's doubts as to whether they could do much about Tibet. Panikkar told the British in conversation in Delhi that 'developments in Xinjiang and in outer Tibet could not fail to influence the people of Tibet proper and

that the present Lama regime was out of date and weak to resist
any real pressure from the Chinese Communists. He said that
even a small expedition could dispose of the present regime (in
Lhasa).' Panikkar was of the view that the opening of diplomatic
relations with the new government in China would strengthen
India's hand regarding discussions on the Tibetan problem.[92] The
Foreign Secretary taking a more 'robust' view, as the British put
it, felt that Panikkar's viewpoint was 'perhaps too realistic' in that
it was 'roughly to the effect that there was nothing India could do
to prevent the Chinese from taking over Tibet'. Without really
being able to influence matters in any way, the British felt that a
'defeatist view' or fatalism on the part of the Government of India
regarding Tibet should be discouraged. The status of Tibet was
important to India because of the eventual threat to her security
across her Himalayan borders. But their advice was equally out of
touch with what was to come. The recipe offered to the Indians
was that they should extend diplomatic support to Tibet and that
in any case, military intervention by the Communist Chinese
government in Tibet was highly unlikely. But, Tibet, Britain also
realized, was now primarily an Indian concern. It would be Indian
moves on the issue that would, along with the counterpoise of
forcible military intervention by the Chinese in Tibet, seal the
region's fate.[93] Stating its opinion[94] on the question of relations
between China and India in view of the establishment of the
Dominions of India and Pakistan, the Foreign Office in London
said that the Indian Independence (International Arrangements)
Order of 1947 clearly defined the principles according to which
treaty rights and obligations would devolve as between India and
Pakistan, and that if 'any of the Treaties now under discussion
have an exclusive territorial application to one or other of the two
Dominions, it will be upon that Dominion that the obligations
and rights of any such Treaty will devolve.' The Foreign Office in
London defined the Indo-Tibetan Agreement of 1914 respecting
the India-Tibet frontier as an example.

3

Fateful Decisions

The local officials and the Tibetan leaders used to come and talk about Gyanak. 'Gya' means foreign, 'Nak' means black, the black foreigner. But an Indian was 'Gyakar' which meant the White Indian, not that we are white-coloured people, but they gave their own sort of colour scheme—those who they called the crystal white-hearted, clear-hearted people, were the good people; and to them, the Chinese were the dark-hearted people.

—Major S.M. Krishnatry, Indian Trade Agent in Gyantse, referring to Tibet before the entry of Chinese troops in 1950[1]

India's Tibet policy post-independence, was spelt out in a note[2] by K.M Panikkar, at that time in between his ambassadorial assignments in Nanjing and Beijing. Panikkar was dismissive about views held by some in the Foreign Office that Tibet be maintained as a buffer state, saying this was completely unrealistic. India had upheld the theory of 'Chinese suzerainty' and the attempts of 'Anglo-Indian diplomatists to make the acceptance of Chinese suzerainty conditional on the assurance that the autonomy of Tibet will be guaranteed to us was never accepted by China even in the days of her extreme weakness'. It was the Chinese position, consistently maintained, that Tibet enjoyed autonomy as an internal relationship with China, he said. Beyond 'trade rights and recognized boundary', India's interests in Tibet were but 'shadowy', Panikkar opined. Any military intervention in Tibet to safeguard the Tibetans was out of question. Panikkar's recommendation to the Prime Minister was that the wisest policy would be give such assistance 'as we can' to the Tibetans but to remain 'strictly neutral' when 'the situation develops' on the grounds that it was an internal affair of China. He also discounted action to safeguard Tibetan interests through the United Nations. He saw the Russians as vetoing any move to help Tibet in the Security Council. As far as the General Assembly was concerned, again, India's position was difficult as the case of Hyderabad was technically on the agenda and India could 'not object seriously to a Suzerain power stepping into an autonomous unit to enforce its authority'. By 1950-51, in the wake of recognition of the People's Republic and the establishment of diplomatic relations with Beijing, Panikkar[3] was telling the British Ambassador there that the Indian attitude to Tibet was that 'apart from cultural and economic establishment of relations, India is not politically interested in Tibet'. It was obvious that the Government of India did not want the development of their relations with China to be adversely affected by the developments in Tibet if they could help it. Reporting from Beijing[4], the British were of the view that there was 'no likelihood of active intervention by India with the Chinese government in Tibetan affairs'.

The view that there was nothing India could do to 'save' Tibet, was endorsed by the Foreign Secretary K.P.S. Menon.[5] He disagreed, however, with Panikkar's premise that India had never regarded Tibet 'as an independent country' saying that India had inherited the commitments of the British government, specifically quoting at this juncture from the Eden Memorandum of 1943 that Chinese suzerainty in Tibet could only be accepted on the understanding that Tibet was regarded as autonomous. According to Menon, to treat Tibet as an 'internal affair' of China was out of the question. Buttressing this argument, the Political Officer in Sikkim, Harishwar Dayal in a telegram[6] to Delhi in the same month, claimed that the Government of India had not acknowledged Chinese suzerainty over Tibet since 1911, asserting and exercising their 'right' to have direct dealings with Tibet and even refusing visas to Chinese travellers to Tibet whose entry was not agreed to by the Tibetan government.

Communicating a summary of Ambassador Panikkar's views on Tibet to the Political Officer in Sikkim and Lhasa on 11 November 1949[7], the Ministry of External Affairs in Delhi was sure that by May or June 1950, the 'Communists would intervene in Tibet.' The inaccessibility of Tibet was a myth, it was stated. If the Chinese regime decided to 'liberate' Tibet nothing would stop them, barring 'miracles or serious international complications'. The idea of maintaining Tibet as a buffer state was completely unrealistic. A buffer state could exist only if such a state were independent. The telegram from Delhi went on to state that it 'has never been our point of view that Tibet is an independent country; we have in fact upheld the theory of Chinese suzerainty'. And on a note of surrender, 'If China decides to make her suzerainty effective, we have hardly any right to intervene so long as our Treaty interests are safeguarded'. Those 'interests', India was defining now as trade rights and a *recognized boundary*. Through careful negotiations it was necessary to defend these trading rights 'though we must be prepared to face the extinction of our political influence'. India intended to remain strictly neutral. 'The establishment of normal diplomatic relations with China is the only way in which we can hope to influence the course of events at that stage'.

Meanwhile, Sumul Sinha[8] the Political Officer in Lhasa was communicating a line very different from Panikkar's in Beijing.

The Foreign Bureau of the Tibetans in Lhasa was anxious to negotiate a new treaty with India, he told Delhi. The desire to negotiate a new treaty was to obtain from the Government of India that the latter regarded 'Tibet as an independent country and NOT (repeat NOT) merely an autonomous region'. The Bureau felt this would strengthen Tibet's position in the world. Similar declarations would be sought from the governments of the U.K and the U.S., it was conveyed. The Tibetans sought modern arms and ammunition with machinery for manufacture of ammunition, and training of troops, Sinha said, and they wanted a visit by a 'Senior Indian Military Officer' to advise them. According to him, diplomatic negotiations on Tibet after recognition of the new government in China 'would be our best line'. Sinha was convinced[9] that Tibet had served as an effective buffer over the last forty years, its commercial value to India was insignificant and in fact the Government of India's policy to Tibet so far had been based entirely on political grounds. The 1914 Simla Convention remained the basis for the determination of relations with Tibet; under it, recognition of Chinese suzerainty was conditional on Chinese acceptance of Tibetan autonomy and of the China–Tibet boundary. The Government of India had not acknowledged Chinese suzerainty over Tibet since it ended in 1911. India had in fact, since 1911, asserted and exercised her right to have direct dealings with Tibet. Significantly, and this would have implications later for the Indo-Tibetan boundary as defined by the McMahon Line, the rights as well as obligations concerning Tibet, were based on the 1914 Convention, 'and we cannot claim the one while repudiating the other'. The boundary between India and Tibet was laid down in 1914 and Sinha warned that 'if the Convention is disregarded, we shall expose ourselves to renewed Chinese claims to Assam tribal area.'

In a meeting Prime Minister Nehru chaired to discuss Tibet policy in December 1949,[10] where the Foreign Secretary, Panikkar and Harishwar Dayal were present, Nehru was of the view that the Indian position on Tibet was 'weak', both in the military and diplomatic spheres. Furthermore, there was no recognition internationally of the autonomy of Tibet. Although the supply of arms and ammunition to the Tibetans as requested by them could be positively considered, great care would have to be taken about the nature of the supplies so as not to foster the impression that India 'was actively encouraging the Tibetans to fight the Chinese'.

Meanwhile, in a conversation with Vice Foreign Minister Zhang Hanfu in Beijing on the 13 August 1950, Ambassador Panikkar told the Chinese that the Government of India 'never had nor do they have now any political or territorial ambition in Tibet' and wished to stabilize the Chinese-Indian border. This statement by Panikkar was welcomed by the Chinese government.[11] There was more to come. On 24 August 1950, the Foreign Office in New Delhi dispatched a telegram to the Indian Embassy in Beijing containing the text of an aide-memoire[12] which they instructed should be handed over to the Chinese Foreign Minister (the post was held by Premier Zhou Enlai, just as the case was with Prime Minister Nehru in Delhi). Interestingly, the message from Delhi to the Embassy contained the following line, that the Government of India 'sincerely hope that the forthcoming negotiations (with the Tibetan authorities) will result in a harmonious adjustment of legitimate Tibetan claims to autonomy within the framework of Chinese sovereignty'. The word 'sovereignty' had inexplicably replaced 'suzerainty'. A few days earlier, on 15 August[13], Ambassador Panikkar had also used the word 'sovereignty' instead of 'suzerainty' in discussing Tibet with Vice Minister Zhang Hanfu. He was conveying Nehru's message that India had no political interests in Tibet. By using the word sovereignty, Panikkar, the geopolitician, who otherwise weighed his words carefully, was implying (perhaps with due deliberation) that Tibet was a part of China. A scholar-diplomat, seasoned by his long years of operating within the complex labyrinth of officialdom, he was not careless with words. Suzerainty, itself a 'chameleon' word, recalling Hugh Richardson's description of this vague concept, had morphed into 'sovereignty' in Panikkar's diplomatese. Suzerainty itself, it must be acknowledged, has had little legal significance or operability in the post-1945 world. Sovereignty is the key word. But could Panikkar have been more elliptical in his communication with the Chinese, leaving the whole issue of Chinese sovereignty over Tibet an open question, not requiring such immediate endorsement by an official representative of New Delhi? Perhaps he could have. But to attribute the mix-up between suzerainty and sovereignty to oversight as many in India do, may not explain this historical riddle. It is quite possible that Panikkar was not speaking out of turn and that he was bolstered by the conviction that Prime Minister Nehru shared the view that suzerainty was a feudal or, an imperialist concept that had outlived its time and that no external force could prevent the Chinese from exercising and enforcing control over Tibet.

In Lhasa, from the end of the Chinese Civil War onwards, the Kashag (governing council of Tibet) had been conscious of the danger of Chinese aggression into Tibet. An appeal was made to the British Government in December 1949 seeking British help for the admission of Tibet into the United Nations.[14] The response from the British Government[15] to the Tibetans was that 'it would be difficult under the present circumstances for Tibet to secure admission to the United Nations' and that the Special Mission the Tibetans proposed to send to the UN be suspended. The British were also clearly placing the onus for a Tibet policy on the Government of India and, were not willing to stake out a position in support of the Tibetans apart from signalling encouragement to the Indians to help the Tibetans with armed resistance against any possible Chinese ingress.

In Delhi, even the usually clear-thinking Secretary General Bajpai appeared to be in two minds about the orientation of India's Tibet policy. In a conversation with the British High Commissioner[16], he was not overly enthused about the Tibetan moves, including an appeal by the Kashag to Mao Zedong to recognize Tibet's special status, labelling them as foolish and unnecessarily provocative. He was against any inconsistency in policy towards China—on the one hand, recognition of the new Chinese government by India (and Britain), and on the other, following a policy in Tibet running directly counter to the proclaimed Chinese position in regard to the territory. If India followed such a policy, she would have to support her position by military force 'or see her bluff called.' The Indian economy was in no shape to permit a military expedition in support of Tibet. Furthermore, no 'appropriate formula' had been found that could incorporate reservations regarding the threat to Tibet by China within the announcement of recognition of the Communist Chinese government.

But in the same meeting Bajpai expressed what he said was his personal opinion, more in line with the views of Harishwar Dayal, the Political Officer in Sikkim, that recognition was 'recognition of an unpleasant fact and should not be blurred by any wishful thinking or appeasement.' The Chinese Communists were prepared to stir up trouble in India and they would react well to firmness but would exploit any sign of weakness. Without provoking the Chinese, 'he was opposed to abandoning any Indian interest in Tibet or elsewhere unless forced to do so.' A retreat in Tibet would have an effect in Nepal and the Communist danger should be kept away from the frontiers of India. Bajpai concluded 'that India must maintain her position in Tibet, stimulate the Tibetan spirit of resistance, maintain her Mission at Lhasa and consider supplying small arms.' His advice to the Prime Minister would be on these lines, he said. The dichotomy of views conveyed by Bajpai during this meeting expressed the fundamental ambivalence within the Indian policy-making establishment in regard to forging a clear approach to the events in Tibet. That there were clear divisions of opinion about how to handle the Tibet issue in the context of relations with China was also evident. These divisions would become even deeper as subsequent developments would show.

Prime Minister Nehru's confidence in Ambassador Panikkar's pronouncements on the new leadership in Beijing and New China remained unshaken despite the skepticism being expressed in the Foreign Office. Panikkar gilded his dispatches with great praise for China and the new government, and he did not deviate from synchronizing his reportage with his assessment of what Nehru's views on dealing with China were. There is no indication that he ever sought a deep dive into Chinese attitudes towards India, which were often coloured by prejudice and patronizing. A biographical note[17] on Panikkar prepared by the Commonwealth Relations Office noted that 'there is a school of thought in the Government of India which holds that he (Panikkar) went to Peking with set ideas and is not reporting objectively but fitting the facts to his theories . . . and accuses him also of reporting what will be welcome to his Prime Minister.'

On 19 August 1950, Nehru in a personal telegram to Panikkar said that in regard to Tibet, India wished to help in a friendly settlement, 'which should aim at the autonomy of Tibet being recognized together with Chinese suzerainty'. The invasion of Tibet, as he termed it, might well 'upset the present unstable equilibrium and let loose dangerous forces. Some of our border states will be affected.' He added, 'Again, for the sake of preserving peace generally, it seems to me path of wisdom for Chinese government NOT to precipitate conflict when especially the Tibetan government is eager to discuss matters with China with view to settlement.'[18] At the same time, the Prime Minister was expressing his irritation with the position taken by the Political Officers in Sikkim and Lhasa who stressed that the Communist domination of Tibet would cause nervousness and unrest among border peoples along the whole of India's northern frontier from Ladakh to Assam and 'policing of that frontier which has hitherto required negligible military effort and expenditure would assume immediate practical importance.'[19] The Prime Minister felt that these messages expressed an unnecessary nervousness and that he did not believe 'any such attempt at pressure tactics is likely to succeed because, ultimately we have no effective sanctions.'[20] India could do little more that give diplomatic support to Tibet in so far as it was feasible.

Ambassador Panikkar's memoirs would suggest that the Chinese were silent about their plans to invade Tibet (the Chinese would deny this).[21] That very month of October 1950, 'rumours of a Chinese invasion' began to circulate, as Panikkar put it in his memoir.[22] On 25 October, Radio Peking announced that the process of 'liberating' Tibet had begun. In Panikkar's words 'the fat was in the fire' and public opinion in India was deeply agitated. He was instructed by Delhi to lodge a strong protest with the Chinese. In Delhi, a similar demarche was delivered to the Chinese Embassy's Counsellor—in the absence of Ambassador Yuan Zhongxian—by Foreign Secretary Menon. In reply, Beijing claimed Tibet as an integral part of China.[23] India was accused of 'blocking a peaceful settlement' in Tibet and of being in league with the imperialists. Exception was taken to the use by the Indians of the word 'invasion' to describe the Chinese move. Tibet had always been a part of China, the Chinese said, to which Menon conveyed[24] that 'the statement that Tibet was always a part of China could be contested.' Meanwhile, the Indian media kept on talking about 'Chinese aggression'. The Deputy Prime Minister and Home Minister, Sardar Vallabhbhai Patel declared publicly in Delhi[25] in November, that a 'peaceful country like Tibet has been invaded and it may not survive. We did not think this would happen. We were maintaining friendly relations with China'. He accused China of not accepting India's advice against military action in Tibet: 'We do not know what will be the outcome of this. Tibet is a religious-minded country. There has been no aggression from its side. But when one is intoxicated with power, one does not realize what one is doing.'

It is intriguing that Panikkar claimed not to know of Chinese plans to enter Tibet before October 1950. In August that year, Liu Po-Cheng, head of the Southern Command of the PLA issued a proclamation to Tibetans stating that the People's Liberation Army would 'soon march towards Tibet with object of driving out the British and American aggressive forces so as to make Tibetans return to the Great Family of the People's Republic of China.' Panikkar himself communicated this development to the Foreign Office in Delhi on 3 August 1950.[26] On 5 August, in a message[27] to Panikkar, the Ministry of External Affairs expressed 'grave concern' about this decision of the Chinese government. Surprise was expressed about the reference in the Chinese statement to British and American interests in Tibet since 'India alone maintains a Mission there', although this was in the charge of a British national Hugh Richardson. India, the response stated, had no designs on Tibet and 'is animated solely by desire to see Sino-Tibetan relations adjusted by peaceful means on basis of enduring friendship among three countries, China, Tibet and India.' The action now proposed by China 'may NOT only be described as aggression but may threaten world-peace'. Panikkar was asked to make representations to this effect to Premier Zhou Enlai, taking into account the possibility of 'a rebuff' but with the satisfaction 'that risk must be taken in larger interests of world-peace'.

Panikkar himself came in for trenchant criticism from the Foreign Office in Delhi about his 'half-hearted' representations to Beijing about Tibet. 'The Ambassador does not appear to have realized that not merely India's honour but her interests are involved in a satisfactory settlement of the Tibetan problem', Foreign Secretary Menon noted. Secretary General Bajpai called the tone of the Ambassador's diplomatic communication 'lamentably weak'. He added, 'Historical parallels are misleading, but anyone familiar with Sir Neville Chamberlain's efforts 'on behalf of' Czechoslovakia in Berlin will find it difficult to resist a comparison that seems obvious'. He felt that 'in this matter of

Tibet, we have been served badly'.[28] The Prime Minister obviously did not share these opinions. Writing to Panikkar he sounded a note of sarcasm, saying 'I am supposed to have 'sold out' to Mao through your bad influence. Panikkar is referred to as 'Panicky'. It really is amazing how great nations are governed by very small people.'[29]

Meanwhile, the situation in Korea was a major preoccupation for Nehru who was making it known that he was aligning neither with Washington nor Moscow on the developing crisis. Given the involvement of the People's Republic of China in the hostilities on the Peninsula, he felt that the only feasible course[30] would be 'to press for acceptance of the People's Government of China by the U.N. and the Security Council' despite the widespread opposition within the U.N. to such a move. As for the Tibetan question, Nehru felt it should be left 'severely alone'.[31] Advocating a policy of non-alignment with reference to Korea, Nehru felt that India should stand squarely against aggression (by either side involved in the conflict) and he made it clear[32] that India was with neither camp. The hostilities in Korea needed to be localized, and the entry of the People's Republic into the Security Council and other agencies and organizations, expedited. In Washington, the Americans were irked by Nehru's non-alignment but they also saw him as a key interlocutor between the Western powers and China. The fact that this channel relied on Panikkar did not reassure the Truman Administration much.

Sure enough, it was Panikkar who became the messenger of a crucially important message on the conflict in Korea from Premier Zhou Enlai to the Americans. On the midnight of 2 October 1950,[33] the Ambassador was awakened by his steward who told him that the Director of Asian Affairs of the Chinese Foreign Ministry, Chen Jiakang was waiting to see him in his drawing room at the Embassy Residence. Panikkar was informed by Director Chen that Premier Zhou wished to see him. At the meeting that thereafter took place at the residence of the Premier, Panikkar was told that

'China would be forced to intervene in Korea' if the Americans crossed the 38th Parallel. But with 'historical insouciance' as the Ambassador termed it, the United Nations passed a resolution to authorize coalition forces led by General Douglas MacArthur to cross the Parallel and bring about the unification of Korea. The Rubicon was crossed. The word that China would intervene, and resist the US-led thrust, as conveyed through the Government of India, fell on skeptical ears in Washington and other western capitals. This worst-case scenario was realized when the Chinese actually entered the conflict—as they had conveyed to Panikkar— once MacArthur had made his move.

Public opinion in India remained primarily focused on Tibet. Giving voice to popular concern across the country, one of the country's most prominent religious leaders, Sri Aurobindo, said on 11 November[34] that 'The basic significance of Mao's Tibetan adventure is to advance China's frontier right down to India and stand posted there to strike at the right moment with right strategy.' The staunchly anti-communist Aurobindo was of the view that the only step that could save India was 'to take a firm line with China and openly denounce her nefarious intentions and stand without reservation with the U.S.A'. India, he said, should be a spearhead of democracy against China. The primary motive of Mao Zedong in invading Tibet was 'to threaten India as soon as possible'.

It was by now clear that the China policy of the Prime Minister did not have unanimous support in his Cabinet. Leading the opposition was his Deputy Prime Minister, Sardar Vallabhbhai Patel. It was not just the Chinese entry into Tibet that brought to the fore the differences between Nehru and Sardar Patel. Gulzarilal Nanda, then Vice-Chairman of the Planning Commission, writing to the Prime Minister in July 1950[35] brought out some interesting contrasts between the two leaders, both towering figures in the country's freedom movement. On the one hand, there was the energetic and vigorous Nehru—the nation's

cherished leader anointed as such by the martyred Mahatma
Gandhi himself, on the other, an iron-willed but physically
ailing, aging Patel—held in the highest national esteem for his
success in building a united, integrated India in the tumult after
Independence and Partition. Nanda said there were two urges at
work in the India of the time: for safety on the one hand and for
social justice and progress on the other. In his view, in the minds
of the people, 'Sardar (Patel) is identified largely with the feeling
for security and you (Nehru) represent the impulse for a better
life.' In times of national danger, in Nanda's view, the urge for
safety came to the forefront. 'People see in the Integration of the
States, the police action in Hyderabad, the defence of Kashmir,
military expenditure and the strong stand against violence and
subversive forces a measure of response to their desire for safety.'
The urge for betterment of living standards, equality and justice
was the weaker impulse. People were willing to suffer if they got
the impression that everything was being done to ensure that the
'least of us' do not suffer 'more than can be helped and that no
one is allowed to exploit our difficulties and to thrive in the midst
of general misery.' The onus was placed on the Prime Minister
to clean up his administration and greater 'accord in action' to
be established between the leadership and the people. Patel had
in this analysis, already established an unimpeachable position
for himself in the minds of the people as a nation-builder during
a crucial phase in the life of new India. But, as a team of rivals
Nehru and Patel had learned to work together, both inspired by,
and deferential to, the unifying, steadying hand of Gandhi and
the memory of their slain leader.

Patel had deep reservations about Nehru's willing suspension
of disbelief about Communist China's strategy and intentions in
the region. The invasion of Tibet confirmed his worst suspicions
and seemed to reveal the weakness of a foreign policy of non-
alignment. Patel's dealings with the Communist uprising in
Telengana had instilled in him a deep aversion for Marxist

ideology and the threat it posed to the young and fledgling Indian democracy. He found a kindred spirit in Secretary General Bajpai when it came to assessing developments in Tibet and the Communist Chinese action. By September 1950, M.O Mathai, the shrewd, suspicious and wily private secretary to the Prime Minister was already putting on record the 'hob-nobbing' between Patel and Bajpai.[36]

By the time of the Chinese invasion of Tibet, this meeting of minds was quite evident. On 3 November 1950, Bajpai gave to Patel a note dealing with the implications of the Chinese advance. The note[37] advocated a strong protest against China's moves in Tibet, and suggested that India's mission in Lhasa and offices in Gyantse and Yadong be withdrawn as a measure of this protest. 'The alternative would be war for which we are not prepared', opined the Secretary-General. India, as a strategic necessity, would have to declare that the McMahon Line was 'our frontier', and the 'necessary dispositions' would have to be made to defend that line. Nepal and Burma were even more vulnerable to 'Chinese aggression' and discussions should be held with both these two countries to develop 'common defence' against China. Advocacy of China's claim to enter the United Nations and the Security Council 'must cease'. At the same time, while advocating a strong Indian response, Bajpai was not advocating an 'immediate breach of diplomatic relations' with China but only a tough diplomatic response—although he knew that this could not preserve Tibet's autonomous (and virtually independent) status as had existed prior to the Chinese invasion.

The Bajpai note Patel read with great interest and 'profit to myself'. In his response to Bajpai on 4 November,[38] Patel was blunt—his view was that the Chinese moves upset all of India's security calculations. India's northeastern approaches would have to be guarded in addition to its northern ones. Chinese irredentism and political ambitions had to be contended with. Boundary disputes would have to be borne in mind. In his view, China was a 'thoroughly unscrupulous, unreliable and determined power practically at our doors'. Any friendly or appeasing approaches to China could 'either be mistaken for weakness or would be exploited in furtherance of their ultimate aim'. Patel also received a briefing from the chief of the Intelligence Bureau (IB), B.N. Mullik.

On 7 November 1950 Patel penned a missive to Nehru—now legendary in the annals of India's China relationship—expressing his grave misgivings about China and his sympathy for the Tibetans who had 'put faith' in India without succor being provided. He said he had studied the problem of Tibet in detail and that neither the Chinese government nor Ambassador Panikkar came out well 'as a result of this study'. The action of the Chinese against Tibet was 'little short of perfidy'. There was a 'lack of firmness and unnecessary apology' in the representations made by the Ambassador to the Chinese. It was clear that the Chinese did not regard the Indians as friends in spite of India doing everything to assuage their feelings, including championing the cause of China's entry into the United Nations. The language China had used against India in response to her protest against the entry of the PLA into Tibet was the language of a 'potential enemy'. It was clear that they would soon disown 'all the stipulations that Tibet had entered into with us in the past' which threw into 'the melting pot all frontier and commercial settlements with Tibet'. The undefined state of the frontier with China and Tibet and 'the existence on the Indian side of that frontier of a population with affinities to the Tibetans or Chinese have all the elements of potential trouble'. The Chinese were Communists with imperial ambitions. In his view what was urgently required was a military and intelligence appreciation of the Chinese threat, the defence of important routes of Chinese ingress into India's frontier areas, raising military preparedness, and reviewing support for Chinese entry into the United Nations. He also advocated strengthening of the northern and northeastern frontier, improvement of communications—road, rail, air and wireless; consideration of the future of the Indian mission in Lhasa and the posts at Gyantse and Yadong; and, finally, a consideration of what policy India should take on the McMahon Line.

A memoir[39] by a former Indian foreign secretary, M.K. Rasgotra makes the argument that Patel and Bajpai would have found little reason to question Nehru's approach toward Tibet if they had known about certain 'informal and personal' initiatives made by the Prime Minister on the same issue. These revelations have not found mention in any other records. Apparently, soon after Indian independence, Nehru sent emissaries on two separate visits to Lhasa to explain to the Kashag the importance of the United Nations and ask whether Lhasa wished to apply for membership to the world body as this would secure Tibet's status as a sovereign member of the comity of nations. This failed to elicit a response from the Tibetans who 'woke up to the significance of Nehru's initiatives too late'. Nehru apparently did not take the Foreign Office into confidence in this matter. There appear to be no other records to corroborate this outreach by Nehru to Tibet except for a reference to a young army officer Zorawar Bakshi (later Lieut. General Bakshi) undertaking strategic military reconnaissance in Tibet disguised as a Tibetan monk in 1949.[40] Dawa Norbu refers to this visit as having been an official mission in which Bakshi was sent by the Government of India to advise the Lhasa government on defence matters.[41] Once the Chinese had occupied Tibet, the latter had missed its chance to secure recognition of an independent sovereign status on the global stage, and Nehru 'the realist' recognized 'the reality' of China's presence in Tibet—with his efforts being then 'focused on negotiating a dignified withdrawal from Tibet of India's extraterritorial privileges.'[42]

This interlude notwithstanding, the historical import of the Patel letter has been stressed by those who contrast its message with what is interpreted as Nehru's unquestioning acquiescence of China's Tibetan moves. But as K.S. Bajpai, the distinguished Indian diplomat and son of G.S. Bajpai, was to note in 2009, almost sixty years after the November 1950 letter[43], 'We need to look beyond the Manichaean oversimplifications to which the Nehru-Patel differences are usually reduced'. The older Bajpai was concerned that India had never dealt with China, and a solidly tenable position from which to negotiate with China was needed. That was essentially the import of what Patel was saying to Nehru, too. 'Bajpai's main point was that we would now have a boundary to negotiate and our ground position would be vital'.[44]

The deep divide in the Indian policy establishment on the nature of the Communist threat from China was wide and open with important political heavyweights like C. Rajagopalachari and K.M. Munshi echoing the sentiments expressed by Patel. The iron discipline and administrative skills of Patel were unmatched by Nehru. In many ways, the centripetal Patel was solidly focused on the essence of the threat that faced India, he knew it backwards, and would be proven right, while Nehru, more protean than Patel, (and reminding one more of the Russian writer, Tolstoy with his love of history and scientific enquiry—'A queer combination of the brain of an English chemist and the soul of an Indian Buddhist'[45]) had a world view infused by ideals and knowledge derived from his internationalism and his readings of world history. Patel was prescient about the threat from China, and the Chinese attitude towards a nascent India and its democracy. On the other hand, Nehru's sympathy for China was a part of his core ideology concerning a pan-Asia. For him, as the historian S. Gopal was to note, 'the frontiers of (India's) national movement lay in Spain and China, for freedom, like peace was indivisible, and in the final analysis it did not matter much where fate had pitched one's tent'.[46]

By any reckoning, both Nehru and Patel were remarkable men, of great depth of character and integrity, leaders who India was fortunate to have at a crucial juncture of her history. While much has been made of the conflict and rivalry between these two brilliant individuals, they had resolved to work together because a leader beloved to both of them, Gandhi, had willed thus. The Earl Mountbatten alluded to this in 1968 when he recalled how Gandhi, a few days before his assassination had asked him to bring about a 'reconciliation' between the two which he conveyed to them after the assassination, as Gandhi lay dead whereupon they 'wept and embraced each other' and how, to 'their lasting credit they achieved, under conditions of utmost stress, a highly effective working partnership'.[47]

It was much later, in 1959 that Nehru was quoted as saying he had visualized from 1950 onwards, 'two powerful states coming face to face with each other on a tremendous border'[48] although even earlier, on the eve of the Communist victory in the Chinese Civil War, he was in communication with Cabinet colleagues like John Mathai, the Finance Minister, on the likelihood of Chinese troops entering Tibet and the resultant implications for India's national security. His views were diluted considerably by the actual advent of the Communist-led regime and his focus turned to early recognition of the new government and bringing the latter into the global comity of nations. In the early years, he was convinced that 'the fact of the change in China' had to be recognized. China could not be left on the margins of the world stage[49]. Till early November 1950, Nehru was telling his Chief Ministers[50] that he had hoped, in view of the friendly advice from India, China would avoid military operations in Tibet. That the Chinese had announced such operations had surprised and distressed India. The action of the Chinese government appeared as 'an act of discourtesy'. Yet, India did not intend to change her general policy towards China 'because it is based on certain principles, as well as our judgement of the world situation'. These were a multiplicity of views on China, with several strands of thought contending in Nehru's mind as on an impressionistic canvas. On the other hand, Patel's was a far more grounded approach to China and to

India's relations with her giant neighbour: he felt India needed a well-defined diplomatic and military strategy to deal with this new force on her frontier.

While Nehru did not reply directly to Patel's letter, in a note[51] marked 'Top Secret', dated 8 November, to Secretary General Bajpai, he spoke of the need to consider carefully India's external policy, both in the UN and in regard to neighbouring countries, including China 'with reference to our defence problems'. He said China's actions in Tibet had been 'rightly resented' by India and that 'we cannot be happy to have a strong centralized and Communist Government in control of the Tibetan border with India' although legally, India's position was 'not a strong one'. If China demanded, the representative in Lhasa and the military escort at Gyantse would have to be withdrawn. It was possible that the frontier would be challenged by China in response to which 'we have to be perfectly clear' and where 'in fact [we are] on strong ground'. He added, 'We consider the McMahon Line as our frontier and we are not prepared, on any account, to reconsider this question'. But Nehru did not anticipate military operations against India by China. What needed to be guarded against was 'infiltration and intrusion of small groups' for which the strengthening of frontier posts was necessary from the point of view of 'watch and ward as well as intelligence.' Communications to Assam and adjoining borders would need improvement, and air-fields erected.

Nehru's letter of 17 November 1950[52] to his Chief Ministers also seemed to paraphrase some of Patel's concerns. Nehru stated that the developments in Tibet had made people realize 'that China might have a long common frontier with India, and this new China was probably very different from the old. Also, the Himalayan barrier was not quite as effective as it used to be'. But then he went on to say that 'it is of high importance' that India understood China. Anything but friendly relations would be bad not only for the two countries but Asia as a whole. However, as a result of the 'wrong and foolish' invasion of Tibet by China, India would 'have to become more frontier-conscious and to take all reasonable steps to guard the mountain passes, which lead to our country. But there was no reason for people to get hysterical or even excited about this matter'. While the developments in Tibet had been a blow to India's China policy, India would continue to work for Tibet's autonomy through diplomatic means while remaining adamant about 'our frontier, the McMahon Line'. But he was not ruling out the basic tenet of friendship with China, and Patel's warnings were overlooked. That was where the fundamental, basic difference lay. In hindsight, Nehru's vision of China lacked precision and high definition. He remained unwilling to articulate, at this early stage, publicly, whatever inner reservations he may have held about the assertiveness and expansionist aims of India's northern neighbour.

But Nehru would not ignore Patel's recommendations regarding strengthening of frontier security in the wake of the Chinese entry into Tibet. As the then Intelligence Bureau chief B.N. Mullik was to write[53], while it has been insinuated that Nehru was unmindful of Patel's warnings, and perhaps no Cabinet meeting was held to discuss the Sardar's letter, a note sent by the Intelligence Bureau on 'New Problems of Internal Security' and Patel's letter were considered by all the Ministries concerned and decisions taken 'within the next seven days' (after Patel wrote to Nehru in early November) the following decisions were taken: a small committee of military experts with an IB representative would visit the Northeast Frontier Agency (NEFA) to recommend points at which units of the Assam Rifles should be posted; a high-powered committee[54] presided over by the Deputy Minister of Defence, Major-General Himmatsinghji, would be formed to 'study the problems created by the Chinese aggression in Tibet and make recommendations about the measures that should be taken to improve administration, defence, communication, etc., of all the frontier areas'; there were other recommendations about strengthening Indo-Tibet frontier checkposts and expansion of the intelligence set-up in the border areas.

The Himmatsinghji Committee would issue a two-part report, the first with recommendations regarding Sikkim, Bhutan, NEFA and the Eastern frontier bordering Burma, submitted in April 1951. The second part had recommendations regarding Ladakh and the frontier areas of Himachal Pradesh, the Punjab, Uttar Pradesh and Nepal which was submitted in September 1951. The Committee also received recommendations from a smaller Assam-based Committee to assess the threat to NEFA and to suggest the placement of Assam Rifles Posts as far towards the frontier line as possible.[55] In a crucial year for frontier management (1951), Indian administrative control was also extended up to the important monastery town of Tawang just south of the McMahon Line, close to the eastern border with Bhutan in February 1951. Earlier, in July 1950, Nehru in a note to Secretary-General Bajpai wrote that he favoured the establishment of a Frontier Administrative Service, a permanent cadre that would train competent young men for service in these areas since the 'NEF (North East Frontier) area is today one of great importance for us from many points of view'.[56] And earlier in September 1949, he had written to his Finance Minister, John Mathai, (copying Sardar Patel on this communication), drawing attention to recent developments that the 'Chinese communists are likely to invade Tibet sometime or other . . . within a year' and that this would mean 'we may have the Chinese or Tibetan communists right up on our Assam, Bhutan and Sikkim border'—areas that would have to be tackled very carefully. Therefore, it was essential that 'these areas should have good communications' and it would be 'a risky business' to ignore this aspect.[57]

It was a crucial year. The Tibeto-Himalayan borderlands were suddenly being thrust into the limelight. For centuries, they had been frontier zones undivided by modern notions of borderlines, not marginal peripheries, but creative spaces where cultures intermingled, trade was transacted and seasonal migrations and pilgrimage within this fluid frontier zone, defined the lives of their peoples. In the early 1950s, all this was changing as both governments—India and China—began to leverage historical claims to operationalize sovereignties in these frontier zones.

. . . .

Tawang is an illustrative case. It is a town that sits astride the gaping fault line in relations between India and China until this day, emblematic of a frontier zone that eludes consensus and paraphrases conflict. Seen as sovereign Indian territory, it was mentioned as a part of the Indian state of Assam under Part 'B' of the 6th Schedule of the Constitution of India in 1950. In February 1951,[58] as the Chinese army was consolidating its presence in Tibet, independent India understood the crucial need to ensure the exercise of her sovereignty in all areas south of the McMahon Line and thus effected the physical extension of Indian administration into Tawang[59].

On a visit to the monastery town in 2017, the 14th Dalai Lama said, 'When I had to flee Lhasa in 1959, it was only once I crossed the border into India here that I felt free of risk and danger. The local people showered me with respect and devotion and treated the many Tibetans who came after me with immense kindness'. As a response to these words, China accused India of 'using' the Dalai Lama to 'undermine' China. It was stressed[60] that 'issues concerning Tibet (of which China sees Tawang as a part[61]) have a bearing on China's core interests'. China increasingly references 'core interests'[62] to define rights it considers sacrosanct and has included the term in the national security law enacted in 2015.

On 6 February 1951, a young Indian Army Second World War veteran from Manipur in India's northeast, Major Ralengnao 'Bob' Khathing (a recipient of the Military Cross) entered Tawang. He was entrusted by the Assam government, on instructions from the Government of India, to go there with a group of men from the Assam Rifles. It was a peaceful event that marked the establishment of the on-ground Indian administration in the monastery town and its surrounding region. It was the Ministry of External Affairs that moved on the recommendations of the Himmatsinghji Committee that civilian administrative control to ensure the welfare and development of the tribal population inhabiting these border regions should be expanded. The core of the argument was that development activities and measures would be far better for the local population than mere military expeditions. With the approval of Secretary-General Bajpai, the Ministry which had been entrusted by the Prime Minister[63] to deal with matters concerning the North East frontier areas, sent out instructions to the government in Assam that administrative presence in Tawang should be established forthwith. This was also fully in accordance with the overall decision to ensure that all areas up to the McMahon Line should be secured and protected. A unilateral occupation of Tawang by the Chinese Communists—which could well have been imminent—could not be tolerated. The Governor of Assam was accordingly informed to take further action in the matter, without delay.[64] The Prime Minister was not specifically consulted before the decision was made, and did express some subsequent unease about this; on the whole, he was to concede that the move was justified given the implications for India of the Chinese occupation of Tibet. In any case, the development also accorded with his general instructions that foreign incursions into these frontier areas (and Tawang was clearly south of the international frontier) should be checked. It was now left to the authorities both in Delhi and in Assam to work out measures to speed up the establishment of administrative presence in order to ensure the welfare of the population up to the international border with Tibet.[65]

Major Khathing had been involved in earthquake relief (in December 1950 a severe and massive earthquake had struck the region, killing several thousands and rendering many more homeless) in the town of Pasighat in the foothills when he was told 'to go to Tawang to establish a new Administrative Headquarters.'[66] His column of men began their journey from the foothills on 17 January 1951, picking up air-dropped rations enroute at Dirang Dzong, and then setting out for Tawang, their mile-long caravan crossing the Sela Pass at 14,200 feet in the morning hours of 3 February. Winter conditions were severe and some of the men were affected by severe mountain sickness and had to be carried on ponies. Pick axes and shovels had to be used to cut their way through snow and ice in the prevailing severe winter conditions, and to clear the way forward for the column. They arrived in Tawang on 6 February, the first day of the Tibetan New Year. That evening there was heavy snowfall in the town, which the villagers took as an auspicious sign. The people of the area were clearly relieved and happy to see the Indian party. Khathing and his men focused considerable effort on earthquake relief work also since Tawang with its stone buildings had been badly affected. The repair of the Tawang monastery and the respect thus conveyed for Buddhism and the faith of the town's inhabitants, also had a very positive impact on the people, helping build trust and confidence in the Indian government. A tour of major Buddhist pilgrimage sites for prominent Monpas in 1952 too went down well.[67] Khathing's tour of the frontier north of Tawang showed in his view that the McMahon Line was no haphazard imaginary line but had been drawn along the 'traditional boundary between the Tibetans and the Monyul (the Tawang area)'. By October 1951 the area had been cleared of the unpopular Tibetan officials who were collecting taxes in the area using the cover of the monastic ties between the Tawang monastery and the Drepung monastery near Lhasa. In Khathing's words, 'the vindication of the McMahon Line in the Tawang area was firmly established'. Tawang, literally, had been liberated.

In March 1951, on the instructions of the Prime Minister, the Tibetans in Lhasa were also officially informed about Major

Khathing's entry into Tawang. The Ministry of External Affairs told the Indian mission in Lhasa that Tawang had come to India under the 1914 Simla Agreement. In view of the 'special relations' between India and Tibet it had not been 'considered necessary' by India to 'send a garrison to Tawang'. The position had changed radically 'when Tibet was invaded' and it became 'imperative to vindicate the McMahon Line and in particular occupy Tawang'. The instructions to the office in Lhasa were that this explanation be given verbally and not in writing 'as it is important to avoid any suggestion that our action needs justification.'[68]

In 2014, a conference[69] was held at Simla to mark the centenary year of the conclusion of the Simla Convention of 1914. A paper presented at the conference discussed the 'status quo rights document of the traditional estate and its subjects of the Tawang monastery' signed by Bob Khathing as the Assistant Political Officer, Sela Sub-Agency based in Tawang, on behalf of the Government of India on 8 July 1952. Unlike the takeover of Tibet by military force and confrontation by China in 1951, the 'peaceful incorporation of Monyul (the region of Tawang) into the union of Indian states was a gradual process' with the last Tibetan official in the area 'accepting the change of situation in February 1951' and leaving for Lhasa soon thereafter. A new agreement was signed by Khathing and the local Mon officials recording their acceptance that Tawang was part of the Union of Indian states. This document of the Water-Dragon year can be compared with the 17-Point Agreement signed by the Chinese with the Tibetans in July 1951 after the People's Liberation Army had entered Tibet. The latter agreement was signed under duress—forced to be 'signed and accepted' while the former signed by Khathing was an agreement to maintain the socio-religious-cultural identity of Tawang.[70] The Agreement of July 1952 in Tawang was titled 'An auspicious endorsement given by the Government of India to the three (traditional) domains of the Tawang monastery: the lands, the houses and the subjects.'[71] Khathing, the 'respected great Indian Commissioner' is described in the document as 'perfect, glorious and exalted.' It basically provided that the 'fruitful, auspicious order' in Tawang be retained and not altered as far as the duties of officials, the priest-patron relationship ('the union of sun and moon'), obligatory monkhood, grain collection, renovation of the Tawang monastery, ownership of lands and estates to be maintained, and that the Indian government would permit the same. The strategic decisions that drew the McMahon Line in 1914—that also respected the customary boundary between Tibet and the local indigenous people of Monyul—were further strengthened and consolidated by the 1952 'acceptance' agreement of Khathing and the smooth transition to practical administration by India. By contrast, the 17-Point Agreement signed by China with Tibet in 1951 is widely seen outside China as having been imposed under duress on the Tibetans and having significantly curtailed their rights and freedoms.

4

End of an Era

The Chinese have entered Tibet. The Himalayas have ceased to exist.

—Sumul Sinha,
Indian Consul-General in Lhasa, 1951[1]

In 1950, the so-called mission of liberating Tibet was entrusted by Mao Zedong to Deng Xiaoping, then First Secretary of the Southwest Bureau of the Chinese Communist Party. By October 1950, a 'Treaty of the Ten Principles on the Liberation of Tibet' had been issued by the Bureau. That Treaty was the precursor to the Seventeen-point Agreement of May 1951 relating to Tibet later concluded by Communist China with the Tibetans. On the Chinese side, these two documents were cited as precursors to the 'One Country, Two Systems' formula proposed by Deng Xiaoping as China's top leader in 1997, in the case of the reversion of Hong Kong to China. The Ten Principles in the October 1950 Treaty spoke of the expulsion of imperialist forces out of Tibet, the exercise of self-governance in 'Tibetan Ethnic Autonomous

Regions', non-alteration of the status, function and power of the Dalai Lama, freedom to practice religion, conducting reform in accordance with the will of the Tibetan people, and much more.[2]

The major phalanx of Chinese troops entering Tibet came through Sichuan. Other groups came through Yunnan, Qinghai and a few through Xinjiang (crossing into western Tibet through remote areas of the Aksai Chin plateau in Ladakh, unbeknownst to India). As far as Xinjiang, often referred to as China's great Northwest, was concerned, Communist troops of the First Field Army had been fighting the Nationalist forces and their supporters there from February 1949 onwards. By September 1949, the control of Xinjiang had fallen to the Communists. By the autumn of 1951, one of the cavalry regiments of the 2d Corps of the PLA 'had reached Ladakh (Aksai Chin) to reinforce the offensive against Tibet.[3] The possibility of Chinese troops entering Tibet from the northwest had been considered in Delhi. There were reports reaching the Indian government that the Chinese had amassed troops in Khotan in Xinjiang. From the operational point of view, however, the Government of India seemed to dismiss the possibility of this route of invasion being the one preferred by China. The Deputy Secretary to the Government of India in the Ministry of Defence, M.K. Ganguli in a note dated 12 June 1950 had the following to say, 'The main caravan route from Khotan to Tibet passes through a portion of North Eastern Kashmir and, although it is possible to go into Tibet without violating Indian territory, it is hardly likely that these tracks will sustain a major military force. From the point of view of the Chinese government there is also a risk of their coming into conflict with us should they violate a part of Kashmir'.[4] The assessment that the Chinese were unlikely to cross the Aksai Chin into Tibet proved to be incorrect. The route from Xinjiang into Western Tibet was strategically speaking, an important one for China, and the later development of the Aksai Chin highway over this territory would buttress this point.

On 7 October 1950, Commanders Wang Qimei and Zhang Guohua led 40,000 troops of the People's Liberation Army to launch an eight-pronged attack on Chamdo—regarded as the eastern gateway to Tibet—on the lower edge of the Tibetan plateau, in the region of Kham. The Tibetans were vastly outnumbered. When Ngapoi Ngawang Jigme, the Tibetan governor of Chamdo, sent three urgent coded messages to Lhasa alerting them to the fact that the Chinese invasion was imminent, there was no response. When finally, a desperate phone call was made to Lhasa on 15 October 1950, the Ngapoi's aide-de-camp was told that this was the time of the Kashag's annual picnic, and the telegrams would be decoded and a reply sent in due course.[5] By 19 October, Chamdo had fallen to the PLA and Ngawang Jigme was captured by the Chinese. This development occasioned a protest from the Ministry of External Affairs in New Delhi which stated that the 'invasion by Chinese troops of Tibet cannot but be regarded as deplorable and in the considered judgement of the Government of India, not in the interest of China or peace'.[6] At this point, the Tibetan government made a move to secure UN mediation, writing to the UN Secretary General on 11 November, appealing for intervention against Chinese aggression.[7] The Tibetan National Assembly in an emergency session requested the fifteen-year-old Dalai Lama 'to assume full authority as head of state'[8] and move his government temporarily to Dromo (Yadong) so he would be out of personal danger. The Dalai Lama addressed a message to Mao Zedong on 17 November saying he wished to revive 'the past harmonious relationship' between Tibet and China with the rider that China should withdraw its troops from Tibetan territory and release prisoners of war.[9] The Indian government was aware of the Dalai Lama's departure for Yadong, a departure that was apparently shrouded in secrecy with the Dalai Lama's friends and supporters insisting 'he leave before escape route was cut off'. The American Ambassador Henderson was given the impression that the Indian government was prepared to give asylum in India to the Dalai Lama with the proviso 'that he remain at a spot remote from Tibet'.[10]

Tibet's appeal of 7 November 1950, for help to the Secretary General of the United Nations, was 'surprisingly sophisticated and eloquent'.[11] It was drafted by Sumul Sinha, India's Political Officer in Lhasa. That appeal, in Sinha's well-crafted words, spoke of the problem in Tibet as the 'outcome of unthwarted Chinese ambition to bring weaker nations on her periphery within her active domination'.[12] China's 'unwarranted' aggression against Tibet, the appeal went on to say, was in 'complete disregard of the solemn assurance given by the Chinese to the Government of India'. Tibetans, it was stated, 'feel that, racially, culturally, and geographically, they are far apart from the Chinese'. Britain, as a member of the Security Council could have asked for this appeal to be placed on the Council's agenda, but chose not to do so. The British examined the issue further from the angle of whether Tibet could be considered a 'state', thereby being eligible to appeal under Article 35, paragraph 2 of the United Nations Charter which requires the appealing party to be a 'state'. This examination concluded, on the basis of the relative independence enjoyed by Tibet from 1911 onwards, that she had a clear international identity of her own. But it did not want the United Nations to pass resolutions it would not enforce, as for example, calling for China to withdraw forces from Tibet to restore the status quo. It was felt that a mere condemnation of the Chinese actions was the best option. Neither did the head of the British delegation at the U.N. support the Foreign Office view that Tibet was a 'state'. It was also cited that the Indian government had strong doubts about the 'absolute independence' of Tibet. India was more keen to pursue the case for China's admission to the UN rather than actively defending Tibet in a time of crisis.

Help came from the most unlikely of sources. On 17 November, El Salvador formally requested that the action by China against

Tibet be put on the agenda of the UN General Assembly. The draft resolution proposed by El Salvador requested condemnation of the Chinese action as well as the 'creation of a special committee to develop proposals for the United Nations regarding actions that could be taken'.[13] The Indian government appeared uncertain about whether to support the Salvadorean move.

As the news of the Chinese military's entry into Tibet trickled in, India seemed hesitant about how to react to these developments. The first unofficial and unsigned diplomatic note handed over by Ambassador Panikkar in Beijing to the Chinese Vice-Foreign Minister on 21 October 1950 weakly suggested that the prospects for China's entry into the UN would be jeopardized by military action against Tibet. There was no questioning of China's move to absorb Tibet, overlooking the Indo-Tibetan Agreement of 1914. On 26 October, after the fall of Chamdo, another note handed over to the Chinese Embassy in Delhi was stronger in phrasing, referring to the 'invasion' of Tibet and that this could hardly be synchronized with peaceful negotiations as assured previously by the Chinese. Calling the Chinese action 'deplorable', it expressed deep regret that the Chinese had decided to seek a solution 'of the problem of their relations with Tibet by force instead of by the slower and more enduring method of peaceful approach'. Four days later, on 30 October 1950, the Chinese government tersely replied stating that the problem of Tibet 'is a domestic problem of the People's Republic of China and no foreign interference shall be tolerated.' As regards the viewpoint expressed by India that the action in Tibet was 'deplorable', the Chinese made the veiled charge that the Indian government had been 'affected by foreign influences hostile to China in Tibet.' In turn, this allegation was strongly refuted by the Indian authorities who stated on 31 October that India's policy was entirely independent and directed at a peaceful settlement of international disputes. Furthermore, the earnest desire of the Government of India to see a settlement of the Tibetan problem peacefully, 'adjusting the legitimate Tibetan

claim to autonomy within the framework of Chinese suzerainty',
was emphasized. It was added that India was anxious to maintain
its establishments in Lhasa, Gyantse and Yadong 'which are to the
mutual interests of India and Tibet and do not detract in any way
from Chinese suzerainty over Tibet'.

Secretary-General Bajpai disclosed to American Ambassador
Loy Henderson on 20 November 1950[14] that the Indian
Representative at the United Nations, Benegal N. Rau was being
instructed to support the El Salvador resolution seeking support
for Tibet only if no 'suitable member of the Security Council'
was prepared to introduce a resolution. This was in order to
emphasize the 'importance of attainment of a peaceable solution
between China and Tibet'. The Government of India 'could not
afford to take an uninterested position regarding Tibet.' But this
approach would not hold. There were worries expressed in certain
quarters in the Ministry of External Affairs that the 'old skeleton
of Hyderabad' could be dragged out by pro-Chinese nations.[15] On
16 November 1950, the Chinese had replied to the Government
of India's note of 31 October. Their tone was determined and
unequivocal. The Chinese forces, it was stated, were in Tibet to
'liberate' it and to defend the 'frontiers of China'. It was a matter
of regret that the Indians had regarded a domestic problem of
China as an 'international dispute'. But the note also conveyed
that 'problems relating to Sino-Indian diplomatic, commercial,
and cultural relations with respect to Tibet may be solved properly
and to our mutual benefit' as long as the two sides 'adhere strictly
to the principle of mutual respect for territory, sovereignty,
equality and mutual benefit'. This was interpreted in Delhi as an
indication that the Chinese were not questioning India's rights
and privileges in Tibet. The decision to support the Salvadorean
move in the U.N. was thus altered. The instructions sent to Rau
were that he was not to support the El Salvador resolution, that
little good would come out of condemnation of the Chinese action
in Tibet at this stage, and indeed, such condemnation might do

much harm.[16] The British, for their part, sought a procedural postponement saying that the legal status of Tibet was unclear. The Indian delegate, the Jamsaheb of Nawanagar made a 'strong speech' stating that India believed a peaceful solution could be found to the Tibetan problem and that it would be best if the Tibetan appeal to the UN was not discussed. All other countries, including the United States, backed this Indian position. Tibet had been effectively abandoned, its protector deities also proving to be of little use.

Bajpai for his part, remained 'openly suspicious and cynical regarding Peiping'[17], as Ambassador Henderson observed. The same month, Nehru expressed his deep disappointment with the decisions taken by the Chinese government regarding Tibet and launching of an 'invasion'. 'He was concerned at the attitude on the part of China which the invasion reflected. This attitude, if adhered to, might result in considerable friction in future'.[18] The Americans were equally concerned about the developing situation, without deciding on a firm course of action ('in view of GOI unwillingness to support Tibet in or out of the UN at this time').[19] In principle, they were opposed to 'Commie occupation'[20] of Tibet and were for checking Chinese advances 'where feasible'.

It is clear that the government in Beijing and the Chinese military leadership particularly, was obsessed with 'an Anglo-American-Indian seizure of Tibet' and had planned at the outset to launch a full-scale military invasion. But supply shortages, military setbacks and logistical difficulties soon imposed their own constraints on a full-scale military campaign. The strategy of 'coerced negotiations' with the Lhasa government was then adopted.[21] This was then re-packaged as a 'peaceful liberation' of Tibet in typical Chinese Communist jargon. Ngapoi Ngawang Jigme and those officials captured by the Chinese in the fall of Chamdo underwent 're-education' in Chinese Communist Party policies and accepted lenient treatment on the condition they would turn collaborators. Ngapoi told the Tibetan government that he could be a negotiator on their behalf with the Chinese in order to stave off a PLA march into Lhasa and to ensure the safety of the Dalai Lama. The suggestion was accepted on the condition that he would negotiate on the basis of a five-point agenda for negotiations set by Lhasa, which included a demand for the return of Tibetan territories seized by the Chinese, and the withdrawal of Chinese troops. The charge made by China that there was imperialist influence in Tibet involving the British and the Americans was also refuted. The Chinese responded with their own five-point agenda, which stated that the Dalai Lama should 'not go to a foreign country' and that once 'national regional autonomy' was granted to Tibet, 'the Dalai Lama's traditional position will continue.' They claimed that they did 'not harbor vindictive desires'.[22] On their arrival in Beijing on 22 April 1951, Ngapoi and his party were greeted at the railway station by Premier Zhou Enlai, Vice-Premier Guo Moruo, Secretary of the Chinese People's Government Lin Beiqu and United Front and Nationalities Affairs Commission Minister Li Weihan. During negotiations in Beijing, the Tibetan delegation was told Chinese sovereignty over Tibet was non-negotiable. Li Weihan, the main Chinese negotiator said that the 'liberation' of Tibet represented the unanimous decision made at the founding of the People's Republic. The PLA troops were there on Tibetan soil and the delegates were asked to decide whether they 'wanted a peaceful liberation or an armed liberation'. The Tibetan negotiators were allowed no contact with the Dalai Lama in Yadong. By 23 May, the 'Agreement of the Central People's Government and the Local Government of Tibet on Measures for the Peaceful Liberation of Tibet' (the 17-Point Agreement)[23] had been signed by the Tibetan and Chinese delegates. The Tibetans claimed that they were signing the document in their personal capacity and that they had no authority to bind either the Dalai Lama or the Tibetan government to it. On 27 May, Radio Beijing broadcasted the full text of the agreement. When the 17-Point Agreement was signed, the Dalai Lama was still in Yadong. He was later to recount how he heard the news of the signing over the Tibetan Service of All India Radio.[24]

Yang Gongsu, then the Chongqing-based department head of the Southwest Department of Foreign Affairs of the Chinese Central Government, enters our story at this point. In 1951, he was directed by the Foreign Ministry in Beijing (after the signing of the 17-Point Agreement) to 'go to Tibet and take charge of all foreign missions in the area'—this meant particularly, the Indian and Nepalese presence in Lhasa. In his memoir, cited below, Yang Gongsu describes his first journey into Tibet and of encountering 'herd owners, chieftains, aristocrats, and herding and farming slaves' reminiscent of the medieval Europe he had studied about in university. Witnessing the great gap between the aristocracy and landowners and the 'farming slaves', he says he was reminded of the dichotomy between heaven and hell.[25]

Sumul Sinha, the Political Officer in Lhasa, like Yang, was of the view that 'Tibet seems to belong to the dead past and barren wilderness', and the life of Tibetan lamas and 'degenerate noblemen' seemed 'to move in the same old grooves' in a chained and tethered fashion.[26] Unlike the Chinese, however, he also possessed an empathy for the 'native intelligence and wit' of the Tibetans he met. He saw himself as having 'strayed into Tibet by some mischance' and he hoped that he would not 'fail' the Tibetan people. With the Dalai Lama in Yadong, and himself under orders from Delhi to remain in Lhasa, Sinha saw life in Lhasa as very dull with everyone awaiting the outcome of talks between the Chinese and Tibetans in Beijing while there was a lull in the movement of Chinese troops into Lhasa. Meanwhile, he noted that the Chinese were making liberal use of the noose and firing squad to eliminate 'state enemies' in the Tibetan capital.[27]

Was there really a serious intention on the part of the Indian government to offer asylum to the Dalai Lama at this crucial juncture? The evidence again points to indecisiveness dictated by uncertain circumstances. On 5 June 1951, after the signing of the 17-Point Agreement, Secretary-General Bajpai was asked by U.S. Ambassador Henderson what the attitude of the Indian authorities would be if the Dalai Lama were to repudiate the Agreement and insist it was obtained under duress without his authority. Bajpai said 'he did not know'. The Government of India 'had taken it for granted Dalai Lama would accept treaty as best terms obtainable' but if the latter refused to accept it, the Indian government 'would find it difficult to regard the treaty as a legal document' and if 'after rejecting treaty Dalai Lama should ask for asylum in India GOI could not well refuse'.[28] What would the course of history have been if the Dalai Lama had refused to accept the 17-Point Agreement? Could he have done so in the absence of any indication of external support from India or the UK or the US? If he had been encouraged to leave Tibet at this point and proclaim his opposition while in India, history may have taken a different course in terms of global condemnation of the Chinese invasion. Ambassador Henderson told Bajpai that it 'would be of advantage to Asia if the Dalai Lama would refuse to accept the treaty. In such an event, aggressive tactics of Peiping would be unmasked'. Bajpai conceded he may be right 'but GOI in the interest of correct relations with Commie China was refraining from attempting to exert any influence on the Dalai Lama'.[29] On 26 June 1951, the US Consul General in Calcutta was reporting that the Dalai Lama 'certainly' did not approve of the 17-Point Agreement and that he would issue such a statement. He would leave Tibet but would prefer to seek asylum in the United States.

In fact, the flight of the Dalai Lama to Yadong resulted in the United States giving serious consideration to the possibility of his going into exile 'and becoming an important Asian symbol/voice of anti-communism'—a 'low risk and high gain' proposition.[30] In the spring of 1951, an unofficial and unsigned letter typewritten on paper purchased in India, from Ambassador Loy Henderson to the Dalai Lama was despatched, urging the Tibetan leader to 'oppose the Chinese and seek asylum abroad' either in Ceylon (Sri Lanka) or the United States.[31] The letter did not have its intended effect, with the Tibetans telling the Americans that they had already begun negotiations with the Chinese. Two days before the signing of the 17-Point Agreement, the Dalai Lama responded to the Henderson letter confirming that negotiations with the Chinese were under way, and that if help was needed in the future it was hoped that the U.S. 'would do its best to help'. Tsepon Shakabpa (1907-89), who had worked tirelessly as Tibet's Finance Minister, and the head of the Tibetan trade mission sent abroad to build commercial ties with various key western nations, and promote Tibet's image as a sovereign, independent state, was the key interlocutor with the Americans. He listed six 'operational questions' to the First Secretary of the American Embassy, Fraser Wilkins in Kalimpong. Several of these questions were concerned with obtaining assurances from the Americans that they would provide strong and sustained support to the Dalai Lama and to the Tibetan cause, in the event of his leaving Tibet. The U.S. response, authorized by Secretary of State Dean Acheson was equivocal—expressing sympathy for the Tibetans, but stressing that whatever assistance, either at the UN or military help contemplated, would essentially be ineluctably conditioned by the position taken by the Government of India, given tradition and geography. At the same time, the Dalai Lama was encouraged to take a firm stand, especially on the question of Outer Tibet where he was not willing to cede control to China. The Americans were unwilling to finance the stay of the Dalai Lama and one hundred of his followers if they sought refuge in the United States, saying that they would have to make their own arrangements for the same from the gold and silver and 'treasure' in their possession. No assurance was given that the United States would lead a coalition of the like-minded and willing to demand Chinese withdrawal from Tibet. The Americans were keen that the Dalai Lama denounce the 17-Point Agreement. The British were skeptical about the American attitude that to them seemed to possess little more than propaganda value.

But by 16 July, events had taken a different course. The Dalai Lama was preparing to return to Lhasa. A large group of his officials in Yadong as well as the most influential abbots of the three great monasteries of Sera, Drepung and Ganden,[32] supported his return to Lhasa. Opposing them were those like Shakabpa and the Dalai Lama's brothers, Lobsang Samden and Taktse Rinpoche. Emotions against India were also high. In his 2014 interview with this author, the Dalai Lama spoke of expecting to see the Indian Political Officer in Sikkim, Harishwar Dayal, who usually travelled to Lhasa via the Chumbi Valley, in Yadong.[33] Separately, it has been said that Tibetan officials in Yadong were 'insulted' that Dayal did not pay a courtesy call on the Dalai Lama despite residing 'only two days away in Gangtok and despite having been warmly welcomed in Lhasa only a little more than a year before'.[34] The fact that he never appeared was evidence about the 'cautious' attitude of the Indian government, according to the Dalai Lama.[35] Sumul Sinha, in Lhasa, was also instructed by New Delhi not to proceed to Yadong.[36] Ultimately, the consensus, after heated debates between those wanting the Dalai Lama to go into exile and those wishing his return to Lhasa ended, after the protector goddess Palden Lhamo had been consulted, was the decision that he should return to the capital. The prevailing view among the Tibetan elite surrounding the Dalai Lama was that the world had deserted them, even the United States had not made any meaningful offers of sustained support, and that the Government of India, most of all, 'was seriously to blame for Tibet's apparent isolation'.[37] Harishwar Dayal in Gangtok came in for strong criticism in this regard for failing to convey to the Tibetans 'any willingness on the part of the Government of India to receive the Dalai Lama should he wish to leave Tibet'.[38] This was unfair criticism of Dayal, who was obviously carrying out instructions from Delhi. Those who knew and dealt closely with him had fulsome praise for him. Arthur Hopkinson, the last British Political Officer in Sikkim, speaking in 1950, had this to say: 'Sir Charles Bell complained that frequently Tibet or the agency dealing with Tibet is the Cinderella of the Indian Foreign Office, and that was too often true, but never during the regime of Mr. Dayal . . .as I know from my own experience; and when my time to swallow the anchor came it was a real pleasure to be able to hand over to an officer so sympathetic to Tibet and the Tibetans'.[39]

In Yadong, after the 17-Point Agreement had been signed, the Dalai Lama had his first contact with Communist Chinese officials in the person of General Zhang Jingwu who came there via India (flying from Kolkata to Bagdogra and thence travelling by road to Kalimpong on his way to the border with Tibet at Nathu La). Writing in 1951, Sumul Sinha had this to say about Zhang, 'I've long suspected General Zhang's purpose for entering by the backdoor (i.e., India) and leaving, as most people expect him to do, by what the Chinese love to call the 'front' door. And yet, history and you will bear me out that the Chinese prefer the back door to the door that opens on China from Tibet, and we helplessly allowed them to get in there by aiding and abetting doubtful characters with—so far as we are concerned—dubious missions'.[40] But Sinha was pragmatic enough to realize that the Chinese were now 'virtual masters of the Lama-land' as he termed it and that the Indians now had no option but to get on with them even if that meant a climb-down, this being all the more important at a time when Pakistan was spoiling for a fight 'for we can't like the Japanese General Tanaka boast that we can fight Pakistan with our left hand and reserve the right arm to deal with those who may seek advantage of our difficulties.'[41]

The Dalai Lama had his first meeting with Zhang on 16 July in Yadong. Zhang was seated at a slightly lower level, after a tortuous debate between the Tibetans and Chinese as to the seating for the meeting. The Tibetans sought precedence for their leader, of course. The meeting was polite and civil with Zhang expressing Mao Zedong's appreciation about the 'patriotic attitude' of the Tibetan delegates who had signed the 17-Point Agreement, and handing over a written message from Mao. The Dalai Lama was himself non-committal about the Agreement. In his memoirs, he describes the apprehension he felt before the meeting, saying 'I was half convinced they (the Chinese) would all have horns on their heads.' They turned out in his words to be 'three men in drab suits', the meeting was 'coldly civil' and he noticed that Zhang was wearing 'a gold Rolex watch'. But having met General Zhang, he was 'a bit happier about the prospect of returning to Lhasa'[42], although his Prime Minister, Lukhangwa Tsewang Rabten (1895-1966) was strong in his opposition to the 17-Point Agreement and felt it was a big mistake to have signed it, that too in 'enemy territory'. The Kashag, meanwhile stalled acceptance of the Agreement saying that they would wait for Ngapoi to return to Lhasa first. The Americans, for their part, were still trying to convince the Dalai Lama that Tibet should not accept the violation of her autonomy by the Chinese and the U.S, would support his going into exile in Ceylon (although there was no American affirmation of support for Tibetan independence). The advance contingent of the Eighteenth Army Corps of the PLA under Wang Qimei was enroute to Lhasa with Ngapoi in tow, while the main force under its commander Zhang Guohua would arrive by the end of October. In the end, the Dalai Lama by returning to Lhasa, had made his choice in favour of exploring the possibilities of maintaining and safeguarding Tibet's unique religious and social characteristics under Chinese paramountcy and control—a strategy of uneasy coexistence with an uncertain future. As far as India was concerned, the impression held by many of the Tibetan elites around the Dalai Lama was that the Government of India's attitude did little to inspire confidence, and that in the absence of any statement from India against the 17-Point Agreement, they favoured cooperation with 'Chinese

Commies (sic) rather than with GOI'.[43] At this critical juncture in the history of Tibet, 'the relationship between India and Tibet was at its lowest ebb. The Tibetans were convinced that India had lost interest in Tibet and was at pains to maintain friendly relations with China'.[44] India for her part, felt marginalized by the Tibetans who were seeking direct aid from the United States without consulting New Delhi. The Indians felt slighted that the Tibetans had approached the Americans first about the possibility of the Dalai Lama repudiating the 17-Point Agreement.

On 24 October 1951, the 17-Point Agreement was formally accepted by the Dalai Lama via a telegram sent to Mao Zedong, which stated that the Tibet Local Government, as it was termed together with the ecclesiastic and secular people, 'unanimously support this agreement' and that they would 'actively support the People's Liberation Army in Tibet to consolidate national defence, drive out imperialist influences from Tibet and safeguard the unification of the territory and sovereignty of the Motherland'.[45] The Tibetans seemed to have little choice but to accept the agreement in the face of the military might of the Chinese and as the rest of the world scarcely walked the talk of support and sympathy for their cause. They accepted it without joy and under compulsion, as Nehru himself noted, writing to his Chief Ministers in 1951. India, herself, had little to offer Tibet in her hour of need.

The Head of the Eastern Division of the Ministry of External Affairs described the terms of the 17-Point Agreement as 'vague' and 'self-contradictory'. While the reference to 'peaceful coexistence' with neighbouring countries and establishment of 'fair commercial relations' was not unsatisfactory, the mention of 'imperialist, aggressive forces' being driven out of Tibet could 'hardly refer to any country except India'. While the provisions for 'regional autonomy' sounded plausible, Article 11 of the Agreement ('in matters related to various reforms in Tibet, there will be no compulsion on the part of the Central Authorities.

The Local Government of Tibet should carry out reforms of its own accord, and when the people raise demands for reform, they must be settled through consultation with the leading personnel of Tibet') could presumably be used by the Chinese to upset the Tibetan regime at any time, and the specious acceptance of the position of the Dalai Lama was called into question by the restoration of the Panchen Lama (the Agreement called for maintenance of the established status, functions and powers of the Panchen Lama). The official told the UK High Commission that the Indian government had told the Tibetans that they hoped their government would be able 'to avoid the stationing of Chinese troops on Tibet's southern border', but 'Article 2 of the agreement was anything but reassuring' (Article 2 stated that 'The Local Government of Tibet shall actively assist the People's Liberation Army to enter Tibet and consolidate the national defences').[46]

Could Prime Minister Nehru reconcile his idealism with 'toleration of a military adventure' launched by China on India's periphery—in Tibet—was the question that many observers asked.[47] The Chinese entry into Tibet, achieved entirely by military means was seen as a serious setback to India's China policy, and as damaging efforts by India to obtain recognition for China in the United Nations. A powerful Communist State was now on India's northeastern border. While Nehru's concern and 'high moral sense' was for peace everywhere, Beijing's action now threatened to 'bring the strife to his doorstep'. The die for India's China relationship was being cast along lines that Nehru, as his country's paramount leader, had scarcely foreseen. Written on the eve of the Chinese takeover, of Tibet, Sumul Sinha's words sound prophetic with the benefit of history's hindsight: 'The present crisis in Tibet is largely the outcome of unthwarted Chinese ambition to bring weaker nations on her periphery within her active domination. I am reminded of prophetic warnings of Chinese friends in 1948 that within three years there will be NO Himalayas'.[48]

But it did not take too long for India's defence and foreign policy planners to gauge the nature of the new threat that loomed on her frontiers. Nepal, Bhutan and Sikkim (together with Ladakh and the tribal areas of Assam, as the northeast frontier was then called), all had centuries of linkage with Tibet; imperial China had at various stages claimed vassalage over Nepal and Bhutan. In the early-twentieth century, one Chinese official had said that in relation to Tibet, the three states of Nepal, Bhutan and Sikkim were like molar teeth in a man's mouth. At one stage, the Chinese 'High Commissioner' in Tibet, Chang Yin-tang, had conveyed to the Nepalese representative in Lhasa that Chinese policy was to build an army in Tibet and form a coalition against India, and compared Tibet, Nepal, Bhutan and Sikkim with five colours: yellow, red, blue, black and green which a skillful artist could arrange 'so as to produce beautiful effects'.[49] The rather fluid state of the frontier could not be denied, although Nepal and Bhutan had established a status independent of China in the decades preceding the end of the British rule in the subcontinent, and Sikkim was firmly in the Indian orbit with no scope for Chinese or Tibetan claims much before India's independence in 1947. Interestingly, the Chinese Nationalist government, before the coming to power of the Chinese Communists, had relinquished 'suzerainty' over Nepal. While supporting Nepal's application of membership of the United Nations, it expressly affirmed Nepal's independent status saying that the suzerainty that China had exercised over Nepal was 'not exactly suzerainty as western international law conceived it. It is the nature of a family connection, symbolized by an exchange of visiting missions at stated intervals. During that period of association we found the people of Nepal to be very independent and peace-loving and Nepal was, in fact, independent.'[50] When required, definitions of the term suzerainty could be moulded by China to fit the needs of policy.

A Cultural Tour and Two Consulates

Zhou Enlai is a handsome man with black hair and tufted eyebrows – hard, strong face with a suggestion of brutality[1]
[Mrs. Vijayalakshmi Pandit] has poise and dignity in repose, Roman more than Greek, with a threat of thunder[2]

—Frank Moraes, diary entry, 1952

The olive branch extended to China by the Nehru Government in 1949/50 was positively received in Beijing—the exchanges over Tibet being an exception. India's painstaking manouevres to ensure that China was not isolated internationally, especially on the Korean situation, highlighted for Beijing the importance of the Indian connection. In the spring of 1952, the India–China Friendship Association was formed, with Tripurari Chakravarty, Professor of Chinese History at Calcutta University, as secretary of the organizing committee. In April, Dr Mohanlal Atal became the first unofficial Indian leader to visit China, going as the Indian delegate to the World Peace Council. An even bigger development was the six-week visit of a high-level unofficial goodwill mission to China led by the Gandhian, Pandit Sunderlal.[3] There was also a visit by an Indian table tennis team.

In April 1952, at the invitation of the Chinese People's Government, the Government of India sent a cultural delegation on a six-week visit to China. It comprised fourteen members, of whom twelve were non-officials, and was led by Vijaya Lakshmi Pandit.[4]

The delegation had been carefully chosen, with great pains being taken to ensure that those selected were 'willing to exercise critical faculties and capable of doing so'.[5] One of the members, the celebrated journalist Frank Moraes, wrote in his diary how on the eve of departure the entire group went to meet the Prime Minister who, in Moraes' words, gave them a two-hour 'wandering talk'. Nehru told them that Pakistan and China were the most important countries for India, and while there was peace along the long border between India and China, 'we must not let China have the upper hand'. The Prime Minister 'deprecated' references to Tibet on which he said, 'the Chinese were sensitive',[6] according to Moraes.

Moraes saw himself as a keen observer of the Chinese. Years later (after the conflict between India and China of 1962), he spoke of what he saw as the monolithic Chinese mind and its difference from the 'Hindu habit of mind'. In his view, the Chinese subscribed to the belief, like Kipling, that 'iron, cold iron is the master of them all'. This passage from Moraes is noteworthy:

Although the Indian mind is often convoluted and sometimes enigmatic, it lacks the curious combination of realism and elusiveness that distinguishes the Chinese mind. The Chinese mind is more nimble than the Indian's, gayer, less sensitive but more practical. Without being fanciful, it likes to express itself in imagery and illustration, and the habit of building up an argument through suggestion rather than statement gives conversation with a cultivated Chinese a curiously evanescent, will-o'-the-wisp quality. It is like Huang Chuan who painted in the 'boneless way', disdaining to imprison his landscapes, flowers and birds within a drawn outline.[7]

'Culture flies in', a headline in the *Daily Express*[8] stated on 28 April 1952. The members of the Indian delegation arrived in Canton (Guangzhou) on that day having flown a four-engine Bharat Airways plane—the first foreign aircraft (with the exception of Soviet ones) to be allowed into Communist China, according to the report in the same newspaper. On 30th April, Premier Zhou Enlai hosted a banquet for the delegation. The British Embassy in Beijing could not but help introduce a sarcastic note into all this by saying that 'even the most critical faculties become blunted by profuse hospitality'[9] which was not borne out by facts. Most of the delegation was not deluded by Chinese propaganda and had an objective view, noting the intense hatred of the United States expressed by their hosts and ordinary people, and the restrictions placed on foreign residents by the Chinese authorities.[10]

Mrs Pandit, the leader of the delegation was, however, impressed by what she saw and who she met. 'Nowhere else in the world can one be so proud of being Asian as in China,' she declared. She felt 'a sense of kinship' with the Chinese people,[11] although she also admitted that the delegation had not been able to see all they desired to. The picture of the New China shown to them was, therefore, a limited one. But Mrs Pandit, the seasoned diplomat, was able to charm her Chinese hosts. 'Immediately after my arrival in Peking,' she noted, 'Vice-Foreign Minister Chang Han Fu sent Chairman Mao's tailor to measure me for a uniform similar to the ones worn by women cadres. This was presented to me by the Foreign Office and I wore it while travelling throughout our stay in China.'[12] Ambassador Panikkar would address her as 'Dear Madam and Leader' and she appeared perfectly at ease during her meetings with an assortment of leading Chinese personalities ranging from Mao Zedong and Zhou Enlai to Chen Yi, the then Mayor of Shanghai.

She found Mao a 'man of few words' when she met him on 16 May. The Chairman was brief but to the point, 'quiet, precise and rather tired - looking' but with a great sense of humour. He offered her a cigarette which she declined, prompting him to ask whether the women of India did not smoke.[13] Ambassador Panikkar answered that some women did, and so did Mrs Pandit, but that it was customary to refrain from doing so in front of elders and those 'who one respects'. Mao's reply was immediate: 'Ah, feudalism dies hard—please smoke to keep me company, Madame, we are in China.' Mao, Mrs Pandit noted, reminded her of Stalin and also of Gandhi (he was 'kind and tolerant')' especially since the Chinese public worshipped him.

By contrast, Vijaya Lakshmi Pandit felt (from her two interviews with Zhou Enlai)[14] that he not only possessed 'great intellectual ability and integrity', but he also valued India's goodwill and friendship. She found him a man of 'great personal charm' who conveyed an 'impression of utter frankness'. Zhou wanted to invite Nehru to visit China saying that the 'Chinese government were anxious that the one statesman who had unwaveringly and constantly spoken up for them should be honoured as befitting his prestige and position.' Speaking to Chen Yi in Shanghai,[15] Mrs Pandit answered questions from the Marshal about the partition of India and Kashmir, to be told by him that it was a 'grave mistake' for India to have referred the Kashmir issue to the United Nations. Chen Yi had praise for the Government of India's action in Hyderabad saying 'one cannot allow a feudal area to exist'. Referring to the constant repetition by the Chinese of references to 'American aggressors' and 'hated American imperialists', Mrs Pandit felt that these were 'just a way of keeping up the public morale' with not much heart put into the exercise. 'In fact, there is less hate for anybody here than in any country I have been in,' she noted. One thing the Chinese were not willing to give in on was what they considered a basic principle—the question of the return of Chinese POWs captured in Korea, being in this category. The Chinese kept insisting that Britain and India should together bring pressure on the United States on this question.[16]

The delegation travelled a by special train, 'in great comfort' from 'Canton to Peking, Mukden, Tientsin, Chu-foo, Nanking, Shanghai and the Huai River Project.' They partook of forty-course banquets and simple village meals. Members of the group like Dr P.C. Bagchi gave speeches in which he analysed the role of Buddhism in bringing India and China together. They met the widow of Sun Yat-sen, Soong Ching-ling (Song Qingling)—a fluent speaker of English—who spoke to the delegation in Chinese and was strong in her boiler-plate condemnation of America, despite having been educated throughout in the United States.

Despite her admiration for much of what she saw in China (like many visitors to the country in that period; besides, the Chinese were lavish in their hospitality as far as their Indian guests were concerned), and the personalities she met, Mrs Pandit also had occasion to be horrified on seeing a film of the San Fan Movement or the Five-anti campaign launched in January 1952 to target the capitalist class. The five-antis were bribery, theft of state property, tax evasion, cheating on government contracts, and stealing state economic information. The film depicted the public trials held in Beijing in February 1952 in which hundreds of persons were sentenced to death after the people voted the 'accused' guilty, by hand and voice votes.

Writing to the Prime Minister on 3 May 1952, Ambassador Panikkar attributed the success of the delegation's visit to the personality of Mrs Pandit, 'and the obvious desire of the Chinese to go all out to please.'[17] The only 'headache' was provided by Raja Hutheesing (writer and journalist) who was Mrs Pandit's brother-in-law. According to the Ambassador,

Hutheesing insisted on travelling with the delegation, despite his not being a member of the group, on the grounds that he was writing a book on China that was authorized by the Prime Minister. Mrs Pandit, the Ambassador claimed, was 'upset' with Hutheesing's behaviour.

The delegation returned after their five-week tour of China on 12 June 1952. Mrs Pandit went on record to state that the 'fine, creative spirit of New China' had greatly impressed all the members. Later, reports surfaced in the press that the delegation had been under 'strict control' during their stay by the Chinese authorities. Mrs Pandit, in a statement, denied these reports.

The year 1952 also saw the formal inauguration of the China–India Friendship Association in Beijing. A contract for exporting 100,000 tons of rice from China to India was signed, and a sum of 2000 million yuan valued then at Rs 4,21,941 was collected and sent to the President of the Red Cross Society of India by the Chairman of the National Red Cross Society of China for relief in famine-hit areas in India.[18]

The Curious Case of the Consulate in Kashgar

The so-called Central landmass—defined as one of the seven theatres of power[19] by civil servants of the Raj like Olaf Caroe—is that region of Central Asia abutting Afghanistan and Kashmir and which includes Xinjiang, known in the days of empire as Chinese Turkestan. Pre-Partition India's borders marched with Persia (Iran), Afghanistan, Nepal, Tibet, and China. Caroe, whose personality reflected both romanticism and paternalism (a fairly typical combination among British colonial administrators), remains a controversial figure, with many scholars implying that he may have facilitated the subcontinent's partition and the creation of Pakistan because of the imperial need to build a 'bulwark' of Islamic states against Soviet expansion, while others argue that he felt the subcontinent's partition represented 'the failure, not the fulfilment of imperial design'.[20] Caroe recognized the 'subcontinent's geospatial centrality when others typically located South Asia on the world's strategic periphery'. India to him was like 'Clapham Junction'[21]—a post-war hub of communications for Asia. He also foresaw the resurgence of China as a great power.

It is to the Central landmass that we must now turn, and to the story of the Indian Consulate in Kashgar in Chinese Xinjiang. The exit of the British from India in 1947 meant that the question of India's consular presence in Kashgar would need to be settled by China agreeing to the continued operation of an Indian office in this Central Asian city which was a major trading serai[22] where the routes connecting both Central Asia and India criss-crossed. Kashgar was historically an important destination for merchants and traders from Kashmir and Ladakh, and a major route used by them was the one over the Karakoram Pass; the other was via the Mintaka Pass, now in Pakistan-occupied Kashmir. K.P.S. Menon, as a member of the Indian Political Service before Independence and Partition, had himself journeyed through these areas over the Mintaka Pass on his way to take up his appointment as agent-general for India in war-torn China during the 1940s. Writing in his tour diary,[23] having traversed Gilgit and Hunza, in the footsteps of the legendary Chinese pilgrim, Xuan Zang, Menon referred to the Karakorams ('What a harsh-sounding name') as singularly forbidding, except by moonlight, but not possessing 'the saving grace of strength. They look moth-eaten; they look as if they are crumbling to pieces'. For years, there had been a slender but useful volume of trade between India and Xinjiang—as Menon found during his rather lengthy halt at Kashgar on his way to Urumchi, the capital of Xinjiang. The 'stream of Indian intercourse' was of benefit to the inhabitants of the region, although the trade was modest in volume. His stay at the Consular residence at Chini Bagh (literally meaning Chinese Garden) in Kashgar, with its lawns and stately poplars and fruit trees, provided a haven of rest to him as it did to many a Central Asian traveller since the time of Sir George Macartney,[24] who had originally established the office in 1891.

The creation of Pakistan and the advent of independence for both India and Pakistan brought the issue of the Kashgar office to the fore. There is little to suggest that the maintenance of the office in Kashgar occupied the Ministry of External Affairs in Delhi at any length, however. The Pakistanis meanwhile seemed anxious to beat the Indians at staking their claim to the erstwhile British consulate in Kashgar. In May 1948, the Pakistan Ministry of Foreign Affairs informed the UK High Commissioner in the country that they wanted Eric Shipton, the British Consul General in Kashgar 'to remain [there] as Pakistan's representative for one year'. Shipton was both a mountaineer and an experienced surveyor, being involved with the Royal Geographical Survey. He had been on a number of unsuccessful Everest expeditions and written an acclaimed book on Nanda Devi (mountain) in 1936. He had conducted a survey of the remote Shaksgam Valley,[25] north of the main Karakoram watershed in the summer of 1937. His 'facility at surveying in remote regions began to see him drawn more closely into the orbit of the agencies of imperial surveillance'.[26] Shipton had done two postings as British Consul-General in Kashgar in the 1940s. Later, he served as the British Consul-General in Kunming, Yunnan, from July 1949 until he was expelled by the Chinese Communist government in April 1951.

The Consular office in Kashgar reported to the Government of India, and not to the British Embassy in Beijing and acted as an 'early-warning station in Central Asia, monitoring Russian expansion, facilitating access to British goods, representing British interests, maintaining a flow of information back to British India'.[27] Halford Mackinder's 'heartland thesis' (in which he posited that the heartland of Eurasia from the Volga to the Yangtse and from the Himalayas to the Arctic lay at the centre of the 'world island') defined British geopolitical thinking in the region. A borderless frontier zone, un-demarcated by either British India or China, helped facilitate the extension of British power into Central Asia.[28] Shipton's own role as Consul-General was ideal for the deployment of his skills as a surveyor and explorer, and the exact ramifications of his mandate tended to be shrouded in some mystery, never disclosed except tangentially in his travelogues and mountain memoirs.

When the request from Pakistan was received in 1948 for Shipton's services to continue under the Pakistani flag, the British were inclined to agree. They had apparently not received any similar request from India. It so happened that when Mrs Diana Shipton, wife of the Consul-General came to the Foreign Office in London in early June asking whether India and Pakistan would both have a consulate in Kashgar, and if so, who would have the consulate buildings, she was told that nothing had been heard beyond the Pakistan approach, and that the matter of the consulate buildings was presumably a matter for India and Pakistan to settle between themselves.[29] It was at this point that the British officials in London determined that they should enquire from India whether the latter intended to send a new Consul-General to Kashgar.

The British did not want Shipton to be the cause for any argument between India and Pakistan on the Consulate issue. On 29 April 1948, a telegram from the Government of India to the UK Foreign Office, and repeated to the Government of Pakistan, conveyed that India hoped to establish her Consulate-General at Kashgar on the expiry of Shipton's contract. It was clear that the argument that the British apprehended was already blowing up over Kashgar. A later message dated 12 June from the Government of India proclaimed that the latter was 'vitally interested in Sinkiang which is a province of China and

borders Russia'. The Indian interest, the message said, was not
be measured only by the number of Indian nationals in Kashgar
or Xinjiang, 'whose protection is by no means the only function
of a Consul'.[30] Further, New Delhi emphasized that the Indian
Independence (Rights, Property and Liabilities) Order, 1947
precluded any claim by the Pakistan Government for transfer of
Kashgar property to Pakistan.

By July 1948, the first (and last) Indian Consul-General to
Kashgar had been selected—Captain R.D. Sathe, who was serving
at the Indian Embassy in Nanjing. Eric Shipton, who knew
Sathe from the latter's school days, was to meet him in Urumchi
and accompany him to Kashgar. The UK mission in Nanjing
meanwhile was making it known to London that 'it would be
more logical for Pakistan than for India to have a representative
in Sinkiang in view of the fact that the Indian community (in
Xinjiang) are predominantly Moslem'. The United States Consul-
General in Urumchi was reported to have said that the Indian
staff at the Kashgar Consulate were disturbed at the report
that their office would be taken over by a 'representative of the
Dominion of India'. However, doubt was also expressed whether
the Chinese government would permit Pakistan to establish its
Consulate in Kashgar when there was no Pakistani Embassy as
yet in China. At the same time, the British seemed to see no way
out but to accede to the Pakistan request that Shipton stay on at
the expiry of his contract to assist the Pakistani representatives
in Kashgar, as a temporary arrangement. The Foreign Office in
London was also said to be conveying to the Indian Government
that as a temporary arrangement they should agree to Pakistan's
suggestion that accommodation and staff in the Kashgar
Consulate 'should be shared'.

The Indian intention was to open the Consulate-General in
Kashgar with jurisdiction over the whole of Xinjiang. Informal
concurrence of the Chinese government, it was said, had been
obtained and formal approval was to follow after the appointment

of Capt. Sathe. But these were changing times. The fall of the Guomindang government and the establishment of the People's Republic were to crucially impact the future of the Indian presence in Kashgar. The matter of the Consulate was taken up with the British government and the view conveyed from New Delhi that 'the so-called British Consulate in Kashgar, manned by Pakistan officials and paid for by Pakistan, is essentially a Pakistan Consulate and that it is a subterfuge for circumventing the Chinese Government's refusal to permit the establishment of a Pakistan Consulate in Kashgar'.[31] 'We do NOT like a Consulate, which calls itself British and is carrying out anti-Indian propaganda'. The British government said in response that the Chinese Government had not refused permission for the establishment of a Pakistan Consulate in Kashgar and the matter was still under consideration. The matter remained unresolved.

Early in 1950, the Chinese Communists gained control of Xinjiang. The new Chinese government was unwilling to accept the accreditation of a new Indian Consul-General in Kashgar. Prime Minister Nehru informed Parliament[32] that Capt. Sathe had left Kashgar on 11 September 1950, although this did not imply that the Consulate had been closed.[33] The ostensible reason given to explain the Chinese attitude was that they were still to settle the question of the establishment of Consulates of other nations in Xinjiang. It was quite clear that the new government's absorption of Xinjiang demonstrated its focus on consolidation of China's Inner Asian frontiers through military build-up as well as the settling of Han population in order to alter the balance vis-à-vis native Xinjiang ethnic groups. The intention was also to remove all vestiges of British imperial history and, as in Tibet, China was determined to see that neither the Indians nor the Pakistanis inherited any right to 'take-over' the old British Consulate in Kashgar whose position astride trading routes connecting Central and South Asia made it an extremely valuable source of intelligence about southern Xinjiang. The non-presence of the Indian Consulate obviously also made it much easier for the Chinese to engage unobserved in their road-building activity connecting Xinjiang and Tibet through the Aksai Chin area of Ladakh, a development which would fundamentally alter the course of India's China relationship post-1958.

The closure of the Indian consulate at Kashgar in 1953 is not an event that is accorded much attention in the annals of India's China relationship. However, the closure of the Kashgar 'window', coming almost simultaneous to the disappearance of the Tibet 'buffer', laid bare the problems of the northern land frontier of India. Partition and the dispute in Kashmir had denuded India of much of its western mountain wall, and the control of Tibet by China had only compounded the problem. A new political geography had emerged along India's northern frontier, with China as a pivot, well-poised—as the early twenty-first century 'Belt and Road Initiative' would later show—to control connectivity and resources in this strategic core.

In their focus on Russia in the coinage of the Great Game theory, the British had nurtured a relatively benign view of Chinese influence or power outreach. However, with the departure of the British from South Asia, Partition and Independence, the advent of Communist China, the Western embrace of Pakistan as a frontline state in the Cold War, all that changed. The closure of the Kashgar chapter signalled the end of Indian traffic into Central Asia through the Karakorams. Pakistan, by virtue of its geography, its occupation of a part of Kashmir—including Gilgit and Baltistan—was quick to step into the space. The spectre of a strong power thrusting down from the north and the fact that India's surrounding seas were empty of any strong naval presence (the British navy had practically disappeared) increased the fear of isolation among many Indian officials, both civil and military— although Prime Minister Nehru did not express whatever reservations he may have had as a result of these developments.

He saw India as being in no position to join issue with China at that point of time in its history as a newly independent state.

In New Delhi, the whole question of links with Xinjiang was treated rather cursorily. Consul-General Sathe had pointed to the difficulties in transacting substantial trade with Xinjiang for reasons such as the Soviet pressure on the Chinese to restrict the movement of foreigners in Xinjiang, the competition from Russian goods, the expense, time and difficulty involved in transporting Indian goods into Xinjiang.[34] At the same time, however, he stressed that from the political and strategic view trade should be continued.[35] But a trade treaty with China on India–Xinjiang trade was rejected by the Commerce Ministry in the Government of India. Strangely, they raised the question whether China was in full de facto control of Xinjiang. Instead, the loss of trade facilities could be used 'as a point to gain concessions in the adjustment of the frontier on the Kashmir side so as to serve our strategic needs.' In the event, such opportunities were not pursued, and the now-forgotten story of India's ties with Xinjiang was relegated to the archives. Today, the visitor to the Chini Bagh, where the old building that housed the Consulate still stands, sees a sign outside the building that states that it housed both the Consulates-General of India and Pakistan before 1953.

Countdown to Panchsheel and a Consulate in Lhasa

After the entry of the Chinese into Tibet, Secretary General Girija Shankar Bajpai had visualized that India would have to negotiate with China 'the conclusion of a Sino-Tibetan agreement regarding our mission in Lhasa, and the two trade posts.' It seemed that a mood of resignation had settled over Delhi regarding Tibet. The focus now turned to ensuring that India's extensive border with the region be defended at all costs. The consolidation of Indian administration in areas south of the McMahon Line had followed, including in the monastery town of Tawang, as recounted in a previous chapter.

The lack of Chinese protest about the Indian move on Tawang, was seen as quiet acquiescence in contrast to the attitude of the Nationalist government which had protested about Indian activities in the northeast frontier areas. Since the mid-1930s, it had been the aim of the erstwhile Foreign and Political Department in Delhi to ensure a frontier with Tibet along the Himalayan crestline as this would provide the best strategic defence against foreign intrusion and safeguard the plains of Assam, which was what the McMahon Line had sought to ensure. The scholar, Karunakar Gupta, writing in the *Economic and Political Weekly* in 1974,[36] noted that the extension of Indian control into Tawang in February 1951 'without any opposition from the Chinese was rightly regarded by the Government of India as indicating that the People's Republic of China was psychologically prepared to accept the McMahon Line as the *de facto* boundary'.

In fact, until 1959, Beijing had no public comment on the Tawang issue. The Chinese government, as the establishment view went, was preoccupied with the consolidation of its authority in Tibet and also with the conflict in the Korean Peninsula. It had not had enough time to study the documents relating to the McMahon Line. 'China's strategy at the time was to avoid making or retracting any explicit border claims', although Mao Zedong, Premier Zhou and other top leaders in Beijing, knew, 'on the basis of an internal military report from April 1952, about the occupation of Tawang and other areas south of the McMahon Line'.[37] New research indicates that Zhang Jingwu (Beijing representative in Lhasa) and Yang Gongsu (director of the Tibet Bureau of Foreign Affairs) after studying documents relating to the Simla Convention and the map showing the McMahon Line signed by the Tibetan and British Indian representatives in 1914, had concluded that 'the Simla Convention and the legality of the McMahon Line were the basis for India's extraterritorial claims in Tibet.'[38] Their advice to the Central government in Beijing was that they should proclaim the old treaties as invalid and ask the Indian side to withdraw from the 'recently occupied areas'.

The decision of the government of China was, however, not to include the border issue in the agenda for talks with India relating to trade, troops and pilgrimage concerning Tibet, because 'the CCP leaders did not yet believe the conditions ripe for settlement' of the border since Tibet had not been brought under full Chinese control, militarily and politically. This was despite the fact that India had explained its position on the McMahon Line publicly, beginning with Nehru himself, on a number of occasions. Even the Foreign Ministry in Beijing had been told by the Ambassador Panikkar's Deputy, T.N. Kaul, in March 1951[39] that unless the McMahon Line was accepted as the boundary, there would be problems in the bilateral relationship. But China was practising, deliberately, a delaying strategy, choosing to conceal rather than reveal its actual position in the matter. It needed India to open doors for the People's Government internationally, and the geography of Tibet entailed an almost insurmountable dependence on India for supplies of food and other essential items. China was clearly buying time.

Ambassador Panikkar left China at the end of his diplomatic tour in June 1952. His successor, N. Raghavan, presented his letters of credence to Mao Zedong on 26 September. Interestingly, in October, the Indian and Pakistan delegations to the Asian and Pacific Peace Conference in Beijing signed a Joint Declaration for cooperation between the Indian and Pakistan peace movements for the peaceful solution of the Kashmir question and other outstanding issues between the two countries.[40] In December, an eight-member Indian table tennis team arrived in Beijing.

On 15 September in the same year, the Government of India announced that the Indian Mission in Lhasa would henceforth be designated as a Consulate-General, and that a Chinese Consulate-General would be opened in Bombay (now Mumbai) in addition to the Consulate-General already functioning in Calcutta (Kolkata). It was also stated that the three Trade Agencies at Gyantse, Gartok and Yadong would function under the general supervision of the Consulate in Lhasa. 'The change in status of the Indian Mission means that the Government of India has now recognized full Chinese sovereignty over Tibet and marks the end of their direct relationship with the Tibetan government', said an inward telegram from the UK High Commissioner in Delhi to the Commonwealth Relations Office in London on 23 September.[41] The Acting Foreign Secretary, R.K. Nehru, however, told the High Commission that there was 'no question of formal recognition' as the new Consul was not accredited to the Chinese government but would be taking letters addressed both to the Dalai Lama and to Lieutenant-General Zhang Jingwu of the PLA, the Chinese Communist Party Secretary for Tibet. But R.K. Nehru's explanation seemed unconvincing, particularly to the Indian media who could not be faulted for interpreting the Indian move on the Consulate-General's establishment in Lhasa as a recognition of Chinese sovereignty (as opposed to suzerainty) over Tibet, as the Chinese had been allowed a Consulate-General in Bombay in exchange.

It was to be over a year before negotiations between India and China on relations between India and Tibet opened in Beijing. These commenced on 31 December 1953. Nehru's approach to frontier questions between India and China was already well-entrenched by then. Tibet had become more a 'psychological' buffer from a political one during British rule—psychological because Nehru was convinced that any military attack on India from Tibet was not feasible. For him, while the status of Tibet and Tibetan autonomy, as also Indian interests in Tibet inherited from the British were issues for discussion with China, the frontier, as his biographer S. Gopal noted, 'was firm, well-known and beyond dispute'.[42] Loosely put, Nehru's attitude was that there was no room for controversy over the McMahon Line: 'Our maps show that the McMahon Line is our boundary and that is our boundary—map or no map. That fact remains and we stand by that boundary, and we will not allow anybody to come across that boundary.'[43] Gopal notes that this assertion of rights was more definite regarding the eastern sector of the boundary.

The problem lay in the fact that, except for Sikkim, the border had not been demarcated—jointly with China—on the ground; the boundary in the western and middle sectors had not been defined in detail by treaty and only, as Nehru stated, by custom, usage and tradition. The McMahon Line was shown only on a map that the Chinese government had initialled in 1914 but not subsequently accepted. The Chinese would set their strategy in such a way subsequently, when the officials of the two sides met in 1960, to seek 'fresh acceptance of every stretch'[44] of the boundary. Panikkar, without the benefit of hindsight, only had this advice to give Nehru: the issue would pose no difficulty. Could Panikkar have sensed the actual Chinese attitude? In retrospect, his advice to Nehru would have serious repercussions for India. As advice, it was fatally flawed.

Throughout his stay in China, Panikkar took the stand that the Tibetan issue was a simple one. Leaders like Zhou Enlai, in his view, recognized the 'legitimacy' of India's trade and cultural interests in Tibet and only suggested that the political office in Lhasa, 'an office of dubious legality' in Panikkar's words,[45] should be regularized by its transformation into an Indian Consulate-General. Other posts and institutions like the telegraph lines set up in the British era, the military escort at Yadong in the Chumbi Valley, 'were to be abolished quietly in time', and the trade agents in Tibet and their subordinate agencies brought 'within the framework of normal consulate relations'.[46] In his seeming obsession with the big picture of two big Asian nations forging deeper understanding and cooperation, Panikkar was content to say that he left 'no outstanding issue' pending at the time of his departure. It was a strategic miscalculation which would have serious consequences. When Zhou Enlai told Panikkar in September 1951[47] in a 'shrouded sentence' that the question of the stabilization of the Tibetan frontier—a matter of common interest to India, Nepal and China—could be settled by discussion between the three countries, it was assumed, in diplomatic guesswork, that stabilization meant that there was no territorial dispute between India and China.

Many records indicate that the view of the officials in the Ministry of External Affairs was that while negotiations for an agreement between India and China on Tibet were necessary, they should also include a border settlement.[48] There should be a quid pro quo for India's recognition of Chinese sovereignty over Tibet.[49] A note by the Foreign Secretary, K.P.S. Menon on 11 April 1952 observed that the Chinese government's attitude was far from straightforward, and could, in fact, be termed 'cunning'. A child could see through the game, said Menon. Zhou Enlai had suggested in September 1951 that India's position in Tibet should be regularized and the 'boundary with Tibet stabilized'. India had said immediately that 'we were ready for discussions' but there had been no response from the Chinese. The latter were saying that 'they [the Chinese] have been in Tibet only for a short while and want more time to study the problem.' Menon was suspicious of Chinese irredentism, and a whispering campaign was already doing the rounds in Lhasa that not only Tibet, but Sikkim and Bhutan, and even the Darjeeling-Kalimpong area 'would soon be liberated.' This would encourage the Tibetans to lay their hands on Tawang and other disputed areas to the south of the McMahon Line. 'The Chinese have long memories; irredentism has always played a part in the policy of the Chinese government whether imperial, Guomindang or Communist.'[50] India was clearly inviting trouble when it was decided that the border issue would not figure in the negotiations on Tibet. Responding positively to the Chinese move for an agreement on Tibet was seen essentially a means of reducing Chinese pressure on the border, and as 'helping' the Tibetans within a larger policy framework of coaxing the Chinese out of their isolation.

The 'knight-administrator' (called thus because of his British knighthood and being a member of the Indian Civil Service) Sir Girija Shankar Bajpai was by now the Governor of Bombay. He continued to be in the picture regarding Tibet. He had noticed that the list of pending issues proposed for discussion with the Chinese did not include the question of the frontier with Tibet. His view, as expressed to the Foreign Secretary,[51] was that 'This business of Sino-Indian relations over Tibet, would, in my judgement, be best handled comprehensively and not piecemeal', implying that the question of the border should not be left aside. Perhaps, as a result of Bajpai's letter, the Prime Minister in a note to the Foreign Secretary on 23 July,[52] expressed his inclination that the frontier should be mentioned in the talks with the Chinese. Panikkar's reasons for not advancing this subject, be what they may, were appreciated but Nehru felt 'that our attempt at being clever might overreach itself' and that it was better to be absolutely straight and frank about the issue with the Chinese.

This was not the first time that Nehru had expressed some misgivings on the issue. In June of the same year, he had in a message[53] to Panikkar said it 'was odd' that Zhou Enlai had made no reference to the frontier in his discussions with the Ambassador. He did not like Zhou's silence in the matter, he added, since the Indian government had made it clear in Parliament that not only the direct frontier with Tibet, but also the frontiers of Nepal, Bhutan and Sikkim, should remain unchanged. Panikkar's response was to state that the Chinese were aware of India's interest in the integrity of Nepal and had not raised any question about it. Neither had they objected to the PM's public statements on the issue. Panikkar said he did not want to make this a subject for further discussion. India should stick to the position that the frontier had been defined 'and there is nothing for us to discuss'. It would be legitimate 'to presume that Chou En Lai's silence on this point and his NOT having even once alluded to Sikkim or Bhutan at any time even indirectly during our conversation would mean acquiescence in, if NOT acceptance of our position.'[54] The Prime Minister did not demur further.

Panikkar did not wait long to reply to Bajpai's letter of 14 July. On 4 August,[55] he wrote to the Governor that the main consideration that weighed with the Prime Minister was the fact that the Indian position had been stated unequivocally as regards the frontier and if the Chinese had 'anything to say about it, it was for them to raise it.' But Bajpai in response[56] was unequivocal in stating that he was neither convinced by Panikkar's argument about what led to the decision not to raise the question of the frontier or by the decision itself. The Chinese had never accepted the McMahon Line and they could not be expected to regard this question as settled. They would raise the issue at their convenience. Bajpai's argument was cogently made:

> The practical difficulty of telling them that we regard the McMahon Line as our frontier and shall treat it as such, without requesting them to answer or commit upon this point, is not quite apparent to me. It they are friendly and accept the present position, they need not say anything about it. If they should do so now, but a dispute arises sometime in the future, we can quote this silence as acquiescence in support of our case. If they are not as friendly to us as we are to them and do not wish silence to be construed as acquiescence, they will have to come out into the open now and we shall know where we really stand: that may possibly leave us sadder men but also wiser.

In retrospect, these words are of great significance. The negotiations on the future of Indian privileges in Tibet would have yielded much greater value if they had been comprehensive and tackled the question of India's frontier—enabling a clear assessment of Chinese attitude as well as inducing awareness and recognition on both sides, of the unsettled nature of the issue. History could have been written differently.

The final imprint was Panikkar's: his view that the frontier should not be raised as the border shown in 'our maps was clear enough and several statements had been made about it in Parliament'[57] carried the day. Neither side was forthcoming to the other about the issue. The Indians felt at the end of the talks that all outstanding issues had been settled, while the Chinese reply[58] was that 'only such questions had been settled as were ripe for settlement.' The fundamental problem was that the stated attitude of the Chinese government was that every treaty and agreement between the Guomindang—and governments prior to them— with foreign governments, would be recognized, or abrogated, revised or renewed[59] 'according to their respective contents' as stated in Article 55 of the Common Programme of the Chinese People's Government.

Let us revert here to Yang Gongsu, the Chinese official in newly 'liberated' Tibet. Like many of his ilk in the establishment in Beijing, he felt it his mission to erase the ignominy of the special privileges enjoyed by countries like Nepal and India in Tibet. Nepalese citizens and merchants enjoyed extraterritorial privileges which exempted them from the operation of the Tibetan law. However, Nepal was regarded differently from India. It was not seen as an 'imperialist' country. India's was a different case. It had inherited imperialist British privileges in Tibet: stationed troops in Yadong and Gyantse, established 'army warehouses' and maintained postal services, telegraph and courier stations, and other 'special services'.[60] But the Chinese wanted 'friendship' with India. Therefore, India's privileges in Tibet, could not be 'lightly abolished'.

Yang drafted three goals for his work in Tibet. Firstly, to recover 'diplomatic power' for China; secondly, to abolish foreign privileges; and thirdly, to normalize relations with neighbouring countries. He was witness to what he called 'insurgent elements' operating against the Chinese army; he wrote how the one-year period from 1952 to 1953 saw an 'open fight with the Tibetan separatist faction'. This challenge having been overcome, the decision to replace the political office of India in Lhasa with a Consulate-General was seen as 'the first step in our execution of the central order to unite our diplomatic power'. The next step was to abolish the 'unequal nature' of the relationship between India and Tibet as established during the British rule of India.

Around the same time, the Chinese demanded of the Tibetan Kashag (executive council) that the latter report to the Central government the previous engagements between the Tibetan government and the British Indian government. The Kashag in response presented two maps to the Chinese: one, a hand-drawn map of the entire Tibetan region, which did not contain any longitude, latitude or elevation markings, only mountains and rivers. The map claimed all territories north of the Ganga in India as Tibetan land. It was rejected out of hand. The other map was a key document. It was the map that showed the McMahon Line. The map presented by the Kashag was the original copy signed by Henry McMahon and Lonchen Shatra, the Tibetan representative, on the scale of 1:500000. In Yang's words, 'there was a red line carelessly scrawled on the map, which demarcated the Tibetan-Indian border. Aside from this map, there existed no border agreement, no explanation of border orientation, and no formal treaty on border demarcation. This carelessly drawn red line map could hardly be the basis of the border assignment.'[61]

Yang recalled that it was the first time a Chinese had seen the McMahon map. The Tibetan officials were demanding, he claimed, the 'return' of territories taken by the British as a result of the 1914 Agreement, even as they agreed to the relinquishing of their previous authority to Chinese diplomatic power. This was a 'challenge', he averred, for China. However, even as the Chinese government set up a Sino-Indian negotiation committee for the talks with India on a Tibet Agreement, which took place from the end of 1953 to April 1954 when the Agreement was concluded, Premier Zhou Enlai had told this team[62] at the start of the negotiations that only issues that 'were close to being decided and consented upon' would be discussed, and 'since the border issue was still very nebulous, the governments would not talk about it at this meeting'.

Meanwhile, the Indian media was not letting Prime Minister Nehru's anodyne remarks about the Chinese entry into Tibet pass without comment.[63] And it was not just the media. The British High Commission in Delhi found Nehru's 'pretence that the Chinese occupation of Tibet had posed no problems for India other than a few petty questions of pilgrim traffic etc., is disingenuous to the point of fantasy'.[64] Most of the Prime Minister's statements seemed to be made off the cuff. The Tibet Day demonstrations outside the Chinese Embassy in Delhi, in which Dr Babasaheb Ambedkar, a member of the Council of States (Rajya Sabha) had reportedly taken part, was dismissed by the Prime Minister as 'extreme folly'.[65] The 'starry-eyed' propaganda about China was attributed 'largely to the effusions of Mrs Pandit.' That the Prime Minister could be deluded about the nature of the internal regime in China or about the ultimate danger of a clash of Chinese and Indian interests was hard to believe. The answer, according to the British, lay almost certainly in Nehru's preoccupation with the Korean situation.[66]

The Indian service chiefs were fully aware, according to this dispatch, that the Chinese were building roads, airstrips and barracks in the frontier regions which caused them to feel anything but complacent. A Reuters News Agency report in the *Scotsman* of 23rd February 1953[67] said that the Chinese had about 100,000 troops in Tibet in frontier posts all along the Himalayan region, particularly in the Chumbi Valley before the Nathula Pass leading into Sikkim. Interestingly, this report mentioned that the 'biggest force of Chinese military labour is employed in building at top speed a motor road from Sinkiang province, in the heart of Chinese Asia, through Western Tibet to Lhasa. A first 500-mile strip of all-weather road is reported already to have been completed.' This is the first recorded reference to the Aksai Chin highway and the appearance of this report seemed to have elicited little or no response in Delhi's officialdom. Tibetan merchants were saying, according to the report, that Chinese military maps showed Sikkim, Bhutan, and Ladakh as part of Tibet. The report on the 'rumoured' Xinjiang–Lhasa Road was corroborated in a letter dated 1 May 1953 from the British Embassy in Nepal to the Foreign Office in London.[68]

The talks on Tibet were held in Beijing after the Chinese government accepted India's invitation to discuss pending matters. Speaking in Parliament, on 16 November 1953,[69] Nehru said that these questions would be considered by the two governments on the basis of mutual respect for each other's sovereignty, independence and territorial integrity. There was no final, or rigid agenda for the talks, he added. Pending matters related to the maintenance of India's long-standing trade and cultural relations with Tibet. Postal and telegraphic communications were another subject on which adjustment was considered necessary. The presence of Indian escort troops stationed in Gyantse and Yadong on the trade route to Lhasa was another pending issue. The Deputy Secretary in the Ministry of External Affairs, Delhi, told the UK High Commission, on the eve of the Tibet talks, that 'India's present relations with Tibet were governed by a number of archaic treaties and agreements which the present Chinese government did not even recognize. The main Indian interest was trade and the position of the Trade Agreements'.[70] The impression that the British diplomat took away from the meeting was that the Indian official was playing down the significance of the talks and 'refusing to admit that there is any strategic or political problem in relation to Tibet.'

Panikkar had told Bajpai in August 1952[71] that excluding the subject of the frontier (the big omission as we know from hindsight), Indian interests in Tibet fell into two categories, viz., representation at Lhasa, and the 'maintenance of certain institutions and privileges in the country' (the use of the last mentioned word, country, was probably a Freudian slip). The sum total of issues to be discussed were: representation at Lhasa; the trade agencies at Gyantse and Yadong; the trade agency at Gartok; the right of Indians to trade in Tibet in places other than trade marts; post and telegraph communications up to Yadong; the maintenance of an armed escort for the protection of the trade marts; and the pilgrimage to Kailash and Manasarovar (the two sacred sites for Hindus and Buddhists in western Tibet). Even before the negotiations had commenced, the Indian side had clearly decided that the maintenance of armed escorts, posts and telegraphs had become untenable in the 'changed circumstances' in Tibet. The Chinese regarded these as 'scars' from British days, but suggested they be gradually removed, with the first step being to replace the Political Officer with the Consulate-General in Lhasa.

On the eve of the talks in Beijing, Prime Minister Nehru was still concerned about the decision,[72] taken on Panikkar's recommendation, not to raise the frontier with the Chinese. The need for alertness and vigilance on the northeast frontier, particularly, appeared to be uppermost in his mind. He acknowledged that he had agreed with Panikkar that the issue need not be raised but added a rider that 'if occasion offers itself and especially if any challenge to the frontier is made, then we shall have to make this particularly clear.' He was also convinced about the geographical factors that gave India a 'strength of position' vis-à-vis Tibet. Tibet needed India for supplies and for logistical reasons. The 'weakest' part of the frontier lay between Bhutan and Sikkim. The policy that India needed to pursue was to strengthen its communication system with the border areas, have well-equipped check posts, strengthen its intelligence system, and bring the border areas within the orbit of India's economic and national life. But he was irked nonetheless by his Consul-General (in Lhasa) Sumul Sinha's not 'taking an objective view of the situation' concerning Tibet. He was dismissive of Sinha's reference to the Chinese 'lust for conquest'[73]. Changes in Tibet would have to be accepted. The only thing India was not prepared to accept was 'any modification of or intrusion across our frontiers.' Thinking 'vaguely' about other matters was futile. There was no question of making India the main route of supply for the Chinese in Tibet. But from the larger political point of view, a trickle of supplies could go through since it signified that Tibet relied on India and thereby had a 'psychological' significance.

This partitioned approach that assumed Chinese acquiescence of the frontier alignment by not raising the issue at all with them ('remiss diplomacy' as the historian and Nehru's biographer, S. Gopal termed it), and what was to clearly be the absence of any 'grand' strategy on dealing with China, was to make India's China diplomacy structurally flawed and increasingly brittle in the years after 1956. The 'bliss' of a 'thousand-year friendship' was short-lived as subsequent events would show—at great cost to the self-esteem and confidence of the young Republic and to the Prime Minister's vision of an Asia integrated by India and China. The chance of 'securing a clear and explicit recognition of India's frontier at a time when India had something to offer in return had been lost,' wrote S. Gopal in his biography of Nehru.[74] Disregarding his inner misgivings on the issue, Nehru had allowed these to be set aside—together with the counsel of his advisers like Girija Shankar Bajpai and K.P.S. Menon—by 'an ambassador [Panikkar] who rationalized a shirking of unpleasantness.'[75] The case for validating India's case on the border she shares with China was thus compromised, with consequences that would prove to be momentous, as the future would reveal.

6

Steep Descent

Semantics alone cannot guarantee an international frontier[1]

—S. Gopal

India's attitude towards China represents the most complex piece in the puzzle of Indian foreign policy. It is the least easy to fathom, and presents many inconsistencies but it is at the same time, I think, the key to the whole. I believe that the explanation is that public declarations of the Indian government are fundamentally out of accord with their real appreciation of the position of China. I suspect that fear is really their basic motive . . . They are horrified at the possibility of war and feel that at all cost they must avoid involvement in any clash with China.[2]

—UK High Commission in India despatch, 1952

Panikkar's successor in Beijing was a man altogether removed from the capricious, China-pandering inclinations of his predecessor. New to China, the unprepossessing Nedyam Raghavan was very different from the flamboyant, vainglorious Panikkar. But once he had settled down to his new assignment, he was observant enough of his host government to transmit objective and clear-eyed assessments of New China to the Foreign Office in New Delhi. Soon after his arrival in Beijing, the Chinese government reacted extremely adversely to a draft resolution on a Korean armistice submitted to the United Nations General Assembly by India. The resolution while affirming that the repatriation of all prisoners of war should be carried out in accordance with the provisions of the Geneva Convention (1949), also advocated that force should not be used against these persons to prevent or effect a return to their homelands. The Chinese were sharply accusatory of the Indians, stating that their stand was no different from the American one that spoke of voluntary repatriation of prisoners of war. Their objections were detailed in a lengthy aide-memoire handed over by Vice-Foreign Minister Zhang Hanfu to Ambassador Raghavan on 24 November 1952.[3] The Resolution itself was openly condemned in a speech at the UN by the Soviet Foreign Minister Andrey Vyshinsky, and the Chinese were seen as being influenced by the Soviets in their approach to the matter.

The Indian Resolution was rejected outright by the Communist bloc even before it had, perhaps, been properly studied. To Nehru, it seemed that the world was determined to commit suicide.[4] He was determined not to abandon the Resolution, telling Vijaya Lakshmi Pandit (Ambassador to the United Nations) and V.K. Krishna Menon, who had been specially sent to the UN to handle the Korean problem on behalf of India, that India's attitude to the Chinese government should 'always be a combination of friendliness and firmness. If we show weakness, advantage will be taken of this immediately.'[5] In fact, from the beginning of the Korean crisis in 1950, while not presuming to shape outcomes, Nehru was clear that however small the part that India could play, it could 'make a difference'.[6] When the hostilities broke out, Nehru expressed no doubt that it was North Korea that had aggressed into South Korea on an extensive scale. But at the same time, he was clear that India should pursue an independent policy, and she would not be hustled, or driven just by the course of events. 'Ultimately, each country in Asia will have to decide its own fate and whether we like that or not, we shall have to accept it.'[7] It was in this light that India had decided to urge both the United States and the Soviet Union to end the war, and also admit the People's Republic of China into the United Nations—one of the benefits of this admission being the creation of a more favourable atmosphere for a solution, as China had also come into the war. India's efforts were not successful, but it had made its position clear even to the extent of being willing to shelve its own prospects of a seat in the Security Council at the expense of championing the candidature of the Communist Chinese.

Ambassador Raghavan was reporting on the hostile propaganda unleashed in Beijing against India in the wake of the Indian Resolution. India was being accused by the Chinese Communist Party organs of getting more and more into the economic stranglehold of the United States. A long letter[8] from Vice-Minister Zhang Hanfu to Raghavan in March 1953 accused India of floating a resolution that was unfair and unreasonable. It went on to state that the Indian Government had 'deliberately misinterpreted' the friendship of the Chinese government. The goodwill expressed by the Indian Government for China 'had not been borne in facts'. Writing to Delhi,[9] Raghavan expressed regret that despite his attempts, there had been little change in the Chinese attitude with their behaviour continuing to be cold. 'They put on the airs of an injured party,' he observed.

Later in the same month, with the death of Stalin, the Chinese attitude was somewhat tempered. They were willing to see the question of all prisoners who were not willing to be repatriated to be handed over to a repatriation commission of five neutral nations (a Chinese proposal, which India lobbied for widely).[10] Nehru could not disguise his satisfaction 'that is all to the good and we need not go about saying that we told you so', and that the Chinese could see that 'we hold our opinions also and cannot be made to change them by pressure tactics. Anyhow, we must always remember our long-range policy, which is of developing friendship with China, subject always to not giving in on any matter that we consider important or vital to our interest.'[11]

Meanwhile, closer home, China was extending her presence in Tibet into the Chumbi Valley, adjacent to the borders with Sikkim and Bhutan. The Chumbi was short on food supplies for Chinese troops, and the Indian Government was requested for transit facilities for 10,000 tons of food grains through India. The request was partially met, with 3000 tons of rice being allowed transit into Tibet.[12] The buzz in Tibetan circles put the estimate of Chinese troops in Tibet at this time at about 20,000 to 25,000. Road construction work was in full swing, with thousands of PLA soldiers being engaged in this activity.

The professing of cordial relations with India notwithstanding, Chinese harassment of Indian personnel in Tibet was an endemic feature. The targets were the Indian wireless operators and mail or dak runners; seizure of arms and cameras from Indian traders and pilgrims entering Tibet was also common. Tibetans were apparently told 'not without hauteur and disdain'[13] that the show of friendliness toward India was a temporary expedient to obtain supplies. There was also bragging about the eventual inclusion of Bhutan, Sikkim, and Nepal within the sphere of Chinese influence. The change in status of the Indian office in Lhasa to a Consulate-General from September 1952 onwards, saw a ceasing of such propaganda. The brother of the Dalai Lama, Gyalo Thondup, meanwhile sought asylum in India claiming persecution in Tibet. Once in India, he claimed great resentment among the Tibetans against Chinese occupation and 'complete violation' by the Chinese of the 1951 Agreement.

Referring to the 'Tibetan border problem', Nehru told his Heads of Mission in the Middle East (who were gathered in Delhi for a conference) that while the '3000 miles or so of border' with China and Tibet did not trouble him, it did make him think 'intensely all the time' because it 'created new problems, new burdens, new financial burdens, new military burdens'.[14] China would continue to be a neighbor and could not be ignored, although it did not mean that 'we should bow down to China'. The Prime Minister was obviously struggling with his own thoughts on China. While it was 'impossible' to do anything about the question of Tibet, the frontier had to be secured, and nothing could be 'surrendered' to China.

It had been obvious since the Communist Chinese takeover in Tibet that what were seen as 'imperial' privileges stemming from the time of the deployment of British power and influence in Tibet were not going to be tolerated by the new regime. It was also clear that Prime Minister Nehru understood the turn of events and was also well aware of independent India's need to adjust to this new reality, while at the same time seeking to secure Indian interests on the long common frontier with China. Principal points at issue were the status of the Indian mission in Lhasa, the post and telecommunication facilities operated by India in Tibet, pilgrimage facilities for Indians, and the Indian commercial offices in Gyantse, Yadong and Gartok. By June 1952, the Government of India had agreed to set up a consulate-general in Lhasa in exchange for a Chinese consulate-general in Bombay.[15] Reporting from New Delhi,[16] in a meeting with Foreign Secretary R.K. Nehru, where they discussed Indian 'privileges' in Tibet, the Chinese Ambassador Yuan Zhongxin reiterated that these privileges were based on 'unequal relationships between Britain and the former Chinese government, and the present Indian government is not liable for these conditions.'

Ambassador Yuan told Nehru that the Chinese view was that privileges established under such unequal relationships 'shall no longer exist', that all issues be 'properly settled through negotiations' and that issues relating to the 'sovereignty of China' like the presence of military 'garrisons' from India, radio stations, carriage of arms, would need to be resolved. Furthermore, Indian personnel could not enter Tibet without visas in accordance with 'international practice' (Travel between India and Tibet had been unrestricted until then). Reiterating the line that India recognized the new conditions in Tibet, and his government's willingness to 'adjust and even cancel' India's traditional rights in Tibet, keeping in mind that India and Tibet 'were historically interdependent on each other', Nehru at the same time said that radio stations were necessary for Indian commercial representatives to carry out their duties. Garrison relief was needed for Indian troops in Tibet. It could not be said that the Chinese government had not interfered with the carrying out of duties of these Indian personnel. The tension between the two sides ran as an undercurrent through the conversation.

The conversation between the two had been preceded by a message[17] addressed to Premier Zhou Enlai from Prime Minister Nehru. In it, the Indian Prime Minister expressed Indian preparedness to 'adapt' to the new situation in Tibet. He reminded the Chinese Premier that the latter had said earlier that there 'is no territorial dispute or controversy between India and China'. No declassified archival material seen by this author contains an actual reference to the Chinese Premier having used these words. It is more than probable that this impression, that there was no territorial dispute, was given to Nehru by Panikkar, based on the latter's reading of Zhou's conversations with him. The truth is that the Chinese gave the impression that the only contentious issues to be discussed regarding Tibet were 'privileges' arising from the exercise of British imperial power in Tibet. The Indians, for their part, seemed to operate on the principle of *qui tacet consentit*, construing that Chinese silence on border issues meant their consent to the border as seen by India. In his meeting of 23 June 1952 with T.N. Kaul,[18] Zhou said that the 'existing situation of Sino-Indian relationship in Tibet, China was a scar left by

Britain' and that 'the relations between the new China and the new Government of India in Tibet, China should be built up anew through negotiations.' In Zhou's view, this was 'the principle that should first of all be stated.'

Nehru informed Zhou that India was anxious to come to a final settlement of pending matters regarding Tibet in order to avoid misunderstanding and friction. His government had agreed to the establishment of a Chinese Consulate-General in Bombay in exchange for the re-designation of the Political Office in Lhasa as the Indian Consulate-General. Nehru was of the view that the pending issues relating to 'other practices' that were seen as 'affecting the dignity of China' could also be modified, as already conveyed to the Chinese by the Indian Embassy in Beijing. This would prevent further 'incidents' with the activities of Indian trade agents in western Tibet, seizure of wireless sets and matters concerning the replacement of the military escorts ('garrisons' as the Chinese termed them) or visits by the Political Officer in Sikkim to the Chumbi Valley and to Lhasa. The Prime Minister suggested to his Chinese counterpart that the two governments take the earliest opportunity to 'consider all pending matters' and to confer 'on all such matters affecting relations between our two countries.' This was followed up with an aide-memoire, drafted by the Prime Minister, which was presented on 5 September 1953 to the Chinese Embassy in Delhi.[19] On 29 September, Ambassador Raghavan was informed by the Ministry of External Affairs that as a 'voluntary gesture of goodwill', it had been decided in principle to withdraw the three platoons in Yadong and Gyantse, provided an early discussion could be held on all pending matters.[20] The decision appears to have caught Indian personnel in Tibet by some degree of surprise, with the Trade Agent in Gyantse calling it 'sober and timely' but at the same time remonstrating that 'we should have thought it better to maintain a small force'.[21] There is no cogent explanation for the Indian move except to surmise that there was anxiety to convey to the Chinese that there was no desire to retain any 'imperial' privileges left over from the British days as far as Tibet was concerned.

The response from the Chinese agreeing to talks on pending matters relating to Tibet came in late October 1953. It was proposed by Premier Zhou that the two governments hold discussions in Beijing in December 1953 'on the problem of Sino-Indian relations in Tibet'. Prime Minister Nehru hastened to thank Zhou for his response, expressing confidence that all 'pending matters between our two Governments can be solved to our mutual satisfaction in the spirit of friendship and cooperation based on equality and respect for territorial sovereignty.'[22]

On the eve of the talks, the views expressed by field personnel in Lhasa were much more granular in content, reflecting views that were laden with suspicions about Indian 'intentions' in Tibet. On 21 October 1953, the Party Secretary for Tibet, Zhang Jingwu sent a lengthy telegram to the Foreign Ministry in Beijing. He was obviously responding to the latter about the matter relating to talks with India on Tibet. The Foreign Ministry had expressed the view, as mentioned in the document,[23] that 'India intends to capitalize this opportunity to have some benefit in Tibet', a view that Zhang, a hard-boiled skeptic about Indian intentions, found 'very accurate'. India, he said, was capitalizing on China's 'temporary difficulties in Tibet, particularly our insufficient understanding of imperialist privileges in Tibet and the ideal solution to border disputes'. And here, the Zhang telegram makes a key observation, one that indicates that the Chinese were fully aware and observant of the question of the border/frontier between Tibet and India. Zhang referred to the Indian claim that 'India and China have no territorial disputes' (citing Nehru's mention of the same in Parliament, too), inferring from this that 'this is where the plot of India lies'. India, he said, had occupied the Tawang region and was claiming the absence of territorial disputes 'just to force us into implicitly acknowledging and legitimizing their occupation. We must stay alert in this regard.' The status quo, he said, as observed by India, was based on the Simla Accord or Agreement between Britain, India and China of 1914. The McMahon Line had been established as a result of the Simla Accord.

Zhang cautioned the Foreign Ministry that the issue of the Simla Accord and the McMahon Line was an important one, and that it was necessary for China to state that it did not recognize these agreements, and had abolished them; further it would need to insist on Indian withdrawal from 'Chinese Tawang and Lower Luoyu' and that China and India should discuss the 'dividing lines' between the two countries. Implicitly acknowledging that the status quo would put China in a disadvantageous position, he stated that 'further' declarations would need to be made, even if the issue could not be settled immediately, i.e., in the impending talks, which should focus on the withdrawal of Indian troops, removal of postal facilities of India, as well as wireless installations. The trade office of India in Gartok could continue, but the commercial representation in Yadong and Gyantse should be discontinued. If India insisted on retaining its presence in Yadong, China should ask for a formal representation in Kalimpong, in exchange.

The Indians were meanwhile getting reports about high-level consultations between the Chinese and the Tibetans prior to the talks in Beijing between India and China. The Indian Consulate in Lhasa reporting to New Delhi said that the Chinese had informed the Tibetan Kashag that they intended to take up the border question, that they would firmly repudiate the 1914 Simla Treaty between India and Tibet. The map showing the McMahon Line was also seen.[24] It was obvious that the Chinese were well aware of the history of the Simla Agreement and having seen the map with the McMahon Line and being cognizant of the Indian entry into Tawang in 1951, were readying themselves to raise these questions at a favourable juncture with India. On the eve of the talks in Beijing, they had assessed that favourable juncture as not having presented itself, as yet. In 1953, Tibet was still not fully controlled, roads and transportation of supplies for Chinese troops were still a problem—entailing a dependence on the Indian route for such supplies, China's preoccupation with the Korean War had not subsided, and recovery would take time. Furthermore, friendship with India was a bridge for China to the world, with Nehru being more than willing to transmit and communicate Chinese aspirations on the global stage. The Chinese were clearly buying time. Opportunities, they had assessed, would present themselves in plenty, to raise the border question, once their strength within the country had been greatly consolidated.

As of early December 1953, on the eve of the talks with China, the Ministry of External Affairs in Delhi was still struggling with the issue of 'Whether the question of our frontier with Tibet should be raised?'[25] If at all the Chinese were to raise the question, the Indians speculated, they should be told that there was 'nothing' to discuss as the frontier was 'clearly defined'. Proposals for 'minor adjustments for the sake of convenience' could at the most be considered, after the Chinese 'had accepted our present frontiers'. If the Chinese were to raise the 'illegality' of the Simla Convention of 1914, they could be told that 'convention or no convention, our frontier is well defined and well recognized by long custom and usage'. Further, if they were to suggest that discussion on the frontier question be postponed in its entirety, since they were not prepared for discussion at this point, one considered option would be to walk out of the talks, 'as suggested by Sardar Panikkar', although this would defeat the very object for which the Conference had been called and could lead to border incidents with China.

Another option, the less extreme one, would be 'maintain our stand about the frontier and refuse to accept the Chinese stand or discuss it, and proceed to other items.' And, if the Chinese refused to do so, then the negotiations should be broken off. (Prime Minister Nehru, for his part, hoped that such an eventuality would not come to pass. If it did, he was sanguine that the matter would be reported to Delhi for a decision. He left the matter there). The Indians would learn the hard way, much later, that diplomacy could not be secured through debating points or unilateral assumption. The internal remedy suggested, in the face of these shadowy uncertainties about the Chinese stand, was the consolidation of positions along the frontier and the occupation of areas right up to the McMahon Line—a policy predicated on the assumption of concerted, focused action that proved difficult to deliver all throughout the remote and inaccessible areas concerned.

There was also some complacency on the Indian side that China needed Indian trade with Tibet more than India did, in view of the dependence on the latter for supplying Chinese troops in Tibet 'for many years to come'. (The argument that the trade agency in Yadong should be retained was built on this premise since the main route to Lhasa from India lay across the Nathu La into the Chumbi Valley where the trade office was located). This proved a flawed prognosis because the Chinese speed in building roads into Tibet revealed the fundamental weakness of this argument. The intention that the Chinese should be asked for the reopening of the Indian Consulate in Kashgar so that trade between Xinjiang and Kashmir could be restored was also not pursued with any seriousness.

The Indian delegation to the talks in Beijing was led by Ambassador Raghavan, and included Joint Secretary T.N. Kaul and Dr K. Gopalachari of the Historical Division in the Ministry of External Affairs. On 31 December 1953 the delegation met with Premier Zhou Enlai in the company of Vice-Minister Zhang Hanfu (leader of the Chinese delegation), Director Chen Jiakang and Yang Gongsu, the head of the Lhasa Foreign Affairs Bureau.[26] Zhou's words to the delegation were noteworthy: he told them that questions that were 'ripe for settlement' between the two sides could be resolved on the basis of mutual respect for territorial integrity, non-aggression and non-interference in internal affairs 'so as to enable peaceful coexistence'. It was obvious that these points made by the Premier were directly related to the issue of Indian interests in Tibet, especially the reference to territorial integrity (read sovereignty) and non-interference. They were subsequently to be written into the Preamble of the Agreement that would be signed at the conclusion of the talks a few months later in April 1954, as the much-vaunted Five Principles of Peaceful Coexistence, or Panchsheel.

The talks commenced on 2 January 1954. The atmosphere was described by the Indians as 'cordial'. The agenda proposed by India covered the Trade Agencies in Gartok (western Tibet), Gyantse (central Tibet) and Yadong (the Chumbi Valley), trade centres, pilgrim traffic and rest houses, posts and telegraph, passports, visas and permits, and the military escorts. The Chinese began by enumerating the five principles referred to by Premier Zhou in his meeting with the Indian delegation stating that if these were agreed to, all pending questions that were ripe for settlement could be discussed and settled.[27] The Chinese listed their agenda as commencing with the Trade Agencies, then the Escorts, followed by posts, telegraphs and telephones, rest houses and trade, pilgrimage traffic and passports, visas and permits.

Of note was the fact that in the discussions about trade and trade facilities, the areas covered were only western and southern Tibet. The Chinese maintained an intriguing vagueness regarding Ladakh, which the Indian side did not seek to probe too deeply, although there was mention in internal communications between the embassy in Beijing and Delhi that India should insist on opening passes at Tashigong in the Spiti Valley of Himachal Pradesh and Demchok on the Ladakh frontier for trade with Tibet. The Chinese response to moves to discuss Ladakh was that if the latter was to be discussed, it would raise the issue of Kashmir which was 'pending settlement through negotiations between India and Pakistan'. They were prepared to allow a channelling of Ladakh trade through Tashigong. The Indian response was that this position could not be accepted as it impinged on the principle of territorial integrity.[28] As it transpired, the Indians themselves decided not to raise the issue of Kashmiri trade with Tibet, as they did not want to discuss 'the disputed Aksai Chin area'[29] which might in turn, steer discussions to border issues. New Delhi agreed, with their embassy stating, 'We do not wish to raise the Aksai Chin question.' It is interesting that the Indian side already saw the Aksai Chin area in eastern Ladakh as disputed—although this was much before the issue of the Aksai Chin highway had erupted, leading to the downhill slide in bilateral relations from 1958 onwards. That they had some inkling about the Chinese being unwilling to discuss the Ladakh sector because of military and security considerations, was obvious. Ambassador Raghavan telegraphed Foreign Secretary R.K. Nehru in March 1954[30] as follows: 'Our view is Chinese are reluctant to concede Rudok or Rawang (both in Ladakh) because of military installations . . .'

The head of India's Intelligence Bureau, B.N. Mullik was to write years later[31] (after the border conflict between India and China had erupted) that on 'two issues the real significance of the Chinese attitude was probably not fully understood at the time'. One, as referred to earlier, was that the Chinese would not discuss the question of trade marts for Ladakhi traders in western Tibet on the ground that this related to Kashmir which was under dispute between India and Pakistan. (China, as early as 1954, was giving the impression that it was maintaining a neutral attitude between India and Pakistan on Kashmir.) The second issue was the Chinese refusal to recognize the traditional trade mart in Rudok without ascribing a reason. In Mullik's assessment, which had the benefit of hindsight at the time he wrote it, this 'was no doubt because the Chinese were building the road from Rudok to Sinkiang via Aksai Chin.'

The negotiations in Beijing slowed down for a few weeks in March–April 1954 when the leader of the Chinese delegation, Zhang Hanfu, fell ill and was hospitalized. By then, both sides had exchanged their respective drafts of the final agreement. The Chinese draft used the words 'Tibetan region of China' with reference to Tibet. There was some discussion in New Delhi on this, which was finally papered over with the Foreign Ministry bureaucracy taking the line that the usage could be accepted since its literal meaning was Tibet and that 'Tibetan region of China' was a rendering from the Chinese. The final agreement referred to Tibet as the 'Tibet Region of China'—essentially meaning the region of Tibet, as administered by Lhasa and excluding other Tibetan-speaking regions in adjacent Chinese provinces like Qinghai, Yunnan, Gansu, and Xinjiang. Differences between the two sides on the issue of immunity for trade agents from search, arrest and detention (the Chinese were insistent that such immunity could not be provided) took time to resolve. The Chinese were intent on the withdrawal of all privileges stemming from the decades of British dominance, especially after 1911. The Indians, anxious to ensure a speedy and successful end to negotiations, agreed to a bulk of the Chinese demands for removal of privileges in Tibet inherited from the British. R.K. Nehru told Raghavan that 'petty points of difference should not hold up the conclusion of Agreement any longer.'[32] Also, the Chinese were insistent that the agreement should not define the 'Tibetan' area covered, and that, in any case, it should not include Tibetan speaking areas like 'Sikang, Chinghai or Sinkiang'[33]. Also, the Chinese were insistent on an eight-year period of validity for the agreement with no provisions for automatic renewal. Three texts of the agreement were prepared, in English, Chinese and Hindi (this being the first international agreement reached by India whose text was recorded in Hindi too).

Prime Minister Nehru was meanwhile pushing for an early conclusion of the agreement before the start of the conference in Geneva to discuss Korea and Indo China. He was anxious that no impression be given to the Americans, in particular, that the talks in Beijing had stalled, indicating a divide between India and

China. The argument appeared to appeal to the Chinese too. The Indians were giving in to most of the Chinese demands on trade arrangements, even agreeing to Kalimpong, Siliguri and Calcutta (Kolkata) as trade centers, although Raghavan claimed he had put up a 'royal fight' in the face of Zhang Hanfu's 'recalcitrant attitude'. The Indians did score some success with the inclusion of the Tashigong route along the Indus as a channel for trade after much negotiation. They agreed to completely withdraw their military escorts in Yadong and Gyantse, hand over the post and telegraph and public telephone services together with operating equipment needed for these services, the twelve Indian rest houses, and the return of all land used or occupied by the Indian government other than the lands within its trade agency compound wall in Yadong. Of interest was the fact that R.K. Nehru advised Raghavan in Beijing[34] that references to withdrawal of military escorts etc., should be avoided explicitly in any public communique regarding the agreement, it being merely stated that 'reciprocal arrangements (were) agreed to in the interest of both sides.' He rightly apprehended that giving play to the concessions made by India would create 'a wrong impression in the minds of the Indian public'.

The Agreement between the Republic of India and the People's Republic of China on Trade and Intercourse between the Tibet Region of China and India was signed in Beijing on 29 April 1954. The Agreement was based on what came to be known as the Five Principles of Peaceful Co-existence or the Panchsheel.[35] The formulation had been proposed by China and accepted by India. Prime Minister Nehru was ready to accept these principles as 'policy that we pursue in regard to those matters not only with China but with any neighbour country, or for that matter any other country.' He called it a statement of 'wholesome principle'.[36] He was confident that the agreement would ensure that the frontier with China would be peaceful, and that peace would prevail to 'a very large extent in a certain area of Asia.'

Most importantly, the agreement conceded that Tibet was a 'region of China'. The Indian side regarded the conclusion of the agreement as a success for India, with T.N. Kaul claiming that a show of 'friendly firmness on matters of principle' had helped India in the negotiations with China. The Indians, he claimed, had stood firm on important points. However, no mention was made at all in the agreement of previous treaties and trade regulations between Britain, Tibet and China. This included the Simla Convention/Agreement of 1914, which was key to deciding the validity of the McMahon Line. The fact was that India had obtained an agreement with an eight-year validity with China on Tibet. This only implied that an uncertain future lay ahead, and that the Chinese having got India to voluntarily dilute her privileges in Tibet, were keeping their options open— especially if either the situation inside Tibet deteriorated because of internal unrest (which it did), or differences arose along the border with India (which happened), or as their own military and strategic situation became stronger, diminishing any dependence on India for transport and supplies. The Chinese had bought time with India. The Indians came away feeling that the question of Tibet having been settled—they had conceded Chinese sovereignty over it—they could now strengthen their posts and presence up to the frontier with China and safeguard their interests more securely. Time would tell that this was a flimsy bargain.

There was one outcome of the agreement which was to have significant ramifications for the whole case of India's boundary with China. Prime Minister Nehru was of the view that the agreement between India and China over Tibet 'marks a new starting point for our relations with China and Tibet.' In July 1954, during a short summer interlude in the hill station of Mashobra, and after seeing a note by K. Gopalachari who had been a member of the delegation that had negotiated the agreement, Nehru recorded as follows in a 17-Para memorandum:

All our old maps dealing with this frontier (with China) should be carefully examined and where necessary withdrawn. New maps should be printed showing our northern and north eastern frontier without any reference to any line. These new maps should also not state that here is any un-demarcated territory.

Both as flowing from our policy and as a consequence of our agreement with China this frontier should be considered as firm and definite one which is not open to discussion with anybody.

Our frontier has been finalized not only by implication in this agreement but the specific passes[37] mentioned are direct recognitions of our frontier.[38]

The observations were portentous. The Prime Minister had concluded that the border with Tibet, and by larger extrapolation, with China, had been finalized as a result of the agreement with the Chinese on Tibet. The issue had not cropped up in the negotiations in Beijing, the Chinese having been silent about it (as a deliberate decision by Premier Zhou, as has been revealed in the Chinese records now available), and the Indians had inferred that that silence meant acquiescence. Guesswork is fatal to good diplomacy and the Indian reading of the Chinese was flawed. The prophetic words of G.S. Bajpai had been overridden by the wishful prognostications of Panikkar who continued to advise the Prime Minister on China from his perch as Ambassador of India in Cairo. In the new maps of India of 1954, as is now reported in the public domain, the unilateral revision of the official maps was completed.[39] 'The legend 'boundary undefined' in the western (Kashmir) and middle sectors (Uttar Pradesh) in the official maps of 1948 and 1950 were dropped in the new map of 1954. A firm, clear line was shown, instead.'[40] The frontier, as messaged by the Indian leadership was 'not open to discussion with anybody'.

The changes in the Indian maps did not go unnoticed by outside observers. The British High Commissioner in Delhi writing to his Foreign Office in July 1955,[41] referred to these as the Indian response to Chinese maps claiming parts of India and Burma for China. Pointing to the then latest Survey of India map published in 1955, it was noted that the northern frontier was depicted in a manner 'significantly different from that of the first edition of 1950.' In the 1950 edition, the whole border from north-eastern Kashmir to north-western Nepal, and part of the Indo-Burmese border was shown as 'undefined', and the McMahon Line and the whole 'East Pakistan border' were 'undemarcated'.

In retrospect, the observation by B.N. Mullik that the 1954 Agreement on Tibet had not served the interests of India is not off the mark. India gave up her stand on the autonomy of Tibet, and subsequently 'restricted all her actions in support of Tibet.'[42] China had conceded almost nothing to India. On the other hand, the Chinese gained new concessions like allowing trade marts in Kalimpong, Siliguri and Calcutta. In the working of the agreement, the Chinese were to make it difficult for the operation of Indian trade with western Tibet, for instance. As it turned out, the Indian Trade Agencies and the Lhasa Consulate were 'gradually isolated and prevented from making contacts with any Tibetans'. As the veteran diplomat Apa Pant was to point out,[43] 'India was geared to do literally nothing in Tibet. The four missions that were functioning there, Lhasa, Gyantse, Yadong, and Gartok were sleepy little pleasant places with neither the staff, the training or the motivation to do anything but play Mahjong, and once in a while attend or give parties to their Nepali or Tibetan friends and the Indian businessmen'.

Significantly, the renunciation of India's historic rights in Tibet was done in favour of a strong and nationalistic China, and not in favour of a 'weak and friendly Tibet'. Furthermore, the question of the northern frontier remained unsettled. The agreement was regarded a 'master stroke of Chinese diplomacy' and Zhou Enlai as 'perhaps the most notable diplomatic conjurer since Bismarck'[44]. But India's domestic situation at the time and the lack of consolidation of Indian administrative and military strength on the frontier with China also placed her in a difficult position that left no alternative but to buy time until the situation improved, by professing friendship with China and readiness to resolve the question of Indian rights and privileges in Tibet. However, the Chinese had clearly retained the option of raising the question of the northern frontier as soon as the situation was 'ripe', which is exactly what would happen down the line.

If India had raised the issue of the McMahon Line, tying it to the issue of settlement of outstanding matters regarding Tibet, the trajectory of India-China relations post-1954 would have been charted on a more realistic, though difficult terrain, teaching India where exactly China stood on matters of vital strategic concern to the young democracy next door. Nehru was prepared to give up the extraterritorial rights inherited from the British on Tibet, but was not prepared to acquiesce in any discussion concerning the McMahon Line decided upon during the Anglo-Tibetan discussions under the Simla Convention of 1914. His own explanation made to Parliament in 1959[45] was that India was merely accepting the reality of Chinese occupation of Tibet which she was not in a position to alter, while the 'raising of the claim to the McMahon Line . . . would have led to a demand for a quid pro quo by Communist China'.[46]

In this brave new dawn, how did the Chinese view the Indians? Ambassador Raghavan, unlike his predecessor, did not suspend judgement so easily. He felt he was taking an objective view of the Chinese. Unlike the Indians, the Chinese were not an emotional lot—their attitude was a matter of fact. Summing up the Chinese approach in a letter to the Prime Minister in March 1954, he said they were 'correct and friendly without being warm and cordial' in their relations with India. The 'people of India' were seen as distinct from the Government of India, and they were waiting for the emergence of a 'People's Government' in India. Until then, they would play down the achievements of the democratically elected government, 'or at least keep the Chinese nation in ignorance of them'. They were keen to project India as a capitalist country bound down by colonialism and feudalism, 'and as such, still not free'. They were willing to make use of India and her independent role in international affairs, but were keen to ensure as far as possible that India did not increase her stature in international affairs so that 'China's ultimate role as the leading Asian power will in no manner be affected or threatened.'

New India, the Ambassador told Nehru, was considered an anachronism, 'a halfway house at best', in transition from capitalism and semi-colonialism to communism and 'popular democracy'. No praise was given in public for the role played by India for a solution to the Korean problem, whereas India had more than her fair share of criticism in the press whenever she did not adopt the Chinese line. In the words of a senior Chinese leader in 1953, as reported by Raghavan, 'India as she is today cannot be considered a friend but is useful as she is more or less certain to remain neutral in any conflict . . . as such friendly relations are to be carefully maintained.' Even references to ancient connections between India and China were studiously avoided 'except in unreported speeches at banquets to visiting dignitaries.'

A few redeeming features in this 'arid desert', according to Raghavan, were: the fact that the Indian Prime Minister was regarded as a sincere friend (though not to be confused with the Government of India); the opinion of the Government of India was valued; personal cordiality was 'occasionally extended' by the Chinese Premier to 'persuasive Ambassadors of India', a matter of paramount importance in a country governed from the top; and an 'inner conviction' gaining ground that India 'is an agency for good in world affairs'.

The Ambassador's rather brave conclusion from all this was one that contradicted his observations about Chinese indifference to India. 'Our relations today are better than ever before,' he wrote, signing off on a letter dated 18 March 1954 to Prime Minister Nehru.[47]

It is true, however, that in the wake of the Tibet Agreement, the scope of functional cooperation in trade, culture and educational exchanges between India and China was sought to be increased, with the Chinese showing a little more enthusiasm about such cooperation than before. Prime Minister Nehru was positively inclined. He was open to the initiation of discussions on a trade agreement, an Indian Government-sponsored cultural troupe visiting China, the visit of a Chinese cultural troupe to India, and the exchange of students, especially so that some young Indians could learn the Chinese language.

Around the same time, yet another incident illustrated the clinical and unemotional attitude of the Chinese towards India and the relationship with India. The repatriation of Chinese prisoners of war (POWs) from Korea had been completed by early 1954. Solely due to Nehru's conviction, India had played a decisive role in the mediation to end the Korean conflict, counter-balancing the influence of the two Cold War blocs.[48] Nehru was willing to take on the Americans in the United Nations in order to push for a speedy end to the hostilities in Korea. Zhou's message to Ambassador Panikkar in Beijing in 1951 warning against UN forces crossing the 38th Parallel had, rightly, been taken seriously by Nehru; the ignoring of this warning by the American-led UN forces had led to a full-blown escalation of the war with the entry of China in the military conflict.

The scale of Chinese intervention in Korea had not been foreseen by Nehru even though India had been a transmitter of the Chinese warning about the 38th Parallel being crossed. Despite this, Nehru was determined to continue his efforts within the United Nations to see an end to the war. It was the Indian Resolution adopted by the United Nations on 3 December 1952, supported by the United States and the Commonwealth countries, and opposed by the Soviet Union and China (the latter called the Resolution, the 'parent of all evil'[49]) that helped pave the way towards the repatriation of the POWs. As discussed earlier, the Chinese displayed great hostility towards India on the terms of the Resolution and the question of voluntary repatriation, although they later signalled (soon after the death of Stalin in March 1953) that they might be able to work with the terms of the document. India was then to lead the Neutral Nations Repatriation Commission (NNRC) on the return of prisoners. Stalin's death and General Dwight Eisenhower's election as US President meanwhile created the conditions necessary for the conclusion of an Armistice Agreement in Korea in July 1953. And India did play a key role in bringing about an end to the conflict with its Resolution of December 1952 on the key question of the return and repatriation of prisoners.

At the end of the Korean War, about one-third of the approximately 21,000 Chinese prisoners of war were repatriated to Communist China; of the remaining number, more than 14,300 prisoners went to Taiwan. It was a significant propaganda disaster for Beijing which had been insisting that all Chinese POWs be returned to China. Zhou Enlai could not have been happy. The head of the NNRC was General K. Thimayya of India. Thimayya had played an impartial role during his tenure in Korea but the Chinese had clearly lost face on the POW issue. It was against this backdrop that in June 1954, on the eve of the signing of the prisoners-of-war agreement between China and the United States, that Brigadier B.M. Kaul (who was later to play a key role in the failed defence of the Tawang sector during the 1962 War) met Zhou Enlai. Kaul was on a private visit to Beijing, and it is extraordinary and reflective of Zhou's leadership style that he should have sought out Kaul to have a discussion about Thimayya, to complain to him and an accompanying officer of the Ministry of External Affairs, Bahadur Singh, about the military chief's attitude. It was an unorthodox move, and it is difficult to understand in retrospect, how it was tolerated by the Indians. A similar move in Delhi by the Indians, hypothetically, would never have been tolerated by the Chinese. Writing to the Prime Minister, Ambassador Raghavan described how 'the whole thing was an attempt to influence the views and opinions of the officers or win them over against the chief under whom they were working.' The incident definitely does throw some light on the personality of Zhou Enlai and the disregard for scruple or diplomatic practice in his method of functioning: his manner of meeting these visitors from India who were not on any official mission, in order to probe them about another serving and senior Indian Army colleague was unorthodox and unprecedented.

In retrospect, 1954 proved to be a memorable milestone in the India-China bilateral relationship. With the Tibet Agreement, a point of no return had been crossed. The very element of certainty that the Indians assumed would now define the relationship proved a chimera. The legacy of empire had been voluntarily and magnanimously relinquished by India in Tibet, but there was much that lay ahead that would prove how unfinished the process of building a solid and stable relationship with China was. For Nehru, the year was one which saw his prestige as an international leader at a high—India's contribution to a Korean settlement seemed to justify her place as a 'third force', as a peacemaker. Then, the Tibet Agreement with China relayed the image that India and China, two newly emergent Asian nations, could be an outstanding example for mature leadership and statesmanship, and pragmatic negotiation against the arid landscape of the Cold War.

Nehru was not unaware about the disappointment the agreement had caused among many people. He defended his position by stating that the agreement was 'quite inevitable'.[50] He was of the view that if 'we had not got that Agreement, the position would have been no better for us in Tibet and a little worse for the Tibetans'. India, he felt, could not have hung on to privileges 'which had no meaning in the present state of affairs.' India's policy should, therefore, be an observance in letter and spirit, of the agreement, while at the same time continuing 'our friendly feelings for Tibet and her people'. And, 'for the rest, we have to be vigilant and wide awake', he concluded. Just a few years later, in 1958, on his way to Bhutan, by the side of a campfire, high in the Himalayas, Nehru would talk about 'misplaced faith' in Chinese 'friendship'.[51] But in the immediate wake of the 1954 Agreement, Indian diplomats were sanguine about its achievements. When in April 1955, the transfer of India's posts and telegraph installations and the 'Dak bungalows' was completed, P.N. Menon, the Consul-General in Lhasa wrote[52] that it represented 'in a decisive fashion the end of the period which began nearly 50 years ago when the then Government of India started to function inside Tibet in an extraterritorial way. But in sharp contrast to the methods of violence and pressure which brought these rights into existence, the final chapter of the giving up of these extraterritorial rights was marked by a harmonious and equitable settlement which is bound to leave no trace of bitterness in any quarter.'

A seal of legitimacy had been placed on China's occupation of Tibet, once and for all, by India with no concrete reciprocity from China. In many ways, for India, the Tibet Agreement of 1954 with China as history has shown, was an unequal settlement. The country that was most closely tied with Tibet, through history, religion, written language, trade, and intellectual debate and dialogue through the monastic tradition, as well as a natural friendship of trust, chose to downgrade these linkages on the assumption that a stable, assured relationship with China was worth much more. It was a strategic error in the higher direction of leadership that would prove costly for India as the postscripts to 1954 would show.

7

Friends with Benefits

The foreign policy of the People's Government does not apparently differ fundamentally from that of the former Nationalist government, or from that which any government of China might be expected to pursue: basically, it is full control over all her own territory and the safety of her borders. Security in Sinkiang and Manchuria having presumably been assured as far as possible by agreement with Russia and by the development of those areas, the principal present objectives, are, the recovery of Formosa, a peace treaty for Japan which will leave that country sufficiently prosperous as a market for Chinese goods but deprived of power as an aggressor or as an industrial competitor, the independence of Korea under a government which is friendly, the full control of Tibet, and the assumption of her own position as a Charter member of the United Nations': other and less immediate objectives doubtless are, the eventual recovery of Hong Kong, the establishment of a friendly government in Indo-China, the protection of Chinese populations in South East Asia, the re-alignment of the Sino-Burmese and the Indo-Tibetan frontiers, the elimination of

*hostile influences in neighbouring states, and the assumption
of political leadership in Asia*[1]

—J.C. Hutchison, UK Chargé d'affaires, Beijing, February 1951

The British called it the billing and cooing phase of the 1950s—
they were referring to the Chinese moves to play along with
India, placing a seeming premium on good relations with their
giant neighbour, and purveying the message that Asia was for
the Asiatics. From their viewpoint, the Chinese had scarcely
moderated their positions, whether it was on the Korean question,
or on Tibet, or as far as their anti-American propaganda was
concerned. The Chinese, they felt, were stringing the Indians
along. On their part, the Chinese were engaged in their own
brand of people's diplomacy toward India. Zhou Enlai personally
delivered over the radio a message to the Indian people in June
1954, where he spoke of the 'profound friendship' that had existed
between the peoples of China and India, and that 'since very
ancient days', a 'borderline covering a great distance of nearly
3000 kilometres links together the two nations'. There had never
been war or animosity, the Chinese Premier said, that had divided
the two nations; they had together been subjected to the evils of
foreign colonialism, 'suffering on the same score and fighting
for the same cause'. A common desire for peaceful development
animated both nations, and the friendship of 960,000,000 people
of China and India constituted 'a mighty force for maintaining
peace in Asia and the world'.[2] Zhou Enlai made his remarks
after completing a visit to India in June 1954. He spoke of his
talks with Prime Minister Nehru, soon after the conclusion of
the Panchsheel Agreement, as having provided a means for the
recognition of the Five Principles of Peaceful Coexistence on the
global stage.

The visit of the Chinese Premier to India was apparently decided at short notice, although the climate for it had been conducive since the conclusion of the April 1954 Panchsheel Agreement. V.K. Krishna Menon, as Nehru's envoy to the Indo-China talks in Geneva, had conveyed a casual invitation to Zhou to stay in Delhi on his return journey to Beijing from Geneva. A day or two before the visit actually took place, the Chinese conveyed to the Indians that they were ready to come to Delhi, taking the Indian Government apparently by surprise. Nehru had to cancel a planned holiday and 'an air of crisis hung over the Protocol Department' of the Ministry of External Affairs[3]. Despite the short notice, however, the trip was billed as historic by the Indian media, and symbolic of the resurgence of Asia, heralding a new phase of Asian diplomacy. Not only would the red carpet be laid for the visiting Chinese leader so that a favourable impression was made on him, but the aim was also to positively impact world opinion about the two Asian giants cementing their friendship.

On the eve of his visit, Zhou chose to give an exclusive interview to the veteran Indian commentator, journalist and political scientist, K.S. Shelvankar.[4] He used the occasion to criticize the policies of the Western powers whom he accused of dividing Asia, citing the examples of Korea and Indo-China. This, in his view, was a threat to peace and security, and more consultation was required among Asian countries to safeguard their interests, 'by assuming obligations mutually and respectively'. The Agreement on Trade and Intercourse between the Tibet Region of China and India and the principles enshrined therein, had set a good example for cooperation among Asian states, he said. Interestingly, the interview included a question addressed to Zhou regarding Mahatma Gandhi. The Premier spoke in reply to state that the Chinese respected the 'life-long devotion of Gandhi and his struggle for national independence'. He said that such a struggle had had 'a profound influence on the Chinese people'. On his part, Krishna Menon was reporting to Nehru from Geneva that Zhou was 'a fine, and I believe, a great and able man' and that he (Menon) did not believe that the Chinese had 'expansionist ideas'. He found the Chinese leader, 'shrewd and observant, very Chinese but modern'.[5]

Writing to his Chief Ministers, on 22 June 1954, Nehru described the visit of the Chinese Premier as a 'matter of considerable significance and historical importance'. Rather intuitively, he then went on to say that there was 'nothing very special' about the visit and it was in line with various developments that had taken place in recent years. The Prime Minister said he had been invited on a number of occasions to visit China by Mao Zedong himself but had been prevented by the war in Korea. After the Korean truce, the deteriorating situation in Indo-China had come in the way. Nehru was clearly conflicted about the importance of the visit, first saying it was not very special, then that it was a very special event. One of the factors on which the future of Asia depended was a stable relationship between India and China, he reiterated. Despite 'great differences' in internal and external policies between the two countries, they had endeavoured to come closer together on the basis of 'live and let live and non-interference'[6].

On his first trip to India, the Chinese Premier arrived in New Delhi in a specially chartered Air-India plane on 25 June 1954. He made the standard stops foreign dignitaries visiting Delhi made, including a visit to the samadhi of Mahatma Gandhi. A distinctive feature was the amount of time the Indian Prime Minister devoted to his VIP visitor—thirteen hours in private conversation alone—apart from attendance at public receptions and extensive ceremonial flourishes[7] to demonstrate the importance of the Chinese guest. 'Mr. Nehru in fact tended to supervise most functions himself, telling the band when to stop playing, the people what to do, and was even seen to be in heated altercation with the Chief of Protocol when a hitch developed in the organization of the State Banquet,' a British diplomatic dispatch of the time noted.[8] Rather superciliously, the British claimed popular interest in the visit remained thin, despite reports in the Indian media to the contrary. [9]

The impression that Zhou gave was 'friendly and disarming', 'lively and sympathetic', but not 'as ready to expand his views in public as he was to expose himself'.[10] When Zhou spoke, the statements were sermons on peace in Asia and Sino-Indian friendship and the application of the Five Principles of Peaceful Coexistence as a remedy for the ills of the world. To reassure his audiences, he emphasized that 'revolution cannot be exported'. Outright condemnation of the Americans was also avoided except references to the 'menace to peace of Asia comes now from outside' in his banquet speech. He only provided written answers to questions at his Press Conference with the Indian media. He told the press that 'I am not prepared to give any extemporaneous answers'. The London *Times* correspondent in New Delhi reporting on Zhou's press conference noted[11] how the meeting did not conclude in the usual applause from the gathered journalists, but was met by silence. Most Indian leader writers in the press had been 'silenced by this sudden Chinese interest in India and patent attempts to reach some kind of accord for some reason as yet not expressed.' Zhou had, however, been an 'intense tourist in spite of the intense heat and long talks' with Nehru. He had attended as many functions as possible and 'shaken hands as vigorously and indiscriminately as any American politician.' Even the Red Fort had taken on 'a very red' hue in the evening sun at a reception given by the citizens of Delhi.

Much play appeared to have been given to the Five Principles with their enunciation at almost every turn, and Zhou even dropping the word 'mutual' in the references to the second (non-aggression) and third (non-interference in each other's internal affairs) principles in the interest, it was said, of 'greater clarity'. Nehru, on his part, seemed to take comfort from the fact that Zhou had assured him of the non-expansionist aims of China.

At the same time, it was felt that he (Nehru) had throughout adopted a 'healthily dispassionate attitude' and was not won over emotionally and unreasonably to the Chinese point of view. Both leaders when seen in public, seemed to exhibit a relative wariness towards each other. Also, Nehru was at pains to emphasize in his public statements, that the course followed by India and China in achieving freedom was radically different—whereas Zhou made no reference to the word 'freedom' in his statements, emphasizing instead 'peace' (a 'Picasso Peace' as the British diplomats termed it, suggesting that the Chinese leader was making a mechanical, sloganeering reference to peace as a pro-forma, clichéd value, comparing it to the Picasso-drawn symbol of peace created in 1949).

This British analysis centred on the inference that the visit by the Chinese Premier, signalled for Nehru a diplomatic point-scoring, that henceforward Asian affairs 'cannot be settled except by Asians themselves'. The 'Big Two' of Asia would be India and China—a special relationship, if not actual 'alignment' even as Nehru was also making it abundantly clear that the communist system was not the political system chosen by India. If this was to be a new balance of power between these two giants, it was also inevitable that in time to come, India and China would seek to extend their respective spheres of influence, and this in turn, would mean increasing friction and difficulties. In the long run, this analysis concluded that India could find parity with China only if it strengthened its ties with the democratic nations of the West.

It was Nehru's first meeting with Zhou Enlai and he went to some length in his banquet speech[12] for the Chinese Premier to explain that he had first gone to China fifteen years earlier hoping to stay there for a month or more as he was keen to meet Zhou but had to leave prematurely because of the outbreak of the Second World War. After fifteen years of 'storm and stress and change' his wish was now fulfilled and he was happy to meet an 'eminent statesman and 'distinguished representative' of a neighbouring country. Both leaders made reference to the two-thousand-year-long traditional friendship between the two countries. In Nehru's words, as the two nations stood 'on the fine edge of the present' in a turbulent world, 'we can learn a lesson from the past' of good relations where they had never come into conflict with each other.

In the frequent enunciation of, and reference to, the Five Principles of Peaceful Coexistence during the visit, the intention of both leaders was to also seek endorsement of these principles from other Asian countries, particularly Burma and Indonesia. Zhou told Nehru that he felt that this would make a 'great difference' for Asia; Nehru added that this would strengthen the area of peace without giving the British or the Americans an opportunity to line up against what India and China were doing. This was especially relevant when it came to working towards an eventual solution for Indo-China. For Zhou, who had spent a good part of the year engaged in protracted negotiations on Indo-China in Geneva, his visit to Delhi was also to continue his diplomacy on seeing how best he could work with Nehru to ensure the neutralization of Indo-China (in keeping with the Five Principles), and keeping it free of Western interference, as a key to Asian peace and China's own security. 'Indo-China was regarded by Zhou as the vital key not only to China's influence in South-east Asia, but also to China's immediate territorial integrity.'[13] China's economic reconstruction after the ravages of the Civil War and the Korean conflict was also tied to this factor. From the Chinese point of view, the major aim of Zhou's visit to India was to talk about Asian peace and focus particularly on Indo-China. In this estimate, the Panchsheel principles could be extrapolated to relations governing countries like Indonesia and Burma, too. Zhou was clear that he would visit Burma after India, to proactively ask the Burmese to accept the principles.

The Chinese were obviously anxious for a return visit by Nehru to China. A visit in between Parliament sessions in New Delhi was discussed. One area of focus for Nehru was the need for India and China to remove fears about their 'bigness' among smaller countries in the region and to create 'friendly confidence' as the Chinese Premier put it. Nehru spoke of securing peace in the world by India and China helping each other. Zhou was frank in acknowledging that 'China's understanding of India is less than India's. The Indian Prime Minister spoke of how the United States, despite being a powerful country was 'afraid' (evoking laughter in the Chinese Premier), creating bases around Soviet Russia and China and thereby, 'a vicious circle of fear'.[14]

Writing to the Prime Minister of Nepal, M.P. Koirala, after the Zhou visit concluded, Nehru said[15] he had been 'favourably impressed' by the Chinese leader finding him a man of 'high intelligence and receptiveness to ideas' and 'by no means the narrow-minded person that communists often are'. Zhou had told him that India 'was economically and industrially more advanced than China'. Nehru seemed convinced of the desire of the Chinese government to live at peace with neighbouring countries. Yet, his advice to the Nepalese Prime Minister, as far as establishment of diplomatic relations between Nepal and China was concerned, was that he 'should not encourage this at this stage or in the near future'. Residual suspicions about China and the Chinese had not been entirely erased in his mind despite the bonhomie of the visit.

In a letter to his Ambassador in Beijing, Nehru spoke of India–China relations being somewhat different and closer as a result of the Zhou visit. This did not mean, he said, 'that we are linking up with China', stressing that 'we retain our position and our policy'. In regard to South-East Asia, Indian policy had become closer to that of China, he averred, than that of the US. In any case, he could speak to Zhou 'much more frankly' than in the past. He had been invited to go to China and he had told the Chinese Premier that he would be happy to accept the invitation.

Nehru's biographer, Gopal, writing much later[16] felt that Zhou was a clever flatterer and had concealed his personality from Nehru, seeking advice about the world and Asia. According to Gopal, Nehru 'was not immune to such deference'. He had been prepared to accept Zhou's reference to the border as being peaceful despite it being long and not fully demarcated, and remained unconcerned about the need to probe such statements in a deeper fashion. Gopal's analysis was questioning of Nehru who, he said, had decided that the question of cooperation or conflict between India and China, on which depended the future of Asia, 'did not now need to be answered fully one way or the other.' A third alternative had emerged, 'of containment of China through friendship'. An environment should be created in which 'China would find it difficult to break her word'.

In this context, the general impression among Western embassies in Delhi, especially the British,[17] was that Nehru had not been taken in entirely by the Chinese Premier, but that the media had given great play to the idea of Asian friendship and the 'historic meeting of the leaders of 960 million Asians'. The press, it was felt, had gone to town with an idea that presumably had its inspiration in official circles. Zhou, for his part, had conveyed a perfectly reasonable impression through his public statements, and pictures of him smiling and talking to Indian leaders 'are bound to convey an impression that the latter do not think Communists are so bad after all'.

Throughout this period, the need to secure the common frontier with China persisted in the minds of Indian officials involved with the China relationship, and indeed, in the calculations of Nehru, too. T.N. Kaul, who had been a member of the delegation that negotiated the 1954 Agreement on Tibet with China, is believed to have expressed the view that the Chinese would push their claims on the frontier, 'within the next five years'[18] which explained their insistence on the eight-year duration of the 1954 Agreement. Kaul's views, in retrospect, are confirmed by a reading of Yang Gongsu's memoir[19] where he speaks of Premier Zhou Enlai specifying to the Chinese officials that the duration of the agreement should only be eight years, saying the country needed three years to recover economically, and then implement its first Five-Year plan. After eight years, the Central government in Beijing could actively start to help Tibet recover and reconstruct its economy—suggesting that close linkages between Tibet and India would become less relevant or necessary after that date. This would also imply that a Chinese presence along the frontier with India would be much more easily managed given a likely consolidation of Chinese dominance in Tibet after eight years.

Kaul's suggestion was that check posts should be established at different points along the frontier to protect against Chinese transgressions. This was especially so in areas like Demchok—an area in Ladakh which appeared to be disputed by the Chinese and about which their attitude during the Tibet Trade Agreement negotiations had aroused suspicion. Nehru's frontier anxiety dictated that he should endorse Kaul's recommendations.[20] On 18 June, 1954, before the Zhou visit, in a note to the Secretary General, Foreign Secretary and Joint Secretary in the Ministry of External Affairs,[21] his skepticism about Chinese goodwill in adherence to the terms and provisions of the agreement was frankly stated: 'No country can ultimately rely upon the permanent goodwill or bona fides of another country, even though they might be in close friendship with each other. . . . Certainly, it is conceivable that our relations with China might worsen, though there is no immediate likelihood of that.' Chinese expansionism, he said, was not an unknown fact: it would have to be considered and policy-fashioned in order to 'prevent it coming in the way of our interests'.

It was after the Zhou visit during which he had not raised the boundary issue with the visiting leader, that Nehru recorded the extensive 17-paragraph memorandum on 'Trade and Frontier with China', referred to in the preceding chapter.[22] He took the decision to proclaim through newly published maps that India's frontier was 'firm and definite.' Whether the Chinese would accept this assumption was not assessed. There was to be no reference to 'undemarcated territory'. This frontier was not open to discussion with anybody. 'There may be very minor points of discussion. Even these should not be raised by us. It is necessary that the system of check-posts should be spread along this entire frontier. More especially, we should have check-posts in such places as might be considered disputed areas.' It was his view (paragraph 16) that 'we need not raise the question of our frontier. But, if we find that the Chinese maps continue to indicate that part of our territory is on their side, then we shall have to point this out to the Chinese Government. We need not do this immediately, but we should not put up with this for long and the matter will have to be taken up.'

There are many who believe that by taking such a decision, Nehru was closing the door on a negotiated border settlement based on mutual give-and-take with China. As historians like Srinath Raghavan point out,[23] the situation confronting Indian policymakers was one of 'great uncertainty about China's claims and intentions'. The answer was to leave no room for doubt as far as stating India's conception of its frontier was 'firm and definite'. Scholars like Hoffmann infer that these instructions stemmed from the fact that the 1954 Agreement 'had not included explicit Chinese acceptance of a border; therefore, compensating action was required—namely, a further hardening of India's public stand on such a border's existence'.[24] The memorandum reflected a belief that no further negotiation would be necessary since border security had been assured 'through friendship'. 'Establishing that friendship, which had required Indian surrender of all British rights in Tibet via the 1954 Treaty, had seemingly strengthened China's desire to avoid making frontier claims'.[25] Or so, Nehru assumed.

In fact, the decision was interpretable both ways. While raising the question with China without any provocation could, in Nehru's view, indicate that India was in doubt about the border line, he was also leaving scope for discussion on the subject with China—if the latter were to publish maps with the frontier wrongly depicted, as the last section of his Memorandum indicated. This view is also echoed by the late Karunakar Gupta who believed that the decision especially to depict the northern boundary of India between Kashmir and Xinjiang/Tibet was 'primarily meant to provide a bargaining counter in boundary negotiations with China which were inevitable at some future date'.[26] Nehru's Intelligence Chief B.N. Mullik, writing in his memoirs, also confirmed that while checkposts were set up in the middle and eastern sectors of the Northern boundary with China, no action was taken to push checkposts in forward areas in the Ladakh sector. The army's attitude was that they could send 'an occasional patrol but they were in no position to open and hold any posts in this area . . . it would be difficult to oust the Chinese from this region. In any case, the army was not in a position to make that effort because of the limited resources available at Leh and of the non-existence of any road communication from Leh to these parts.'[27]

The decision to define the territorial integrity and 'nationhood' of India on the basis of confirmation that the boundary lines involved were defined and demarcated presupposes, however, that Nehru's move was more in the character of seeing the nation as an encompassed cartographic space, and 'to weave a structure of sentiment' around it which is reverential and worship-worthy.[28] Here is the case of the map teaching the eye 'to see' the nation[29]. Built upon the earlier, underlying attachments to seeing India represented as a mother-goddess deity rising from the peninsula and towering over the northern mountain ranges with her flowing tresses, her red sari and spear in hand, these new maps became part of popular, enchanted, patriotic cartography serving the reverential patriot. On the Chinese side, similar maps from the 1950s depict the nation as the Great Mother Country (Fatherland) exhorting the citizen to serve the country.

The Return Visit: Not Seizing Pigtails

Nehru's visit to China came in October 1954, fifteen years after his curtailed tour on the eve of the Second World War. The invitation to visit the People's Republic had come soon after the establishment of diplomatic relations in 1950 with Madame Sun Yat Sen as the conveyor of the message, but Nehru had put off his visit taking the view that the war in Korea and the unsettled nature of East Asian affairs went against a visit at that time. After the conclusion of the Panchsheel Agreement and the visit of Zhou Enlai to Delhi, circumstances seemed more propitiate for a visit.

If the India-China relationship were a morality play, then the two protagonists would be Jawaharlal Nehru and Zhou Enlai. In their heyday, both enjoyed incomparable prestige with their people. Nehru, for instance, was often compared to Bharat Bhushan, India's jewel, a quality that some of his biographers like Walter Crocker found 'magical'.[30] At the core of Nehru's pan-Asian feeling, was his discerning of a 'common element in the struggles against imperialism, of whatever shade, in various parts of the world' that awakened him to 'a sympathy' with China.[31] As a young, emotional romantic during the struggle for freedom, the frontiers of India's national movement lay in Spain and China, 'for freedom, like peace, was indivisible, and in the final analysis it did not matter much where fate had pitched one's tent'. This was his formative ideology and accounted for his half-liberal, half-Marxist position and his experiments with democratic socialism. The fifties were the heyday of Indian foreign policy under Nehru who succeeded significantly in creating a credible image of what Kingsley Martin, the British journalist and editor of the *New Statesman,* called 'a third force, as if he could act as a peacemaker'. This was particularly in evidence during the Korean War and the Indo-China problem. Nehru was ambitious about his foreign policy, and India's role in the world, navigating between two opposing blocs, confronting issues of war and peace, and leaving an indelible global imprint on the politics of his time. His view of the world was based on a sense of imbued morality, a view that stemmed from the zeitgeist—the *yugadharma*[32]—of India's freedom movement, and the experience of having eliminated the British Raj through non-violent resistance. Scholars have termed it as Nehru's conviction of 'moral efficacy'[33] as opposed to confidence in the military sphere—an area where the contrast with China's first-generation Communist leadership is apparent.

It follows that Nehru's main Chinese interlocutor, Zhou Enlai, did not bring to the ambit of the Sino-Indian equation any special, emotional attachment. Zhou was adept in the ways of diplomacy; a man of 'cunning, of tenacity and of charm',[34] he adapted himself to different audiences, a study in ambivalence and seeming sincerity. One of those he impressed deeply was Henry Kissinger who first encountered Zhou in July 1971 and called him 'one of the two or three most impressive men I have ever met.' In Kissinger's adulatory words, Zhou 'moved gracefully and with dignity, filling a room not by his physical dominance (as did Mao or De Gaulle) but by his air of controlled tension, steely discipline, and self-control, as if he were a coiled spring.'[35] Zhou's biographer, Gao Wenqian[36] shows Zhou as far from perfect, often fallible, but with a 'deft talent for finding some tiny crack in the wall that would allow him to appear even-keeled in his judgements'.[37] Throughout, he eternally deferred to Mao, and was 'forced to carry Mao's execution knife'. Here was a man in whom 'Taoist-like concealment and endurance were combined with obedience and strategic defense, along with a two-timing personality and the face of Janus revealed to all'. He saw diplomacy as theatre, as a stage for the deployment of Chinese capabilities vis-à-vis the world. He is described by Gao as 'trailing like a faithful dog' behind Mao, and using 'rhetorical babble' whenever the situation demanded as a self-protective measure, employing 'voluminous and disgusting flattery'. In the words of China scholar Andrew Nathan, Zhou was 'unique . . . in his capacity to endure abasement', an 'enabler' of Mao with a 'servant mentality'.[38] An example of such servility was his betrayal and denunciation of another revolutionary leader, Liu Shaoqi, during the Cultural Revolution, on Mao's orders.

The veteran observer of China, Simon Leys describes Zhou as 'the kind of man who could stick a knife in your back and do it with such disarming grace that you would still feel compelled to thank him for the deed', a 'compulsive seducer' for whom no interlocutor ever appeared 'too small, too dim or too irrelevant not to warrant a special effort on his part to charm them and to win their sympathy and support.' He could show 'tolerance, urbanity and a spirit of compromise to urbane Western liberals; spitting fire and hatred to suit the taste of embittered Third World leaders, displaying culture and refinement in front of artists, being pragmatic with the pragmatists, philosophical with philosophers, and Kissingerian with Kissinger.'[39] There is of course, no disputing Zhou's brilliance of mind, his intelligence, and a personal magnetism that left a lasting impression on foreigners who met him. But as Leys also notes, the enigma of Zhou lay in the paradox of his personality: 'that, with all his exceptional talents, he should also present a sort of disconcerting and essential *hollowness*. Some 2,300 years ago, Zhuang Zi, giving advice to a king, pointed out to him that, when a small boat drifts in to the path of a huge barge, the crew of the barge will immediately shout abuse at the stray craft, if however, coming closer, they discover that the little boat is empty they will simply shut up and quietly steer clear of it. He concluded that a ruler who has to sail the turbulent waters of politics should first and foremost learn how to become an empty boat.'[40]

But during the period of our narrative, there is no doubt that Zhou's voice carried great weight in China's leadership councils on foreign affairs and the conduct of foreign policy. He was considered the Party expert on foreign affairs, a shrewd and pragmatic practitioner of the 'diplomacy of the possible',[41] and he and Mao Zedong cooperated very well - 'one making plans inside, and the other negotiating outside'.[42] There is no doubt that Zhou left an indelible imprint on China's foreign policy from 1949 till his death in 1976. In this, the similarity with Nehru is obvious. They were both many-sided personalities even though the historical circumstances conditioning them were obviously different. In Nehru's case, it is apposite to recall the words of Louis Mountbatten in 1968, that the predominant characteristics of the 'other great protagonists' involved in India's freedom struggle were contained in him: 'He was truly Gandhi's disciple in his emphasis on personal and moral values. He was not without (Vallabhbhai) Patel's toughness of fibre, (Mohammed Ali) Jinnah's remoteness or Liaquat (Ali)'s equanimity. But his individuality was not simply the sum of theirs. He had very rare qualities of his own—the artist's insight and the philosopher's wisdom.'[43]

In 1954, in the wake of the Agreement on Tibet and the enunciation of Panchsheel, whose principles Nehru saw as closely mirroring the soul and spirit of Gandhian non-violence and the philosophy defining India's place in the world, he was convinced of India's potential as the fourth power in world politics, besides the United States, the Soviet Union and China. It was the 'urge for Peace' and public welfare that expressed the identity of India; the Five Principles of Peaceful Coexistence in his view, provided a way out of the mired politics of the Cold War. So, when the invitation addressed to Nehru from Zhou Enlai arrived towards the end of August 1954, and he hurried to accept it almost immediately, he was doing so, he felt, because his meeting with the Chinese leadership in Beijing would be a 'world event' of the greatest importance. He would go to China, alone, he decided, not in the company of the Burmese leader U Nu, who had requested Zhou that he visit along with Nehru, because he, Nehru, needed to have 'full talks' with the Chinese.[44]

The visit to China took place from 18 to 30 October 1954. Arriving in Canton (Guangzhou), Nehru flew to Hankow (merged today into Wuhan), then to Beijing where he drove with Zhou Enlai through the streets, and was received by Mao Zedong. Zhou threw a cocktail party for his Indian guest with 500 attendees, followed by dinner. Nehru's programme included a visit to Asha (the elephant he had presented to the children of China in the previous year), the National Institute of Minorities, and places of tourist interest. He was invited to lunch by Madam Sun Yat Sen (Soong Ching-ling), met with Vice Premiers Chen Yun and Li Fuchun, and visited a cotton mill and prison. He was hosted to a public meeting by the Mayor of Beijing, Peng Zhen, where 20,000 people were present. Mao Zedong threw a banquet, preceded by a meeting. In Manchuria, he visited steel plants. Returning to Beijing, he had his third meeting with Mao which lasted for one-and-a-half hours. He held a press conference and gave a radio broadcast. He then flew to Shanghai, then to Hangzhou and on to Guangzhou from where he departed for India. It was a visit conceived on a grand scale by the Chinese, and Nehru had reason to be pleased.

The consolidation of an 'area of peace' in the midst of the Cold War was a vision that propelled Nehru's visit to China where he was the first foreign head of government to be received by the People's Government.[45] Addressing a press conference on 15 October 1954 at the Government House, Calcutta,[46] on the eve of his visit to China, he stated that it was essential that two countries like India and China should understand each other for the sake of peace not only of Asia, but of the world. The avoidance of war should be an international priority. Nehru was urging China's neighbours to assume that Communist China, 'if assured of reasoned understanding, would concentrate on the gigantic priorities of development. In advancing this thesis,

Nehru was transposing his own intellectual approach for India to what would be his priority if he were the Prime Minister or final decision maker in China.'[47]

Writing to U Nu on 14 November 1954, on his China visit,[48] Nehru talked about discussions that ranged from economic matters to flood control and cultural subjects. His 'real discussions' had been with Chairman Mao Zedong and Premier Zhou, he said. Nehru told Mao that he had been greatly moved by the welcome 'by the great masses' that he had received on arrival in China.[49] Mao's view was that the overriding 'common point' that both countries had to cope with was 'imperialism'. Nehru told the Chairman that the 'human factor' of a combined population of over one billion was what made India and China great powers. Mao commended India for having the 'courage' which powers like Britain and France did not have, to cast an affirmative vote for the restoration of China's status in the United Nations. Mao invited Nehru to discuss the utility of war as an instrument of securing policy goals. Friendly countries need not guard against each other, he said. Nehru told him that 'technology used in modern warfare has made alertness in guarding one's own borders meaningless.' Nehru's view was that 'on every count, war has to be avoided' because of its brutalizing effect on humanity. Mao was clear that victory or defeat in war depended on the 'scope of destruction suffered.' China had positioned 'only a small number of troops in Tibet', Mao said. They were there for 'road construction'. When the road was built, he added 'they will leave'. Nehru did not make a response.[50] Ambassador Nedyam Raghavan did, with these words, 'What China does in Tibet is China's own business. India trusts China' and that when he was appointed Ambassador to China, Nehru had 'instructed him to trust China just as China trusts India', to which Mao said, 'Yes, we trust India. With India there, we can sleep well'.[51] He was effusive in his parting words to Nehru, quoting the classical Chinese poet, Qu Yuan against a moonlit sky at Zhongnanhai, his official residence, 'There is no greater sorrow than the sorrow of departing alive. There is no greater joy than the joy of first meeting'[52]. China and India, he added were not two countries who would 'seize each other's pigtail'—they were not on the alert against each other. China was in need of friends like India.

Nehru's long conversations with Mao, spread over three meetings during the visit offer a fascinating insight into the contrasting personalities of these two leaders, each a product of their national milieus of independence and liberation. Scholars like Andrew Kennedy[53] have focused on the 'strikingly ambitious' courses in foreign policy that both charted and attributed each to the 'national efficacy beliefs' they held. Despite the poor material power possessed by either nation in the early 1950s, both Nehru and Mao were imbued with deep convictions about the 'ability of one's state to accomplish specific military and diplomatic tasks, as opposed to the estimates' of material power. Having come to power after achieving victory in armed combat with his opponents (the Nationalist Chinese), Mao had a sense of 'martial efficacy' that enabled him to challenge the United States in Korea and in Vietnam but his weak sense of 'moral efficacy' resulted in greater caution in the diplomatic sphere. In the case of Nehru, a strong sense of moral efficacy borne out of the non-violent nature of a Gandhian freedom movement in which he played a key part, enabled him to take bold decisions in the diplomatic arena, as in approaching the United Nations on Kashmir in 1948, and in his ambitious, visionary approach to nuclear disarmament. His weaker sense of martial efficacy resulted in his being far less assertive in the military realm, as Kennedy notes.

The Nehru–Mao meetings[54] began with Mao speaking about the obstructions being placed in the path of China by the Western powers and the US policy of 'increasing tension right around China'. He wanted Taiwan liberated. He conveyed insecurity about the encirclement of China because some nations 'did not like to leave China alone'. Nehru, on the other hand, spoke of the great need for peace in the world, but he also referred to the 'fear' in the smaller nations in Asia of two large nations like India and China. There was fear of communism too. Even America was affected by this fear complex. India on the other hand, was 'not afraid of any country in the world'. India followed her own policy, and what she considered 'right and just'. If the principles of Panchsheel agreed upon between India and China could be applied in world affairs, then much suspicion and fear could be removed between nations. Mao said they would have to 'watch and see' if these principles were implemented, although it would be wrong to make war an instrument of state policy. On this he wished to speak more with Nehru.

At their second meeting, Mao conveyed that countries like Britain were worried about the Chinese populations being too large and this meant aggression from China. Nehru mentioned that even some Southeast Asian nations had similar apprehensions. Mao was of the opinion that it was necessary 'to study the questions of the advantages of war'. If war came, people were mobilized and kept under constant tension, and this in turn, could create conditions conducive to revolution. The 'revolutionary force' of the people always 'needed to come up', he told Nehru. If a third world war started, then the major proportion of the world would be 'in a revolutionary stage' much to the disadvantage of America. Nehru responded saying that what he understood from Mao's statements was that war, even if it was bad and should be avoided, should be welcomed if it came. He also did not agree with Mao's view that in war, it was quantity, in terms of people and weapons that mattered, since no country could profit from killings on a large scale. War had a brutalizing effect on humanity. Mao was in general agreement but he qualified his response by saying even if tens of millions of people were killed by war, if one government went away, there would be another and the surviving people would find a way to keep themselves alive. It was 'difficult to sink entire China into the sea and so too India, no matter how many people are killed.'

His thinking seemed to incorporate the inevitability of war (or the strategy of protracted struggle) as much as an advocacy for peace— but the latter almost as an afterthought. Nehru's rejection of war as an instrument of policy appeared far less ambivalent, although Mao appeared to be fully engaged with the arguments made by his Indian guest.

Nehru's talks with Zhou Enlai[55] were extensive and detailed. The subjects covered a wide spectrum of issues, including Taiwan, the South East Asia Treaty Organization (SEATO), Indonesia, Thailand, Ceylon, Nepal, Laos, Cambodia, Korea and Pakistan; the latter was criticized by Zhou for allying itself with Britain and the U.S. Zhou told Nehru that he had told the Pakistani leaders that they should settle the Kashmir question with India, to which Nehru stated that he had always been willing to talk things over with Pakistan and that things became different when Pakistan accepted American military aid. Zhou claimed to understand very little about Pakistan and its origins. He said that China would be willing to participate in an Afro-Asian Conference since it would work in the interests of peace in Asia. The first references to the Bandung Conference (1955) were beginning to figure in the dialogue between India and China. Zhou suggested that Indian experts on public health and sanitation visit China and was agreeable to supply silk cocoons to Kashmir, telling Nehru that Kashmiri experts should visit China to make their choice of what they wanted. The atmosphere of the talks was cordial, and Zhou told Nehru that they should continue their contacts without any formality. Nehru was in agreement.

Asked at a press conference in the Chinese capital as to how he had been convinced about the Chinese desire for peace, Nehru said his view was based on the talks he had with the Chinese leaders, the 'vast number of smiling Chinese faces' and the 'appreciation on the part of the Chinese government and people that any kind of war would come in the way of peaceful reconstruction in their country.'[56]

In his note on his China visit, referred to earlier,[57] Nehru also states that in talks with Zhou, he referred to Chinese maps which still showed portions of Burma and of India as if they were in Chinese territory. As far as India was concerned, he commented, 'we were not much concerned because our boundaries were quite clear and were not a matter for argument'. But people had argued that China had an 'aggressive intent'. This had also caused apprehension in Burma. He said Zhou had replied that these maps 'were old ones and China had not done any surveying to draw new maps.' Nehru said he repeated that as far as India was concerned, 'there was no doubt about our boundaries and I was not worried about them. But I wondered how China would feel if a part of Tibet had been shown as part of India in our maps.'[58] That apart, his reception in China had been most cordial, reflecting 'almost an emotional upheaval' and a basic urge for friendship with India. He felt that the idea 'that this great nation [China] could be ignored or bypassed' was 'completely irrelevant'.

Ambassador Nedyam Raghavan in his appraisal of the visit called it the 'most important' diplomatic exchange to take place since China's liberation and that it was 'admirably timed'.[59] India's contributions to the resolution of the Korean impasse, the 'diplomatic triumph' at Geneva despite being kept out of the Conference (to discuss Korea and Indo-China), the conclusion of the Agreement on Tibet and the adoption of the Five Principles, all had helped to make a successful visit. Raghavan was convinced that this was, for India, 'a diplomatic triumph of the greatest possible significance'. It had served to set the seal on the 'correct Chinese understanding' of India where relations had been 'correct and friendly without being warm and cordial'.

The account of Nehru's visit to China cannot be complete without a mention of his meeting—his first—with the Dalai Lama. The young Tibetan leader was himself in Beijing for the first time where he had met several times with Mao Zedong and built a relationship with the latter which in his own words, was like 'son and father'.[60] He met Nehru at a dinner party hosted by Zhou Enlai. When Zhou introduced Nehru to the Dalai, in the latter's words, 'Pandit Nehru became motionless. Speechless. At least, I think fifteen, twenty seconds. . . . I think Pandit Nehru was reflecting on past history and Sardar Patel's prediction.'[61] The Dalai Lama, in conversation with the author in 2014, referred to Zhou Enlai as an 'attractive' personality but 'much too polite' in contrast to Mao, who he termed as 'straightforward' and a person with whom trust could be developed. With Zhou, and his excessive politeness, in his view, it was 'difficult to develop trust.'[62]

Throughout the early- and mid-1950s, Nehru had been a vociferous advocate of bringing China into the comity of nations. While it is commonly held that this stemmed from his misplaced notions about Asian solidarity, and his idealism, there is some weight in the argument that much of this approach had to do with Nehru's 'reading of history and his views on the salience of power among nations'. Great power politics in the early years of the twentieth century had convinced him that great powers ought not to be shunned as they could thus become threats to global stability as had happened to Germany after the First World War. It was essential that China be brought into the UN and 'enmeshed in international norms and regulations.'[63]

That Nehru was not however, completely swept away by the cordial reception he had received in China was noted in diplomatic quarters. A British dispatch from the High Commission in Delhi, noted how in his first public speech on returning to India from China, after emphasizing his belief in China's pacific intentions, Nehru himself questioned, 'How can I guarantee what will happen afterwards?'[64] The same dispatch noted that Nehru had come back even more convinced that India had adopted the right path for its political and economic development, although he had been particularly struck by the sense of unity of purpose of the Chinese people. In fact, a nationalistic streak was also evident in some of his pronouncements following his return—he spoke of shedding Western influences and imitation of foreign methods. There seemed a latent realization in him that greater unity and enthusiasm for the national purpose and agenda, to create a progressive nation (as he had witnessed in China) was needed. The British view as stated was that 'Mr. Nehru's visit to China and the evidence which he saw there of Chinese achievement and surging development have convinced him to a very practical extent that, despite the comfort and protection afforded by the Five Principles, China now represents a real and disturbing—if as yet latent—challenge to Asia.'[65] There would be increasing watchfulness of Chinese intentions, the dispatch predicted.

The Secretary General in the Ministry of External Affairs, N.R. Pillai told the British High Commissioner that as a result of his visit, Nehru was now more than ever convinced 'of the peaceful intentions of the Chinese regime'.[66] In a long talk with the UK High Commissioner, Pillai praised the 'well-administered and well-disciplined' nature of Chinese society, saying that at the same time, 'the people were not dragooned. [The] Chinese had found a compromise between the regimentation of Russia and the individualism of the democracies'. The regime of the Chinese Communist Party was firmly established and it was utterly illusory to imagine that there could be 'any prospect of Chiang Kai Shek returning to the mainland.' The one thing that was clear was that India would have to redouble her development efforts since 'it would be fatal if China were to go ahead faster than India since this would spell the doom of the democracy here'. Much greater momentum would have to be imparted to the Indian development process if India was 'to keep her lead in the race.'

The Secretary General was deeply impressed by the 'friendliness', the 'veneration' and 'affection' of the Chinese people saying that he had never seen such large gatherings of people to greet the Prime Minister even in India. The exchange of visits between the two Prime Ministers had resulted in a 'growing personal friendship' between Nehru and Zhou Enlai.

Nehru's personality had made a big impact, and his influence throughout had been for patience and restraint (especially on Korea) and he had been 'extremely skillful and successful in correcting (the) somewhat one-sided version of affairs' of the Chinese. Nehru had also discussed the subversive methods of international communism (he received a 'general and categorical' assurance that 'it would be no part of Chinese policy to support Communist parties in other countries') as also the problem of the overseas Chinese (often considered as a tool for interference in the internal affairs of countries in southeast Asia by China) with Zhou. Pillai claimed that Nehru did not raise the question of the India–China boundary[67]. While eventually, India would ask for 'formal Chinese concurrence in India's claim', it believed that the longer the claim went unchallenged by China, and the more effective Indian occupation of the border area became, 'the stronger becomes India's position'. As a result of the visit, Nehru was 'more than ever convinced of the peaceful intentions of the Chinese regime.'

Speaking in the Lok Sabha on 22 November 1954, the Prime Minister felt the visit fitted in with a gradual change in the world situation. He was assured that the year had passed without the disaster of war which had appeared to be imminent 'on a big scale' earlier, and he was appreciative of the role that had been played by the United States in this regard. Credit had to be given to the 'big powers', in his view. The political consequences of his visit to China, he said, were 'a clearer understanding between India and China and what they stand for and what they work for, and a knowledge that there is much in common in the tasks that confront them.' India, as she was situated 'geographically and politically can be of some service in interpreting some countries to others and thus helping to remove misunderstandings'. He suggested that his visit had helped to ease existing tensions in Indo-China and Southeast Asia and that 'as such it helped in the larger and vital problem of world peace'.[68]

Nehru's visit to China came at a time when the latter's perception of international politics was being defined as not only consisting of the bifurcation into East and West in the Cold War format, but also recognizing a vast 'intermediate zone' between these two blocs. Both India and China were seen in the Chinese analysis, as part of this intermediate zone. India was useful to China because of 'its Asian identity, historical experience, and territorial proximity with China'.[69] The relationship with India in the 1950s, before the differences on the border transformed these ties, was defined as a partnership for promoting peaceful coexistence between countries with different political and social systems. Internally, Beijing's approach on relations with India in this period was to avoid raising territorial issues and just focus on securing India's goodwill, not only for maintaining smooth bilateral relations, but also 'mainly for consolidating Beijing's legitimacy in the international scene.'[70] Internal analyses within the Chinese policy-making structure seemed willing to concede the 'progressive' steps taken by the Indian government to reform state institutions, and to reduce feudal and foreign influence. Nehru's domestic offensive against the Communist Party of India was however, labelled as 'reactionary'. Nehru, in this analysis, wanted a peaceful international environment for the development of the Indian bourgeoisie. The test of being seen as a friendly government was also met by India's recognition of Taiwan as a part of China and supporting the PRC's entry into the United Nations. China's 'friendly diplomatic initiatives' like supplying food grains at a time when India was facing shortages was seen as having improved relations after the initial misunderstandings over Tibet. Towards the closing years of the Korean War too, relations had made progress. India's ties with the West, with Britain and the 'ambiguous' relationship with the United States however, did not find favour with Beijing. If there was imperfection in the India–China relationship, India was to blame for this because she remained fearful of a communist revolution in India and Asia, 'suspicious of alleged hidden motives behind China's promotion of peaceful coexistence principles, and ambiguous about how the Taiwan question should be solved.'[71]

The problem of Tibet lingered too. There was always suspicion about Indian involvement in Tibetan affairs. Border issues remained to be settled. The Chinese Ministry of Foreign Affairs' approach was to solidify 'unity' with India through 'reasonable, beneficial, and restrained' struggles whenever necessary. The metaphor of class struggle on the international stage comprehensively informed Chinese foreign policy perspectives at this stage of history. Existing in that intermediate arena between the two Cold War camps, India had a special place in Chinese grand strategy, both as a neighbour as well as a significant global presence. The year 1954 in many ways marked an ascending slope in India–China relations to a high point achieved in 1956 at the zenith of 'Hindi–Chini Bhai Bhai' (Indians and Chinese are brothers) understanding and bonhomie, although the subterranean undercurrents of wariness and sub-optimal levels of mutual trust lingered below the surface. When relations began a downward spiral from 1957–58 onwards, bilateral differences over the boundary, and later, Tibet, subsumed any sense of global understanding that the two countries may have shared in the post-Panchsheel period of interaction, often at the highest level of leadership. But at the time of Nehru's visit, the Chinese needed India's cooperation on the international stage. Beijing's approach to the Indians was governed by realpolitik. 'There was ample room to focus on what the two countries had in common'.[72] According to this analysis, the 'two parties used their shared experience of Western oppression to lay philosophical grounds for cooperation.' The legacies of history and the economic problems faced by the two countries 'provided a basis for sympathy and cooperation.'[73]

In New Delhi's diplomatic circles, those watching Nehru were of the view that he had not been won over emotionally or unreasonably to the Chinese point of view, as a result of his meetings with the Chinese, although the interactions had established India and China as the 'Big Two' of Asia. Nehru had come back to India impressed by the efficiency of the Chinese government, by the 'unity, order and sense of purpose' of the country as a whole, although the methods used to achieve this were undesirable. At the same time, he was convinced that the Chinese leaders, in spite of being communists, were not doctrinaire fanatics but responsible people who wanted peace to continue their development. In Nehru's view, a deeper understanding between India and China had developed as a result of his visit and that of the Chinese Premier to Delhi earlier, and it was desirable for them to cooperate to as large an extent as possible. Nehru had shown no inclination to sacrifice India's interests, as for example, in Nepal, where the Chinese had reluctantly said they would not press for the early opening of a Chinese mission. The presence of the Dalai Lama in Beijing had served as a clear reminder to him of the changed status of Tibet and the potential danger of communist infiltration over India's northern frontier. Obviously, he did not trust assurances he had received that the communist revolution was not for export, and 'cooperation' in this case would involve keeping an eye on the Chinese. Even if the Five Principles of Peaceful Coexistence (Panchsheel) had been mutually accepted, there was no guarantee that China would stick by these faithfully.

As far as the Western powers were concerned, there could be no harm done by Nehru serving as a bridge to China. At the same time, he was prepared to guard Indian interests, and even as he spoke against 'spheres of influence', it was clear that in practice, India was not in favour of Chinese influence in Nepal, or for that matter, even in Burma. But in the field of internal policy, Nehru (even while emphasizing the rightness of the path chosen for India's political and economic development and its difference from Communist China) had been struck by the sense of unity and purpose of the Chinese people, 'since they are the very characteristics that he finds to be conspicuously lacking in his own country'.[74] The China visit had quickened the realization in him that if democracy had to be securely rooted and thrive, it must show itself to be capable of producing material advantages at least comparable to those achieved by China. How to match the disciplined determination of China was the question. Nehru's nationalistic streak was ever more in evidence, consequently. A stronger sense of nationalism was required in India, he seemed to suggest, if the unity and sense of purpose seen in China had to be achieved.

8

A 'Short' History of
Sino-Indian Friendship

*We have for centuries praised your art and culture. We have for
ages prized your friendship and neighbourliness. Chairman Mao
Zedong expressed our feelings succinctly and aptly when he said
'The Indian nation is a great nation, and the Indian people is an
excellent people'... This mutual exchange of respect has through
millennia engendered peaceful contact between our countries
which is indeed unique in the annals of man. I venture to say
that it has rarely been matched in history over such an expanse
of time.*[1]

—Soong Ching-ling, New Delhi, December 1955

China scholar and Harvard University academic Arunabh Ghosh
authored a paper in 2017 where he argued for an approach in
bilateral relations between India and China that went beyond
'high political' life and focused instead on the cultural, scientific
and economic factors that can provide fresh perspectives on
the history of the relationship. For instance, many Indians who

have travelled to China know the Chinese enthusiasm for the Hindi film *Awaara* (The Vagabond) released in 1955 in China and re-released in the 1980s. Indian soft power, especially Indian films, have made a tremendous impact on the Chinese and the first connections in this regard were made during the era of 'Hindi–Chini Bhai Bhai', post-Panchsheel. Ghosh argues that the 1962 conflict between the two countries, which is the subject of geopolitical and strategic analysis, has served as a 'teleological end-point for China-India studies of this period' because of an obsession with the 'causes, course, and legacy of the war'.[2]

Comparisons were often made between India and China in that early era just as much as they are made today, and implicit competition was frequently implied by visitors and scholars alike as far as these two countries were concerned. The fact is that the 1950s opened up a new era of real-time contact between Indians and Chinese, one that was very different from the past because it was not confined to scholars of history, philosophy, religion or literature. Journalists, writers, artists, theatre personalities, dancers and musicians, scholars, students, athletes and sportsmen, scientists, and economists, from India and China, were all coming into contact with each other through exchanges of visits between the two countries. It was an unprecedented opening up to each other that was thus created, mainly driven by the wider climate of political understanding and cordiality. The China-India Friendship Association was set up in 1952, two years before the establishment of the Chinese People's Association for Cultural Relations with Foreign Countries.[3] The India-China Friendship Association was set up in 1951, a year before its Chinese counterpart. Its aim was to promote friendship and solidarity between the two countries. Large numbers of friendship delegations were exchanged. Newspaper reports from 1953 speak of Asha, the baby elephant gifted by Nehru to the children of China. The Hong Kong press reported in April that year that the three-and-a-quarter-ton elephant 'left Hong Kong by train today for Peking, when she will curtsy on one knee before the Chinese Premier, Mr. Zhou Enlai, and present him with a message from the Indian Prime Minister, Pandit Nehru.' Asha was transferred on a freshly painted railway wagon, an official of the Indian Commissioner's office in Hong Kong saw her off, and an officer of the Indian Embassy in China met her on the China side of the Hong Kong border.

In a chronology of exchanges between Indian and Chinese cultural/non-political delegations from 1950 to 1960 prepared by the Center for History and Economics of Harvard University,[4] the list for 1951 includes an exhibit on the PLA in New Delhi; in 1952, Chinese films, including the classic *White-haired Girl,* were warmly received in India. In September that year, an Indian table-tennis team visited China. In July 1953, an Indian Arts Delegation arrived in China and its music and dance performances were attended by Mao Zedong and other leaders. In October 1953, Harindranath Chattopadhyay, the author of the song on brotherly friendship (*Hindi Chini Bhai Bhai*), visited Beijing. An agreement to commence student exchanges was reached in October 1954. Dr Raghu Vira, the linguist and scholar of ancient Buddhist history, extraordinarily, made a three-month tour through China and Inner Asia collecting ancient literary materials and artefacts. In August 1955, Beijing hosted a meeting attended by over 5,000 people in support of India's claims to Goa. In September that year, Chinese Muslims on pilgrimage to Mecca were received in India. In October, an Indian Film Week was held in China with four films, including *Awaara* shown in 20 cities.[5] In December 1956, the Deputy Director of the Chinese State Statistics Bureau, Wang Sihua, led a delegation of Chinese statisticians to the Indian Statistical Institute, which spent a month there studying statistical methods. In July 1957, Kalidasa's classic story *Shakuntala* was staged in Chinese in Beijing and watched by Premier Zhou Enlai and Indian Ambassador R.K. Nehru.[6]

In 2008, Mira Sinha Bhattacharjea, a former Indian Foreign Service officer, recounted her experiences of working in China during her posting in Beijing in the mid-1950s. She spoke of being drawn to China as a young girl because of Chinese poetry and the experience of interacting with 'Chinamen' selling embroideries to Bengali houses and the discipline, exactitude and precise manner in which these embroideries were done. Ms Bhattacharjea was posted in China in the mid-1950s when the friendship with India was at its height. She spoke of how food shortages in China were managed, and that her impression of China 'was that of a Gandhian Society (because in her words, 'it was very human-oriented') where the focus was on making available basic necessities to the people.' She was impressed with the way the Chinese cared for their children. She added: 'In the 1950s, India was the model and the Chinese were keen to learn from us. They admired our technical capacity and wanted the technology but not our economic policy. They wanted practical knowhow . . . China's interest in us has been more political and strategic rather than economic. They want to learn from other countries' experiences and build their own model which is free from the problems of other models.'

China in the fifties had neither money nor material resources nor technology, but 'what they lacked they just made up for by this human effect and human warmth and cooperation.' Vestiges of the old society were visible, the 'story-teller at the street corner was still there, the little woman who would repair a torn garment was still there'. Further, 'India was never unknown', it was 'prevalent as a civilization in their everyday life', as part of their 'cultural, historical and mythological background'. Bhattacharjea bemoaned the fact that in India, there had been no serious attempt to study China, there were only 'impressionistic views of China'[7].

This honeymoon period in relations was highlighted by the visit of Nehru to China in 1954 and the visits made by Zhou Enlai to India in 1954 and 1956–57. The atmosphere in bilateral relations was further improved by the exchange of numerous delegations,[8] including the visit of Soong Ching-Ling from December 1956 to January 1957. A 38-member troupe of the Peking Variety Theatre gave performances in various Indian cities. Other delegations from China included a cultural delegation—a delegation of the Union of Chinese Stage Artists and from the China-India Friendship Association—and a military goodwill delegation led by Marshal Peng Dehuai which visited military centres in various parts of India from 23 January to 2 March 1958. Delegations from India visiting China included those from the Young Men's Christian Association of India, the All India Trade Union Congress, film delegations, the All India Federation of Educational associations, medical and teaching professions, the India-China Friendship Association and the Indian Youth Congress. The leading economist and statistician P. C. Mahalanobis and the prominent Buddhist scholar Rahul Sankritayan were also guests of the Chinese government. Scholarly exchanges during this period covered many development-related fields of work, including statistics (Premier Zhou Enlai was very impressed with the work of the Indian Statistical Institute), water and power, state planning, agrarian cooperatives, irrigation, steel production and small-scale industries.

The demographer Dr Sripati Chandrashekhar's four-week visit to China in late-1958 during the early months of the Great Leap Forward campaign launched by Chairman Mao Zedong,[9] merits special mention. His observations on birth-control techniques in China, including postpartum sterilization for women, diaphragms, and intra-uterine devices,[10] remain a fascinating and unusual record of the era, while his views on the country in general were seen as influenced by his perceived closeness to the United States. Chandrashekhar, himself, was not a welcome visitor in China, because unlike other visitors from India, the authorities regarded him with some suspicion perceiving him as someone close to the Americans, and ideologically different, and therefore less inclined to suspend disbelief about China and the Chinese under the Communist Party. When he finally did visit China, after some years of waiting for permission from the government of China, he had to go there in his private capacity; he did not receive state hospitality which irked him no end, as his letters to friends and acquaintances indicate.[11]

Returning Indian visitors were infused with admiration about the progress made in China and the enthusiasm of the Chinese people for their nation's progress. The Foreign Office in Delhi received reports from the Embassy in Beijing about new experiments like the backyard furnaces promoted by Chairman Mao Zedong as part of the Great Leap Forward, and the organization of communes. Delegations from India studied these projects. Streets in both countries resounded to the cries of 'Hindi Chini Bhai Bhai' with scarcely any premonition of the clouds gathering on the horizon. Hemanga Biswas (the Bengali poet and singer who was a founder of the Indian People's Theatre Association), who spent two years in China between 1957 and 1959, wrote in 1960: 'What I saw in the streets of Peking were . . . cheering crowds waving greetings to those going for voluntary labour to Ming Tombs, in trucks decorated with flags and festoons, singing and dancing to Chinese drums and cymbals.'[12] He had learnt Chinese, and lived in communes.

Archives in the Tata Institute of Fundamental Research (TIFR) contain a letter written in 1948 from Homi Bhabha (the father of India's nuclear programme) and D.D. Kosambi (the mathematician) to S.S. Chern (1911–2004), the renowned Chinese mathematician in then war-torn China, offering him the hospitality of the TIFR as Visiting Professor for a year, as also any close collaborators. Chern had spent time at the TIFR in 1946–47 but by the time Bhabha's letter reached him, he had accepted a position at Princeton University. He was in his reply to Bhabha, grateful 'for the concern of my foreign friends, which has never failed me'.[13]

In September 1957, the Vice-President of India, S. Radhakrishnan visited China as the country went through a period of 'rectification', confessions, self-criticism which were acquiring a sinister tone, as the young Indian diplomat, K. Natwar Singh, was to note in his diary. The theatre of Sino-Indian diplomacy was, however, undisturbed. Radhakrishnan was accorded a high-profile welcome by a constellation of Chinese leaders including Chu Teh, Liu Shao Chi, Zhou Enlai, Soong Ching-ling, Chen Yi, Peng Chen and Ho Lung. In his remarks on arrival in Beijing, he was less diplomatic than direct; he told his hosts that they should not forget lessons from the past, that they should 'practice moderation and seek virtue and righteousness.'[14] He was housed at the Zhongnanhai, home to the top Chinese leadership.

Soon after his arrival, the Vice-President was taken to meet Chairman Mao Zedong, and Natwar Singh writes how Radhakrishnan patted Mao on his left cheek after shaking hands. Mao was momentarily taken aback, to which the Vice-President is believed to have said, 'Mr. Chairman, don't be alarmed, I did the same thing to Stalin and the Pope.'[15] These gestures apart, the Vice-President chose to lecture his Chinese audiences on the importance of 'morality', the way of 'humanity and love' and the way of 'Tao'. He advocated that China should maintain its traditional values as much as it followed new values. As a British dispatch notes: 'On arrival at Beijing airport, for example, he ended his speech by expressing the wish that the Chinese Government would exercise its power with moderation and humanity'.[16] The Chinese could not have been pleased, although no diplomatic incident was noticed. The English versions of Chinese press reports on the visit are believed to have carried considerably doctored and condensed versions of the Vice-President's remarks.

Radhakrishnan could have had in mind the militaristic content of Chinese life under the Communist Party's control. India and China are different societies. As scholars have noted, the idea of 'popular sovereignty' and the practice of resistance of politics against government, a hangover from the anti-colonial struggle, is very strong in India[17]. Disobeying the law despite the structure of constitutionalism in Indian democracy, and challenging the sovereignty of the state dictates the 'everyday language of politics' in India. China's masses cannot do that. The engagement with the modern or modernity in China differs from that in India. Critics of modernity in China are regarded as people opposed to progress and freedom.[18]

The Chinese had made detailed preparations for the visit including a performance of the ancient Sanskrit story of Shakuntala (by the poet Kalidasa), and the Vice-President was also invited to address the National People's Congress. In his address, Dr Radhakrishnan, again, made bold to say that the people must 'be allowed a sense of democratic participation', adding after paying tribute to the leadership of Chairman Mao, that if the people felt frustrated, they could with 'raw courage' challenge the government[19]. His hosts did not protest, although there was little coverage of these extraordinarily candid statements in the Chinese language press.

At the banquet hosted by Mao Zedong, the Vice-President expressed the hope that under the former's leadership, socialism would become democratic and humanistic. He spoke about democracy and its role in international affairs. On another occasion, he exhorted his Chinese hosts to observe the principles of morality and not to look at problems from a purely material angle for 'if in seeking for material preservation we abandon spiritually valuable moral principles, then our future will be dark indeed.' His last words before he left the country were good wishes to the Chinese people to progress 'towards a democratic, liberal and humane Socialism'.[20]

Rabindranath Tagore, often seen as the icon for Sino-Indian friendship both in India and China, and who visited China in 1924, had in many ways personified the emphasis on civilizational leadership and fraternal partnership, in his writings on friendship between the two countries. The bonding of the 1950s would have pleased Tagore, although he was not alive to witness it, having died in 1941. He saw no fundamental contradiction in their good relations since the importance attached to the concept of harmonious, inclusive development seemed common in both cultures—*vasudhaiva kutumbakam* (the world is one family) and *shijie datong* (the world in grand harmony) being synonymous. In his youth, Tagore had been a spirited opponent of the opium trade with China especially since that opium was mostly grown in British India, and this had been the subject of his famous essay 'Chine Maraner Byabasay' (the Commerce of Killing People in China). His establishment of the Cheena Bhavana (China House) in Santiniketan—the site of the Viswa Bharati University he founded in Bengal—was also an embodiment of his desire that the youth of India and China should know each other better. The image of the *amrakunj* (mango grove) was the metaphor favoured by Tagore—a field of inspiration for these young people, with their personalities developing in harmony with the environment around them. This is not to deny that Tagore did not have his critics in China. The May 4th 1919 movement in China had stirred the youth of the country deeply, and there was criticism of Tagore's language as being 'the dialect of another world' and advocacy on the part of these students, not of Oriental culture and civilizational harmony, but of 'the machine gun to drive out the machine-gun wielding imperialist aggressors.' Spiritualism was not needed according to this point of view. This was quite the opposite of Tagore's view that 'the clearing of a passage for machines or machine guns cannot be the most memorable fact of history'.

On balance, however, Tagore's warm affection for the Chinese people is not forgotten, and Zhou Enlai speaking at Santiniketan in 1956, during a visit to India, recalled the poet's 1924 visit to China saying that his support for the struggle for national independence of China would not be forgotten. Nehru was himself greatly taken with Tagore's vision of India–China harmony and fraternity. The leading Indologist of twentieth century China, Ji Xianlin (1911–2009), writing in 1983, said Tagore was an anti-imperialist, a patriot, as also a mystic. Ji is believed to have seen Tagore in person at Jinan, his hometown, when he was thirteen as he told the then Indian President K.R. Narayanan in 2000.[21] A scholar of Hindu and Buddhist scriptures, he translated the Ramayana into Chinese while incarcerated in a cowshed for over a decade, during the Cultural Revolution. To him are attributed the famous words, 'China and India have stood simultaneously on the Asian continent. Their neighbourliness is created by Heaven and constructed by Earth'. Ji is a figure of considerable importance in the context of modern Sino-Indian relations. He was a scholar of Sanskrit, and was asked by Hu Qiaomu, secretary to Mao Zedong at the time, to establish a Department of Oriental Languages and Literature in Peking University in 1949. He emerged as the doyen of Indian studies in China, thereafter.

The Indian Sinologist, Prabodh Chandra Bagchi, writing in 1944, was similarly effulgent in his description of the ties between India and China. In his view, the records of ancient ties were more than of historical interest, but would evoke the 'gratitude which we should feel for our ancestors who had sacrificed themselves for the selfless work of building up a common civilization for the two largest agglomerations of people in Asia.'[22] Bagchi, who was serving as the Vice-Chancellor of Viswa Bharati University at Santiniketan before his death in 1956, was fond of quoting the words of a seventh century message from the Indian monk Prajnadeva to the Chinese pilgrim, Xuan Zang, as a metaphorical expression of the long distances yet to be traversed in relations between India and China: 'the road is long, so do not mind the smallness of the present'.[23]

When scholars like Bagchi referred to the 'common civilization' that India and China shared, theirs was a perspective about the influence of India or 'Yindu' having permeated popular Chinese outlook down to the smallest human settlements across the vast country. Buddhist cosmology had for centuries, before the advent of New China, influenced Chinese conceptions of cartography, global geography, oceans and continents, and links with the outside world. The world was conceptualized as one inhabited continent surrounded by water—the Buddhist *Jambudvipa*, with Mount Sumeru at the centre. Jambudvipa 'in its form resembled the Indian subcontinent and Tibet, being narrow at the bottom and wider near the top, split in the middle by the mountain chain of Himavat (the Himalayas). North of those peaks lay Anavatapta, a sacred lake usually identified with Lake Manasarowar in western Tibet, from which was said to emerge the Indus, Ganges, Oxus (Amu Darya), and Śita (Tarim) Rivers.'[24] Northern India, particularly Bodh Gaya was presented as the centre of the world. Orthodox Confucian scholars disliked this Buddhist bias, but the images persisted, cross-pollinating with indigenous Chinese beliefs. 'Anavatapta, lodged within high mountains at the center of Jambudvipa, began to be conflated by some authors with Kunlun, a legendary peak regarded in pre-Buddhist Chinese sources as a central pillar supporting the heavens.'[25] Buddhist precepts about giving India central prominence clashed with the entrenched impulse to give China that core importance. It was during the late Qing dynasty, during the nineteenth century, that a greater geopolitical awareness of India began to transcend traditional beliefs and outlooks. A more integrated perspective was considered necessary, given that the far-flung Qing frontiers in the west were encircled by Russian and British-influenced territories and regions. Geographic agnosticism about India and its location was replaced by more scientific cartographic studies and the gathering of intelligence. The Qing conquest of Eastern Turkestan (today's Xinjiang) opened up overland trade routes to India from Yarkand to Ladakh, Kashmir and the Punjab. Indian merchants were regular visitors to Xinjiang, part of the Indian trading diaspora scattered across Central Asia and through their presence, the Qing 'gained a pool of political intelligence.'[26] Ladakh was a well-situated listening post. The Qianlong emperor (1735-1796) delighted in 'Hindustani jade,' writing seventy-four poems about India inspired by his love for this precious import, whose intricate carving and extreme thinness achieved through the technique of water polishing by skilled Indian craftsmen enchanted him completely and in his view, was 'far beyond the reach of jade craftsmen of Suzhou.'[27]

Beyond popular mythology drawing reference from Buddhist tradition and legends, in the nineteen-fifties, however, by and large, the average Chinese knew little of India. Ambassador K.M. Panikkar wrote in his memoir,[28] that the Chinese he met in Beijing, apart from Premier Zhou Enlai and a handful of Chinese leaders, knew nothing about India. They had only a vague idea about India's political position or historical development. They had romantic notions about India, about the inheritance of the Buddhist traditions, but their knowledge of modern India was mostly non-existent. Panikkar blamed this not on the 'notorious egocentrism' of the Chinese, but on their education in the past having been controlled by Americans and Western missionaries. He recounted how he had spent time talking to Chinese audiences, trying to dispel this ignorance and even some of the communist views that India was a 'reactionary' and 'capitalist' country.

Panikkar's account of life in Beijing in those early years is revealing in the details it conveys of the systematic way in which the government was eliminating those perceived as enemies of the state, including religious sects that had large followings, and also Christian missionaries and nuns. Even foreigners were not spared and sentenced to long incarceration, with exit visas to leave China being hard to obtain. The Chinese government gave the Ambassador permission to travel in the country, including chaperoned visits into villages where he found that land reform had 'broken the chains, made the village' (he wrote glowingly of visiting the one-room tenement of a worker, a clean and spacious room in which there was a beautiful vase— 'a sign to me of inherent culture'[29]). Another point of interest was his visit to the interiors of northwest China—to the ancient site of Dunhuang on the ancient Silk Route, where he was witness to the ravages inflicted on this place of world heritage by western archaeologists like Aurel Stein, who had acquired and brought away from Dunhuang 9,000 ancient manuscripts (Buddhist sutras and scrolls) and paintings for a paltry sum of 500 rupees. The French scholar Pelliot followed to complete the ransacking systematically, so that 'no manuscript of value was left there for anyone to acquire'.[30]

Panikkar was always effusive in his pronouncements about friendship between India and China. Prime Minister Nehru was also known to be similarly affirmative in his expressions about friendship between India and China. But such affirmativeness was not the case, always. The Delhi bureaucracy was formal and distant with the Chinese Embassy, and the authorities were watchful of the Chinese diplomatic entourage. The British newspaper, *The Observer* of 25 February 1951 reported thus in its 'Delhi notebook': 'The relations between the Ambassador from Peking and India's External Affairs Department remain starchily formal. When I called at the Embassy recently, the latest signature in the visitors' book was dated three weeks back. It happened to be that of an Indian friend of mine. He explained the position: "Did you see those two outside the gate, with *pagris* (turbans) as conspicuous as a London bobby's boots? They take the number of every car that goes in. It tends to discourage the Great Friendship".'[31]

Chinese indifference to Indian sentiments could also have resulted in a diplomatic faux pas when in 1954,[32] immediately after the signing of the Panchsheel Agreement, a Russian film on India began to show in a fairly large circuit of cinemas in Beijing. The film reportedly depicted the worst social conditions in India, showing poverty and placing India in a bad light. The commentary in Chinese was as bad as the film itself. Indian Ambassador Raghavan took the issue up with the Chinese asking them what their reactions would be if he were given freedom to take moving pictures of China wherever he went, and took pictures of slums and those of people living in caves. The film was promptly taken off the screens, although it was suspected that given the huge advertising campaign for the film, the Chinese authorities must have known beforehand that the film was derogatory to India. The matter formed the subject of a dispatch from the British embassy in Beijing to the Foreign Office in London.

From the British in Beijing, there were also reports rather dismissive of the Indian inclination to accept at face value the 'nauseating reiterated Chinese rigmarole that "we are of course still very backward and we have many shortcomings, so please give us the benefit of your advice and experience."' In 1956, these reports took the view that in industrial output, China was ahead of India and that its powerful and centralized system of government and control, its racial and linguistic unity, and the working capacity of the people were operating in its favour. Of course, the conclusion that such a lead and India's losing the race could spell doom for democracy in India, seems far-fetched in hindsight. But the impression was growing about the pace and speed of Chinese economic growth and development. British economist Nicholas Kaldor who spent some time in China after a longer stay in India is believed to have said privately: 'While China is racing ahead to industrialization, India is crawling with much too low a rate of investment and the 'race' has already become a procession.'[33] The question was raised as to whether India was concerned that the prospect of Chinese economic penetration of Cambodia would be a threat to India in Southeast Asia. The evidence did not suggest that, since it appeared that the first visit of Prince Sihanouk to Beijing had been arranged through Indian good offices. Could it be that the Indians were accepting of Chinese advances in the region, just as they had with the 'liberation' of Tibet? Were they not concerned about Chinese expansion, even if not by calculated aggression but 'by sheer uncontainability, by—as it were—a monster's natural lurch or sprawl or spill or flux?'

However, not all Indians were impressed by what they saw in China. In 1955, the delegation of Rajkumari Amrit Kaur, Minister of Health, and one of the students led by Dr C.P. Ramaswamy Aiyar, the Vice-Chancellor of Benares Hindu University, while being polite in their public utterances about their visits, spoke more pungently in private conversations. The health minister was not altogether complimentary about Chinese medical standards and the Vice-Chancellor had some good digs about Chinese discipline, and ignorance of the outside world. His speeches also focused on the lack of freedom in China. In private, they drew attention to the large numbers of Russians to be seen in Beijing and the dislike they saw among the Chinese for the growing Soviet influence in their country. Both visitors while commenting on this, also said they got the impression that the Chinese were secretly yearning for closer ties with the West. As for the young Indian students, they, too, had not been impressed with the regimentation and the fact that they could not look around for themselves. But the Indian press, the British diplomats in Beijing reported,[34] did not report all this as they preferred to sugar the bitter pill when it came to China!

Frank Moraes, the prominent editor and commentator, was even more blunt in his assessment. Writing in 1963,[35] he was of the view that India's relations with China had been built more on illusion than on fact. Of course, the 'eruptive' fact of China's attack on India in 1962 enabled this conclusion in large measure. Moraes wrote about the fundamental difference between the Hindu mind and the Chinese mind. The Hindus were products of a religious tradition animating Indian society and the quest for the divine. Divinity was not a notion that troubled the Chinese. The mystical, the speculative and the divine were not aspects that they dwelt on. Where the Hindu mind was not monolithic, the Chinese mind was. The Chinese were accustomed to dealing with absolutes. Nehru was an emotionally eruptive man but violence had no place in his thinking.

Tan Chung (the Chinese academic whose family ties as the son of Tan Yun-shan brought him to Santiniketan and to India in his youth after growing up in China during the war years) contrasts the Chinese diligence in preserving historical memory with the Indian lack of emphasis on keeping historical records.[36] Chinese civilization in his view is highly integrated, in contrast to the Indian, which has also been the recipient of far greater external influence than China. India's past is heterodox and its present, pluralist as is widely believed. Indian religious thought did leave a considerable impact on China through the influence of Buddhism brought through Central Asia. A similar impact of Chinese culture on India was not as palpable.

In fact, the image of India in the modern Chinese mind has been influenced, in not insignificant part, by British India's opium trade with China—this was an encounter 'mediated' by the British 'that brought the two nations face to face in a strange, almost unwanted, partnership'. Even as the Chinese were evolving their own system to regulate and restrict foreign trade in their country— in an endeavour to keep the foreigner out as far as possible, they were also aware of the extinction of India's nationhood under creeping British colonialism. The unfortunate image of India as 'a petty accomplice of powerful imperialist interests' propagated by Parsi and Marwari merchants trading in South China, was thus reinforced. The presence of native regiments in the British expeditionary force fighting the infamous Opium War and the countless Indians serving the expedition in a menial capacity, sealed Chinese views about a subjugated nation. Sikh policemen, hired by the British, were also ubiquitous on the streets of China's treaty ports. India was on the wrong side of history in China's struggle against the foreigner.[37] In the wake of the Chinese rout in the Opium Wars, there was an attempt however, among Chinese intellectuals like Wei Yuan (1847) to advocate a simultaneous policy of contention and collusion with countries like India in order to offset the threat from the West and for tactical gain, in a manifestation of realpolitik which seems to be an early avatar of the present-day Chinese strategic outlook on the world.[38] The 1958 study by the Chinese scholar Jin Kemu, 'A Short History of Sino-Indian Friendship'[39] speaks of the Sepoy Rising of 1857 in India and the Second Opium War in China as having 'lent influence to each other.' In the course of the Taiping Rebellion or 'Revolution' as the study terms it, 'some Indian troops sent by the British to suppress the revolutionary forces went over and fought side by side with the Taipings, writing a glorious page in history when our peoples united against a common foe. During the Boxer Revolt, an Indian soldier noted down in his diary his indignation at the atrocities of the imperialists and his sympathy for China.'[40] The study then waxes on to say, 'Just as the Himalayas could not separate us in ancient times, modern imperialism is powerless to destroy our friendship.'[41]

It was left to Tagore to talk about Asian identity and oneness, and for an awakening in India about China to register in the early years of the twentieth century, as the freedom movement gathered momentum and nationalist sentiment in favour of other Asian countries struggling against foreign aggression and domination grew. When Indian indentured labour was sent by the British to South Africa, they encountered Chinese labour working in the gold mines there. Both these sets of people were subject to severe racial discrimination and restrictions. Mahatma Gandhi's early work in South Africa had him engaged with both Indian and Chinese labour, and Chinese and Indians were imprisoned as a result of these campaigns.[42] The medical mission sent by the Indian National Congress to war-torn China, saw the first real contacts being established between them and the Chinese communists. Hitherto most interaction had been with the opposing Nationalists or the Guomindang. The saga of one Indian medical doctor, Dwarkanath Kotnis (the doctor without borders[43]) who was attached to Communist units deep inside Communist-controlled terrain, and who died in China during this period, is still venerated in China. It was the subject of a Hindi movie—*Dr. Kotnis ki Amar Kahani* (The Immortal Story of Dr. Kotnis) released in the late-1940s on the eve of Indian independence and which was a box office success. The music composer, Vasantrao Desai studied Chinese music for the songs in the film and its background score.[44]

In a small way, Indian audiences were becoming aware of the struggle waged by the Chinese people, although the exposure which was mainly through popular media like newspapers and film was in no way deep or substantive. In August 1958, Yin Hua and Guo Qinlan (Kotnis' son and widow) visited India and were warmly met by Nehru. While Kotnis is not widely remembered in India today, in China he commands adulation, even veneration, as the scholar Vinay Lal notes. The PRC issued two postage stamps on his 40th death anniversary in 1982, and a large statue of a handsome young Kotnis stands in the Martyr's Memorial Park at Shijiazhuang where he is buried.[45]

An interesting account of a young Indian woman's sojourn in war-torn China in the 1940s comes from the account of Parvathi Thampi,[46] the daughter of the veteran diplomat K.P.S. Menon who was posted as Agent-General of the (British) Government of India in Chongqing. Flying with her parents from Kolkata to Kunming, over 'The Hump'—i.e., over the Eastern Himalayas from Assam into Yunnan, and then to Chongqing, she proceeded to Chengdu where she joined a college for her studies. Economic conditions under war were in a very poor state, food was scarce, and airplane tickets could be bought with a bar of soap, and 'half a silk saree', as Thampi recalled. The Chinese treated foreigners as outsiders, despite being polite and courteous. 'For three years, I shared their hardships, worked and played with them, laughed and even fought with them but never knew their innermost thoughts, never really found who was for the government in power and who was not, who was for Mao and Zhou Enlai or who was not.'

In the 1950s, it was as if the two countries were engaged in encounters of rediscovery. These exchanges peaked by 1957–58; however by 1959, with the outbreak of the revolt in Tibet and rising border tensions, the number of such visits plummeted sharply. Herbert Passin[47] writing in 1961, analysed the objectives of the Chinese as far as cultural diplomacy was concerned in Cold War terms. The aim, he noted, was to win India over to communism, and China's relations during this time with the Communist Party of India were particularly important. (The latter itself by the early 1960s split into pro-Russian and pro-Chinese factions.) Passin expressed the view that even Gandhians—in spite of their advocacy of and belief in non-violence—were 'vulnerable to the appeal of Chinese communitarianism, mass persuasion techniques and puritanical morality'.[48] Even religious leaders and the so-called 'saints' of Hindu society returned from China impressed by what they had seen there. For such Indians, ideological conformity in China was not viewed adversely but as a mark of national unity and discipline which contrasted powerfully with the divisions of politics, caste and other interest groups in Indian society. The Chinese practice of celebrating historical anniversaries was also very appealing as for instance when in September 1955, the 1500th anniversary of the paintings of the Ajanta caves was celebrated in Beijing with a number of distinguished Indian guests. Between 1952 and 1955 seven exhibitions of Indian art were held in China, while from 1951 to 1955 there were eleven exhibitions of Chinese art in India[49]. Indians were also greatly flattered by the manner in which the Chinese feted and greeted visiting Indian cultural groups, in contrast to the cursory way in which they were treated on visits to Western countries. Indian artists and literary figures often felt that they were given far more weightage in China than in their own country—which by contrast seemed quite disorganized and directionless, despite being (or because it was) a democracy. Chinese artists on visits to India also seemed to reap the propaganda advantage in comparison to westerners who may have visited in larger numbers. Because of the way their visits were organized by the Chinese authorities, they made the news. An example was the publicity surrounding a 6000-mile tour of Indian historic sites that three Chinese artists made in early 1959.

In any case, China's energy and dynamism made a deep impression on visiting Indians—it exerted an almost magnetic attraction. And those visiting China from India were often drawn from the elite strata of society, and what they said and wrote on return made a very significant impact on public opinion regarding China. They also came back with the 'glow' that resulted from the VIP treatment they received in China—meeting Chinese leaders of the top echelon and being given hospitality as state guests. Thus, China had created a 'sounding board' in Indian society.[50]

In the academic sphere, during the 1950s, Chinese scholars on India generally focused on traditional fields in Indology, i.e., the languages, literature and religions of the subcontinent. The awareness of Indian multiculturalism and multilingualism must have been thus instilled, and the contrasts with China must have been revealed. A second area of focus was the study of Sino-Indian cultural exchanges from which stemmed the idea of China–India fraternity or the 'bhai-bhai' concept in relations—first enunciated in 1924, during the visit of Tagore, by the Chinese scholar Liang Qichao (although at that stage, India was seen more as an elder sibling of China, having 'given' much in terms of cultural borrowing to China). The contribution of scholars like Ji Xianlin was very important in this regard since he wrote extensively on the impact of Buddhism (from India) in China, and the impact of Chinese material culture, imports like paper and silk, on India. From India, Bhaskar Anand Saletore, former Director of the National Archives, New Delhi, did a study entitled 'India's Diplomatic Relations with the East' published in 1960. This was perhaps one of the few studies in India that looked at India–China relations from the very beginning to the thirteenth century.[51] Thirdly, travelogues of India written by Chinese scholars visiting India in the fifties provided information on India's historical sites, culture and customs, art, and society. In the assessment of Chinese scholars these appraisals tended to be 'over-positive and unanimously uncritical'.[52] This was also a period of translation of literary works from each country into the language of the other—mainly Chinese and Hindi. From India, these included Sanskrit and Pali classics, the works of Tagore and 'progressive' literature, such as the works of Premchand and Mulk Raj Anand which were translated into Chinese. Writers like Premchand had a special appeal because of his desire to 'revolutionize' social realities which was somewhat synchronous with what Chinese proletarian literature set out to do, with the approval of the Chinese authorities. Raj Kapoor's film *Awaara* held a similar appeal in China with its representation of social problems like caste, poverty, and injustice—an appeal that endured as the renewed popularity of the re-released film showed in the late 1970s.[53]

One feature of the India–China relations during the 1950s was the personal 'touch' provided by Mao Zedong in his contacts with Indian ambassadors in Beijing. An instance of this is provided by his acceptance of the invitation from Rajan Nehru, the wife of R.K. Nehru, the Ambassador of India, to dine at the embassy. He is believed to have told the guests present that 'Every Chinese wished to reincarnate in India in his/her future life' much to the surprise of the Indians present.[54] This hortatory phase in bilateral relations was also the era when the friendship societies and associations sang the 'Hindi-Chini Poem'—a composition of actor, poet and politician Harindranath Chattopadhyaya— and the 'India–China Friendship Song' written by the composer He Luting. The latter song spoke of the tall Himalayas not being able to split the friendship between the two countries, and that their people 'got along better than brothers'. The Chattopadhyaya composition in turn, extolling the Panchsheel agreement, spoke of this 'mighty pact, which shall ever be intact, Pandit Nehru, Zhou Enlai, Hindi-Chini bhai-bhai'. The two governments certainly did not discourage these displays of enthusiasm and the 'bhai-bhai' sloganeering.[55]

Amidst this effulgence of cordial ties between the two nations, one account stands out for the contrary signals it conveys. It is the account of the visit to China of the Hindi poet, Ramdhari Singh 'Dinkar' (1908-1974) who traveled to China in October 1957 'during a particularly fraught historical juncture when China-India cultural diplomacy rubbed up against the literary persecutions of the Anti-Rightist Campaign in China.'[56] Dinkar wrote a travelogue of his visit that offers interesting insights about the China he encountered. By mid-1957, Mao's Hundred Flowers movement had come to an end and the large-scale of persecution of intellectuals had commenced in an atmosphere of insecurity, censorship and paranoia. While Dinkar's itinerary was similar to that of other literati from India visiting China at the time, with visits to places of historical and touristic importance, a meeting with Zhou Enlai, dinners and banquets, seeing plays and theatrical performances, his travelogue also contains his understanding of the Hundred Flowers and Anti-Rightist campaigns. The references stem from his quest to meet the Chinese poet Ai Qing whom he saw as the country's 'greatest' poet. Ai Qing had fallen victim to the Anti-Rightist campaign and been sent to the countryside to perform manual labour. When he, Dinkar, heard about this, he writes that he was shocked and distinctly uncomfortable. This incident was Dinkar's first glimpse of the 'disjuncture between the image of literary openness the Party attempted to outwardly project, and the anxiety and insecurity that permeated the Chinese literary sphere during these early months of the Anti-Rightist Campaign.'[57] Dinkar then expresses the view that the Ai Qing, 'the great poet' had 'voiced his dissent. Perhaps he said: this communism foisted upon us, this is not what we had made sacrifices for. If this is communism, then we have no interest in this communism.'[58] Dinkar's quest for Ai Qing revealed his sensitivity to the 'silences and absences' created by literary persecution. Writing in his travelogue, he asked the question: 'Why should despair not be written of?' He offers an answer whose connotations continue to be relevant for the China of today: 'Because the state wants to encircle and contain all minds so as to lead society towards a single aim, these are chains with no chinks. The state ensures that individuality can never pierce through. For if a hole appears, water may flow through it in unwanted directions.' Here he was challenging a rethink of the whole premise of India-China cultural diplomacy, and friendship, of the inherent nature of the difference between these two systems encountering each other. Dinkar was to go on to become a harsh critic of the Nehru government and its China policy in 1962. His epic poem, 'Parasuram ki Pratiksa' (Awaiting Parasuram, 1963) was an epitome of nationalism targeting the government for 'luring Indians into a slumber resulting in India's defeat in the war.' It was poetry serving the national cause and Dinkar is today a poster-child for all those who critique Nehru for his 'failure' in regard to China and India's China policy, and who champion strong nationalistic approaches in dealing with India's neighbour to the north.

No account of this period in relations would be complete without a reference to Vasant Paranjpe (d. 2010)—Indian diplomat, Sanskrit scholar and fluent Mandarin speaker, who had perhaps the closest and longest exposure to China than any Indian of his generation. Beginning as a student at Beijing University in the summer of 1947, on the eve of Indian independence, he was witness to the 'liberation' of the city by the Chinese communists in January 1949. Later, he was interpreter to Prime Minister Nehru in his various meetings over the years with the Chinese leadership, until 1960. His years of exposure also made him a keen observer of Chinese and Indian psychology and behaviour. He saw them as two very different sets of people. He contrasted the emotional, idealistic, voluble, 'rather vague and brash' Hindu, with the pragmatic Chinese wedded to 'reason'. The Hindu was fond of speculating about life beyond death, of the concepts of atma (individual soul), Brahman (cosmic soul), and the ideal of moksha (emancipation of the soul). The average Chinese was more rooted in the mundane affairs of the world, and the conduct of an individual in society. Ethics and etiquette were important to them. An interesting aspect that Paranjpe observed was that the Chinese, unlike the Hindu/Indian, observed strict reciprocity in human relations. Such reciprocity also worked 'in a vicious way' as in wars or feuds, where it was always an eye-for-eye and a tooth-for-tooth, and while they could be good friends, they were bad enemies. The Hindu was more casual, and more tolerant. Hindus, in his view, placed an excessive faith in the written word and elevated it to the level of a 'cosmic force' (shabda-brahma) whereas for a Chinese an oral assurance was enough. The Chinese were long-term planners while the Indian seemed often swayed by short-term benefit. In negotiation, Indians would lay all their cards on the table, while the Chinese would take a much longer time to reveal their true hand.[59] These somewhat essentialist observations require more in-depth examination, even if coming from a seasoned observer of China. They would make a subject for a longer study of relevance to twenty-first century relations between India and China.

9

The Other Neighbour

During the early period of diplomatic relations between India and the People's Republic of China, links between the latter and Pakistan were correct and formal, but hardly indicative of or presaging the 'iron brother' relationship that exists between the two countries today. Pakistan recognized the People's Republic on 4 January 1950, a few days after India did, stating that it wanted to develop cordial and mutually advantageous relations with China. In September 1950, Pakistan supported the Indian resolution in the United Nations seeking to replace the delegation of Nationalist China with that of the People's Republic of China. Pakistanis felt that China was not only a large neighbour, but also that it contained 'a large Muslim population'.[1] In June 1951, Pakistan's Foreign Minister, Zafrulla Khan, announced that the country would shortly nominate an ambassador to the People's Republic. He said Pakistan would not let pass any opportunity that might arise for 'furthering understanding with China'. On the question of Tibet, and the entry of Chinese troops, he said that if the Sino-Tibetan Agreement had 'settled' relations between Tibet and China, he would 'not be disposed to cavil at it on account of stationing of Chinese troops in Tibet.' The presence of Chinese troops on the borders of the subcontinent 'would not necessarily constitute a threat to India and Pakistan.'[2] The fact that contacts between China and Pakistan were slowly on the rise was evidenced by the invitation extended to six Pakistani left-leaning intellectuals and lawyers to attend the second anniversary of the People's Republic in Beijing, and the setting up of the Pakistan-China Friendship Society in August–September 1951.

The country's first Ambassador to Beijing was a retired Army General, N.A.M. Raza, who presented his credentials to Mao Zedong in November 1951. The British in Beijing described him as having a 'forceful and forthright' approach towards the Chinese Government and being "manifestly surprised at their lack of good manners and at their unorthodox practices and ethics".[3] The Chinese government was rather surprised that the Ambassador's letters of credence were signed by the British monarch, King George the Sixth, and Mao Zedong is believed to have displayed 'considerable ignorance of the differences in race, historical traditions, and political status of India and Pakistan' (as reported by the British, who had, if these dispatches are to be taken at face value, a soft corner for Pakistan vis-à-vis India). In London, the Foreign Office seemed much taken with the attitude displayed by the Pakistani Ambassador, saying that 'Gen. Raza is going to be a rival to Panikkar by the looks of it, though the fact that his credentials were signed by the King may make the Chinese suspicious of him and of Pakistan's independence.'[4] Meanwhile, tensions were endemic on the Gilgit/Xinjiang frontier—in August 1950, a detachment of seventeen Chinese Communist troops had moved up to the Mintaka Pass, north of the Hunza region to relieve fifteen others who were holding an outpost on the pass. Having taken over their predecessors' weapons, the relieving force proceeded to desert toward Pakistan; their predecessors objected, and the relieving force shot and killed them. They then crossed the pass and surrendered to the Pakistani forces. One of the mutineers was a Muslim and all seventeen were sent to

Gilgit Jail. The Pakistanis were embarrassed by the incident and concerned that the Chinese would accuse them of having caused the murder of the garrison. The Ministry of Foreign Affairs in Karachi wished to hand the group back to China, as they were deserters under international law but were in no hurry to do so, presumably seeking to obtain what intelligence they could from them before they were handed back.[5]

Pakistan's increasing dependence on the United States during these years saw it voting with the Americans to postpone China's entry into the United Nations, after that early vote to support the replacement of the Nationalist Chinese delegation in September 1950. The Chinese must have regarded this an indication of Pakistan's compromises with the West, but do not seem to have made an issue of it. Pakistan, however, was also careful not to cross some lines—with regard to Korea while terming North Korea an aggressor, it did not apply the same term to the Chinese.[6] In 1954, Pakistan joined the Southeast Asia Treaty Organization (SEATO), very much a part of the anti-Communist bloc. The Chinese Embassy in Karachi at the time, 'sent annual work reports back to Beijing, consistently complaining of their indifferent treatment by the Pakistan government.'[7]

In September 1951, *World Culture*, a magazine published in Beijing, reported on a secret trial held in Pakistan of several prominent Pakistanis including the poet Faiz Ahmed Faiz, Pakistan Communist Party member Syed Sajjad Zaheer, Syed Sibtey Hassan of the Progressive Writers Association, and many others who had been implicated in an alleged 'plot' for supporting a peaceful solution of the Korean problem.[8] The article referred to a statement signed by more than a hundred prominent Indian writers and artists, explaining how the Pakistani Government under 'imperialist' influence, was endeavouring to suppress the popular fight for a peaceful solution in Korea. The article was an attempt to draw attention to the alleged 'reactionary tendencies' of the Pakistan government which took a 'jaundiced' view of this 'gratuitous declaration of Chinese solicitude for the rights of Pakistanis in their own country.'

Of greater concern was the issue of Chinese claims to Pakistani territory. The existence of Chinese claims over Pakistani, Indian and Burmese (Myanmar) territory was becoming known. In January 1952, the British Foreign Office addressed a top secret note to the Map Office in London, forwarding two maps showing such Chinese claims. The first map illustrated Chinese claims on 'Kashmiri', Afghan and Tajik territory. The second concerned Chinese claims to Indian and Myanmarese territory. The first map showed that the Chinese claimed all territories up to and including the Karakoram Range in Kashmir. A major part of Hunza in Kashmir, including Killik and Mintaka Passes on the Karakoram Range, were depicted as Chinese. The entire Shimshal region was claimed, as also the whole of Baltistan and the area east of the Indus, above the India–Pakistan 'cease-fire line' as it was then termed. Indian territory claimed by China included the greater part of Ladakh, including Leh. The British surmised that the Chinese Communists intended to 'take root' in the Kashmir region and convert the whole area to communism. Therefore, they felt, further 'delay' in settling the Kashmir issue between India and Pakistan would only help the Chinese further their ideological aims to spread communism into South Asia.[9] The correspondence quoted a 'special source' in Tibet who had informed London of a movement gaining ground in China for the creation of a strong and united 'Greater Tibet' comprising of all Tibetan-speaking territories stretching from China to Kashmir. Of special interest was the fact that this source conveyed that the Chinese were reportedly building a 'motorable road from Tibet to Xinjiang via the border of Ladakh'. And the second map clearly showed the Chinese claim dipping from the southeast corner of the Bhutan boundary along the edges of the plain of the Brahmaputra River.

The Chinese Embassy in Pakistan, meanwhile, continued to be active in promoting 'people' diplomacy as was evidenced by the visit,[10] for the first time, of a delegation of eminent Pakistani women to China in 1954 at the invitation of the All-China Democratic Women's Federation to attend the National Day celebrations of the People's Republic. (Four Indian delegations reportedly attended the same event.)[11] A member of the Pakistani Constituent Assembly, Begum Shah Nawaz, was the leader of the seven-member delegation. On their return to Pakistan, Begum Husein Malik, one of the members, delivered a talk at the Pakistan Institute of International Affairs recounting the delegation's first-hand experiences of China. Like Indian visitors to China at the time, what seemed to strike the Pakistanis most was the 'discipline and patriotism' of the Chinese, together with the role of Chinese women in the life of the country. The visitors had also come away with the impression that overall, the Chinese administration was of 'higher standard and less corruptible than the Pakistani' one. Premier Zhou Enlai met the delegation at 11.45 pm in the evening during their stay in Beijing and the meeting lasted until 3.15 am. The Pakistani ladies were full of admiration for the 'achievements of the people of China'.

Early in February 1956, Soong Ching-ling (the widow of Sun Yat Sen) made a visit to South Asia that covered India, Burma, and Pakistan. In Pakistan, where she visited Karachi, Lahore, and Dacca (in the erstwhile East Pakistan), she was accorded top-level treatment, being greeted by the Prime Minister, the Foreign Minister, the Foreign Secretary and other senior officials. She attended a number of public functions and had interviews with the Prime Minister and the Foreign Minister, and invited the former to visit China. She spent two hours attending the debate on the Constitution in the Pakistan Constituent Assembly. The level of treatment accorded to Mrs Soong Ching-ling was that normally assigned to countries with which Pakistan, at the time, had far more cordial relations. In her public speeches, she made reference to the success of the Bandung Conference 'which had exploded the myth that such a conference could not be held without the participation of the West'; furthermore, peaceful coexistence between countries with different political systems, as China and Pakistan, was a 'practical possibility'. The Foreign Office spokesman in Karachi was at pains, however, to emphasize that the visit was an expression of 'Pakistan's desire to have friendly relations with all countries' and advised the Press 'not to try to read more into it (the visit) than that.'[12] The British envoy, reporting from Karachi, remarking on the tenor of Pakistan's foreign policy noted that, 'The sense of isolation and of being surrounded by powerful enemies and supported by uncertain allies, who are too far away or unwilling to render immediate assistance, remains strong'. Mrs Soong did not hold any press conference where she could have been asked searching questions about where China stood on Kashmir or Afghanistan and Pakistan's disputes about these matters, which would run the risk of causing some embarrassment to her hosts.

In 1956, it was announced that Pakistani Prime Minister H.S. Suhrawardy would visit China availing himself of the invitation originally extended by Zhou Enlai to his predecessor Mohamed Ali Bogra during the Bandung Afro-Asian Conference in 1955. The Chinese, according to the British diplomats in Pakistan, were seeking to improve Sino-Pakistan relations 'by an appearance of sweetness and light.'[13] Suhrawardy's own party, the Awami League, was in favour of a revision of Pakistan's foreign policy by withdrawing from military alliances and 'adopting a more neutralist line'.[14] The visit to China fitted into this scheme. The Chinese were wooing Pakistan, too. They were also anxious of securing a prime-ministerial visit from Pakistan to China before the projected visit of Premier Zhou to Pakistan. (They were of course at variance with the Pakistani stand that the Anglo-French attack on Egypt during the Suez Crisis in 1956 was not colonialism but intended to maintain peace in the area. Zhou Enlai termed it 'colonial aggression'.[15]) An article in *The Times*, London, of 16 November 1956[16] described Zhou's Asian peregrinations (to

India, Pakistan, Afghanistan, Nepal, Burma, Laos, and Cambodia) as influenced by perspectives gained by China at Bandung. The 'urbane handshakes and the friendly dinner-table discussions of Bandung' had been followed by a stream of visitors to Beijing, making the Grand Tour, as it were. Could it be that China perceived South Asia as a 'zone of exclusive Indian influence', the paper speculated. Was that why there was this spate of visits being undertaken by the Chinese Premier to the region? China was already competing with Russia to be seen as the backer of anti-colonialism, and they could not but be secretly pleased that the Russians had now 'to explain away Hungary and all the simmerings and discontents of Eastern Europe.' They would sail under the flags of trade and friendly relations and coexistence, which still resounded well in Asian ears, except in Burma where the frontier question with China was proving bothersome. At the same time, China did not see itself solely as an Asian power, sharing influence with India, just as it had never seen itself as a unit in 'the Communist Empire ruled from Moscow.'

Mr Suhrawardy was in China from the 18 to 29 October 1956. He arrived in Beijing in a British Viscount aircraft flown by the Pakistan Air Force, spoke to a mass rally in the Chinese capital, visited a jet aircraft factory and 'attended the requisite number of banquets'.[17] He had conversations with Mao Zedong and Zhou Enlai, and Mao 'bestowed the rare honour' of attending the banquet given by the Pakistani Prime Minister. The latter reportedly displayed frankness and straight-talking in his public statements in China and did not indulge in 'flattery' as was the case with other visiting leaders, for instance, the Indonesian President Sukarno. Briefings received from the Pakistan Embassy by British diplomats suggested that the Chinese had made it clear to the visitors that they disliked Pakistan's membership of the SEATO and the Baghdad Pact, to which the Prime Minister apparently said that America had no aggressive intentions in Asia and its intention was only to contain the spread of communism in Asia, which was 'an aim fully shared by Pakistan'.[18] (Foreign Secretary of Pakistan S.A. Baig told the British in Karachi that exchanges on this issue were 'lengthy and vehement' and fear and hatred of the United States seemed to dominate Chinese thinking. In the end, the Chinese leaders had said in effect, 'We might manage to trust the Americans with less suspicion if there is any response on their side. Would the Pakistanis see what they could do to achieve this?'[19]) Mr Suhrawardy reminded his Chinese hosts of the tradition of Sino-American friendship and said he hoped it could be resumed. To this, Zhou Enlai reportedly said that 'if Pakistan could contribute to improving Sino-American relations, he would be very pleased.' It was a remark with its eye on the future and the role that Pakistan would come to play in the eventual normalization of Sino-American relations.

The Chinese apparently kept off Kashmir but the matter was brought up by the Pakistani Prime Minister who said that China's talk about the unity of Asia and the Bandung spirit was meaningless so long as a problem of this nature existed. He was told by the Chinese that they hoped Pakistan would be able to reach an acceptable solution with India, to which Mr Suhrawardy responded that he hoped they would 'give the same advice to India.' The Chinese were 'careful' not to commit themselves on 'the merits of the question.'[20] It was to be noted that Chinese press comments on the visit were positive and enthusiastic about the prospects of improved relations between the two countries, although the 'adulatory' tone customary in articles about India 'was never quite attained.'[21] Of interest also was the impression made on the Pakistani delegation that the Chinese government was thinking of moving in the direction of family planning, with Foreign Secretary Baig saying that the ghost of Malthus 'might be said to have been present at most of the conversations.'[22]

Mr Suhrawardy's candour in statements made to the Chinese during his visit apparently had struck a raw nerve, for very soon after this visit, negative comments about him began to appear in the Chinese press which published reports from the opposition press in Pakistan, critical of the Prime Minister.[23] Alleged differences in foreign policy with the Awami League in East Pakistan were reported and the general aim appeared to be to suggest that public opinion in Pakistan was against the country's continued adherence to SEATO and the Baghdad Pact. Pakistan's vote in the United Nations in favour of a continued moratorium on entry of the People's Republic into the UN was also attacked. Suhrawardy seemed undeterred by these affectations, telling the British in early 1957[24] that Pakistan was in a 'very special position' since it had a foot in South Asia as well as the Middle East. He was not troubled about Indian ambitions as the Chinese would 'keep these in check' and that he had been at 'special pains' to develop what he called 'a feeling of personal friendship' with Zhou Enlai and to 'make a link with China'. He said India had abandoned Laos and Cambodia to the Chinese, and her 'influence had ceased in Tibet'. China and Nepal were signalling the establishment of relations which was embarrassing for India which would 'find her work cut out' to maintain her position in the region.

But the direction in China–Pakistan relations towards building better trust and understanding was not abandoned. Premier Zhou went to Pakistan for ten days in December 1956 and visited Karachi, Peshawar, Lahore, and Dacca. Asked about Kashmir at a press conference in Karachi, he said that he needed to 'make a full study of the question' and that 'Before that I hope Pakistan and India will settle this question directly between themselves because the people of Pakistan and India have lived together for such a long time throughout history. We believe that they will be able to find a solution.'[25] The Premier chose to refer to the 'many centuries'-old linkages between the two countries (referring obviously to the Buddhist pilgrims between ancient India and China) as 'precious evidence of our long existing friendship'. A joint statement issued at the end of the visit placed on record 'that there is no real conflict of interests between the two countries', downplaying Pakistan's relationship with the Western bloc. An editorial in the *People's Daily* of 26 December 1956 stressed the continuous progress in economic relations and cultural exchange between the two countries.

These exchanges between China and Pakistan took place at a time when relations between India and China were at an apogee that would soon diminish as the border problems between them acquired greater salience. China under the watchful, calculating gaze of Zhou Enlai was no doubt aware of the space occupied by Pakistan on the strategic calculus between China and the West, and the need to cultivate a relationship with this neighbour of India. The investments in this relationship were certainly being made from the early fifties onwards, and they would prove their utility before long.

. . . .

In 1954, Indonesia suggested the holding of a conference of Asian and African states. Nehru was not initially enthused as he felt that such a meeting would end up as a 'forum for heated discussion on local and regional matters'[26] such as Israel and Palestine. He was not impressed by the 'intellectual calibre' of leaders like Nasser.[27] But he also saw the utility of such a conference as helping to refute the US policy of imposing military alliances on Asia and Africa. Holding together, India, Indonesia, and Burma could form an 'area of peace' that could symbolize a principled challenge to such policies. He was also clear that China should be invited to such a conference even if the United States and the United Kingdom objected. Also, China was eager to be invited. It was decided that all the independent countries of Asia and Africa should be invited, which gave the conference importance by virtue of its wide membership. Topical relevance was provided by the outstanding issue of the crisis in East Asia arising out of the detention of American prisoners from the Korean War in

China. As it transpired, the prisoner issue became the subject of discussion outside the Conference, complicated by US–Taiwan relations, and China's insistence that it was being provoked by American actions that were regarded in Beijing as belligerent. But Nehru was determined that the Bandung meeting should succeed and busied himself with attention to the smallest details regarding its organization including the 'adequate provision of bathrooms and lavatories'.[28]

A dramatic curtain raiser to the conference involved the sabotage of the Air India Constellation plane, the 'Kashmir Princess', carrying some members of the Chinese delegation to the Bandung conference in early April 1955. The crash took the lives of sixteen passengers (Chinese and East European media personnel slated to attend the Bandung conference) and crew members of the ill-fated aircraft. It is widely believed that the act was carried out by Taiwanese intelligence with the help of some ground handlers at Hong Kong airport. The target was the Chinese Premier, Zhou Enlai, who did not travel on the doomed flight. It is also believed that the Chinese Communist authorities knew that the flight was targeted for sabotage by the Guomindang authorities in Taiwan who assumed that Zhou would travel on it to Indonesia, which led to their Premier not traveling on the plane. The period was a trying time for the Taiwanese, diplomatically; they were concerned about Zhou wishing to open negotiations with the United States and isolate Taipei, and also the prospects of China even joining the United Nations. Recognition of the regime in Beijing would be the worst blow possible. There was concern also about Britain's improving relations with the PRC. All this, from the Taiwanese viewpoint, was worse than any direct military confrontation with Beijing in the Taiwan Straits. A successful Afro-Asian Conference in Bandung with Zhou as a leading light, pushing Beijing's 'peace offensive', and the cynosure of world attention, would not suit Taiwanese interests. The incentive to assassinate Zhou was, therefore, strong.[29] After the incident, Beijing was quick to exploit the propaganda value of Taiwanese involvement in the plot to destroy the plane, and it did win the upper hand in this contest with the Nationalist regime. The fact that Zhou and his cohort knew about the sabotage plans beforehand and could have easily cancelled the flight thereby saving the lives of the passengers, received little play.

Bandung marked in many ways a diplomatic debut on the global stage for Zhou Enlai. Taking the 'honours in diplomatic acuity'[30] at the Conference, Zhou clearly stole the limelight among 600 leaders and delegates of the twenty-nine newly independent countries from Asia and Africa—a veritable theatre of diplomacy—that congregated in the Indonesian city from 18 to 24 April 1955. Both Nehru and Zhou were crowd-pullers at Bandung. Zhou's visual impact was impressive, with an Indonesian Chinese magazine gushing that 'people could not stop talking about Zhou's eyebrows which were thick and black'. The Premier became a quick-change artiste, wearing a Mao suit at the conference, and a Western suit when meeting the local Chinese population.[31] From the onset, Zhou's name appeared more times in the Western media coverage of the Conference than Nehru's as a 'primary delegate of interest'.[32] At the Conference, Zhou presented himself as upholding respect for sovereignty, stressing that communism posed no threat and downplaying ideological differences. He said he had come to Bandung 'to seek unity, and not to quarrel', attempting to strike a note of moderation.[33] In the media, no other delegate was studied so comprehensively. China's Western detractors, all gunning for communism, were also taken aback when on the penultimate day of the Conference, Zhou (viewed as the shrewdest Asian diplomat of his time[34]) offered to engage in bilateral talks with the United States on the Taiwan Straits issue, saying that the Chinese people were friendly to the American people. The Australian journalist, Peter Russo, summed up Zhou's Bandung performance thus: 'We must be brave and face up to the horrible disappointments of the Afro-

Asian conference at Bandoeng. Our greatest let down I suppose was that (Zhou) did not behave like the savage we know him to be. Cunningly and with subhuman restraint, he upset our anticipations by refraining from howling aggressively at the other delegates or threatening to infiltrate them.'[35]

However, to suggest that Zhou's grasp of the limelight correspondingly amounted to Nehru's stature being eclipsed at Bandung may miss the mark. This is borne in the view expressed by the Lebanese representative, Ambassador Charles Malik, to an unreceptive US Secretary of State John Foster Dulles. Malik asserted that 'the US press was dead wrong in concluding that Nehru's stature was diminished substantially. Nehru retains power because of India's position in the area, his personal relationship to communist China, and India's membership in the Commonwealth'.[36] Walter Crocker, then the Australian Ambassador to Indonesia, decried the assessment that there was power rivalry between India and China at Bandung leading to a decline in Nehru's prestige. Nehru had aimed at initiating China into the larger community of Asian nations, it was therefore natural for China to be the main focus, and it would therefore be wishful thinking to regard China as having 'supplanted' India. Also, Nehru also saw his emphasis on neutralism in world affairs as having been fulfilled by the tenor of proceedings and outcomes of the Conference.[37] Nehru's policy of cautious friendship with China (and his not being oblivious to the threat to India on its borders with China) proceeded on the argument that 'an isolated and inward looking China can pose a serious threat to peace in Asia, but a China susceptible to outside world opinion and friendship of countries such as India may feel less encircled by a hostile world.'[38] It was this approach he pursued at Bandung where China was concerned.

In the early years of the People's Republic, Mao Zedong had characterized China as being in the 'intermediate zone' between the two superpowers—the United States and the Soviet Union.

This was a position that gradually metamorphosized as the Sino-Soviet rift grew increasingly wider from the 1960s onwards, and after the opening to the United States in 1972. Friends and enemies were determined according to circumstances as per this political stratagem. But in the early years after the founding of the PRC, the Chinese leadership pursued an 'orientation of taking the initiative in actively seeking friendship' over the Himalayas, with the focus being to 'put India at ease'.[39] Troublesome border issues were not raised by China in the discussions leading to the Tibet Agreement of 1954 contrary to the advice received from Party officials in Tibet. When the Bandung Conference came a year thereafter, this sunshine period persisted—with the two countries making the Five Principles of Peaceful Coexistence their co-sponsored project at this gathering of Afro-Asians. Internal Chinese documents[40] termed the Indian state as bourgeois, with leaders like Gandhi and Nehru as its leading representatives, and being two-sided in domestic and international politics. At the same time, the stratagem was to highlight the 'progressive' side of the Indian government while not losing sight of such 'reactionary' measures as the offensive against the Indian Communist Party (even after his China visit of 1954, Nehru did not hesitate to label the Communist Party in India as obsolete revolutionaries who followed the diktats of the Soviets and the Chinese). The Chinese were appreciative of the Indian government being 'realistic and sensitive enough to awaken to the fact that the United States was conducting expansionist power politics and was heading toward a new world war'.[41] Also understood was the fact that in a world situation characterized by polarization, Nehru's belief that India could benefit only from a position of neutrality and advocacy of peace was sensible.

In the Chinese view, India valued the genuine friendship shown by the socialist camp as opposed to the partiality shown by the United States to Pakistan, the setbacks suffered by the US in the Korean War, and the position taken by the Western powers on Kashmir. In this analysis, the Bandung Conference marked a high point where the 'maturity' of Indian foreign policy was amply demonstrated. Furthermore, Beijing regarded India as having 'met (the) test for a friendly government in supporting the PRC's legitimate status in the United Nations and recognizing Taiwan as part of China'.[42] The relationship between China and India was seen thus as a model of peaceful coexistence between states with different social systems. Nehruvian neutralism was also exerting its influence on newly independent Asian and African countries to follow a similar orientation of peace and neutrality in their foreign policies. Most importantly, securing India's friendship toward China would not only help bilateral relations between the two but consolidate Beijing's legitimacy on the global stage. Until the complications emanating from differences over the border manifested themselves from 1958–9 onwards, this view of friendly ties with India having useful international ramifications, prevailed in Beijing.

At Bandung, Zhou was careful not to raise such issues as China's entry into the UN, or questions of ideology or political systems; his focus instead was to establish for the audience of the other twenty-eight nations present that China wished to seek common ground while reserving differences—thus providing the 'organizational basis for the application of the five principles of peaceful coexistence.' He was flexible about the usage of the term 'peaceful coexistence', stating his willingness to substitute it with 'living together in peace', given the fact that some of the nations present were suspicious about the term as originally phrased. The pragmatic and outwardly conciliatory Zhou declared that the wording could be 'revised, and the number of principles may be increased or reduced; for what we seek is to identify our common aspirations.'[43] Economic and cultural relations among Afro-Asian nations, he felt, should be on the basis of 'mutual benefit and equality'.[44] This was an era in which the leadership of the Chinese Communist Party placed emphasis on the diplomacy of peaceful coexistence and united front with the aim of breaching the 'political isolation, economic embargo, and strategic containment instituted by the US'.[45] In the conclusion to his speech at the Conference, he said that 'peace and independence' were what the countries of Asia and Africa wanted and that 'it was not our intention to make the Asian and African countries antagonistic to countries in other regions. We want just as well the establishment of peaceful and cooperative relations with countries in other regions.' He hoped the conference could become 'a treasured page in the history of Asia and Africa'.[46]

Nehru recorded his own impressions[47] of the Bandung Conference on 28 April 1955. He noted that Zhou Enlai had attracted the most attention both in public and in the conference and that this was natural 'as he was not only playing a great part in the crisis of the Far East, but was rather a mysterious figure whom people had not seen.' In his view, Zhou had conducted himself with 'ability and moderation', spoken with authority, took pains to meet delegates and 'went to many parties given by Heads of delegation.' Zhou had displayed patience even when he encountered offensiveness and lost his cool once when in a committee meeting he said, 'China would not be bullied.' On the whole, he had created a very good impression. He, Zhou, had been at pains to emphasize that China wished for no special privileges, but only wanted equality of treatment and was prepared to settled international disputes peacefully. Asked about Tibet at one of the committees, he had said it would be 'thoroughly impracticable to establish a communist regime in Tibet and the Chinese government had no such wish . . . Tibet was an autonomous region of China and they had no desire whatsoever to interfere with its customs or ways of life.' But Tibet was an integral part of China and the Chinese had gone there (in 1951) because 'it had been used for imperial intrigues, meaning thereby the British recently and previously Czarist Russia'. The communist Chinese also wanted to treat Taiwan as an autonomous region. Asked if he could use force against Taiwan, according to Nehru, Zhou said that 'force is being used by Chiang Kai-shek and the Americans all the time. He, for his part, wanted a peaceful settlement and he thought this was possible provided the foreign element was removed, that is, America withdrew. But he could not give a one-sided assurance about not using force in the circumstances.'

In Nehru's view, Zhou 'came out well from that questioning and even some of his greatest opponents, who were present, realised that his case was not a bad one'. The Chinese Premier had been frank, courteous and 'to the point' and was 'prepared to give every assurance to remove apprehensions'.

The Bandung Conference also provided the stage for explorations of the possibilities of opening a dialogue between China and the United States. Krishna Menon—Nehru's troubleshooter on the diplomatic stage—told the US Ambassador in Delhi[48] after the Conference that he had met Zhou Enlai many times at Bandung, 'sometimes with Nehru present, oftener alone, and that at least one talk lasted five hours.' These confabulations had left Menon convinced that China was 'not expansionist,' given the latter's seemingly reasonable approach at the Conference. China was prepared to negotiate with the US on Taiwan, and the Government of India was willing to use its good offices to enable this if requested, although regardless of this, it would continue to explore the possibilities of negotiation. Menon suggested that as preliminary steps, even before it was agreed to start negotiations, the two sides should take steps to relax tensions, including the release of US airmen held by China, and US restraining the Taiwan regime from firing on the Chinese Communist forces. Menon told the Ambassador that the Indian government believed 'Communist China will never be Russian satellite and that possibility of US-Communist China settlement greater than US-Soviet settlement.'

Krishna Menon was to recount his experience at Bandung to Michael Brecher in the late 1960s. He summed up Zhou Enlai's role at the Summit as that of a 'good liberal who wanted a settlement (of outstanding issues with the United States, particularly). He wanted to be Asian—and to be accepted as such—and to play the role of a statesman . . . I would not have believed at that time that he would be Prime Minister of a country that would invade India.'[49] A recent biography of Krishna Menon recounts how Zhou and Menon 'sat next to each other for a long time in Bandung.' Zhou invited Menon to visit China to discuss the release of the imprisoned American pilots and also the Taiwan issue. Menon made his maiden visit to China in May 1955 for a duration of ten days when he had six rounds of talks with Zhou on the release of the imprisoned pilots and the bombardment of the Quemoy and Matsu islands by the Chinese. On his return to Delhi, he briefed Nehru who immediately informed US President Eisenhower that the Menon–Zhou talks had yielded result, and that China had offered to release the detained airmen. The meetings with Zhou had lasted a total of eighteen hours, with the record running into one hundred and fifty pages. Bilateral relations between India and China did not figure in the discussions except on the issue of increased air services, and when Menon briefly referred to Tibet saying India had not 'capitulated' on the issue 'because Tibet had never belonged to India anyway.' The focus was on the possible normalization of Sino-US relations. Zhou, the polished diplomat, was adulatory in his references to Menon as enjoying the full confidence of Nehru, and also 'one of the people who are very close to us.' Of significant interest is the fact that Zhou seemed prepared to use Menon as a catalyst to facilitate channels of communication with the United States, a process that Kissinger was to open and bring to fruition some seventeen years later in 1972. Zhou told Menon: 'you have to remain the go-between because although you have said you were not a negotiator, you cannot as well shake-off the responsibility of a go-between as you understand the situation of different parties and that facilitates the solution of the question.' On his return, Menon held a press conference where he announced the decision of the Chinese government to release the four airmen, and that Zhou had himself termed his talks with Menon as very useful and that one could look forward with hope. One of the obstacles, Menon told journalists, between China and the United States was the lack of contact. A day after the press conference, the four American pilots were released in Hong Kong.[50]

From 1950 onwards, Nehru had been an advocate of the entry of China into the United Nations and the Security Council. When the Korean War broke out in June that year, India had supported the UN Resolution condemning North Korean aggression on South Korea and urging the withdrawal of North Korean forces to the north of the 38th Parallel. Support was also extended for UN intervention to restore peace and security in the area. Nehru's advocacy at the same time for a negotiated settlement also saw him urge both Stalin and Dean Acheson, the then US Secretary of State, to allow the admission of China into the Security Council so that it could work with the United States and the Soviet Union for a negotiated solution to the problem in Korea. Nehru was convinced that no solution would be possible without China's concurrence. He spoke on these lines in Parliament on 3 August 1950[51] when he said that the entry of China into the UN could well have prevented the Korean crisis.

A 'peculiar atmosphere of rumour', as has been noted,[52] surrounds the whole question of the events that may have transpired regarding India versus China on entry into the Security Council in the 1950s. Nehru is vilified by his opponents as having refused offers from the United States and the Soviet Union to join the Security Council and overlooked the national interest. The Vijaya Lakshmi Pandit papers at the Nehru Memorial Library in Delhi speak of an offer by the US in August 1950 to assist India's entry into the Security Council. Reporting to the Prime Minister about a conversation she had with the U.S. Secretary of State John Foster Dulles, she refers to Dulles talking 'of the possibility of finding a way to amend the Charter by which China could be deprived of her permanent seat in the U.N. after which there would be no objection to India's admission. He hinted that American might be happy to see India as a permanent member and I interrupted to say that in view of our relationship with China, we had no desire whatsoever to be a party to this move.' A related conversation with Philip Jessup, who was Deputy Chief of the U.S. Mission to the United Nations said the same: 'He also spoke in terms of an attempt to remove China from a permanent seat and put India there.'[53]

A similar move was made by the Soviet leadership in 1955 for India's entry as a sixth member of the Security Council.[54] However, Nehru was driven in his approach to the issue by the conviction that unseating China to allow India's entry (which is what the US offer involved) 'would be bad from every point of view. It would be a clear affront to China and it would mean some kind of break between us and China.'[55] In the case of the Soviet offer, Nehru felt that the issue of China's entry should be first resolved before India's case was taken up. Nehru did not deny that India was certainly entitled to a permanent seat in the Security Council as a great power, but 'we are not going at the cost of China.'[56] The momentary convergence between India and the United States, by the former's support for the first two UN Resolutions on the Korean crisis in June 1950, was however, soon replaced by divergence when India refused to support a third resolution, giving the Americans full command over the UN forces in Korea. By July, differences were even more in evidence when India tried hard to persuade all parties that the PRC taking the Chinese seat at the UN would greatly defuse tensions in East Asia. On the US side, the offer to India appeared to emanate from the desire to trade support for India joining the UNSC with an end to India's advocacy of the communist Chinese joining the UN and the Council. As a staunch believer in the crucial role that the UN was meant to play in global affairs (despite the treatment of the

Kashmir issue), Nehru was against destabilizing the organization with a move that would involve a change to its charter, which India taking China's seat would entail. China, in his view, needed to be integrated into the international community instead of the isolation which Cold War politics dictated. The Soviet Union had been similarly ostracized by the United States during its early history, generating bipolar tensions and confrontation. The lessons of this history needed to be learnt so that China was not isolated in a like fashion. China's centrality in a postwar world could not be denied as it was a key constituent in Asian resurgence. Despite the fact that China was to 'betray' Nehru's trust as the steep descent into conflict from 1959 onwards was to demonstrate, his concerted efforts to see the integration of China into the international community in the period preceding this certainly helped initiate engagement between Beijing and opposing parties to de-escalate tensions in East and Southeast Asia. The refusal of the US offer in 1950 is comprehensible from the point of view that Nehru did not want to see China being unseated from entry into the Security Council in favour of India. However, the summary rejection of the (tentative) Soviet offer of 1955 to push for India's entry as a sixth member (without taking away China's 'seat') is more difficult to justify or defend in the crucible of history until the archives reveal more details.

10

Buddha Jayanti: An Anniversary Remembered

Following the hooves of yak singing a sad song.
Let me ask you:

Do you know the troubled tales of your forefathers?
Did you see their footprints in the mountains you roam?[1]

—Dhi Lhaden: 'Do You Know
the Tales Of Our Forefathers?'

The year 1956 came with the crises in Suez and Hungary and witnessed an intense phase of the Cold War. Nehru was worried. 'I do not like the look of things in the world today. I cannot mention any particular thing—we have had of course many things but at the present moment I cannot mention any particular thing—but the whole look of it and many small things taken together produce a feeling of grave anxiety in my mind.'[2] Against this tense backdrop, the Government of India's decision to commemorate the 2500th anniversary of the birth of the Buddha stood as a contrast. Nehru described it in a communication to Krishna Menon as 'sticking to the right path', in a situation that hovered between the 'atom and the Buddha'[3]. This was at a time when the state of affairs along the border with China was beginning to occupy some of Nehru's attention, too. Apart from incorrect delineations, from the Indian point of view, of the border that were increasingly seen on Chinese maps, on the ground, Chinese activism was increasingly in evidence. Activities included Chinese usage of the caravan route from Xinjiang into Tibet across the Aksai Chin (which was clearly on the Indian side of the border as marked on Indian maps); visits by Chinese patrols to Demchok, a Ladakhi village; and Chinese soldiers being spotted at Nilang in what is now Uttarakhand, but was then a part of Uttar Pradesh. Chinese claims were also being asserted in the area of Bara Hoti, south of the pass of Tunjun La which was identified clearly as a border pass between the Tibet Region and India in the 1954 Agreement.

Again, in his correspondence with Krishna Menon, Nehru expressed his disquiet about not having raised the question of the border with the Chinese during the 1954 talks.[4] He tried to assuage his doubts by expressing the conviction that the Chinese would take no action to unsettle matters on the border while they were preoccupied with internal matters within the country. He was unsure of the terrain ahead in India's dealings with China, even as the external impression of cordial friendship was maintained. To quote his biographer S. Gopal, Nehru was 'insufficiently alert to possible Chinese encroachments on a major scale. Curiously, the reported presence of Chinese personnel in Aksai Chin, and the defiance of Indian sovereignty that this implied, roused no marked reaction in Delhi'.[5] Nehru wished to avoid confrontation with China. Writing to his Defence Minister, K.N. Katju, he expressed himself, thus: 'I am not at all sure of what China may do ten or twenty years hence. But to protect ourselves against possible developments, we have to do other things and not try to put up a useless Maginot Line. In particular, we have to have peace, quiet and contentment on our side of the border.'[6]

At the same time, where neighbouring countries like Nepal and Burma, and their relations with China were concerned, Nehru's views were infused with more realpolitik. His discomfort about Nepal initiating dialogue with China with the intention of establishing closer bonds, was candidly expressed to leaders of both countries. With Burma, however, he did not want the latter's relations with China run into difficulties, since he felt that this would disturb his vision for peace in Asia. This was at a time when U Nu was expressing his apprehension about possible Chinese imperialist designs. Nehru encouraged the Burmese leader to hold talks with Zhou Enlai on the question of the China–Burma frontier, even conveying to Zhou that he should be accommodating in his approach to Burma. He told Zhou, 'I would like also to mention that, by and large, in these sparsely inhabited frontier mountain areas, frontiers and positions which are based on previous agreements and have also been accepted by usage, custom and tradition for appreciable periods, should not be disturbed or altered except by friendly agreements'.[7] This was an approach that Nehru obviously would have liked to see applied to the Indian border with China, too. To Burma, the Chinese stated that they regarded the McMahon Line (a stretch of the line covered the Burmese frontier with China too, extending eastwards from its Indian section) as 'immoral' and based on what they regarded as an illegal treaty (between British India and Tibet), but that they were prepared, for the sake of an agreement, to accept it as the de facto boundary.

In the summer of 1954, the Dalai Lama accompanied by his family and an entourage of some five hundred people,[8] including the Panchen Lama, visited Beijing at Mao's invitation to be present at the signing of China's new Constitution at the National People's Congress. Many Tibetans feared for his safety in China, believing he had been taken there against his will. He arrived in Beijing on 4 September 1954 after a journey by car, horseback, plane, and train, and was personally met by Premier Zhou Enlai himself. The

Chinese government lavished hospitality on their Tibetan guests with Mao Zedong hosting a reception in his honour. During his stay in Beijing, the young Tibetan leader met Mao and Zhou on a number of occasions and also interacted briefly with Nehru during the latter's visit to Beijing in October that year. The Dalai Lama was informed by Mao, who discussed everything from culture to religion with him, that the Chinese authorities intended to proceed with Tibet's full integration into the 'motherland'. A Preparatory Committee of the Autonomous Region of Tibet (PCART) was set up in March 1955 at a ceremony attended by the Dalai Lama and the Panchen Lama. The new Constitution also included an amendment prohibiting minority groups from secession. In his own words, his discussions with Mao gave the Dalai Lama, however, 'a lot of hope and reassurance'. The book, *A History of the Liberation of Tibet*, published in Beijing in 2008, contains a poem that the Dalai Lama wrote after meeting Mao, a verse of which ran thus:

> *Only limitless blessing could create such a leader*
> *like the sun radiating across the land.*
> *His writings are as precious as pearls.*[9]

The Dalai's views about Zhou Enlai were somewhat different. He told this author in 2014[10] that Zhou was a 'very attractive' personality, a survivor; he did not 'suffer' under Mao like Liu Shaoqi, or Peng Dehuai or Peng Zhen or Deng Xiaoping, all of whom he characterized as 'straightforward'. Zhou was politeness itself, he said, but not someone with whom you could develop 'trust'.

The Dalai Lama's intention, it would seem, was to develop a personal relationship with Mao Zedong, having seen his paramount position as leader of the Chinese people. During his stay in Beijing, it was announced that he would be Chairman of the new Tibet Autonomous Region (TAR) that was to be created eventually, with the Panchen Lama as his deputy. The word 'Autonomous' was especially appealing to the Tibetans.[11] The Dalai Lama, as his interpreter Phuntsog Wangyal observed, seemed especially interested in socialist reform of Tibetan society, seeing this as necessary for Tibetan progress.

Mao Zedong had in fact set out the Communist Party policy towards minority regions from the early years of the inception of the People's Republic. In June 1950, he had stated that social reforms in minority areas were of great importance and needed cautious handling. Impetuousness should be ruled out on all accounts. Reforms should be implemented only when conditions were ripe. This did not mean of course that no reform should be carried out. He also made public pronouncements that the Chinese Communist Party had adopted a policy of protecting religions. He told a group of people from the Chamdo region of Tibet in October 1952 that land redistribution in areas inhabited by minority nationalities would be decided by minorities themselves. 'The Communist Party puts into practice [the principle of] the equality of nationalities: it does not wish to oppress you or exploit you, but rather to assist you . . . The Agreement must be implemented, but since you are afraid, implementation will simply have to be postponed. If you are afraid this year, we will wait until next year to implement it. If you are still afraid next year, then [we] will wait for the year after next before implementing it.'[12] Subsequent events in Tibet would show that the implementation of these assurances was a completely different story. In fact, also in 1952, in an inner-party directive to the Central Committee of the Communist Party, Mao's suspicion of 'bad elements' in Tibet surfaced frequently. He saw 'the Dalai and most of his clique' as unwilling to accept the 17-Point Agreement of 1951. He was undeterred by this, stating that delay in implementing the Agreement's provisions could be to China's advantage since the Tibetan upper classes would continue to perpetrate their 'atrocities' against the people while the occupying Chinese would continue to do their 'good works' to bring development to Tibet. Care should be exercised, Mao said, that the Panchen Lama should not fall under the influence of the Dalai Lama and his 'clique'. When conditions were ripe, the Chinese could, and would, go on the offensive to implement the 1951 Agreement, Mao concluded.[13] According to the Dalai Lama's older brother, Gyalo Thondup, on the eve of the Dalai Lama's departure from Beijing, the Chairman's mood was different. In that final meeting, Mao declared that Buddhism was poison. As quoted by Thondup, he said, 'It reduces the population because monks and nuns must stay celibate, and secondly it neglects material progress.' The Dalai Lama was reportedly left shocked, concluding that Mao was 'the destroyer of the Dharma after all.'[14] His biographer, Alexander Norman, recounts that at that moment, the young leader realized how Mao had completely misjudged him, taking his interest in reform and his 'scientific turn of mind'[15] for skepticism about religion. However, the impression that His Holiness conveyed to this author in a personal interview in the summer of 2014[16] was that he saw his relationship with Mao almost on father-and-son lines and that in his view, Mao felt his (the Dalai's) thinking was 'modern, progressive, revolutionary-minded and then, scientific-minded.' According to the Dalai, it was because Mao trusted him that he told him at their last meeting that 'religion is opium'. It was a view he said formed over twenty to thirty meetings he had had with Mao, of which at least ten were private, personal meetings.

The Dalai Lama's journey back to Tibet took him to his birthplace in Qinghai, Taktser, where the local population was prevented from seeing him. As he made his way home, westwards, many he met recounted tales of Chinese brutality. On his return to Lhasa in June 1955, to a joyous welcome from his people, the Dalai Lama was to recall how that brief summer was the last in a period of uneasy coexistence between the Chinese and the Tibetans; by the autumn of that year, reports of harsh implementation of reform by the Chinese in Tibetan areas of

China (Kham and Amdo)[17] were beginning to reach Lhasa.[18] In the words of Jianglin Li in her book *Tibet in Agony*: 'The widespread, desperate opposition that the Communist Land Reform programme engendered in the Tibetan regions of China stands as eloquent testimony to its excesses.'[19] Furthermore, the majority of the 'rebels' it was believed were members of the masses rather than the old Tibetan ruling classes. The reforms foreshadowed the period of the Cultural Revolution, a decade later. They also led up to the crisis of March 1959 and the final exile of the Dalai Lama from Tibet and his seeking asylum in India. Monasteries were destroyed, large estates confiscated, and landowners punished. Monks and nuns were harassed. Young Tibetans were forcibly drafted into the People's Liberation Army. Striking at the very foundations of Tibetan tradition and social structure, nomadism was targeted as being barbaric and repugnant, and nomads rounded up and forced to settle on assigned lands. 'The clash of cultures and traditions left little room for harmony.'[20] Khampas, a section of the Tibetan population, who traditionally carried swords and personal weapons were forced to hand these over. A rebellion in response was inevitable. By the end of 1955, uprisings had broken out in Kham and Amdo, resulting in heavy Chinese casualties. The Chinese reportedly used their air force to bomb the Sampeling and Lithang monasteries[21] which were centres of the rebellion involving both the Khampas and monks. Isolated in Lhasa, in the Potala Palace, the 21-year-old Dalai Lama was naturally deeply disturbed and left despondent by these reports. He wrote two letters to Mao Zedong, protesting the use of force to which he never received replies. In August 1955, he gave a speech[22] in Lhasa saying that Tibet was advanced in religious affairs, and that the Chinese were not 'masters' of the Tibetans. All Tibetans should remain united and rise above sectarian or regional divisions. The only exceptional object that the Tibetans possessed was their religion. 'It is like our heart', he said. Its long existence and propagation were necessary.

Le Yuhong, a senior Chinese official in Lhasa at the time, noted in his diary[23] that most Tibetans did not understand the 17-Point Agreement and were 'poisoned by imperialist culture', emphasizing that 'both the Tibetan script and the Buddhist religion originated in India, a longtime conduit for foreign culture into Tibet. Even now, they point out . . . India is the most convenient place for Tibetan aristocrats to send their children for schooling. "Why can't Tibetans be counted as an Indian ethnic group?" is the question they ask.'

In July 1955, R.K. Nehru, the then Indian Foreign Secretary, visited the Chumbi Valley in Tibet on his way to Bhutan. The lack of access from India directly into Bhutan necessitated his taking a route via the Chumbi into the mountain kingdom with whom India was now taking steps to establish a mutually beneficial bilateral relationship. Until 1792, the Valley (that exists as a wedge between Sikkim and Bhutan, directly abutting northern Bengal) had been a part of Sikkim, but then lost to Tibet. Its strategic importance lies in the fact that it is situated south of the great Himalayan ranges that separates India from Tibet along the rest of the long mountain frontier. The Foreign Secretary in a report[24] on his visit was to note the palpable suspicion displayed by the Chinese officials present in the Chumbi in regard to direct contact between Indians and Tibetans. He did not interact directly with any Chinese officials during his visit, probably in his view due to the fact that he was on his way to Bhutan which at the time China historically claimed as a vassal state, a position also that of the Tibetan Kashag (government). R.K. Nehru mentioned that on the high cliffs overlooking the town of Yadong—the main population centre and the location of the Indian Trade Agency—various Indian regiments that had served in the Chumbi Valley since the time of the Younghusband Expedition had engraved their names and emblems, the Chinese having made no attempt to remove them at the time. He wrote that Chinese relations with Tibet 'are based on conquest and domination' and there was 'an innate dislike of the Chinese among the Tibetans'. In his view, there was 'a strong undercurrent of resistance to the Chinese in Tibet which is perhaps confined at present to certain classes, but might assume larger proportions in future.' The main concern of China was to overcome Tibetan resistance and 'to break the nexus between India and Tibet.'

It was to India, indeed, that the Tibetans turned at this juncture. The 2,500th birth anniversary of the Buddha was being celebrated across the nation and an invitation to the Dalai Lama was deemed appropriate by the Indian establishment. Reaching out to him was not easy. The idea of the visit was first broached with Prime Minister Nehru by the Chogyal (hereditary ruler) of Sikkim in July 1955. He was advised by the Prime Minister that the invitation would need to be sent through the Chinese government. The Chogyal, who had met the Dalai Lama before he went to China in 1954, told Mr Nehru that the Dalai was dissatisfied with the course of events in Tibet and that the people there were agitated with the formation of the Preparatory Committee for the creation of an autonomous Tibetan region. He was of the view that trouble was brewing in Tibet and could also spread to Tibetan ethnic areas in China. After the meeting, the Prime Minister recorded[25] that while the Chogyal's appraisal could not necessarily be correct, it did indicate that 'things are not well in Tibet.'

The invitation carried by the Chogyal to Lhasa from the Mahabodhi Society of India did not have the desired effect. There was no response. The message had obviously to be routed through Beijing, as correctly anticipated by the Foreign Office in Delhi. The recommendation of India's Political Officer in Sikkim, the diplomat Apa Saheb Pant,[26] was that there should be no feeling in Lhasa that the Government of India was hesitant about extending a 'straight-forward invitation' to the Dalai Lama. Apa Pant was himself an impressive personality, described by his colleague Nari Rustomji[27] as 'a brilliant diplomat who reflected the best in eastern and western culture . . . a man of enthusiasms, with the capacity of absorbing his environment like a sponge.' His special interest was Mahayana Buddhism.

The relations between the Dalai and Panchen Lamas were of particular concern. There were both protocol and metaphysical issues to be sorted out. Rustomji, an Indian Civil Service officer who spent the bulk of his career in India's northeast, summed it up well: 'Our task was not made easier by the fact that the Lamas' followers were explosively sensitive to the smallest niceties of protocol and were ready to draw daggers at the merest suspicion of a slight. Though the Dalai Lama was popularly held to be the supreme authority in Tibet, the Panchen Lama's followers wished it to be understood that, in the earlier incarnations, it was the Panchen who was the Guru, or Spiritual Teacher, of the Dalai, and that, whatever the position might be regarding secular authority, the Panchen's status in the celestial hierarchy was no lower than that of the Dalai himself.' It was thus in August 1956 that the embassy in Beijing was informed[28] by the Foreign Office in Delhi that it had been decided that formal invitations would be sent to the Dalai and Panchen Lamas to participate in the Buddha Jayanti celebrations. These would be handed over to the Chinese authorities to be transmitted to the two Lamas.

Apa Pant was to later record in his memoir that a great deal of diplomatic insistence was required from the Indian side before the invitations were finally accepted, including 'a personal letter from Dr (Sarvepalli) Radhakrishnan (at that time India's Vice-President and Chair of the Buddha Jayanti celebrations Committee) before the Chinese Government could bring itself to acquiesce in the visit by passing the invitation to Lhasa'.[29] 'The visit', as Pant was to separately state, 'was a miracle in itself.'[30] It was believed that the monasteries of Sera, Drepung and Ganden made strong protests to the Chinese as well as to the Dalai Lama about this invitation from the Government of India which lay undelivered for some months. When delivered, it was immediately considered by the Tsongdue Geypa (the Tibetan National Assembly) and within a period of twenty-four hours it was unanimously recommended that the Dalai Lama should accept the invitation. (In 1953, the same Tsondue Geypa had deliberated for six months over the invitation given by the Chinese to the Dalai Lama to visit China and finally advised him for 'health reasons' not to go).

The inclusion of the Panchen Lama[31] in the invitation, had its own significance, as Pant was to note, since he had 'always been regarded as being under special Chinese patronage'. In 1956–57, both the Lamas were virtually of the same age, although historically the previous Panchens had been senior in years to the Dalai Lama. The Panchen Lama, whose predecessor had fled to China in the 1920s after a dispute with the Thirteenth Dalai and died there, had been 'discovered' as a child, not through elaborate traditional procedures but selected by the Chinese and had remained in China during his early years under their watch. His credentials had not been fully accepted in Lhasa. Nonetheless, the Dalai Lama, especially after his exile to India in 1959, knowing the pressures that the Panchen became subjected to by the Chinese government and the CCP to toe the party line, spoke of him (in Apa Pant's words) 'with compassion, well realizing the pressures of his situation'. In fact, during his 1956 visit to India, the Dalai mentioned to Foreign Secretary Subimal Dutt[32] that the Panchen's party could be a 'bit offended' by the fact that while Prime Minister Nehru had spoken to the Dalai on a few occasions, he had not talked to the Panchen Lama even once.

The invitation to the Dalai Lama was finally handed over to him via Beijing on 6 November 1956. The Chinese government had taken its time to agree to its acceptance. Many Communist Party cadres in Tibet opposed acceptance of the invitation. The armed opposition in Kham to the so-called reform of Tibetan society and life had not died down, and there were apprehensions that the revolt could spread to central Tibet and Lhasa. Of course, to refuse the Dalai Lama permission could have risked an escalation of an already tense situation. There was the possibility that an alienated and unhappy Dalai Lama would never return to Tibet. Mao conceded the point but felt this would not go against the Party's interests as it would provide the opportunity to resume the reform process again in Tibet. In his words, 'We will never initiate the offensive and will instead allow them to initiate the offensive. We will then launch a counteroffensive and mercilessly crush those who started the offensive.'[33]

In order to facilitate travel of the Tibetan VIP delegation, the Government of India conducted a trial flight from Delhi to Lhasa and back.[34] Ultimately, however, the party travelled by road over the Nathu La pass on 24 November 1956 into Sikkim. Both the Dalai and Panchen were treated to a rapturous welcome once they reached Gangtok (capital of Sikkim) by crowds waiting to greet them with coins, currency notes, ceremonial scarves and amulets. This was not before a representative of the Chinese Embassy in Delhi had removed the Tibetan flag of the Snow Lion from the blue Buick ferrying the two Lamas into Gangtok ('as if the soul of Tibet, too, could as easily be spirited away!'[35]).

Despite the much-vaunted divine immanence attributed to both the Lamas, interlocutors like Rustomji found them very charming and sensible young men (the Dalai Lama was twenty-one and the Panchen eighteen years of age), 'of gentle and considerate manner, inquiring and vigorous mind and irresistibly attractive personality'[36]. The Dalai, particularly, possessed a quality that was ethereal and ageless that moved even Rustomji, the seasoned bureaucrat. Apa Pant's description of the young Dalai Lama is worth reproducing in full:

He is a unique personality, he combines boyish exuberance with grace and dignity and has a sharp irrepressible sense of humour with maturity and clarity of thought. He is conscious of the odds that he has to fight against. He knows that the Chinese Communists are highly organized and that they are hard fighters and very efficient workers. He also realizes the weaknesses of his own people. He knows that they are lazy, lethargic and often very corrupt and treacherous to their own cause.[37]

The situation in Tibet apparently was weighing heavily on the mind of the Dalai Lama. He told Apa Pant soon after crossing the Nathu La into Sikkim that he wanted to speak with Prime Minister Nehru on a matter of 'great importance', about the 'danger to India, in the situation developing in Tibet.'[38] The Prime Minister appeared none too pleased to receive news that the Dalai wished to speak to him, pulling up Pant for 'trying to dictate to us how our foreign policy should be run from the heights of the Himalayas.'[39] But he did meet the Dalai Lama.

The Tibetan delegation was flown in a special aircraft to Delhi and accorded a ceremonial welcome (including a military Guard of Honour) reserved for heads of state. They were received by Vice-President Dr S. Radhakrishnan and Prime Minister Nehru at Palam Airport. A thirty-nine-minute film posted online by Tibet TV[40] provides riveting historical footage of the tour across the length and breadth of India. Two days after his arrival in India, the Dalai Lama met Prime Minister Nehru. A record of the meeting survives in the form of notes jotted down by Nehru himself.[41]

A further meeting followed on 28 November. The Dalai Lama told the Prime Minister that the Tibetans had vested their hope in India, had grown desperate, and were 'prepared to die'. Nehru told him that Tibet could no longer remain the forbidden land. In his brief to Foreign Secretary Subimal Dutt after the meetings,[42] Nehru said he had advised the Dalai Lama to accept Chinese 'suzerainty' (the Prime Minister did not use the term 'sovereignty') and try to secure 'maximum internal autonomy.' Apart from other considerations, India was not in a position to give any effective help on Tibet, nor were other countries in a position to do so. The Dalai Lama told Nehru that China was not following the terms of the 1951 Agreement with Tibet, and that the Chinese were gradually tightening their grip on Tibet. The Prime Minister, on his part, advised the Dalai to take a lead on reforms in Tibet and be the leader of his people. He told Dutt that his impression was that the Dalai Lama was still 'thinking in terms of Tibetan independence and looked to India for guidance.'

Subimal Dutt then spoke to the Dalai Lama along similar, emollient lines. He told the latter that the 'very fact that China had agreed to his visit to India showed that they respect both Tibetan as well as Indian feelings on the subject and it was also a sign of their confidence in the Dalai Lama and [of] other friendly relations with India.'[43] He noted that the Dalai agreed with the advice of the Government of India and believed that 'the Gandhian way was the only possible way open to Tibet.' The young Lama also had advice for the Indians. He told Dutt that it was important that the representative of the Government of India in Lhasa should not be pro-communist or pro-Chinese and that his subordinate staff should be absolutely reliable. He said the Chinese were putting out their own version of the events in Tibet and giving the impression to the world that Tibet had willingly 'gone back to the great motherland'. That, however, was not so. Tibet had unwillingly accepted Chinese sovereignty, he told the Foreign Secretary.

There were ample indications that the Chinese sensed that the Dalai Lama did not wish to return to Tibet. Despite the show of initial bravado, Mao was concerned. The image of international communism had not been helped by the events in Hungary, and should the Dalai not return to Tibet, it would only harden world opinion against the Chinese presence in Tibet as occupiers rather than a legitimate presence. Preferring discretion and caution, Mao dispatched his Premier Zhou Enlai to India to talk to the Dalai Lama and persuade him to return. Zhou arrived in Delhi on 28 November almost as soon as the Dalai had arrived in India. Shrewd and probing, he tackled the

Dalai with silken ingenuity. He told him that the message he was
conveying from Mao was that reform could wait for another six
years and would be carried out according to the wishes of the
Tibetan leadership. He was asked searching questions by the
young Tibetan leader, too. The latter was particularly concerned
about the destruction of temples and monasteries, and the lack
of respect for religion under Chinese occupation. Zhou admitted
that there had been flaws in the implementation of land reform
work in Kham, that matters had been handled 'imperfectly'.[44] He
also told the Dalai that the Chinese government would be happy
to give him foreign exchange that he could pass on to his two
brothers, Gyalo Thondup and Jigme Norbu (known as Taktser
Rinpoche), already living in exile outside Tibet and suspected
by the Chinese of encouraging the Dalai not to return home. In
his typical and skilled diplomatic style, Zhou reassured the Dalai
that China regarded India as a friend, that his visit to India at
this juncture was a good development, that 'we should persevere
in Sino-Indian friendship, strengthen Sino-Indian unity . . .
India declares that Tibet is China's sovereign territory. This is all
very good.'[45] He hosted a banquet for the Dalai Lama and sent a
'guardedly optimistic' report to Mao on their meeting. The Dalai
had apparently agreed to return to Tibet. But matters did not rest
there.

Kalimpong is a small town that nestles in the Himalayan
foothills in West Bengal state. In the 1950s, it was a meeting ground
for Tibetan émigrés and refugees as well as people from the plains
and a number of foreigners, including Chinese Guomindang
elements. Premier Zhou Enlai spoke for the Chinese establishment
when he told Prime Minister Nehru that activities for Tibetan
independence were being carried out from Kalimpong. The town
had acquired the sobriquet of being a 'nest of spies' by that time.
The Dalai Lama's intention to visit Kalimpong during his sojourn
in India was not looked at favourably by the Chinese government.
He and the Panchen Lama were encouraged to accompany

Premier Zhou on a visit to Nepal, instead. The Lamas were not keen to do so and the proposal fell through, whereupon Zhou sought another meeting with the Dalai Lama which took place on New Year's Day, 1957. According to the Dalai Lama's account of this meeting,[46] Zhou told him that the situation in Tibet was worsening (obviously meaning that he, the Dalai Lama, should return to Lhasa) and that he would best not visit Kalimpong. The Premier mentioned that the Chinese would deploy force, if necessary, to quell the resistance in Tibet. The next day, General Ho Lung who had overseen the PLA campaign in Tibet in 1950, spoke stern words to the Dalai Lama repeating Zhou's message. He cited an old Chinese proverb to the young leader: 'The snow lion looks dignified if he stays in his mountain abode, but if he comes down to the valleys he is treated like a dog.'

The Dalai Lama did not alter his programme and did visit Kalimpong. He stayed at the stately Bhutan House, (where the Thirteenth Dalai Lama had also resided in 1912 for three months as the guest of Raja Ugyen Dorji).[47] His two brothers Gyalo Thondup and Jigme Norbu, as well as their mother, a number of friends and well-wishers, former members of the Kashag, were all there with him. Most of them were of the view that he should stay in India and not return to Tibet. But return, he did, in March 1957, believing that it was what the gods wished. His brothers were worried about what would befall him on his return because he had been forthright in expressing his fears about the direction of events in Tibet. They felt that Nehru had been taken in by Zhou's sweet talk and betrayed the Tibetan cause. Gyalo Thondup even accused the Indian officials of 'murder', questioning them about their 'compassion, their morality, their principles'.[48] They were convinced that they would never see their brother again.

The hurt they felt about Nehru stemmed from his insistence that the Dalai Lama return to Tibet and work for Tibetan autonomy from within, at a time when it was increasingly clear that Chinese policy towards the region was increasingly hardline. At the same time, the euphoric tenor of the Indian Prime Minister's welcome of Zhou Enlai on this his second visit to India, and the exaltation of Indians and Chinese being brothers in a new Asian order founded on the Five Principles of Peaceful Coexistence rang a hollow note, especially with the Dalai Lama's party. It was a sad moment. The Dalai Lama retained his equanimity, despite all this. Bidding farewell to Gyalo Thondup on the Nathu La pass,[49] he said that he was facing the truth, the Buddha himself, that he was going back for the people of Tibet, and that he was not fearful. This was no ordinary man.

Nehru's attitude was not devoid of sympathy for the Tibetans. Idealist, dreamer, champion of democratic freedoms, or romantic, as he is often typified to have been, he nonetheless proclaimed that this sympathy could not be 'allowed to interfere with a realistic understanding of the situation and our policy'. Encouraging the Tibetans to oppose Chinese 'overlordship' over Tibet would be to raise false hopes among the Tibetans which India would not be able to fulfil. Moreover, this would be opposed to the Five Principles laid down in the Agreement with China on Tibet, as he told Foreign Secretary Dutt in 1954.[50] The Tibet Agreement was a recognition of a factual situation that could not be altered by India. The Chinese could never be driven out of Tibet. If Tibetans were to seek refuge in India, the government would not hand them over to the Chinese because 'they have a right of asylum in our country and we can give them the fullest assurance about this.' But India would not allow her territory to be used as an operational base against China. The real argument in favour of Tibetan freedom or autonomy was the 'nature of the country'. It was most inhospitable to others and could not maintain large numbers of foreigners. If the Tibetans were 'stout enough to keep up a spirit of freedom, they will maintain a large measure of autonomy and the Chinese will not interfere. If the Tibetans actively rebel, they will be ruthlessly put down by the Chinese and even their autonomy will go.' Of course, India would have to remain vigilant and wide awake—both China and the Soviet Union were expansionist, and it was conceivable that relations with China might worsen. The possibility of such change should always be anticipated, and adequate precautions would have to be taken.

Nehru's reputation with the Tibetans, however, remained one of veneration. Apa Pant, writing to him in January 1957, said: 'The very attraction that the Tibetans feel towards India and towards you in particular is often overwhelming and not a little embarrassing.'[51] To them, he was 'Chogyal Nehru, Dharma Raja and the Protector of Religion.' A note by India's Consul-General in Lhasa, P.N. Menon, attached with the same letter from Pant to the Prime Minister, expressed the opinion that the bane of Tibetan nationalism was the real lack of a 'sense of unity and political consciousness in the way we understand it'. Menon was of the view that the Dalai Lama and his retinue that accompanied him to India, wanted greater freedom from Chinese control than the latter would be prepared to concede at any time. To that extent they represented 'the genuine national sentiment which desires Tibet's complete independence.' At the same time, they were conscious that Tibet would need to lean on some 'important neighbouring nation' to modernize itself if it was to become a factor on the global stage. Chinese suspicions of India were very real in this regard and they had been further fuelled by the manner in which Tibet was described as a country in the welcome addresses given to the Dalai and Panchen Lamas in various parts of India. Menon concluded that 'in all matters concerning Tibet we must keep in mind the extreme suspicion and susceptibilities of the Chinese.'

The Panchen Lama had returned to Tibet[52] before the Dalai, since he opted not to go to Kalimpong. Nehru had not been able to spare the time to meet him for a substantive discussion, and the young Lama met Special Officer Border Areas P.N. Luthra[53] instead, on 8 January, before he left India. It was a long and frank conversation.[54] Luthra had accompanied the Panchen during his trip through India and described him as exuberant and outspoken as well as a profound scholar of Tibetan Buddhist scriptures and religion. He felt the Panchen was capable of independent thinking and possessed a domineering personality. The Panchen told Luthra it was futile to fight the Chinese as the Tibetans did not have the resources to do so. At the same time, the impression spread by those close to the Dalai Lama that he, the Panchen, was in league with the Chinese was completely wrong. No one could have stopped the entry of the Chinese into Tibet. If the Chinese meddled in the religion and the Tibetan way of life, he would take a strong stand. In the past, it was the Lhasa government (meaning the Dalai Lama's establishment) that had wreaked 'unprovoked oppression on the Shigatse (seat of the Panchen) people'. The Chinese had put an end to this and for this, he was thankful to them. The Panchen told Luthra that he wanted friendship with the Lhasa government, but the latter also needed to respect him and recognize the status of the Shigatse government. He had tried to speak frankly with the Dalai Lama but the latter was 'under the strong influence of his officials and his brother (Gyalo) in Kalimpong.' He wanted unity with the Dalai Lama because he believed this to be in the best interests of Tibet.[55] He felt he had been misunderstood in India. He reiterated that it was useless to fight the Chinese to gain independence. Turning to the issue of relations with India, the Panchen said he wanted friendly relations. He put forward some suggestions for strengthening trade ties between Shigatse and India 'on an enduring basis'—sending scholars to study Sanskrit in India, and Hindi and English too, although he would not like to tell the Chinese about this aspect of training'. He wished to build a monastery in Calcutta on a plot of land given to one of his predecessors by Warren Hastings.

In retrospect, one can only ask why the Panchen Lama was virtually ignored by the Prime Minister with the spotlight being on the Dalai Lama throughout the visit. With our knowledge of the later tragic history and trajectory of the Panchen's life (his torture and imprisonment from the early 1960s onwards, following 'struggle sessions' led by the Communist Party after he authored the famous 70,000 Character Petition denouncing the PRC government's Tibet policies, and his death at a relatively young age in 1989), would a more expansive approach to the Panchen by the Government of India have been in order so that he was not left completely isolated, and possibly, alienated? The manner in which the eighteen-year-old religious figure repeatedly asked Luthra to convey his sentiments to the Prime Minister who had not had the time to meet him to discuss Tibetan matters, as reflected in the written record of his meeting, has more than a fleeting touch of pathos.

Both Luthra and P.N. Menon were realists in their approach to Tibet, seeing the irrevocability of Tibet's merger with China and the eventual disintegration of the old monastic theocratic order that had defined the region for millennia. For instance, Menon's assessment of Ngapoi Ngawang Jigme who accompanied the Dalai Lama to India in 1956, merits mention. In his words, 'He (Ngapoi) is clearly the brainiest and most capable member of the Tibetan Cabinet. He is an extremely difficult person to analyse . . . I am convinced he is playing an extremely difficult game of trying to balance himself in Tibet without completely falling either into the Chinese net or the alternative net of older Tibetan officialdom. He seems to have the confidence of the Chinese in the way they showed him the highest respect in all their dealings with him.'[56] Apa Pant called Ngapoi 'easily one of the most hated persons today in Tibet', although 'very courageous' and 'now worried about his part in cooperating with the Chinese in Tibet.' Ngapoi had apparently been 'advising secretly (sic) the Dalai Lama not to give in to the Chinese demands, especially regarding colonization of Tibet by a large number of Chinese settlers.' But Pant also called him 'a dark horse'[57].

Apa Pant's affection for the Tibetans was less inhibited and more spontaneously expressed. With his abiding belief in Buddhist dharma, Pant was also a true believer in the 'identity' of Tibet as a distinct entity—unique and quite apart from China—even if he did not champion Tibetan independence and was fair and unbiased in his assessment of Chinese officials he met in Tibet. With his extensive knowledge of the terrain there, based on three visits he made during his tenure as Political Officer in Sikkim, his reports are rich, detailed and fascinating in their depth, despite the passage of over six decades. For instance, in an early evidence of the beginnings of the Sino-Soviet split, he records how in early 1956, it appeared that the communist monolith in Tibet was 'not so monolithic as, at that very moment in time, Russian advisors in Tibet were being confined to their quarters and silently, in the dead of night, removed swiftly to their home country.'[58] In 1957, he made his third and final visit to Tibet, one that lasted for forty-seven days and took him to both Lhasa and Shigatse, and the main monasteries, and involved meetings with both the Dalai and Panchen Lamas.

Pant was frank in expressing the view that Tibet was a 'country' forcibly, with the might of military strength, 'occupied' by the Chinese. Noting the rapid pace of development and roads and communications linking Tibet with inland China, he also observed that 'it is evident that the Tibetans have no love lost whatsoever for the Chinese. The impressions that the Chinese have made on the Tibetans' mind is negligible and at best, very superficial.' The Chinese were destroying the family life of closely-knit Tibetan communities, 'taking away children from the peasants'. He stated that it was a fact that 'beyond Kongbo 350 miles east of Lhasa, no Chinese civilian can travel unless he is in a convoy of at least 100 vehicles with full military escort and the Sikang highway constructed at such heavy cost is now not under general use.' In contrast, the people of Tibet considered India as 'the only country which can and will help in their plight and the

Prime Minister as the 'Chogyal' Nehru, Dharma Raja Nehru – who would protect religion not only in Tibet but in the whole outside world.'[59] He reported that after his historic visit to India for the Buddha Jayanti celebrations, the Dalai Lama was anxious that Prime Minister Nehru should visit Tibet. Pant reported that the Dalai felt that 'At the moment, all (Tibetan) hopes are centred on India. Everybody feels that a great miracle will be performed by India and Nehru.' The invitation from the Dalai to Nehru was 'passionately sincere' in Pant's description of it. It was, of course, not appreciated by the Chinese, although the Dalai also intended to invite Zhou Enlai, too, to Lhasa while Nehru visited. In Pant's words: 'He wanted the agreement between India and China for his survival.' Prime Minister Nehru also agreed with the view that a joint visit by him and Zhou would remove suspicion and fear out of the situation and help to 'construct lasting peace all along the Himalayan Frontier.'[60]

Pant was fair in his assessment of the top Chinese officials in Tibet—Zhang Guohua, Fan Ming, and Yang Gongsu. He said they were 'extremely intelligent and capable persons. They were no doubt convinced and fighting communists, but were none the less alert and receptive to new ideas . . . It is indeed interesting to see how the "atmosphere of Tibet" affects even those hardboiled and highly intelligent communist materialists from China.'[61] At the same time, it did not escape him that the Chinese were highly suspicious of the Indian presence in Tibet and they made things extremely difficult during his trip to Shigatse by imposing all sorts of controls on whom he could meet. Time limits were placed during his meetings with the Panchen Lama, who later sent Pant a message apologizing for the inconvenience thus caused.[62] The Panchen requested that his 'difficulties' be conveyed to Prime Minister Nehru and that he, the Panchen, 'really and sincerely desired for the good of the Dharma and for the good of Tibet, the Prime Minister of India should visit Tibet. He said it was only Pandit Nehru and India who could help Tibet and no one else.'

The Chinese had obviously not succeeded in winning the Tibetans over to their cause. They, Pant said, were also keeping a watch across the border with India and establishing their contacts with Bhutan and with the North East Frontier. At the Samye monastery in southern Tibet, Pant 'found many Monpas, that is, people from Tawang travelling from the Lhoka side, that is the southern side of Tibet to Samye and to Lhasa for trade and porterage. I learn on good authority that these Monpas are contacted by the Chinese and given all facilities for trade and also given some special work.'[63] He continued, presciently, 'If one day, Tibet really is 'absorbed and digested' by the Chinese, and if in Tibet, the rule of Tibetans who are properly indoctrinated and are pro-Chinese is established, I have no doubt that the tendencies for expanding the frontiers of Tibet especially towards Ladakh, Tawang and Nepal areas would be encouraged.' Tibet, together with the Indo-Mongoloid people residing in Sikkim, Bhutan and other frontier areas, had a definite emotional and cultural pull towards India. Pant concluded that once China shut the 'back door' and the connection with Tibet was lost, as the old saying went, the Dharma would 'escape into the rice valley to the south', and the situation would be forever changed—and later events did indeed bear him out.

No account of those historic days would be complete without a reference to Gyalo Thondup, the Dalai Lama's older brother. Apa Pant's reports contain more than a passing mention of this colourful and controversial figure. Thondup was often in Gangtok to whisper his version, as Pant said, of what the Chinese wanted to do in Tibet. The Chinese were deeply suspicious of him. It was through Thondup and his sources that in early 1956, the pamphlets printed in China of a map showing large areas of Ladakh, Himachal Pradesh, Nepal, Sikkim, Bhutan and the North East Frontier Agency (NEFA), the 'five fingers' (the palm being China) were available in Gangtok.[64] Beginning in 1951–52, Thondup had been in touch with the American Consulate-

General in Calcutta to discuss the situation in Tibet, including the steady encroachment of communist rule. Declassified records from the US National Archives testify to this point.[65] The Indian Government was reluctant to be identified with any evidence of American assistance to the Tibetans, although Nehru's Intelligence Chief B.N. Mullik was strongly anti-communist and kept in regular touch with Thondup, and was seen as sympathetic to the anti-Chinese cause. The Dalai's brother, together with a few trusted supporters, was determined to organize opposition to the Chinese presence in Tibet from Indian soil. They founded an Association for the Welfare of Tibet which was a cover for a political group that called for Tibetan independence. After the bombings in Kham in 1956, they prepared a communication addressed to President Eisenhower, Prime Minister Nehru and, interestingly, the Prime Minister of Pakistan[66] detailing the tragedy and destruction unfolding in Tibet. As the Dalai and Panchen Lamas arrived in India, the *New York Times* published a lengthy article detailing the 'program of colonization in Tibet that is slowly changing the entire political and security picture in the strategic Himalayan zone'. The Far East Bureau of the State Department also prepared a comprehensive report on the subject bringing the implications of China's 'liberation' of Tibet to the notice of the higher echelons of the US Administration.[67] By early 1957, Gyalo Thondup was working with the Central Intelligence Agency to train Tibetans on American bases to carry out a clandestine programme of resistance in Tibet.[68]

The question that persists, after these long years, is what defined the core of Nehru's attitude towards Tibet? Throughout the archives, the image of Nehru—especially prior to the Tibetan Revolt of 1959 and the flight of the Dalai Lama to India—as somewhat short in his attention span on Tibet in contrast to his focus on the 'big picture' involving China, persists. The consolidation of India's northern frontier with China to him was worthy of consistent focus, although here, too, he often mistakes the trees for the forest. A larger, strategic focus of what India rubbing up against China meant, appeared to elude him. He never assumed that China could pose a clear and present military danger to India from the territory of Tibet. He was naïve to assume that China would concede Tibetan 'autonomy' and that the Tibetans could convince and persuade the Chinese to grant them an idealized autonomy from within, only if they tried hard enough. While he could be a hard-boiled realist in some of his references to China (as with the head of the Intelligence Bureau, B.N. Mullik and with journalist Frank Moraes in 1952, about the true nature of Chinese expansionism and the fact that the only country which could resist Chinese moves would be India), he could not get over his inclination to stress the paramount importance of friendship between India and China. Tibet could not get in the way. But his sporadically expressed realism about China did have a positive effect in terms of moves made to consolidate Indian presence in the border areas, and the administrative takeover of Tawang in early 1951.

Here again, Apa Pant is generous in his assessment of the Prime Minister. Nehru, he felt, sought peace, 'not acquisition, special position or war over Tibet.' While Pant was in Tibet in 1957, the situation in Kham had turned steadily graver. Andut Sang, one of the rebel Khampa leaders travelled to Lhasa in November 1957 to meet with Pant who was in the Tibetan capital. Sang placed before Pant a petition signed in blood by the Khampas appealing to Nehru to help 'liberate their land of the oppressors.'[69] Destiny however willed otherwise. At that very moment, as Pant noted, Gangtok, Darjeeling, Kalimpong were 'teeming with spies, black-marketeers and even armament dealers, who were meddling in Tibet on behalf of the Big and Small powers.' The Chinese attributed a lot of the blame to Prime Minister Nehru for this, believing him to be a stooge of the imperialists, according to Pant.

Ultimately, Nehru did not visit Lhasa, although he transited the Chumbi Valley, staying two nights at the Indian Trade Agency in Yadong, on a trek into Bhutan in September 1958. He was also reluctant to go to Lhasa pending a clear enunciation of the views of the Chinese government on such a visit. By the autumn of 1958, the climate in India–China relations had begun to change with the sunshine period of the friendship of 'one billion' entering a terrain of long shadows. Thus, it was that musing over a campfire high up in Himalayas on this trip, Nehru wondered what had gone 'wrong' with India's policy of peace and friendship with China.[70] He answered the question himself—while he felt deeply for peace, 'China, Russia, America, were striving for power, domination, grandeur and of course the world's resources of minerals, land, oil, markets, etc.' He talked about his 'misplaced faith' in Chinese 'friendship'. Earlier that day, 23 September 1958, he had been 'welcomed' by the People's Liberation Army on the top of Nathu La, the 14,500 feet high pass between Sikkim and Tibet.

Sixty-eight-year-old Nehru was the first high-level dignitary to visit Tibet after the Chinese entered the region in 1950. Premier Zhou Enlai had not done so. The Chinese were not welcoming of the Nehru visit, and no protocol courtesies like a guard of honour was offered when the Indian Prime Minister crossed into Tibet. Nor were any ceremonial scarves given to him, as is the practice in Tibet. The Chinese had taken care to blacken all insignias carved on the mountain rocks by Indian Army soldiers who had visited the Chumbi Valley over the years (contrary to what R.K. Nehru saw in 1955). They wanted no trace of an Indian presence. But the humble Tibetans who lined the path of his journey to greet him with 'burning juniper' were immensely enthusiastic in their welcome of the Prime Minister, and when he visited the Yatung bazaar on the day of his arrival, many of them sobbed and cried and prostrated themselves before him. 'There was Tibetan disapproval of the Chinese at every stage.'[71] He also met the small Indian community of traders there. Tsarong Shape or Tsarong Dzasa, the former Defence Minister of Tibet, was one of the Tibetans who came to meet him. He and other Tibetan dignitaries told Nehru over a dinner conversation that the 'Chinese were committing atrocities' and that the Seventeen-Point Agreement of 1951 was being violated.[72]

Nehru elaborated on the issue of Chinese expansion in his report on his visit to Bhutan[73] via Tibet. He said he had told the Bhutanese King Jigme Dorji Wangchuk that the world was now seeing the emergence of a strong Chinese state which was following the policy of all previous strong Chinese states which 'tended toward expansion'. What was being experienced was the 'revival of Chinese expansionism under cover of Communism.' It had been inevitable, he felt, for India to recognize Chinese sovereignty over Tibet and it had been explained to the Tibetans that they should not get India into difficulties over an urge for independence. He admitted that there was much discontent in Tibet over Chinese 'occupation.' Tibet, he conceded, was 'an occupied country and no one could doubt that this was done against the will of the Tibetans.' But Tibet was 'exceedingly backward' in political and economic matters. To expect the old order to continue was not justified. Violent rebellion would lead nowhere, in his view. The Tibetans should insist on the autonomy that had been promised to them by China without challenging Chinese sovereignty.

Nehru's view about the inevitability of the Chinese presence in Tibet was, in a way, a postscript to what Olaf Caroe had noted in his Mongolian Fringe essay of 1940 about the Chinese exerting 'an incessant force on Tibet' and through Tibet (as the map of the 'five fingers' would suggest) placing 'pressure upon the 'Mongolian' peoples directly along the Indian border.'[74] Caroe's policy prescription had been to give effect on the ground to the McMahon Line of 1914 and to resist Tibetan encroachments south of that line. This was what Nehru's government had done in the immediate aftermath of Independence. The Chinese communists for their part lost little time in consolidating their hold and presence in Tibet. Tibet was a vast and underpopulated tract of territory, rich in minerals, forests and animal reserves which were virtually untapped. The security dilemmas[75] confronting both India and China were different: for India it was the consolidation, protection and confirmation of her northern frontier against external aggression or encroachment (and simultaneously disengaging from inherited interests in Tibet); for China it was shutting the backdoor of Tibet to prevent any recrudescence of 'imperialist' influence and threat to China's national security as well as control of a vast and rich territorial expanse. The clash of these two conflicting interests would have a profound impact on the future trajectories of relations between the two nations, as impending events would show.

11

Borderlines

The biggest force of Chinese military labour is employed in the building at top speed a motor road from Sinkiang (Xinjiang) province, in the heart of Chinese Asia, through Western Tibet to Lhasa. A first 500-mile strip of all-weather road is reported already to have been completed.[1]

As regards roads, there have been rumours of the construction of a motor-road from Sinkiang to Gartok, and a connecting link from there to Lhasa – in fact one rumour last year said that the Gartok-Lhasa portion had been completed.[2]

—A Reuters report in *The Scotsman*, 23rd February 1953

In 1954, while preparations were on to finalize the Agreement on Trade and Intercourse between India and the Tibet Region of China, the view of officials charged with conducting the negotiations with China was that while an agreement was worthwhile, it should include a border settlement between the two countries. This view held that there should be some quid pro quo for India's recognition of Tibet as a 'region of China'.[3]

Prime Minister Nehru preferred, however, to settle for the advice received from Sardar Panikkar (who had, till recently, been India's Ambassador in China) that this question should not be raised as the border 'shown in our maps was clear enough and several statements had been made about it in Parliament.' Nehru's view was that Indian possession of these border areas should be made 'effective', although in implementation, this policy failed—a failure arising from the formidable difficulties of terrain and also the 'slow-moving machinery' of the Indian state. R.K. Nehru, himself a former Ambassador to China and India's top diplomat as Foreign Secretary and Secretary General of the Foreign Office, was to say years later that in his estimation, if border negotiations had taken place in 1953, 'some settlement might have been reached on the basis of Chinese acceptance of our border, subject to some adjustments in Aksai Chin[4] and one or two other places.'[5]

It was not as if the Prime Minister did not anticipate that relations with China might worsen as he wrote in the wake of the Tibet Agreement's conclusion. He did not want the country to be taken unawares if that were to happen. An agreement with China on Tibet could not provide a permanent guarantee; the Chinese like the Soviet Union, in his view, were 'expansionist'[6]. India would have to be vigilant and wide awake, he wrote. India had only 'given up' what it could not hold—certain rights it had previously exercised in Tibet, but had gained a 'friendly frontier and an implicit acceptance of that frontier'[7]. At the level of officials in the Ministry of External Affairs, the signing of the Tibet Agreement was not taken to mean internally that all issues with China had been settled. T.N. Kaul, then Joint Secretary in the Ministry, had this to say in 1954:

> It remains however to be seen how far and how long new China will continue this policy of peace and friendship towards its Asian neighbours while there is no reason at the moment to apprehend any threat of aggression towards India from the side

of China. The danger of infiltration of ideas and agents is there
and it can only be met by strengthening the social and economic
conditions of our border people and by establishing an effective
and sympathetic administration all along our border.[8]

In response, the Prime Minister noted that check posts should be
established at all 'disputed points' along the border, together with
the extension of administration 'right up to these borders.' The
matter, he said, had been delayed and 'we should try to expedite
it.' But the undercurrent of concern that the Chinese could well
raise issues pertaining to the border, despite the assumption
on the Indian side that the 1954 Agreement had settled such
issues for good, persisted. Doubts emanated, particularly, from
Premier Zhou's assertion that only issues considered 'ripe for
settlement' had been raised.[9] However, when told that there had
been informal feelers from the Chinese side that the desirability
of a non-aggression pact between India and China should be
considered, Nehru was of the view that no step should be taken in
that direction. He felt that the Agreement on Tibet 'goes half way
at least toward a non-aggression pact and that is quite enough.'[10]

As discussed previously, Chinese officials in Tibet were well
aware, even before the conclusion of the 1954 Agreement, of
Indian movements south of the McMahon Line and particularly
about the extension of Indian administration into Tawang in early
1951. Officials like Yang Gongsu (director of the Tibet Bureau of
Foreign Affairs) and Zhang Jingwu,[11] after studying documents in
the possession of the Kashag about the Simla Conference of 1914,
had stressed to Beijing that 'the Simla Convention and the legality
of the McMahon Line were the basis for India's extraterritorial
claims in Tibet'.[12] Their recommendation to Beijing was that the
latter should insist on Indian withdrawal from areas occupied
south of this 'illegal' line before any understanding was to be
reached on a common border: 'India must withdraw from
Chinese Tawang and Lower Luoyu which it currently occupies.

China and India may discuss the dividing lines between both countries.'[13] These officials were of the view that 'one of the main Tibet issues facing India involves these treaties and the bilateral borders, i.e., the Simla Accord and the so-called McMahon Line.' Abolishing of these old 'accords' was necessary, they concluded. The proposals were not accepted, and Yang and his colleagues in Lhasa were told that the border issue was not on the agenda. The Central establishment in Beijing wanted to settle only those issues relating to Tibet that were ripe for settlement because 'Tibet is not brought under the complete control by us militarily and politically' and therefore 'our position in Tibet will be unstable for the next one and two years.' The recovery of areas south of the McMahon Line, they continued, should only be raised 'after we are well prepared.'[14]

T.N. Kaul, then the Counsellor in the Indian Embassy in Beijing did, indeed, raise the issue of the McMahon Line with the Chinese Foreign Ministry in March 1951. There would be a problem in the bilateral relationship if the Line was not accepted by the Chinese, he told Chen Jiakang, Vice Director General in the Department of Asian Affairs. Kaul was referring to Chinese maps showing territories claimed by India as a part of Tibet. Chen said he would report Kaul's 'personal opinion' to Premier Zhou since he did not believe the statement represented the official view of the Indian government.[15] Zhou Enlai instead told Indian Ambassador Panikkar in September of the same year that 'there was no territorial dispute or controversy between India and China.'[16] He added that stabilization of the Tibetan frontier was in the common interest of India, Nepal and China, and could be achieved through early discussions.

Meanwhile, legal experts in China were evaluating the documents on the Simla Convention and were advising their government that in the absence of ratification of the Convention by the Chinese authorities, it was an invalid document even if the reasons for not accepting it was because of disagreement over the line between Inner and Outer Tibet and the line between Tibet and neighbouring Chinese provinces.[17] Despite these preparatory steps towards understanding the nature of the dispute, the matter was not raised with India. At that stage in relations between the two countries, India was becoming China's channel to the Western world, it was helping China on the repatriation issue of Korean War prisoners, and enabling China's entry onto the global stage provided by the Bandung Conference of Afro-Asian Nations, besides facilitating the establishment of the informal Sino-American talks in Geneva and later Warsaw. It was a honeymoon period in the bilateral relations between India and China, and border issues were not allowed to intrude upon this happy state because China saw India as a valuable interlocutor for its global entry. Further, India was vital for the sustenance of the Chinese troop presence in Tibet because it was the source and conduit for the supply of food and other essentials. Nehru himself realized this; he said that this difficulty of providing supplies for the Chinese presence would ultimately force the latter to be withdrawn since it was 'very difficult to send food across the Gobi desert and through a good bit of China.'[18] But India had decided not to question or confront China on the legitimacy of the latter's presence in Tibet because, in the Prime Minister's words, it did not want to 'assume an aggressive role of interfering with other countries.' There were many things in the world that India did not like 'but we do not go like Don Quixote with lance in hand against everything that we dislike. We put up with these things because we would be, without making any difference, merely getting into trouble.'[19]

In the wake of the signing of the Tibet Agreement of 1954, Prime Minister Nehru did, as discussed earlier, take the decision to have new maps of the frontier with China issued which showed this frontier as definite and firm and not open to discussion. It was a political decision, especially taken because India did not want any doubt to arise about the McMahon Line. The Line should no longer be referred to by its British name (which for Nehru was an unfortunate reference that hearkened back to the British days of expansion) but should simply be the frontier of India with Tibet in the eastern sector of the border. No impression of uncertainty or indefiniteness should be conveyed regarding this line. It was to be shown as a demarcated boundary even if some geographers could question that. Larger national interests were involved. Flowing from this came the decision of September 1954 that the international boundaries of India should be shown in one continuous line with no reference to whether such boundaries had been demarcated or not.

Almost immediately after the conclusion of the 1954 Agreement, a hitherto quiescent border was to show signs of stirring in a foreshadowing of bigger troubles to come. On 17 July 1954, the Chinese Ambassador in Delhi in a note addressed to the Ministry of External Affairs complained that Indian troops had intruded into the 'Wuje region of China' north of the Niti Pass (one of the passes mentioned as a point for border trade in the agreement) in the central or middle sector of the boundary. A further note followed on 13 August. The area in question was known to the Indians as Bara Hoti, a small grazing plain used as a pasture ground south of the Himalayan watershed and the traditional boundary as claimed by India which was understood to be the pass of Tunjun La. Traditionally, the Indian authorities policing this ground had raised no objection to Tibetan graziers using this pasture in accordance with local custom where people on both sides had built their own patterns of coexistence over the centuries. However, in the summer of 1954, when the Indian policing party arrived at Bara Hoti, they found a Chinese contingent had already entered the area and pitched a presence there. The Indian side was mulling the issue when the Chinese made their protest in July 1954. India's response of 27 August[20] stated that the Chinese had entered the area without proper documents and that the action was not in conformity with principles of non-aggression and friendly coexistence between China and India. The Indian note expressed the hope that the Chinese would withdraw from the area as they had crossed into Indian territory. A similar pattern of Chinese behavior was repeated in the summer of 1955 with another intrusion into Bara Hoti. In 1955, India complained to China that the Tibetan officials had realized grazing tax from Indian herdsmen in the area, which was a new development. By September that year, Chinese soldiers were seen south of the Niti Pass when they stopped an Indian patrol at Damzan, ten miles south of the Pass. Precise coordinates of the area in longitude and latitude were conveyed to the Chinese to show that it was well south of the international border on the Indian side. In May 1956, armed Chinese soldiers were seen at the area of Nilang, again in Indian territory as claimed by India. The Chinese, for their part, continued to deny these crossings and insisted that there was no historical record showing Tunjun La (the pass which the Indians claimed as being on the border) as a border pass between China and India. They said they were open to a joint investigation of the matter relating to Wuje/ Bara Hoti and that both sides should refrain from sending their troops into the area. The Indian side was agreeable to the joint investigation but did not commit themselves to the proposal that neither side should send troops into the area. The Chinese on their part refused to accept the Indian contention that the grazing ground in question was south of Tunjun La and that the latter pass was the border between India and China.

The incidents did not seem to worry Nehru who regarded this as the transgression resulting from the excessive zeal of local Chinese and Tibetan officials. What concerned him more were the continuing depictions of Indian territory as Chinese on the latter's official maps. This led him to raise the matter with Zhou Enlai during his October 1954 visit to China—in response to which he was told by the Chinese Premier that the maps in question were based on the old Guomindang maps which had not yet been revised by the People's Government. In September 1956, the Chinese were seen taking up positions south of the border at Shipki La Pass—again, one of the six border passes mentioned in the 1954 Agreement. Nehru was still unperturbed and he wanted the language of diplomatic notes addressed to the Chinese to be low-key and restrained so as not to raise temperatures or tensions.

During the visit of Zhou Enlai in December 1956 and January 1957, the matter of the McMahon Line came up in the discussions between the two Prime Ministers. Premier Zhou began by raising the Tibet question explaining that China was taking a 'careful attitude' in dealing with the issue and how the regions of Outer and Inner Tibet and Chamdo would soon come together as an autonomous government under the Central government in Beijing. Zhou did touch upon the existence of opposition to China in Tibet, the Tibetan exiles in Kalimpong, and their attempts to influence the Dalai Lama. He told Nehru that in the past he had not known much about Tibet: for example, 'I knew nothing about McMahon Line until recently, when we came to study the border problem after liberation of China.' Nehru then referred to the history of the Simla Conference which had decided the McMahon Line and the Chinese government had not raised any objection to it. 'Surely, the Chinese Government always knew about it (i.e., the McMahon Line)', he told Zhou.

The Chinese Premier told Nehru that in the case of Burma, his government had decided to accept the McMahon Line as 'an accomplished fact'. They would consult the Tibetan government in the matter as the latter had wanted the Line to be rejected. They had written about this matter to the Indian government, too, immediately after 1947. The question was still undecided and was 'unfair' to China, but Zhou said 'still we feel that there is no better way than to recognize this Line'. To this, Nehru referred to the border being high and mountainous and sparsely populated. If both sides could agree, he said, on 'some principle, namely the principle of previous normal practice or the principle of watershed, we can also settle these other small points (about two miles here and two miles there).' Perhaps trying to set his guest at ease, he added that 'this has nothing to do with the McMahon Line', probably implying that the nomenclature of the McMahon Line, but not its definition of the mountain border between India and Tibet, may not be given currency. Zhou agreed that the 'question can be solved and we think it should be settled early.'[21]

Zhou's statements bordered on the vague and had a sufficient element of ambiguity, and the incidents of border transgressions by Chinese patrols persisted in the central sector. The two sides met to discuss their differences over Bara Hoti in April 1958. Here the Indians defined the location of Bara Hoti by exact latitude and longitude, but the Chinese refused to give corresponding details of the location of the place they referred to as Wuje, saying that such terms as latitude and longitude were 'imperialistic terms'.[22] No publicity was given to these discussions which went round in circles for four weeks and ended without a solution to this small dispute in sight. Two years later during the Officials Talks of 1960 on the boundary question, the Chinese did define the area of Wuje with latitude and longitude details and laid claim to an area of 300 square miles. But the first attempt to 'probe the Chinese mind on the question of the international frontier failed', as Subimal Dutt noted in his memoir.[23] The 'inflexibility' and the 'sloganeering' of the Chinese at these talks upset their Indian counterparts; the Chinese seemed unsure of the alignment of the boundary and did not want to commit themselves to a definite line.[24] As far as the border situation was concerned, the Defence Secretary M.K. Vellodi was advised by the Foreign Secretary to avoid provocations. A policy of peaceful coexistence was still advocated. But Dutt was concerned. He wrote in his diary on 1 May 1956 that he had advised the Prime Minister that the truculent attitude taken by the Chinese at Bara Hoti and Nilang could not be attributed to the local patrols; 'they must be acting on instruction. We should take up these local disputes with the Chinese even if we do not take up frontier demarcation as a general issue.'[25] He was also to observe in 1958 that the discussions on Bara Hoti had 'revealed that the Chinese Government are not prepared to accept our northern border as shown in our maps, because these maps are supposed to have been prepared by the British colonialists surreptitiously. They are also not prepared to accept the passes mentioned in the 1954 Agreement as border passes and thereby, indirectly repudiate the principle of watershed marking the international boundary. We cannot afford to make concessions on either of these points',[26] he concluded.

Meanwhile, the fact that differences relating to the border were going beyond Nehru's description of 'two miles here and two miles there' was established by September 1957, immediately after the visit of Vice-President Radhakrishnan to China, when the news broke of a new highway constructed by China linking Xinjiang and Tibet through the Aksai Chin plateau in northeast Ladakh, claimed by India as a part of Jammu and Kashmir and falling within its territory in the definition of the frontier with China. The news report in the Chinese media about the opening of the road was greeted with 'baffled concern' on the Indian side.[27]

The building of the road should not have come as a surprise. From 1952, there had been media reports of such activity by the Chinese in Tibet and Xinjiang. The London newspaper The Times[28] reported at that time that there were reports from western Tibet suggesting that the Chinese were developing communications throughout their border regions to the north and west of China. Specifically, the newspaper reported that a 'great highway will run through country south of Kashgar and then cross border of western Tibet on way to Lhasa. The new system would enable transport to reach Lhasa from Soviet territory.' The same report from 1952 also spoke of the 'enterprise' shown by the Indian Air Force in building landing strips—said to be the highest in the world—in helping 'link Kashmir's frontier with Tibet and Sinkiang more closely with civilization.' This meant, the report went on to say, that 'information about what the Chinese are doing on the other side of the frontier now comes far more quickly to the authorities in Srinagar and Delhi.' The information for this report came interestingly from Ladakh and not from the Chinese side and these Ladakhi sources told the paper that as for the highway being built in western Tibet by China, it would run roughly parallel to 'frontier between Kashmir and Sinkiang before it turns east through Tibet on its way to Lhasa.' The main purpose, they added was to 'give the Chinese easier access to Tibet by forming a southern branch of the system of communications now being developed in southern Sinkiang'.

In geopolitical terms, the development of these roads and highways was essential for the Chinese, given the distances that separated Tibet and Xinjiang from the industrial heartland of China and the difficulties that posed for regular supplies being transported for Chinese troops and for the defence of these regions. As noted by John Garver,[29] the western route into Tibet from Xinjiang though passing through formidable terrain, offers a continuous rise in elevation unlike the northern or eastern routes, so that once an altitude of 4,600 meters is reached, the route stays on that level without any steep descents unlike the others. The road through the Aksai Chin plateau receives very little snow or rain, so terrain and weather made it a preferred route for the Chinese at that time. It was also an old caravan route taken by the Dzungars, and a PLA detachment had followed this route in 1951 to carry out the Chinese entry into Tibet, although this was disputed by Indian intelligence[30]. By mid-1957, the Aksai Chin highway had been completed by the Chinese. In 1960, Zhou Enlai was to aver during the talks he held in New Delhi that 'the People's Liberation Army went to Sinkiang in 1949. From there it went to South Sinkiang in 1950, and thence to the Ari District of Tibet through this area by the end of 1950. This area is on a high plateau. In 1950, the PLA transported its supplies on horses. Later, a highway was also built.'[31]

Apart from the early press reports, it was not as if the construction of the highway was a complete surprise for the Indians. B.N. Mullik, the then Director of the Intelligence Bureau, was to write later how the Bureau had been collecting ground-level intelligence from the early fifties onwards about road building in northeastern Ladakh by the Chinese. By November 1952, the IB was reporting that the Chinese were developing a jeep track from Yarkand via Aksai Chin to Tibet, and had also alerted the government in Delhi that this track had been completed up to Rudok by 1953—which was why the Chinese had refused the Indian suggestion that a trade mart be opened in Rudok during the Trade Agreement talks on Tibet. In September 1955, the Indian Trade Agent in Gartok, Laxman Singh Jangpangi, had written to the Ministry of External Affairs about the construction of the road. This 'unsung hero' as he was referred to[32] had close knowledge of the frontier areas. 'The 1955 report of the road was overlooked or deliberately suppressed in the mood of cultivating China.'[33]

Mullik was to write[34] that the road from Xinjiang to the Ladakh border was being improved all through 1953–54, reaffirming the fact that Jangpangi was reporting these developments and that the Chinese Vice-Chief of the Foreign Bureau in Ngari or Ali had told him that the Chinese would construct the Xinjiang–Gartok road via Rudok. In August 1957, the Indian Trade Agent reported that the Gartok–Rudok road was almost complete and that the Chinese were hoping to run a thorough, motor service from October onwards. On 6 October 1957, the Xinjiang–Gartok road was formally opened with a ceremony and twelve trucks on a trial run from Yarkand reached Gartok. The road was believed to be 1,170 kilometres long. By January 1958, the Xinhua News Agency was reporting that the highway had been opened and that the road was being fully utilized.

Although information about the construction of the road had been available to the Indian side from 1951 onwards, as seen from

Mullik's account, the implications for Indian national security were 'not properly comprehended.' Neither the Army Headquarters nor the Ministry of External Affairs raised any questions in this regard on the basis of the reports from the Intelligence Bureau. By August 1956, the Bureau's patrols had seen signs of Chinese survey parties near the Lanak La and staking a claim to Khurnak Fort in southern Ladakh. It was not clear whether the Chinese were attempting to fix their boundary or surveying terrain for the road. But what was clear was that much of the tell-tale signs left by the Chinese were well within territory claimed by India. The report of a patrol party that had visited the upper section of the Aksai Chin east of the Karakoram Pass and found clear signs of Chinese occupation—including an area near the Qarakash river with an area marked on the dry river bed for small planes to land—was available in early 1958 and the Bureau recommended that a protest be lodged with the Chinese government against 'this serious trespass'. But the Foreign Office took the line that the 'exact boundary of this area had not been demarcated and so any protest' lodged 'could not be on firm grounds'. Army Headquarters felt that 'they were in no position to open and hold any posts in this area. Moreover, this road was not of any strategic importance and it would be difficult to oust the Chinese from this region.' This is not to discount the fact, however, that General K.S. Thimayya who had been appointed Chief of Army Staff in 1957, distrusted the Chinese from his experience in Korea, and by their behavior in Tibet. Even prior to his appointment as COAS, Thimayya had, as the Western Army Commander, encouraged the collection of military intelligence on the Chinese in Tibet and Xinjiang, including the Aksai Chin. Sidney Wignall, the Welsh mountaineer who led an expedition to climb the Gurla Mandhata peak in Tibet, wrote in his memoir[35] about gathering photographic data on Chinese road construction—specifically on the Xinjiang–Tibet road—on the request of an Indian Army Officer in the Indian High Commission in London in 1955. In Wignall's words,

Thimayya had 'set in motion intelligence-gathering operations to obtain proof the Chinese were building up a huge army in Tibet and had ambitions to wrest territory from India by force if necessary.'[36] In the course of his expedition, Wignall was able to gather detailed information about the construction of the highway and its alignment into western Tibet out of Xinjiang across the Aksai Chin.

Speaking many years later, R.K. Nehru, then retired from the Ministry of External Affairs, expressed doubts as to whether India or China had 'any strong claims' to Aksai Chin, though the Indian claim he admitted 'may be somewhat stronger.' He recalled how until 1954, the boundary of Kashmir with Xinjiang had been shown as 'undefined in our official maps.' In 1954, the Prime Minister had himself decided 'to change that to an international boundary.' The Chinese did not question the Indian claim at that time. To that extent, they misled the Indians who assumed that all was well. Nehru, on the other hand, had made statements in Parliament about the McMahon Line being the boundary with Tibet in the eastern sector of the boundary 'map or no map', but had never said anything about Aksai Chin. R.K. Nehru was of the view that the Chinese were (and on this he agreed with Neville Maxell,[37] otherwise reviled by most Indian experts as having taken an unreasonably anti-Indian stand on boundary matters with China) 'thinking in terms of a quiet exchange in the sense, that "you occupy NEFA (the North East Frontier Agency, now Arunachal Pradesh), we will keep on making our claims on our maps, etc. We will occupy Aksai Chin, then sometime later we will settle it."'[38]

R.K. Nehru corroborates the fact that reports about the construction of the road were available to India from at least 1955. He adds, however, that the Indian Ambassador in Beijing was never informed of the fact and that even the Prime Minister was not aware of it. It was left to the Indian Embassy in Beijing to discover on the basis of a report in the *People's Daily* that a road had been constructed in the Aksai Chin running through what was on the basis of the small map attached to the report, Indian territory. More than just the publication of the map, the fact that India had, while in possession of at least some knowledge about the construction of the road from the early 1950s onwards—and despite the decision taken by Nehru to show the external boundaries of India as firmly defined and delineated—not followed up with actual occupation of the areas falling within claimed Indian territory in the western sector of the boundary is not easily understood.[39] Was it the inhospitable terrain involved which would have made occupation difficult to sustain on a permanent basis, or was it just oversight? In either case, the repercussions would prove to be significantly consequential for India. The existence of the Chinese-built road could no longer be a secret; it was now in plain sight of the world.

The matter was now brought to the attention of the Prime Minister who, in a note addressed to Foreign Secretary Dutt on 4 February 1958, said that a reconnoitering party should be sent to the Aksai Chin area in the spring of that year 'with clear instructions that they should not come into conflict with the Chinese'. This would be ground reconnaissance only and even Nehru doubted if it would be 'very helpful'. In his words, 'I do not see how we can possibly protest about the alignment of the road without being much surer than we are . . . It is suggested that our maps (showing the boundary alignment) should be sent to the Chinese . . . rather informally'.[40] The first diplomatic Note Verbale addressed to China on the Ladakh boundary was sent in July 1958, when the Ministry of External Affairs made a protest about the entry of Chinese troops into the Khurnak Fort area claimed by India as being within 'Indian frontiers of the Ladakh region of Kashmir' which China had occupied. The note expressed the hope that unilateral action was not being taken by China 'with whom . . . relations are of the friendliest, to enforce alleged territorial claims in the region'. There was no mention of the road. But the note did mention that the Indian government proposed to send a reconnaissance party to the area 'with clear instructions that the party will remain within the Indian side of the frontier.'[41]

The year 1958 also saw Nehru's triumphant visit to Bhutan. The Dalai Lama's visit to India had preceded it, and there was a brewing revolt in Tibet. The Chinese could not have been pleased. The differences over the border pointed to a deterioration in the proclaimed friendship between the two countries. Nehru, in a letter to Krishna Menon in October 1958 said as follows, 'The general Chinese attitude to us in many small matters has not been at all friendly or even sometimes courteous. I realize that this is probably due to the petty officers, but there can be little doubt that the new turn in internal policy in China has had one effect on their external contacts.'[42] A coolness was developing towards India and India's role in promoting world peace. Earlier the subject of praise, it was minimized in public statements made by leaders like Zhou Enlai. The Chinese perception was that the 'usefulness of Nehru to their cause was over.'[43] The rift between China and the Soviet Union which was beginning to be felt also impacted the attitude towards India. In China, the disastrous effects of Mao's Great Leap Forward policy were having ruinous effects on the country and its economy. Famine engulfed the country and millions died of hunger. 'No period in Chinese history parallels the economic decline that occurred at this point of time.'[44]

In the wake of the publication of the report in the *People's Daily* about the opening of the Aksai Chin highway, the Indian Government decided to dispatch two patrol parties—one from the Army led by Lt. Ram Iyengar and the other a police party led by a veteran Intelligence Bureau official (Karam Singh) who knew the area extremely well—to confirm that the newly built Chinese highway passed through Indian territory. The Army patrol chose to cover the northern part while the police patrol covered the eastern part of where the highway was presumed to run. The first patrol was taken prisoner by the Chinese at Haji Langar and removed to Xinjiang where its members were detained for two months. The second patrol proceeded eastward unhindered by any encounter with the Chinese, saw numerous heavy tyre marks of trucks at Sarigh Jilganang Kol, crossed the Aksai Chin road 'up to Ladakh's boundary and planted our flag'.[45] It was a hazardous trip that confirmed without doubt that the road cut across Indian territory.

The IB now made recommendations to the government that Indian presence should be increased through the setting up of posts, including the Army, in various parts of the disputed territory in Ladakh, especially to safeguard the route to the Karakoram Pass and also to check Chinese infiltration in the Aksai Chin. When these recommendations were discussed in early 1959 at a meeting in the Ministry of External Affairs, the Chief of Army Staff, General Thimayya, 'quite categorically states that he did not consider that the Aksai Chin road was of any strategic importance'.[46] He did not respond positively either to the suggestion that the Army open posts in what was now contested territory. His views were endorsed by the External Affairs Ministry—the Foreign Secretary felt that such posts would be of little use to check Chinese infiltration and 'might even provoke Chinese intrusions.'[47] The Prime Minister agreed with the Foreign Secretary that no new posts needed to be opened in the area. The IB protested the decision after which Nehru agreed that a few posts could be opened, but not in the vicinity of the Aksai Chin road because this might provoke tensions. Of the five new posts sanctioned, only two could be opened because the Chinese had already moved to occupy the area where these posts were intended to be located.

The Chinese were engaged in road-building activity connecting Tibet to mainland China at a frenetic pace through this period. Arterial and radial roads were being laid out so that Tibet was no longer dependent on supplies from India and the

Chinese Army could be adequately fed and maintained. The reports were of concern, no doubt, to the Indian side and led to the establishment of the Border Roads Organization (BRO) to tackle the need for construction of better roads and communication infrastructure in the Indian border areas adjacent to Tibet. The Indians, of course, faced a far more formidable task in completing this task because the mountainous terrain on the Indian side was far more challenging to the road-builder than the high plateau of Tibet (although to reach Tibet from the mainland, the Chinese had to tackle equally difficult and treacherous terrain in Sichuan and Qinghai). The Chinese pace of road construction outmatched the Indian by many leagues.

The disappearance of the Army patrol sent in the summer of 1958 into the northern part of the Aksai Chin was of course worrying. At the time, the Indian side was not aware that they had been captured by the Chinese. It was time, therefore, to raise the matter of the highway constructed by China with the Chinese. An 'informal' note[48] on the subject was given to the Chinese Ambassador in New Delhi by the Foreign Secretary on 18 October 1958. In it, the matter of the construction of the highway 'across the Eastern part of the Ladakh region of the Jammu and Kashmir State' was raised. The India–China boundary, the note said, was 'traditionally well-known and follows well marked geographical features'. It observed, rather lamely, that the Chinese government had constructed a road through the area 'without first obtaining the permission of the Government of India and without even informing the Government of India . . . No applications for visas from Chinese personnel working on the road or from Chinese travellers traversing this road have ever been received by the Government of India.' But it added that the Government of India was 'anxious to settle these petty frontier disputes so that the friendly relations between the two countries may not suffer.' It hoped, it said, that an early reply would be received. And lastly, the note drew reference to the missing Army patrol asking the Chinese for information that they may have of the party.

The Chinese reply[49] handed to the Indian Embassy in Beijing on 1 November 1958 spoke of an 'unlawful' intrusion by the Indian patrol party and the latter's detention by the 'Frontier Guards of the Chinese Liberation Army'. It also complained about Indian aircraft penetrating into Chinese airspace over the 'south western part' of Xinjiang—that this was 'inconsistent with Sino Indian friendly relations'. The Chinese demanded that the Indian government 'guarantee that no similar incidents will occur in the future.' It said that the detained Indian personnel had been 'deported' through the Karakoram Pass.

Interestingly, the Indian reply in the form of a Note[50] given by the Ambassador of India in Beijing to the Vice-Minister in the Chinese Ministry of Foreign Affairs, acknowledged, on the basis of the Chinese reply of 1 November, that it was now clear that the area where the patrol had been apprehended was a 'matter of dispute' in terms of whether it was in Chinese or Indian territory. It expressed concern about the manner in which the Indian patrol had been pushed across the border without previous intimation to the Indian side, posing a grave risk to their lives and that it was providential that they had been rescued at the Karakoram Pass in time. Foreign Secretary Subimal Dutt was to write later[51] that it was particularly shocking that the arrested patrol should have been physically pushed across a pass which was already close to blocked by heavy snowfall, given the time of year (October) and that it was fortunate 'that the half-famished prisoners were discovered by an Indian search patrol which had been sent to the area as a precaution.' No publicity was given to the incident as India still 'did not suspect any hostile design' by the Chinese. With the benefit of hindsight, this observation seems completely misplaced. It was, however, still possible to keep such incidents under wraps—away from the public eye—in that time and era, in contrast to the impossibility of maintaining such discretion today.

It was obvious from these developments that China was refusing to accept the frontier as India defined it. Nehru was not oblivious to this fact. He knew that the mere fact that China had stated that the old maps were not reliable was not sufficient to denote their acceptance of the Indian version of the border. As far back as 1954—even as he had ordered all old maps to be withdrawn and new ones published by the Survey of India showing India's frontiers as defined without the shadow of any doubt—he was aware of the force of Chinese nationalism that existed beneath the outward confines of a Marxist-Leninist state. He told a meeting of senior officials in the Ministry of External Affairs at the time that 'sooner or later this nationalism would assert itself and when that happened, China would pose a problem for the whole of Asia.'[52] In March 1958, the Prime Minister warned the Ambassador-designate to Beijing, G. Parthasarathy, that China was 'arrogant, devious, hypocritical and thoroughly unreliable'.[53]

The Chinese had lost no time in strengthening their ground advantage in the areas that were now clearly revealed as part of a disputed frontier with India. The latter's slowness in this regard was contrasted with the speed with which China had consolidated her position. From the PRC's First Five Year Plan (1953–58) onwards, 'China spent a staggering US $4.3 billion on 'transportation and communications' that constituted some 11.7 per cent of the total development expenditure, the bulk of which was spent on building roads to connect mainland China with Tibet.'[54] As John Garver points out, 'The very few roads linking Tibet to the rest of China have thus been vital to every Chinese central government concerned about asserting its authority over Tibet.'[55] By 1955 the Lhasa–Chamdo and the Xining–Lhasa highways had been completed. By April 1956, 4,300 km of road had been completed in Tibet, including some that reached up to the Indian border. The strategic intent of such road construction was clearly missed by India, and the publication of the Chinese map with the Aksai Chin road was a wake-up call. The Chinese had grasped the crucial nature of this western artery linking Xinjiang with Tibet which did not pass through terrain beset with rebellious activity by Tibetan ethnic groups as the other road links to Tibet did. They had used this route to move troops from Khotan in Xinjiang to Tibet during the invasion of 1950. Later in that decade, the route was developed into an all-weather road even as the Chinese knew that it passed through territory shown as Indian in Indian maps. Today, the world knows it as China's National Highway 219 (NH219). Once the road was a fait accompli, China was ready to publish its alignment on her maps. India's shortcomings in failing to consolidate control over areas along the frontier with China that she claimed as hers on her maps were exposed. Nehru's decision to show the boundary as a firm line was not buttressed by action on the ground to make good this claim.

China's occupation of Aksai Chin was to become the fundamental grievance that India nourished against China in the boundary dispute. In Nehru's mind, the occupation challenged, the concept of an age-old Indian nation whose boundaries had been well-defined before colonial times, that rested on the assumption of an idea of India that pre-dated modern colonialist history. India's claimed boundary in Ladakh was not, therefore, to be based on British surveys and exploration, or on the suggestions put forward by the British to the Chinese in the nineteenth century,[56] but on where Ladakh's traditional customary boundary lay, as the conquests of the Dogra ruler Gulab Singh of Jammu had established. Independent India was just asserting these rights in a spirit of 'nationalist self-enlightenment'.[57]

Nehru had assumed the primary responsibility of deciding where India's boundary should be drawn on her maps. It was an 'intensive' and 'detailed' involvement with decisions to be taken in the matter.[58] This was not so much as his having acquired knowledge of the precise historical details that made up the dispute or, for that matter, the nature of these borderlands, but his predilection for making the 'sweeping political conclusions to be drawn from history'.[59] In making these judgements, hindsight would reveal that Kashmir and its importance for the defence of India against Pakistan after Independence and Partition, would overshadow the position of Ladakh. Ladakh's age-old connections with Chinese Central Asia across the Karakoram Pass were not given the attention they deserved and were largely bypassed. The rise of the People's Republic of China on India's strategic horizon and developments in Xinjiang and Tibet should have occasioned deeper introspection on India's part. That the possession of these two regions by China 'made it possible to use the arid wastes of northeastern Ladakh to link together into an all-weather communications system routes that previously could be traversed only seasonally'[60] was not sufficiently addressed. The realization that with Xinjiang and Tibet under Chinese occupation, 'the addition of the Aksai Chin area of Ladakh could outflank Leh and offer strategic possibilities that—to put it at its mildest—no Government of India could ignore'[61] dawned on Indian policy makers too late.

The northern frontier of Kashmir with China had caused little concern during British times. The Indian contention has always been that Chinese jurisdiction had never extended into the Aksai Chin, although the British views were more indeterminate in their approach to Chinese claims to this elevated table land in the northeast portion of Ladakh. But even the British had come to regard the Kunlun Range that bordered the plateau on its northernmost limits as the border between Kashmir and Xinjiang. However, in 1899 they had conveyed to the Qing government of China that they were prepared to concede the Aksai Chin to China in exchange for the latter's recognition of the Mir of Hunza's claim to the western end of the Taghdumbash (to the west of the Karakoram Pass). The offer was ignored by China. The boundary along the Kunlun Range therefore continued to be depicted on British Indian maps with no suggestion of this having been mutually determined with China. Post-independence, British strategic assumptions and tradition were upheld and the claim on Aksai Chin was maintained since giving it up to China, it was felt, would 'set a precedent in the whole question of Kashmir and relations with Pakistan, thus increasing the threat to India's security.'[62] But the reality was that the situation had changed with the exit of the British, and the defence lines[63] that 'held' the subcontinent had been altered with the 'external' defence line of Tibet—a natural buffer—having been eliminated once the Chinese had occupied the region in 1950–51.

The British approach had placed more emphasis on security rather than political boundaries. Leading British voices like Sir Henry McMahon, the Foreign Secretary in Delhi in the early 1900s, distinguished between 'frontier and boundary' with the first signifying a wide strip of land which served as a barrier between two countries, and the second being a specifically defined line 'delimited verbally in an agreement or, in a series of demarcations, on the ground itself.'[64] Independent India seemed to accept British geo-strategic ideas without much questioning, and very little insight and re-evaluation seemed to have been exercised in the matter post-1947 as was to be expected. In Ladakh, until 1954, no formal border with China had been marked, and the matter was not raised with China. It was only in 1958 that formal claims regarding this section of the border were made known to the Chinese. In fact, even thereafter, until the public mood made it impossible for him to exercise any maneuverability on the subject, Nehru would express doubts about the location of the border, seeing no importance in Aksai Chin where, he famously said 'not even a blade of grass grows' much to the outrage of the opposition in Parliament. In 1958, Foreign Secretary Subimal Dutt was to offer the following advice to the Prime Minister while expressing his doubts about the Indian claims to the area, but also advising Nehru not to submit to the Chinese claim, as this would 'serve as an encouragement to the Chinese authorities to take unilateral action in other concerned areas also.' He added, presciently, 'In the long run there is bound to be a stalemate. That is to say, the Chinese will continue to use the road and we shall merely be going on record as having asserted our claim to this area without being able to enforce our right or obstruct the use of the road by the Chinese.'[65]

Nehru had first visited Ladakh in 1949. In a letter[66] addressed to Provincial Premiers (as the Chief Ministers were then termed) he described the region as a 'far away corner of India, yet it is India', one of the 'greatest seats of old Indian culture'. For him, three impressions of Ladakh stood out. The first was flying over the Himalayas and 'looking down at a magnificent spectacle of ice-covered peaks, glaciers and snow-fields'. The second was that of 'a vast wilderness of sand and rock with occasional oases on the banks of the Indus or where water came down from the glaciers', and the occasional monastery perched on a hill, fitting in with the 'bare and bleak scene.' The third memory was of a 'moonlit night on the banks of the Indus' where 'the river shone like burnished silver and in the background there were mountains with snow on their peaks, also glistening in the moonlight.' The Indus, 'which gave India its name, and which, in its later stages, becomes a mighty river', was here 'a mountain stream with something of the frolic and playfulness of youth.' Writing these words, he had not envisaged that Ladakh would be at the epicenter of a contested border with China as events emerged in 1957–58.

It was against this backdrop that in August 1958, the Indian government decided to take up the frontier issue formally with their Chinese counterpart. The map published by the *China Pictorial* magazine in July 1958 had included large areas of Indian territory, including four out of five divisions in India's then North East Frontier Agency (now Arunachal Pradesh) and a considerable stretch of many thousand square miles in north and eastern Ladakh, within the territorial confines of China. The time had come, Nehru decided, to take up the boundary issue formally with China. A note from the Foreign Office in Delhi to the Chinese

Embassy on 21 August 1958[67] asked that necessary corrections be made in these maps. The reply of 3 November[68] from the Chinese claimed that the Chinese had not as yet undertaken a survey of the Chinese boundary nor consulted with the countries concerned. It concluded that the Chinese government believed that 'with the lapse of time and after consultations with the various neighbouring countries and a survey of the border regions, the new way of drawing the boundary of China would be decided in accordance with the results of the consultation and survey.' In response, Nehru decided to write personally to Zhou Enlai. His letter of 14 December 1958[69] to Zhou expressed his disbelief and surprise that the Chinese were now talking of new surveys as there was 'no dispute' about these large parts of India that were now shown as Chinese in China's maps. These boundaries were well-known and fixed, he said. Nehru also referred to his conversation with Zhou in December 1956 when the latter had told him that China proposed to recognize the McMahon Line as the border with India just as it had been accepted by China as the border with Burma.

Zhou's reply of 23 January 1959[70] repudiated Nehru's view that the McMahon Line represented the boundary with China in the northeast, adding that a friendly settlement could be reached for this section of the boundary. Referring to the boundary in the western section (Ladakh), Zhou took issue with the delineation on Indian maps. He was of the view that the two countries should maintain the status quo (keeping to the border areas under their jurisdiction). He concluded by saying that the Chinese government and people valued their friendship with India and 'would never allow any dispute between our two countries to affect this friendship'.[71]

Within the foreign office, Nehru asked Foreign Secretary Dutt to focus on the boundary dispute. The latter formed a team consisting of Director of the Historical Division Sarvepalli Gopal and his Deputy K. Gopalachari, and Joint Secretaries

K.L. Mehta and Jagat S. Mehta, together with Under Secretary V.V. Paranjpe.[72] The Chinese were also taking similar steps. In May 1958, the Chinese Communist Party (CCP) established a 'Boundary Committee' under the State Council to coordinate work on boundary issues, starting with the Sino-Burmese boundary. The new committee was chaired by Vice Foreign Minister Zeng Yongquan and comprised members from the key departments and ministries dealing with national security issues. 'It was required to justify fully every major decision on the exact line of the border to the CCP leadership.'[73] A major undertaking was to study the situation along the border with India. Chinese survey teams investigated the western and eastern sectors of the Sino-Indian border.

12

The Unravelling

'What aim did Chinese comrades pursue in attacking Nehru so uncompromisingly? According to Comrade Mao Zedong, they unmask Nehru as a 'double-dealer', 'half a man, half a devil', 'half a gentleman, half a hooligan'.[1]

—Mikhail Suslov, Soviet Communist Party
ideologue reporting on a visit to China, 1959

If 1958 displayed signs of an unforeseen turbulence in India's relations with China, the events to come in 1959 portended far worse. To the troubles brewing in the context of an unresolved boundary question, were to be added the aftermath of a widespread revolt against Chinese presence in Tibet, and the resultant flight of the Dalai Lama to India. Together with this came the first incidents of bloodshed involving the loss of life of Indian personnel in the border areas. All these events contributed to deepening anti-China public sentiment within India. The halcyon days of the 'friendship of one billion' were clearly over. The internal situation within China was also far from normal.

Mao's Great Leap Forward had proved disastrous for the country with widespread famine, rural distress and deprivation, drastic economic decline and millions of deaths from hunger and starvation. The Indian Embassy in Beijing reporting on the situation surmised that 'China may resort to diversionary tactics and assume an international violent posture to wade over internal difficulties'.[2]

Internal political struggles within the leadership of the Communist Party also resulted in Mao Zedong adopting far more radicalized policies both on the domestic and foreign policy fronts. Tensions with the Soviet Union were growing over the latter's espousing a policy of greater dialogue with the United States. Nor did Soviet warmth towards a non-aligned India please the Chinese. Nehru's successful visit to Washington for talks with President Eisenhower in the winter of 1956 was another cause for concern in Beijing. The US and its western allies were now more willing than before to assist India's economic development plans despite prior differences over its non-aligned status. They were also aware of the growing differences with China over the border issue. The failure of China's economic programme and the disastrous Great Leap had lowered Chinese prestige. In the words of Allen Dulles, the CIA Director, the 'image of Mao as the 'all-wise father' has been somewhat impaired.'[3] In such a situation, it has been argued that it suited China to bring the differences with India over the border and over the Aksai Chin into the open, in order to 'underline the power of China and show its importance' and to show India as a 'soft target.'[4]

Meanwhile in Tibet, tensions were mounting. The Chinese communists led by Mao, for their part, saw Tibet as a profoundly backward place, ridden with feudal societal values, and needing the reform-minded policies of the Chinese Communist Party. Insensitivity to Tibetan culture and history was a given. There was therefore, an inbuilt rift between the Chinese and the Tibetans that widened in the years from 1950 onwards.

In early March 1959, Chinese Foreign Minister Chen Yi spoke to the Charge d'Affaires at the Indian Embassy in Beijing, I.J. Bahadur Singh, saying that Premier Zhou Enlai hoped to visit India in the autumn while returning from a trip to Egypt and could then 'accompany' Prime Minister Nehru to Tibet. This was in response to a long-standing proposal for Nehru to visit Tibet in response to an invitation from the Dalai Lama (and after the Prime Minister had already traversed the Chumbi Valley on his visit to Bhutan and back, in the autumn of 1958). The Tibet visit of course, did not materialize as subsequent events would indicate.[5]

After the Dalai Lama returned to Lhasa from his trip to India in early 1957, his brother Gyalo Thondup who had been in touch with the CIA, delivered what he called 'the first group of (six Tibetan) resistance fighters' across the Indian border in March 1957, into what was then East Pakistan and is now Bangladesh. There they were met by Pakistani and American officials and taken for training to the island of Saipan in the Western Pacific. Four months later, they were air-dropped back into Tibet. Gyalo's first contacts with the CIA, as he claims, were made through his brother Norbu who had spent time in the United States and Japan. Some 'unnamed Americans' also visited him in Darjeeling and Kalimpong[6], 'wanting to know what was happening in Tibet, expressing concern and saying that they wanted to help'.[7] But the American mission to help Tibet did not receive any direct support from the Dalai Lama who was still officially committed to the implementation of the 17-Point Agreement with China on Tibet. According to Gyalo, the resistance movement, regardless of the training of a few Tibetans and support in some arms and ammunition from the United States, was 'completely spontaneous and independent, both from the Tibetan government in Lhasa and from any foreign power.'[8] Neither, he claims, was the Indian government—including the Intelligence Bureau headed by B.N. Mullik—informed of the fact that Gyalo was using his presence in Kalimpong to recruit members for a Tibetan resistance movement to be trained by the United States (it is however difficult to assume that the Indian intelligence authorities did not know about these activities). The 'trainees' for the resistance were recruited from Kalimpong and Darjeeling, and were followers of Andrug Gompo Tashi, a trader from Lithang in Kham. Gompo Tashi, outraged by the Chinese bombing of Lithang monastery in 1956, founded a resistance organization called Chushi Gangdruk (meaning 'Four Rivers and Six Ranges'), the traditional Tibetan name for Kham. These were years when Kham was descending into chaos with thousands of Khampas fleeing to Lhasa and camping on the outskirts of the Tibetan capital. By early 1958, the number of refugees in Lhasa had mounted to some fifteen thousand.[9] On 16 June 1958, the flag of Tibetan resistance was unfurled and the Chushi Gangdruk transformed into a National Volunteer Defence Army.[10] By mid-1958, the resistance fighters, whose numbers had swelled within Tibet, had driven the Chinese out of southern Tibet, an area called Lhokha. The Khampas had traditionally been considered pro-Chinese since Kham had been under Chinese rule from the time of the late Qing dynasty. They had not aligned themselves with Lhasa at that time, but now they had identified with a larger cause—that of Tibet.[11] Trust in the Chinese was at an all-time low.

The Chinese leadership meanwhile was prepared for a protracted war in Tibet. Mao Zedong directed the CCP Tibet Work Committee in January 1959 to be ready to settle 'the Tibet question through war', seeing Tibet as a 'training and proving ground for his armed forces and as a lead-in to a final showdown to settle the Tibet question.'[12] The tenuous bonds of goodwill— if any—between the Chinese and Tibetans in Lhasa, were close to a breaking point. The Chinese had greatly improved their position in Tibet in terms of logistics and connectivity. Two all-weather highways had been constructed, an airport completed, the Korean War was behind them, and they had also begun the secret development of nuclear weapons. Mao was signalling his eagerness for war in Tibet.[13] By 15 March 1959, a few days before what came to be called the Lhasa Incident, and the flight of the Dalai Lama out of Lhasa, the PLA was fully prepared for what would become an armed onslaught on the people of the Tibetan capital and the destruction of several key religious, residential and monastic buildings, including parts of the Potala Palace and the Norbulingka where the Dalai Lama lived. PLA troops from Chengdu, Kunming, and Lanzhou would fan out into various parts of Tibet. Troops of the battle-honed First and Fourth Field Armies were also on stand-by.

The tumultuous events of March 1959 in Lhasa leading to the escape of the Dalai Lama to India are best recounted in his autobiography published a few years after these events. The uprising in Kham, the influx of the Khampa revolutionaries into Lhasa, coupled with many thousands of ordinary people from various areas of Tibet entering the capital to watch the religious Monlam ceremonies offset against the growing intransigence of attitude of the Chinese administration, created the tinder that was waiting to be set alight. The Dalai Lama found that the situation left him with little room for maneuver. He could not, as the Chinese demanded, turn his official Tibetan 'army' against the rebels. At the same time, he would be ill-advised to proclaim open resistance against the Chinese. Meanwhile, the crowds surrounding the Norbulingka were getting increasingly restless since rumors were afoot that the life of the Dalai Lama was in jeopardy and that the Chinese intended to harm him. The latter, on the other hand, were accusing the Dalai and his Kashag of being in league with the rebels and showing 'a lack of logic and balance.'[14] The catalyst was an invitation sent by the Chinese to the Dalai to attend a cultural performance in the PLA headquarters in Lhasa on 10 March, which he had accepted in principle. The crowds in Lhasa, and those surrounding the Norbulingka, were convinced that this was a ploy to lure the Dalai literally into a trap from where there was no escape for him and that he would be spirited away from the performance to imprisonment in China. They were determined to prevent his leaving the Norbulingka. The fact that the Chinese had stipulated that none of his security detail could accompany him to the performance only intensified the concerns of the people. Ultimately, it was decided that the Dalai Lama would not attend the cultural performance as it would have been impossible for him to leave his palace through the agitated crowds that thronged around it.

By 16 March, the news was that the Chinese were making preparations to destroy the Norbulingka and that they were surrounding the place with guns and artillery. There were rumours of Chinese troops arriving in Lhasa by air. The crowds who were determined to protect the Dalai Lama were getting increasingly panicky and restive. Two shells fired in the vicinity of the Norbulingka seemed to suggest that 'the end had come and that something drastic had to be done without delay'.[15] The uncertainty of the situation and the 'compelling anxiety' of his people to see that the Dalai Lama should get away before 'the orgy of Chinese destruction and massacre began' resulted in the decision taken by the Dalai's closest advisors that he should leave Lhasa immediately—where that journey would lead or end, seemed unclear, but leave he must. On the dawn of 17 March, the Dalai Lama, accompanied by those members of his family who were still inside Tibet, including his mother, younger brother and sister and his personal assistants and bodyguards, left the Norbulingka in disguise, under a veil of the utmost secrecy since any leakage of information about their escape to either the crowds surrounding the palace or to the Chinese would have disastrous consequences. It was a most dramatic escape— the Dalai himself dressed in the simple attire of a humble foot soldier and with a fur cap, leaving the surroundings associated with all the majesty of his office, seeking the blessings of the Buddha and leaving his prayer room, his mind 'drained of all emotion.'[16]

It would be a long journey, southwards of Lhasa, across lakes, roadless mountains and passes, the river Tsangpo, and desolate and forbidding terrain. At the outset of this passage, no decision had been taken that the party of 100 escorted by about 350 Tibetan soldiers, would seek refuge in India—plans were still crystallizing. On the journey, the devastating news of the bombardment of Lhasa was brought to the Dalai Lama. The destruction had commenced within forty-eight hours of his departure, the Norbulingka had been shelled and even the Potala had not been spared. Thousands of people had been killed. There had been wanton devastation in the ancient monastery of Sera, too. It seemed inevitable now that the Dalai Lama should leave Tibet and the only choice would be to seek refuge in India. It was a sad journey as the group moved forward and it was not helped by the fact that towards the end, as the frontier with India neared, the Dalai was ill and barely able to ride a horse. A dzo (a cross between a yak and a cow) was found for him—a most primeval but a safe form of transport—and transported thus, he crossed the border into India at Chhuthangmu (Khinzemane) on 31 March 1959, 'in a daze of sickness and weariness and unhappiness deeper than I can express.'[17]

The Chinese versions of the story of the Dalai Lama's disappearance differed considerably from the Tibetan account of events. Two versions did the rounds on the Chinese side. One, that the Tibetan religious leader had been abducted by Tibetan 'reactionaries' and forcibly taken to India; the other suggesting that Mao Zedong had himself ordered that no obstacles be placed if the Dalai Lama attempted to escape. The balance of evidence as available, based on published Chinese memoirs and records, would suggest that Beijing did not have precise intelligence or information about the Dalai's departure from Lhasa on 17 March. It is difficult to give much credence to some Chinese claims that PLA artillery were actually trained on the escaping party on the night of 17 March as they took the ferry to cross the Lhasa

(Kyichu) River.[18] It was more than possible for a Tibetan religious personage to slip away unnoticed by the Chinese and the Dalai Lama was not the only such person to have done so. The Sixteenth Gyalwa Karmapa, Rangjung Rigpe Dorji (d. 1981) also fled Tibet through Bhutan in March 1959, unnoticed and with no hindrance to his escape.[19]

It is indeed a fact that on 12 March 1959, Mao Zedong had addressed a cable to the CCP Tibet Work Committee declaring the Dalai Lama was involved in a counter-revolutionary conspiracy, and that they had inferred 'from our gentle exterior and military restraint that we Chinese are cowards'. He said the rebel elements should be drawn out through a few small victories into an all-out battle. But for the moment, Mao felt, it would be better to 'hold out for a major showdown.' If the Dalai Lama and his cohort attempted to flee, 'we should not attempt to stop them if they do ... We should just let them go, no matter where they are headed to Shannan (Lhokha) or to India.'[20] The cable helped buttress later rumors that the Chinese in Lhasa were merely following Mao's diktat when they 'allowed' the Dalai Lama to flee. It was a story that appealed to the Chinese imagination; it was cited as an example of Mao being a 'superior strategist', exemplifying his 'knack for thinking a step ahead of most people.'[21] It has been a clever propaganda tool within China, persisting all these years. It coexists, ironically, with another theory that the Dalai Lama was forcibly abducted and taken to India, that he had no choice in the matter, that he was not a 'traitor' (so that at any time he could 'repent' and return).

Less well known is the fact that by the afternoon of 17 March, Mao had changed his mind and issued fresh instructions to the Politburo of the CCP 'to make every effort to prevent the Dalai Lama's escape.'[22] While the full text of Mao's instructions have not been released, their gist was preserved in the notes of Yang Shangkun, Deputy Secretary General of the Central Committee of the CCP and Director of its General Office. Mao's mind had changed and he now wanted that every effort be made to prevent the escape of the Dalai Lama (although if such efforts were to fail, he still felt the damage would not be too great to tolerate). But whether these instructions reached Chinese military commanders and party officials in Tibet in time, before the Dalai Lama's escape, is unclear. Between 17 and 19 March, the Chinese had no reliable intelligence about the Dalai's whereabouts. The PLA Tibet Military Command reported his escape belatedly and Yang Shangkun seems to have been notified about this development late on 19 March.[23] The fact that the Chinese authorities in Lhasa did not know of the Dalai Lama's absence from Lhasa until 19 March was further corroborated by the Political Officer in Gangtok, Apa Pant, in a message to the Foreign Secretary in New Delhi on 31 March.[24]

By 15 March 1959, having been briefed in extensive detail by the Indian Consulate in Lhasa about the rising revolt in Tibet—which the Consul-General described as 'nothing short of total national uprising'[25]—the Foreign Office in New Delhi had conveyed to both the Political Officer in Sikkim and the Lhasa Consulate that Prime Minister Nehru 'was quite clear in his mind' that asylum would be provided to the Dalai Lama, if he sought such protection.[26] (Coincidentally, on 17 March, as the Dalai Lama fled Lhasa, Mr Nehru spoke in Parliament about the situation in Tibet saying it was not easy to get a full picture of events there, although there had been 'difficulties and conflicts, sometimes on a small scale and sometimes on a somewhat bigger scale'. He was careful to avoid any criticism of the Chinese or expression of sympathy for the plight of the Tibetans.)[27] On 18 March, the Consulate in Lhasa informed New Delhi about the departure in secret of the Dalai Lama from Lhasa on the night of 17 March and that if at any stage, hostilities should commence against the Tibetans and his safety was threatened, the Dalai would seek shelter in India. By 20 March, a proclamation of the Tibet Military Area Command of the PLA stated that the army 'had been ordered to take punitive action to put down the rebellion.'[28]

On the 26th March, the Dalai Lama in a message to Prime Minister Nehru explained the circumstances of his flight from Lhasa.[29] He referred to the 'religious relations' that had existed for a thousand years between India and Tibet and that the two were 'like brothers without any differences'. Citing India's support for humanitarian causes, he told the Prime Minister that in view of the critical situation faced by Tibet, he intended to cross the border into India.

On 28 March 1959, Zhou Enlai, representing the PRC State Council, ordered the dissolution of the Tibet 'local government', the dismissal and punishment of 'traitors' associated with the rebellion, and the formation of a new Preparatory Committee of the Tibet Autonomous Region with the Panchen Lama as the acting chairman.[30] On 31 March, Beijing Radio announced that the Dalai Lama was 'abducted by rebels against his wishes' on 19 March and publicized the texts of six letters exchanged between the Dalai and General Tan Guansan, the Political Commissar in Tibet, in which the former had pleaded his inability to attend the cultural show on 10 March due to the 'unlawful action of reactionaries' and that when conditions improved he would 'try secretly to come to the military area'. The Chinese were obviously keen to portray that the Dalai Lama was rendered helpless because of reactionary elements surrounding him, although Pant read the Dalai's reference to these elements as being deliberately made in order to put the Chinese on the wrong track and gain time before he got away from Lhasa.

Events in Tibet were being closely watched in the Soviet Union, as on 31 March, the Central Committee of the Soviet Communist Party issued a report under the signature of Yuri Andropov, then head of the party's department for ties with communist and worker parties in socialist countries. The report was based on briefings from the Chinese Communist Party. It attributed the troubles in

Tibet to 'Anglo-American intelligence' which, it said, had always been active in Tibet, including around the Dalai Lama. Based on what the Chinese had told them, the Russians believed that the uprising in Tibet had a 'national-religious tint'[31]. The Chinese, it was stated, were of the view that 'Indian circles were mixed up in the Tibetan events' which would affect 'Chinese-Indian relations in some measure.' They had observed that Nehru had so far 'separated himself from the events in Tibet' and they had, therefore, for the moment decided to 'withhold from publication the information in their possession on the interference of India in Tibetan affairs'.

On 3 April 1959, the Prime Minister informed Parliament that the Dalai Lama had crossed over into India at the border post of Chhutangmu in the North East Frontier Agency on the evening of 31 March. The Tibetan leader could have also escaped Tibet through Bhutan. But the Bhutanese local authorities who made contact with the Political Officer in the Kameng Frontier Division, Har Mander Singh told the latter that the route was difficult. Bhutan was obviously worried about the repercussions from China if the Dalai Lama indeed entered Bhutan from Tibet on his way to India.[32] Once he had entered India, at Chhutangmu, the Dalai Lama walked one and a half kilometers to Grong-Kukpa where, according to local historians, he planted his walking stick firmly on the ground. 'In its place now a large tree has grown' and a stupa has been built. He blessed his new security detail, the Assam Rifles with these words: 'May your luck increase to the size of a mountain. May your name and fame be such as to cover the whole universe.'[33] He and his party of around eighty persons then headed to the monastery town of Tawang. The same day, on 3 April, the Prime Minister addressed a message to the Dalai Lama welcoming him to India, and indicating that necessary facilities for his stay in India, and that of his family and entourage, would be provided. 'The people of India who hold you in great veneration will no doubt accord their traditional respect to your person,'

Nehru added.[34] Separately, the Dalai Lama was advised through P.N. Menon, a senior official of the Ministry of External Affairs and a former Consul-General to Lhasa himself, that he should not issue any long statement to the press so as to avoid embarrassment to the Government of India and to himself.[35] At a press conference on 5 April, the Prime Minister acknowledged that 'Tibet had disappeared', that Tibetan autonomy had disappeared,[36] and that the 17-Point Agreement had broken down. He said he was not sure what the impact of developments in Tibet would be on India's 1954 Agreement with China on Tibet.[37] Nehru emphasized that India had not wanted to interfere in Tibetan affairs since Independence but had not given up her 'sentimental interest' in Tibet, and that the enormous feeling that had been aroused in India by the recent developments was testimony to this.[38] Tibet, 'culturally speaking, is an offshoot of India', the Prime Minister went on to say.[39] Asked whether relations between India and China would deteriorate as a result of the granting of asylum to the Dalai Lama, Nehru stated, 'Naturally, conditions are such that difficult, delicate and embarrassing situations are created', and that the factor of India's security was a major factor. Also, India desired to have friendly relations with China. However, there were strong feelings about developments in Tibet as far as India was concerned. The situation would require balance and adjustment, and sometimes difficult choices'.[40]

On 5 April, the Political Officer in the Kameng Frontier Division, Har Mander Singh, reporting from Tawang where he had brought the Dalai Lama, and where the large Tawang monastery arranged a reception for the Tibetan leader, said he had formed the impression that the latter did not appear to have any planned intentions to escape from Tibet. But the Chinese had left him with little option. His principal advisors who had accompanied him had come to realize that 'they have no future in a Tibet dominated by China'.[41] They would ask for the Government of India's help 'in promoting their claim for complete independence of Tibet by negotiating on their behalf with the Chinese and by building up world public opinion in their favour.'[42] The Dalai Lama told Singh about the circumstances leading to his escape from Lhasa, in a long conversation on 6 April.[43] He said he and his closest advisors and family members had 'come to India in the hope that as India and Tibet had friendly relations and historical, religious and cultural ties, the Government of India would not spurn them in their moment of need.'[44] He was prepared for a long struggle of liberation, he added.

The import of the decision to grant the Dalai Lama asylum in India was obviously preoccupying the Prime Minister. Writing to C. Rajagopalachari on 8 April, he described the Tibet situation as difficult and 'embarrassing' for India. He realized now that the inherent contradictions in Tibet since 1950 made conflict with China inevitable. The Tibetans had been denied autonomy. The fact that Indian public opinion had expressed itself so strongly in favour of the Dalai Lama, and their sympathy for the difficulties he had faced, coupled with the decision to grant him asylum in India, was 'not going to be liked by the Chinese.'[45] The Prime Minister was at a loss as to what more India could do. Yet, he also realized that 'during the last year or so, the Chinese government has become progressively more rigid and there has been even a touch of arrogance in their dealings with other countries.'[46] The disillusionment with China had set in, and the bedrock of engagement since 1950 was beginning to display pronounced fissures.

On 8 April, the Chinese Foreign Minister Chen Yi spoke to the Indian Ambassador in Beijing, G. Parthasarathy, at a reception for an Indian steel delegation. The atmosphere, as described by the Ambassador, was 'friendly.' Chen Yi described the present state of bilateral relations with India as an 'ordeal'. His government, he said, had studied the various statements made by Prime Minister Nehru and had welcomed the intent not to interfere in the internal affairs of China and stressing age-old friendly ties with China.

True to the Chinese line, he described the Dalai Lama as having been 'abducted and taken to India by Tibetan nobles'.[47] Autonomy was not the issue in Tibet as the Chinese government had already begun work on the subject, with a Preparatory Committee set up under the Panchen Lama. Religion was not an issue either. These rights were being safeguarded and the monasteries receiving protection. The 'crisis arose because 'Upper strata' wanted to declare Tibetan independence, drive out the Han people and get rid of the Chinese People's Liberation Army.'[48]

At this point, the Prime Minister thought it opportune to advise the Dalai Lama on what the latter should say to the press. Huge numbers of correspondents—national and international—had flocked to Tezpur in the Assam foothills awaiting the arrival of the Dalai and his party from NEFA on their way to Mussoorie where arrangements had been made by the Indian government for their stay. It would be best, Nehru said, if a brief statement were released to the correspondents with a more detailed statement deferred for the future. Later, the Foreign Secretary sent P.N. Menon, who was accompanying the Dalai Lama, a revised version of a statement that had been prepared earlier by the Tibetan side. This was the statement that was subsequently released to the press on 18 April 1959[49] with one significant addition—it was stated categorically therein that the Dalai Lama 'left Lhasa and Tibet and came to India of his own free will and not under duress.'[50]

The Tibetan leader's sojourn through the Kameng Frontier Division of NEFA, had obviously left a deep impression on him. He had been greeted with deep devotion by the people, and seen how the residents of the area had realized that 'as Indians living in the Frontier Lands, they have liberty to acknowledge the Dalai Lama as their spiritual head without prejudice to their nationalism.' The granting of asylum to the Dalai had made a 'deeply favourable impression' on their minds.[51] Meanwhile, Ambassador Parthasarathy, writing to the Foreign Secretary, advised that every effort be made to preserve the friendship with China 'as it has world significance' although 'the phase when it was an emotional expression has ended with the emergence in a sharp form of concrete issues like Tibet and our frontier.'[52] The Chinese, in his view, were skillfully organizing their propaganda in 'such a way that they can switch over to either line to approve of our official policy of non-interference or to attack us for supporting Tibetan reactionaries and meddling in Chinese affairs.' The final outcome would depend on how successful they would be in consolidating their position in Tibet, he concluded. But it was necessary to reject any Chinese claim that India wanted Tibet as a buffer state and that as far as the frontier issue was concerned, it was holding or claiming territories 'occupied by British imperialism.'[53]

Prime Minister Nehru met the Dalai Lama in Mussoorie on 24 April 1959. He grilled the latter intensively about the origins of the Tibetan revolt in Kham, the extent of Chinese casualties, from where the Khampas got their arms and the spread of the revolt to Tibet proper from Kham. Nehru also wanted to know about the three letters written by the Dalai to General Tan Guansan. Nehru was told that there was no intention to blame the Tibetan people for the troubles in Lhasa, but that the intention was, to delude the Chinese as the option of leaving Lhasa was being considered from 10 March onwards, although specific plans were made only in the late afternoon of the 17th when the situation regarding reaching any understanding with the Chinese seemed irretrievable. When told by the Dalai that Tibetans expected to achieve independence in the long run, the Prime Minister who seems to have adopted a rather interrogatory tone, bordering on irascibility during the meeting, told him, 'Let us face facts. One cannot bring heaven to the people in India even if I wish it. The whole world cannot bring freedom to Tibet unless the whole fabric of the Chinese state is destroyed.' He advised the young Tibetan leader to be 'more realistic,'[54] and added it was no good complaining: 'Only old

The Unravelling
301

women complain!' He said the Dalai Lama 'should be under no illusion and, therefore, should fashion his policy with reference to actuality.'[55]

Meanwhile, the Chinese response to Indian moves to help the Dalai Lama was undergoing a change from the more ameliorative tone adopted earlier. On 24 April, the *People's Daily* reporting on speeches made by delegates at the National People's Congress said that these contained 'strict warning to Indian expansionist elements'. The mood was acquiring vicious overtones. Opinion expressed by an Indian newspaper, the *Hitavada*, that India should convene a conference of Zhou Enlai and the Dalai Lama came in for strong condemnation as 'blatant intervention'. Ambassador Parthasarathy reported that Tibet was being discussed in Street Committees and that the tone of speeches was very critical of India. News of Nehru's impending meeting with the Dalai Lama was also not viewed favourably: 'for the sake of China-India friendship and also for the sake of the prestige won by India in the international field, we hope that the Prime Minister will make a wise decision by choosing a road of abiding by the five principles of peaceful co-existence and not interfering in the internal affairs of China.'[56] Towards the end of April, criticism against 'Indian expansionists' was in overdrive.[57]

In June 1959, the Dalai Lama, staying in Mussoorie, made a detailed public statement[58] with a distinct political meaning. He said the harassment and persecution of the Tibetan population in the hands of their Chinese rulers was increasing and that he could not keep silent about these events any longer. His duty now was to tell the world the truth about Tibet and to appeal to the conscience of all peace-loving nations. In 1950, the Chinese had flagrantly violated the territorial integrity of Tibet 'at the point of the bayonet' and compelled the leadership in Tibet to sign the Seventeen-Point Agreement. They, the Chinese, had unleashed a 'reign of terror' in Tibet. Through this time, the Dalai Lama said, he had tried his best to persuade the Chinese to adopt a policy of conciliation but he had not succeeded. He was making these assertions in full knowledge of their gravity 'because I know them to be true.' If the Chinese were not prepared to accept these charges, they should agree to an investigation by an international commission. He was already frustrated about the situation in Tibet when he had visited India in 1956 and had wanted to stay back, but had been persuaded by Prime Minister Nehru—who had always shown 'utmost kindness and consideration' to him—to return to Tibet on the basis of assurances given to the Prime Minister by Premier Zhou Enlai. But the situation had worsened upon his return. He understood that the reforms needed to be introduced to change old and ancient methods of societal functioning in Tibet, but his attempts to introduce such reforms, especially in land tenure, had not succeeded in the face of Chinese obstacles. He wished for the return of peace and goodwill in Tibet but such a solution should guarantee 'the preservation of the rights and powers which Tibet has enjoyed and exercised without any interference prior to 1950.'

More than a hundred journalists attended the 20 June press conference in Mussoorie; such meetings with the press were an entirely new phenomenon for the Tibetan leadership. Purshottam Trikamdas (a former secretary to Mahatma Gandhi) and D.K. Sen, who became a trusted advisor to the Dalai Lama and helped write his autobiography *My Land and My People*, were called upon to prepare the English version of the Dalai Lama's June statement. It was during this press conference, as later recounted by Gyalo Thondup,[59] during the question-and-answer session, that the Dalai Lama said: 'wherever I am, accompanied by our government, the Tibetan people recognize us as the government of Tibet.' The Indian Government, meanwhile, was at pains to clarify that it did not take responsibility for various statements made at the time, including the statement of the Dalai Lama. Reportedly, Nehru was angry about the press conference. While the Government of India were prepared to show the respect due to the Dalai (keeping in view his high position), there was no reason to believe 'that he will do anything which is contrary to international usage and embarrassing to the host country'; additionally, they did not recognize any separate Government of Tibet, and therefore, there was 'no question of a Tibetan government under the Dalai Lama functioning in India.'[60] The Chinese were angry, too.[61]

As a direct response to the Dalai Lama's press statement, inviting a Commission to look into the Tibet problem, the Geneva-based International Commission of Jurists conducted an international investigation into the situation in Tibet.[62] The conclusions of the Commission were adverse for the Chinese, reporting that the Chinese had violated the understandings of the Seventeen-Point Agreement, committed human rights abuses, and placed restrictions on Tibetan religious practices. On 2 September, the Dalai Lama addressed a letter to the UN Secretary-General Dag Hammarskjold requesting the immediate intervention of the United Nations and consideration of the Tibetan issue and Tibet's claims to independent status. 'Lhasa, the capital of the State, is now a dead city', he told Hammarskjold.[63] Later in 1959, the case of Tibet was brought before the United Nations. A mildly worded UN resolution, sponsored by Ireland and Malaya, condemning China's violation of human rights in Tibet was passed, with forty-five countries voting in favour, nine opposed, and twenty-nine (including India) abstaining. Efforts to introduce a similar resolution in 1960 did not succeed, because of reasons connected with worsening US–Soviet relations following the shooting down of a US U2 plane over Soviet territory which diverted attention from Tibet. A more strongly worded resolution sponsored by Thailand and Malaya was passed by the UN General Assembly in 1961 but did not materially change the situation in Tibet.

In recapitulation, the question of Tibet being brought before the United Nations in 1959, saw a bitter and acrimonious debate in the General Assembly 'far more bitter than Hungary or anything else' in the words of Krishna Menon, the Indian Permanent

Representative at the United Nations.[64] The Russian delegation was insistent that India should vote against any resolution on the subject. The general feeling in the Government of India was that discussion of the Tibet issue in the UN would not serve any purpose. It could be exploited to promote 'cold war purposes' was the view of the Foreign Secretary.[65] At the same time, public opinion in India would strongly disapprove of any action which shut out discussions of recent happenings in Tibet in the United Nations. It would be best not to stand in the way of a discussion if that was the wish of the overwhelming majority of members of the UN. In the event, as instructions from Delhi arrived late, the Indian delegation did not vote on inscription of the Resolution.[66]

Making a statement in the United Nations General Assembly on the 21 October 1959, Krishna Menon clarified that while India did not support the inscription of the resolution, there was no intention to put forward legalistic objections or procedural barriers to its introduction or passage. Consideration of the problem should centre on the interests of the Tibetan people and 'of the Dalai Lama himself'.[67] India would have liked to see the changes taking place in Tibet to have happened 'more peacefully with less cruelty, perhaps with less upset.' India's broad policy on the issue, quoting the Prime Minister, was predicated on three factors: firstly, the preservation of the security and integrity of India, secondly, on the desire to maintain friendly relations with China, and thirdly, on 'our deep sympathy for the people of Tibet.'[68] However, it was India's view that the Seventeen-Point Agreement still stood, unlike what many other delegates had said while discussing the draft resolution. And, because India wanted reconciliation in Tibet in the future, and since the resolution 'does not promote constructive steps at all' it could not have India's support. India decided, therefore, to abstain on the resolution, but this abstention was in no sense 'a lack of concern or a lack of feeling in regard to the Tibetan people or any reflection upon our relations with China.'[69] Was this a case of diplomatic cold-feet?

In 1960, the Dalai Lama and his entourage were relocated from Mussoorie to Dharamshala, a more remote location, about five hundred miles from Delhi. Writing to him in August 1960, Prime Minister Nehru said there were two questions facing India on the Tibet issue: one was the proper rehabilitation of the Tibetan refugees who had come to India, and the other was 'the larger and more difficult issue of what is happening in Tibet itself.'[70] By 1960, India had given asylum to more than 20,000 Tibetans with numbers mounting as more such persons streamed across the frontiers with Tibet. This was a cause of considerable friction between India and China, as Nehru said, but India had gone ahead with receiving the refugees and granting them asylum, assuming 'full responsibility' for them, and was committed to their rehabilitation. India had not sought any help from other countries in this regard, though assistance had been offered by Australia, New Zealand and the United States. The only condition was that the refugees should not use India as a base for hostile propaganda or activities against China. However, this still left the larger question about what should be done about the situation in Tibet. On this count, Nehru told the Dalai Lama that he had not always been happy with some decisions taken by him or the harmful advice he had received from those close to him, like his brother Gyalo Thondup. Nehru also sought to counsel the Dalai against attempts to seek 'mediation by the United Nations' as this was not likely to produce practical results. 'I can hardly be expected to encourage you to follow a course of action which I consider unhelpful and possibly harmful.'[72]

By the end of April 1959, the mood had distinctly changed and the chill in India's relations with China was to become pronounced. The trigger was not only the crisis associated with the flight of the Dalai Lama, but the agitated mood of Indian public opinion, no doubt egged on by different political interests opposed to the government which had always been deeply skeptical and questioning of the Nehruvian approach to China.

A demonstration outside the Chinese consulate in Mumbai protesting the events in Tibet, saw a portrait of Mao Zedong being pasted on the consulate walls following which the crowd hurled 'tomatoes and rotten eggs' on it. The Chinese embassy in Delhi pronounced this as a 'huge insult to the leader' of China in a written Note to the Ministry of External Affairs on 27 April.[73] The next day, the Foreign Ministry in Beijing had escalated the level of protest further when Vice-Minister Ji Pengfei summoned Ambassador G. Parthasarathy to express concern over what he termed a 'malicious act insulting the Head of State and beloved leader of the Chinese people'. The 'reactionaries in India are hot-minded', Ji told Parthasarathy. The Chinese note handed over by Ji was 'offensive in tone and unreasonable in demand', Parthasarathy told Delhi.[74]

On 28 April, the National People's Congress while condemning the revolt in Tibet noted, 'with regret that certain people in Indian political circles have recently made extremely unfriendly statement (sic) and committed extremely unfriendly acts which interfere in China's internal affairs' and hoped that this 'abnormal situation' would quickly disappear and friendly relations between China and India would be further 'consolidated and developed.'[75] The response to Parthasarathy from Foreign Secretary Dutt was to convey that the Prime Minister had already expressed his regret over the incident involving the Mao picture, in Parliament, and would like his 'personal regrets' conveyed to Mao as well. He did not propose to send a direct message to the Chinese leader. In India, under the Constitution, the people enjoyed the fullest freedom of expression and it would be 'an embarrassing precedent for the Prime Minister to take direct responsibility for the behaviour of a small group of irresponsible people belonging to an insignificant party'.[76] The Indian attempt to explain the situation did not seem to alter the Chinese stance—the incident involving Mao's picture had aroused 'extreme indignation' among the Chinese people and under these circumstances 'what is the use of talking of Sino-Indian friendship'?[77] Mr Nehru's reply to Ambassador Parthasarathy was that while India realized the importance of friendship with China, this friendship 'cannot be obtained by threats and coercive attitude.'[78] Parthasarathy told Nehru that the 'ferocity and venom of the anti-Indian campaign' had surprised many among the diplomatic circles in Beijing, even the East Europeans. He added that in the last year or so, the 'Chinese in national exaltation and fanaticism have bordered on insolence in their treatment of some foreign countries.'[79] This 'aggressive nationalism' was giving China 'an unlovely visage', he said. In their reactions, the problems—'hidden currents and issues' as Parthasarathy termed them—in the India–China relationship had also shown up.[80] Wild charges had been made about 'Indian imperialists' having inherited the legacy of British imperialism and that Independent India had tried to obstruct the exercise of Chinese sovereignty in Tibet from 1950 onwards. And, as Parthasarathy put it, opportunities for a face-to-face in-depth discussion with leaders like Zhou Enlai were also becoming increasingly difficult.

In China, there remained persistent suspicion and doubt about the Indian government's approach towards Tibet. Even if India had recognized Chinese sovereignty in Tibet, it still nurtured the idea that Tibet was ideally meant to be a 'buffer' between India and China—essentially an 'imperialist' vision—and that Nehru had always believed that given Tibet's remoteness from the Chinese mainland, and the difficulties associated with terrain, China would never be able to exercise complete and effective control over the region. If Nehru advocated no hostile actions against Beijing, it was only because he wanted Tibet to retain its autonomy which could best be achieved by speaking out in favour of Tibet's geographical and cultural (and religious) uniqueness. Of course, these subtleties made little sense to the Chinese leadership in Beijing. Also, there was little or no appreciation of India's democratic political system which led Mao to regard 'all criticism from India (including from the Indian media) as indications of the Indian government's support for the rebels'. Senior Party leaders like Deng Xiaoping asserted that the Indian government, and Nehru especially, 'had been deeply involved' in the rebellion in Lhasa.[81]

The experience of this downturn in relations was proving quite epiphanic for Nehru, himself. Addressing Parliament on 4 May 1959, talking about the 'tragedy' in Tibet (also a term the Chinese took exception to) he said the deeper tragedy, 'that something that we have laboured for, for all these years which is maybe said to be enshrined, if you like, in the Panchsheel or in Bandung, has suffered very considerably'.[82] He said he was 'aggrieved beyond measure at these various recent developments and at what is being said in China, the charges made against India.' It was difficult, he said, for the general public in India not to be affected by these charges, charges which 'do not stand the slightest scrutiny'. Very serious charges were being made against India in China, in an irresponsible manner 'by the leaders of a people whom we have not only honoured and respected but who we have considered particularly advanced in culture and politeness and the gentler art of civilization. It has been a shock to me beyond measure because, quite apart from everything else, I have looked up to the Chinese . . . that this kind of thing should be said and done in the excitement of the moment.'[83]

Adding insult to Nehruvian injury was the publication in the *People's Daily* on 6 May 1959 of the editorial entitled, 'The Revolution in Tibet and Nehru's Philosophy'. It accused India and Nehru, of interference in Tibet both during the 1950 Chinese takeover and also during the Tibetan revolt of 1959, where the Indian reaction of 'instinctive sympathy' and feelings of kinship with Tibet could not be accepted as Tibetan sentiments and feelings should not be considered as separate from those of the whole Chinese people and such expressions amounted to interference in China's internal affairs. Furthermore, the Chinese accused Nehru of seeking a kind of semi-independent status for Tibet, when the latter spoke of Tibetan autonomy.[84] The piece had the imprimatur of Mao himself as subsequently released information reveals. After the flight of the Dalai Lama to India, and the warm and cordial reception he received on arrival in India, Mao proposed at a high-level meeting in Hangzhou that China launch 'an open counteroffensive' justifying policy towards Tibet.[85] On 25 April, he instructed that the emphasis on propaganda relating to Tibet should be shifted from blaming the 'bandit gang' of Chiang Kai-shek and the Chinese Nationalists to the 'British imperialists (who) have acted in collusion with the Indian expansionists to intervene openly in China's internal affairs, in the hope of taking over Tibet.' Mao's directive was that the blame should be directly focused on Britain and India and there should be no circumvention in this regard.[86] The Chinese emphasis was now on conducting a big campaign of criticism against India and Nehru. The CCP Politburo directed that a special group be organized under Hu Qiaomu and Wu Lengxi, Mao's political secretaries, 'to draft a comprehensive essay explaining Beijing's perspective on India's involvement in the Tibetan rebellion'. Mao is believed to have personally worked on the main points of the essay, which would emphasize how Nehru and his government had sought to block political reform in Tibet, harboured territorial ambitions towards Tibet, and the contradictions in Nehru's approach towards the region: recognizing on the one hand, Chinese sovereignty over Tibet, and on the other, looking upon Tibet as a buffer between China and India. This was the background to the venomous diatribe in the *People's Daily* of 6 May 1959.[87]

The onslaught was maintained with the Chinese Ambassador in New Delhi, Pan Zili, telling the Foreign Secretary that various sections of opinion in India including members of the government were slandering China and sabotaging friendship. The Tibetan 'rebels' were being encouraged. The 'temporary' difference between India and China concerned only the region of Tibet. But what was in the Indian mind, the Ambassador asked: 'Will you be agreeing to our thinking regarding the view that China can only concentrate its main attention eastward of China, but not southwestward of China?' India could not have 'two fronts' (was this a reference to the implications of an unquiet border with China compounding India's troubles since the 'front' with Pakistan was already conflict-prone and a threat?)[88] Foreign Secretary Dutt quite justifiably found the language of the Ambassador's statement 'unorthodox and extremely irritating'.[89]

Meanwhile, there were increasing reports of the harassment of the staff of the Indian Consulate in Lhasa and in the Trade Agencies in Gyantse, Gartok and Yatung as also of Indian nationals in Tibet. The government in Delhi saw this as deliberate Chinese policy to 'squeeze out Trade Agencies out of Tibet.'[90] A large number of Indian nationals including Muslims and some Lamas from Jammu and Kashmir had been residing in Lhasa and Shigatse from before the conclusion of the 1954 Agreement. They had not been required to carry Indian passports in the past but were anxious to retain their Indian nationality; they were also not being permitted to contact the Indian Consul-General in Lhasa. The Government of India was also concerned about the 'persistent propaganda' describing Indians as 'imperialists, who have inherited the British traditions and continue to exploit the Tibetans.'[91] On the functioning of the Trade Agencies in Tibet, the Indian Government sought a clear answer from the Chinese side, 'as the continued functioning of the Trade Agencies in China and India (stipulated under the 1954 Agreement) on a reciprocal basis will depend on the answer.' In India, the Chinese Trade Agencies were located in New Delhi, Kolkata and Kalimpong.

The reaction of the Soviet Union to the events in Tibet forms an important segment in our consideration of the history of these times. The Soviet government and party were kept fully in the picture about the happenings in Tibet by the Chinese and were generally supportive of the latter. The diary of the Soviet

Ambassador in Beijing, P.F. Yudin, records a conversation with Deng Xiaoping—then General Secretary of the Central Committee of the Chinese Communist Party—in June 1959 where briefly touching on the issue of the Dalai Lama, Deng told Yudin, 'Nehru calculated the Dalai Lama would play a huge role in the Indians' plans (sic) and that chaos would begin in Tibet without the Dalai Lama. Quite the opposite, in Tibet, things are going well without the Dalai Lama. The Dalai Lama has turned out to be a burden.'[92] In a conversation with diplomat and Sinologist Ambassador S.F. Antonov on 14 October 1959, Mao said the Tibet situation was different from other minority areas. 'The Dalai Lama is a god, not a man. In any case he is seen that way by the majority of the Tibetan population' and that it was better he had left for India.[93] But criticism of Nehru and India engendered divisions between Moscow and Beijing. The Chinese were upset when instead of focusing the spotlight on Nehru's alleged communion with the rebel elements in Tibet, the Soviets tended to play up Western media reports that criticized Chinese policies in Tibet and towards India.[94] 'Who is Nehru?' asked an irate Mao. 'He is a middle-of-the-roader of the Indian bourgeoisie.'[95] This was also a time when Soviet officials told the Chinese that over 'the next two years' they would not be able to 'honor some of the obligations specified in the agreement signed by the two countries on 15 October 1957, including the requirement to give nuclear bomb prototypes and technical data to the PRC,'[96] since US–Soviet negotiations to ban nuclear weapons testing had commenced in Geneva and there was an upcoming summit between Khrushchev and US President Eisenhower. The rift was to widen even more as the border problems between China and India came more and more to occupy the public space. On Tibet, meanwhile, the Soviets were clear that while the Chinese had been right to suppress the revolt, and that even if some 'reactionary' circles in India may have supported the rebellion, the revolt would not have erupted if the PRC had 'implemented timely democratic reforms and appropriate measures to improve [Tibet's] economy and culture while taking account of the historic specifics of Tibet, and had been duly vigilant with regard to reactionary elements . . .'[97] In a conversation between Khrushchev and Mao, where Liu Shaoqi, Zhou Enlai, Zhu De, Lin Biao, Peng Zhen, Chen Yi, and Wang Jiaxiang were present, Khrushchev told Mao, 'As for the Dalai Lama's departure from Tibet, had we been in your place, we would not have given him the chance to leave. It would have been better if he was in the grave.'[98]

The manner in which an atmosphere of friendly relations between India and China was transformed in a time-span of a few fateful months in 1959, represented 'one of the most dramatic turns in state-to-state relations during the Cold War era.'[99] The flight of the Dalai Lama in March was followed by the deterioration of the border situation involving Indian casualties in clashes with the Chinese both in the eastern and western sectors. By the end of the year, the edifice of friendship and cooperation between the two countries had collapsed. In the fifties, both China and India had developed visions of their place in the world as two great civilization-states. Nehru saw India's rich history and cultural values, her geographical size and plural democracy, the advocacy of peace and non-violence, together with the Five Principles of the Panchsheel as undergirding the authenticity and credibility of India's naturally-ordained leadership role in world affairs. Mao and the Chinese Communist Party also envisaged a central and similarly ordained role for China on the international stage with the goal being to promote a global revolution. These differing world views were antithetical to each other, with a collision waiting to happen—Tibet, and an unsettled frontier ignited the fire. Writing in December 1959, the head of a Soviet Party-Governmental Delegation to the PRC, M. Suslov said, 'We are getting an impression that, while recognizing formally the principle of peaceful coexistence between two global systems, the

Chinese comrades tend to regard this principle just as a temporary tactical maneuver.'[100]

But as far as Tibet was concerned, the tragic events of the year 1959 had proved cataclysmic. The Indian Trade Agent in Gyantse summed it up in stark terms:

> While the heart of Tibet was bleeding the free world only made speeches. With the end of the debate on Tibet in the United Nations, Tibetans lost all hopes of their survival, (they) stare at the sky with blank eyes and ask – (a) Where is God? (b) Where is (the) Buddha? (c) Where are the defenders of human rights? (d) How can the world witness such brutal acts on a race that has always wanted to live in peace? Buddha, they say, has disappeared from the world and (they) are fast losing hopes of survival of their race. From all appearances, Tibet is finished.[101]

Six decades of subsequent history do not take away from the anguish and despair expressed in those words.

13

Disputed Frontier, Divided Histories

China was seeking to assert a claim, never made before, to the Indian Olympus[1]

—Olaf Caroe

The finest combination of boundary and barrier that exists in the world; never was such a God-given boundary set to such a vast, impressive and stupendous frontier[2]

—Thomas Holdich on the Himalayas

The year 1959, which was at the centre of the tragic events in Tibet, also became the setting and stage for the full-blown appearance in the public domain of a serious boundary dispute between India and China. The flight of the Dalai Lama from Tibet to India and the tensions it generated were but a prelude to a succession of events that widened the India–China rift. It became increasingly clear that most of these events were centered around the question of what was a long and disputed boundary. India under Nehru had long regarded that this boundary was not open to discussion. After the 1954 Agreement with China on Tibet, the Prime Minister had unilaterally decided that this India-defined boundary of close to 4,000 km would be shown as a firm and definite line on all published Indian maps. There could be no ambiguity, Nehru felt, about this boundary. Peace on these borders could be maintained, in his view, by pursuing a policy of friendship with China. The slogan of 'Hindi–Chini Bhai-Bhai' became the siren-call. It was delusional diplomacy and its wages would prove costly for India. For the Chinese, border problems and differences 'left over from history' needed to be resolved through negotiations and—unlike India at the time—they were prepared to take the line that a boundary dispute did exist.

By 1958, the existence of the Aksai Chin highway across territory shown as a part of Ladakh in India's maps, had been raised by India with China in the informal diplomatic note of 18 October 1958. The Chinese had replied to counter the Indian claim that the road passed through Indian territory. The dispute now revealed was just the beginning of a long sequence of diplomatic exchanges between the two countries, and would uncover the wide perceptional gap in approaches to the definition of the concepts concerning the boundary they shared. In his first letter on the dispute to Zhou Enlai, of December 1958, Nehru said there was no question of 'large parts of India being anything but Indian'[3]. Nehru had suspended disbelief when he took Zhou at his word when the latter told him during their meetings from 1954 onwards that China had not had the time to revise boundary alignments shown in old maps or that China intended to accept the McMahon Line as a reality after consulting with the Tibetan authorities. Nehru's illusions would be shattered as 1959 ran its course and in the years that followed. The experience would destroy him.

Speaking in Parliament (the Lok Sabha) on 28 August 1959,[4] in answer to a question regarding the occupation of Ladakhi territory by China, Nehru disclosed that an Indian reconnaissance party had been detained by the Chinese at Khurnak Fort inside Indian territory, a claim disputed by China. The Prime Minister was still reluctant to concede that the Chinese had occupied Indian territory in Ladakh saying that 'it would be hardly correct to say that our area is under occupation of the Chinese, that is, under any kind of fixed occupation.' But he did agree that China had built a road across the Aksai Chin which India claimed as a part of Ladakh. However, he added that the area involved was 'extraordinarily remote, almost inaccessible'. Asked by an irate Member of Parliament whether any nation 'can come and build roads and camp there', the Prime Minister seemed to draw a distinction between borders and frontiers, saying that in some areas, there was no doubt 'from any side' about the alignment of the border, but in other parts 'it is very difficult even in a map to indicate it', and there were parts where 'there had been no demarcation in the past'.

All this seemed to fly in the face of, and directly contradict, the decision taken in 1954 by Nehru himself to show every part of India's border with China as fixed and well-determined and not open to discussion. But Indian policy making circles were clearly perturbed by the launch of 'an active policy of violation of the international frontier and intrusion into our territory' as a message from the Foreign Secretary to Indian Missions abroad would indicate.[5] He attributed the Chinese moves on the border 'to serious misunderstanding of our intentions towards Tibet'. The Prime Minister himself, writing to his sister Vijaya Lakshmi Pandit, the High Commissioner in London,[6] said India intended to take a firm line on the issue but would 'try to avoid any step which might lead to a break with China.' In September 1959, he told Parliament that his government was preparing 'a kind of a white paper' which would detail all the correspondence with the Chinese government since 1954 and that this would soon be placed before the House. It was a fateful decision made no doubt in the interest of full transparency of approach, as Nehru, the life-long democrat, would have willed, but it would, as subsequent events showed, completely do away with any scope for flexibility or give-and-take in India's approach towards China on the question of their shared boundary. The first white paper was released to Parliament on 7 September 1959.

The Chinese approach, as outlined in several letters addressed by Premier Zhou Enlai to Nehru, was that the 'boundary question is a complicated question left over by history.'[7] The onus for the problem was placed on British machinations in Tibet when India was under British rule. What China objected to was that India 'demanded' that this British policy of 'aggression against China' should now be recognized 'as the foundation for the settlement of the Sino-Indian boundary question.' The Chinese view was that India and China should arrive at a settlement of this question taking into account both the historical background and existing actualities, and that pending this, the status quo along the border should be maintained. Zhou maintained that the boundary had never been formally delimited. The boundary in Ladakh, he stressed, had never been agreed upon between the two countries, citing Nehru's own statement in Parliament in August 1959[8] that 'nobody had marked' the boundary of the old Kashmir State with Tibet and Chinese Turkestan. Zhou said that the boundary line marked on Chinese maps was the 'customary line derived from historical traditions'. And, as far as the McMahon Line and the boundary east of Bhutan was concerned, Zhou maintained that this Line had been 'determined by the British Representative and the representative of Tibet local authorities behind the back' of China, and was a 'product of the British policy of aggression against the Tibet Region of China and has never been recognized by any Chinese Central Government, and is therefore decidedly illegal.' This was an approach that contrasted markedly with what Zhou had told Nehru during their meetings in 1956. Zhou added that it would not be wise to mount pressure through public opinion 'to force China to accept India's unilateral claims' on the boundary. While China did not recognize the McMahon Line, its troops had 'never crossed' the Line although Indian troops had, after the rebellion in Tibet, begun to cross this Line and occupied the area of Longju (where the first armed clash between Chinese and Indian troops occurred in August 1959).

The 'malicious campaign' in India against China over Tibet was a subject raised by Zhou Enlai in a meeting with Indian Ambassador Parthasarathy[9] in Beijing on 9th September. China was not pleased with the fact that the 'treatment accorded to the Dalai Lama exceeds the scope of political asylum'; Zhou cited instances of the Dalai receiving foreign envoys in Delhi and meeting senior Indian political leaders. Zhou said he had told Nehru that a border problem existed between India and China, but the latter had held an opposite view, although now he seemed to be 'accepting that there are border questions.' While the status quo along the disputed boundary should be maintained, it was another thing 'to inherit the policy of British imperialism' which, he said, India had done. As far as the 'illegal' McMahon Line was concerned, in 1947, the Tibetan authorities had 'asked for its revision demanding the return of all territories south of the line.' The Indian representative in Lhasa, Hugh Richardson, had conveyed in December 1947 that the 'Government of India would be happy to have an assurance that existing relations would be maintained till new agreement was reached between both sides'. In contrast to this willingness to conclude a new agreement, India was 'now trying to impose these treaties on China.'[10] Zhou expressed his regret over Nehru's 'statements over Tibet and the Sino-Indian border' saying they seemed to be 'made in an excited state and not in a sober way.' China, on its part, sought a 'reasonable settlement' of the boundary 'on the basis of peaceful friendliness and the five principles and negotiations after good preparations.' Zhou said Nehru had misunderstood his references to the McMahon Line during their talks in 1956—he maintained that what he said was that 'there was a border dispute and that the McMahon Line was unacceptable'. In the Ambassador's report on the meeting, the Premier 'expounded his case vigorously with the help of maps and documents' and 'was full of confidence in the correctness and strength of the Chinese stand on the border question.'[11]

The Government of India was anxious that its case on the boundary be heard in foreign capitals. An important focus was the Soviet Union. The Ambassador in Moscow, K.P.S. Menon briefed General Secretary Khrushchev personally on the matter during a meeting on September 12. The Soviet leader told Menon that it was his country's desire that the dispute with China be settled peacefully 'and not by guns or machine guns' and 'did a few kilometers matter?' The land in dispute, he supposed, was of little value and the danger was that 'both sides might treat (it) as one of prestige. But what higher prestige could a country (aspire to) than a good friend and a tranquil frontier?'[12] Khrushchev informed Menon that his response to the Chinese when they would raise the matter with him, would be on similar lines. Indeed, in October 1959, the Soviet leader raised the matter with Mao Zedong during a discussion held in Beijing in the presence of Politburo members from both countries including Liu Shaoqi, Zhou Enlai, Zhu De, Lin Biao, Peng Zhen, Chen Yi, and Secretariat member Wang Jiaxiang. Khrushchev referring to the bloody clash in Longju in the eastern sector in August, queried that even if Nehru was a 'bourgeois statesman', who could replace him? The events in Tibet, he then said, were the fault of the Chinese, that it was a failure of Chinese intelligence that the intentions of the Dalai Lama and his plans had not been known earlier. He told Mao that the Chinese should have exercised restraint on the border and 'solve disagreements without spilling blood.' A thoroughly exercised Mao retorted, 'You pasted two labels on us, saying the conflict with India was our fault and that the Dalai Lama's escape was our fault. We pasted one label on you – time servers. Here.'[13] Khrushchev said it was difficult to understand China's conflict with India, citing Lenin's example where he gave to Turkey 'Kars, Ardahan and Ararat', and that territorial issues were not surmountable. One of the Politburo members present, Peng Zhen, remarked that 'The McMahon Line is a dirty line that was not recognized by any government in China.' China was also peeved that the *Tass* statement on the border differences between India and China 'was in support of India.' Chen Yi, the Foreign Minister told the Soviet side that he was 'outraged by your declaration that the aggravation of relationship with India was our fault'. Mao then sought to calm the atmosphere by saying that the events in Tibet and the border conflict were 'temporary developments'.

Meanwhile, the Chinese propaganda arm was in overdrive. An editorial in the *Peking Daily*[14] lambasted the Indian media, public opinion and Nehru for their 'inappropriate remarks' on the border dispute. It contrasted the Indian reactions and approach with the 'fair and reasonable' attitude of the Chinese government which was summed up in three points: firstly, a willingness to seek an overall settlement through friendly negotiations; second, that pending a settlement, the two sides maintain the 'long existing status quo of the boundary' and third, as far as local disputes were concerned, negotiations be held on 'provisional measures of solution'. The article questioned India's demands that Chinese maps showing the boundary differently from India's depiction be revised saying that before 1930, even British maps had not depicted the McMahon Line and, in fact, had shown the boundary in a manner similar to China's 'traditional line' (i.e., in the foothills of the Himalayas and not along the highest watershed of the Himalayas, as McMahon defined it). All that the Chinese wanted, the paper said, was to stress that the resolution of the issue depended on 'negotiations between two sides with reasonable conciliatory and amiable attitude and taking considerations (sic) of historical background and actual situation.' Western imperialism, it was claimed, was now using the opportunity to sow tension and 'fish in troubled waters' between India and China, and create 'opportunities for imperialism and its agents in India'. China wanted the 'ship of Sino-Indian friendship' to 'weather the storm and pursue a steady course on the ocean of peace', the commentary concluded. This did not stop the tempo of the anti-Indian campaign in the Chinese press including coverage of an event in Lhasa in September 1959 where 'Tibet personalities affirmed that Tibet never accepted McMahon Line' and a statement by a nephew of the 13th Dalai Lama asserting that the Tibetan representative at the Simla Conference of 1914 'had not dared to sign' the Indo-Tibetan Agreement confirming the Line as the boundary between British India and Tibet. The Panchen Lama's statement accusing India of expansionist activity and 'unilaterally' claiming large tracts of Tibetan territory as India's was also given prominence.[15]

The growing tensions on the border, in both the western (Ladakh) and eastern Sectors (North-East Frontier, now Arunachal Pradesh), were obviously a source of great preoccupation for Prime Minister Nehru. On the eve of his departure on a visit to Iran, he recorded a 'Note on the Border Dispute with China' in which he enjoined both civil and military officers to 'avoid actual conflict unless it is practically forced down upon us. That is to say, we must avoid armed conflict not only in the big way but even in the small way.'[16] The three sectors of the frontier 'with 'Tibet-China' as he termed it, were, firstly, the McMahon Line from Burma to Bhutan; secondly the frontier between Tibet 'and Uttar Pradesh, Himachal and the Punjab'; and thirdly, the Ladakh frontier. Each of the three in his view involved 'a slightly different approach.' Indian forces should keep to 'our side of the frontier, that is, the McMahon Line or elsewhere.' Any Chinese armed detachment coming over to the Indian side of the Line 'should be told to go back' and should be fired at only if they fired first. In the second, the middle or central sector of the boundary, there were understandings reached during the 1954 Agreement with Tibet and these should be adhered to, although check-posts should be 'vigilant' and reinforced where necessary. The Ladakh frontier could be divided into two parts: one, the area around the Chushul and, the second, covering the Aksai Chin. Strong detachments were necessary to defend Chushul and its airfield but conflict should be avoided as far as possible. The Aksai Chin area would have 'to be left as it is', the Prime Minister felt. India had 'little means of access' there. 'Any questions relating to it can only be considered, when the time arises, in the context of larger question of the entire border.' But he was clearly not thinking of making large-scale concessions to China in such an eventuality. 'Minor deviation', as he called it, from the border shown on Indian maps could be considered, when the time arose, but 'any question relating to major changes such as are envisaged in the Chinese maps cannot be considered by us in this way.'[17] In the meantime, 'attacks on China should be avoided' in the media.

Meanwhile, the Indian case on the boundary dispute was spelt out in a letter addressed by Prime Minister Nehru to Premier Zhou on 26 September 1959. In this long missive, Nehru sought to refute Chinese allegations that independent India was trying to reap the fruits of British aggression against China. He emphasized that the boundaries of India had been 'settled for centuries by history, geography, custom and tradition. While India favoured the maintenance of the status quo on the border, it was the Chinese government that had 'repeatedly' violated it through the construction of the Aksai Chin highway, and through numerous other transgressions into India's border areas. Nehru went on to lay down the historical evidence for India's boundary depiction in Ladakh, in the middle sector of the boundary, and in the eastern sector covered by the McMahon Line. The Prime Minister went into considerable detail about the Simla Conference of 1914 and the decisions reached on the definition of the eastern boundary through the 'binding' agreement reached between Henry McMahon, the then Foreign Secretary of India, and Lonchen

Shatra, the Tibetan representative, who had participated in the conference 'on an equal footing' with the Chinese and British Indian representatives. This agreement, he added, should be regarded as binding on both China and Tibet in accordance with established international practice. It was now a matter of great surprise to India that China had put forward large claims to Indian territory. No government could agree to discuss the future of such large tracts, although India was prepared to concede that across such a long border of 'more than 3500 kilometers', some disputes may arise which could be peacefully and amicably settled. When the 1954 Agreement on Tibet had been concluded between India and China, Nehru said he had 'hoped that the main problems history had bequeathed to us in the relations between India and China had been peacefully and finally settled. But years later, you have now brought forward, with all insistence, a problem which dwarfs in importance all that we have discussed in recent years and, I thought, settled.' The promise and hope of a border of peace and friendship that Premier Zhou had spoken of as the ideal could only be achieved if 'China would not bring within the scope of what should essentially be a border dispute, claims to thousands of square miles of territory which have been and are integral part of the territory of India', he concluded[17].

At a Conference of Governors in October 1959, the Foreign Secretary elaborated the Indian position.[18] 'The Indian frontier along the whole of the north of India from the epic times has been practically where it is today . . . This is the frontier which has been the traditional, natural, geographical frontier of India.' This frontier had been defined by the geographical principle of 'the major watershed' except for a few variations. In the past, small disputes had arisen with the Tibetans over grazing grounds and 'a few monasteries' but these disputes were not over the whole frontier. The Chinese had come into the picture, too, at times: specifically, in Ladakh and in the area of the McMahon Line. They had been party to the agreement reached in Ladakh when the Tibetans had appealed for their intervention following the war with the then Dogra ruler of Jammu, Gulab Singh, in the 1840s. Similarly, they had been present at the Simla Conference of 1913–1914 when the boundaries between Inner and Outer Tibet and between Inner Tibet and China were being discussed.

The Chinese, however, had not accepted the result of the Simla Conference. In the years following, the British had tried to secure Chinese agreement in the matter but had not succeeded and had withheld publication of the map showing the McMahon Line for that reason. The confusion over whether the Chinese exercised 'sovereignty' or 'suzerainty' over Tibet had persisted. According to the Foreign Secretary, in 1936 'the British informed the Chinese that they would accept Chinese sovereignty over Tibet. There was no condition attached to it.' But in 1943, Antony Eden as the British Foreign Secretary, writing to his Chinese counterpart, had 'again referred to Chinese suzerainty over Tibet', using the expression 'that the British would accept Chinese suzerainty over Tibet, and this was conditional on the recognition of Tibetan autonomy.'

Foreign Secretary Dutt explained that the difficulties in maintaining access and presence in the areas along the border were 'practical and stupendous'. Both terrain and geography helped the Chinese. This difficulty was compounded by the fact that the Chinese had not defined this frontier and 'merely indicated it by a line in their map and that line also they have shifted from time to time.' Their policy as it appeared, was 'to extend their occupation up to the line which they claim is the border.' It had therefore been a matter of 'great wisdom' for India to extend administration in the eastern sector of the border up to the McMahon Line. Dutt also listed the various patrols sent by India into the now-Chinese-occupied areas of Ladakh, claiming, rather vaguely, that it was only in 1958 that the Chinese were found 'gradually coming into the area' without making any mention of the Aksai Chin highway. He referred to Premier Zhou Enlai having said in September 1959 that he was prepared to settle the matter in accordance with 'actual realities of the situation.' He then said one could speculate that the Chinese government 'may take the line that the realities of the situation may mean somewhat like this. We are in occupation up to the McMahon Line frontier. They are in actual possession of certain areas of Ladakh. If we recognize their occupation, they might make a practical settlement by recognizing the McMahon Line.' He underlined that this 'is only speculation.'

Nowhere in the elucidation of the Indian position was there evidence of any recognition that boundaries between nations are fixed and determined on the basis of mutual agreement between the sovereign governments concerned. India adhered to the line that she had defined her frontier, geographically 'and in other ways.' The Chinese, India felt, had 'at no time defined their frontier.' To infer from this set of observations that, all that was left to do was to secure China's agreement to, and acceptance of, the frontier as defined by India, was unrealistic and bound to be elusive. Terms like 'Chinese betrayal' would suffuse the Indian public imagination in the following years, with an inevitable descent into conflict as differences in approach and position became increasingly more difficult to reconcile. Both nations have accumulated greater national progress and international prestige since the 1950s, but on the question of their high frontiers they are essentially in the same place. Immobility on the issue is pervasive and this legacy dispute has extended into the twenty-first century.

The subject of the border, weighing on the mind of the Prime Minister with the increasing pressure—brought on him from within his own party (the Congress), the Opposition, media and public opinion—figured in his letter to Permanent Representative to the United Nations in New York, Krishna Menon in November 1959.[19] The retired Chief of the Army Staff General Cariappa came in for an irate comment from Nehru who criticized him for making 'foolish statements about our settling problems with Pakistan immediately and of having a joint defence policy' (Cariappa was responding to a proposal to Nehru from Pakistan's military leader Ayub Khan in April 1959 for such a joint defence policy between Pakistan and India). Nehru dismissed the possibility (as he had also done in Parliament in May 1959) of such a joint defence between India and Pakistan, given the fact that defence policy was closely aligned with foreign policy where there was no meeting ground between India and Pakistan (India being strictly non-aligned and Pakistan a Western ally). The question of a joint defence with Pakistan 'had no practical meaning under the circumstances.' Of course, Ayub Khan had himself confirmed in September 1959 that a pre-requisite for his joint defence proposal was the solution of the problem of Kashmir and the (Indus) canal waters.[20]

During these crucial months, two serious armed clashes had taken place between Indian and Chinese armed personnel: the first in Longju, in the eastern sector in August, and the second at the Kongka Pass in October 1959. Both these incidents involved the loss of lives of Indian soldiers and triggered strong reactions and anti-China emotions in India. The clash at Longju was the first time that troops of the two sides had exchanged fire. The Indian side had always held that Longju was south of the McMahon Line and had never assumed that this would be contested by China. A month before the incident, India had informed the Chinese Foreign Office[21] that it intended to para-drop a doctor to Longju, requesting that 'necessary immediate warning be issued to neighboring Chinese posts of this operation.' The exact coordinates and grid references of Longju's location had also been conveyed to the Chinese 'who responded that it was "not necessary to bring activities in Indian territory to their notice." This elliptical response from China was contradicted by subsequent Chinese action when their armed personnel crossed south of the McMahon Line. The fact of this crossing was also recognized as a Chinese transgression by the Americans—Allan Dulles, head of the CIA, told a meeting of the National Security

Council in Washington on 10 September 1959 that the Chinese attack in Longju 'resulted in a penetration three miles beyond the McMahon Line.'[22]

The clash at Kongka La in Ladakh on 20 October 1959 killed five Indian police personnel, wounded four and resulted in the capture of ten Indian policemen. To illustrate the wide difference between Indian and Chinese claims of where the frontier lay, Kongka La as seen by India was located 'at least 65 kilometers inside the traditional frontier' on the Indian side.[23] To rub further salt into India's wounds, the captured personnel were released by the Chinese (who accused the Indians of arrogance and being 'incited' by the Soviets) on 14 November 1959— Nehru's birthday—together with the bodies of those killed in the encounter. Battle lines in Ladakh were being clearly drawn. The Chinese were steadily encroaching on Indian territory far west of India's claimed boundary, and beyond the Aksai Chin plateau across ridge lines and river valleys that brought them much closer to the Ladakhi heartland and the passes that led into traditional trading routes with Tibet from south-eastern Ladakh.

The British journalist and *New Statesman* editor Kingsley Martin and his partner Dorothy Woodward, who were good friends of Prime Minister Nehru, observed the effects of the escalating crisis with China on the Prime Minister during this period. They were to tell the historian B.R. Nanda in a recorded interview from August 1967[24] that the change in Mr Nehru was marked after 1959. In Woodward's words:

I think he really 'died'. I think Nehru 'died' at the Kongka Pass, because after that time he . . . realized that they (the Chinese) were not honest about the maps. He knew about the road over the Aksai Chin. He also told me . . . how when he had been travelling by train from Lucknow down to Delhi with Zhou Enlai, how they had discussed the boundary questions and the McMahon Line and Zhou Enlai had really given Nehru to believe that they would accept the McMahon Line.. I am not sure that Nehru had really followed any developments in the Aksai Chin. If Nehru had realized what the Aksai Chin might mean, I believe he would have discussed the Aksai Chin as well as the McMahon Line with Zhou Enlai.

Woodward and Martin felt that there had existed a window in 1956 during the Zhou–Nehru discussions to reach a 'compromise' on the boundary. In their words, 'After all, the Aksai Chin was not that important to India. The McMahon Line was, in fact, much more important.' They observed that after the Kongka Pass incident, Nehru began to mistrust the Chinese 'more and more and more.' This was coupled with the fact that Indian public opinion 'became hysterical about China.' Under the pressure of this public opinion, and as his health failed, Nehru was 'a very tired man', a disillusioned man. He was never himself again after the Kongka Pass incident.

From January 1959, taking account of the steady advance of Chinese in areas east of the Aksai Chin highway in Ladakh, the Indian Government had been considering the augmentation and strengthening of Indian check posts in the area. The prime mover of this policy was the chief of the Intelligence Bureau, B.N. Mullik. This was an early manifestation of what was later to be termed the 'Forward Policy' of India in the western sector of the border. At a meeting held in the office of the Foreign Secretary on 8 January 1959,[25] Mullik suggested a new policy of company headquarters at Phobrang, with sections posted at Tsogstsalu, Shamal Lungpa and Shinglung (on the Chinese side of the claimed Chinese boundary). Mullik also suggested that two army posts be established at Sarigh Jilganang Kol in the east and at Palong Karpo (close to the Aksai Chin road). The proposal to establish a post at Shinglung was given a go-ahead based on the argument that 'reconnaissance reports do not indicate that the Chinese are as yet exercising active possession in the area.' It was therefore considered a definite advantage in opening (the) post at Shinglung in order to 'clearly emphasize that we do not accept the international boundary as shown in the Chinese maps.' However, the proposals to establish posts at Sarigh Jilganang Kol and Palong Karpo were not agreed to, the logic being that 'since we do not propose to have a major clash with Chinese forces already in occupation of this area'. But it did not end there. In order to prevent Chinese incursions to the south and west, it was however recommended that after establishing the new police outposts at Tsogstsalu and Shamal Lungpa, reconnaissance parties should be organized from these outposts toward the Lanak La in the east, along the Chang Chenmo Valley, with a view to patrol the area and also to find a suitable spot for a fourth police outpost in the locality.

On 7 November 1959, Zhou Enlai wrote[26] to Nehru urging that the 'disquieting' situation along the border be improved speedily and an appropriate solution worked out to prevent border clashes from occurring. He proposed that pending a settlement, the status quo should be maintained and that neither side should seek to alter the status quo by any means. Elaborating on this further, he suggested to Nehru that 'the armed forces of China and India each withdraw 20 kilometers at once from the so-called McMahon Line in the east, and from the line up to which each side exercises actual control in the west', and that neither side send their armed personnel into this zone of disengagement, although civil administrative personnel and unarmed police could be stationed there for 'maintenance of order'. Zhou's letter carried the reference to a 'line of actual control', a term that has now passed into common usage in the lexicon of the India–China boundary dispute. Nehru felt that the proposal from Zhou was disadvantageous to India.[27] India was not prepared to abandon all check posts on the McMahon Line. As the Foreign Secretary termed it in a message[28] to the Indian Ambassadors in Moscow, Washington, London, and

Cairo, 'Abandoning our forward posts would mean that in the frontiers of NEFA and in the frontiers of Sikkim, UP, Punjab and Himachal Pradesh a large majority of the passes which open from Tibet into India would be thrown open to intruders, and in case no settlement of the boundary is reached, it would be impossible for us to restore the status quo in these areas and extremely easy for the Chinese to come in and occupy them.' In Ladakh, it was conceded that the 'facts of occupation themselves are in doubt.' Further, the Chinese claim line was a shifting one and India did not accept 'the assertion that they have extended their occupation up to the line which they show on their maps.' The Indian suggestion in response to the Zhou proposal was that the Chinese withdraw to the east of the Indian claimed boundary in Ladakh and that India withdraw to the west of the Chinese claim line. These two lines were separated by 'hundreds of kilometers' and there would not be 'the remotest risk of any border clash.' India was prepared to make a concession in Aksai Chin 'where in the past we have not sought to exercise any active occupation.' The Foreign Secretary, however, added that the delay on the part of the Chinese in handing over the prisoners taken during the Kongka Pass incident together with the dead bodies of Indian personnel was 'most objectionable and disproves the Chinese Premier's profession of friendship.' A formal reply to Zhou Enlai's letter of 7 November was sent on 16 November.[29] It expressed willingness—in addition to responding to the Chinese proposals on the lines outlined by the Foreign Secretary in his message to the Ambassadors—that the Prime Minister was always ready to meet and discuss with the Chinese Premier the 'outstanding differences between India and China and explore avenues of friendly settlement.' However, it was added, immediate efforts 'should be concentrated on reaching an interim understanding which will ease present tensions' after which a meeting of the two leaders could be fixed.

As regards proposals for demilitarization and the creation of a zone of separation in the border areas being discussed by the two Prime Ministers, Ambassador Parthasarathy in Beijing expressed a sensible view to Foreign Secretary Dutt[30] that demilitarization to be effective 'cannot precede the definition of the frontier but must follow an agreement on the course of the frontier.' He suggested that the two questions of definition of the frontier and demilitarization be taken up 'together'. A 'firm' agreement that armed forces of either side would not resort to firing was also advocated. 'The agreement should be that both parties should hold their present positions (and) if the patrols of either party come across patrols of the other side, they should stop at the point they have reached. On no repeat, no account should they shoot'. Meanwhile, news from Washington that US Secretary of State Christian Herter had expressed doubts about the validity of the Indian case on the border with China in a public statement in November 1959, caused some embarrassment between India and the United States. State Department officials, however, hastened to clarify that 'all the intricate details' about the dispute had 'confused' the Secretary who himself expressed 'sincere regrets' for the misunderstanding caused. Herter told the Indian Deputy Chief of Mission[31] that there was a 'strong feeling of sympathy' for India on the part of both the administration and the American people for India, while strongly criticizing 'the aggressive actions of China.' A press release was subsequently issued by the State Department to remove the misconceptions caused by Herter's statement.

In the midst of escalating tensions along the border, there seemed to be little change in India's policy seeking the representation of China in the United Nations. India, in fact, put the item down again for discussion in the United Nations as it had done every year from 1949 onwards. Krishna Menon, speaking in the plenary meeting of the General Assembly on 22 September 1959 said that India's position in the matter was not determined by emotional concern about the plight of Tibet and the Tibetans or by questions of her sovereignty being violated by China in the border areas. It was a question of principle that China should be represented in the United Nations, 'in the interests of world peace and co-operation.' He continued that 'Friendship with China is something that we regard as necessary for them and for us.' If the 'affairs of the world' were to be settled, 'we cannot have a great part of the world out of it.' This seeming intent to respect 'principle' however lofty and high-minded, may have sounded incongruous to many observers, given the growing hostility between India and China and the mounting opposition to the Government of India's China policy within India. The meeting of minds between Menon and Nehru on the issue of Chinese representation in the United Nations, seen with the hindsight of history, struck a note of discordance—extending such a favour to China at this particular time did not secure any particular advantage for India with the Chinese, or with its friends and well-wishers on the global stage (save the Soviet bloc).[32]

The proposals for withdrawal put forward by Nehru to Zhou Enlai for prevention of clashes in the western Sector (exclusively), were rejected by the Chinese in the Premier's letter to the Indian Prime Minister, of 17 December 1959.[33] Zhou said he was 'perplexed' by the Indian stand and termed the proposals 'a big step backward' and 'unfair.' It entailed the withdrawal of Chinese forces from territory which had 'long belonged' to China. Would India be willing, similarly, to withdraw personnel 'from the area between the so-called McMahon Line and the eastern section of the Sino-Indian boundary as shown on Chinese maps?' Attention was also drawn to the boundary being shown on Indian maps as a delimited (marked as a fixed boundary) one when until 1952, these boundaries were 'indicated as delimited.' Zhou agreed that talks on the boundary issue be held between the two Prime Ministers 'to reach first some agreements of principles as a guidance to concrete discussions and settlement of the boundary question by the two sides.' In response to this last point, Ambassador Parthasarathy advised the Foreign Secretary[34] that adequate preparations were necessary before such a meeting was held and that it would be best to begin with an official level preliminary meeting either in Beijing or Delhi. Nehru then replied to Zhou[35] that their meeting would be of little use since an agreement 'on principles' could scarcely be reached 'when there is such complete disagreement about the facts.'

The mood within the Indian public and Parliament in response to perceived Chinese 'aggression' along the border, coupled with concern about the events in Tibet was, meanwhile, steadily worsening. Until early 1959, the people of India had been largely in the dark about events concerning the border with China. The 'friendship' of China toward India, and Nehru's policy, had not come under the public scanner. From March 1959, that changed. Members of Parliament like Hem Barua (Praja Socialist Party), Atal Bihari Vajpayee (Jana Sangh) and Braj Raj Singh (Socialist) were among the first to raise the issue of the concentration of Chinese troops on the border. Nehru dismissed their concerns saying he had not even 'heard a rumor to that effect, leave out the facts.'[36] The publication of Chinese maps showing large chunks of Indian territory as Chinese was another issue raised. The Prime Minister sought to downplay the matter saying only small areas of territory were in dispute. On another occasion, in August 1959, he denied that the Chinese had questioned the validity of the McMahon Line reiterating that 'the McMahon Line is the firm frontier, firm by treaty, firm by usage, firm by geography.'[37] The Prime Minister was trying his best to downplay the whole issue, being 'reluctant to tickle the dragon's tail.'[38] His guarded responses on Chinese incursions in the eastern sector, especially Longju, irked the members further. Nehru, while deploring the use of force by the Chinese, took the line that he did not think these incidents were a precursor to something more serious, although he said the government was prepared for any eventuality, and had placed the border area of NEFA under the army. On 12 September, Nehru was considerably less equivocal in his condemnation of the Chinese claims saying 'there can be no mediation, conciliation or arbitration about these demands of the Chinese about large chunks of territory.'[39] But he sought to distinguish the Ladakh sector of the boundary from the middle and eastern sectors where nothing more than minor rectification of the boundary could be considered. In the Aksai Chin, he argued, 'It is a matter of argument as to what part of it belongs to us and what part of it belongs to somebody else. It is not at all a dead clear matter . . . That particular area stands by itself.'[40] But the outcry in Parliament and among the public rose to a crescendo after the incident at Kongka Pass. Indian fury was at a new pitch. Anti-Chinese demonstrations were held all over the country. *The Hindu* newspaper noted in a commentary that 'in the present conflict with China, the resentment against the Chinese is taking the form of a personal attack against Nehru.'[41]

During a debate held in Parliament on 25 November 1959 after the Kongka Pass incident, while referring to the Opposition's persistent demand that the Chinese troops should be ejected from sovereign Indian territory, an increasingly beleaguered Nehru said, 'People seem to think that we need not go to war, but we may have some kind of petty campaigns here and there. I do confess that this is beyond my understanding'. In Nehru's assessment, such steps would demand full-scale war being launched against China. Members criticized the Prime Minister for conceding that Tibet was a part of China, and for his 'infantile exhibition' of friendship and fraternal links with that country. Krishna Menon, by now the Defence Minister, was accused of pro-Communist leanings and lacking the trust and confidence of the nation, and its people. It was also advocated by the Opposition, particularly the Jana Sangh, that India should cease support for the People's Republic of China's admission to the United Nations. Only the Communist Party of India endorsed the government's China policy. The Defence Minister struck a rather unrealistic note, when seen in retrospect with the benefit of hindsight available to us today, that the frontier with China 'had been like the United States–Canada frontier and as it had been hoped that no case for military action would arise, only checkposts had been maintained mainly to guard the trade routes.'[42] Some Congress members, on the other hand, sought firmness in the government's dealings with China. In remarks that reflected the Indian public's view that Tibet should be a buffer state between India and China, they said that this was what the British had established and they questioned why India should 'withdraw all our extraterritorial rights out of idealism.'

In the face of mounting belligerence within the Opposition, Nehru sought to induce restraint and moderation. Speaking in Parliament on 21 December he said 'so far as I am concerned and so far as this Government is concerned, we will negotiate and negotiate and negotiate to the bitter end. I absolutely reject the approach of stopping negotiations at any stage.' He added that 'There are . . . only two ways in which nations deal with each other, diplomatic or war, there is no third way.' The Opposition refused to concede the point, however, that there was no space between diplomacy and war. The Jana Sangh's Vajpayee advocated breaking off diplomatic relations with China as an expression of Indian ire against Chinese expansionism. The intransigent Opposition was not prepared to countenance any suggestion that India's case was not one hundred per cent watertight. There was an uproar when Nehru said, 'to imagine that what we think is inevitably and hundred per cent right is not necessarily correct. Sometimes we may be a little wrong too.'[43]

By the end of 1959, relations between India and China had seen a steep decline. The years gone by when the two countries had sought to build a bilateral relationship seemed a waste of time, and the years to come immersed in the prospect of a kinetic frontier situation and pervasive uncertainty. The events in Tibet and the asylum granted by India to the Dalai Lama had rapidly eroded China's belief in whatever credentials India may have had as a reliable or trustworthy partner, while the growing rift on the boundary issue had convinced India that China's true face as an aggressive and expansionist neighbour (with overtones of imperialistic intent) had been exposed.

The differences regarding the boundary were to prove the most complicated and difficult to unravel, or resolve. Seasoned observers have noted, 'the India-China boundary conflict arose primarily because the two concepts, the Chinese one of strategic borders, and India's of historic borders, could not be reconciled. While the Chinese were prepared to use diplomatic and, if necessary, military methods, in pursuit of their concept, the Indian approach from 1950 was primarily declaratory and ineffectively military.'[44] Nehru's 'discovered' India, that he wrote about with eloquence and idealism, was founded on the idea that the nation's frontiers were handed down to its people by tradition, geography, custom and usage, and by history. Whether India's case was infallible or not, these were borders to be defended, if the need arose, to the last drop of Indian blood. India had existed as a unified and composite whole, a consolidated territorial space hemmed by the highest Himalaya, from time immemorial. India had not been 'created' by the British during colonial rule—its existence predated British rule, by thousands of years. The fact that the Himalayas rimmed the Indian subcontinent proved, when seen through the prism of this opinion, that this was a God-given boundary as sung and spoken of in epic poems and the mythology that had been embedded for millennia in the Indian psyche. These were not borders to be questioned by any country, 'map or no map', as Nehru famously said in 1950.

On the other hand, the Chinese post-1949, had also embraced pre-People's Republic definitions of the extent of Chinese territorial sovereignty, together with the claims on areas like Xinjiang and Tibet dating back to previous, imperialist Chinese dynasties, and the frontier 'definitions' that accompanied them. Securing the peripheries of these regions in order to ensure a defensible frontier also became a strategic necessity in the early years of the PRC as Tibet was militarily occupied, and secure connectivity and infrastructural links to this remote region became a crucial requirement. The difference was that the pursuit of ambiguity and stealth in advancing their interests—before the extent of their claims were revealed—were preferred approaches as far as China was concerned. In India's case, the neglect to physically secure her claims in the Aksai Chin, while showing all of this area as within its boundaries in its maps, was to come at great cost to national prestige and confidence, with far-reaching implications that have proved difficult to erase even to this day.

During the British era, colonial India had been obsessed and absorbingly preoccupied with the security of its northwest frontier. The advance of Russia into the heart of Asia was to be prevented, and this was a policy priority. Post-Independence, the focus of India's policy makers turned to safeguarding the northeast frontier of the country as an area of imminent danger, given the emergence of an expansive communist China and its clear intent to militarily occupy Tibet. That occupation would make China's borders coterminous with India's. Chinese maps already showed a wide swathe of territory south of the Himalayan watershed in this region stretching to the upper banks of the Brahmaputra River. Chinese intentions, therefore, were assessed as a clear and present danger. In New Delhi, the government was firm in its understanding that the McMahon Line constituted the boundary on India's northeastern frontier with Tibet. In their view, the 1914 Agreement between British India and Tibet at the Simla Conference had yielded this line and even if the consent of China to this agreement had not been received, the lack of such consent did not detract from its validity. The McMahon Line, according to this view, provided the best frontier for the defence of India, particularly its potentially vulnerable eastern and northeastern areas, running as it did along the crest of the high Himalaya—the high watershed. This was an area, therefore, of the highest strategic importance for India.

After 1914, the British had not moved with sufficient alacrity to ensure the proper defence and administration of this frontier, and it was only in the 1940s that they had begun to ensure effective occupation in a slow and gradual manner. The Tibetans in Lhasa had expected Britain to secure Chinese agreement to the frontiers of Tibet, but that had not been achieved. There were thus signs of Tibetan restlessness about the line and that this was not a win-win situation for both sides. However, post-1947 and particularly by 1950, as the Chinese began to move into Tibet, the Government of India was clear that a 'defensible' frontier was vital to the country's security. It was anticipated that no time should be lost in order to secure these interests, and that the McMahon Line provided for the best frontier under these circumstances.

The land frontier of India with China, following the occupation of Tibet in 1950–51 would bring the two countries into cheek-by-jowl juxtaposition with each other. This frontier was 'defined' by a patchwork of custom and usage, historical treaties and tradition, but there was no agreement between India and China that had 'settled' this boundary across its entire length. It was anticipated that New China was bound to question this frontier and perhaps occupy some disputed areas, even presenting India with a fait accompli. The vulnerability of India's heartland, its densely populated regions and industrial centres, would stand exposed as a result.

Apart from the northeast frontier, Ladakh was also a preoccupation. In the early days, links between Ladakh and west Tibet had been particularly strong, although from the nineteenth century onwards, the region had been integrated into the dominions of the Maharaja of Kashmir. Eastern Ladakh was geographically a continuation of the high plateau that also covered Tibet. Ladakhis were Buddhists like the Tibetans, and their religious and social customs, their language and attire reflected affinities with Tibet. Further, no natural geographical barriers existed between Ladakh and Tibet. But the times had changed. Where earlier, China had hardly counted as a factor in determining India's policy in the region,[45] by the mid-twentieth century, the situation was different. Various boundary lines had been mulled over—with one of these interpretations, of an alignment along the Karakoram watershed, being proposed to the Chinese in the late nineteenth century (1898), without a response from the latter. The school of thought within the British Indian establishment for a frontier that would create a barrier of barren and inhospitable terrain between India and 'hostile' Russian territory, ultimately prevailed. This frontier, unilaterally conceived, but based on the recommendation of Sir John Ardagh (the Director of Military Intelligence), and exploration of these regions by British surveyors in the second half of the nineteenth century, defined a northern boundary along the Kun-Lun mountains—largely along the lines shown in the Survey of India maps of today.

The intention was to have a strategic frontier with difficult terrain being on the Indian side of the line, as a further barrier for defence against extraneous forces and interests. But this was not an easy frontier to define. Much of Ladakh's external borders lay across uninhabited, forbidding terrain. In the north, the region was ringed by high mountain ranges, but in the south and southeast there were no clear watersheds with the River Indus flowing northwest from Tibet into Ladakh. The coexistence between Ladakh and Tibet rested on the belief that the customary boundary had been fixed from ancient times. Trade missions from Ladakh into Tibet were a regular feature and any small disputes about the boundary were no barrier to the transaction of regular trade contacts, pilgrimage and people-to-people interaction. As far as the northeastern corner of Ladakh was concerned, the actual state of physical occupation was not easily ascertained—even less so for the Chinese since no evidence existed of their administrative or physical presence. But of the two watersheds east of the Karakoram Pass, one running southeast along the Karakoram Range, and the other east along the Kunlun Mountains and taking in the Aksai Chin plateau, the latter was the line that came to be depicted as the international frontier of India, even if it was shown as an 'undefined' boundary in Indian maps prior to 1954.[46]

It would not be off the mark to say that like the histories of many other international land borders, traditionally there tended to be frontier zones rather than linear, fixed, predetermined boundaries between India and China, pending delineation of these borders through mutual agreement or bilateral treaty. Tibet and Xinjiang, once absorbed through the sweep of Chinese colonizing power, brought China to the frontier zones that separated these regions from India. For many Indians, however, the boundary dispute appeared to signal that China was questioning the historical authenticity of the Indian nation.

When the boundary dispute surfaced between India and China in the late 1950s, it revealed fundamental differences in approaches of the two countries to the issue. The Government of Prime Minister Nehru was emphatic that the boundary did have a treaty basis (citing various historical agreements) whereas the Chinese maintained that the boundary had not been delimited and was only a 'traditional, customary' line. India took the stand that the boundary was fixed, not in dispute and that it had a legal basis. There is a wide gulf in positions between the two countries, particularly with regard to the historical basis of the boundary in Ladakh with India citing the Treaties of 1684 and 1842 with Tibet, and China disputing the existence of the 1684 Treaty and saying that the 1842 agreement only refers to both sides agreeing to hold to their confines and not encroaching on each other. In the middle sector of the boundary, the 1954 Agreement on Tibet between India and China mentioned six passes for the conduct of border trade with India maintaining that these passes are border passes while China denying that these were accepted as such. That agreement lapsed in 1962. In the Sikkim sector of the border, China accepts the boundary alignment on the basis of the Anglo-Chinese Convention of 1890. As for the eastern sector covered by the McMahon Line, as mentioned earlier, China has refused to recognize the legal validity of the Indo-Tibetan Agreement of 1914 which sanctified this line, on the grounds that Tibet did not have the right to conclude separate Treaties.

In late 2014, during a discussion with a senior Chinese academic in Beijing, this author was told that the Chinese Communist Party 'was never aware when they took over, that India and Tibet shared anything in common'. The leaders of the party, he claimed, 'were not scholars but farmers and workers', and they did not realize the 'international implications' of a 'minority issue' like Tibet. They had no knowledge of the special character of Tibet, about the Dalai Lama and the religious system prevailing in Tibet. According to him, 'Even Zhou Enlai did not know of the McMahon Line'. The Guomindang, he maintained, had taken away most of the government archives to Taiwan. When the Xinjiang–Tibet Highway (across the Aksai Chin) was built, they did 'not know about disputed territory. They realized it only in 1954'. When they learnt of the McMahon Line, their first reaction was 'to keep that line—let it be there'. Zhou Enlai felt the western sector was 'more military (strategic)' because of the road, and he also felt that the eastern sector/ the area south of the McMahon Line, could be controlled by India. But Nehru had not accepted it, my interlocutor said. The leadership of the two countries had not understood each other, and 'did not communicate properly' and 'the ambition of Nehru was as big as Mao Zedong's. One felt that China was a revolutionary country, the other that India was a modern, great country.' He added that Mao did not understand Indian democracy and the difficulties that Nehru faced. Turning to the Zhou Enlai factor, his view was that Zhou had ceased to influence Chinese policy after 1957 when he had been 'criticized' by the Party and from 1958, he was merely 'the CEO of Chairman Mao'.

The much-vaunted friendship between India and China, as the events of 1959 showed, was transient, fading quickly as the differences relating to the border accumulated and events in Tibet culminated in the flight of the Dalai Lama to India.

14

The River of No Return

The border dispute is a heady cocktail of history, law, morality and expediency[1]

—A.G. Noorani,

Zum Lein:
Zum Indische Lein
Fest steht und treu
Die wacht am McMahon Lein
To the line:
The Indian line
Faithful and vigilant stands
The watch on the McMahon Line[2]

—Jagat Singh Mehta
(based on Heinrich Heine's *A Watch on the Rhine*)

In the spring of 1960, Prime Minister Nehru decided that the time was opportune to accommodate a visit to Delhi by Premier Zhou

Enlai. The Prime Minister's mood was not hopeful or optimistic. He was under duress, convinced that tensions with China would be a continuing phenomenon and that there was 'complete disagreement about the facts'[3] on the boundary question between the two countries. The *People's Daily* article of 6 May 1959 titled 'Nehru's Philosophy and the Revolt in Tibet' had contemptuously overlooked Nehru's decade-long efforts to personally husband 'faith in friendship with China' and was shot through with a 'lack of political understanding of the functioning of a parliamentary system and democratic polity' in India.[4] In the opinion of some who had worked closely with Nehru on the bilateral relationship with China,[5] the publication of the article accusing Nehru by name as responsible for the problems with China, was a 'fatal turning point in Sino-Indian relations.'[6] Nehru also knew that the torrent of opposition from within his own Cabinet and which stretched across the spectrum of political parties into the arena of public opinion—in which China was seen as oppressor of the Tibetan people, an aggressor causing bloodshed and violating sacred Indian ground in Ladakh and along the Northeast Frontier—would leave him with little room for maneuverability or compromise. There was limited or no scope for 'sagacity' or restraint.

The Prime Minister's involuted sophistry in an attempt to explain the rationale for the invitation was that 'talks' with the Chinese leader were not 'negotiations', and that he would stand firm and unyielding where the Indian case on the differences with China were concerned. He had also been encouraged by the expression of 'heavy moral support' for India as it faced tensions on the front with China, from President Eisenhower, who had visited India in December 1959 (no specific material assistance was sought at this point from the United States). These statements of solidarity had 'struck a deep chord' at a special hour, especially the private assurance from Eisenhower that the United States would not allow Pakistan 'to stab India in the back' if India was to face China in a conflict situation.[7] The Soviet leader Nikita Khrushchev also made two brief visits to Delhi in February 1960 where he urged that both India and China resolve their differences, bilaterally, saying that the boundary dispute represented a 'most embarrassing question' for his country as it involved two 'friendly peace-loving countries'.[8]

Meanwhile, on another front, China and Burma agreed on a boundary settlement in which one section in the far west covered a part of the McMahon Line, and which China agreed to accept as a final alignment, setting aside any notions of its 'illegality'. The impression that had gained ground within the Indian establishment was that the Chinese were similarly willing to accept the McMahon alignment in a settlement with India, too. The Agreement between China and Burma, in the words of Premier Zhou, laid to rest a problem 'inherited from history, a product of imperialist policies of aggression' and symbolized a 'brilliant model' of peaceful coexistence among Asians. For long years before the Agreement, the Chinese government, Guomindang first and then, Communist had published maps depicting large parts of northern Burma as China, 'as if the northern triangle of Burma were part of the bulging belly of a large dragon sprawled lazily over a caving-in roof.'[9] The western section of this boundary from the Isurazi Pass to the trijunction point of India, Burma and China were covered by the McMahon Line, but neither side referred to this Line in their negotiations with the understanding being that the boundary would be delimited along a 'traditional customary line', a concept that signaled inherent flexibility of approach. The Burmese interest was in delineation of a boundary line along the watershed and they stuck to this line with the Chinese finally relenting, as part of an overall border settlement. When the Agreement was signed in 1960, Premier Zhou praised Burma as being 'one of the first countries to recognize the People's Republic of China, the first country to sign a Treaty of Friendship and Mutual Non-Aggression with China, and the first country to bring about a settlement with China of the boundary question left over by history, on the basis of the Five Principles of Peaceful Coexistence, through mutual understanding, mutual accommodations and friendly consultations.'[10] The Burmese did give up small portions of territory in sections of the boundary well away from that covered by the McMahon Line, but in essence they obtained what they had wanted—the British-defined boundary which was now most importantly, recognized by China.

In October 1959, Mao Zedong and Liu Shaoqi reportedly told Ajoy Ghosh of the Communist Party of India that 'they wanted to exchange NEFA for their claim in Ladakh' and 'would put pressure on India to negotiate'. A 'proper atmosphere' needed to be created in this regard and Foreign Minister Chen Yi proposed to Ambassador Parthasarathy that Vice-President Radhakrishnan should visit China as a 'starting point' for negotiations. The letter of invitation arrived on 24 October 1959 and Radhakrishnan turned the proposal down as the clash at Kongka La had already taken place by then (21 October).[11] This notwithstanding, present-day Chinese researchers maintain that the clashes at Longju and Kongka La induced a 'major change' in Chinese policy. In November 1959, Mao chaired an important meeting in Hangzhou wherein he instructed Zhou Enlai to make two proposals to Delhi: firstly, the creation of a demilitarized zone by the withdrawal of troops of both sides by 20 km from each side of the Line of Actual Control, and secondly, talks between the two Prime Ministers.

There was Chinese 'frustration' at the Indian unwillingness to negotiate. Beijing wanted a 'compromise' solution. A report by the Intelligence Department of the PLA General Staff from September 1959 stated that the Chinese leadership had decided that they were 'willing to accept Indian control over the disputed territories at the eastern sector if India in return accepted China's control over parts of Aksai Chin.'[12] In short, the Chinese were apparently willing to apply the principle of 'give and take' in order to achieve a border settlement in the main because rising tensions with India on border issues further compounded the difficulties in Tibet in the wake of the revolt there. Therefore, Zhou's brief for his Delhi visit was to resolve the border dispute with India on the basis of a package deal.[13] But there was an underlying condition to all this: the core suggestion of the PLA report of September 1959 being that if 'New Delhi would come up with a proposal whereby India would forsake its claims to Aksai Chin in the western sector in return for China's recognition of Indian claims in the eastern sector', then China would communicate its willingness for such a package deal.[14]

Ambassador Parthasarathy was meanwhile reporting from Beijing that the Chinese foreign office had told the Egyptian Ambassador that Prime Minister Nehru represented a progressive force in Asia and that it was their intention to strengthen good relations with India. The Indian Ambassador's advice to Foreign Secretary Dutt was, however, that 'we should clearly say 'no' to any attempt to persuade us to accept joint discussions to delimit the entire boundary or sections thereof, while remaining friendly in our approach and showing readiness to reach settlement of specific disputes. I feel, politically, we are in a strong position to maintain our clearly stated policy.'[15]

Did Zhou Enlai come to Delhi with the intention of offering a compromise settlement of the boundary question with India? It is plausible that the revolt in Tibet was a source of insecurity for China at the time and heightened the necessity of settling boundary disputes with countries bordering Tibet—Nepal, India and Burma. Peaceful borders were necessary, it has been argued, in order to enable a more concerted focus on sorting out the situation in Tibet. 'The presence of territorial disputes threatened to complicate consolidation of central authority in Tibet because neighbours might provide support for rebels or even seek to intervene in the conflict.' This accounted for the Politburo meeting held by Mao in September 1959 where it was decided that China should seek a negotiated border settlement with India. This was carried forward in January 1960 when the Politburo Standing Committee discussed the dispute with India and 'agreed that the border with India should be settled swiftly through negotiations based on the principle of 'give and take' (*huliang hurang*).' This process, it was agreed, should involve both countries making 'concessions'. Stability on China's external frontiers (in this case with India) was necessary if stability was to be brought to Tibet internally. Of course, Zhou's visit to Delhi was an out-and-out failure. But 1960 provided an opportunity to both countries to settle their boundary problem, given China's vulnerabilities in Tibet, and the need for external balancing to counter threats to internal stability through the interference of outside forces (in this case, India).[16]

Compromise on the issue was unthinkable in Delhi. The situation along the border with the loss of lives of Indian personnel, and the assumption that India's policy of friendship for China had come apart because of Beijing's perfidy, only deepened the sense of encircling gloom. Nehru could only maintain that a war with China was unlikely, that in any case a no-war policy towards China was imperative, and talks should not be abandoned because the difficulties of terrain and logistics in Tibet would make it impossible for the Chinese to transact a full-blown conflict on the border. China, in this view, did not constitute a military threat to India in the short term and only, perhaps, in the long term as her strength and capabilities were augmented through greater industrial capacity and the establishment of military bases in Tibet. It was a strategic assessment that top military leaders like General K.S. Thimayya, the Army Chief, did not disagree publicly with. The latter's estimate was that 'the Karakoram Range crest-line in the west and the crests of the Himalayan main range in the east provide effective land barriers against a major Chinese military push.'[17] However, Thimayya was also clear that the northern border had to be defended and his encounters with the Chinese as Chairman of the Neutral Nations Repatriation Commission (NNRC) in Korea had not left a favourable impression or inspired much trust. Although such views were not expressed publicly by him, he was concerned by Chinese behaviour in Tibet.[18] He had sought intelligence assessments of Chinese strength in the

Aksai Chin soon after he became Army Chief in 1957. But his differences with Defence Minister Krishna Menon would spill over into assessments of the Chinese attitude. Menon resented the 'international reputation and popularity' of Thimayya[19]. When the latter argued for better defensive measures in a strategy of 'dissuasion' against the Chinese, saying that they would otherwise play 'Chinese Checkers' along the length of the border with India (because of better road communications), he was overruled by Menon who instructed that the army 'ignore China and focus on the enemy on the other side' (Pakistan). By August 1959, just as tensions along the border with China were beginning to rise alarmingly, differences between Thimayya and Menon had reached the point where the former tendered his resignation to Nehru who made a personal appeal to the General to withdraw it.

Both Menon and Nehru shared the view that there was no threat from China, militarily. It was a 'bedrock premise.'[20] This lulled the Indians into a sense of complacency and misplaced confidence that even if the Chinese were to use force in Ladakh, the defensive capabilities of the Indian military forces would be formidable. This was without any corresponding action to raise the force levels necessary to maintain such a capability. (General Thimayya's advice to the government was that 'we should look offensive only when we are capable of an offensive.' Bases along a line of defence well away from the border which would stretch Chinese supply lines in case of a conflict, as recommended by him, were never established.)[21]

At the same time, to assuage national feelings, publicly, no soft line would be taken with the Chinese, with Parliament keeping a close watch for any signs of weakness in Nehru's approach. The Prime Minister played to the gallery when he said there was presently 'no bridge between the Chinese position and ours. There is nothing to negotiate at present.'[22] Foreign Secretary Dutt was reported as telling the Americans on 16 February 1960[23] that Nehru 'did not expect anything tangible to come out of the meeting' with Zhou Enlai. The purpose of the meeting would be to ascertain first, why the Chinese had behaved in such a hostile way and second, what China 'really wants.' At best, the meeting 'might provide a basis for further talks.' On the Indian side at least, there appeared no sense of urgency about reaching a border settlement or about achieving some meeting ground as a result of the Zhou visit. From various quarters, including from President Rajendra Prasad, Nehru was receiving counsel that he should not 'capitulate' to any Chinese demands, and being reminded about the sacrifices made by India to gain its freedom from foreign occupation which should not be forgotten for a moment.

Additionally, S. Gopal, Director of the Historical Division in the Ministry of External Affairs (and later to be Nehru's biographer), had returned from London after a study of the India Office Archives and other documentary evidence on the boundary issue. Briefing Nehru on his findings, he had conveyed that India's case on the Ladakh-Xinjiang/Tibet boundary (the western sector) was as strong and justifiable as the evidence supporting her claim to a boundary along the McMahon Line in the east. Nehru's earlier 'doubts' about the western sector boundary (which he had also alluded to, publicly, including in Parliament) were eclipsed from this point. In his mind, even more from then on, 'no retraction from the notified and affirmed frontiers of India was seen as politically feasible.'[24] But, even as incensed voices in Parliament and in the public arena were talking of 'throwing' the Chinese out of Ladakh, no one in the government or outside ventured 'to even speculate on the hazards of military operations aimed at evicting the Chinese from the Aksai Chin'.[25]

In early April, the British High Commissioner in Delhi, Malcolm MacDonald, reported on a conversation he had with the Indian Finance Minister in Nehru's cabinet, Morarji Desai.[26] The latter told MacDonald that the talks with Zhou were bound to fail on the first day, and that the Chinese did not understand this. Desai said that the 'official Chinese estimate of Nehru is that he is a 'weak man' who could be talked and persuaded' by Zhou's 'charm and adroitness into a compromise agreement about the border.' But Nehru, he said, could not make any concession whatever 'in way of yielding Indian territory to China' for two reasons. Firstly, Indian parliamentary and public opinion would not permit it. If Nehru tried to cede territory to China, 'he would be put out of office as Prime Minister.' Secondly, Nehru was himself averse to any such bargain. He was 'hurt' by the Chinese attitude, partly by Zhou 'having misled him and let him down completely on the border issue, and partly by the criticisms of many of his own countrymen suggesting that he might give way weakly to the Chinese.' The Chinese were guilty of 'unvacated aggression' against India. Asked by the High Commissioner whether India would be ready to permit the Chinese to go on using the road through Ladakh, Desai said 'this would be easy' as India 'fully appreciated the importance of the road to the Chinese.' But this would have to be accomplished without any surrender of Indian sovereignty to the Chinese. Desai agreed with the High Commissioner that the Chinese were unlikely to accept such an offer and said this was why there could be no settlement of the dispute 'in the foreseeable future'. Also, nobody— neither Nehru nor his cabinet colleagues—trusted the Chinese, and they believed that even if a small concession was made, the Chinese would take it 'for the time being, only to return with more ambitious demands later on.' India was 'not prepared to let the Chinese make the Ladakh road the thin end of the wedge.' In his personal opinion, he said, the Chinese were apprehensive that India would make better progress than China, they wished to retard India's progress, and had started the frontier troubles as a means of 'diverting the Indian government's attention, energy and resources'.

Zhou Enlai was in Delhi for seven days from 19 to 25 April, 1960, accompanied by a large delegation, which included his Foreign Minister, Chen Yi, that arrived by three special aircraft. Before his departure for Delhi, he had presented a 'Plan for the Talks between the Chinese Premier and the Indian Prime

Minister on the Border Problems' to the leadership of the Chinese
Communist Party, in which the prospects for the visit were
analysed. The Premier was not confident about the full success
of the plan but he did not anticipate total failure, either. He was
hopeful that the two sides could at least arrive at an understanding
or agreement to reduce tensions.[27]

'Zhou Enlai was the least garlanded V.I.P. who visited Delhi
that spring.'[28] The atmosphere in Delhi was distinctly strained and
cool, and Zhou received a markedly restrained welcome. In his
welcome speech at the airport, Nehru referred to the events that had
given 'a shock' to the Indian people and 'imperilled relations in the
present and for the future'. Zhou was described as 'incongruously
platitudinous' in his remarks on the occasion, in an assessment by
the British High Commission in Delhi which appeared in favour
of the Indians taking a hard line on the dispute with China.[29] But
it was difficult to deny even for the Indian officials present, that
there was an air of 'serious purposefulness'[30] where the Chinese
visitors were concerned. Regrettably, as it transpired, the visit was
an exercise in futility, and marked for disaster from inception to
conclusion. The talks between the two Prime Ministers ended in
deadlock. It was a classic example of two ghost ships passing each
other in the night, on separate voyages that drew them further
apart, a case of all reason spent. Where earlier, prior to the events
of 1959, Nehru was master of his policy towards China, now
public opinion was giving him the lead.[31] In a telegram to the
Ambassador in Kathmandu, at the end of the talks, on 25 April
1960, Foreign Secretary Dutt announced, 'We have firmly rejected
all the Chinese suggestions.' He continued, 'Our impression is
that the Chinese have been impressed by the firmness of our stand
and the consistent narration of our case by our Ministers whom
they met individually.'[32] In another message to Heads of Indian
Missions on 27 April, Dutt announced that the 'views of the two
Governments remain as far apart as before' and that we have
disagreed with the Chinese stand on every single point.'[33]

This was to be the last encounter between Nehru and Zhou, the two men meeting against a background of mounting complications in the India–China relationship. In the words of Nehru's biographer, S. Gopal, they had 'so much in common— intelligence, finesse, sensitivity to wider issues; easily, at that time, the world's two most intellectual Prime Ministers'. But Zhou possessed a 'clearer idea than Nehru of where power and interest lay' and by 1960, when they met for the last time, they were 'paired antagonists locked together.'[34] Nehru and Zhou were to have seven one-to-one meetings during the visit, at the Prime Minister's official residence at Teen Murti House—away from the glare of the press, assisted only by their interpreters. The Indian Prime Minister preferred an approach of direct talks with his Chinese counterpart. Key members of his Cabinet like Home Minister G.B. Pant and Finance Minister Morarji Desai, who were strongly realist and deeply suspicious of China and Defence Minister Krishna Menon met the Chinese Premier, individually, for discussions. Nehru subsequently came under attack in Parliament, particularly for the meeting between Krishna Menon and Zhou.

Nehru also asked Swaran Singh, a senior Cabinet colleague (and not Krishna Menon) to have simultaneous talks with Foreign Minister Chen Yi who told Singh (in the face of being told that India would not compromise on its claims in Aksai Chin) that China would never accept the McMahon Line as the basis for a border settlement. 'If the Chinese recognized the Simla Convention and the McMahon Line, there would be an explosion in China. The Chinese people would not agree. Premier Zhou Enlai had no right to do so.'[35] When Singh asked Chen how the Chinese could have accepted the McMahon Line in their boundary settlement with Burma, Chen said that 'the line was agreed upon as a result of joint surveys. An agreed line similarly reached with India after taking into account the actual control and historical conditions would not necessarily mean that India would lose large parts of territory.' Burma, he said, had understood that China would not accept the McMahon Line and this had made it possible to achieve a 'settlement which was reasonable and practical.'[36] To elaborate further, Vice-Foreign Minister Zhang Hanfu told Swaran Singh that China and Burma had taken a 'realistic attitude while discussing this problem (of the McMahon Line)' and that in the agreement with Burma, no mention of the 'so-called McMahon Line has been made'. China, he said, had clarified its reservations and Burma had 'understood and sympathized with it' and it had, therefore, been easier to bring about a settlement which was 'reasonable and practical'. Zhang said, 'China did not recognize the McMahon Line and Burma understood the position and, therefore, we had a treaty of friendship.' Chen Yi rounded this off by telling Singh, 'We thank the Burmese friends for not forcing the McMahon Line. The Burmese are thankful to us for recognizing the line of actual jurisdiction.'[37]

Chen appeared to advocate a similar approach where India and China were concerned, saying that 'after we have drawn a line based on actual jurisdiction, historical data, surveys, etc. by mutual understanding, we may call it the Zhou-Nehru Line or the Peace and Friendship Line . . . We do not mean that all Tibetans must go to China. In future, Tibetans should be living on both sides of the Sino-Indian border.'[38] He referenced the purpose of the Zhou visit saying that by coming to Delhi with a large delegation, the Chinese were not asking India 'to give up any territory' and that 'otherwise, we would not have come. We have come here for the sake of friendship, and, I see that it is not possible to settle this question if we depend on archives and quote a letter here and there.'

At their very first meeting on 20 April 1960, Prime Minister Nehru informed Zhou Enlai that there was a 'great deal of perturbation and distress' caused by 'difficulties' created by the Chinese side. As far as India was concerned, her frontiers were clearly defined 'apart from a few minor questions.' For nine years, the Chinese had said 'nothing'. If they had not agreed with India, 'they should have told us so.' Nehru told Zhou that friendship with China had been the 'cornerstone' of India's foreign policy, from the beginning of her independence. The Chinese claims to Indian territory, he said, had 'produced a feeling of great shock, as happens when firm beliefs are upset suddenly.' Feelings towards the Himalayas were 'powerful' in India, and it had all along been assumed that the border would remain peaceful with 'only policemen to check the people coming in.' India could not agree with the Chinese proposition that the 'entire frontier is undefined and not delimited.' Even if the boundary was not marked on the ground, if 'delimitation can take place by definition of high mountain areas and watersheds and if it is (a) normally accepted principle of demarcation, then it is precisely defined in the past', thereby suggesting that the very fact that the boundary, as seen by India, ran along the highest Himalayan crest line or watershed, that in itself pointed to a fixed, delimited boundary.

Nehru said that as for Tibet, India had no extraterritorial interest there, these having been given up willingly after independence. 'We were merely interested in Tibet not as a government but as a people and more culturally', Nehru told Zhou. The Dalai Lama had been received with due courtesy because of the fact that he was a highly respected figure among the people of India. Zhou was not moved. His reply was that the 'activities of the Dalai Lama and his followers have far exceeded the limits of political asylum.' He maintained the line that as far as the border was concerned, modern nations needed to have boundaries 'defined in terms of latitude and longitude, but this was not done and this precisely is the situation.' On the McMahon Line, while China did not recognize it, she had not put forward territorial claims and only advocated 'maintenance of the status quo'. Zhou said that China was willing to take a 'realistic view' on this issue. As far as the western sector was concerned, no question 'had been raised in the past' and it was assumed that there would be no problem. 'New China' had 'inherited this area', and in 'the early days after the foundation of the People's Republic of China we sent troops and supplies to Tibet from Xinjiang through the Aksai Chin area.' The delineation of the western sector of the boundary had a basis, 'namely, the Karakoram watershed'. Zhou defined the 'status quo' as implying that this meant the situation 'prevailing after independence and this would also show the friendliness of our attitude.'

Zhou told Nehru that India 'had made changes in its maps' after 1947. At the time of Independence, no boundary line was shown but the 'area was shown in colors', then, 'the boundary was marked as undefined'; after 1954, however, the same boundary was shown as 'defined.' He suggested formation of a 'Joint Committee' to 'look into the material we both have' and that this 'may be useful for the sake of our friendship', and that while the work of the Committee was in progress, 'we should maintain a distance between the forces of the two sides.' Reverting to the Simla Convention and the McMahon Line, he told Nehru that it would have been better if this had 'not been brought up as a legal basis for India's claim. But the Government of India did it in the past year and that is why the problems became complicated.' This could never be accepted by China, but, 'is it impossible to settle our dispute in the eastern sector? No.' The thinking in China was 'that there is a dispute and we think that if both sides take into account not only the historical background but the actual situation, a reasonable solution is possible.' The Chinese position on the actual situation was that the McMahon Line could not be recognized, but China would not cross that line since India had already reached it, and as regards the two or three points where India had 'exceeded the McMahon Line, we are willing to maintain the status quo pending negotiations.' In seeking 'common ground' both sides must have 'common understanding' on whether the boundary was determined or delimited or not. Zhou's advice to Nehru was 'the boundary line has to be fixed by negotiations . . .

we must seek a solution which brings no defeat to any side and that it should be reasonable, equitable and friendly.'[39]

Zhou maintained, as he had done earlier during his correspondence with Nehru in 1959, that while the boundary was not formally delimited or fixed, there existed a line of actual control, and that in the eastern sector, this was the McMahon Line and in the western sector, it was the line—rather vaguely defined by him— as lying along 'the Karakoram and the Kongka Pass'. He further elaborated that by the line of actual control, he meant that 'the administrative personnel as well as patrolling troops of one side have both reached up to that line.' This, in his estimate, was the 'common ground' which could be 'considered as a basis for determining our boundary dispute.' Zhou told Nehru that the watershed principle was not the only geographical principle to be applied while determining the boundary alignment and that the principle of 'valleys' and 'mountain passes' should also apply. Further, neither side 'should put forward claims to an area which is no longer under its administrative control.' There were, of course, individual places 'which needed to be readjusted individually', although these were 'not a territorial claim'. Zhou was of the view that 'national feelings' were important, for instance, the 'deep feelings' of the Indians towards the Himalayas and the same feelings that the Chinese, particularly those in Xinjiang, towards the Karakoram. Taking a position that would be reiterated without exception by the Chinese thereafter, Zhou said that he would not talk about the area of the border west of the Karakoram Pass, 'as it involves Pakistan.'[40] According to the Chinese Premier, it was not his intention to ask the Government of India 'to entirely agree with our stand point or explanation.' He told Nehru, 'the stand and the view points on both sides as well as the facts differ greatly and, therefore, there is need for negotiation'. In both the eastern and the western sectors of the boundary, there existed 'a dispute of the same nature.'[41]

Nehru differed with Zhou, drawing a distinction between administrative activity and military patrolling, although he agreed with Zhou that 'we cannot go on arguing about this endlessly.' He repeated his previously stated position that the Chinese knew about the Indian maps and that India had expected China to raise the issue if there was objection to the boundaries shown therein, and that it was only in September 1959 that 'you told us of your objection to our maps'. He told Zhou that India had been 'led to believe all through these years that broadly speaking, our maps were acceptable to you except for minor border disputes.'[42] Drawing a distinction between the eastern and western sectors, and responding to the Chinese Premier's suggestion that patrolling of borders be stopped in order to avoid contact, he said that the 'no patrolling' regime should pose no real difficulty in the eastern sector (implying that India was already exercising jurisdiction and military patrolling and administrative presence up to its claimed international border, i.e., the McMahon Line), but it could not be the same case in the western sector. Here, the answer to avoiding conflict or contact, was not 'no patrolling' but that 'patrolling should not be done in a direction where conflict may arise.'

The grim and somber mood within the Indian leadership about China's perceived betrayal of Indian goodwill, trust, and friendship was in evidence during Zhou's other meetings, too. Vice-President Radhakrishnan said he was 'speaking more in sorrow than in anger'[43] when he told Zhou that while he was not a student of history and did not want to go into details, the important question was the fact that the two countries should be 'not just neighbours but friends' and that 'it should not matter if it was necessary to give up some territory here or there but the important thing was to bind the Indian people closer to the Chinese people.' Chinese Foreign Minister Chen Yi was in a militant mood. He told the Vice-President that both China and India had been bullied by imperialist countries; India had been bullied by just one power, but China by a number of them. China would not be bullied by imperialists but when 'our Indian friends want to bully us, then we do not know what to do.'

In a conversation with R.K. Nehru (the former Ambassador in China) on the night of 21 April, Zhou Enlai brought up the question of Tibet and the Dalai Lama. He expressed the view that the unfortunate events in bilateral relations between India and China of the last year were a 'dark cloud' that needed to be dispelled and that 'we maintain that all that has happened is not what we expected. But it was a logical outcome of the revolt in Tibet and the coming of the Dalai Lama to India.' He told R.K. Nehru that the Dalai Lama had deceived the Chinese with the three letters that he had written to them before his escape, and after his arrival in India, he had been carrying out anti-Chinese activities and encouraging the 'movement for independent Tibet, beyond the definition of political asylum'. The developments in Tibet, the Chinese Premier said, had 'a direct bearing on the border problem'. Importantly, Zhou seemed to suggest a hardening in Chinese attitude towards the border issue having been an outcome of a confluence of events—one, the Tibet revolt, and two, India 'having mentioned the Simla Convention and asked us to accept the McMahon Line and also the 1842 Treaty (Ladakh-Tibet).' He said to R.K. Nehru, 'We are not willing to accept either of them and we resent this new development.' This Indian 'demand' he said was 'both new and shocking'. However, China was 'willing to consider settling the eastern border, accept the Indian jurisdiction up to the McMahon Line and assure that we will not cross it.' But in the past two years, matters had become 'very complicated'. Non-settlement of this problem would harm both China and India, he concluded. Zhou said China considered the southern boundary (with India) as a boundary of peace. He quoted Mao to say that China's 'enemy lies in the east, and will come from the sea.' Chen Yi speaking with Swaran Singh suggested that if an overall settlement could not be reached, 'some interim arrangement should be made.' He did not elaborate.

The emphasis on the 'illegality' of the McMahon Line was emphasized by the Chinese, throughout. Chen Yi was the chief spokesman for this position. He told Swaran Singh (and his words were unequivocal in their messaging):

> Supposing the so-called McMahon Line is recognized, that would mean that we would recognize that McMahon had the right not only to delimitate (sic) the boundary between China and India but also the boundary between Inner and Outer Tibet. We have no reactionary words as Inner and Outer Tibet. We have only provincial boundaries between Sichuan, Tibet, Yunnan, Qinghai and Xinjiang. The Tibetan reactionary elements have an idea of 'Greater Tibet'. [If this happened] about one-fourth of the total Chinese area would be handed over to the Dalai Lama. Our non-recognition of the Simla Convention and the McMahon Line should not be misunderstood as our having any intention of making territorial claims over India.[44]

This line was repeated by the Chinese to many of his Indian interlocutors during the visit, including the Finance Minister Morarji Desai. To the latter, Zhou's words were: '(while not recognizing the McMahon Line) *we accept your jurisdiction and have no territorial claims south of the Line* (italics added)'.[45] Desai asserted that China must withdraw troops before talks could begin. When Zhou complained about 'political' activities by the Dalai Lama, the Finance Minister said, 'not so gently, that Zhou Enlai was being unjust. The Dalai Lama was not preparing to march into Tibet.' There were heated words exchanged about the campaign in each country against the other. The meeting was acrimonious[46].

On the recommendation of Prime Minister Nehru, Zhou Enlai met both Home Minister Govind Pant and Defence Minister Krishna Menon. The first meeting with Krishna Menon lasted two hours—there was a dinner conversation between the two ('informal and old style' in Menon's description to Nehru)—and a further meeting on 22 April at a private dinner hosted by

Menon at his residence. The Defence Minister also met Chen Yi on 23 April for a meeting of almost two and a half hours, and they met again 'for some ninety minutes' on 24 April. Krishna Menon was seen as an advocate of a give-and-take, negotiated settlement on the boundary issue with China, or 'horse trading' as he put it, but it is not known whether he discussed the contours of any such 'deal' with his Chinese interlocutors.[47]

Krishna Menon recorded a fourteen-page note[48] on his meeting with Zhou Enlai on 20 April, and also a brief summation of his conversation with the Chinese Premier at the official banquet the same day. There is no record of his purported third meeting with Zhou or his conversations with Chen Yi. His lengthy note on the first meeting does not contain any substantive detail. Menon seems to have followed the line taken by Nehru and the rest of the cabinet, speaking of the 'deep sense of shock' that India had suffered, 'not a shock of fear but of friendship outraged.' Zhou, too, repeated the Chinese position on both the McMahon Line and the Aksai Chin road. On Tibet, he said that while China did not object to the grant of political asylum to the Dalai Lama, it was 'shocked with the reception and the treatment given to the Dalai Lama and that the Dalai Lama was using India as his base of operations and maligning China.' According to Menon, Zhou 'spoke, I thought, with some feeling on this matter and gave the impression that the Chinese view was that the Dalai Lama was functioning as a great propaganda centre.' He 'constantly referred to this as an irritant.' He was also concerned 'about a considerable amount of talk against China in India.' But he 'expressed both in words and in his countenance a very genuine friendship and admiration about Nehru,' and 'to find a way out, something about sincere desires and an attempt to place things in what they regard as a proper perspective.'

Menon told Zhou that India knew where 'our boundaries were and so did the world. The Himalayas were the boundary of India. How could we escape this fact?' The situation on the border had not been caused by India who 'had no troops' in these areas (at the time when the incidents of violence and confrontation had occurred), but had been 'an initiative' of China's, and therefore China had to restore confidence in the relationship. But Menon also came away with the impression that in the eastern sector of the border, the Chinese position was 'more or less to let things be and to obtain some definition of frontiers.' Zhou told Menon that he had 'come with a very sincere desire to settle matters and we must find a settlement and should not leave things for a long time.' Menon told him that no Indian government could make compromises with regard to Indian sovereignty and territory. A 'repair' to Indian 'injury' was required, he stressed. The essential factor was to achieve a 'meeting of minds'. In the informal dinner conversation with Menon, Zhou spoke of finding 'principles for a settlement' and appeared to give the impression of 'trying to discover whether we could find some basis.'[49]

It is beyond the realm of possibility to speculate whether an agreement or solution to the boundary dispute could have been reached during the Zhou visit. Yet, the records make clear that the Chinese seemed to still consider a solution possible. They had come to Delhi to negotiate and not just to talk. Their opposition to the McMahon Line may have been unrelenting, but obversely they had also not rejected the reality of administrative and military presence that had come to define actual control of the border areas by India and China. They were in a probing mode; theirs was a gambit, testing the mood and the stance of the Indians, and they encountered seeming rejection. Nehru, in the words of veteran diplomat K.P.S. Menon,

> did not assert himself vis-à-vis Parliament and vis-à-vis what we regard as public opinion. Members of Parliament or some of them took a heroic posture, that not an inch of our territory should be surrendered and that sort of thing. But we lacked the wherewithal to back up such demands. Actually, the people

who talked loudest against any kind of solution were the people who were most emphatically against Panditji [who] took the voice of these people to be the voice of the public. After all, what is public opinion? George Kennan once said 'Public opinion is the opinion which is manufactured by some politicians, journalists and publicity-hunters of all kinds'. If at that time, Panditji [Nehru] had put his foot down, we could have had a fair solution of our frontier problem with China.[50]

As far as the Chinese 'barter' offer, where 'Chinese claims to NEFA would be abandoned in return for India's foregoing any claims to the Aksai Chin and all other parts of the Western Sector already under Chinese control'[51], Zhou Enlai was to make at least two public references to it: in a written statement issued to the press and while speaking at a press conference in New Delhi on 25 April. 'Six Points' of purported proximity between the Indian and Chinese positions were articulated in the statement, but Zhou—ever adept at hedging—spoke elliptically and with caution, ambivalence replacing the categorical in the manner in which he put these points across. India was, in any case, unwilling to accept negotiations which implied that the entire length of the border was not delimited, or defined by custom and tradition. However, it was open to a discussion about the entire boundary, its historical background, and a bilateral settlement with China, especially since the Chinese occupation of Indian-claimed territory in the Aksai Chin needed attention. 'Barter' and 'horse-trading' were unacceptable, Nehru said. There was a profound sense of injury and grievance on the Indian side. Where he had previously appeared to consider permutations for a border settlement, the Kongka Pass incident of October 1959 had destroyed such prospects and 'Nehru's rejection of the Chinese position during the April talks brought to a final decision the Indian process of considering alternatives'.[52]

Basically, discussions to consider these alternatives had been ongoing between Nehru, some of his senior cabinet colleagues, and a few officials in the Ministry of External Affairs. A 'compromise' solution that was sought to be achieved 'would not involve formal relinquishment of territory'. As earlier stated, this was elaborated by Morarji Desai in a conversation with the UK High Commissioner, Malcolm MacDonald on 5 April when he said that India 'was prepared' to allow the Chinese continued use of the Aksai Chin area, considering the importance of the road, but this would have to be done 'without any surrender of Indian sovereignty over the region.'[53] Vice-President Radhakrishnan also disclosed to the High Commissioner in a later conversation, that India would want China to accept the McMahon Line. The way forward, Radhakrishnan said, would be for 'the Chinese to concede to us the shadow whilst we concede to them the substance' of Indian sovereignty in Ladakh.[54] Krishna Menon himself told the press a few years later that 'all sorts of ideas' had been discussed internally on the Indian side. In his words, 'Actually the Prime Minister and I had talks on what could be done but other people, some of them senior men, although they did not veto it, said, 'why all this now, we will see when it comes'. It was not understood that in diplomacy if you take the initiative, your action has far greater effect. Perhaps they thought it was not necessary.'[55] Given Zhou's insistence during the talks that China had all along been in physical and effective control of the contested territory in Ladakh, and seeking a barter where China recognized Indian claims and presence in the eastern sector in return for India recognizing Chinese control in Ladakh—an idea that was rejected by India—the proposal outlined by Desai and Radhakrishnan, was a non-starter. In Menon's words, 'I believe that in 1960 China had made it very difficult for those of us who wanted to do anything.'[56] Apart from parliamentary and public opinion against Nehru's China policy—and the perceived 'deceit' in Chinese actions—by 1960, any barter of territory with China would have proved an almost insurmountable task given that in March 1960, the Supreme Court of India had ruled in the Berubari case that would have entailed transfer of territory to East Pakistan, stating that 'the executive did not have the authority to cede or accept territory' without seeking an amendment to the Constitution. Such an amendment would have entailed approval of two-thirds majority in Parliament and at least half of the 14 state legislatures.[57]

After the talks between the two Prime Ministers had concluded, the definition of outcomes itself became a subject of considerable argumentative discussion between the senior officials of the two delegations. The Indian preference was to solely focus on the two leaders having agreed that the officials of the two sides would meet to examine the documentary material on which each country based their case. The officials would then draw up a report for submission to the two governments which could reflect points of agreement; it would also list the points where there was no agreement which would require further clarification and examination by both sides. The Chinese wished also that where necessary, the two sides dispatch personnel to the border areas to carry out surveys so as to record areas of agreement and disagreement on which proposals could be made to the two governments, separately or jointly. The Chinese suggested that this group of officials be called a Sino-Indian Boundary Working Group. The terms of reference for this group, they added, could be the 'points' of 'proximity', as detailed by Zhou Enlai. These were: (1) The boundary between the two countries had not been delimited and that the two parties have a dispute over the boundary; (2) There exists between the two countries a line of actual control up to which each side exercises actual control; (3) In determining the boundary between the two countries certain geographical principles, such as, watersheds, river valleys, mountain passes, etc., will be equally applicable to all sectors of the boundary; (4) The settlement of the boundary question between the two countries must take into consideration the national feelings of the two peoples towards the Himalayas and the Karakoram mountains; (5) In the process of settling the boundary question between the two countries through consultations, both parties will abide by the line of actual control and not raise territorial claims as pre-requisite conditions. However, individual adjustments may be made.[58]

These suggestions were not accepted by the Indian side led by Foreign Secretary Dutt, in line with the position taken by Prime Minister Nehru himself in talks with the Chinese Premier. To accept that the boundary with China had not been delimited across its length would have been tantamount to accepting that there was a 'dispute' with China on the issue.[59] The Indians had all along maintained that for most of the length of the boundary, there was really nothing to discuss in terms of delimitation as this boundary was already determined by treaty, tradition, custom, and usage. Secondly, accepting the existence of a line of actual control would have implied that India would have to tacitly acknowledge the gains made by China in her encroachments across India's defined boundary on maps, in the western sector deep into Ladakhi territory. Thirdly, India was firm in its view that in a Himalayan boundary, only the watershed principle— that of the highest watershed—should be applied to define the boundary line. This had key implications for the interpretation of the McMahon Line, as modern aerial surveys had helped describe and delineate this line along the highest watershed, removing the vagueness and lack of granular data in McMahon's description of the line in the small-scale map of 1914. Acceptance of mountain passes and river valleys as terms of definition were unacceptable, given the primacy of the principle of the watershed, as India saw it. Fourthly, the reference by China to the Karakoram mountains was seen as an attempt to secure recognition of a boundary claim in the western sector that aligned itself on the Karakoram Range, including the Aksai Chin within its remit, and important features like the Depsang Plains close to the Karakoram Pass, the Chang Chenmo Valley, and the important Pangong Tso Lake, and pushing the alignment west from the Lanak La to Kongka La Pass.

There were differences between the two groups of officials on whether the statement issued at the end of the talks should be titled 'Joint Statement' or 'Joint Communique'[60]—the Indian preference being for the latter. Foreign Secretary Dutt was also clearly reluctant to accept Chinese suggestions of inclusion of such phrases as the talks having promoted 'mutual understanding' between the two sides even while mentioning the existence of differences on the boundary question and that discussions should facilitate the exploration of 'avenues' for a 'reasonable settlement'. In Dutt's view, it was 'too early, at least on the results present of the present talks to find a reasonable settlement of the boundary question.'[61] To this, Assistant Minister Qiao Guanhua's reply was that 'it is necessary to mention here the prospect of a reasonable settlement. We do not consider it too early to mention it. We never take that kind of pessimistic attitude.'[62]

In the event, a Joint Communique was issued at the end of the talks between the two Prime Ministers on 25 April. The document made reference to the purpose of Premier Zhou's visit being to discuss 'certain differences relating to the border areas'. It stated that the two leaders had explained their respective stands and that this had led to 'greater understanding of the views of the two Governments but the talks did not result in resolving the differences that had arisen.' It had therefore been decided that 'further examination should take place by officials of the two sides of the factual material in the possession of both the Governments.' Historical documents, records, accounts, maps, and other material relevant to the boundary question in the possession of each side would be examined, checked, and studied, and a report drawn up for submission to the two governments, listing the points of agreement and disagreement, 'or which should be examined more fully and clarified.' During this period of examination of material, 'every effort should be made by the parties to avoid friction and clashes in the border areas.'[63] One 'gaping hole' was the absence of reference in the document to the Panchsheel/Five Principles of Peaceful Coexistence.[64]

At his press conference during which he fielded questions from the Indian and foreign press, Zhou Enlai reiterated the

Chinese opposition to the McMahon Line with the familiar coda that territorial claims had not been put forward by China in this context—which he claimed was an attitude of 'understanding and conciliation'. Because of this, he added, 'the dispute regarding the Eastern sector has become a smaller one'[65]. He contrasted this with the situation in the western sector where he said that China had asked India not to cross the line up to which 'China has exercised jurisdiction to which the Indian Government had not entirely agreed'. In his view, therefore, 'there is this bigger dispute with regard to the Western sector of the boundary.'[66] He expressed the hope that after the officials of the two sides had studied the factual material, the 'Indian Government will take an attitude similar to that which the Chinese Government has taken in the Eastern sector, that is to say, an attitude of mutual accommodation. In this way, we believe settlement of the question can be reached.'[67] Zhou put across these proposals in a 'cautious' and 'elliptical' way, perhaps signalling also that they were not completely set, and could, if the situation changed for the worse in bilateral relations, be withdrawn at Chinese will.[68] It can be construed that Zhou was alluding to implicit acceptance of the McMahon Line when he suggested that territorial claims should not be put forward regarding areas no longer under administrative control of each side. But Zhou was also careful to say, especially after seeing the reaction from Nehru, that no preconditions could be attached to these suggestions, that nothing could be taken for granted.[69]

Very soon after the departure of the Zhou for Kathmandu, Nehru was facing Parliament. He distanced himself from the points of 'proximity' outlined by Zhou at this press conference. He conceded that there were 'disputes' between the two sides, by which he meant that there were pockets of dispute but did not concede that the boundary itself was in dispute. He did not agree with the point that geographical principles like river valleys and mountain passes should apply to the definition of the boundary in addition to watersheds, saying that the latter principle was very important, while 'river valleys, etc.' did 'not carry us anywhere.' As far as 'national feelings' of the Indians to the Himalayas and of the Chinese to the Karakoram were concerned, he had no objection. The point regarding adherence to the Line of Actual Control pending settlement, and not putting forward territorial claims, he said was 'an odd way of putting it'. Nehru also said that he did not agree to the suggestion that both sides should refrain from patrolling along all sectors of the boundary. Also, during the talks, he said that 'basic disagreement about historical and actual facts came up again and again.'[70]

This rejection couched in candid terms by the Indian Prime Minister, occasioned an adverse reaction almost instantaneously from the Chinese. On arrival in Kathmandu, Zhou commented that the statement made by Nehru was 'not so friendly towards China.' Nehru had not reacted in such a fashion 'face to face, but as soon as we left, he attacked the Chinese government as aggressor. This is not an attitude to take towards guests. We were very much distressed by such an attitude.'[71] There was never any acknowledgement by China of the challenges facing Nehru in navigating the public space of political and popular opposition to Chinese 'aggression'—as it was perceived to be—in Ladakh. In fact, as the discussions in Parliament of the Chinese Premier's visit gathered tempo, there were calls from the parties outside the government to secure 'early vacation of Chinese aggression'. Atal Bihari Vajpayee of the Jana Sangh criticized the Prime Minister for 'falling into the trap of prolonged talks.' He said that while he did not want war, he did not rule it out 'as a means to safeguard the nation's welfare and integrity, which would be welcomed by the entire nation except the Communists.'[72] Most of the political opposition, barring the communists, urged toughness of approach in policy towards China, wanting effective steps to be taken to drive away Chinese intruders from Indian soil. 'Parliament's hostility to any kind of negotiations with China until it vacated all Indian territory occupied by it, remained unchanged.'[73] There was also criticism of the government for having supported China's membership of the United Nations, and for not having supported the efforts by some countries to seek condemnation by the United Nations of human rights violations in Tibet. The Government's alleged unpreparedness in defence matters also came under the scanner—with Krishna Menon as Defence Minister being the target of much suspicion and adverse comment.

Nehru's loyalty to Krishna Menon has over the years been a subject of prolonged scrutiny. He saw Menon as one who helped elucidate issues which required such illumination and better understanding. He had also gauged the depths of Menon's frail emotional balance, his insecurity and 'frightful' sensitivity which required him to be treated 'gently and understandingly.'[74] For Nehru, the strategist, Krishna Menon was the 'rationalizer and operator.' He valued Menon's contributions to the national cause in the pre-independence years when the latter was in London. For him, Menon supplied 'intellectual stimulation, intellectual fire.'[75]

In July 1960, General Thimayya in a conversation[76] with UK High Commissioner MacDonald said: 'the Prime Minister's loyalty to Mr. Krishna Menon springs from the fact that Mr. Menon is his only colleague with whom he can discuss intelligently international affairs' and that Nehru was 'determined not to lose his colleague', despite the latter's unpopularity with other cabinet colleagues and a controversial image as being pro-communist. The Prime Minister had even defended Menon when he said that the Indian forces were 'not adequate' to take on the Chinese. Speaking of the situation on the frontier with China, the General said that the 'military defences of India' were greatly improved. In Ladakh, the 'build-up south of the area now occupied by the Chinese' was proceeding apace and had already 'reached a strength which is reassuringly formidable'. The two weak spots were Nepal and Bhutan, and one of the difficulties was 'Mr. Krishna Menon's dislike of the Bhutanese and the Bhutanese' intense dislike of him.' Another difficulty was that the 'present

Indian cabinet does not look far ahead about frontier problems, but is inclined to deal with situations as and when they arise.' The Prime Minister had himself said to Thimayya that there would be no danger 'whatsoever' of Chinese military action against Nepal.

As far as Sikkim was concerned, the General said that the Political Officer in Sikkim, Apa Pant, was pursuing a 'very shortsighted policy', opposing the Royal House, encouraging political agitation within the Opposition, and undermining the loyalty of the people of Sikkim to their government. The ruling establishment in Sikkim, he said, 'hated' Mr Pant. Thimayya admitted in answer to a query from MacDonald that it would require 'a major military operation' to push the Chinese out of the Aksai Chin. MacDonald noted: 'He had evidently written that off. He said that if the Indians had been alert five years ago in occupying that region themselves, they would have prevented the Chinese ever getting in. But now it is too late.' This military assessment conveyed by Thimayya was a sober one, even as in Parliament and the press, the calls to 'vacate Chinese aggression' grew louder and Prime Minister Nehru became increasingly isolated and besieged by such opinion.

The contestation between India and China over their Inner Asian frontiers had become graphically evident following the events of 1959 and 1960, as we have outlined. As the two newly established countries sought to secure their claimed borders through the 1950s, frontier zones had been replaced by linear border alignments as outlined on the maps of each nation. In the absence of mutual agreement between the two, the differences over boundary claims were only bound to intensify. It has been said that the 'Sino-Indian boundary dispute must be regarded as the culmination of a long process of boundary-making, the concluding act of an ancient political drama in which the behavior of the actors is conditioned not only by the final stage setting but by the plot and action of earlier scenes.'[77] In the early stages, in the imperial phase of Chinese history and during British colonial domination of India, frontiers had been 'broad and zonal'; until in the nineteenth century, rival empires began to jostle for position in these areas.

The British never finalized boundary arrangements with China. The 'God-given boundary' across the Himalaya—'the vast, impressive and stupendous frontier'—made precise boundary delimitation an almost impossible task. And China had been a militarily weak, indecisive power through this phase of history. The British had instead preferred the 'screen' of buffer states and administered tribal territories along the Inner Asian frontier. However, the effect of this policy was 'fossilizing the structure of the frontier zone for over half a century, thus reducing the force of direct contact and the necessity of boundary-making. The Inner Asian frontiers of India remained frontiers rather than boundaries.'[78] Post-Independence and liberation, both India and China respectively advanced into these buffer zones. In India, the entry of Chinese forces into Tibet sounded the warning for speedy action to secure the northeastern sector of the frontier with China in 1950–51. China, on its part, secured access into Tibet from Xinjiang through the Aksai Chin plateau—in a significant erosion of Indian claims—thus securing a strategic advantage for itself in the Ladakh and Kashmir region of the subcontinent. A turbulent frontier had come into existence, and that turbulence persists until the present day.

It has been argued that it is easy to fault Nehru for his lack of flexibility in approaching the boundary problem during the talks with Zhou in 1960, in the 'flat glare of hindsight'.[79] The decision to table the White Papers, as they were published, in Parliament exposed the country to the tangled web of the dispute, and all concerted and clearly well-intentioned attempts by the Prime Minister to explain the complexities of the situation to opinion makers came to naught. The Chinese propaganda machine and its attacks on him alienated the Prime Minister and deepened the chill in bilateral relations. Any 'give' on the dispute, or acceptance of the principle of 'barter', had too high a political price as mounting public opposition against any show of flexibility blocked the way forward. Where at one stage, Nehru gave the impression that there existed some ambiguity and haziness about the Indian claim to Aksai Chin, after the historical evidence had been collated, he dropped all references to such ambiguity and was convinced of the strength of the Indian case put together as a result of the research done by S. Gopal (Head of the MEA's Historical Division) in 1959–60. He also took the view that Chinese claims regarding their boundary alignment seemed weak and unsupported by solid historical evidence, and were being advanced only by stealth and military occupation.

The stage for an ultimate, full-scale military showdown with China was being set but it was not a scenario that was anticipated in Delhi. War with China, for Nehru, seemed unthinkable—it was not what his policy approach of cementing understanding and coexistence with Beijing had been about all these years. Further, he had always dismissed the possibility of any Chinese logistical and military capacity to launch such a conflict against India from the highlands of Tibet. In retrospect, history can teach us many lessons, but the light of experience is often that 'lantern on the stern, which shines only on the waves behind.'[80] A fateful two years beckoned, as Zhou Enlai left Delhi in April 1960. Convinced of the correctness and sanctity of India's approach to the boundary question with China, Nehru believed that any accommodation of China's position did not arise—all that was necessary was to persuade the Chinese about the validity of the Indian case. It was a flawed assessment, further hamstrung by the growing stridency of voices in the Opposition and within public opinion that were against any give and take on the issue. A Chinese government note of 31 July 1960 reviewing Zhou's visit concluded that India was disinterested in a border settlement and that it wanted to provoke incidents on the border to incite the Chinese into a reaction. It concluded that the Indian Government was 'afraid' of Indian public opinion who were complaining about their 'own government's inability' and that the latter was 'facing up difficulties and resembles a mother who lacks milk . . .'[81]

15

The Decline

The Himalayas have always dominated Indian life as they have dominated the Indian landscape. The stirring of the Indian spirit was directed towards these fastnesses, Shiva was the blue-necked, snow-crowned mountain God; Parvati was the spring-maiden, daughter of the Himalaya; Ganga was her elder sister; and Meru, Vishnu's mountain, was the pivot of the universe. The Himalayan shrines are still the goal of every Hindu pilgrim.

—Historical Background of
The Himalayan Frontier of India[1]

The leader of the Indian team at the Officials' Talks with China, which were held between June and December 1960 in Beijing, Delhi and Yangon, was Jagat Mehta. He was to reminisce years later how the assignment entrusted to the team by the government was 'impossible not only because of the chasm of differences but because, at least the Indian side, was hemmed in by imposed political constraints.'[2] These were talks, not negotiations, and the end goal was to elucidate each side's positions, not to arrive at any set of principles on the basis of evidence presented that could form the basis for political-level discussions leading to a mutually acceptable settlement. It was certainly not to seek common ground for negotiation. The consensus within the Indian establishment was that their case on the boundary question with China was strong and infallible: that China had aggressed into sovereign Indian territory; that China had to vacate its occupation of this territory (the Aksai Chin); and that India could hold to this firm position, prevent and withstand further Chinese ingress into Indian territory, without any, or at least negligible, risk of Chinese reaction in the form of full-scale armed conflict across the border.

Numerous theoretical reasons for the Indian attitude have been advanced over the years. They included that India (and for that matter, China) would not accept the national humiliation of losing territory that it regarded as sovereign and integral to its 'sacred' geo-body, especially after having been subject to colonial occupation for three centuries; the loss of territory during the Partition of 1947, as well as the Pakistani occupation of a section of Jammu and Kashmir (the 'cartography of national humiliation'[3]). To this belief was added the deeply-held conviction that the Indian nation had existed much before British structuring of the subcontinent through conquest and colonial-era cartography, and therefore, India's modern boundaries were not an 'imperial' legacy as the Chinese claimed.[4] At the same time, independent India had come to regard her boundaries as linear (as the Survey of India maps showed), replacing the frontier 'zones' of yore where peoples had come and gone without joining crossing points into regular borderlines.

A similar argument regarding the sense of 'victimhood' in both India and China—stemming from 'past suffering and anti-colonialist credentials' and linking disputed territories to past history—is made by Manjari Chatterjee Miller in her 2013 study[5]. Miller terms this phenomenon as 'Post-Imperial Ideology' or PII and attributes the actions of both India and China leading up to and during the conflict of 1962 as stemming from this cause. The same ideology, it is explained, led to the two countries competing with each other to be key players in the newly decolonized community of nations in Asia and Africa, and resulted in Nehru and Zhou Enlai each claiming their countries were victims of imperialism, and denying they were making territorial claims, saying their claimed boundaries had always been sacrosanct parts of their nations, historically.

One recent study speaks[6] also of the 'reputational imperative' for Nehru, and for India, as not being seen as having succumbed to their own weakness before a stronger power (China), and giving up sovereign territory and thereby violating the country's territorial integrity. The scope for negotiating flexibility had become further constricted by 1959 with the decision of the Prime Minister to release all documents and missives relating to the boundary as exchanged with China. Public opinion had been 'educated' but not enlightened. It now saw the case entirely through the prism of nationalistic fervour against China for having betrayed 'trust' and 'friendship,' and therefore felt the need to protect fixed, pre-determined boundaries against Chinese transgression and occupation. The White Papers thus became a testament to reference Chinese culpability rather than a means to reckon more deeply and questioningly, the whys and wherefores on how the dispute arose in the first place.

At the same time, the government had no clear solutions as to how the territory occupied by China was to be recovered. Writing to the Burmese leader U Nu in 1960, Nehru said, 'I do not myself see any kind of settlement which we can accept, though we shall work for it. The Chinese have dug in their toes, and we are not prepared to accept this position at any cost. Indeed, no Government in India will accept this position now or in the foreseeable future'.[7] Nehru wished to avoid 'cognitive failure' on the issue; he felt strongly on the matter, but he seemed increasingly torn between the correctness of India's case and the contrasting imperative of not resorting to a military solution to regain lost territories and losing himself in a 'sea of hatred'.[8]

When the two sides met for talks between the officials after Zhou Enlai's mission to Delhi in April 1960, there appeared little room for 'meaningful negotiations', as Jagat Mehta was to note.[9] 'The essence of the Chinese case was that a boundary line had no validity if it was not jointly surveyed, described, or negotiated—in other words, formally delimited; for India, the traditional limits were declared as clear and publicly affirmed in an official map.' This was a yawning chasm between the two sides in their fundamental approach to the problem. As affirmed in the Joint Communique issued at the end of the Zhou visit, the officials of the two sides were to 'examine, check and study all historical documents, records, accounts, maps and other material relevant to the boundary question, on which each side relied in support of its stand, and draw up a report for submission to the two governments.' There was no room for 'an iota of discretion'[10] here, or, give and take. While the Indians were operating under clear political constraints and answerable to parliamentary and public opinion for every move made, the Chinese came from a system of government not democratically accountable to its people or to a probing, argumentative legislature. The Indian approach to boundary-making—while understanding the concept of frontier zones rather than linear boundaries straddling the Karakoram and the Himalaya—had thought it eminently justifiable that the watershed principle, historical evolution and evidence of administrative jurisdiction (even if sporadic in areas of the Aksai Chin and Ladakh's frontier marches with Xinjiang) should legitimately form the basis for linear boundaries drawn on official maps. The Chinese had little to show of contact or historical familiarity with the area when compared to the rulers of Kashmir. Mehta, citing Francis Watson's book *Frontiers of China*,[11] points to the Chinese predilection to looking down on neighbours from a high frontier, which explains how, from the

Qing dynasty onwards, and continuing with the Nationalists and the Communists, old maps of China—even as late at 1954—showed Nepal, Bhutan, Sikkim, northern Burma, and Arunachal Pradesh as part of the Chinese domains. In the absence of consultation with China, the Indians on their part moved ahead with a linear definition of external boundaries with their largest neighbour, and there was little scope thereafter for any modification of this definition given the constitutional 'rigidities' that disallowed such modification.

The officials of India and China had a deadline of six months in which to complete their 'joint' report. The entire length of the boundary between India and China had to be covered. The scope and intensity of the assignment was unprecedented. The Indian delegation was headed by Jagat Mehta, with S. Gopal as deputy head, and including boundary experts like T.S. Murty and G.N. Rao. V.V. Paranjpe with his formidable language skills as a Chinese-speaker, was interpreter. The pace of discussions was intense. But that the crisis in relations would eventually terminate in conflict between the two countries was unforeseen at the time. The report of the discussions though released in a single volume, had distinct Indian and Chinese submissions of evidence put forward by each side to support their claims covering the eastern, middle and western sectors of the boundary.

There was scarcely any meeting ground between the two sides in the description of their boundary lines and claims. The Indians put forward a precise, point-to-point definition of the boundary shown on their maps, while the Chinese description was much more vague—confirming, in Mehta's view, that they 'were not really familiar with the southern limits of what was considered China.'[12] S. Gopal, as the lead on the historical research that marshalled the evidence to support the Indian case, had strengthened the Indian policy brief. It may, as some have argued, have been a maximalist stand, but in consonance with Gopal's acknowledged reputation as a historian, it was impeccably researched, a focused marshalling of fact, and imbued with certitude. It was a task, as a later historian, Srinath Raghavan, put it, that stood at the intersection between history and foreign policy-making—where frontier history met foreign policy. Under Gopal's stewardship, the Historical Division of the Ministry of External Affairs which did the research for the Officials Talks of 1960 with China, rose 'to the peak of its performance and influence'[13]. Gopal's contributions on the historical inputs provided on the boundary question with China, 'throughout remained crucial'.[14] This required a mastery of fact and argument, and this scholarship was the progenitor of an academic industry of sorts, globally, on the Sino-Indian boundary question in the years that followed.

The Indian case, as summarized in the concluding section of the six-hundred page Report of the Officials (which was approved by Nehru personally in its draft form in his study at his residence at Teen Murti House, 'next to the original Tang Dynasty horse presented to him by Zhou Enlai during 1956–7'[15] and presented to Parliament on 14 February 1961[16]) argued that boundaries, 'unless artificially altered by force or agreement' were charted across natural features like mountain barriers, which was why the Indian alignment was based on the highest Himalayan watershed. Geography had shaped history and cultural and ethnic divisions along this frontier, and gradually these had evolved into linear boundaries. The McMahon Line, for instance, was not an artificially imposed one, but 'ran along the natural traditional divide between Tibet in the north' and the Indian and Burmese territories to the south of the water parting. In the western sector, as Mehta notes, the evidence was 'comparatively meagre'; the fact was that this—the Aksai Chin—was a barren, uninhabited area and over history, it had been 'left as a no man's land'. But evidence, on the other hand, as asserted by China, that it had been under the control of Xinjiang, was non-existent. In the nineteenth century, the Dogra rulers of Kashmir had maintained administrative posts there. Until 1950, there had been a 'total absence of historical control' by China in the area.

The Indian arguments supporting the McMahon Line rested on the assumption that in 1914 Tibet had treaty-making powers separate from China, and that between 1911 and 1950 Tibet had functioned independently. In 1954, India had recognized Tibet as a part of China and in the 1960 talks while asserting Indian territorial claims south of the McMahon Line, India did not repudiate the agreement of 1954. The argument put forward by India rested on the fact that Tibet had attended the 1914 Conference with China and British India on the basis of the former's acceptance of Tibet's full powers to participate in the meeting as a separate and distinct entity. Therefore, Tibet had acted within its rights and powers to conclude an agreement with Britain in regard to the boundary across the Himalayas with northeastern India. The evidence put forward by the Chinese regarding territorial claims south of the McMahon Line was meagre, although emphasis was placed on the Tawang Monastery and its lands (all areas south of the McMahon Line) as having been under Tibetan influence and 'control' until 1950 by virtue of connections (of a theological and revenue-collecting kind) with the great monastery of Drepung in Tibet. On the other hand, the North East Frontier Agency (NEFA), as Arunachal Pradesh was then called, is mentioned in the Indian Constitution, and in 1950 Nehru had in Parliament asserted that McMahon Line alignment constituted the international boundary of India. The Chinese stand on this same boundary had remained 'evasive, ambivalent and deliberately misleading'[17] in those early years. The Chinese claim was contrary to the spirit of mutual confidence and respect for territorial integrity which was integral to the Panchsheel principles.

While the Indian officials could take satisfaction from their presentation of their case in a detailed, comprehensive and well-argued manner, Mehta observes that in their 'heart of hearts' they hardly believed that these talks 'could lead to an acceptable denouement'. For them 'it was an exercise in advocacy in defence of the position already taken by the government when the crisis was precipitated by Chinese insensitivity to India's political ethos.'[18] The fact was that the 'Sino-Indian boundary had become a major political problem.'[19] There was, however, a small silver lining— during the period of these talks from June to December 1960, the boundary had remained quiet without even a single border incident. On the report itself, *The Hindu* newspaper summed up the general response in the public space with its observation that 'the irresistible conclusion that will be drawn from any reader of the officials' report . . . is that the prospect of a settlement either in the immediate or even the distant future is indeed very, very dim . . . Neither the present Chinese temper nor the atmosphere in India lends encouragement to the prospect of another round of talks at Prime Ministers' level in the foreseeable future.'[20]

Yet what exercised public opinion was a different development. In June 1960, the Chinese pulled a proverbial rabbit out of the hat when they produced a new map which added 'two thousand square miles of Ladakh to their territory.'[21] Chinese Foreign Minister Chen Yi, when asked about the discrepancy, clearly dissembled when he 'stated the boundary was the same as on their earlier map published in 1956'[22]—an untrue statement. In fact, during the Officials' Talks, the Indian side was to draw attention to the 'bewildering variety of alignments shown by official Chinese maps published in the course of a decade' which led to the conclusion that 'one could not be certain as to what was the alignment claimed by China, let alone be convinced that it had a traditional and customary basis over a period of centuries.'[23]

China did not publish the report until April 1962. As a compilation of the evidence put forward by both sides, the report was 'an extraordinary compilation of historical and geographical data which needed a great deal of specialized knowledge to make any responsible evaluation.'[24] The Indian case had been meticulously prepared, and the evidence was carefully documented and impressive. The Chinese, expectedly, given the spotty nature of their evidence, were quick to use the taunt of imperialism to label the Indian documentation, ignoring the fact that 'the advance of Chinese imperialism was an important motivating force in the formulation of British policy'.[25] The containment of Russia had led to British interest in the Karakoram mountains, as had the containment of China having led to the exploration of the hill tracts in the Northeast and the resultant McMahon Line. In answer to the Chinese critique that the Indian arguments were to be seen through the prism of imperialism, historian and member of the Indian delegation, S. Gopal said firmly:

> We hold, as we have again repeatedly stated, no brief for imperialism . . . in considering the boundary alignment it is not necessary to consider or analyse the motive of the past unless of course there is definite evidence to prove that it has a bearing on the alignment under consideration . . . we . . . have always tried to concentrate on the facts and to deal with them objectively even when they concern the period of British imperialism in India. . . . I am glad that Director Yang [his Chinese counterpart] agrees with me that not every Englishman is an imperialist. This only proves my point that it is not sufficient to state or to prove a general motivation of British imperialism. What is necessary for our purpose is to show that every particular individual who has been cited has been describing the alignment in a particular manner because he was motivated by imperialist intentions . . .To rebut our evidence it would be necessary to prove what the Chinese side said that every Englishman who confirmed the traditional Indian alignment was therefore an imperialist.[26]

The Chinese elided the fact that Imperial (Qing) China's claims to Tibet and occupation of Xinjiang were not dissimilar to the actions of the Western colonial powers' in various parts of

Asia and Africa, or of Tsarist Russia in regard to Central Asia. Rationalizing this later, as bringing the 'five races' under one flag (*Wu Zu* 五祖) was a convenient fig-leaf, used even by Sun Yat-sen and the nationalists. The imperial periphery required political domination in this scheme of things.

The conclusion of scholars assessing the report soon after its publication was that 'the case the Chinese presented was a shoddy piece of work, betraying—if only to those in a position to consult the sources cited—a fundamental contempt for evidence.'[27] The presentation did not do them any credit. The question that arises is why they agreed to have these talks when they were so ill-prepared. Was it just to examine the Indian evidence? Were internal developments within China the cause and the need to divert people's attention outwards? Did they need to deflect attention from the turbulent developments in Tibet that pointed to the unpopularity of their regime among the Tibetan populace by dialling up the border dispute with India? 'By advocating border talks, they could play the role of a party most anxiously seeking peacefully to settle the dispute, while at the same time they could approach the talks in a manner that precluded any actual settlement'.[28] In the event, they appeared to use, for propaganda purposes, the contents of the Indian submissions as evidence of the latter's 'reliance' on British imperialist history, a trope that would harmonize with communist ideology and among those who 'would not easily believe that a government (China's) would sponsor demonstrably false assertions.'[29]

Writing after the Zhou Enlai visit to Delhi in April, the British High Commissioner in Delhi observed that the firmness displayed by the Indian side and their refusal to make any concession to the Chinese, was remarked upon in diplomatic circles in Delhi as at least having the temporary effect on 'smaller Asian nations to resist Chinese pressure'. The case of the Nepalese and that of Prince Sihanouk in Phnom Penh (who had not similarly succeeded in forestalling the Chinese) was mentioned in this regard. Yet, at the same time, the Chinese remained in physical occupation of the Aksai Chin, as well as Longju, which had been vacated by the Indians. There was 'nothing' the Indians could do to force them out. Therefore, even if 'discussions ended in moral victory for the Indians, they in effect produced a physical victory for the Chinese'. The Chinese political and military 'march which swept first across Tibet and then intruded into Indian territory' had not been driven back. This could have significance and consequence for the future.[30] This observation could have applied *mutatis mutandis* to the situation post the Officials Talks, too.

The two Prime Ministers—Nehru and Zhou—never met again. There was also no follow-up action on the Officials' Report, and the dust on it has accumulated over the ensuing decades. In retrospect, the words of Olaf Caroe, who would fall within the Chinese definition of arch-imperialist, conveyed the most apposite critique of the report. Writing in 1961, on the immense document of 555 closely printed pages, packed with comment upon comment, as 'Pelion piled on Ossa and Ossa on Olympus.'[31] Caroe highlighted the contrasting intellectual approach to a dispute by representatives of 'the two maturest civilizations in the world, each in the bloom of a renaissance.' The Chinese argument, he said, was 'shot through with a sly mockery' of the Indian evidence, while the Indian argument, in Caroe's words, was marshalled with a lucid clarity and respect for logic worthy of any Oxford cloister. 'Save perhaps on the ground of prolixity, a Socrates could hardly fault it.' And, concluding with a statement that the true boundary of the Indian world is on the crest of the northernmost crinkle of the Himalaya where it overlooks and falls to the Tibetan plateau, Caroe noted the lack of common ground in the two reports—Indian and Chinese. China, he said, was seeking to assert a claim, never made before, to the Indian Olympus.[32]

In July 1961, the Secretary-General of the Ministry of External Affairs, R.K. Nehru who had also served as Ambassador in Beijing, visited Beijing and Shanghai. R.K. Nehru, in the assessment of the CIA[33] was believed to be close to Krishna Menon and according to this view, subscribed to the belief that a way out of the prevailing impasse should be found with the Chinese. The occasion provided by the fortieth anniversary of the founding of the Mongolian People's Republic, which R.K. Nehru was attending on behalf of the Indian government, was utilized by him to stop over in China to meet with Chinese leaders. The trip seems to have been arranged essentially as an initiative of R.K. Nehru, through the offices of the Chinese Ambassador in Cairo where the former had served previous to his return to New Delhi. The Chinese are believed to have agreed to the visit on the assumption that R.K. Nehru wished to discuss the border issue, although it would appear that he had not been assigned to spearhead any such mission by his government. The Prime Minister approved the visit, saying it could do no harm, 'may do some good', but made it clear that R.K. Nehru had no brief to negotiate. Officials like Foreign Secretary M.J. Desai opposed his stopover, since it was felt that he 'had been influenced by (Krishna) Menon in this course and that, in any case, Menon was interfering too much in MEA policy formulation.'[34]

The Chinese apparently anticipated a 'bargaining gambit' where none existed. R.K Nehru was given top-leadership-level access on arrival when he met Liu Shaoqi and he also held extensive discussions with Zhou Enlai and Chen Yi. The Chinese were apparently 'aroused and lashed out angrily' at their visitor when he reportedly demanded that the Chinese withdraw from the Aksai Chin; Liu told the Secretary-General that it was 'ridiculous' for him to make the long trip in order to 'restate a position which China had previously indicated was "unreasonable, unjust and unacceptable"'.[35] If the Indian demand was that the Aksai Chin be vacated, then it was necessary for India to simultaneously vacate NEFA, Liu added. This was the 'only' condition on which China would consider looking at the Indian proposal. In a six-hour exchange with Zhou Enlai and Chen Yi, R.K. Nehru was met with a 'somewhat more tactful but equally solid rebuff'. Nehru left Shanghai on 17 July, followed three days later by Ambassador Parthasarathy who was leaving China on the completion of his tenure. The next Indian Ambassador to China would take up position only in 1976. Parthasarathy was replaced by career diplomat Purnendu Kumar Banerjee who would be Charge d' Affaires for India in Beijing from 1961 to 1963.

Banerjee who had arrived in Beijing as R.K. Nehru's visit was unfolding and Parthasarathy was preparing for his departure for India, was to record how the Ambassador had not kept a record of the Secretary-General's meetings with Chinese leaders on specific instructions from R.K. Nehru himself. The latter said 'he would be reporting to the Prime Minister personally'. Transiting through Hong Kong on his way back to Delhi, R.K. Nehru held a press conference claiming that he had taken a 'strong and clear stand against Chinese violation of Indian territories' and he had given the Chinese 'a suitable warning'[36]. The Chinese could not have been pleased. In this, the Secretary-General was also playing to the Indian gallery as there had been an uproar in Indian Parliament when the news of his unannounced visit to China had been broken by the Hong Kong papers.

The exact purpose of R.K. Nehru's misbegotten stopover in China in 1961 is difficult to ascertain. R. K. Nehru had always prided himself on his 'access' to, and the confidence he enjoyed with the Chinese leadership dating back to his years as Ambassador in Beijing. But there was little he could have done to stem the worsening tide in relations with China, given the fact that he had no negotiating brief to utilize in his meetings with the Chinese leadership, and since Prime Minister Nehru himself was no longer able to 'lead' on the issue in the face of crippling domestic opposition to any settlement with China on the boundary problem. Years later, when the Chinese Foreign Ministry briefly opened its archives, only to shut them again, the record of three conversations that the departing Ambassador Parthasarathy had with Zhang Wenjin, Director in the Asian Department and a veteran of the Officials' Talks with India on 17 July 1961, surfaced. These conversations[37] provide, inter alia, a useful and illuminating insight into R.K. Nehru's visit and its impact on the Chinese. In them, Parthasarathy probes the Chinese on their policy towards Bhutan, Sikkim, and Pakistan in continuation of what R.K. Nehru had done during his meetings. The Indians wanted confirmation from China that the latter respected India's right to 'represent Bhutan and Sikkim in handling foreign affairs'. All the Chinese would say was they respected the 'proper' relations between India and Bhutan, and India and Sikkim. The question raised by the Ambassador, they said, was 'beyond the scope of border issues.' Referring to reports about China and Pakistan discussing the Kashmir issue, Parthasarathy said India was 'very sensitive' about Kashmir, and China's discussion of border issues concerning Kashmir and Xinjiang with Pakistan was unacceptable to India since these border issues were being discussed 'with a country that has no right to negotiate' on issues that only concerned India. China responded that India was trying to expand rather than reduce differences of opinion between themselves. China could, when necessary, be in 'temporary contact with the local authorities' to handle 'practical problems' thereby spinning an argument that dealing with Pakistan, which was in actual control of the territory concerned, should be taken by India in its stride.

On the boundary between India and China, Zhang suggested there were two ways of approaching the issue. One, where each side presents the factual evidence regarding their case, after which this evidence was objectively compared in order to see 'whose information is relatively more logical, and finally parceling the [land] out to [the country] whose [version] is more beneficial to the two countries' friendship'. Second, where 'the two sides' views differ greatly and it is impossible to bring them into line, each side can keep to its own position and consider, from a political standpoint, what kind of resolution would be more beneficial. To this, Parthasarathy suggested that the two sides consider the second option where each side kept to its own views, and 'depending on the facts of the situation, we will make some compromises and resolve the issues.' The difficulty, he added, lay in swaying public opinion on such a 'big gesture'. He took care to state that this was just his personal view. Zhang said it was not necessary to speak 'of which side was wrong in the past' since 'this is an issue of mutual concessions.'

During a subsequent meeting with Parthasarathy on 19 July, Zhang Wenjin said Premier Zhou had mentioned that R.K. Nehru had suggested that a way forward would be for both sides to 'reconsider [the issues]'. Zhang asked Parthasarathy to explain this, to which the Ambassador said that the Secretary-General had not received [new] directives or suggestions (from the government)—implying thereby, that R.K. Nehru did not carry any negotiating brief. The idea was 'just to make use of the opportunity to exchange views on current Sino-Indian relations.' Parthasarathy expressed the view that there was a necessity 'to take the issues out of the icebox' and look for a way to break the stalemate. He was also of the view that using the Officials' Report as a foundation would not lessen differences of opinion. His suggestion was that methods like 'a kind of gesture that would change the atmosphere', restoring contacts at all levels, seeking a mutually satisfactory solution 'to lesser issues', not adopting 'rigid attitudes' and to stop 'conceiving of each other in a hostile way' could be possible ways forward. It was necessary to have 'a basic trust'.

Zhang asked whether the Ambassador thought it possible to start by 'supplementing and revising Premier Zhou's proposed six points of consensus' (put forward in Delhi in April 1960). Parthasarathy demurred saying the time had not come for such an adjustment. But he noted that the fifth point put forward by Zhou, which referred to both sides maintaining the status quo without making territorial demands, had aroused fears on the Indian side—

that 'if we agree to this point, it means we agree that China has sovereignty over Aksai Chin.' To this, Zhang said that what Zhou had meant that each side should not make the acceptance of their territorial claims a pre-requisite for the conduct of negotiations, since maintaining the status quo and the final resolution were 'two different things.' He told Parthasarathy that China had 'consistently' adhered to 'two principles in handling relations with others'. The first was: 'Do not be the first under heaven', that is, 'do not take the first step in causing harm'. The second was: 'It is improper to take but not give', that is, 'if others treat us unfairly, we cannot fail to give answer.' Likewise, 'if others are good to me, I will be even better to them in return.' India's criticisms of China, he claimed, had been far more numerous than China's of India. While it was alright to have differing opinions, it would be 'best if the leaders of the two countries stay behind the frontlines.'

But the fallout and controversy from the R.K. Nehru visit did not recede easily. The new Indian Charge d' Affaires, Banerjee, was summoned to the Chinese Foreign Office on 24 October 1961[38] to meet Vice-Foreign Minister Geng Biao who delivered a 'very strong protest' against 'incorrect and untrue' statements made by R.K. Nehru about his visit. During his meetings with the Chinese leadership, R.K. Nehru had 'not made any claims about the disputed border' unlike what he had stated in his interaction with the media in Hong Kong. Statements made in Parliament in Delhi about the visit by the government, were 'equally untrue, slanderous and misleading.' Criticism was directed both against Prime Minister Nehru and Defence Minister Krishna Menon in this regard. Banerjee who had no information about what had transpired during the R.K. Nehru visit, was left in an awkward position, unable to substantively refute the Chinese charges.

Years later, R.K. Nehru spoke of his participating in what he called the 'last dialogue' between India and China during his visit to Beijing and Shanghai in July 1961.[39] He recounted that he had spoken to the Chinese about Kashmir and their relations with Pakistan and that their reply had been, 'We regard you as a more important neighbour, we want to have friendly relations with you; the border problem should be settled peacefully and as for Kashmir, where have we said that we do not recognize your rights?' He felt the Chinese had clearly implied that as 'part of an overall settlement, they would accept our sovereignty over Jammu and Kashmir.' When he had raised the matter with Zhou, the latter had said, 'We have never said that we will not recognize your sovereignty; but then of course, we must have relations with Pakistan, too.'

R.K. Nehru was of the view that the basis for a reasonable boundary settlement had to be based on an approach of give and take—'some exchange'. History is a fickle judge, but there is the possibility that he had gone to China on the basis of some unwritten exchanges of views with the Prime Minister and the Defence Minister that such an approach could be considered as the foundation for a settlement. But this can never be confirmed given the passage of time and the deaths of these principal players. R.K. Nehru observed that 'the negotiations did not proceed because after I came back here there was a violent denunciation in Parliament and the Prime Minister, too, said the visit was infructuous.' R.K. Nehru always maintained, however, that his visit had been of some value and that the Chinese suggestion was that quiet talks should continue at a diplomatic level on the basis of the Officials' Report, or 'on the basis of new proposals'. Zhou Enlai had said that India should appoint an ambassador (after Parthasarathy had departed) for this purpose.

R.K. Nehru claimed that among the proposals 'tentatively' put forward by the Chinese, were 'that on the basis of recent administrative control, they should accept our (India's) sovereignty over 'southern Ladakh' and over NEFA, subject to some adjustments, and that on the same basis, we should accept their claim to the northern areas, i.e. Aksai Chin and Linzithang.'

But the pressure of public opinion on the Prime Minister was so great that he had no option but to dismiss the talks as infructuous and to decide on a 'forward policy' in Ladakh for which India was militarily unprepared. But India, R.K. Nehru claimed, had a 'clear enough warning that the forward policy would lead to armed conflict'. In July 1962, R.K. Nehru met Chinese Vice-Minister Zhang Hanfu in Geneva. The latter warned that the mounting tensions and differences between China and India were 'bound to lead to a serious military conflict.' R.K. Nehru said his suggestion to the Prime Minister was that 'unless we were prepared for a serious military encounter with the Chinese, it would be better to initiate talks, as proposed by the Chinese in 1961, if only to gain time. It was not too late for such a move even in July 1962, but the mounting demand in Parliament for strong action, fed by China's aggressive language and activities, came in the way of any new initiative.'[40]

The 'Forward' Policy

> 'Nehru's forward policy is a knife. He wants to put it in our heart. We cannot close our eyes and await death'.

Was the Forward Policy a misnomer and actually only a policy of continuous surveillance of the Chinese forward positions in Ladakh, by India? In early 1971, an interesting debate took place between Neville Maxwell (the Australian journalist and Nehru's nemesis on frontier policy) and the Indian scholar and legal luminary A.G. Noorani on the pages of *The China Quarterly*. Maxwell claimed that the Forward Policy was designed to dominate the Aksai Chin Highway and ultimately to evict the Chinese from occupied territory. Noorani, on the other hand, maintained that the Forward Policy was not aimed at evicting China from territory Indian considered hers, but to check the continuing Chinese advance in Ladakh. He added that it was not the intention of the Indians to provoke clashes with the Chinese, the objective being containment and not war.[41]

It is logical to accept that the deployment of such a policy by India in its initial stages was aimed at drawing attention to the fact that the Chinese had wreaked a logistical advantage by building the road through Aksai Chin. Given the Chinese push westward in the area, if India had not set up outposts east of the upper reaches of the Shyok river and in Chushul in Ladakh, no obstacle would have been placed before the Chinese in occupying more vacant areas without even a modicum of resistance from the Indian side. The 'Forward' Policy, seen from this perspective, was amply justified, although in its later stages before the denouement of 1962, not anticipating adverse Chinese reaction, it can be argued that it became more venturesome as the signalling from the Chinese was bypassed. Before 1961, although the Chinese had moved into the Aksai Chin, a wide swathe of territory separated the forward Chinese posts from Indian positions in eastern Ladakh. With the Chinese steadily pushing eastward, and extending their occupation of these areas, the decision was taken to push forward Indian posts in order to remove this vacuum that the Chinese seemed intent on occupying. In all this, the underlying, and in hindsight, flawed, basic assumption backed by civilian intelligence—if residual wisdom is to be believed—was that the Chinese were unlikely to deploy force against these Indian outposts because of the fallout on diplomatic relations, and also because reports of the domestic political and economic challenges faced by China— food shortages especially—would make it difficult for China to do so. In first flush, this conclusion may have appeared valid since the setting up of Indian posts appeared to deter the Chinese. This spurred the Indians to quickly establish more posts—little posts that were too small to withstand any real attack, and crucially, were not backed up by suitable reinforcements. Soon, the empty areas between the forces of the two sides was to diminish entirely. By 1962, when some Indian posts in the Galwan Valley (scene of a bloody skirmish in June 2020 in which twenty Indian soldiers including their commanding officer, lost their lives in a clash with the Chinese) were established, outflanking Chinese posts, the Chinese attitude acquired more threatening proportions. The posts were surrounded by the Chinese cutting off their land route of supply, and even opening fire. This appeared to invalidate the basic assumption behind the decision to implement the Forward Policy, necessitating a reappraisal. Unfortunately, no such reappraisal was done.

Logistics were weighted in favour of the Chinese. Their troop strengths were large and their transportation and road networks were also vastly more developed, growing steadily in the decade before 1962, after the occupation of Tibet. Logistic difficulties had prevented the Indians from augmenting their troops' strength. The Srinagar–Leh Road had been completed only in October 1961 and snow cover prevented operation of the road in winter months. The airlift capability of the Indian Air Force was also limited. Small airfields or advanced landing grounds had been established at Chushul, Thois (in the Shyok Valley) and at Fukche near Dungti in the Demchok area in Ladakh as also at Daulat Beg Oldi near the Karakoram Pass. Immense courage and ingenuity were displayed by the Indian Air Force and the Army in creating these air strips in extremely inhospitable terrain.

The airfields merit a special mention. In 2011, when the Air Force reactivated the air strip at Daulat Beg Oldi and successfully landed an AN-32 transport aircraft at Fukche after close to four decades, an Army veteran was to recall the creation of the strip in 1960. A decision was taken to construct the strip in order to provide administrative cover to the Indian posts at Galwan, Sultan Chusku and Trijunction (the name of the post and not to be confused with any trijunction of three borders on a map) in northern Ladakh. Aerial reconnaissance was carried out and the site at Daulat Beg Oldi surveyed. Thereafter, a team of two officers and seventy-five men were sent to prepare the landing ground which they did in twenty days. The area was marked with the bleached white bones of traders from Ladakh who had perished in blizzards at the Karakoram Pass while transiting to Xinjiang, in order that the ground could be seen from air, by Air Force pilots—the advice from the Air Force team from the Western Air Command led by Air Marshal Pinto was 'for heaven's sake mark the bloody Landing Ground!'. The altitude of the strip was at 16,200 feet. Similar landing grounds were established at Fukche and Chushul. In fact, from 1948 onwards, the Indian armed forces built landing grounds at Leh (1948), Kargil (1951), Thoise (1956), Chushul (1959), Daulat Beg Oldi (1960) and Fukche (1961). In the words of a retired Army veteran: 'The Landing Grounds were built on grounds that were hard, barren and sandwiched between almost a range of parallel running mountains. At most places it was a question of removing boulders, filling potholes and generally leveling the ground. The good old infantry equipment of a pick axe, shovel and crow bar came in very handy . . . When the first Dakota plane landed at Leh (11400 feet) in December 1948 the locals brought with them hay, gram and water as they thought it was some big flying animal!'[42]

Most of the forward posts established to deter the Chinese had to be supplied by airdrops, and the distribution of the Indian defences in what essentially were penny packets in forward areas made them crucially vulnerable to being overrun by the Chinese in the event of a full-scale attack. The fatal flaw inherent in Indian policy responses, especially in the top echelons of leadership was the belief that the Chinese would abstain from a full and frontal attack on Indian positions in order to dislodge and overrun them, this despite what could have veritably been seen by China as a throwing of the Indian gauntlet. Events after 8 September 1962 along the western and eastern sectors of the border would provide testimony to this.

To call these moves a 'Forward Policy' itself may of course have been a misnomer. The Indian side had its justifications for seeking to safeguard its claims along a disputed border as the Chinese were seen to making inroads into what India regarded as sovereign territory. There were inconsistencies in the Chinese definition of the Line of Actual Control as were evident from 1959–60 onwards. The alignment shown on the Chinese map given to the Indian delegation at the Officials Talks of 1960 was quite different from that shown on a Chinese map printed in 1956 of the same area, which Zhou Enlai had endorsed as being the Chinese claim line and Line of Actual Control in 1959. The new claim line or alignment of 1960 ran generally much to the west of the line on the 1956 map, taking in some 5,180 sq. km (2,000 sq. mi) more of Indian territory in Ladakh. By end-1959, the Chinese had enforced their control both west and south of the Aksai Chin highway in Ladakh and improved their logistical advantages by building feeder roads and transport links, and opening new all-weather posts in order to prove their presence up to this new, and changed, claim line. Accentuating Indian concerns, by May 1962, China and Pakistan agreed to start negotiations to settle the portion of the India–China boundary west of the Karakoram Pass between Pakistan-occupied Kashmir and Xinjiang despite strong Indian protests. This did not deter India in continuing its efforts to resolve these mounting tensions at the political and diplomatic level with China.

The compulsions of national economic development had constrained the growth in and development of military strength by India; a lack of roads and logistics were particular weak points in the border areas which prevented supply and movement of troops. Sabre-rattling with China, despite the unrealistic and aggressive calls for swift and firm action both in Parliament and the press, did not help. Diplomacy and political contact provided a more reasoned pathway to resolve problems with China. But Nehru was under growing pressure from the public arena—especially as the White Papers had placed all actions vis-à-vis China under the scanner—to be seen as resolute and even muscle-flexing on India-

China border matters. On the policy front, it was an imperative that no further inch of territory should be yielded to the Chinese who were seen as continuing their land grab in Ladakh. While no offensive was planned against the Chinese, it was necessary to protect positions taken up by Indian personnel to stop the Chinese advance, so that if they were attacked, self-defence on India's part was the only way. In November 1961, it was directed that patrolling by Indian personnel should be undertaken (with a view to 'establishing our posts which should prevent the Chinese from advancing any further'[43]) as far eastward as possible in Ladakh in order to prevent the Chinese from advancing further and also dominating Indian positions.[44] The emphasis on 'dominate' has been commented on by scholars—'it was a military term, understood by any commander to mean 'observe and cover'. The idea was that an Indian post should be better situated tactically than an opposing Chinese post'.[45] Defence Minister Krishna Menon's explanation to Cabinet officials was that the new additional posts would be 'positioned to cut off the supply lines of targeted Chinese posts; they were to cause the 'starving out' of the Chinese, who would thereafter be replaced by Indian troops in the posts. These posts would serve as advanced bases for Indian patrols assigned to probe close to the (Aksai Chin) road.'[46]

Speaking to the Canadian author Michael Brecher some years later, Menon said India's policy on the frontier with China was not to wage war. The Indian moves to establish forward posts were in response to China's 'policy of expanding frontiers'. That explained why, he said, 'from 1959 onwards we started moving forward and why from '59 to '62 we established ourselves in Ladakh in a parallel position to (the Chinese) in something like 4000 sq. miles of territory, planting posts and so on. I started it myself.'[47] Menon also conceded that there was factual recognition of the financial, economic, political, and moral commitments (as he termed them) of the country, implying thereby that this policy had its limits. In plain speak, the intention was not to wage war, but to provide a means to withstand Chinese encroachments that were steadily advancing into Indian-claimed territory and to block their further advance. Menon had an ally in the Intelligence Bureau Chief B.N. Mullik who was also briefing the Prime Minister about the extent of Chinese ingress since October 1959.

The strategic affairs analyst, K. Subrahmanyam, writing on the Forward Policy argued that critics of the policy ignored the fact that 'the Chinese were constantly moving forward during the years 1959–1961 up to their 'claim line'. At that stage they put forward two 'claim lines', the second one claiming more area than the first. Given the fact that the Chinese were brazenly lying that they were already in occupation of this area, when the Government of India were aware that they were not, it would have been imprudent on anybody's part to accept the second Chinese claim line was a final one.' The new Indian posts fell 'somewhere between the old and new Chinese 'claim lines', and were sited not so much from a tactical point of view but more as observation posts to keep an eye on Chinese movements.' In Subrahmanyam's words, 'This was the essence of the so-called 'Forward Policy'. In fact, the more appropriate name would be intensive or continuous surveillance policy.'[48] But no overall plan to implement this Forward Policy in Ladakh was formulated by Army Headquarters who also told the civilian establishment that 'it could not send reinforcements to Ladakh until a road link was completed between Ladakh and India proper.' Also, a key directive to position major concentrations of forces in select locations behind the forward posts, from where they could be maintained logistically, was never implemented. Verbal and written orders were intermixed, and these were issued by General B.M. Kaul in consultation with Mullik. Prime Minister Nehru, Krishna Menon, General Thapar (the Chief of Army Staff) and Foreign Secretary M.J. Desai were also involved in the formulation of these orders in a highly unorthodox fashion as it is usually the discretion of local area commanders to determine 'small-unit troop dispositions.'[49] In December 1961, the Forward

Policy was applied to the eastern sector/NEFA as well. The policy was 'sold' to the public with the claim that India was standing 'firm'.

As far as the Army was concerned, the policy was seen as a direction to push ahead into territory claimed by India but occupied by China in Ladakh, with the intention of showing the flag and asserting the Indian claim. 'If the Chinese could set up posts, why not us? The DIB (Director, Intelligence Bureau)'s assessment was that the Chinese would not react if we moved forward and set up the posts. The Foreign Office shared this view.'[50] Later, both the Intelligence Bureau's Mullik and Krishna Menon would explain that setting up posts in Indian territory could not be termed a forward policy. But it can be argued that 'the substance of the policy was more important than its nomenclature.' There was no adequate back-up in terms of infrastructure and logistics for the posts thus set up. It was left to Lt. Gen. Daulat Singh, the Army Commander for the Western Area, to express reservations in writing. He saw the Forward Policy directive as a political one, not based on a proper military assessment of the situation.

That no military conflict with China was anticipated, 'or even sought as a solution to the boundary question', seemed borne out by the fact that the Indian defence budget declined between 1957–1960 from US $539.11 million to US $481.81 million.[51] The military challenge to China from India could not have been regarded as serious given these statistics which spoke of the very real constraints that Krishna Menon was to allude to much later, with Brecher. In fact, the Defence Minister had publicly stated as far back as 1956, when he was still representing India at the United Nations, that India had no reason to think China was either expansionist or belligerent 'or imperialistic in any way.'[52] Even Mao Zedong had told the Soviets in 1959 that the Chinese would abide by ('maintain') the McMahon Line and also that 'we will never, under any circumstances, move beyond the Himalayas.' A similar assurance was conveyed in Zhou Enlai's letter of 17

December 1959 to Nehru that the Chinese government would not allow its armed personnel to cross the McMahon Line pending a 'friendly settlement' of the boundary question.[53] Even after the events of 1959, when Indian perceptions of China became increasingly negative, and India saw China as increasingly pre-disposed to harm India, the conviction that there would be no military counteraction from China on the border was firmly held. Intelligence shared with India by the Americans in 1961, after the capture of documents by Tibetan rebels in Tibet, 'indicated that China's domestic difficulties had produced extremely low morale and physical fitness in the People's Liberation Army'.[54]

The Chinese response to the forward moves along the border by India from 1961 onwards, was to be expected. They saw these moves as a deliberate disturbance of the status quo. From January 1962 onwards, they were threatening armed counteraction through their diplomatic contacts with third countries who were also friends with India. The Burmese ambassador in Cambodia was told by his Chinese counterpart that if India wanted 'to bully, pressure, or fight' the Chinese, the latter were 'quite willing to use troops to resist attack'. The threat was apparently conveyed to the Indian Ambassador in Phnom Penh who must have informed New Delhi. But the Indian flanking operations continued.[55] The Chinese response was to resume patrolling from the Karakoram Pass to the Kongka Pass. It was as if each side had launched its 'forward policy' in these disputed areas. A political quarrel was mutating into a military confrontation. The number of protest notes exchanged between the two sides rose exponentially in the summer of 1962. But the Indians continued to misread the signals from the Chinese. The events in the Galwan Valley (where Indian forces had regularly patrolled and the lower reaches of which 'were twenty-eight miles beyond the Chinese claim line'[56] in the 1956 map which they had shown to the Indians at the onset of the dispute) in Ladakh in the summer of 1962, when the post was surrounded by the Chinese who then withdrew without opening fire, were wrongly assessed as signalling that the latter would not use force against the Indian posts. But what the Chinese were conveying was that they 'could eliminate any Indian post at any time'. They also accused the Indians of attempting to establish 'a new base for aggression'[57]. Nehru and the Delhi establishment believed that the Chinese were facing a difficult position internally—on the economic front as a result of food shortages and famine and also the failure of the Great Leap Forward, as well as on account of the withdrawal of the Soviet experts, and military harassment by the Taiwanese. They hardly foresaw any prospect of a military invasion by China on India.[58]

On 2 June 1962, the 1954 Agreement on Trade with Tibet lapsed— it was as if, with this development, the Panchsheel principles had themselves been annulled. China had left India little room or scope to carry on with the agreement, although the loss of the Consulate in Lhasa was unfortunate—till date, the Chinese have resisted all moves by India to seek the re-establishment of this office in the Tibetan capital.[59] As far as the agreement was concerned, the Chinese had clearly violated it through harassment of Indian pilgrims, traders, and nationals in Tibet. A Note from the Ministry of External Affairs in New Delhi to the Chinese Embassy of 17 July accused the Chinese government of not only violating the Five Principles of Peaceful Coexistence but also of having systematically and arbitrarily contravened 'each and every provision of the Agreement itself.'[60] The Indians rejected charges that they had not respected Chinese sovereignty in Tibet or interfered in China's internal affairs. 'The Sino-Indian Agreement of 1954', the Note said, had 'run its course' and that during 'its currency it was systematically whittled down with the result that the centuries old trade and cultural ties between India and Tibet have been disrupted.'

It has been argued that the Agreement's being allowed to lapse and the termination of cross-border trade as a result, cut off food supplies to the Tibetan plateau, causing a famine in Tibet in 1962. This school of thought claims that the famine was caused not just by the disastrous agricultural policies of Mao's Great Leap

Forward but also because of the decision to terminate the 1954 Agreement on Tibet between India and China resulting in food shortages for Tibetans.[61] For the policy makers in Beijing, this hardly made a difference. Food shortages in Tibet were a localized issue. Trade along India's Himalayan frontiers with Tibet had gone on for time immemorial. Mid-century geopolitics had cut off the oxygen summarily. Freedom of movement across borders was a thing of the past. India's decision not to seek a renewal of the 1954 Agreement may have been validated by the difficulties caused to the functioning of the offices in Tibet by Chinese policy makers in Beijing, but with the benefit of historical hindsight, perhaps patience would have served as the best prescription. Perhaps there was some realization also to this effect. The Chinese archives speak of a meeting on 6 June 1962 between Sumul Sinha, then the Director in the East Asia Division/Department of the Ministry of External Affairs and Ye Chengzhang, a diplomat at the Chinese Embassy in Delhi where apparently Sinha conveyed that 'it was not as if the Indians had rejected the negotiation of a new agreement, but that they wanted to find common grounds for the new agreement; they welcomed the words for it.' Sinha is identified in this conversation as Shen Shumei, his Chinese name. Sinha's thinking was certainly rational, after all, could a relationship that was time-tested and deeply oriented towards the welfare of border peoples be terminated so arbitrarily? The Chinese of course cold-shouldered this tentative move by Sinha.[62] The opportunity for India to restore its consular ties with Tibet has never really presented itself since, except for a brief window in the mid-nineteen eighties when the Chinese appeared open to the idea of restoring the consulate in Lhasa, and India was as yet unready to accept the offer. In 1962, India also thought that trade was a leverage that could be used against the Chinese in Tibet. One account speaks of a meeting of Indian traders in Yadong in April 1962 when one trader declared that the problems in relations between India and China had been created by the

Chinese government and that China must recognize this. To PRC officials the inference was that 'India was trying to scare China into abandoning its legitimate territorial claims by raising the specter of a trade embargo' and this was unfriendly conduct. But what 'was clear was that border peoples in both China and India depended on the trade relationship for sustenance.'[63]

The opinion has been expressed that the Chinese decision to go to war with India was occasioned primarily by their suspicions and misgivings about India's Tibet policy from its inception in 1950–51, once Chinese forces entered Tibet. In the mind of Chinese leaders like Mao Zedong, India was a legatee of British imperialist policy that sought to make Tibet a buffer zone where Indian influence would be easy to spread, and that it was a co-conspirator with Tibetan rebels supporting the Dalai Lama. The Dalai Lama's decision to seek refuge in India in 1959 did not help matters. The Chinese attitude was misplaced given the fact that India gave up all the privileges enjoyed by Britain in Tibet in 1954 and also acknowledged Chinese sovereignty over the territory, even if Delhi called for respect for Tibetan autonomy. The CIA's activities in Tibet from 1955–56 onwards were transacted with little official knowledge of the Indians, even if the Intelligence Bureau was perhaps aware of the broad contours. From conversations between Chinese Communist Party leaders and their Soviet counterparts from 1959 onwards, the Chinese animus towards India on the Tibet issue was on clear display. Once India's 'Forward Policy' was deployed from late 1961 onwards, the Chinese read this as an additional provocation by the Indians to seize what they (the Chinese) saw as sovereign Chinese territory in pursuit of the former's 'reactionary' aims.[64]

As the game of zig-zagging of posts of the two sides continued (Mao's eight-character comment called it 'armed coexistence, jigsaw pattern'[65]) and tension escalated, on 17 August 1962, Indian troops were authorized to fire at the Chinese in order to prevent encirclement of their posts in Ladakh. The gauntlet had been thrown. At the same time, the GOC-in-C, Western Command, Lt. Gen. Daulat Singh 'bitterly complained of the inadequacy of the defences in Ladakh to hold a full-scale attack by the Chinese.' He maintained that the deployment of the existing Indian force in Ladakh had involved claiming territory by 'show of flag' rather than by tactical considerations, and that the situation had worsened since the launch of the Forward Policy as the 'Chinese reaction to that policy had been sharp and significant.' The Chinese had built up a full division in Ladakh as against India's two regular and two militia battalions. He added that India's forward posts, anchored to DZs (dropping zones from air), were tactically dominated by Chinese posts on higher ground. His grim conclusion was:

> I would be failing in my duty if I did not draw attention to the size and shape of this potential threat and the means required to contain it . . . Finally, I submit that this is an issue which permits of no delay in decision-making at the highest national level. I concede that the military means asked for appear to be of somewhat considerable size, but that is not so when viewed in the context of safeguarding national security in this theatre.[66]

In fact, this cautionary approach had been reflected also in the three-tier defence plan for the eastern sector recommended by Lieutenant General S.P.P. Thorat in October 1959. The Thorat Plan, as it came to be known, suggested the establishment of small early warning outposts as close to the McMahon Line as possible—these outposts were not meant to engage the Chinese in battle but to fall back before a Chinese advance. A second tier behind them would represent 'strong delaying positions, which would force the enemy to halt, deploy and fight.' The third tier would prepare tactical ground where Indian troops 'could take up positions that would have supply lines that could be maintained from the plains, thus turning the difficulties of the terrain to their advantage' so as to leave the Chinese with no choice 'but to fight with their lines of communication extended.' This defensive plan of Thorat was however politically unpalatable as the prospect of surrender of any territory to the Chinese even at the first line of defence was unthinkable and 'no one in India was willing to lose even one square inch of ground.'[67] Meanwhile, Krishna Menon and Nehru were growing increasingly dependent and trusting of another senior Army officer, B.M. 'Bijji' Kaul, who had no previous combat experience. Kaul was promoted to the rank of Lieutenant General and brought to Delhi as Quarter Master General (QMG) in 1957, against the wishes of the then Army Chief Thimayya.

Nehru was also not deterred by the predictably hostile Chinese response to the Forward Policy moves. Beijing was obviously rankled by the policy. The Chinese press called it a 'policy of *can shi*, that is, roughly translated, a policy of 'nibbling' of another country's territory', a term also used by Chinese negotiators. *Can* is the Chinese ideograph for silkworm, which fits the image of 'nibbling away' with the literal translation of *can shi* being food or forage for the silk worm, 'which would destroy a leaf or whole plant by gradually consuming it.'[68] Nehru was still convinced that Beijing would not retaliate on any large scale, militarily. The Chinese response on Galwan seemed to confirm this. Chinese military personnel had clear-cut instructions on how to react to the Indian forward presence in the 20-km band inside their line of actual control: 'a Chinese unit had first to issue a warning and try to push them into retreating: if this did not work, it had then to confiscate their weapons according to international custom, and after an explanation, return their weapons and allow them to leave.' Also, in May–June 1962, China's main concern was focused on a possible invasion from Taiwan and there was therefore reluctance to provoke 'hostilities in the Himalayas' which would have meant a diversion of resources and a two-front war situation. From July 1962, once the threat of a Guomindang invasion had lifted after American assurances to this effect, the focus shifted to the border with India. At the same time, the

Indian establishment, particularly the military, were aware of 'China's military superiority on the ground' if any small clash were to develop into full-scale hostilities. Perhaps, this was why around the same time, there developed a distinctly conciliatory tone in New Delhi's diplomatic communication with Beijing. At a lunch he hosted for the departing Chinese Ambassador, Pan Zili, Nehru indicated that 'India would be prepared to hold discussions without demanding withdrawal from disputed areas as a pre-condition.' On 26 July, a note to the Chinese reiterated this position and spoke of a willingness to talk once the 'current tensions have eased and the appropriate climate is created.'[69] Nehru's discussion with Ambassador Pan seemed to have elicited a hard-nosed reaction in the Chinese Foreign Office. A note sent to the Chinese delegation in Geneva on 16 July assessed India as having entered a stalemate with China both politically and militarily because of economic difficulties, poor relations with neighbours, and factional political conflict within (the Congress Party), especially regarding the issue of the successor to Nehru. Under these circumstances, the Chinese felt that India wished to see a relaxation of tensions with China. India was seen as adopting a two-pronged approach—on the one hand, showing willingness for peace talks and to 'test China', while on the other, filling up 'gaps' in the western sector by advancing on the Chinese, setting up more posts and 'occupying areas, in an attempt to make it a reality so as to carry out bargaining.' The proposal, therefore, from India was a 'delaying tactic to consolidate already occupied areas, and to make preparation for further annexation.'[70] In this situation, China, it was felt, 'should intensify military confrontation in the western sector and stop Indian side from further advancing. However, China has to be careful not to provoke military conflict'.[71]

On 22 July, the Chinese delegation in Geneva sent an urgent report to the Foreign Ministry seeking instructions and stating that Krishna Menon had visited the delegation for discussions with Vice-Premier Chen Yi and said that if the boundary problem was not solved before Nehru's death, it would drag on further. Menon stated that since the dispute between the two countries started with the Aksai Chin road, the resolution of the problem should also begin with this road. Past history should be 'forgotten' and the two sides should 'start drawing a fresh line in the western sector, i.e., the relevant territory including the road and the areas on the two sides of the road could be drawn as Chinese territory, and in exchange, China can demarcate to India a part of territory in the eastern sector which is considered by everybody as Chinese territory'. (Was Menon alluding to the Chumbi Valley, abutting Sikkim and Bhutan and overlooking the strategic Siliguri Corridor in West Bengal?) The size of this territory, he continued, 'may not necessarily be equal' (to the territory conceded in the western sector by India). Turning to the sector covered by the McMahon Line, Menon noted that China had already withdrawn from Longju (claimed by them as being north of the McMahon Line) and India had also not re-occupied it 'as a gesture of peace'—therefore there was 'no problem' in this sector 'any more'. If 'the boundary problem could be resolved like this, the two sides can sign a Treaty of Friendship for 50 years, and start trade, etc.'

Was Menon speaking on instructions from Nehru? We will never know. Menon would refuse to speak on the issue when subsequently asked whether any such offer had been made to the Chinese in Geneva in 1962. For years, rumours have persisted about the Chumbi Valley 'ask' from Menon to Chen Yi. If the Chinese archives are to be relied on (there is no reason to discount them) then, indeed, Menon did make such an 'offer'. Chen Yi's response was, however, dismissive. He asked Menon if the proposal made by Nehru to Ambassador Pan on 16 July to continue discussion between the two countries on the basis of the Officials' Report was 'official'. Menon replied in the affirmative. On being asked whether what Nehru told Pan about a symbolic withdrawal by the two sides in the western sector amounted to what Menon had proposed to Chen, Menon said that, in his opinion, withdrawal by the two sides would not resolve the problem, and that 'territory must be exchanged.' To this, Chen replied 'India wants China to relinquish 90,000 sq. kms in the eastern sector (Chinese claimed territory south of the McMahon Line) and some portions of territory in the western sector and also wants China to return a piece of territory at a different place to India. How could this be considered?'

Chen asked Menon if he had any other proposal, to which the latter replied:

> In order to prevent border conflict, it can be considered as a temporary arrangement while the two sides maintain their respective positions. The two sides could agree to let border security forces of both the sides freely set up sentry posts in the disputed areas in the western sector. However, a 'gentlemen's agreement' will stipulate a definite restriction on the strength of both side's sentry posts. The strength of one side's sentry post ought not to be several times that of the other side's sentry post, the two sides should not attack each other, and a distance of 1–2 miles should be maintained between the sentry posts of the two countries. After 2–3 years, some territorial adjustments could again be considered. However, the issue of use of the Aksai Chin road by China needs to be considered irrespective of the circumstances.[72]

The Chinese appeared willing to consider a temporary arrangement to avoid conflict but Chen told Menon in a subsequent meeting on 23 July that the proposal for the two sides to clarify their respective claim lines in the western sector, and then treat the area between the two lines as disputed territory could not be agreed to, as this was Chinese territory that was involved. The only common point, Chen said, was that China and India 'are not willing to fight'. He proposed that he and Menon issue a communique in Geneva announcing discussions between China and India on prevention of a border conflict, with the time, venue, and level of discussion being decided later. Menon demurred, saying there was enough time. The two sides could report this proposal to their respective governments who could then issue the communique.[73] That communique was never issued.

Reporting on these talks, the Associated Press dispatch of 25 July said Krishna Menon had accused China of firing first in the latest confrontation in Ladakh—an accusation that was denied by Chen Yi, also as stated in the same report. Chen told AP that he considered the 'border dispute with India as a localized problem which would not lead to war.' Krishna Menon meanwhile returned to India on 25 July—he kept his silence on what had transpired in Geneva but briefed the Cabinet six days later. When asked by Michael Brecher on the subject, he would say that he had had no negotiations with Chen Yi, only 'informal talks' and that Chen had been 'anxious' to see him. Arthur Lall, the Indian diplomat who was with Menon in Geneva, would write about the 'three very important meetings' which took place between Chen Yi, Zhang Hanfu, Qiao Guanhua and Krishna Menon. He said there had been a 'serious exploration' of the border dispute during these conversations and that at the end, Chen Yi 'surprised us with his proposal that a communique be issued to the press' and had suggested the following language: 'Two senior Ministers of the Governments of the People's Republic of China and the Republic of India have met and discussed the border situation between the two countries. These discussions have been constructive and fruitful, and it is the intention of the two governments that they should lead to further talks in the near future.'[74]

Against the backdrop of a border stalemate, China was increasingly assessing India's foreign relations as rightist and reactionary, dependent on 'monopoly capitalism' and tied to America. Nehru, it was felt, was engaged in a policy of long-term opposition to China. Linking this latter stance to the

Soviet Union and the United States, India's policy was seen as seriously compromised. India was serving as a 'hatchet man' for America's 'new colonialism' in the Congo, for instance, where it had sent 6,000 troops and 'let Indian soldiers die unjust deaths in Katanga'. India was also 'brazenly wooing and influencing' and 'making use of' the Soviet Union, the Chinese felt. The Soviets, for their part, were 'using India to support Soviet-American talks, disarmament to pressure China' and cooperating with India's anti-China stance. India was using 'all kinds of shameless tactics to sabotage anti-colonialist and anti-imperialist struggles', depending on America and 'expanding in Asia and Africa' to get the 'leftover soup and rice'. Military contacts had been established between India and the US. The value of India—'this big country sporting a non-aligned label'—to America had already surpassed that of Pakistan. All this demonstrated Nehru's 'craftiness and cunning'. In the end, Nehru's 'whole reactionary face' would be 'known to all'.[75]

Dark days beckoned.

16

The Fall

The Assyrian came down like the wolf on the fold[1]

As tensions mounted with India, China was moving to settle its boundary issues with various neighbouring countries. It has been argued that these settlements were in consonance with China's larger strategic concerns and not to isolate India (although that impression is hard to discount and indeed Indian policy makers were convinced that this is exactly what China intended, and that this policy of conciliation towards India's neighbours was to suggest India was intransigent). This policy was seen as pragmatic, and defined as *Sanhe Yishao* or Three Conciliations and One Reduction. The concept was formulated after the failure of the Great Leap Forward, against a backdrop of domestic challenges and also in order to ameliorate tension between China and the three categories of adversaries: the 'modern revisionists' (the Soviet Union), 'imperialists' (the United States), and 'reactionaries' (India, Pakistan, Burma, etc.) and, in an attempt to improve relations with China's neighbours, to reduce China's support for national liberation movements in neighbouring countries.

Given the imperatives of the strategic environment surrounding China, which overwhelmed ideological or domestic objectives, 'pragmatic policies seeking accommodation were necessary.'[2] During this period, China concluded boundary agreements with Burma (where the agreed boundary alignment broadly followed the McMahon Line in its western portion), Nepal, Pakistan, and Afghanistan, either before, or following the conflict of 1962 with India. Closer relations with these countries were thereby achieved, and they provided balance to the threats from worsening ties with India and the Soviet Union.

In the words of Wang Jiaxiang, director of the Chinese Communist Party Central Committee International Liaison Department, 'it was necessary to relax and restrain the struggle on several fronts according to Comrade Mao Zedong's consistent call to "win over the majority, isolate the minority and take advantage of contradictions to defeat them one by one."'[3] It was a policy derived from a sense of vulnerability and it received the support of leaders like Zhou Enlai. Mao was in agreement with it until he disavowed it at the 10th Plenum of the 8th Central Committee in September 1962 and embraced the more radical approach to 'sit tight in the fishing boat despite the rising wind and waves'[4]. Wang Jiaxiang was the leading formulator of the policy calling for restraint. If the policy had prevailed, and Mao had not engineered a volte-face, scholars have argued that Liu Shaoqi and Zhou Enlai may not have chosen to teach Nehru 'a lesson' in light of their support for the *Sanhe Yishao* or the policy of 'three accommodations (with the Soviet Union, the United States, and India) and one reduction', that is, reduction of support for national liberation movements in neighbouring countries.[5] Zhou's own visit to Delhi in April 1960 was seen as an exposition of this policy of seeking 'mutual understanding and mutual accommodation' with India, although this endeavour was unsuccessful and bore no fruit. That visit must be viewed as stemming from the decision by China in January 1959 (at the level of the Communist Party's Central

Committee) to settle border issues with neighbours by 'ultimately erecting a distinct, strict border . . . as well as constructing normal relations between our sides.'[6]

In the period from November 1961 until November 1962, a total of 196 diplomatic Notes on the boundary question, border incidents and violations of territorial air space were exchanged between India and China illustrating the worsening state of relations between the two countries. Of these, the Indian Note of 26 July 1962[7] stands out for a few reasons. Firstly, the Government of India said it wished to settle the issue with China through peaceful negotiations. Secondly, in referring to the aggressive patrolling by China west of the 1956 Claim Line, and conceding the fact that China was inclined to contest 'the correct international boundary in the Ladakh region' (as claimed by India), the note asked why the Chinese Government was not restraining their forces 'from going beyond even their 1956 map claim line which is capable of easy and quick verification.' It was the first time that India had diluted its previous insistence that China should withdraw from all the territory in Ladakh claimed by India even if the latter was willing to allow China the 'use' of the Aksai Chin road. India was conveying to the Chinese, implicitly, a willingness not to insist on Chinese withdrawal east of the 1956 Claim Line provided Chinese forward posts west of this line were withdrawn, and to start negotiations (as opposed to mere talks) on this basis.

The Chinese did not take the bait and the Menon–Chen Yi talks in Geneva (discussed previously) did not yield any progress on this front, either. Even the communique that would announce a resumption of talks to resolve border differences was never issued. It was an opportunity missed, when seen through the hindsight of history and of subsequent developments. The Chinese reply of 4 August 1962 insisted that China had never crossed its national frontier and it could not consider any 'one-sided withdrawal'. It sought the resumption of discussions on the border question without preconditions. On 6 August, when Nehru placed the latest

White Paper on the dispute before Parliament (which contained details of these exchanges), members of opposition political parties including the Jana Sangh and Swatantra parties felt 'there was no ground for peaceful negotiations'. Nehru defensively took the stand that India did not accept either the 1956 or 1960 claim lines of China, although he did affirm that he was prepared to 'discuss what measures should be taken to remove the tensions that exist in the region and to create the appropriate climate for further discussions.' He was obviously preparing the ground for talks with China, but in the parliamentary debate on 13 August it was clear that this was not all acceptable to the non-Communist Opposition with the Jana Sangh MP U.M. Trivedi moving an amendment on behalf of his party that 'under no circumstances any talk on border dispute with China be made till Chinese forces have withdrawn from the Indian territory which has been recognized by law and history.'[8] Trivedi urged for the recruitment of more army personnel so that within six months, 'a well-trained army will march to the Himalayas and throw back the whole Chinese force'.

Other members urged the breaking off of diplomatic relations with China and that the government accept military aid from either the United States or the Soviet Union; also that the Prime Minister take over the defence portfolio as the Defence Minister Krishna Menon 'had forfeited the confidence of the House and the country.' Nehru refused to admit to the argument that India would rely on any foreign army to defend its territory, although he still thought it 'absurd' that the Chinese would indulge in an invasion of India. The very thought of China 'swooping down the whole of India and swallowing it has, I submit, nothing to do with reality or possibility, even remote possibility'. At the end of the debate, with no conclusion reached, Nehru sought agreement from the members that 'nothing should be done which, in the slightest degree, sullies the honour of India. For the rest, I want a free hand.'[9]

Fateful decisions precede fateful events. In the early phase of the dispute with China in 1958–59, India had sought to deploy a policy of 'persuasion and argument'. After the Kongka Pass incident of October 1959, public opinion in India became a strong pressure point on the Indian Government leading to a distinct element of unwillingness to yield on the border question. A shifting Chinese claim line in Ladakh then occasioned the launch of the Forward Policy of 'non-violent military pressure' from November 1961. Was India's conflict management hobbled by an unwillingness to negotiate with China and to understand that such negotiations would involve an element of give-and-take? By a repetitive insistence that China should withdraw from territory in Ladakh in order to consider 'border claims in the light of historical evidence', was the problem further accentuated? On the other hand, China had developed a different conception. The Chinese approach was to seek Indian acceptance of China's military occupation of the Aksai Chin and eastern Ladakh and then achieve a barter arrangement involving the western and eastern sectors of the boundary (China being the 'beneficiary' in the west and India in the east, south of the McMahon Line).[10]

Were the Chinese preparing for war with India? Contrary to the belief among Indian policymakers that war was most unlikely, the historical record as revealed today, suggests otherwise. Here again, the Tibetan connection is intrinsic to our understanding of the problem. The Chinese had begun to augment their military presence and capabilities (including logistical) with the advent of the Tibetan resistance in 1956. The military action taken to quell the revolt lasted almost six-and-a-half years from 1956 to 1962. 'Military action in Tibet is a key to understanding the border conflict with India', this author was told in 2014[11]. For the Chinese, this was the largest military action involving the PLA after 1949. It involved the use of Soviet-made aircraft to bomb the Tibetan rebels and monasteries in Kham and Amdo. The 54th Army that had fought in Korea was sent to Lanzhou in western

China in 1958 and trained there for action in Tibet. After two months of training, they were sent to Qinghai (Amdo), operating between altitudes of 2,000 to 4,000 m. In 1959, according to the same source, the 54th Army was sent to central Tibet and areas close to the Indian border. In March of the same year, Lhasa itself was the scene of fierce battles involving Chinese troops and Tibetan rebels around the time of the flight of the Dalai Lama to India. Mao Zedong himself is understood to have sent three telegrams to force commanders in Tibet, welcoming the Tibetan rebellion because it was an opportunity to 'train our army', the army in focus being the 54th Army.

By the summer of 1962 the army was fully trained, its endurance levels at a high, and adequate ammunition stocks available for use in new combat situations. A report from the Consulate of India in Lhasa for the month of April 1961 noted that 'the Chinese cadres and troops in Lhasa are reported to be casually discussing the invasion of India by the Chinese.'[12] A further report for May of the same year said, 'a casual source mentioned having heard that Mon-Tawang area (NEFA border) was concentrated with Chinese troops, guns, heavy artillery and anti-aircraft guns. The impression in the area, according to this source, was that the Indian side is well-defended and that many Tibetans were escaping from Tsona area into NEFA without the Chinese bothering them.'[13] A report for July 1961 stated that 'It is more or less confirmed that two three Dakotas have been landing daily with troops and goods at Dam air field. The planes, it is stated, do not halt there for long but take off immediately. On July 16, three Dakotas are stated to have landed there with armed PLA, who also carried some weapons answering the description of small mortars. The said PLA . . . left for unknown localities presumably in Western Tibet.'[14]

This is where the theory that India's so-called Forward Policy 'provoked' the Chinese into conflict bears scrutiny. Contradicting the 'deeply flawed' arguments put forward by authors like Neville

Maxwell, in 2014 the media correspondent, commentator and author Bertil Lintner called for putting the 1962 border war in context and keeping the internal political situation in China always in focus[15]. In 1959, Mao had launched the Great Leap Forward, a disastrous foray into 'modernizing' China. By 1961, millions of people (estimates vary from 18 to 32 million) had died as a result of Mao's policies. As Mao's power faced eclipse, his stratagem was to unify the country against an outside enemy. India was a 'soft' target, having granted the Dalai Lama asylum for one. Attacking India was not a spur-of-the-moment decision provoked by the Forward Policy. Lintner points to what China did in the years before the 1962 war, besides military action against Tibetans inside Tibet. In January 1961, 'a combined force of three divisions, of 20,000 men, of regulars from the Chinese PLA launched a very similar attack across the northeastern border of Myanmar. The target was a string of secret, Nationalist Chinese Kuomintang camps on the Myanmar side of the border from where they had launched raids against China.' No Myanmar government had acknowledged this operation, Lintner observed. The operation was code-named 'Mekong River Operation', it was swift and over within weeks. Once it was finished, the Chinese troops withdrew to their side of the border. In Lintner's view, the Mekong River Operation was a 'rehearsal' for what happened with India in 1962.

Meanwhile, the relations between China and the Soviet Union were increasingly challenged by factors relating to Soviet–US relations, Soviet overtures of aid—including military assistance to India—as also the Soviet stance on Sino-Indian border tensions. The 'monolithic unity' that Mao Zedong had spoken of when referring to relations between China and the Soviet Union in 1957 had developed fissures. From 1959 onwards, the Chinese leadership had begun to warn the Soviets about the 'reactionary' nature of the Nehru government which was 'provoking' a border conflict with China. The *Tass* news agency carried a statement by the Soviet government on

9 September 1959 which deplored the latest border incident between India and China and stressed that the Soviet Union maintained friendly relations with both China and India—with 'fraternal friendship' characterizing relations with China and 'friendly cooperation' being the byword for relations with India 'in keeping with the ideas of peaceful coexistence'. As the conflict intensified, and relations with India worsened, the Chinese felt that Moscow was being partial to India while pretending to claim neutrality and impartiality, saying in early 1963: 'Here is the first instance in history in which a Socialist country, instead of condemning the armed provocations of the reactionaries of a capitalist country, condemned another fraternal Socialist country when it was confronted with such armed provocation.' The Soviets sent a verbal missive to the Chinese National People's Congress in February 1960 that 'one cannot possibly seriously think that a state such as India, which is militarily and economically immeasurably weaker than China, would launch a military attack on China and commit aggression against it.' From the Soviet point of view, the Chinese handling of the issue was 'an expression of a narrow nationalist attitude.' Incidents of Chinese shooting at Indian border forces it was felt, was designed to embarrass the Soviet Union in its moves to seek détente with the United States. There thus 'developed a parallel yet interlinked deterioration of relations between China and the Soviet Union and China and India'.[16]

Between November 1960 and October 1962 when China launched its military offensive against India, there was a lull in the differences between China and the Soviet Union on the India–China boundary question. But Moscow did finalize an arms deal with India on the eve of the conflict, and the Indian Air Force was also interested in the acquisition of Soviet MiG-21 aircraft together with helicopters and transport planes[17]. On 29 August 1962, India and the Soviet Union signed an agreement for the delivery of twelve MiG-21 aircraft and eight AN-12 transport planes.

Yet, in the summer of 1962, the Soviets 're-published maps of the Sino-Indian border showing both the Aksai Chin and NEFA as parts of China'. The 1959 edition of *Atlas Mira* showed Sikkim as an independent state.[18] Then, in April–May 1962, about 60,000 disaffected ethnic Kazakh Chinese Muslims fled from Xinjiang into bordering Soviet territory, arousing Chinese suspicions that these asylum-seekers were being encouraged and helped by the Soviet authorities. This running-with-the-hares and hunting-with-the-hounds approach of Moscow was held in abeyance during the Cuban missile crisis which escalated just as China was preparing its full-scale attack on Indian positions in October 1962. The postponement of the delivery of the Soviet MiGs to India ostensibly to de-escalate the situation was also in consonance with Moscow's need to win Chinese support during the Cuba crisis. On 13 and 14 October, Khrushchev told the Chinese Ambassador in Moscow, Liu Xiao, that the Soviet Union sided with China on the Sino-Indian boundary question and that his government would 'consider suspending the sale of MiG aircraft to India' while saying that the sale of these aircraft was of 'no military significance and would not tip the balance of power between China and India.'[19] China assessed Khrushchev as 'double-dealing on the Sino-Indian boundary question.' On 25 October, *Pravda* in an editorial said that the 'infamous' McMahon Line had been imposed on the Chinese people by the British colonialists. But China opposed what it termed as the Soviet 'surrender' to the Americans in Cuba as of 28 October and this opposition angered the so-called Khrushchev 'clique'.

From 5 November onwards, the Soviet tune changed and China was accused of playing for prestige and also 'creating a hotbed for the bacillus of nationalism and war mania' and pushing India into the arms of the West, and for implying that the responsibility for the conflict rested on India.[20] The Chinese response was deeply condemnatory: 'The CPSU and the Soviet government supported and encouraged the Indian government opposition to China on all three fronts—political, military and economic, giving aircraft and money to India to beat its brother China . . . Weren't Indian reactionaries and American imperialists wild with joy to take advantage of the opportunity to drive a wedge between China and the Soviet Union?'

By July 1962, top-levels of Chinese leadership were focused on dealing with the growing tensions on the border with India, with every move going to Mao for approval.[21] Chinese units were divided into three commands to handle the situation—one for the Aksai Chin area under the command of the southern Xinjiang military district; the second under the commander of the Tibet Military Region, Lt. Gen. Zhang Guohua; the third in Lhasa was under the region's political commissar, Tan Guansan, which would indicate that there were still worries about controlling a restive Tibetan population.[22] The Chinese were leaving nothing to chance, although their numbers were overwhelmingly superior to the Indians. In fact, in August 1962, the Indian Army's Western Command warned Delhi 'that political decisions were not being based on military means' referring to this imbalance in numbers and logistics support.[23] The allocation of commands by the Chinese to cover Aksai Chin and the eastern sector suggested more serious fighting was expected in the east. As the summer progressed, both Chinese and Indian 'words and deeds' matched each other in belligerence. The establishment by India of forty-five new forward posts in NEFA, thirty-five of them on the McMahon Line, 'could have been construed in Beijing as legitimate grounds for Chinese reaction.'[24]

In June 2011, the *People's Daily Online* posted an article on 'Why did Mao Zedong decide to start the India–China War?'[25] The article itself was an extract from *The Red Wall's Testimony* by Yin Jiamin (a former PLA Air Force officer) first published in 2004 and reprinted in 2009. The piece referred to Mao as saying that

India had 'really bullied us to the extreme. Since Nehru insisted on conflict, we have to play on and not step back ... However, our fight back is only in the nature of a warning and a punishment. It is only to tell Nehru and the Indian government that it is not right to solve the boundary issue through military means.' The article referred to Mao as having 'always considered territory as his flesh and blood'. In the Chinese view, Nehru had assessed the Chinese as weak and he assumed that 'China would not dare to go to war with India'. Mao after resolving to launch the attack against India, also informed Khrushchev, who did not display open opposition to the decision and recognized that if the Chinese faced an attack from the Indians, it would only be natural to counterattack. On 18 October, a meeting of the Politburo Standing Committee was convened by Mao to discuss the border dispute with India. Mao Zedong, Zhou Enlai, Liu Shaoqi, Zhu De, Deng Xiaoping, Chen Yi and He Long were present, in addition to a host of military generals including Civil War veteran Lei Yingfu and senior diplomats like Zhang Hanfu and Qiao Guanhua. Speaking after a presentation on the border situation had been made by Qiao and Lei, Zhou Enlai recommended a 'defensive counterattack' against India and this recommendation received unanimous approval of all present at the meeting. When Mao asked Zhang Guohua, the commander of the Tibet military region whether China could win the war, Zhang reassured him that it could. Mao said the worst outcome in case China lost would be occupation of Tibet by the Indian army (revealing China's continuing suspicions about India's motives regarding Tibet). 'But Tibet is China's sacred territory', Mao continued to state, 'There will be one day when we will win it back.'

The same piece by Yin Jiamin continues to state that at the suggestion of the Chief of General Staff, the 'counterattack' was timed for 20 October. The decision was to attack with overwhelming force. Mao, who was standing beside a large map made a gesture of embrace and said, 'We will penetrate inside, not fight'. Pointing to the Indian posts he said loudly, 'Sweep them off'. Zhang Guohua claimed, 'We are facing the royal army of India. They cannot be compared to the force of Chiang Kai-shek. They have not fought a war for a long time whereas we have had ones frequently; they have not crossed high mountains whereas we have often stayed in high mountains . . .'

Throughout September and early October 1962, the Chinese did not hide their preparations for war, in a direct signal to the Indians. Equipment, weapons and construction materials were moved to the forward areas where they could be observed easily. Tactical deployments and manouevres were however, concealed. Commanders enforced radio silence while other units broadcast misleading transmissions 'from and to phantom units deploying in the wrong direction.'[26]

Coup de grâce

On Saturday, 8 September 1962, a unit of armed Chinese troops advanced over the McMahon Line, contrary to previous assurances, crossed the Thagla Ridge—the watershed that in Indian maps marked the international boundary—and came down to the Dhola post, an encampment of soldiers from the Assam Rifles. The Chinese disputed the alignment of the boundary along the Thagla Ridge, claiming that the McMahon Line, as drawn in 1914, lay south of the area. The Forward Policy moves by India had resulted in the establishment of the post of Dhola. Following the development of 8 September, the Indians launched a 'Thagla Ridge Operation' with the modest aim of 'persuading' the Chinese to leave. Minimum force was to be used and fire was to be 'permitted only in self-defence'. This became the curtain-raiser to the NEFA campaign that ended in the disastrous rout of the Indian army in the eastern sector by 20 November. 'The Thagla incursion was gradually allowed to become the battle for the survival of those responsible for India's China policy including the Generals who had associated themselves with the tepid military response to the Chinese threat.'[27]

Nehru and Krishna Menon expected the operation to succeed. They felt the Chinese would not react massively, and that India would suffer 'only minor losses from the PLA's circumspect countermoves.'[28] The Army Chief, General Thapar, was believed too skeptical about such assertions but was overruled by the Defence Minister and by Foreign Secretary M.J. Desai, who 'described his opinions as being in keeping with those of Mr. Nehru.'[29] On 18 September, the Indian Government announced that the Army had been instructed to drive the Chinese out of the Dhola area. As firing intensified and there were growing reports of a Chinese build-up in the area, the Army pointed to the possibility of the Chinese retaliating elsewhere in NEFA and in Ladakh. H.C. Sarin, Joint Secretary in the Ministry of Defence, then issued a written order on 22 September 'that the Army should prepare and throw the Chinese out as soon as possible.'[30] Chief of Army Staff General Thapar was accordingly directed to evict the Chinese in the Kameng Division of NEFA where the Dhola post was located. Brigadier John Dalvi, who was commanding the 7th Brigade charged with securing Dhola, prepared a plan that would require proper logistical support. The build-up was not possible within the short time given to evict the Chinese. Differences between the Eastern Command of the Army and the XXXIII Corps charged with the defence of NEFA came out into the open.

On 21 September 1962, a note given by the Ministry of External Affairs to the Chinese Embassy stated that Chinese soldiers had opened fire on an Indian patrol post east of Dhola. A Chinese note of the same date accused the Indians of having attacked Chinese troops in the Namka Chu valley (immediately adjacent to the border with Bhutan), south of Thagla in the Che Dong area. It said that a 'most serious and the strongest protest' was being lodged with India and said that the Chinese side would be compelled 'to take the necessary defensive measures'.[31] The

Indians, for their part, continued to maintain that all areas south of the Thagla Ridge were part of Indian territory. Prime Minister Nehru meanwhile stated he continued to be prepared to hold talks with the Chinese. Congratulatory messages were sent to Beijing on the thirteenth anniversary of the founding of the PRC.

On 4 October, India announced the formation of a new army corps, the '4th', to defend NEFA under the command of Lt. Gen. B.M. Kaul who took himself off personally to the Dhola area to 'direct' operations. With no previous combat experience, the General began devising his plans to evict the Chinese. The possibilities of Indian troops, still in cotton uniforms, being frozen at Yumtso La (west of the Thag La peak) or being starved to death if their line of communications was cut off by the Chinese was brought home to him, in military briefings. On 6 October, the Chinese accused the Indians of willfully distorting facts and 'calling black white', charging Nehru with 'irresponsible statements' and that India should stop playing with fire and that the Indian side was 'advised to consider carefully the consequences',[32] that India had 'intruded to the north of the illegal McMahon Line.' On 9–10 October, heavy fighting broke out in the vicinity of Dhola post. General Kaul, who was camping in NEFA, said that the eviction of the Chinese was imperative 'in the national interest and the country was prepared to lose 20,000 lives if necessary, for the achievement of this aim.'[33] It was thus on 10 October 1962 that 'regular soldiers of China and India fought a pitched battle in the remote Thagla area,' in the area of Tseng-Jong or Chedong, at a height of 15,000–16,000 ft. The Chinese suffered heavy casualties in this encounter. On 12 October, the Sino-Pakistan boundary talks began in Peking. Also, on 12 October, Prime Minister Nehru, who was leaving for Colombo on an official visit, when asked by the Press as to what order had been given to troops in NEFA said: 'Our instructions are to free our country'. This was played up in the media as Nehru having ordered the army to throw the Chinese out.

On 14 October, President Radhakrishnan called for unity among the Indian people to meet Chinese aggression, while Defence Minister Krishna Menon said India would not negotiate a surrender, but would fight to the last man to expel the Chinese from NEFA. On the same day, the *People's Daily* in an editorial declared that a 'massive invasion of Chinese territory by Indian troops in the eastern sector . . . seems imminent' and proceeded to issue 'an implicit warning'. On 16 October, the Military Affairs Commission in Beijing 'decided to annihilate Indian troops north of the McMahon Line; the following day the operational order was given 'liquidate the invading Indian army'.[34] In the dawn of 20 October 1962, a massive, and obviously preplanned, Chinese attack was launched in the Namka Chu sector and other parts of NEFA as well as in Ladakh. From 20 October to 18 November, in Ladakh, Indian posts at Daulat Beg Oldi, the Galwan Valley, Hot Springs, Demchok, Spanggur, Rezangla to name a few areas, were overrun. The Chushul airfield was attacked but was not taken. Chushul was eight to ten miles west of even the Chinese claim line of 1960.

Despite severe logistical shortcomings, the lack of preparedness, the suddenness of the Chinese attack, and manpower shortages, Indian troops in Ladakh fought courageously and on many occasions, to the last man, in the defence of their positions. The situation was different in the eastern sector, where the Army defences collapsed and disintegrated without much resistance and the shortcomings in strategic planning and the higher direction of war were tragically exposed. In NEFA, the Chinese attacked in force in areas south of the McMahon Line across the breadth of this sector. Tawang was threatened and fell on 25 October, Asaphila to the south of Longju was captured, and Kibithoo fifteen miles south of the eastern section of the McMahon Line was also taken. South of Tawang, the Indian defensive position at Sela was attacked and overrun. On 18 November the town of Bomdila, over forty miles south of the McMahon Line was attacked and fell to Chinese forces. Similar Indian reverses took place in the Subansiri, Siang and Lohit Frontier Divisions of NEFA.

The tide of defeat could not be reversed. By their onslaught in the eastern sector, the Chinese were obviously trying to demonstrate 'once and for all that they did not accept the McMahon Line'.[35] As equipment shortages were glaringly revealed, Nehru told Krishna Menon on 29 October, 'I do not know how I shall explain to Parliament why we have been found lacking in equipment. It is not much good shifting about blame. The fact remains that we have been found lacking and there is an impression that we have approached these things in a somewhat amateurish way'.[36] But despite the pall of gloom that enveloped New Delhi and the rest of the country, there could be no doubt that the Chinese attacks had not cowed the Indians; the sense of solidarity and unity among the people in defiance of what was seen as naked aggression could not be denied.

On 20 October, Soviet leader Khrushchev reportedly asked Nehru to accept China's conditions for a border settlement and urged him not to introduce the question in the United Nations since the USSR would have to support the Chinese.[37] In his reply, Nehru denied that it was India that was attempting to settle the dispute with China by force. At the same time, India could not accept any claim that 'is contrary to history, treaties and its own traditions, more especially when this is occupied by aggression.' India had always been prepared for discussions towards a peaceful settlement but how could such a course be pursued when Chinese armies were present on Indian territory, Nehru asked. China would need to restore the status quo prior to 8 September, he insisted.[38] On 21 October, the United States government expressed shock over Chinese aggression against India and stated their sympathy for India.

On 24 October, Premier Zhou Enlai in a letter addressed to Prime Minister Nehru put forward a three-point proposal for settlement of the dispute. Firstly, that pending a peaceful settlement, both parties respect the line of actual control along the border, and that the armed forces of each side withdraw 20 km from this line, and disengage. Secondly, if India was in agreement with the first point of the proposal, the Chinese would withdraw their frontier guards to the north of the McMahon Line, while both sides should at the same time undertake not to cross the line of actual control in the middle and western sectors of the border. Thirdly, talks should be held once again by the Prime Ministers of China and India. Nehru's reply was sent on 27 October. In it he expressed his hurt and grief over the fact that his 'hopes and aspirations for peaceful and friendly neighbourly relations' with China had 'been shattered by the hostile and unfriendly twist given in India-China relations over the past few years.' He said India was not able to understand 'the niceties of the Chinese three-point proposals' and that India wished to see a reversion to the status quo along the entire boundary, as it prevailed before 8 September 1962. If China could agree to the latter, then India was prepared to resolve differences by talks and discussions. Meanwhile, a *Pravda* editorial of 25 October supported the Zhou Enlai proposals of 24 October, and the Soviets—for the first time—took a position on the McMahon Line, calling it 'notorious'.[39]

On 26 October, a state of emergency was declared in India while Nehru pledged that India would fight the Chinese until 'final victory is achieved.' On 27 October, he said that India was at war with China in every sense of the word although war had not been declared. Writing to his chief ministers, Nehru spoke of the need to concentrate 'on this great struggle which threatens our integrity and freedom. Everything else will have to take second place.' He called the conflict 'a supreme national issue'.[40] On 31 October, Krishna Menon tendered his resignation as Defence Minister. 'The lack of preparedness of the army under his leadership now made Menon look 'like Cardinal Wolseley, left naked to his friends and enemies".[41] His political eclipse was greeted with delight in both Washington and London who had all along assumed that Menon had a Machiavellian hold over Nehru which seemed a naïve assumption since the Prime Minister exercised his individual judgement on matters of external policy and strategic direction. As *The Economist* noted in January 1962, the 'idea of Jawaharlal Nehru as the empty vehicle of any other man's policy is a curious one, and only such assumptions make the 'Menon' theory of Indian policy tenable.'[42] Menon was to assert some years later that he had been neither 'a buffoon nor a Rasputin'[43]. Mercurial, insecure, temperamental, sharply intelligent and calculating, it is difficult however to term him an evil genius, his reputation as one was more a Western creation.[44]

Returning to the tumultuous autumn of 1962, of interest was the American endorsement of the McMahon Line which came on 27 October. It was a fortuitous occurrence that slipped through a wall of official reservations about recognition of the Indian position. The initiative was taken by the American Ambassador John Galbraith in Delhi. He had received a message from the State Department basically expressing skepticism about the Line and instructing the Ambassador that 'because Nationalist China did not accept the McMahon Line as the legitimate border, neither should Galbraith and the United States.'[45] Ignoring this guidance, Galbraith issued a statement endorsing the Indian position, after obtaining permission from National Security Advisor McGeorge Bundy and the White House to do so. This high-visibility gesture in the thick of the conflict, put the Americans on India's side much to the chagrin of the US Embassy in Taiwan which protested bitterly. Washington was, of course, totally preoccupied with the Cuban missile crisis at this time. The US Embassy in Delhi was sending off 'telegrams on various urgent matters without the slightest knowledge of whether they are being received or acted upon. It is like marching troops out of the trenches and over no man's land without knowing whether they get through or get shot down en route,' Galbraith observed.[46]

On 27 October 1962, the Indian Ambassador in Washington B.K. Nehru met US President John Kennedy to deliver a letter from Nehru concerning the serious developments on the frontier with China. The letter expressed the confidence that in this hour of crisis for India, the country would have the 'sympathy and support' of the President and his administration. Kennedy assured the Ambassador of the full sympathy and support of the US and that his government was 'prepared to demonstrate this attitude in ways which might be helpful . . . within our capabilities.' The thrust of the President's remarks was that the US was ready to be of assistance and 'when Indians told us what would be most useful we would work out terms and procedures.' The American discomfort with Krishna Menon was on display when the President asked what the effect of the reverses suffered by India would have on Menon's future, adding that he was an 'Indian problem'.[47]

In his desperation, Nehru, already a figure shrunken by the weight of circumstances surrounding the imploding of a carefully-fostered China policy, turned to the United States for help in arms, equipment and defence support. The Americans also tacitly supported the groundswell of opinion within the Congress Party and the Opposition for Krishna Menon's removal. Nehru was to comply on October 31 when 'it became clear that the Congress Party was willing to accept the Prime Minister's resignation if Menon was not let go.'[48] The US commenced delivery of military assistance in early November. C-130 Hercules aircraft carried out drops of arms and ammunition supplies as well as essential clothing to Indian soldiers on the battlefront. American aircraft regularly landed in Delhi and also carried out photo missions over the Indo-Tibetan border. The then US Assistant Secretary of State Roger Hilsman, a veteran of the Burma campaign in the Second World War, personally coordinated the aid effort.[49] The United States also worked to restrain Pakistan against taking any 'political or military action that would require India to divert focus or forces' from the China border.[50]

As Nehru himself was to concede after the war was over, 'There is no nonalignment vis-à-vis China.'[51] Large segments of the Indian political class, and public opinion, saw the rationale for India to turn to the United States in this hour of need. On 7 November the Prime Minister wrote to U.S. Ambassador Galbraith expressing gratitude for the American arms lift underway. On 19 November, he addressed two letters in quick succession to President Kennedy asking for assistance.[52] The first spoke of the 'grim situation in our struggle for survival and in defending all that India stands for against an unscrupulous and powerful aggressor'. He said there was need for transport and jet fighters to stem the tide of aggression. The second letter spoke of the further deterioration in the situation with the retreat of Indian forces from the Sela defence line and the threat to the oil fields in Assam. All sections of the border were threatened, he said. In view of the 'desperate' situation, the Prime Minister asked for immediate support from the US to strengthen India's air force—the 'ask' was for a 'minimum of 12 squadrons or supersonic all-weather fighters' and also radar cover. These needs were immediate, he added. The Prime Minister wanted that US Air Force personnel 'man these fighters and radar installations' while Indian personnel were being trained. These fighters and transport planes would be used to protect Indian cities and installations from Chinese air attacks, and also, if it was possible that the US planes manned by US personnel 'assist the Indian Air Force in air battles with the Chinese air force over Indian areas where air action by the I.A.F. against the Chinese communication lines supplies and troop concentration may lead to counter air action by the Chinese.' The assistance requested would be used entirely against the Chinese, and Pakistan had been reassured on this matter.

Nehru's letter was an extraordinarily desperate one, a tragic exposition of anguish and defeat. The response from Washington, on the eve of the Chinese ceasefire, contained in a telegram from Secretary of State Dean Rusk to Ambassador

Galbraith[53] was that the message from Nehru 'in effect proposes not only a military alliance between India and the United States but complete commitment by us in a fighting war' and that it was 'a proposal which cannot be reconciled with any further pretense of nonalignment'. Rusk underlined the importance of not pushing Moscow to support Beijing in the event of full-scale American support for India. It was necessary for India to mobilize its own diplomatic and political resources to seek 'the broadest base of support throughout the world'. In the event, even as Nehru expressed his readiness to discuss India's requirements with a group of American officials dispatched from Washington, the unilateral ceasefire announced by China on 20 November over Beijing radio, was a development that altered the situation.

During the weeks of the crisis enveloping India, the Chinese propaganda onslaught on Nehru was vicious. A *People's Daily* editorial on 27 October titled 'More on Nehru's Philosophy in the Light of the Sino-Indian Boundary Question',[54] blamed the conflict on the 'deliberate provocations and aggression by the Nehru government.' It claimed that it was 'no accident' that the 'interference in Tibet' and the 'provoking' of border incidents by 'India's ruling circles headed by Nehru' should have both transpired as part of the 'expansionist philosophy' of India. This philosophy was essentially that 'The places that I have occupied are mine, and so are those I intend to occupy. Since I was able to occupy an inch of your territory yesterday, I certainly can occupy a yard of your territory today.' The editorial claimed that Nehru was no spokesman of the Indian people and India had not freed itself from 'dependence on imperialism'.

The Soviet government's concern over the hostilities did not abate. Indian officials were also sensitive to the need to enlist greater Soviet support for the country in the conflict with China. The Soviet ambassador in Delhi, I. Benediktov left a detailed account of a conversation with Secretary General R.K. Nehru where the latter said that the crisis with China was no mere border conflict but 'part of a general strategy of Chinese leftist dogmatists-sectarians who obviously now have the upper hand in the leadership of the CCP (the Chinese Communist Party)' and who were trying to force India to abandon its policy of non-alignment. Nehru told the Soviet envoy that he was convinced that these actions were an extension of the CCP's ideological disputes with the Communist Party of the Soviet Union (CPSU).[55] The Indian Ambassador in Moscow, T.N. Kaul, kept the Prime Minister informed of his conversations with Khrushchev and other senior Russian leaders.

After the end of the Cuban crisis, the Soviet tilt towards China seemed to correct itself with the adoption of a more understanding position vis-a-vis India. Khrushchev spoke of the need for 'compromise' on the Sino-Indian question, citing the example of the Cuban crisis where he said, 'There was no victor and no loser. Only humanity and reason were true victors.' Kaul spoke of senior Soviet officials being 'almost apologetic about their inability to take our (India's) side openly.'[56] In December 1962, Nehru in a meeting with Soviet Ambassador Benediktov discussed the situation with China.[57] The Soviet envoy repeated his government's line that the border conflict between India and China be resolved through peaceful means. Nehru said that General Secretary Khrushchev had given the world 'a great example during the incident with Cuba'. He said India had not begun the war with China; it had been thrust on India. India wished that the problem was settled. But the entire Indian nation, including 'simple peasants, workers and employees' felt 'the harshest feelings toward China, toward what it did against India'. The Indian people 'insist on the liberation of territory that belongs to India.' India wished to sit at the negotiating table with China, but 'for this it is necessary that the position on the border that existed 3 months ago be restored—the position on 8 September.'

The Chinese announced a unilateral ceasefire on 21 November. In the eastern sector, they began their withdrawal from the occupied areas to the north of the McMahon Line. India's morale lay in tatters, and shibboleths about the impregnability of the Himalayan frontier stood exposed. In the western sector, the Chinese had aimed at and largely succeeded in reaching their 1960 claim line and ensured that there was no Indian threat to the Aksai Chin highway. But the Indian Army had fought bravely and fiercely against the Chinese in this sector. Unlike in the eastern sector, they had not suffered a rout even if there were military reverses. In the east, the 'Fighting Fourth', the 4 Mountain Division, which had won laurels in Italy fighting the Germans in the Second World War, had virtually disintegrated. Even after announcement of the ceasefire, the Chinese continued to ambush and fire at withdrawing Indian troops and even at road workers of the Border Roads Organization.

In Ladakh, many battlefields where dead Indian soldiers lay, fell within the Chinese claim line of 1960. It was only in the spring of 1963 that their bodies were retrieved and cremated with full battle honours. The battleground of Rezang La (depicted on the front jacket of this book) is etched in the memory of many Indians as one such instance where Major Shaitan Singh and men of the C Company of 13 Kumaon (Kumaon Regiment) of the Indian Army fought to the last man in an epic struggle against the Chinese who outnumbered them many times over.[58] Veteran journalist and commentator Inder Malhotra summed up the tragic history of this battle in the following words in 2012 when he said that the Battle of Rezang La was the 'brightest of the bright spots in the pervasive darkness of 1962'.[59] In the Namkha Chu area of NEFA, skeletons of Indian soldiers were spotted as late as 1987–88. In 1965, when India released final casualty figures for the war, they were: 1,383 dead, 1,696 missing and 3,968 taken prisoner by the Chinese. Twenty-six of those taken prisoner died in POW camps in China from battle wounds, the rest were repatriated to India in May 1963. The vast majority of casualties (90 per cent) were in NEFA. There is no authoritative account of Chinese losses, but it is noteworthy that India did not capture even one Chinese soldier during the conflict.[60]

In early November 1962, the British Embassy in Beijing writing to the Foreign Office in London on the Chinese attitude to India said, 'As such, she (India) constitutes both in herself, and as an alternative pole of attraction in Asia, an obstacle to achievement of China's objectives, and the Chinese have obvious interest in weakening and humiliating her. They no doubt calculate that if Nehru is driven openly away from his non-aligned position, which they have just formally declared a sham, this will also reduce his attraction for others and serve their ultimate purpose. They may also hope that external troubles will set up strains leading to revolutionary change inside India. The border war is nicely calculated to serve these ends.'[61]

The rout suffered by India had effectively dethroned the country's position as a leader of the non-aligned world, and destroyed Nehru's image as an influential world statesman and arbiter between the East and the West. China had demonstrated its military superiority and strength and had succeeded in its intent to 'teach' India 'a lesson'. The decision to withdraw from areas overrun in NEFA was also to demonstrate that China was no self-aggrandizing aggressor and that having won its 'victory' and achieved the aim of showing its military superiority, it had no desire to retain territory forcibly captured from neighbours.

For Mao himself, after the disasters of the Great Leap Forward, the Anti-Rightist campaign launched in 1957 and ravages of the widespread famine that consumed China in the late 1950s and early 1960s leading to the death of at least 40 million, which had shaken his leadership position, 1962 became that turning point to salvage his fortunes. The power struggle within the Chinese Communist Party between Mao and his supporters on one side and his opponents on the other, came to a head during that year and ended with the ultra-leftists supporting Mao and the Chairman himself winning this 'class struggle'. The victory against India further consolidated Mao's position. Mao was now intent on being seen not only as the revolutionary leader of China but of revolutionary movements worldwide.[62]

The Maoist strategy during the brief onslaught on India had focused on 'robust logistics, strategic surprise, a dramatic shift from defence to offence, terrain advantage' in the East, and troop morale, plus the fleeting opportunity provided by the Cuban missile crisis which diverted attention away from the India-China theatre. Nehru had expected restraint from China, but it was a gross miscalculation, ignoring Sun Tzu that 'humble words and increased preparations were signs that the enemy was about to advance.'[63] The pattern of Chinese operations which echoed those in Korea in 1950, applied the teachings of Sun Tzu: 'exhibit a maiden's coyness. Afterwards emulate the running hare, it will be too late for the enemy'—first displaying a deceptively weak image and then exploding in overwhelming force—'Beijing combined the orthodox with the unorthodox to confuse' the opponent both at command and ground level. Once tactical success was achieved, Chinese commanders 'chose not to pursue whether the enemy fled in panic or retreated in order', ancient strategies embedded in Chinese strategic culture, which even the Communists under Mao relied on heavily.[64] The chastisement and punishment of India, without conquest or domination, transformed Mao's internal difficulties in the 1959-60 period and raised China's international profile especially in the developing world, expanding on Zhou's Bandung forays.

It is often speculated that the outcome of the conflict may have been different for India, if the Air Force had been inducted into the military operations against China. Writing in 2006, a senior Indian Air Force (IAF) officer[65] noted that the omission of the Air Force had been 'costly and catastrophic' as a result of multiple factors 'that impinged on the decision-making process at the highest level.'

A significant factor had been the advice of Intelligence Bureau Chief Mullik that Chinese bombers would attack Indian cities if the IAF were used in combat. American Ambassador Galbraith shared a similar opinion based on an over-estimation of the capabilities of the Chinese Air Force. Another factor was the absence of joint planning between the Indian Army and Air Force. The American analyst George Tanham opined that 'The Indian government, although in a desperate state and calling for massive American air support, did not investigate what its air power might do to redress the situation.'[66] The IAF was apparently quite confident about using its air power against China, and as a fact, their Canberra planes flew 22 photographic reconnaissance missions between 13 October and 11 November 1962 over Aksai Chin, Tawang, Sela and Walong areas, with some sorties at '300 feet above Chinese concentrations', without any damage to the aircraft from Chinese anti-aircraft artillery. But despite advice from the Air Force about the modest capabilities of Chinese Air Force operating from Tibet and beyond, Nehru was apprehensive of even a single bomb falling over Delhi 'and the war escalating out of control'. The Air Force could have been used 'for interdiction, battlefield air interdiction, attack on areas captured by the Chinese, attack as a retribution on deeper targets'. There is a distinct possibility that the use of combat air power by India could have mitigated to some extent the nature of the defeat inflicted on the country by the Chinese.

On 14 November 1962, India's Lok Sabha adopted a resolution[67] expressing regret that despite India's gestures of goodwill and friendship towards China and the principles of *Panchsheel*, the Chinese had committed aggression and 'initiated a massive invasion of India'. Nehru called the resolution a 'resolution of resolve, of determination and of dedication'. The House placed on record its high appreciation of the 'valiant struggle of men and officers' of the Armed Forces and noted that the 'flame of liberty and sacrifice has been kindled anew' among the people of India in their response to the crisis. It also acknowledged the moral and material support received from a large number of friendly countries. Most notably, 'the firm resolve of the Indian people to drive out the aggressor from the sacred soil of India, however long and hard the struggle may be', was solemnly affirmed. What this implied was that in the popular will, India's historically claimed boundaries were sacrosanct, and the nation remained committed to seeking the relinquishing by the Chinese of their hold over territory claimed by India within these boundaries as shown on Indian maps. That position endures to this day, nearly six decades after the conflict. Speaking in the Lok Sabha in the debate on the resolution, the Prime Minister asked members to take a 'realistic view'. His words were:"I have said that in a war between India and China, it is patent that if you think in terms of victory and defeat—there might be battles and we might push them back, as we hope to— but if either country thinks in terms of bringing the other to its knees, it manifestly cannot and will not happen. Let us be realistic. Are we going to march to Peking?'[68]

Nehru himself drew a distinction between battles won or lost, and a country's defeat. Countries, he said, 'cannot run away from geography' and the basic struggle between India and China was 'going to last a very long time.' But to say that China was going to defeat (or had defeated) India 'in the sense of a real defeat' was difficult to imagine from his point of view. India had not been defeated in the manner in which Germany had been defeated in the Second World War. Neither, he felt, had India been humiliated: 'I refuse to say India has been humiliated, even to some extent. I refuse to consider India such a country as to be humiliated solely by a battle being lost. A country is a much bigger thing.[69] But he spoke from a wilderness, with his opponents unwilling to concede such finer points of understanding. The Prime Minister remained steadfast too about India's frontier alignments and the arguments buttressing their case. For instance, the North East Frontier Agency (NEFA) as he said, 'theoretically and constitutionally' had always been a part of India, and from the very first day when the Chinese came into Tibet, India had adapted her policy to 'consider this fact of a great, dynamic and powerful country, aggressive and expansive, coming nearer to our borders.' The fact was that 'we were always working in NEFA, developing NEFA, sitting on the borders there' which the Chinese interpreted as India having entered NEFA in the nineteen fifties, and that it 'was theirs all the time.' This was a 'remarkable way' of stating their case which was a different matter. It was a 'little difficult for some of us trained otherwise to keep pace with the perversities of truth that they (China) utter.'[70] Referring to his remarks soon after the 1962 conflict had begun, that India had been 'living in a world of unreality', he clarified a year later that what he meant was the 'world is cruel. We thought in terms of carrying the banner of peace everywhere and it has betrayed us. China has betrayed us; the world has betrayed us. Our efforts at peace and following the path of peace have been knocked on the head. Now we have to take to war; we are forced to, much against our will.'[71]

In September 1963, India's Defence Minister Y.B. Chavan made a statement in the Lok Sabha[72] about the results of the enquiry to investigate reverses in the operations against the Chinese in October–November 1962, in both Ladakh and NEFA. The enquiry in question was the Henderson Brooks–Bhagat Report believed to be in seven volumes, along with appendices, which has still not been officially released by the Indian government. In March 1963, Mr Chavan had disclosed to the Lok Sabha the terms of reference of the enquiry conducted by two senior officers of the Army Lt. Gen. Henderson Brooks and Brigadier P.S. Bhagat into the 'debacle' of 1962, on the directive of the Chief of Army Staff. The scope of the enquiry had dealt with training, equipment, the system of command, the physical fitness of Indian troops, and the capacity of the Army's Commanders at all levels to influence the men under them.[73] For the Defence Minister, the Report was a 'real hot potato'.[74]

Mr Chavan said the government had decided against release of the report as it 'endangered our security' and could 'affect the morale of those entrusted with safeguarding the security of our borders'. Briefing the Lower House about the findings of the report, the Minister said that one of its conclusions was that the Indian troops 'did not have a slant for a war being launched by China', they had 'no requisite knowledge of the Chinese tactics, and ways of war, their weapons, equipment and capabilities'. Also, the 'concept of mountain warfare' as understood by the higher commanders needed to be put right. 'Training in leadership' was another problem. Equipment shortages were an issue. A crucial difficulty was that equipment could not be reached in time to the forward formations in the mountains because of logistical difficulties. There was an overall shortage of vehicles, and of these, what was available were too old and their efficiency not adequate for operating in mountain terrain. However, the army's weapons were 'adequate to fight the Chinese and compared favourably with theirs'. The enquiry was critical of the practice among higher Army formations 'of interfering in tactical details even to the extent of detailing troops for specified tasks' instead of leaving it to commanders in the field to make on-the-spot decisions. As far as physical fitness of the troops was concerned, the problem had arisen because many were not acclimatized to fight at high altitudes. Where acclimatization had taken place, as in Ladakh, 'the height factor presented no difficulty.' The capacity of commanders was a mix of good and 'not-so-good' as had obtained in any army 'in the last World War'. Some higher commanders did not depend on the initiative of the lower commanders who 'alone could have the requisite knowledge of the terrain and local conditions of troops under them.'[75]

As far as intelligence gathering was concerned, Mr Chavan revealed that the collection of intelligence was not satisfactory and that the acquisition of intelligence was slow and the reporting of it vague. A clear picture of the Chinese build-up was not made available. There were shortcomings about the dissemination of intelligence, too. He then came to the key point regarding the higher direction of operations. Here he alluded to the lack of proper policy guidance and major directives by the government to the Army. But overall, the troops in Ladakh had done 'an excellent job even when overwhelmed and outnumbered.' In the eastern-most part of NEFA, the withdrawal from Walong had been orderly in the face of a 'vastly superior enemy'. But in the Kameng sector in the western edge of NEFA, the battles were at heights 'not known to the Army and at places which geographically had all the disadvantages for our troops and many advantages for the enemy.' As to the famous 'Fourth Division', the sad fact was that this was the Fourth only in name, for it was not fighting with its original formations intact. Troops from 'different formations had to be rushed to the borders to fight under the banner of the 'Fourth Division' while the original formations of the Division itself were deployed elsewhere.'[76]

A crucial segment of the Defence Minister's statement referred to the 'Direction of Operation' or essentially, the 'Higher Direction of War'. The Opposition in Parliament wanted the enquiry to expose faulty political direction in the conduct of the war and to hold the Prime Minister and Krishna Menon accountable. Chavan had this to say on the subject: 'Even the largest and best equipped of armies need(s) to be given proper policy guidance and major directives by the Government whose instrument it is.' Implied in this was an admission of the failure of political leadership. Army Chief General Thapar, in an article written in January 1971, attributed the decision to evict the Chinese from the Thagla Ridge in the eastern sector and the publicity given to it, and not the so-called Forward Policy, as responsible for the start of the war. (*The Statesman*, 9 January 1971). 'Krishna Menon's 'Higher Direction of War' was based on a basic assumption that China would never go to war with India. It was Pakistan alone that posed a threat.'[77]

Nehru has long been criticized for the statement he allegedly made at Madras (now Chennai) airport on 12 October 1962 to the effect, 'Throw the Chinese out'. What he actually said was 'Our instructions are to free our territory . . . I cannot fix a date, that is entirely for the army to decide'. The Prime Minister had been fully briefed about the situation in the Thagla and Namkha Chu area, and his statement was not a public order to the Army who were empowered to exercise tactical judgement based on military considerations.

Perhaps the most dignified and sober response to the Defence Minister's statement—in an otherwise disturbed and accusatory mood in Parliament about the ignominy of the defeat India had suffered and fixing responsibility for failures in leadership and the 'Higher Direction of War'—was from Congress Member K.C. Pant who while commending the Defence Minister for a 'great and sober speech', quoted a few words of wisdom from Winston Churchill after the defeat at Dunkirk in June 1940: 'They seek to indict those who were responsible for the guidance of our affairs. This also would be a foolish and pernicious process. Of this I am quite sure that if we open a quarrel between the past and the present, we shall find that we have lost the future.'[78] Presciently, for all future generations, Pant noted that this enquiry should be regarded 'not as a post-mortem, but as a diagnosis. It is but an incident in a developing situation.' Neither the Prime Minister nor Krishna Menon intervened in the debate. The Prime Minister had, however, hand written the concluding paragraph of Chavan's statement when it had been shown to him prior to its presentation in Parliament. His words were as follows: 'What happened in Se La and Bomdi La were severe reverses for us, but we must remember that other countries with powerful defence forces have sometimes suffered in the initial stages of a war. The aggressor has a certain advantage, more especially when the aggression is sudden and well-prepared. We are now on the alert . . .'[79]

In China, histories of the conflict with India refer to it as the 'Sino-Indian Border War of Self Defence and Counter Attack'. In August 1994, a history of the war was published by the Chinese—

by a so-called Chronicler Group of the History of the Sino-Indian Border War. It describes the 1962 conflict as a war fought by 'Chinese Tibetan and Xinjiang frontier guards in an attempt to fairly and justly conclude the Sino-Indian border dispute.' It describes many areas along this border as 'highly contested territories', and that the war was 'not fortuitous', blaming the Indian government as having 'tried relentlessly to interfere with the Chinese government's effort to peacefully liberate Tibet, safeguard its privileges in Tibet, continue the Tibetan feudal serfdom system, support mutiny among Tibetan higher officials, and attempt to turn Tibet into a Sino-Indian buffer zone.' The 1962 conflict is seen as 'a continuation and development of the disputes and struggles along the border and the inevitable result of the Indian government's inheritance of the imperial ambitions of Britain, its expansionist goals, regional hegemonic agenda, and its deliberate attempt to create destructive tension and encroach and invade Chinese territory.' The study says the Indian Government concluded that any 'Indian aggression, no matter how violent and threatening, would not be met with any Chinese resistance. They thus embarked on a hazardous journey of military gamble and risk-taking.'[80]

The Chinese response is described as an 'anti-encroachment struggle' against India, the strategy being used to neutralize as 'pushback, close in, surround, and blockage' and the formation of an 'interlock situation'. The experience of the 'war of self-defence and counter-attack' is enumerated as: endeavor for a complete political and military victory, attain the military goals of the war of self-defence and counter-attack, execute the Chinese Communist Party's principles and policies with absolute resolution and political dedication, enforce logistical and rear-base development, focus on transportation; ensure logistical support, promote political security and economic development in border areas and 'fight a people's war in a modern era'.

In 2012, a number of articles appeared in the language press in China on the fiftieth anniversary of the conflict. One of them, prepared by the Academy of Military Sciences talked of the war as having 'cast a shadow for half a century'.[81] India was blamed for having caused the war as a result of the implementation of the Forward Policy. It quoted Chen Yi as saying 'Nehru's 'Forward Policy' is a dagger, with which he hopes to pierce out our heart. But we can't just close our eyes and die'. It referred to emotions from the trauma caused by the war still engulfing Indian minds and that 'anxiety is still the dominant emotion in India'. China, the article continued, had withdrawn from territories occupied during the conflict despite obvious military advantage, and even the Indians had 'failed to understand why the Chinese side took this decision.'

The prevalent international and domestic view was that this decision had been driven by economic considerations since China was coming out of three years of very difficult times. Also, the Chinese wanted to avoid a long-term war since logistical difficulties were involved given the 'complex geographical barriers and harsh climatic conditions'. There were analysts who believed that the intervention of the two superpowers—the US and the Soviet Union—forced the Chinese army to retreat. The Soviets had 'secretly' supported 'the dirty tactics' of the Indian side providing arms and equipment to the Indian army and air force. The United States also provided 'massive' military support to India apart from the aircraft carrier *USS Enterprise* setting sail from the Pacific to the Indian Ocean and entering the Bay of Bengal. But all these theories were 'guesswork'—the Chinese Government and Army had never been afraid of 'ghosts' and 'horror stories', and China had 'imposed a unilateral withdrawal, mainly because this was in accordance with the clear-cut war aims that it had set for itself. The goal of the 1962 War of Self-Defence was not to regain the territory that had been eroded but to give a fitting reply to Indian provocations at the border.' The retreat of the Chinese army 'was in keeping with the consolidated and balanced considerations of the larger strategic direction that we (China) wished to take in China's neighbourhood'. Mao had sent word to Nehru, long before the conflict began, 'That the main focus of China's attention and struggle lay in the East, in the Western Pacific region, in order to combat the ferocious and aggressive Western imperialism and was not aimed against India.' Talking about the 1962 War, Mao said that 'this war has ensured at least ten years stability on the Sino-Indian border' and history had shown how correct he was, since his expectations had been exceeded by a long margin.

On 1 November 2012, the Chinese television outlet, Phoenix TV carried a report by Yang Zhifang[82] which said that the flight of the Dalai Lama to India 'was the initial spark that finally ignited the Sino-Indian border conflict.' The report said that the 'Dalai's fleeing to India was a gift from Nehru to Mao' since once the Tibetan religious leader fled to India and a large number of his followers also started fleeing to India, it 'provided China with a situation where military interdiction became the natural course to take.' Indian troops on the border thus came into contact with intercept operations against Tibetans that had been launched by Chinese forces and this resulted in a quiet situation on the border being quickly transformed into a tense and sharp standoff. Thus, the 'flight of the Dalai to India in 1959, acted as a detonator that set off the fuse on the Sino-Indian conflict.' Another article by Liu Zongyi, a research fellow at the Center for South Asia Studies in Shanghai, attributed divergences over the alignment of the McMahon Line also as one of the fundamental reasons for the border war.[83]

Shan Zhiqiang, writing in the *National Geography* in December 2012, spoke of travelling along the Aksai Chin highway and visiting a 'martyrs cemetery' built at Kangxiwar in Aksai Chin to honour Chinese soldiers who had lost their lives in 1962. It described the cemetery as having 'rows upon rows of graves with tombstones' of soldiers from various parts of China—a total of 106 soldiers, many of them 'in the age group of 20 years or so'.

China could never give up Aksai Chin as 'this would have meant a severe rupture in the relationship between Xinjiang and Tibet'. But the region where China gained the biggest victories was in the eastern sector, Shan went on to say, and after the unilateral withdrawal, 'the area where we lost the most territory was also in the East.' This was a region of 'great strategic significance'. And then the writer goes on to quote the Chinese military writer Jin Hui who stated, 'With regard to the border conflict of 1962 between India and China, it was very clear who was the victor and who was the loser. But looking back after 30 years [the piece was written in 1995], the person who was the winner was winner only in name, while the loser walked away with everything on the table'. Shan then concludes: 'Today, while some people call the Chinese actions as the most virtuous move on the battlefield', some others refer to it as the 'biggest blunder'. The war of 1962 had provided China in his view with 'a historic opportunity to regain most of our lost territory' but by unilaterally withdrawing 20 k.m. north of the 'illegal McMahon Line', China had 'lost the initiative'. 'We gifted back what all we had gained without a quid-pro-quo'. The model of Chinese action which was also mirrored in the war with Vietnam could be summed up as follows: 'Encounter provocation –> Military Action –>Victory –> Unconditional Withdrawal –> A Return to Normalcy'. It could be concluded with a 'deep sense of disappointment' that 'China has lost this territory (south of the McMahon Line) forever.'[84]

A Chinese academic who specializes in border issues and conflicts, in conversation with this author in 2014 maintained that Mao Zedong did not want war with India but China's internal problems at the time and the fact that the PLA was 'very aggressive and felt the Indian army was bothering us and wanted to teach the Indians a good lesson' propelled Mao forward. 'The war was raised by the military side', he said, and 'Mao was forced to agree'. His strategy (Mao's) was to have a 'quick, short war to make the Indians to agree to sit down and talk'. But the decision after the conflict to withdraw from NEFA came as a real surprise to the PLA who were apparently assuming that the captured territory was now theirs to administer, and 'had found people to be county leaders and local officials/identified them in the Eastern Sector'. Suddenly, Mao had ordered them to come back. 'Our soldiers were really surprised when they were ordered to go back—they thought this was not real news', my interlocutor told me.

In the summer of 2017, when there was a prolonged standoff between Chinese and Indian forces on the Doklam Plateau in Bhutan, among the hostile reactions circulated in the Chinese media was a statement by the deputy director of the Defence Ministry, Colonel Wu Qian warning 'certain persons in the Indian army to keep historical lessons in mind.' Dai Xu, a retired colonel of the PLA Air Force and a pronounced hawk, wrote in a blog that in 1962 'China only used a knife to kill a chicken' [part of an idiom: 'no need to slaughter a chicken with the knife used to slaughter an ox'] to deal with India the ox and that was enough to make it run like a mad cow.'[85] The tone of obvious triumphalism cannot be missed six decades down the line from 1962.

The epitaph for 1962 cannot be written before giving an account of the China-Pakistan relationship that grew out of the embers of the failed India–China one. In the early months of 1963, China and Pakistan forged an alliance which has weathered the ups and downs of history since then. It has been said that the 'rise and fall of Sino-Indian relations have long been the most effective barometer of Sino-Pakistan relations.'[86] When relations between India and China were warm in the mid-fifties, relations between Pakistan and China were cool. Pakistan had never been comfortable, however, about the intimacy that marked India–China relations in their heyday. During the Bandung Conference, Prime Minister Mohammed Ali met Zhou Enlai and told Zhou that 'Pakistan's participation in the Manila Treaty (SEATO) was not intended to oppose China'. Mao Zedong told the Pakistani

Ambassador in Beijing in 1955 that there were no disputes between the two countries and they should become friends. Mao told the Chinese Ambassador in Pakistan in 1956, 'One thing for sure, we must continually enhance the friendship and cooperation with Pakistan.'[87] In Mao's calculation, Pakistan occupied a very strategic position, linking West Asia and Southeast Asia, and Sino-Pakistani friendship could break the encirclement of China by imperialist forces, and secondly, Pakistan's location between China and West Asia, Europe and Africa, made it China's doorway toward the world, and opening the door could help 'break the economic embargo imposed (on China) by imperialism.'[88] Developing ties with Pakistan, a Muslim country could also help China develop contacts with Muslim nations, in Mao's view. Pakistan was therefore, China's 'western gate' and China was determined to unlock this gate.

From 1956 onwards, a readjustment was to take place in China's relations with Pakistan and there were distinct moves to put India and Pakistan on an equal footing as for instance, Premier Zhou's visits to New Delhi and Karachi on one trip in 1956. The readjustment was also a response to the Chinese 'disquiet' over India, and the Tibetan issue and suspicions about India's attitude as the situation in Tibet deteriorated and the Dalai Lama visited India. In one Chinese scholar's viewpoint, Zhou Enlai 'raised' the border issue with Nehru during the Dalai visit and 'clearly signalled a linkage of the McMahon Line and India's attitude toward Tibet'.[89] As Sino-Indian relations deteriorated after 1959, Pakistan's first reaction had been to utilize the situation to seek a settlement on Kashmir. When the revolt in Tibet worsened in 1959, Pakistan voted for a resolution that criticized China's actions in Tibet (India abstained). President Ayub suggested to Prime Minister Nehru in 1959 that India and Pakistan should form a joint defensive front to defend the subcontinent. This was rejected by Nehru. Thereafter, the improvements in India–US relations under the Eisenhower and Kennedy administrations only increased Pakistan's isolation and deepened its unease. The Soviet Union was also cultivating deeper relations with India. The solution was for Pakistan to turn its attention to China and make it the 'strategic counterweight' to India. President Ayub also made Pakistan's unresolved border with China as a launch pad for strengthening relations with China by expressing readiness to negotiate a border settlement which was seen by the Chinese as a contrast to India's unwillingness to negotiate on border issues. In March 1961, Pakistan formally proposed border negotiations with China. In March 1962, it clarified to the Chinese that its membership of the SEATO and CENTO was not directed against China. Pakistan also changed its position on the Tibet issue. In May 1962, the two nations announced that they would hold border negotiations.

Three years before the conflict between India and China, in September 1959, Pakistani attention was drawn to a Chinese map showing parts of Hunza as Chinese territory. The Pakistani Foreign Minister Manzur Qadir said his government would take no official notice of the map, 'for maps, by themselves, did not constitute violation of territory.'[90] But the Foreign Office said that the government was collecting 'authentic, internationally acceptable material to have a clear line demarcated between Pakistan and China.' President Ayub announced that Pakistan would soon propose border talks with China. On a visit to Washington in 1961 he told the press: 'The Chinese have their ideology, and we have our ideology. But we are neighbours and we would like to live as good neighbours. We have no cause to quarrel over our undemarcated border'.[91] The year 1961 was a lean one for Pakistan's foreign policy. Relations with Afghanistan worsened, and efforts to dissuade the United States from sending arms to India failed. India's liberation of Goa worsened Pakistan's sense of insecurity about India's military aims. The Pakistani tilt towards China became more pronounced. In December 1961, it voted in favour of seating China in the United Nations. In March 1962, the Chinese who were obviously taken with Pakistani overtures to them, agreed to discuss the border question, immediately after their first demarche to India over the Forward Policy in February 1962. It was announced in Karachi that Pakistan and China 'had agreed to negotiate a provisional demarcation line between Sinkiang and 'the contiguous area,' the defence of which is under the actual control of Pakistan.'[92]

In the same month, Premier Zhou told the Pakistani Ambassador in Beijing that 'Sino-Pakistani friendship is not an expedient measure, but it is long-standing. We also want friendship with the Indian people, but Indian authorities refuse to act accordingly and they support an attitude of opposition.'[93] Later, in September on the eve of the conflict with India, Liu Shaoqi while receiving the credentials of the Pakistani ambassador N.A.M. Raza,[94] referred to India's 'great power chauvinism', with Vice Minister Geng Biao adding that 'India's great power chauvinism is also very severe'. Liu said that India 'believes erroneously that China is easily bullied.' He brought up the issue of Tibet referring to India cautioning China about not advancing militarily in Tibet and how India 'did not speak again' after being chastised by China that 'liberating Tibet is China's own matter'. But India had 'stirred up armed rebellion at its border with China's Tibet' because she 'regarded Tibet as part of India's sphere of influence, or even Indian territory, and instigated Tibetan rebellion'. India had similarly tried to interfere where China's relations with Nepal were concerned. As far as China and Pakistan were concerned, China had already considered India's viewpoint on the issue; China was 'not intervening in Pakistan and India's dispute over Kashmir' and therefore, there 'is no reason whatsoever for India to oppose Sino-Pakistani negotiations'. In October 1962, the Pakistani Foreign Secretary told China's ambassador Ding Guoyu that India deserved to be taught a 'lesson' by China and that Pakistan hoped that 'China will severely punish India and drag India down through a long-term struggle'.[95]

In fact, when China announced a unilateral ceasefire on 20 November, the Pakistanis were unhappy that 'not only had the war brought about an increase in Western backing for the Indians, but with India facing crushing defeat, Beijing had pulled back rather than taking advantage of the situation to press for a border settlement that could have included Kashmir.' Pakistan's president lamented, 'I wish the Chinese had consulted us before they ordered the cease-fire and in future, too, I hope that before they take any precipitate steps they will consult us, as we may be able to give them sound advice.'[96]

On 26 December 1962, China and Pakistan announced 'complete agreement in principle' on aligning their 'common border'.[97] In March 1963, Zulfiqar Ali Bhutto, the Foreign Minister of Pakistan signed the finished agreement with his Chinese counterpart Chen Yi in Beijing. The agreement covered a 200 mi long alignment beginning at the Afghanistan trijunction and running in generally southeastern direction to just west of the Karakoram Pass. China transferred 1,942 sq. km of territory that it controlled to Pakistan. Pakistan claimed that it did not surrender any territory under its control. Agha Shahi, then Director General in the Pakistani Ministry of External Affairs, briefing the British High Commissioner in Karachi in February 1963, said that when maps showing each country's claim line were exchanged between Pakistan and China, it was found that both sides claimed the Taghdumbash area in the extreme north, the Oprang Valley area, and the Shaksgam Muztagh area.[98] The total area in 'dispute' amounted to 3,400 sq. mi. Shahi said Pakistan did not regard its claims to the Taghdumbash and Shaksgam areas as 'particularly well substantiated'. The Indians, he said, claimed the Shaksgam area but the latter was 'virtually inaccessible from the Pakistan side and was militarily untenable.' The Pakistanis, therefore, felt that 'they had done well to trade what they regarded as rather shadowy claims for these two areas for the Oprang Valley where possession gave Pakistan 'important salt deposits and grazing areas'. The upshot was that 'of 3400 square miles in dispute Pakistan would have 1350 square miles and China 2050.' Shahi claimed that the settlement was better than Pakistan had hoped for.

In February 1963, the Chinese Foreign Ministry in a note[99] addressed to the Indian Embassy rejected Indian charges that the 'reaching of an agreement on the boundary between China and Pakistan manifests a desire to exploit the differences between India and Pakistan on the Kashmir question' as 'preposterous to the extreme'. The note claimed that the Chinese government had 'never involved itself in the India-Pakistan dispute over Kashmir' and that the Sino-Pakistan boundary negotiations had 'not at all touched on the question of the ownership of Kashmir'. China hoped that 'the two sister countries India and Pakistan will be able to solve their dispute peacefully.'

The 'Agreement Between the Government of the People's Republic of China and the Government of Pakistan on the Boundary Between China's Sinkiang and the Contiguous Areas the Defence of Which is Under the Actual Control of Pakistan' of March 1963 saw the conceding by Pakistan of the Tagdumbash and Shaksgam areas to China in return for the Oprang Valley to which the Mir of Hunza attached importance. This area lay outside the main watershed. With the exception of this, the alignment of the 'border' agreed upon followed the main watershed of the Hindu Kush and Karakoram mountains and gave Pakistan control of the principal mountain passes. The agreement made headline news in Delhi. An objection voiced by the Indian Foreign Office in conversation with the British High Commission[100] was that the Pakistanis had accepted the Chinese contention that the Karakoram Range marked the boundary in the eastern part of the alignment agreed to and thereby strengthened the Chinese argument that the Karakoram range also formed the 'boundary' further east of the Karakoram pass contrary to the Indian claim line/boundary that ran along the Kunlun Range to include the Aksai Chin within Indian territory. India alleged that Pakistan had ceded not less than 2,000 sq. mi of territory that was India's, in Kashmir, to China whereas Pakistan claimed to have gained 750 sq. mi and not ceded any territory under its control to China. Chinese Foreign Minister Chen Yi declared that the speedy settlement reached by China and Pakistan had been made possible because they had adopted an attitude of 'mutual understanding, mutual accommodation, equality and cooperation and not one of arrogance, unreasonableness and profiting from the other's loss.'[101]

In India, the *Times of India* called it a 'shady agreement' that had been announced two hours after the Indian delegation in Pakistan for talks on Kashmir had called on President Ayub. The talks were happening under the stewardship of the Americans and the British who had seized the opportunity to push this through, taking advantage of India's vulnerabilities after the disastrous outcome of the events of 1962 with China. In sum, these were dark days for India. The agreement smacked of opportunism on the part of both Pakistan and China. Both countries knew fully well that it would never be accepted by India, even if it purported to be provisional in nature pending a settlement of the Kashmir issue between Pakistan and India. Despite Chinese protestations to the contrary about the Kashmir dispute being separate from the agreement, China had become 'a factor in the eventual settlement of the Kashmir dispute.'[102] Prime Minister Nehru saw it as 'interference on the part of China in India's sovereignty over Kashmir'.[103]

The point remains about China's salience in the India-Pakistan conflict. The Chinese approach was summed up presciently by Vijaya Lakshmi Pandit after 1962, when she said 'Chinese attitudes towards the Indo-Pakistani conflict also demonstrate that alliances, collaborations and supporters do not have to be with like-minded progressives, much less communists. There may be any political hues and the Chinese would use opportunities on the basis of a marriage of interests.'[104] What China did was to 'take a leap to psychologically purchase the friendship of the people of Pakistan regardless of the fact that they are not Communists and the government is conservative.'[105] Sino-Pak friendship was justified, particularly in Pakistan, as providing a common front against India and even when Pakistan was a member of the U.S.-led alliance system in the nineteen fifties, China correctly assessed that 'Pakistan did not share the declared purpose of the sponsors that these pacts were to contain and defeat the communist countries but primarily to increase her military strength vis-à-vis India.'[106] Ultimately, it can be stated that hostility to India was and has been a meeting point between these neighbours. Any position of neutrality on the Kashmir issue was also abandoned by China after the Agreement of 1963 with Pakistan. China's attempts to side with Pakistan during the India-Pakistan war of 1965 also indicated that the future of Kashmir was a matter of interest to the Government of China, and that it 'cannot be settled behind her back.'[107]

At the end of this story, the question still remains about Nehru's policy towards China and the reasons that led to the collapse of that policy. India's first Prime Minister is seen as having betrayed the nation's interests vis-à-vis China and also been betrayed by the Chinese as the events of 1962 showed. In the aftermath of the conflict, Nehru did not seek to shift the blame or seek to apportion responsibility for the debacle thrust on India; he wrestled with his own demons within, on the entire construct of his China policy, and died, for all intents and purposes, a lonely and vanquished man. But, one of his close advisers did write many years later that

the body of higher professional civil servants did not truly exert themselves to volunteer professional dissent on issues which eventually were to lead to grave damage to national interests and prestige . . . the general surrender to the hypnosis that 'Panditji (Nehru) knows best' was an extensive phenomenon since our independence . . . It cannot be wholly disowned that the professional advisers, not just the political ones, rendered less than their duty to their beloved Caesar.[108]

In December 1962, Nehru writing to his chief ministers spoke of a lack of preparedness on the part of the Indian Army, the laggardness in building roads and communications in the border areas to enable more logistical preparedness, the fact that the operations in Tibet and the Korean War had made the Chinese more battle-toned and ready for the showdown with India, and that the Chinese attack was not so much about a border dispute as to keep the 'Cold War going'.[109] The Chinese believed in the 'inevitability of war', they did not want tensions in the world to lessen. They preferred polarization. India's humiliation would drive it into the Western camp spelling the end of non-alignment, and the Soviet Union—whose revolutionary ardour had cooled from the Chinese point of view—would then have to help China to a much greater degree. It has been argued elsewhere[110] that the Chinese were blind to comprehending India's parliamentary system, and that Nehru, even while being a powerful leader, was constrained by democratic opinion; and that dissent and the tradition of protest were an intrinsic part of India's open political system. The Chinese completely misunderstood India's policy on Tibet, the treatment of the Dalai Lama and the decision to grant refuge to thousands of Tibetans—perhaps because the Dalai Lama's presence in India was a stark advertisement of their policy failures in Tibet. Nehru's internationalism and his vision of India's role and relevance in bringing China to the global stage in a world divided between the United States and the Soviet Union, obscured many facets of New China seeking its place in the world and balking at India being seen as a political equal. He also did not weigh the consequences of the political isolation resulting from China's rapprochement with India's neighbours from 1959 onwards—particularly the border agreements with Nepal, Burma and Pakistan. China's opening to Pakistan and the agreement of 1963 (the 'alliance of animus' as Nehru termed it[111]) had ramifications for India that persist to the current day. Should India have paid more attention to relations with Pakistan once the climate in relations with China began to deteriorate from 1959 onwards?

The historian Ramachandra Guha cites H.V. Kamath, author of the book *Last Days of Jawaharlal Nehru*, describing Nehru in September 1963 as 'an old man, looking frail and fatigued, with a marked stoop in his gait, coming down the gangway opposite with slow, faltering steps, and clutching the backrests of benches for support as he descended'—recalling Isaiah Berlin's description of a dying Tolstoy, a tragic, isolated figure, consumed by the ghosts of his abandoned dreams, and like Oedipus 'beyond human aid, wandering self-blinded at Colonus.'[112] Kamath added, 'India's defeat, nay, military debacle in that one-month war not only shattered [Nehru] physically and weakened him mentally but, what was more galling to him, eroded his prestige in Asia and the world, dealt a crippling blow to his visions of leadership of the newly emancipated nations, and cast a shadow on his place in history.'[113] The diplomat, Purnendu Banerjee, who headed the Indian Mission in Beijing after the departure of Ambassador Parthasarathy, wrote in his memoirs about meeting Nehru in early 1964, a few months before his death in May that year. Banerjee found that the Prime Minister's powers of concentration were greatly reduced. Nehru launched into a long and painful monologue about relations with China, his friendship with Zhou Enlai, and the Chinese 'betrayal'. In another meeting a few weeks later, the Prime Minister's health had deteriorated further. 'His eyes had lost their sparkle, his face was shallow, and his expression like that of a baby. There was no trace of his vitality, agility and youthfulness; it was a frail shadow of the former Mr. Nehru.'[114]

A few months after the 1962 conflict, in January 1963, Zhou Enlai had asked to see Banerjee. During their meeting, the Chinese Premier called Mr. Nehru 'a man of high philosophy and great vision' and while he understood the latter's political predicaments, the Indian Prime Minister should understand the Chinese Premier's position also and strengthen his hand which

was 'extended in friendship and cooperation.' Zhou suggested
two steps for Nehru's consideration; one, that both sides should
stop making negative statements about each other's country and
secondly, that both should meet as soon as possible away from
the media glare, in 'total privacy' in a mutually agreed venue to
exchange ideas 'for an agreed and joint action to defuse the current
situation.' Banerjee transcribed this conversation and conveyed it
to Nehru when he visited Delhi a short while later. Nehru asked
him 'what game Zhou was playing'. Then, he struck a match,
held the paper on which Zhou's points had been written down by
Banerjee to the flame and 'burnt it over a large crystal ash tray'. He
told Banerjee that 'from the Indian side it would take more than
a quarter of a century to return to any substantive negotiation,
provided the Chinese refrained from another attack on India.'[115]

If the 1950s was a period of fulfilment, the 1960s was a
period of disillusionment for India. A lecture by one of India's
most distinguished diplomats, K.P.S. Menon in 1969[116] makes a
reference to the common criticism that Nehru's government had
'no notion of India's permanent interests in dealing with China'.
There is the charge of India having 'given away' Tibet to China.
But Tibet was never India's to give away, to begin with. Even
the British did not own Tibet at the height of their power and
imperial reach.

Menon argues, quite reasonably, that independent India did
not want to start on the wrong foot with China. But China was
never happy with the constant comparison with India, especially
when India's friends said that 'in the contest between India and
China lay the success or failure of democracy versus communism'.
Did India, on its part, contribute to the deterioration of relations
with China? For instance, it withdrew its ambassador in 1961
unilaterally and when the Tibet Agreement came up for renewal,
refused to renew it at least in order to keep its consulate in Lhasa
and keep the trickle of trade between Tibet and India going—it
has not been possible thereafter to revive those linkages. The

Zhou Enlai mission of 1960 to India also offered the opportunity to improve relations and scope for negotiation of a boundary settlement that would have involved some degree of mutual accommodation and adjustment instead of declarations of absolute right—most importantly Chinese recognition of a frontier in the east aligned along the McMahon Line in return for Indian concessions of Chinese claims in the disputed Aksai Chin. While there is no evidence to suggest Nehru was prepared to negotiate along such lines, his inflexible posture was also the result of opposition within the Cabinet, criticism in Parliament (occasioned equally by burning patriotism as well as a burning desire to embarrass Nehru) and 'zealous officials of the Ministry of External Affairs' who carried on 'an increasingly angry missive warfare with China'.

The best foreign policy is a combination of firmness and flexibility. India adopted a full throttle approach of firmness towards China as the border dispute erupted from 1959 onwards. Firmness, without strength, cannot fulfil its desired aims. Soviet leader Khrushchev told K.P.S. Menon when the latter was India's Ambassador in the Soviet Union in the early 1960s, that the legalities and intricacies of India's frontier dispute with China were beyond his grasp, but he knew that such disputes were often the most difficult to deal with because they were always dealt with from the point of view of national prestige and not the national interest. China continues to be India's central problem externally. The opportunity to create a stable frontier between the two countries was effectively bypassed in the 1950s and the responsibility for this is not exactly defined—there were acts of omission and commission implicating both India and China. But an unresolved boundary problem with China and a growing developmental and economic gap between India and China today, pose a greater challenge for India than for China.

Nehru died on 27 May 1964. A condolence book was opened in the Indian Embassy in Beijing to be signed by local dignitaries and diplomats. No Chinese appeared at the embassy to sign the book for two days until the embassy received a message from the Foreign Office that 'an important visitor would be coming'. The visitor was Zhou Enlai accompanied by senior Foreign Ministry officials. He signed the condolence book (no record seems available of his exact remarks) and stayed on for about ten minutes to talk without 'the slightest hint of acrimony' about his 'long and extremely eventful association with Jawaharlal Nehru'. That was the impression he made on A.K. Damodaran,[117] one of the Indian diplomats who was present. Of course, Zhou Enlai's comments about Nehru in conversation with President Richard Nixon during the latter's visit to Beijing in 1972, showed no such understanding.[118] The Nehru–Zhou association from 1954 to 1960 was a complex gambit of moves and counter-moves and the verdict of history has not been kind to Nehru in its assessment of these maneuvers. Suffice to say that the lack of a stable frontier between India and China, and China's close relationship with Pakistan (which was an offshoot of the India–China tensions of the early 1960s) are specters that continue to haunt the world's largest democracy till this day. The hindsight of history is both revealing and sobering.

If making Asia was an idea, then India and China struggled over its creation. In the early years after India's independence, Nehru's challenges were enormous and unlike any facing other world leaders because an international identity had to be crafted for India, together with a strategy of national development. As Sunil Khilnani[119] has said, Nehru was struggling to create an idea of India. There was an audacity about this quest, an audacity of hope that he would and could set the direction of India's global trajectory. He was not one to lose himself in atavistic musings about an overarching Greater India; about connections that extended from 'Bamiyan via Bodhgaya to Borabadur', but had a vision to place India and Asia in a world of modernity and interconnectedness based on science and development and away from militarism and bloc politics. Did Nehru read China correctly? In parts, yes. He had no illusions about China's propensity to seek greatness through expansionism and expropriation. He saw the need to restrain its potential to assert its interests through force and revolution. But he also believed that communist China's exclusion and exile from the global comity of nations would harm the interests of an emergent India as part of an Asia that had struggled long and hard to liberate itself from the shackles of Western domination and exploitation. Through all this, he remained a firm and steadfast proponent of the ideals and principles of participatory democracy, liberty, and the fundamental freedoms. Where he misjudged China was to assume that the charter of the Five Principles of Peaceful Coexistence and a friendship of 'brothers' would pre-suppose that China would never use force to advance territorial aggrandizement against India. The juxtaposition of two political systems, one guided by the rules of constitutional democracy versus one based on the 'coercive apparatus of the State' persists to this day. Nehru also feared compromise with China on the boundary question because the country would not accept it. Diplomacy foundered in a whirlpool of political rhetoric in the democratic and public space where reason and foresight were sacrificed. India has still to extricate itself from these currents. Moulding domestic consensus on the issue of a territorial settlement with China should have been Nehru's priority and the true test of his mettle. That call was never made—it was a tragedy for which both Nehru, the leader revered by millions of his people, and the country paid the price.

Coda

'In geopolitics, the past never dies and there is no modern world.'[1]

Today, India and China are essentially competitors and rivals as they jockey for positions of influence in both continental and maritime Asia.

Their bilateral relationship will always be complex. Mutual suspicion and alienation have only deepened in recent years. China's reaction to India's growing ascendance on the global stage is at best, articulated with ambivalence and at worst, with unconcealed hostility. The overarching compass of India-China relations therefore, points to a complicated future. The fragility of ties is constantly exposed, the fabric stretched by persistent and underlying regional rivalries, shadowed by the memory of past conflict, hostile public opinion and low levels of political will and equilibrium. And between India and China, the politics of history also translates into a constant reminder of how the past shadows the present in their relations, how it has shaped current policy options and approaches. 'Letting go' is not a question, it is heresy. All of this often contributes to the impression that this is a voyage on a river of no return, that the renewal of conflict is foretold, and only a matter of time.

If there is one conclusion that could be a take-away from the history of the period from 1949 to 1962 for India and China, it is that there can be no easy explanations for what went wrong in their relationship. Jawaharlal Nehru saw the need for friendship and mutual understanding between the two nations but within himself, he also sensed the challenge posed to India by a China wishing to assert itself on the global stage and 'reclaim' what were seen as historically ordained, sovereign rights on her periphery, and steadily advancing on the borders with India. Why did Nehru not tackle this threat differently? The counter-question could be whether there were realistic options before India to have acted differently. Senior Indian diplomats like Girija Shankar Bajpai were uneasy and suspicious about the Chinese and many in Nehru's cabinet were of a similar cast of mind—the leading voice of this school of thought being Vallabhbhai Patel—but could India have resisted the Chinese advance on Tibet, militarily? An Indian strategy spelling a hard-line, combative approach to Communist China, could not have been easily actioned, given India's own constraints in a time of nation-building and internal political and economic challenges. Yet, the question of giving asylum in India to the young Dalai Lama as the Chinese advanced on Tibet, and supporting the Tibetan appeal for help to the United Nations, deserved Indian support. This would have entailed the immediate onset of a hostile relationship between India and Communist China, and also the possibility of an early entente cordiale between China and Pakistan, but would have compelled India to grasp the hard reality of China on her frontiers. It would also have meant the choice of a foreign policy path of much closer alignment and concert with the United States and the West, a choice very different from the Nehruvian vision of India and China symbolizing the new voice of independent, decolonized Asia. But the fall-out would have entailed India to confront two tense relationships with neighbours to the west and east—Pakistan and China—indefinitely.

Nehru erred, in an act of omission, in ignoring his better instinct to raise the issue of India's border with China and its confirmation during the negotiations for the 1954 Agreement that acknowledged Chinese sovereignty over Tibet. Nehru listened to advice from K.M. Panikkar—India's Ambassador in Beijing—advice that was seriously flawed and misguided. Acts of omission were also involved in the failure of Indian diplomats in senior positions, as policy formulators, to exercise proper judgement, and also to candidly counter the Prime Minister's own preferences and choices in China policy. In retrospect, was the 1954 Agreement little more than a 'scrap of paper'? Its high-sounding tenor of peaceful coexistence between India and China, has little by way of substance or meaning for their relationship today—a relationship characterized by 'combative' coexistence. The Agreement's shelf-life was also limited and furthermore, it showed Tibet as a pawn on the chess-board of the Indians and the Chinese. Did India understand that even if provocation is to be avoided, grasping the nature of 'power' is the golden rule of successful diplomacy? Did Nehru understand the 'art of the deal', that diplomacy must combine a healthy dose of reason with emotion? He seemed to display irascibility when encountering cautionary points of view about China expressed by officials like Sumul Sinha—the Consul-General in Lhasa— effectively silencing them rather than taking their views on board. The historian S. Gopal buttressed through rigorous research the Indian case on the boundary, but it was not his responsibility to provide a political perspective to the problem, which was entirely a calculation that Nehru—as political leader—should have made. At the other extreme of this spectrum, in an act of commission, Nehru deduced wrongly that the way was open after the Agreement had been concluded, to direct his officials to show the external boundaries of India as defined and settled, despite the fact that this was a unilateral decision not confirmed by any bilateral agreement to help consolidate such a move. Having taken this decision, unlike at the time of the Chinese entry into Tibet, when Indian presence and administration was extended along the north eastern frontier—including the monastery town of Tawang, close to the Tibetan border—similar attention was not paid to securing India's borders with China in the Aksai Chin area of Ladakh. If the belief was, as the archives would suggest, that the Aksai Chin was a 'grey' area, then why did not India consider the policy options available to seek a settlement in this area with China—as part of an overall border agreement—that would see the Chinese relinquishing their claims south of the McMahon Line? India's frontier policy of 'firm boundaries' was transacted in a walled space segregated from a foreign policy on China that stressed conciliation, dialogue, and accommodation—a non-sustainable exercise in policy contradiction. Again, when Chinese Premier Zhou Enlai visited Delhi in April 1960, the opportunity for negotiations for a settlement was neither grasped nor recognized as such. Later, India's policy planners in the Defence, Home and External Affairs Ministries, did not foresee the scale of the Chinese reaction to the surveillance/'forward' policy in Ladakh—a policy that wreaked its own consequential costs—as the aftermath of the conflict showed—in terms of the loss of global and national prestige for India.

China's own acts of commission in plotting the grid of this history cannot be ignored. The Chinese moved with deceptive stealth to secure their claims in Ladakh—once Tibet had been militarily taken—and waited to unveil their approach to the boundary question, until the time was 'ripe' to raise this with India in 1959. The 'pacification' of Tibet was achieved by military means and the alienation of the Tibetan people was a clear offshoot of China's heavy-handed approach to 'reform' Tibetan society—an approach that continues to this day. The flight of the Dalai Lama to India was a severe indictment of the failure of

Chinese policy in Tibet. From the outset also, China, did not see India as long-term friend or equal, but rather, in a time-serving, opportunistic fashion, as a convenient enabler to propel the PRC's debut on the world stage. The Chinese consummation of ties with Pakistan as the war clouds of 1962 with India gathered, was another example of such 'strategic' opportunism. (Today, Pakistan's geostrategic location, sacrificed long ago by India at partition, leverages 'China's search for dominance in the Indian Ocean as well as on land with the Belt and Road Initiative'[2]). The contrast in leadership between India and China was also striking. Their leaders were many worlds apart. Mao Zedong and Zhou Enlai were the offspring of revolution, war, internecine purges, civil strife and violent political struggle, personifications of the old adage that iron, cold iron is the master of them all. Nehru's code of conduct, his vision of Asia, his cosmopolitan approach to the world—formed by his exposure to ideas of the enlightenment, fundamental rights and democratic values—evolved further in an environment of civil disobedience, and the non-violent struggle for Indian freedom led by his idol and mentor, Gandhi. Zhou Enlai came across in his meetings with Nehru as the practitioner of the practical, devoid of sentiment or misplaced idealism, in contrast to his Indian counterpart's utopian 'vision' for India and China that sought to bridge vast divergences in history, ideology, and national character. Nehru's mistake was to assume that the Chinese leaders thought and acted in ways he could understand. The United States was to make the same error in the years to come, assuming that China would change as the policy of reform and opening-up gathered momentum. Why do democracies think the rest of the world is made in their image? The learning curve is long.

Issues of war and peace between India and China continue to remain suspended on the razor's edge of inherited frontiers.[3] Over a century ago, Archibald Rose, the British Consul at Tengu-yueh in the Yunnan Province of China, spoke of India having acquired a 'Chinese neighbour along the whole stretch of that 3000 miles of frontier from Kashmir, past Nepal, Sikkim, Bhutan, Assam, and Upper Burma'. The 'Chinese colossus' had moved, he said, presciently.[4] China's 'core' interests, including Tibet and Taiwan, and its approach to territorial disputes with neighbours, including on the borders with India and Bhutan, have been stridently expressed by its 'wolf warrior' diplomats in recent years. The Chinese Communist Party and Chinese State are increasingly inflexible about the handling of these issues. It has been said that Xi Jinping's global ambitions exceed those of Mao Zedong and Zhou Enlai and that China today, is the flag-bearer of a new imperium in Asia.

The centrality of margins and peripheries in this framework of frontiers is scarcely recognized today. Although specific country situations differ, the borderlands of India and China, be they Kashmir, northeastern India, Tibet and Xinjiang, are not the primary focus when it comes to understanding frontiers and their 'fractured geographies'[5]. Frustrations among the youth, ethnic nationalisms, issues of identity, self-determination, human rights, geographical isolation, the use of armed force by the state, cross-border terrorism and questions about governance straddle these borderlands.[6] They have tended to be viewed as targets of central government policy radiating from national capitals rather than as areas that possess their own ecosystems of existence, where policy must focus on local issues that directly impact the lives of people. The concept of frontier zones which historically provided for 'an intermingling of peoples'[7], allowing the retention of close integration across borders between communities in terms of language, custom and religion, has been lost. Geopolitics trumps all. Borders congeal and conceal transnational borderlands that cannot speak for themselves since Delhi and Beijing 'must quit playing ventriloquist'[8] in order that these distinct voices are heard.

This concept of connector zones, or recognition of a shared habitat was once common to the Himalayan ranges that border India and the Tibetan plateau, is alien to the diplomatic negotiating agendas of India and China. It is unrealistic to assume that these ideas will occupy the consideration of the two governments in the future, either. The Himalayan Fringe that marks the frontiers between South and Central Asia, including Tibet, holds the key to the future of close to three billion people—in terms of climate, water, sustainability, preservation of intangible heritage, disaster management and prevention, and human security. But contested sovereignties and cartographies have prevented the coordinated, sustainable development of these areas and their opening to the world. A Himalayan Consensus is as yet a visionary and elusive dream, even as largely Occidental notions of centre and periphery, mainland and margins dominate the discourse on sovereignty and dictate the closure of borders and traditional points of interaction and movement of peoples. Today, the map precedes everything. It becomes the anchoring geometry for a nation. The emblem of the Survey of India, the official cartographer of India, 'A Setu Himachalam'—from the Palk Strait to the Himalaya—mahasagara to Shambhala⁹—essentially evokes the image of Bharat Mata (Mother India) with her outstretched hands, feet firmly planted on peninsular ground, surrounded by the waters of the Indian Ocean, the Arabian Sea and the Bay of Bengal, her flowing tresses encompassing the Himalaya, and her smiling mien dominating the headwaters of the Ganges and the Indus. This is the junction of modern cartographic science with traditional belief and mythological precept, an inviolate meeting ground. The subconscious attachment of all Indians to the Himalayas, that emotional bond which Nehru described as being 'something more precious than a hundred or thousand miles' and bringing 'people's passions to a high level'—together with the fact that many in this country regard Tibet as included within India's 'religious geography'¹⁰—is another key factor. These are emotional attachments that continue to this day.¹¹

Each country continues the steadfast pursuit of agendas to consolidate power and presence in contested border regions. The moves include infrastructure building and the quest for strategic advantage in the event of conflict through the occupation of disputed areas. China's renaming of claimed areas in Arunachal Pradesh as 'South Tibet' could be a part of an effort to create leverage over India on the boundary dispute, as some experts point out.[12] India has also renamed a number of places in the State. What do the locals—the people of Arunachal Pradesh want? They want for one, their local, indigenous place names to be preserved. The Monpas of Arunachal Pradesh are an example of border peoples in the Himalayas who have existed for centuries on the periphery of the Tibetan Buddhist world. Their internalized concept of that world coexists with their strong and distinct ethnic and tribal identity. Their history is tied up with both Bhutan and Tibet.[13] Their habitat which includes the town of Tawang, is a crucial border land, a meeting place for a number of cultures, a Himalayan zone of interaction, and a place of trade and pilgrimage. Centuries ago, Tawang was the target of the 'Buddhist diplomacy' conducted by the fifth Dalai Lama to spread the dominance of the Gelukpa sect of Tibetan Buddhism, in an exercise of ritual and cultural 'sovereignty', a cosmological vision[14]. But this ritual or cultural 'sovereignty' is totally different from the Westphalian concept of sovereignty that China seeks to impose on these areas through a convenient transitioning from ritual concepts that connected tribal areas in Arunachal Pradesh to Tibet's past as an independent theocracy. China's attempts include the incorporating of the 6th Dalai Lama who was born near Tawang as a 'national treasure' of China, a move that should encounter principled opposition from the people of Tawang, particularly, since he is an intrinsic part of the religious and cultural heritage of the Monpa people.

But what remains as our takeaway is that the trans-Himalayan circuit constructed by the relatively unhindered movement of people and commodities continued until 1962. The true moment of transformation, when the doors on Tibet from India closed, was that watershed year, after which the loss of access for India's border peoples to trans-Himalayan circuits was re-oriented from both north and south-bound connections, only southward. The instinctive identification among the people of these borderlands, as in Tawang, with the cultural and imagined Buddhist geography of the Himalaya, is submerged by modern cartographies of closed borders in these zones today.[15]

While the imperative of addressing underdevelopment and the building of infrastructure are no doubt priorities to be addressed, the trans-boundary ecological factors that impinge on the world of the Himalaya also need attention. The issue of trans-boundary waters, as China builds dams on the upper reaches of the Brahmaputra/Yarlung Tsangpo River in Tibet— triggering deep concerns in lower riparian areas in India, Bhutan and Bangladesh—needs resolution. As hydropower projects in Arunachal Pradesh are also taken up, there is a pro-dam and anti-dam discourse happening there that transcends boundaries, as for instance, between Tawang and eastern Bhutan. The dilemma facing policy makers is to ensure that there is no displacement of marginalized borderland communities or the exclusion of grassroots voices as agendas driven by national security are implemented.[16]

Turning to the larger regional space, the Indo-Pacific world today is riven by the emerging axis of confrontation between China under its supreme leader, Xi Jinping, and the United States. A legacy of maritime and land disputes have shown the face of a country–China—unabashed about flouting the established rules of international order. China's position on such disputes has tended to become much less flexible and more stridently hard line when it comes to seeking solutions. We are, as Henry Kissinger said recently, in the foothills of a new cold war. The future is uncertain. That makes the task of India's policy makers and negotiators so much more complex and formidable.

It is easy to play winners and losers, as far as 1962 is concerned. But after six decades, the dust settles better. Battlefield losses did not cause India to change the stand on the boundary question with China. On its part, China withdrew from territories overrun south of the McMahon Line and consolidated its position in Ladakh with the strategic intent being to secure the highway linking Xinjiang and Tibet, across the Aksai Chin plateau. India was able to restore presence in the territory vacated by Chinese troops south of the McMahon Line, and the people who inhabit the region have remained loyal and patriotic Indian citizens. Were the much-vaunted Chinese 'victories' real or pyrrhic? This history has endeavoured to explain that the brief conflict of 1962 was avoidable and that if any lesson is to be learnt, it is that both countries should display the maturity and good sense to ensure the experience is never repeated. Ultimately, a solution will have to be driven by concessions made by both sides, although what these concessions could be cannot be a simple exercise of academic modelling. They will involve decisions made at the very highest political level in both countries, the underlying logic being that peaceful borders are best for all. If there is one lesson that this history teaches us, it is that only a political solution can work which may necessitate both India and China to 're-fashion'[17] their claims.

The question remains: does India have a boundary problem with China, or is there a territorial question that divides the two countries? Embedded in this conundrum is the history of India's relations with Tibet, the 1914 Simla Agreement, the McMahon Line, and the widely-held belief among the Indian people that the so-called liberation of Tibet was unfortunate (together with the mistaken conviction that India (meaning Nehru) should 'have done something about it'). Yet the assumption that prevails is that there is only a boundary or frontier problem with China (unlike the Kashmir issue with Pakistan which is viewed as a territorial problem). Boundary issues and problems are easier to resolve than territorial questions. India's claim to the Aksai Chin in Ladakh is a territorial claim just as China's claim on Arunachal Pradesh is a territorial claim—both these claims are political problems for each country. Political problems need negotiations and each side must have a clear idea of what they want to achieve from such negotiations. India-China relations in the fifties and sixties of the last century deteriorated over the fixing of boundaries, but the territorial issue both in the West and the East of the boundary generated the political divide. Each country must have a purpose in approaching this conundrum—is peace the goal, and the aim to reduce military confrontation, promote economic development and sub-regional integration of our borderlands, enhance regional and global stability—the list could go on—or, is it a game of wait-and-see, of tactical gain and jockeying for positions? New ideas, new analyses, enlightened perspectives and viable ways forward, are needed. As time has gone by, positions have hardened and flexibility and the willingness to adjust and seek 'win-win' solutions seem increasingly in short supply in both countries. The widening asymmetry of power between an ascendant China and an ascending India only complicates the situation further. China's near-autistic sense of entitlement which her adversaries can only view as hubris fired by insecurity, and her abandonment of the Panchsheel principles in relations with India (as with most countries), has only accentuated with time.

The two countries are still writing the second act in the story of the life of their relationship. Around them and within their own borders, worlds have changed unalterably. But a clear and unbiased reading of the history of the fifties and early sixties of the last century in their bilateral interaction yields useful pointers. Diplomacy may be life without maps, but an understanding of its history enables us to chart new paths and address fault lines. Only a combination of hindsight about history, and foresight, can help illuminate the pathways to an ultimate solution. This must involve rationality of approach, combining with strategies of conflict management, tension de-escalation and disengagement in order to secure a final boundary settlement that is built on strategic defensibility, the interests of populations in the borderlands and connectivity that enhances the all-round economic development of these far-flung regions, thus ensuring what has been termed the 'centrality of marginality'. In a democracy like India's, the contours of a possible settlement can be finalized only in an atmosphere where political polarization does not stifle a constructive debate between the Government and the Opposition. Losing the future because of our ongoing quarrel between past and present in the quest for vengeful indictment, can yield little by way of value. Beyond emotion and sentiment, the space for mutually acceptable solutions does exist and must be explored. But the possibilities and the prospects of realizing such a scenario may increasingly be fewer and fewer, if we do not learn from the lessons of history. Because of this, optimism is a scarce commodity and the road is long. We must for now, accept the smallness, and the restricted, confining nature of the present. Perhaps, one can visualize the dramatis personae in our history, most of them taken by the Grim Reaper, congregating one last time in some galactic hideaway as they take stock of the enormous liabilities that stem from the gambles they made—and the burden this inheritance imposes on future generations, yet unborn.

Maps

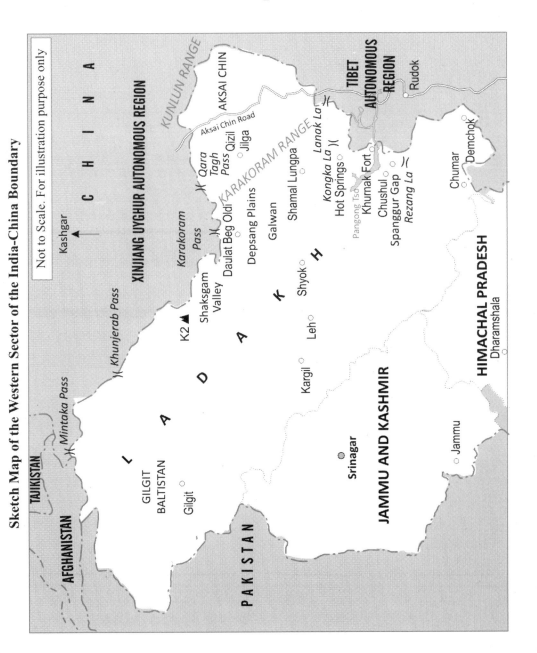

Sketch Map of the Western Sector of the India-China Boundary

Not to Scale. For illustration purpose only

TAJIKISTAN

AFGHANISTAN

Mintaka Pass

Khunjerab Pass

PAKISTAN

GILGIT BALTISTAN

Gilgit

CHINA

Kashgar

KUNLUN RANGE

XINJIANG UYGHUR AUTONOMOUS REGION

Karakoram Pass

K2

Shaksgam Valley

AKSAI CHIN

Aksai Chin Road

Qara Tagh Pass

Qizil

Jilga

KARAKORAM RANGE

Daulat Beg Oldi

Depsang Plains

Galwan

Shyok

Shamal Lungpa

LADAKH

Kargil

Leh

Lanak La

Kongka La

Hot Springs

Khurnak Fort

Pangong Tso

Chushul

Spanggur Gap

Rezang La

TIBET AUTONOMOUS REGION

Rudok

Chumar

Demchok

HIMACHAL PRADESH

Dharamshala

JAMMU AND KASHMIR

Srinagar

Jammu

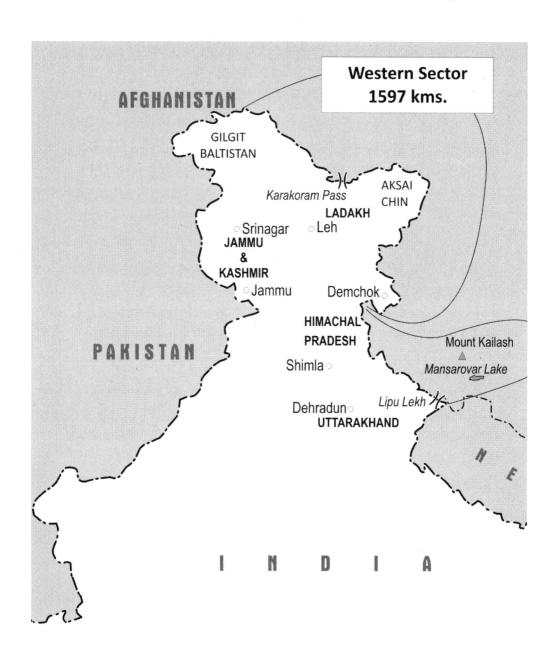

AFGHANISTAN

GILGIT
BALTISTAN

Western Sector
1597 kms.

Karakoram Pass

AKSAI
CHIN

LADAKH

Srinagar   Leh

**JAMMU
&
KASHMIR**

Jammu   Demchok

**HIMACHAL
PRADESH**

Mount Kailash

Shimla

Mansarovar Lake

Dehradun   *Lipu Lekh*

UTTARAKHAND

N
E

P A K I S T A N

I   N   D   I   A

Sketch Map of the Northern Boundaries of India
India-China Boundary - 3488 Kms.
Not to Scale. For illustration purpose only

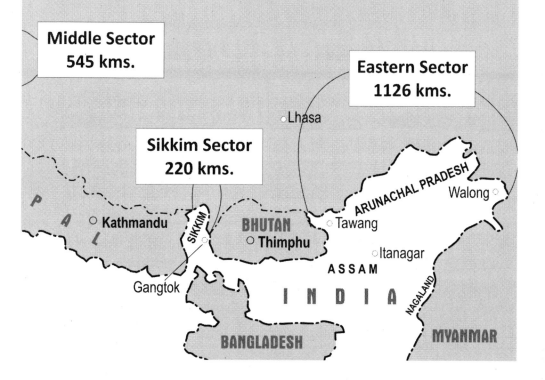

CHINA

Middle Sector
545 kms.

Eastern Sector
1126 kms.

Lhasa

Sikkim Sector
220 kms.

ARUNACHAL PRADESH

Walong

NEPAL

Kathmandu

SIKKIM

BHUTAN

Tawang

Thimphu

Itanagar

ASSAM

Gangtok

INDIA

NAGALAND

BANGLADESH

MYANMAR

Sketch Map of the Middle Sector of the India-China Boundary

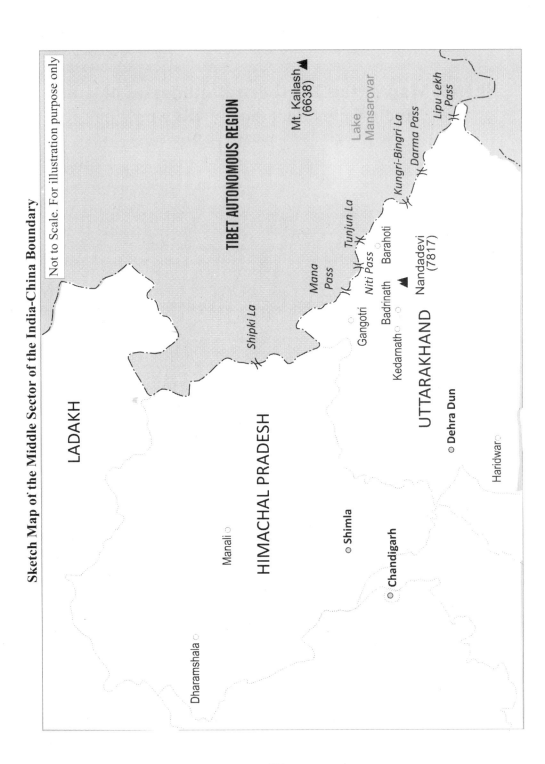

Not to Scale. For illustration purpose only

LADAKH

HIMACHAL PRADESH

TIBET AUTONOMOUS REGION

Dharamshala

Manali

Shimla

Chandigarh

Shipki La

Mana Pass

Tunjun La

Niti Pass

Gangotri

Barahoti

Badrinath

Kedarnath

Nandadevi (7817)

UTTARAKHAND

Dehra Dun

Haridwar

Kungri-Bingri La

Darma Pass

Lipu Lekh Pass

Mt. Kailash (6638)

Lake Mansarovar

Sketch Map of the Sikkim Sector of the India-China Boundary

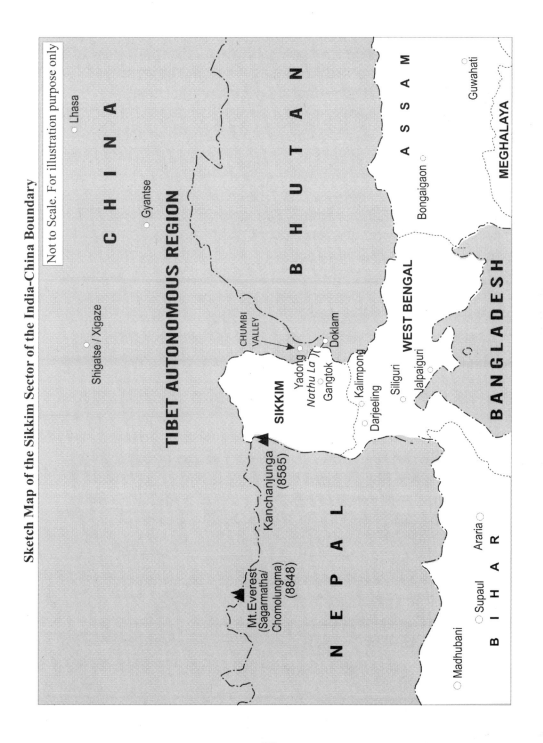

Not to Scale. For illustration purpose only

CHINA

Lhasa

Gyantse

TIBET AUTONOMOUS REGION

Shigatse / Xigaze

BHUTAN

CHUMBI VALLEY

Yadong

Nathu La

Doklam

SIKKIM

Gangtok

Kalimpong

Darjeeling

Siliguri

Jalpaiguri

WEST BENGAL

ASSAM

Bongaigaon

Guwahati

MEGHALAYA

BANGLADESH

Kanchanjunga (8585)

Mt. Everest (Sagarmatha/ Chomolungma) (8848)

NEPAL

BIHAR

Supaul

Araria

Madhubani

Sketch Map of the Eastern Sector of the India–China Boundary

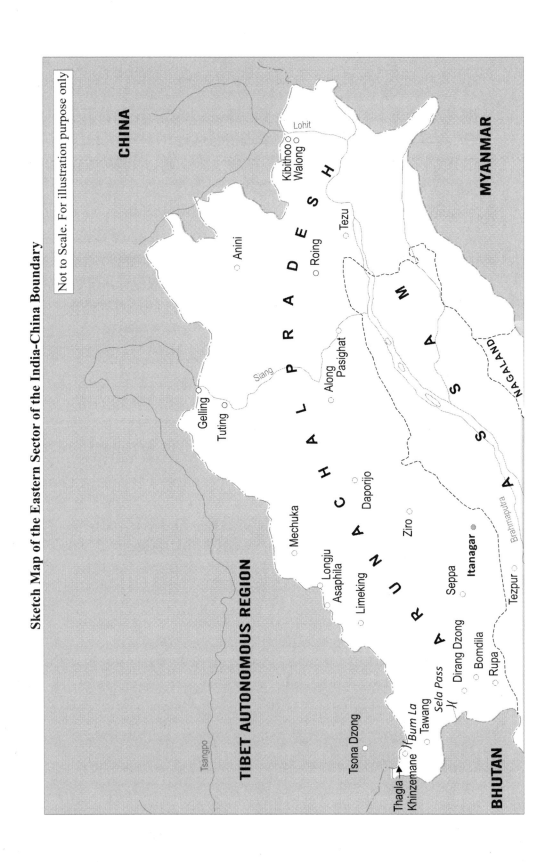

Not to Scale. For illustration purpose only

Notes

Introduction

1. Martin Luther King, Jr.: 'The past is prophetic in that it asserts loudly that wars are poor chisels for carving out peaceful tomorrows.'
2. See Melvyn Bragg, Simon Schama and Antonia Fraser, 'Relevance of the Study of History in the 20th Century' (the quote is from Simon Schama on the same podcast), 'In our Time', *BBC Sounds*, 3 December 1998: https://www.bbc.co.uk?sounds/playp00548g accessed on 27 February 2021
3. Srinath Raghavan, *War and Peace in Modern India*, Permanent Black, 2010, p. 4
4. See Philip Zelikow, *The Nature of History's Lessons in the Power of the Past: History and Statecraft*, edited by Hal Brands, and Jeremi Suri, Brookings Institution Press, 2015, p. 302: 'Hindsight is not 20/20. In fact, as the 9/11 Commission report observed, hindsight blinds. It blinds because the path of what happened is so brightly lit that all the other possibilities are cast even more deeply into shadow. History lessons should try to overcome that blindness'.
5. See T.G. Otte, 'The Inner Circle: What is Diplomatic History? (And Why We Should Study It): An Inaugural Lecture', *History*, Vol. 105, Issue 364, January 2020

6. Frank Moraes, Entry in personal diary, 1952, Frank Moraes papers, The School of Oriental and African Studies, University of London. Also finds a mention in Moraes' book, *Witness to an Era: India 1920 to the Present Day*, London: Weidenfeld & Nicholson, 1973

7. William A. Callahan, The Cartography of National Humiliation and the Emergence of China's Geobody, *Public Culture* 21:1, Duke University Press, 2009

8. Manjari Chatterjee Miller, *Wronged by Empire Post-Imperial Ideology and Foreign Policy in India and China*, Stanford University Press, 2013

9. See Mahesh Shankar, *The Reputational Imperative: Nehru's India in Territorial Conflict*, Stanford University Press, 2018

10. The proverb means to further complicate something that is already challenging

11. *Times of India*, 24 April 1960

12. See Margaret Macmillan, Patrick Quinton-Brown 'The uses of history in international society: from the Paris peace conference to the present', *International Affairs*, Volume 95, Issue 1, January 2019

Chapter 1: Freedom, Liberation and Nationhood

1. V.L. Pandit (I) Sub F-62, Nehru Memorial Museum and Library (NMML), New Delhi.

2. Humayun Kabir, 'Rabindranath Tagore'. Lecture at the School of Oriental and African Studies, 1962. A more detailed account of Tagore and China can be seen in this author's 'Geo-civilizations: India and China in Tagore's Century', King's College London, 2014. https://www.nirupamamenonrao.net/uploads/4/2/6/7/42673355/tagore_lecture_final.pdf

3. *Visva-Bharati Quarterly*, April–July 1929.

4. Even earlier, the Younghusband Expedition to Tibet of 1904 had been strongly condemned by Henry Cotton, the then President of the Indian National Congress as an 'act of wanton violence and aggression.' (See Willelm Van Eekelen, *Indian Foreign Policy and the Dispute with China: A New Look at Asian Relationships,* Brill, 2015)

5. Nehru was particularly conscious of the issue of Indian troops being used in China in the period since the Opium Wars (*Jawaharlal

Nehru: A Biography by Sarvepalli Gopal, Vol. 1, 1975). In fact, the Ghadar Party (the movement founded by Indian expatriates in San Francisco in the early 1900s) placed the opposition to the use of Indian troops in China at the forefront of its agenda.

6. Guido Samarani, 'Shaping the Future of Asia: Chiang Kai-shek, Nehru and China-India Relations during the Second World War Period', Working Paper, 2005, Center for East and South-East Asian Studies, Lund University, Sweden.

7. K.R. Narayanan, the then President of India, speaking in New Delhi on 7 November 1998, on the occasion of the centenary of the Chinese scholar Tan Yunshan, referred to the letter written by Zhu De, the Commander of the Eighth Route Army, to Jawaharlal Nehru, thanking him for the Congress Party's support for China and the rallies organized in such support. (Reproduced in *China Report* (1999) 35:205)

8. 'Jawaharlal Nehru's Urgent Appeal to You', Poster, Congress China Medical Aid Committee, London, 1938, V.K. Krishna Menon Papers, Box no. 4, File no. 4/1, NMML, New Delhi.

9. Message from Dr T.V. Soong, President of the National Economic Council, to Jawaharlal Nehru, April 1938, V.K. Krishna Menon Papers, ibid. The offer to send the medical unit was communicated by Krishna Menon (representative of the Indian National Congress in London) to Shelley Wang, who in turn communicated it to T.V. Soong who responded thus: 'We are most grateful to Nehru and Congress for their sympathy and assistance, the symbol of international solidarity.' Shelley Wang told Menon, 'I am sure the Chinese people, with me, will always regard this unselfish action as the first step towards the present and future cooperation of the Indian people with ours.' The original request to send this mission came in 1937 from Zhu De who along with Mao Zedong commanded the Eighth Route Army which, during the fight against Japanese forces, came nominally under the military structure headed by the Guomindang in a united front against Japan.

10. Indian opinion tended to be more sympathetic to the Communist Party's forces, seeing the latter as fighters for China's liberation and the Guomindang as totalitarian. This was a view also expressed by the philosopher-statesman Dr S. Radhakrishnan who toured China in 1944.

11. Gandhi (Mahatma), *Collected Works of Mahatma Gandhi,* New Delhi, 1999, Icon Softec, p. 269.

12. These were Nehru's words: 'As I descended (into Chongqing) the pleasant and familiar sound of Bandemataram greeted my ears and looking up in some surprise, I saw an Indian in uniform. He was Mukherji of our Congress Medical Unit', (*Selected Works of Jawaharlal Nehru,* Series 1, Vol. 10, July 1939–March 1940), p. 121.

13. Radio broadcast to the Chinese people, 31 August 1939. FO371/123535, The National Archives, London (TNA).

14. Letter from the British Consulate General in Saigon to the Secretary to the Government of India, External Affairs Department, Simla, 25 August 1939. FO 371/123535, TNA.

15. Ibid.

16. FO371/123535, ibid.

17. In 1942, Chiang Kai-shek visited India with his wife Soong Mei-ling much to the irritation of Winston Churchill who did not want the Generalissimo to meet Gandhi and Nehru 'and spread the pan Asian malaise through the bazaars of India'. Chiang did not make a good impression on Gandhi who referred to him after a five-hour meeting in Calcutta as 'that inscrutable man' (S.K. Arora, 'Indian Attitudes Towards China', *International Journal,* Vol. 14, no. 1 (Winter 1958/59).

18. As also with Qin Bangxian and Wang Ming (cited in Guido Samarani, ibid.)

19. https://archive.org/stream/in.ernet.dli.2015.174465/2015.174465. China-Spain-And-The-War_djvu.txt : Nehru's account of his journey to China, Kitabistan, 1940.

20. While informing the public in India about the request received from Zhu De for the dispatch of the medical mission, *The Hindu,* 25 December 1937. Even though Nehru did not meet Mao during his China visit, he had exchanged correspondence earlier with the Chinese leader expressing admiration for the feats of the Eighth Route Army. Mao also wrote to thank him for the dispatch of the Medical Unit.

21. Edgar Snow in Foreword to D.F. Karaka, *Chungking Diary.* Bombay, 1942.

22. Ibid.

23. Letter 12 November 1942 from the External Affairs Department reporting a conversation with Sir Mohammad Zafrulla Khan, FO 371/31691, TNA.
24. Ibid.
25. These connections were not enduring. The pro-left nationalism of leaders like Nehru diverged from the U.S. and Europe-oriented leanings of the Guomindang by the end of the Second World War. Talk of civilizational affinities between the two countries, sentiments that encouraged the formation of the Sino-Indian Cultural Society and the foundation of Tagore's Cheena Bhavana in Santiniketan in the 1930s was already losing some of its appeal by the end of the Chinese civil war. See Brian Tsui, 'The Plea for Asia, Tan Yunshan, Pan-Asianism and Sino-Indian Relations', *China Report* 46:4 (2010).
26. Telegram to Chongqing, 19 August 1942, FO 371/31691, TNA.
27. Ibid.
28. Ibid.
29. Ibid.
30. FO371/131691, TNA.
31. Ibid.
32. Ibid.
33. Ibid.
34. Interview: K.P.S. Menon (interviewee) recorded by B.R. Nanda (interviewer), 8 November 1976, New Delhi, NMML, Oral History Project, Transcript.
35. As Nehru was popularly known. Pandit—meaning scholar as also the Kashmir Pandit community to which he belonged.
36. It is quite plausible that Nehru had received glowing reports about the Communist Party forces in the Anti-Japanese War from the members of the Indian Medical Mission. The latter had returned with messages of gratitude from Communist Party leaders like Mao and no word of gratitude from the Nationalists. (Arora, 'Indian Attitudes')
37. Inaugural Speech at Asian Relations Conference, 1947. Jawaharlal Nehru, *Speeches*, Vol. 1.
38. Ibid.
39. Nicholas Mansergh: 'The Asian Conference', *International Affairs*, Vol. 23, no. 3 (July 1947).

40. Ibid.

41. Literally, 'China House'—a centre for Chinese language and culture, set up by Tagore at Santiniketan, Bengal, in 1937.

42. Yun-yuan Yang: 'Controversies over Tibet', *The China Quarterly,* No. 111 (Sep 1987).

43. Quoted in Yun-Yuan Yang, 'Controversies over Tibet.'

44. Fang Tien-Sze, 'An Assessment of Ambassador Luo Jialun's Mission to India: 1947-9', *China Report* 50: 3 (2014): 189-201.

45. Ibid, p. 192.

46. Ibid, p. 193, citing Luo's memoir: The design of Indian National flag and I' (印度的國旗制定和我), in Compilation Committee for Collection of Mr. Luo Jialun's Works (羅家倫先生文存編輯委員會; ed.), *A Collection of Mr. Luo Jialun's Works,* Vol. 2 *(*羅家倫先生文存第二冊*)*. Taipei: Academia Historica and Commission for the Compilation of the History of the Kuomintang, 908–15.

47. See http://loksabhaph.nic.in/writereaddata/cadebatefiles/C22071947.pdf which carries the text of the whole debate on the Constituent Assembly Resolution that was adopted on 22 July 1947 approving the design of the Flag.

48. Fang, ibid, p. 193.

49. For a narrative on the genesis of the design of the Indian Tricolour, see Laila Tyabji, 'How the Tricolour and Lion Emblem Really Came to Be', *The Wire,* 14 August 2018. https://thewire.in/history/india-national-flag-emblem-suraiya-badruddin-tyabji

50. Letter from Jawaharlal Nehru to Vijaya Lakshmi Pandit, 2 July 1949 (V.L. Pandit (II Instalment) Sub. F-20, NMML.

51. Ibid.

52. Ibid.

53. Letter from V.L. Pandit to J. Nehru, 23 September 1949, ibid.

54. This was a view extant in Nehru's writing from the early nineteen forties at least. See Jawaharlal Nehru, *China, Spain and the War: Essays and Writings* (Allahabad: Kitabistan, 1940).

55. Giri Deshingkar: 'The Nehru Years Revisited', in *Across the Himalayan Gap,* http://ignca.nic.in/ks_41046.htm (Accessed 3 March 2014).

56. Ibid.

57. Ibid.
58. This view of the Communists in China as nationalists was also echoed by John Hutchison, the British Ambassador in Peking who wrote in February 1951 that 'The doctrine of the Chinese Communist Party is thus not only predominantly a Chinese product, but it is the product evolved in the light of experience, often bitter, of practical men who have themselves applied it during long years of actual experience to Chinese populations in a Chinese environment.' Hutchison quotes Mao in this context: 'Whatever is useful must assume our national form', 'Chinese culture ought to have its own peculiar form, national according to the principles of Chinese democracy.' (Sir John Hutchison's report on conditions in China (1951): FO 371/92220, TNA).
59. Note by A.A.E. Franklin, 29 January 1951: FO 371/92248, TNA.
60. Ibid.
61. K.M. Panikkar, *In Two Chinas: Memoirs of a Diplomat.* London, George Allen and Unwin, 1955.
62. Ibid., p. 27.
63. Ibid., p. 61.
64. See Rajmohan Gandhi: *Patel: A Life,* Navjivan Trust, 1990.
65. Ibid, p. 509.
66. FCO7/1429, TNA, p. 48.
67. Ibid.
68. Telegram from Foreign New Delhi to *Indiadel*, New York, 21 November 1949; J.N. (S.G.) Papers, 1st Part, File no. 31, Pt. I, NMML.
69. Telegram from Foreign New Delhi, 20 November 1949; J.N. Papers, ibid.
70. Letter, 3 December 1949 to Tan Yun-Shan; J.N. (S.G.) Papers (1st Part), File no. 32 (Pt. I), NMML.
71. Text of Note on File FCO 7/1429, TNA.
72. Ibid., p. 16.
73. J.N. (S.G.) Papers, (1st Part), File no. 32 (Pt. I), NMML.
74. J.N. (S.G.) Papers, (1st Part), File no. 32, (Pt. II), NMML.
75. Note by the P.M. dated 7 February 1950, J.N. (S.G.) Papers, (1st Inst.), File no. 36 (Pt. I), NMML.
76. Telegram from Nehru to K.P.S. Menon, 11 January 1950; J.N. (S.G.) Papers (1st Inst.) File no. 34, NMML.

77. Secret and Personal Letter of 7 January 1950 to Thakin Nu; J.N. (S.G.) Papers (1ˢᵗ Inst.) File no. 34, NMML.

78. Quoted in telegram from Bharat, Nanjing to Foreign New Delhi, 4 November 1949; J.N. (S.G.) Papers (1ˢᵗ Part) File no. 30, NMML.

79. Ibid.

80. Ibid.

81. Report in the *Hindustan Times,* New Delhi, 24 May 1950.

82. FO371/83558, TNA.

83. Ibid.

84. FO 371/99378, TNA.

85. Note by A.A.E. Franklin, 26 May 1950: FO 371/83558, TNA.

86. Letter to Vijaya Lakshmi Pandit (VLP), 21 August 1950, V.L. Pandit (I), Sub. F-62, NMML.

87. Letter to VLP, 10 September 1950, ibid.

88. Letter from J. Nehru to Vijaya Lakshmi Pandit, 14 September 1950. V.L. Pandit (II Inst.), Sub. F-20, NMML.

89. Ibid.

90. Panikkar, *Two Chinas*, pp. 78–79.

91. Written in the 18ᵗʰ century, one of China's Four Great Classical novels.

92. Panikkar, *Two Chinas*, pp. 78–79.

93. Ibid., p. 80.

94. VLP 1ˢᵗ Inst. 1951–63, Letter to Jawaharlal Nehru, 5 February 1951, NMML.

95. Note by J.N. to the Secretary General and the Foreign Secretary, 15 June 1949; J.N. (S.G.) 1ˢᵗ Inst. File no. 24, Pt II, NMML.

96. R.K. Nehru: Transcripts (Oral History), NMML.

97. S. Gopal: 'India, China and the Soviet Union', *Australian Journal of Politics and History*, Vol. 12, Issue 2, p. 241–57.

Chapter 2: Top of the World

1. Note, 17 February 1988, Richardson Papers, Bodleian Library, Oxford University.
   Hugh Richardson, a Tibetologist, served long years in India and was the Indian representative in Lhasa before and immediately

after Indian Independence. See http://tibet.prm.ox.ac.uk/tibet_Hugh_Richardson.html
2. Interview in The *Newsweek* magazine, 25 September 1972. See Richardson Papers, Bodleian, MS. Or. Richardson 8.
3. Conversation with the Dalai Lama, Dharamshala, India, April 2014. Also see next chapter where this aspect is discussed in more detail.
4. The three traditional areas of Tibet are U-Tsang in the west, Kham in the east (bordering Sichuan and Yunnan) and Amdo (in Qinghai) in the north-east. Amdo is the birthplace of the current Dalai Lama.
5. Dalai Lama, interview, 2014, April 2014.
6. VL Pandit papers (II Instalment), Subject file F-19, NMML, New Delhi.
7. On 8 November 1950, the Tibetan authorities in Lhasa also appealed to the United Nations against the Chinese 'aggression'.
8. Tsarong Dzasa (1888–1959), commonly known as Tsarong and military commander, diplomat, close aide of the 13th Dalai Lama.
9. Huber, Toni: 'A Tibetan Map of Iho-kha in the South-Eastern Himalayan Borderlands of Tibet', *Imago Mundi,* Vol. 44 (1992).
10. K.C. Johorey, Transcript Pt. II, NMML.
11. 'India and the Mongolian Fringe': Note by the Foreign Secretary, 18 January 1940 *India Office Records, L/P and 5/12/36/23, Part I.* The Note is reproduced in Parshotam Mehra, *The North-Eastern Frontier: A Documentary Study of the Internecine Rivalry between India, Tibet and China* (Oxford University Press, 1979, 1980) pp.111–24.
12. Defined by the Merriam-Webster dictionary as a territory historically or ethnically related to one political unit but under the political control of another.
13. Led by Francis Younghusband at the behest of the Viceroy Lord Curzon, this expedition/assault was aimed at securing British commercial and strategic interests in Tibet and primarily ensuring that it became the buffer to the perceived advance of Tsarist Russia on India's frontiers, which remained an obsessive British concern at the time.
14. Letter to Mr Arnott, 15 November 1988. Copy given to this author by Dr Michael Aris, London 1990.

15. 'The word suzerainty has been used for some years to describe the British view of the relationship between China and Tibet. It has never been defined and, indeed, appears to be incapable of absolute definition and takes its colour from the particular circumstances of each case. It is not surprising that this chameleon word has caused confusion.' (Hugh Richardson, *Tibetan Precis*, Pg 64 http://pahar. in/wpfb-file/1945-tibetan-precis-by-richardson-from-high-peaks-pure-earth-maps-added-pdf/ accessed 14 November 2017). The British intention was to deal with Tibet directly, if necessary, as an autonomous entity under the nominal control of China. The dictionary meaning of the word suzerainty is that one nation state (in this case, China) exercises influence and power and the right to conduct foreign relations of a lesser state (in this case, Tibet) over which it is 'suzerain', although the latter largely enjoys self-rule. Suzerainty is not a term in usage today. Sovereignty is the prevailing term. A state exercises sovereign power over all territories within its boundaries, and concepts of suzerainty or vassalage are anachronisms in international legal parlance today. See also chapter 4 for a further discussion on the subject of 'suzerainty' as it pertained to the question of Tibet.
16. Rumbold letter, ibid.
17. These 'escorts' were small, military contingents providing security to the trade agencies and British political representatives in Tibet.
18. Tubten Gyatso (1876–1933), see https://treasuryoflives.org/biographies/view/Thirteenth-Dalai-Lama-Tubten-Gyatso/3307 The 13th Dalai Lama's life was an extremely eventful one—he was reform-minded, and a flag-bearer of Tibetan nationalism, although he developed close friendly ties with British representatives like Charles Bell, the Political Officer in Sikkim. Tibet's tentative opening to the outside world commenced under his watch.
19. Thupten Jampel Tishey Gyantsen, (1911–47) who died in still-unexplained circumstances in the wake of the so-called Reting Conspiracy, in prison in Lhasa in 1947. See Gyalo Thondup and Anne F. Thurston, *The Noodle Maker of Kalimpong: The Untold Story of My Struggle for Tibet,* Random House, 2014; Thondup (brother of the 14th Dalai Lama) renders an account of the events surrounding the Conspiracy and the Reting's death as also a rather

negative assessment of the role of Hugh Richardson for allegedly 'manipulating' ignorant Tibetan officials.

20. Although the 14th Dalai Lama has stated on record that while the relationship between the 9th Panchen Lama and the 13th Dalai Lama was 'difficult and negative, in private there was a deep, special spiritual connection', Thomas Laird, *The Story of Tibet: Conversations with the Dalai Lama*, Atlantic Books, London, 2006.

21. Richardson notes how even if it had been possible to prise the Panchen Lama out of Chinese hands, it is unlikely that the Tibetans would have approved of a British excursion to their distant frontier. In his words, 'They regularly tried to appear to balance any concession made to one of their great neighbours by a similar concession to the other; and they preferred to make none to either.' Hugh Richardson, Papers, Bodleian Library, Oxford University MS. Or. Richardson 2.

22. *Tibetan Precis*, Hugh Richardson, p. 64.

23. Hugh Richardson Papers, ibid.

24. Dekyilingka, or the Grove or Garden of Happiness housed the British and later the Indian mission in Lhasa from 1936 to 1962. It was not far from the Norbulingka, the summer palace of the Dalai Lama.

25. Richardson Papers, ibid.

26. Accompanying Gould on his mission was the young Indian artist Kanwal Krishna (1910–93) whose portraits of the Tibetan high clergy and nobility offer a brilliant visual record of many historical personalities in Lhasa at the time. (Clare Harris and Tsering Shakya: *Seeing Lhasa: British Depictions of the Tibetan Capital, 1936–47*, Serindia Publications, Chicago, 2003).

27. Richardson Papers, ibid.

28. Potala Palace, built in the 7th century CE, the winter seat of the Dalai Lama, sacred to Tibetan Buddhism and a UNESCO World Heritage site. The word 'Potala' is believed to be derived from the Sanskrit 'Buddhalaya' or Buddhist temple.

29. Richardson Papers, ibid.

30. The Shandong Peninsula in northeastern China, under German occupation prior to the First World War, was pledged by the Allies to be returned to China for her support to the Allied cause during the War. However, this pledge was not redeemed and Shandong,

which was occupied by Japan in 1914, was allowed to remain under Japanese control under the terms of the Treaty of Versailles. This occasioned great outrage in China and triggered the student demonstrations of 4 May 1919, a historical watershed.

31. Richardson, *Tibetan Precis*, p. 26.
32. Charles Bell (1870-1945) spoke Tibetan fluently and it is 'no understatement to compare Sir Charles' part in Tibetan affairs with that of T.E. Lawrence in Arabia.' (Lars-Erik Nyman, 'Tawang-A Case Study of British Frontier Policy in the Himalayas', *Journal of Asian History*, Vol. 10, No. 2, (1976), pp. 151-171.
33. *Tibetan Precis* Ibid., p. 29.
34. Ibid.
35. Interview with the Dalai Lama, Dharamshala.
36. Richardson, *Tibetan Precis*, p. 83.
37. 'No one contested Chinese suzerainty over Tibet', Churchill to Soong at the Pacific Conference in Washington D.C., 1943, quoted in *Tibetan Precis*, p. 84.
38. https://sites.google.com/site/legalmaterialsontibet/home/eden-memorandum (accessed on 15 November 2017).
39. Inward Telegram from the External Affairs Department, New Delhi, to the Secretary of State for India, 4 October 1944; FO 371/41588, TNA.
40. Quoted in Letter from A.J. Hopkinson, The Residency, Gangtok, to the Joint Secretary, External Affairs Department, New Delhi, 8 April 1946, F.O. 371/53661 TNA.
41. Shenchi Liu, 'China's Relations with Tibet', *The China Weekly Review*, 12 June 1948; ProQuest Historical Newspapers: Chinese Newspapers Collection (1832–1953), p. 50.
42. Ibid.
43. Ibid.
44. The Manchus or the Qing dynasty occupied Mongolia by the late 17th century. Inner Mongolia and Outer Mongolia were the two 'regions' of Mongolia. Inner Mongolia was the southern part, contiguous to China, while Outer Mongolia was the region bordering Russia. Outer Mongolia (today's independent nation of Mongolia) declared independence with the support of Soviet Russia in 1921, and its independence was further confirmed on the basis of a national referendum in 1945. Even as late as 1995, Chinese leaders like Deng Xiaoping were expressing their unhappiness

that Mongolia was no longer Chinese territory. Previous to the separation, the territorial contours of China had resembled a 'maple leaf' which had now been 'nibbled' away. Inner Mongolia has remained a part of China and is now called the Inner Mongolia Autonomous Region. See: https://thediplomat.com/2015/10/the-truth-about-mongolias-independence-70-years-ago/

45. Richardson Papers. Neither did the occasion elicit any comment from China. In their note to the Tibetan government on the handing over of power to India, the British government promised to take 'a friendly interest in the future prosperity of the Tibetan people and in the maintenance of Tibetan autonomy.'

46. Speaking of the Reting Rinpoche's rebellion, the British reading was that in Lhasa traditionally the monks (clergy) were supportive of China while the laity was British-inclined. F.O. 371/76318, TNA. The big monasteries in Tibet—Sera, Ganden, Drepung and Tashi Lhunpo—were traditionally the nuclei of political intrigue, and infiltrated by Chinese interests.

47. Richardson Papers.

48. For a detailed exposition of the Tibetan Mission of 1947, see Lezlee Brown Halper and Stefan Halper, *Tibet An Unfinished Story*, Oxford University Press, 2014, Chapter 8.

49. Telegram from Indian Mission in Lhasa to the Political Officer in Sikkim and Foreign, New Delhi (the Ministry of External Affairs), 27 March 1948 , Foreign Department File No. 7/2/NEF/48 Secret; in A.S. Bhasin: India-China Relations 1947-2000, Vol. 1, A Documentary Study, 2018.

50. Telegram from Foreign New Delhi to the Mission in Lhasa, 30 July 1948 in Foreign Dept. File no. 7/2/NEF/48 Secret; in Bhasin, ibid. Vol. 1.

51. Ibid.

52. Inward telegram from the External Affairs Department to the Secretary of State for India, 7 January 1946 with text of aide memoire which was handed over by Hopkinson in Lhasa on 22 January. FO 371/53613 TNA.

53. FO 371/46123, TNA.

54. Ibid.

55. Writing in his book *Tibet, Past and Present* (Oxford: Clarendon Press, 1924), Charles Bell said the following: 'We want Tibet as a

buffer to India on the north. Now there are buffers and buffers, and some of them are of very little use, but Tibet is ideal in this respect. With the large desolate area of the Northern Plains controlled by the Lhasa Government, central and southern Tibet governed by the same authority, and the Himalayan border States guided by, or in close alliance with, the Indian Government, Tibet forms a barrier equal, or superior, to anything that the world can show elsewhere.' (Quoted by Foreign Secretary, Government of India, Olaf Caroe in his note of 19 September 1945 to the Indian Office in London. FO 371/46123 ibid.)

56. Telegram from Nanking to Foreign Office, London 13 October 1948. F.O. 371/69739, TNA.

57. F.O. 371/76314, TNA.

58. Ibid. Around the same time, Secretary-General Bajpai mentioned to the UK High Commissioner in Delhi that the Chinese Ambassador had called to protest about a map that appeared in a recent film on Kashmir showing Tibet as separate from China. Bajpai said he had dismissed this as a 'flimsy protest.' The British also learnt from sources in Delhi that the Chinese had also asked whether they might establish a Consulate in Kashmir. Whereupon, the somewhat difficult circumstances of that unhappy State were gently pointed out, and the matter was left there.' (F.O. 371/76314, TNA.)

59. F.O. 371/69739, Ibid. Secret Letter from CRO to HCUK, Delhi dated 29 October, 1948, TNA.

60. Yun-yuan Yang, 'Controversies over Tibet: China versus India, 1947-49', *The China Quarterly*, No. 111 (Sep., 1987), pp. 407-420.

61. Government of India, *Notes, Memoranda and Letters Exchanged and Agreements signed between The Governments of India and China 1954-1959*, White Paper II, p. 39.

62. *The Times*, London, 28 July 1949.

63. Yun-yuan Yang, ibid.

64. Richardson Papers, Ibid., Folder 21, Fols. 1–129.

65. Robert Ford (1923–2013) was a radio operator for the British mission in Lhasa before he was asked by the Tibetan government to start its first broadcasting service in 1947. He was captured by the invading Chinese Communist forces in 1950 and held in prison in China until 1955.

66. Richardson Papers, Folder 32, Fols. 1–99.

67. C.F. Greenwood, Far Eastern Department, Foreign and Commonwealth Office, to Richardson, 28 April 1993. Richardson Papers.

68. https://publications.parliament.uk/pa/cm200708/cmhansrd/cm081029/wmstext/81029m0001.htm 29 October 2008 (Accessed on 19 November 2017).

69. Robert Barnett, 'Did Britain Just Sell Tibet?', *New York Times*, 24 November 2008.

70. 'Britain's Suzerain Remedy', *The Economist*, 6 November 2008.

71. 'The McMahon Line, validity of', Note by P.L. Bushe-Fox, 20 November 1962. F.O. 371/31961, T.N.A.

72. Charles Henry Alexandrowicz-Alexander, 'The Legal Position of Tibet', *The American Journal of International Law*, Vol. 48, no. 2 (Apr., 1954), pp 265-274.

73. R.S. Kalha, 'Tibet as a Factor in Sino-Indian Relations Past and Present', *Journal of Defence Studies*, Vol. 6, no. 4, (2012) pp. 7-26.

74. Note by Olaf Caroe, Foreign Secretary, 19 September 1945 in FO 371/46123, ibid.

75. Amanda J. Cheney, 'Tibet Lost in Translation: Sovereignty, Suzerainty and International Order Transformation, 1904-1906', *Journal of Contemporary China*, Vol. 26, Issue 107 (2017).

76. Okamoto Takashi, ed. 岡本隆司 編. *Sōshuken no sekaishi: Tōzai Ajia no kindai to hon'yaku gainen* 宗主権の世界史：東西アジアの近代と翻訳概念 [A world history of suzerainty: A modern history of East and West Asia and translated concepts]. Nagoya: Nagoya daigaku shuppankai, 2014. 399 pp. ISBN: 9784815807870.

77. Dibyesh Anand, 'The British Imperial Scripting of Tibet's Geopolitical Identity', *The Journal of Asian Studies*, Vol. 68, no. 1, (2009) pp. 227-252.

78. Ibid.

79. See A.J. Hopkinson, 'The Position of Tibet', Lecture, 25 April 1950 at the Royal Central Asian Society, London, *Journal of the Royal Central Asian Society*, 37:3-4, pp.228-239 where he says: 'Sir Charles Bell complained that frequently Tibet or the agency dealing with Tibet is the Cinderella of the Indian Foreign Office, and that was too often true'.

80. Ibid.

81. Letter from British Embassy in Washington D.C. to Ernest Bevin, M.P., 6 January 1951, enclosing Aide-Memoire from the State

Department tracing American views on Tibet from 1943 until 1951. FO 371/10310, TNA. In fact, the State Department also declined to receive a Tibetan mission seeking assistance on the grounds that the arrival of such a Mission would be harmful rather than helpful 'since it might strengthen the hands of those who advocate an immediate invasion of the country.' (Message from Ambassador Loy Henderson in Delhi, conveyed to the Indian Mission in Lhasa asking that the Kashag be given this message in response to their communications of 22 December 1949 to the President of the United States and the Secretary of State on plans to send a special mission to the U.S.), J.N. (S.G.) Papers (1st Part) File no-35, NMML.

82. A.J. de la Mare, Note, 19 December 1962. F.O, 371/31691, T.N.A. Mare notes that the term 'illegal McMahon Line' had become a 'sort of convention, like that in the southern states of America after the Civil War, when a northerner was always known not as a 'Yankee' but as a 'god-damn Yankee'.'

83. Telegram from Pol. Sikk. Lhasa to Foreign New Delhi, 14 November 1949, J.N. (S.G,) Papers, 1st Part, File no. 31 (Part I), NMML.

84. Jawaharlal Nehru to Secretary General Bajpai, Top Secret, Note, 9 July 1949. J.N. (S.G.) 1st Instalment. File no. 26 (Part 1), NMML.

85. Cable from the Chinese Foreign Ministry, 24 December 1950, 'Report on Negotiations regarding the Tibet issue between China and India', Digital Archive, The Wilson Center (digitalarchive. wilsoncenter.org).

86. Ibid.

87. J.N. (S.G.) 1st Instalment. File no. -26 (Pt.-1), NMML.

88. J.N. (S.G.) Papers, 1st Part, File no. 31 (Part I), NMML. 'Proceedings of a Press Conference addressed by Prime Minister Nehru on 16 November, 1949'.

89. Telegram from the UK High Commissioner in Delhi (UKHC) to CRO London, rptd. Nanking, 18 September 1949, FO371/76314, TNA.

90. Telegram from the UK High Commissioner (UKHC) in Delhi to CRO London, 17 November 1949: FO 371/76314, TNA.

91. The Ambassador in India (Henderson) to the Secretary of State, 10 January 1950. Foreign Relations of the United States, 1950,

East Asia and the Pacific, Volume VI 793B 00/1-1050 – Telegram-https://history.state.gov/historicaldocuments/frus   1950v06/d132 accessed 15 November 2017.

92. Telegram from the UKHC in Delhi to CRO, 6 November 1949; FO 371/76314, TNA.
93. UKHC Delhi to CRO, 26 November, 1949; ibid.
94. F.O. 371/69739, TNA.

Chapter 3: Fateful Decisions

1. Major S.M. Krishnatry (1922–2015), an officer of the Maratha Regiment, was the Indian Trade Agent in Gyantse in the Chumbi Valley, at the time. (see https://www.orfonline.org/expert-speak/indian-frontier-administrative-service-unexplored-ace-india-deck/) Oral History Transcript, (Vol.1), Acc. no. 863, NMML.
2. Note by K.M. Panikkar on Tibet Policy, 4 November 1949', Avtar Singh Bhasin: *India-China Relations 1947-2000, a Documentary Study*, Vol. 1, Geetika Publishers, 2018, pp. 164-167.
3. Telegram from British Embassy, Peking to Foreign and Commonwealth Office, 21 January 1951, reporting on a conversation with the Indian Ambassador. F.O. 371/10310, TNA.
4. Ibid. Panikkar's volte-face in his attitude on Tibet is intriguing. In Nanjing as Ambassador to the Guomindang, he had been more a votary for Tibetan autonomy and separate existence, but his approach to the issue as Ambassador to the People's Republic veered more to the acknowledgement of Chinese sovereignty over Tibet and he made it clear to his British interlocutors that he did not cling to the Curzon policy of buffer states even if the Indian Foreign Office did not entirely agree with him.
5. Note by K.P.S. Menon, 12 November 1949 in Bhasin, *India-China Relations,* pp, 167-169.
6. Telegram from Political Officer, Lhasa to Foreign, New Delhi dated 14 November 1949, marked 'Top Secret': Foreign Department File no. C/13/NEF/49-Pt-II), NAI.
7. J.N. (S.G.) Papers, 1st Part, File no. 31 (Part I), NMML Ibid.
8. Telegram from Political Officer, Sikkim, Lhasa to Foreign, New Delhi, 4 November 1949. J.N. (S.G.) Ibid.

9. Telegram, 14 November 1949 from Political Officer, Sikkim, Lhasa to Foreign New Delhi. J.N. (S.G.) Ibid.

10. 'Note on the meeting held by the Prime Minister with Foreign Secretary (KPS Menon), K.M. Panikkar and Political Officer (H. Dayal) on 30 December, 1949 to discuss 'Policy on Tibet', Foreign Department File no. C/13/NEF/49-Pt-II), NAI.

11. Note handed by the Foreign Minister of China to the Indian Ambassador, 21 August 1950 in *Treaties Signed and Memoranda Exchanged between the Governments of India and China. 1949-1959*, Ministry of External Affairs, New Delhi, 1959.

12. Telegram marked 'Top Secret' from Foreign New Delhi to Indian embassy, Beijing dated 24 August 1950 cited in Bhasin, op.cit, Vol 1, pg. 329.

13. 'Discussion on Tibetan Problems During Vice Minister Zhang's Reception of Ambassador Panikkar' in 'Record on India's Interference of our Liberation of Tibet and our Replying Documents', 15 August 1950, Archive no. 105-00010-01(1), Ministry of Foreign Affairs of the P.R.C. , cited in Halper & Halper, *Tibet.*

14. Telegram from the Kashag 3 December 1949, FO 371/76314, TNA.

15. FO 371/76314.

16. Ibid.

17. FO 371/83558, TNA.

18. Telegram: Personal for Panikkar from Prime Minister, 19 August 1950. J.N. (S.G.) Papers File no. 52 (Pt I), NMML.

19. Telegram from Political Officer in Sikkim, Gangtok to Foreign, New Delhi, 17 August 1950, ibid.

20. Note by Prime Minister to Secretary General and Foreign Secretary, 18 August 1950, ibid.

21. Halper & Halper, *Tibet.*, p. 106 quoting declassified Chinese Foreign Ministry documents, cites Director General Chen of the Ministry of Foreign Affairs as claiming that he had specifically informed Panikkar on 30 August 1950 that the PLA 'was going into Sikang'. Chen called it a 'determined plan' and not a new one.

22. Ibid., p. 112.

23. V.L. Pandit (II Instalment) Sub. F-19, 1950, Chronology of Events, Invasion of Tibet, NMML.

24. Note by the Foreign Secretary on his meeting with the Chinese Counsellor, 26 October 1950. J.N. (S.G.) Papers, File no. 61 (Pt I), NMML.

25. 'Tribute to Swami Dayanand' (speech at the Rishi Dayanand Nirvan Utsav), Delhi, 9 November 1950 in *For a United India: speeches of Sardar Patel 1947–50.* Publications Division, Ministry of Information and Broadcasting, Government of India, 1967.

26. Telegram from the Indian Embassy in Peking to the Ministry of External Affairs, 3 August 1950. J.N. (SG.) Papers (1st Pt), File no. 50 (Part I), NMML, p. 31.

27. 'Top Secret' Telegram from Ministry of External Affairs to the Embassy in Peking, 5 August 1950, J.N. ibid., p. 29–30.

28. Bhasin, *India-China Relations*, Vol. 1, p. 385–7.

29. Letter from the Prime Minister to Ambassador Panikkar, 25 October, 1950 in Bhasin, ibid. p. 389.

30. Letter to Ambassador Sarvepalli Radhakrishnan in Moscow, 8 July 1950; J.N. (S.G) Papers, File no. 47 (II), NMML.

31. Note to the Foreign Secretary K.P.S. Menon, 12 July 1950; J.N. (S.G.) Papers, File no. 48 (Pt. I), NMML.

32. Telegram from Krishna Menon to Nehru, 5 July 1950 regarding statement issued by the Government of India on 29 June; J.N. (S.G.) Papers, File no. 47 (Pt. II); NMML.

33. Panikkar, *Two Chinas*, p. 109–10.

34. As quoted by Shyam Kumari of the Aurobindo Ashram, citing the last testament of Sri Aurobindo, Letter to the Editor, *Border Affairs*, New Delhi, October-December 2001. http://www.reversespins. com/aurobindo.html. (Accessed 18 April 2018). Also quoted by Sudhir Ghosh, MP in a letter to Prime Minister Nehru, 1 December, 1962. J.N. (S.G.) Papers.

35. Letter to the Prime Minister from G.L. Nanda, 11 July 1950; J.N. (SG) Papers (1st Pt) File no. 49 (Pt I), NMML.

36. 'Memorandum for self': Note by Mathai, 8 September 1950, J.N. (S.G.) Papers; File no. 52 (Pt. I), NMML.

37. 'Nehru, Patel and China', NMML, Chandrashekhar Dasgupta, audio file http://nehrumemorial.nic.in/en/digital-archives/61-workshop/detail/775-4-mr-chandrashekhar-dasgupta-19-04-2014. html?tmpl=component (Accessed 21 April 2018)

38. Letter from Sardar Patel to G.S. Bajpai, 4 November 1950; Dasgupta, Ibid. Also, *Patel A Life* by Rajmohan Gandhi, Navajivan Publishing House, Navajivan Trust, 1990, pp.511–12 Also in J.N. (S.G.) Papers (1st Inst) File no. 62 (Pt II), NMML.
39. M.K. Rasgotra, *A Life in Diplomacy*, Penguin Books, 2016, ch. 1.
40. Chitleen K. Sethi, 'General Zorawar Chand Bakshi: The greatest wartime hero who 'just faded away'', The Print, 28 May 2018 (https://theprint.in/theprint-profile/lt-gen-zorawar-chand-bakshi-the-greatest-wartime-hero-who-just-faded-away/63532/).
41. Dawa Norbu, 'Tibet in Sino-Indian Relations. The Centrality of Marginality', *Asian Survey*, Vol. 37, no. 11 (Nov., 1997), pp. 1078-1095.
42. Rasgotra, *Life in Diplomacy*, ch. 1.
43. K.S. Bajpai: 'Weightlifting', https://www.outlookindia.com/magazine/story/weightlifting/262753 , (Accessed 20 April 2018).
44. ibid.
45. Isaiah Berlin, 'The Hedgehog and the Fox' in *Russian Thinkers*, Penguin Books, 1979.
46. S. Gopal, 'The Formative Ideology of Jawaharlal Nehru', *Economic and Political Weekly*, Vol. 11. No. 21, 1976, pp. 787-792.
47. The Earl Mountbatten of Burma: 'Reflections on the Transfer of Power and Jawaharlal Nehru', Nehru Memorial Lecture, Trinity College, University of Cambridge, 14 November 1968.
48. Michael Brecher, *Nehru, A Political Biography*, Oxford University Press, 1959.
49. Sarvepalli Gopal, 'India, China and the Soviet Union', *Australian Journal of Politics and History*, Vol. 12, 1966.
50. Jawaharlal Nehru, *Letters for a Nation: From Jawaharlal Nehru to His Chief Ministers, 1947–63*, ed. Madhav Khosla, Penguin, 2014. Patel's health had meanwhile taken a turn for the worse; his condition rapidly deteriorated, with the end coming on 15 December 1950.
51. Prime Minister's Note of 8 November 1950. J.N. (S.G.) Papers (1st Inst.). File no. 62 (Part II), NMML.
52. Ibid.
53. B.N. Mullik, *The Chinese Betrayal*, Allied Publishers, Bombay, 1971
54. Also called the North and North-East Border Defence Committee, Mullik, *Chinese Betrayal*, p.

55. Mullik, *Chinese Betrayal*, p.

56. J.N. Note to S.G. No. 851-P.M., 4 July 1950. J.N. (S.G.) Papers, File no. 47-II, NMML.

57. Letter to Dr. John Mathai, 10 September 1949. J.N. (S.G.) 1st Instalment. File no. 29(I), NMML.

58. For an excellent rendition of events surrounding the extension of Indian administration into Tawang in 1951, see Sonia Shukla: 'Forging New Frontiers: Integrating Tawang with India, 1951', *China Report* 2012, 48:407.

59. Tawang houses the largest Gelugpa or Yellow-Hat (a sect of Tibetan/Himalayan Buddhism founded in the 14th century by Lama Tsongkhapa) monastery in India and is a site of Mahayana Buddhist pilgrimage. The Monastery is known as the Tawang Ganden Namgyal Lhatse i.e., 'the celestial paradise of divine site chosen by the horse' and was founded by Merag Lodroe Gyamtso in the year 1680-81. It was originally a large and fortified complex strategically sited where the caravan routes from Tibet, Bhutan and West Kameng met. (See https://tawang.nic.in/tourist-place/tawang-monastery/). The 6th Dalai Lama, Tsangyang Gyatso (1683–1706) who lived a tragic and short life, and whose poetry is his enduring legacy, was born near Tawang in the seventeenth century. The 14th Dalai Lama, Tenzing Gyatso, who entered India as a refugee from Tibet, crossed the border into India at Khinzemane in the vicinity of Tawang in March 1959. Monyul, or land of the Mon people, is the traditional name of the region of which Tawang is the centre and its inhabitants are called the Monpas.

60. Chinese Foreign Ministry spokesperson Hua Chunying in April, 2017. See: https://timesofindia.indiatimes.com/india/china-vows-necessary-measures-after-dalai-lama-visits-arunachal/articleshow/58028406.cms

61. The entire state of Arunachal Pradesh, with the exception of Tirap district, is claimed by China which refers to the area as 'South Tibet'.

62. The three sacrosanct rights of the Chinese nation are seen as firstly, maintaining the current one-party political system, secondly, the defence of sovereignty and territorial integrity, and, thirdly, people's livelihoods and economic development.

63. 'Note on Assam Frontier Tracts', 6 February 1949, J.N. (S.G.) 19 (Pt. I), NMML. The Prime Minister noted, 'There are so many

international problems involved in these areas that, inevitably, the External Affairs Ministry would have to deal with them . . . The fact that the frontier is not clearly defined and accepted by the countries on the other side also makes it necessary for these tracts to be dealt with by External Affairs'.

64. See also Lobsang Tenpa, 'McMahon Line (1914–2014) and the Status of Monyul until 1951–52': in *The Tibet Journal*, Vol. 39, no. 2 (Autumn/Winter 2014) pp. 57-102, Library of Tibetan Works and Archives http://www.jstor.org/stable/tibetjournal.39.2.57 (Accessed 5 August 2017).

65. Nehru never visited Tawang. One account this writer has heard is that in October 1952 on a tour of the frontier areas, the Prime Minister wished to visit the monastery town but in the absence of an air strip and roads, the intention was not realized. A plan that his plane should overfly Tawang at a low height and drop flowers over the monastery also did not fructify because of cloud cover.

66. Note by Major Khathing on 'The Assam Rifles and the McMahon Line', describing his historic entry into Tawang. (Unpublished, circa 1987).

67. Bérénice Guyot-Réchard, *Shadow States India, China and the Himalayas, 1910–1962*, (Cambridge University Press, 2017), citing records in the NAI and records of the NEFA Secretariat, Itanagar, p. 102.

68. Telegram to Lhasa, 14 March 1951, *India–China Relations*, Vol. 1, p. 496.

69. The conference was titled 'Re-visiting Shimla Convention 1914' and was held on 12 May 2014. It was organized by the Himachal Pradesh University in cooperation with the Tibet Policy Institute Dharamshala.

70. Tenpa, *Centenary of the McMahon Line*, p. 66.

71. Ibid, p. 67.

Chapter 4: End of an Era

1. This is the statement famously attributed to Sumul Sinha, the Indian Representative in Lhasa, 1951. See *Venkat Forever: A Tribute to Ambassador A.P. Venkateswaran* (Ed. T.P. Sreenivasan and James M. Peck, Konark Publishers, 2015) p. 157, in which

Mr Venkateswaran recalls a telegram with these words sent by Consul-General Sumul Sinha to the Ministry of External Affairs in New Delhi. Venkateswaran called this 'one of the most powerful telegrams I have ever seen in my entire life. Yet such a powerful telegram did not shake the Indian establishment as it should have.' This view was greeted with irritation by Prime Minister Jawaharlal Nehru who felt the larger picture of good relations with China should take precedence over any perceived threat of China's entry into Tibet. Venkateswaran opines that this reflected 'rather negatively on our idol who happened to be Jawaharlal Nehru and who continued to harbor very fond images of China and India leading Asia forward'.

2. See *Nine Decades of Vicissitudes: The Memoir of Ambassador Yang Gong Su*, Haikou: Hainan Chubanshe, 1999, ch. 7, p. 188.

3. W. Whitson with Chen-hsia Huang, *The Chinese High Command A History of Communist Military Politics 1927-71*, Praeger Publishers 1973.

4. Foreign Department File no. 7/13/NEF/49-Pt. II Secret, NAI.

5. Halper & Halper, *Tibet,* p. 98.

6. Department of Information and International Relations, Central Tibetan Administration, *Facts About The 17-Point 'Agreement' Between Tibet and China*, Ganchen Kyishong, Dharamshala, 2001.

7. Ibid.

8. Ibid.

9. Ibid.

10. Telegram from the Ambassador in India (Henderson) to the Secretary of State, 27 December 1950 (https://history.state.gov/historicaldocuments/frus1950v06/d3674) (Accessed 15 November 2017)

11. Melvyn Goldstein, *A History of Modern Tibet, volume 2: The Calm Before the Storm: 1951-1955*, University of California Press, 2007, Part One, Ch 3.

12. Ibid.

13. Goldstein, *History*, p.63.

14. Telegram from The Ambassador in India (Henderson) to the Secretary of State, 20 November 1950 (https://history.state.gov/historicaldocuments/frus1950v06/d350) (Accessed 15 November 2017).

15. Tsering Shakya, *Dragon in The Land Of Snows*, Pimlico Books, 1999, p.98.

16. Goldstein, *History*, p.75.

17. Telegram from Henderson to the Secretary of State, 30 November 1950 (http://history.state.gov/historicialdocuments/frus1950v06/d356) (Accessed 15 November 2017). The Americans continued the usage of 'Peiping' for Peking/Beijing until the Nixon opening to China in 1972.

18. Telegram from Henderson to the Secretary of State, 3 November 1950 (https://history.state.gov/historicaldocuments/frus1950v06/d338) (Accessed 15 November 2017).

19. Telegram from the Secretary of State to the Embassy in India, 6 January 1951 (https://history.state.gov/historicaldocuments/frus1950v06/d379) (Accessed 15 November 2017).

20. Ibid.

21. Robert Barnett, Benno Weiner, Francoise Robin, Ed., *Conflicting Memories: Tibetan History under Mao Retold: essays and primary documents*, Koninklijke Brill NV, 2020, p.23.

22. Facts About The 17-Point 'Agreement', ibid.

23. For the text of the Agreement see http://www.tibetjustice.org/materials/china/china3.html.

24. Dalai Lama conversation with the author, Dharamshala, 2014.

25. Yang, *Nine Decades,* ibid.

26. S.M. Krishnatry Papers, Correspondence with Sinha, S., Manuscript Section, NMML.

27. Ibid.

28. Telegram from Ambassador Henderson to the Secretary of State, 5 June 1951. (https://history.state.gov/historicaldocuments/frus1951v07/d103) accessed 15 November 2017.

29. Ibid.

30. Goldstein, *History,* p. 119.

31. Ibid, p. 120.

32. It is often speculated that the pro-Chinese elements in Tibet resided mainly in these great monasteries.

33. The Chumbi Valley is a wedge-shaped tract of land, once Sikkimese, but now Tibetan, between Sikkim and Bhutan. The land route into Tibet from Sikkim crosses into the Chumbi Valley over the pass of

Nathu La. Yadong, the site of the Indian Trade Agency until 1962 is in the Chumbi Valley.

34. Goldstein, *History*, p.144.
35. Dalai Lama Interview, 2014.
36. Writing to Krishnatry, Sinha said in October 1951 that while it was true that 'we did not invite the Dalai Lama to India, but if we had done so we would have prejudiced the chance of a fair settlement between Tibet and China'. Krishnatry, ibid.
37. Goldstein, *History,* p. 146.
38. Ibid.
39. A.J. Hopkinson: 'The Position of Tibet', ibid.
40. S.M.Krishnatry Papers, op.cit.
    Referring to the Chinese methods with the Tibetans, Sinha wrote 'You may recall that a certain General Peng once sent a packet full of dung in reply to the Kalon Lama's message to stop hostilities in Kham. We can't really even if so inclined, emulate the Chinese in these matters.'
41. Krishnatry, ibid.
42. The Dalai Lama, 'Freedom in Exile', HarperCollins, 1990, cited in Goldstein, op.cit, p. 153.
43. Shakya, *Dragon,* p 114, quoting 129 FRUS, Vol VII, Part 2 (1951), p. 1751, telegram from Evan Wilson, Consul-General in Calcutta to the State Department.
44. Shakya p. 134, the reference to India feeling marginalized came up in a conversation that Secretary-General Bajpai had with the UK High Commissioner, Archibald Nye on 4 July 1951.
45. Shakya, p.141.
46. Inward telegram to the C.R.O. from the UKHC in New Delhi 30 May 1951. FO 371/10310, TNA.
47. Robert Trumbull, 'India Reconsiders Her Peiping Policy', *The New York Times,* 29 October 1950.
48. Telegram from Lhasa to the Political Officer in Sikkim, 27 October 1950; Bhasin, *India China Relations,* pp. 399-401.
49. 'Chinese Interests in the Territories on India's Northern Frontier'; Research Department, British Foreign Office note, 'Secret', SEA/13/50 3 March 1950, TNA.
50. Security Council Official Records 1949, No. 39, p. 7, quoted in Research Department note, ibid.

Chapter 5: A Cultural Tour and Two Consulates

1. Frank Moraes (1907-1974), Editor, The Indian Express, diary entry, on eve of departure of Cultural Delegation for China, April 1952, Moraes Papers, School of Oriental and African Studies, London.
2. Ibid.
3. Herbert Passin, 'Sino-Indian Cultural Relations', *The China Quarterly*, No. 7 (Jul–Sep 1961), pp. 85–100.
4. The full list of the delegates was as follows: Vijaya Lakshmi Pandit, Leader; Acharya Narendra Deva, Vice-Chancellor, Banaras Hindu University; Amaranatha Jha, educationist; P.C. Bagchi, scholar of Oriental History, Literature and Languages; Durga Bai, advocate and social worker; Nawab Zain Yar Jung, architect and engineer, Hyderabad–Deccan; S. Bhagwantam, Director, Physical Laboratories, Osmania University; M. Chalapathi Rau, President, Indian Federation of Working Journalists' Organisations and Editor, *National Herald*; Frank Moraes, Editor, *The Times of India*; B.N. Ganguli, Professor, The Delhi School of Economics; N.S. Bendre, artist; Shanta Rao, dancer; N.P. Chakravarti, Ministry of Education (Archaeological Dept.); and Leilamani Naidu, Ministry of External Affairs.
5. Telegram from Foreign Office, London to British Embassy, Beijing, 22 April 1952, FO 371/99270, TNA.
6. Ibid.
7. Frank Moraes, 'India and China', *The American Scholar*, Vol. 32, no. 3 (Summer 1963), pp. 445–50.
8. 'Daily Express', London, 28 April 1952, FO 371/99270, TNA.
9. Ibid.
10. A Telegram of 14 May from the British Embassy in Beijing to the Foreign Office noted that when Frank Moraes asked the Chinese girl who was acting as an interpreter to direct the driver of the motor car placed at their disposal to go to the British Embassy, 'he was informed that there was no such place'. (Ibid.)
11. Report on the visit of the Cultural Delegation to China, Ministry of External Affairs, New Delhi, 1952, J.N. Papers (S.G.), File no. 820, NMML, New Delhi.
12. V.L. Pandit, (II Inst,) Sub. F-20, NMML, New Delhi.
13. Ibid.

14. Ibid.
15. Ibid.
16. Telegram from Mrs Pandit to Jawaharlal Nehru, May 6, 1952, Indian Embassy, Peking to Foreign New Delhi, VL Pandit Papers, S. no. 23, NMML, New Delhi.
17. K.M. Panikkar, letter to the Prime Minister, 2nd May, 1952, V. L. Pandit, Ibid.
18. *A Chronology of Principal Events Relating to India-China Relations, 1949–1961*, Ministry of External Affairs, New Delhi, 1962.
19. Peter John Brobst, *The Future of the Great Game: Sir Olaf Caroe, India's Independence and the Defence of Asia,* (Univ. of Akron Press, 2005) map, p. xv.
20. Ibid, p. xviii.
21. Ibid., p. 16.
22. A resting place at crossroads, a watering hole, for travellers along ancient merchant routes.
23. K.P.S. Menon: *Delhi–Chungking: A Travel Diary*, Oxford University Press, 1947.
24. George Macartney (1867–1945), first British Consul in Kashgar. Born in Nanjing, he was half-Chinese.
25. 'Shaksgam, with its potent mix of imperial masculinity, exploration in uncharted territory, high adventure and the aesthetics of the mountain sublime sparked a wave of romantic longing among British mountaineers, explorers and geographers', Jonathan Westaway, 'That Undisclosed World: Eric Shipton's Mountains of Tartary (1950)', *Studies in Travel Writing*, 2014, 18:4, 357–73, https://www.tandfonline.com/doi/pdf/10.1080/13645145.2014.964 457, (Accessed on 23 May 2018).
26. Ibid.
27. Ibid.
28. Ibid.
29. FCO 7/1429, TNA.
30. Ibid.
31. Telegram from Ministry of External Affairs, New Delhi to Indian Embassy, Nanking, 14 February 1949. J.N. (S.G.) Ist Instalment, F. no. 19 (Pt.-II), NMML, New Delhi.
32. Prime Minister Nehru in a written reply to a Parliament Question on 19 December 1950, FCO 7/1429, TNA.

33. The question of Indo-Xinjiang trade was discussed in 1950–51 and the conclusion reached was that since 'almost all the Indian merchants had returned from Xinjiang, there was nothing much that could be done in the matter'. Trade had always been limited on account of geographical reasons, carried on through the most difficult route in the world over the Karakoram mountains. Goods exported from India were mainly cotton cloth, dye stuffs, woollen goods, medicines, tea, spices, and artificial silk cloth. Goods imported were blankets, carpets, raw wool, and silk yarn.

34. There were three routes through which trade was normally carried on between Xinjiang and pre-Partition India. Two of these routes were via Chitral and Gilgit now occupied by Pakistan. The third route through Leh, across the Karakoram Pass, was the most important of the three trade routes.

35. Historical Division, Ministry of External Affairs, Note, 18 November 1953, Subimal Dutt Papers, Subject File no. 78, Miscell. Files, 1953–54, NMML, New Delhi.

36. Karunakar Gupta, 'Hidden History of the Sino-Indian Frontier I—1947–1954', *The Economic and Political Weekly*, Vol. 9, no. 18 (4 May 1974) pp. 721–26.

37. Chinese academic Dai Chaowu (quoting from the Archive of Ministry of Foreign Affairs of the People's Republic of China, 'Collections of the current military, political, and economic conditions in Tibet', 12 April 1952), 'From 'Hindi-Chini Bhai-Bhai' to 'international class struggle' against Nehru: China's India policy and the frontier dispute, 1950–62', *The Sino-Indian War of 1962: New Perspectives,* Ed. Amit R. Das Gupta and Lorenz M. Luthi, Routledge, 2017.

38. Dai Chaowu, 'From 'Hindi-Chini Bhai-Bhai''.

39. PRC, Foreign Ministry Archives, 105-00119-02 (1), 'Summary of the conversation between Director Chen Jiakang and Counsellor Kaul, 26 March 1951, quoted in Dai Chaowu, "From Hindi-Chini Bhai-Bhai", p.71.

40. Ministry of External Affairs, Chronology of Principal Events Relating To India-China Relations, 1949-1961.

41. F.O. 371/99664, TNA.

42. Sarvepalli Gopal, *Jawaharlal Nehru: A Biography,* Vol. 2, *1947–1956* (Oxford University Press, 1979) p. 176.

43. Parliamentary Debates, 20 November 1950, Vol. V, Pt. I, pp. 155–6.
44. Gopal, *Jawaharlal Nehru,* p. 176.
45. Panikkar, *In Two Chinas,* p. 175.
46. Ibid.
47. Gopal, *Jawaharlal Nehru,* p 176.
48. See B.N. Mullik, *My Years with Nehru* (Allied Publishers, 1971) pp. 155–56.
49. R.K. Nehru, 'Our China Policy: A personal assessment', 30 July 1968, R.K. Nehru Papers, Correspondence with B.K. Nehru, NMML, New Delhi.
50. K.P.S. Menon, Note, 11 April 1952 in V.L. Pandit papers, (II Instalment), Sub. F-19, NMML, New Delhi.
51. Letter to N.R. Pillai, Foreign Secretary dated 14 July 1952, J.N. (S.G) Papers, File 138, Pt. II, NMML, New Delhi.
52. Ibid.
53. Telegram to Panikkar, 16 June 1952, Ibid.
54. Ibid.
55. J.N. (S.G.), File no. 142-I, p. 106–07, NMML, New Delhi.
56. Letter to Panikkar, 7 August 1952. J.N. (S.G.) Papers, F.no. 134-II, pp. 222–23.
57. R.K. Nehru, 'Our China Policy'.
58. Ibid.
59. Note, January 25, 1954, File no. FO/371 105627, TNA.
60. Yang Gongsu, Cangsang Jiushinian: Yige Waijiao Teshi de Huiyi, *Nine Decades of Vicissitudes: The Memoirs of Ambassador Yang Gongsu,* Haikou: Hainan Chubanshe, 1999.
61. Yang, *Nine Decades.*
62. Ibid.
63. Frank Moraes in an article in the *Times of India* of 30 September 1953 remarked on the danger of India becoming an unconscious accessory to Communist China. *The Statesman* criticized Mr Nehru's statement in the Rajya Sabha about not desiring to claim any position in Tibet 'which may not be in keeping with the full sovereignty of China'. F.O. 371/105627, TNA.
64. F.O. 371/105627, 'Talks on Tibet', TNA.
65. Ibid. Addressing the Council of States, 23 September 1953, Nehru stated that India 'did not claim any position in Tibet which was

not in keeping with full sovereignty of China but sometimes petty incidents had occurred which were rather irritating and for this reason the Chinese government had been asked to open conversations to settle all these pending small problems so that local officials may know exactly how things stand.'

66. Ibid. 'Ever since 1950 he has given first priority to a Korean settlement because of his fear of the results for India of an extension of the war and now that the good offices of India have at last been accepted by both sides, he is more than determined to avoid any public references to China which could conceivably be represented as partisan.' F.O. 371/105627, 'Talks on Tibet', TNA.

67. F.O 371/105628, report from the *Scotsman*, 'Chinese Troops in Tibet', TNA.

68. Ibid.

69. F.O. 371/105627, TNA.

70. Ibid.

71. J.N. (S.G.), File no. 142-I, p. 106-07, NMML.

72. 'Situation on the North Eastern Frontier': Note of Prime Minister Nehru to Secretary General, MEA; *Selected Works of Jawaharlal Nehru* (*SWJN*), Vol. 21, p. 555–58.

73. Note by Prime Minister to S.G. and F.S, 5 March 1953. (J.N.) (S.G.) File 169 (Pt.-II) NMML. In fact, the Chinese were moving systematically and with deliberation to establish their full control in Tibet. Logistically, they were dependent on India for supplies at this point. Thousands of gallons of petrol for instance came across the Nathu La Pass from Sikkim into the Chumbi Valley. Steel, corrugated iron sheets, tin sheets for roofing and cement came from India. 'The Chinese Army was coming into Tibet in a big way': K.C. Johorey, Transcript, Pt.-II, NMML.

74. Gopal, *Jawaharlal Nehru*, Vol. 2, p. 181.

75. Ibid.

Chapter 6: Steep Descent

1.   Gopal, *Jawaharlal Nehru*, Vol. 2, p. 179.

2.   *India in the Mirror of Foreign Diplomatic Archives*, Ed. Max-Jean Zins and Gilles Boquerat, Manohar, 2004 (a publication of the

French Research Institutes in India; distributed by Foundation Books) p. 138, quoted in A.G. Noorani, 'Our Secrets in Others' Trunks', *Frontline*, 15 July 2005: https://frontline.thehindu.com/books/article30205364.ece, (Accessed 5 May 2021).

3. J.N. (S.G.) F. no. 152 (Pt.-II), pp. 231–32, 241, 241A, 242, NMML.
4. Gopal, *Jawaharlal Nehru*, Vol. 2, p. 146.
5. Ibid.
6. Speech to Parliament, 3 August 1950. J.N. (S.G.), F. 50 (I), NMML.
7. Ibid.
8. Letter from Chinese Vice Foreign Minister to Ambassador Raghavan, 8 March 1953. J.N. (S.G.) F. 169-II, p. 406–09, NMML.
9. Letter from Ambassador Raghavan to the Prime Minister, 17 March 1953. J.N. (S.G.) F. 169-II, p. 361, NMML.
10. Gopal, *Jawaharlal Nehru*, Vol. 2, p. 148.
11. Ibid.
12. Annual Report for 1952, Consulate General of India, Lhasa. J.N. (S.G), File 170-I, p. 189–200.
13. Ibid.
14. Extract from the speech of the Prime Minister to Heads of Indian Mission in West Asia, 27 March 1953. J.N. (S.G.) File 172-II, p. 145–7.
15. 23 June 1952: Meeting Minutes between Chinese Vice Foreign Minister Zhang Hanfu and Deputy Chief of Mission, T.N. Kaul, History and Public Policy Program Digital Archive, PRC FMA 105-00025-03, 18–20, The Wilson Center.
16. 06 September 1953, Cable from Ambassador Yuan Zhongxin, 'Minutes of Meeting between R.K. Nehru and Ambassador Yuan', History and Public Policy Program Digital Archive, PRC FMA 105-00032-03, 12–14, The Wilson Center.
17. Telegram from the Prime Minister to Ambassador Raghavan, 01 September 1953. J.N. (S.G.) F. 199-I, 274–80), NMML.
18. 'Summary of Conversation between Chinese Premier Zhou Enlai and Indian Commissioner T.N. Kaul', PRC FMA 105-00025-03, pp. 28–32, Wilson Center Digital Archive.
19. 'Raghavan from Prime Minister', 01 September 1953. Telegram to Indian Embassy, Beijing. J.N. (S.G.) F. 199-I, pp. 274–80, NMML.
20. Telegram from Foreign New Delhi to Indian Embassy Beijing, 29 September 1953. J.N. (S.G.) F. 203, p. 218, NMML.

21. Telegram from Gyantse, 05 October 1953. J.N. (S.G.) F. 204-II, p. 201, NMML.
22. Telegram from the Prime Minister to the Chinese Premier Zhou Enlai, 22 October 1953, ibid.
23. 21 October 1953, Cable from Zhang Jingwu, 'On Issues of Relations between China and India in Tibet'. History and Public Policy Program Digital Archive, PRC FMA 105-00032-23, pp. 76–81, The Wilson Center.
24. Telegram from Consulate in Lhasa to New Delhi, 27 November 1953. J.N. (S.G.) F. 217-I, p. 23, NMML.
25. Note by the Ministry of External Affairs, on 'Main Points which may arise during discussions at the Peking Conference', 3 December 1953 J.N. (S.G.), F. 2187, pp. 200–08, NMML.
26. Telegram from the Indian Embassy, Beijing to Delhi, 31 December 1953. J.N. (S.G.), F. no. 226-I, p. 14–15, NMML.
27. Telegram from the Indian Embassy, Beijing to Delhi, 08 January 1954, J.N. (S.G.), F. no. 227-II, p. 190.
28. Telegram from Indian Embassy, Beijing to Delhi, 20 January 1954. J.N. (S.G.) F. no. 230-II, p. 247–48, NMML.
29. Telegram from Indian Embassy, Beijing to Delhi, 23 January 1954. J.N. (S.G.), F. no. 230-II, p. 82, NMML.
30. Telegram from Indian Embassy, Beijing, Raghavan to R.K. Nehru, 23 March 1954. J.N. (S.G.), F. no. 241-II, p. 418, NMML.
31. Mullik, *Chinese Betrayal*, p. 153.
32. Telegram to Indian Embassy, Beijing, 9 April 1954. J.N. (S.G.) F. no. 245-IIp. 189–90, NMML.
33. Telegram from Indian Embassy, Beijing, 8 April 1954. J.N. (S.G.) F. no. 245-II, p. 169–73. NMML.
34. Telegram to Indian Embassy, Beijing, Raghavan from R.K. Nehru, 27 April 1954.
35. The Five Principles were:
    1. Mutual respect for each other's territorial integrity and sovereignty
    2. Mutual non-aggression
    3. Mutual non-interference in each other's internal affairs
    4. Equality and mutual benefit, and
    5. Peaceful co-existence.

36. Speech of Prime Minister Nehru in the Lok Sabha on the Agreement on Tibet, New Delhi, 15 May 1954.

37. The specific passes mentioned in the 1954 Agreement were all in the Himachal Pradesh, and (then) United Provinces sections, of the border and did not include Ladakh, Sikkim or the northeastern sections of the border. The passes were: Shipki La, Mana, Niti, Kungri Bingri, Darma and Lipulekh. The Prime Minister assumed that the border had been 'finalized' on the basis of these passes being named in the agreement. Subsequent developments did not bear him out. In any case, these passes were all in a specific, limited section of the boundary—the Middle Sector. The Western and Eastern Sectors of the boundary, as well as the Sikkim–Tibet frontier were not covered.

38. Note by the Prime Minister on the Report of Dr. Gopalachari, 1 July 1954, J.N. (S.G.) F.no.265-I, pp. 34–36, NMML.

39. A.G. Noorani, 'Nehru's China Policy', Review Article of Vol. 26, Second Series, *Selected Works of Jawaharlal Nehru*, edited by Ravinder Kumar and H.Y. Sharada Prasad, in *The Frontline*, Vol. 17, Issue 15, 22 July–04 Aug 2000.

40. Ibid.

41. Office of the High Commissioner for the United Kingdom, New Delhi, 22 July 1955, FO 371/115204, TNA.

42. Mullik, *Chinese Betrayal*, p. 154.

43. Apa B. Pant, 'A Himalayan Tournament', in R.K. Nehru Papers, Writings/Speeches by others, S.no. 7, NMML.

44. Coral Bell in *Foreign Policies of the Powers*, ed. F.S. Northedge (1974), p. 128, quoted in Karunakar Gupta: 'Sino-Indian Agreement on Tibetan Trade and Intercourse: Its Origin and Significance', *Economic & Political Weekly*, Vol. 13, no. 16 (April 22, 1978) pp. 696–702.

45. Nehru in Rajya Sabha, 9 December 1959.

46. Karunakar Gupta, 'Sino-Indian Agreement', p.702.

47. Letter from Ambassador N. Raghavan to Prime Minister J. Nehru, 18 March 1954, J.N. (S.G.) F.no. 241-1. pp. 79–85.

48. Robert Barnes, 'Between the Blocs: India, the United Nations, and Ending the Korean War', *Journal of Korean Studies*, Vol. 18, no. 2 (Fall 2013) pp. 263–86.

49. Raghavan from Prime Minister, 25 January 1953 (Telegram); J.N. (S.G.) Vol. 161-II, p. 315.

50. Note by the Prime Minister 18 June 1954, Subimal Dutt Papers, Subject File S. no. 6, Tibet Files (1954–59), NMML.

51. Apa Pant, 'Himalayan Tournament' in R.K. Nehru Papers.

52. Consul-General in Lhasa, Reports on Tibet, monthly report for the period ending 15 April 1955, File no. 55-R&I/55, 1955, No. 3 (6)-5/55, NAI.

Chapter 7: Friends with Benefits

1. 'Conditions in China': F.O. 371/92220, TNA.

2. FO 371/110226, TNA.

3. Ibid.

4. Interview with the Chinese Premier by Dr K.S. Shelvankar in *The Hindu*, 23 June 1954, titled 'India's Work for Peace: Mr. Chou En-Lai's Tribute'.

5. Menon's telegram to Nehru, 21 June 1954, quoted by S. Gopal in *Jawaharlal Nehru,* Vol. 2, p. 194.

6. Letter to Chief Ministers from J.N. dated 22 June 1954. J.N. (S.G.)—File 263, Pt.-I, NMML.

7. The Premier even found time to see a Hindi film, 'Jhansi ki Rani' (Queen of Jhansi) about one of India's women freedom fighters in the First War of Independence of 1857.

8. Letter from Acting U.K High Commissioner in New Delhi, G.H. Middleton, 1 July 1954, FO 371/110226, TNA.

9. One such report in the *Hindustan Times* (of 27 June 1954) spoke of the public enthusiasm with which Zhou was greeted everywhere he went in Delhi, including in the refugee colonies that still dotted the city, with crowds shouting 'Bharat-Cheeni Maitri Zindabad' (or Long Live India-China Friendship) and his eyes being 'wet with tears of joy' at the reception he was being given by women and children of the city.

10. Ibid.

11. 'Cooperation in Asia, Mr. Chou's Recipe', *The Sunday Times,* London, 28 June 1954; FO 371/110226, TNA.

12. *The Hindustan Times,* 28 June 1954.

13. Kuo-kang Shao: 'Zhou Enlai's Diplomacy and the Neutralization of Indo-China, 1954–55', *The China Quarterly,* no. 107 (Sep. 1986) pp. 483–504.

14. J.N. (S.G.) Ibid.

15. J.N. (S.G.)- File 264-Pt. II, NMML.

16. Gopal, *Jawaharlal Nehru,* p. 195.

17. Letter dated 22 July 1954 to CRO from UK High Commission, New Delhi, F.O 371/10385, TNA.

18. Srinath Raghavan, 'Sino-Indian Boundary Dispute, 1948–60: A Reappraisal', *Economic and Political Weekly,* 9 September 2006, pp. 3882-3891.

19. Gongsu, *Nine Decades of Vicissitudes,* Chapter 8, 'Diplomatic Negotiations with Our Neighbours'.

20. Raghavan, 'Sino-Indian Boundary Dispute', p. 3885

21. Note on 'Tibet and China', 18 June 1954, *Selected Works of Jawaharlal Nehru* (SWJN), Second Series, Vol. 26, pp. 476–80.

22. Memorandum on 'Trade and Frontier with China', *SWJN,* Second Series, Vol. 26, pp. 481–84.

23. Raghavan, 'Sino-Indian Border Dispute', p. 3885.

24. Steven Hoffmann, *India and the China Crisis,* (University of California Press, 1990) p. 34.

25. Ibid.

26. Karunakar Gupta, 'The Hidden History of the Sino-Indian Frontier' II, 1954–1959, *Economic and Political Weekly,* 11 May 1974.

27. Mullik, *Chinese Betrayal,* p. 201.

28. Sumathi Ramaswamy, 'Visualizing India's geo-body: Globes, maps, bodyscapes', *Contributions to Indian Sociology* (n.s) 36, 1&2 (2002).

29. Ibid., quoting Christopher Pinney (1994). Nehru's own description of the greatness of India in *The Discovery of India* reflected this reverential embrace of the mystique and magic of the country.

30. Walter Crocker, *Nehru: A Contemporary's Estimate,* Oxford University Press, 1966. In Crocker's words, 'It was based in part upon the fact that the people believed that he had been chosen by Gandhi as his political heir; in part upon his devotion to the national interest as he saw it, so self-evident and so marking him off from the run of Indian politicians . . .'

31. S. Gopal, 'The Formative Ideology of Jawaharlal Nehru', *Economic and Political Weekly,* Vol. 11, no. 2,1 22 May 1976, pp.787-792.

32. Dharma—or faith—that is tied to the yuga, or epoch or age, as defined in Hindu tradition.

33. Andrew Bingham Kennedy, *The International Ambitions of Mao and Nehru*, Cambridge University Press, 2012, p. 142-59.
34. Jonathan D. Spence, 'The Mystery of Zhou Enlai', *The New York Review of Books*, 28 May 2009.
35. Quoted in Peter Martin, *China's Civilian Army The Making of Wolf Warrior Diplomacy*, Oxford University Press, 2021, p. 110.
36. Gao Wenqian: *Zhou Enlai Zhuan* (Biography of Zhou Enlai), 1998; 'Zhou Enlai: The Last Perfect Revolutionary', *Public Affairs*, 2007.
37. Spence, 'Mystery of Zhou Enlai'.
38. Ibid.
39. Leys Simon, 'The Path of an Empty Boat', *The Times Literary Supplement*, 26 October 1984.
40. Ibid.
41. Qiang Zhai, 'China and the Geneva Conference of 1954', *The China Quarterly*, No. 129 (Mar 1992), pp. 103–22.
42. Kuo-kang Shao, 'Zhou Enlai's Diplomacy and the Neutralization of Indo-China, 1954–1955', *The China Quarterly*, No. 107 (Sep 1986), pp. 483–504.
43. The Earl Mountbatten of Burma, 'Reflections on the Transfer of Power and Jawaharlal Nehru', Nehru Memorial Lecture, Trinity College, University of Cambridge, 14 November 1968.
44. J.N. (S.G.) File no. 277, Part I, pp. 181–82, NMML.
45. Shen Quanyu, 'Sino-Indian Friendship in the Nehru Era: A Chinese Perspective', *China Report,* 41:3 (2005).
46. SWJN, Second Series, Vol. 27, p. 4.
47. Jagat Singh Mehta: 'Nehru's Failure with China: Intellectual Naivete or the Wages of a Prophetic Vision', Paper presented at a conference at the University of Toronto, October 1989.
48. J.N., 'Note on Visit to China and Indo-China', 14 November 1954, History and Public Policy Program Digital Archive, National Archives Department of Myanmar, Accession Number 203, Series 12/3, 'Letter from Jawaharlal Nehru to U Nu, relating to Note on Visit to China and Indo-China (16.11.54)'. Obtained by You Chenxue, http://digitalarchive.wilsoncenter.org/docunent/121651
49. 19 October 1954, Minutes of Chairman Mao Zedong's First Meeting with Nehru, History and Public Policy Program Digital

Archive, PRCMFA 204-00007-01, 1–10, Obtained by Chen Jian and translated by Chen Zhihong. http://digitalarchive.wilsoncenter. org/document/117825

50. Ibid.
51. Ibid.
52. V.V. Paranjpe, 'How to Understand China', in *Across the Himalayan Gap: An Indian Quest for Understanding China,* Ed. Tan Chung, Gyan Publishing House, 1998.
53. Kennedy, *International Ambitions,* Introduction.
54. J.N., 'Note on Visit to China and Indo-China' ibid.
55. Ibid.
56. Press Conference by the Prime Minister, Beijing, 26 October 1954.
57. J.N., 'Note on Visit to China and Indo-China', 14 November 1954, ibid.
58. Ibid.
59. J.N. (S.G.) File 299- Pt. 1, pp. 66–70, NMML.
60. Interview with the Dalai Lama by author, Dharamshala, India, 2014.
61. Ibid. The Dalai Lama was obviously referring to the views expressed by Sardar Patel to Prime Minister Nehru in November 1950 about the true nature of the Communist Chinese regime.
62. Ibid.
63. Nabarun Roy, 'Why Did Nehru Want the People's Republic of China in the United Nations?', *The Diplomat,* Tokyo; 6 April 2018.
64. Letter from G.H. Middleton, High Commissioner for the U.K. in India, FO 371/115018, TNA.
65. Ibid.
66. Inward Telegram from the U.K. High Commissioner in India, 4 November 1954: FO 371/110226, TNA.
67. Ibid.
68. Inward Telegram to the Commonwealth Relations Office from U.K. High Commissioner in India quoting Nehru's speech to Lok Sabha, dated 22 November 1954; FO 371/110226, TNA.
69. Xiaoyuan Liu, 'Friend or Foe: India as Perceived by Beijing's Foreign Policy Analysts in the 1950s: *China Review,* Vol. 15, no. 1 (Spring 2015), pp. 117–43.
70. Ibid.
71. Ibid.

72. See Sulmaan Wasif Khan, 'Cold War Cooperation: New Chinese Evidence on Jawaharlal Nehru's 1954 Visit to Beijing', Cold War History, Vol. 11, no. 2 (May 2011) pp. 197–222.

73. Ibid.

74. Letter from the U.K. High Commissioner in New Delhi, 15 January 1955, FO371/115018, TNA.

Chapter 8: A 'Short' History of Sino-Indian Friendship

1. Soong Ching-ling, Speech at New Delhi reception, 21 December 1955, *New China News Agency*; FO 371/115018, TNA.

2. 'Before 1962: The Case for 1950s China-India History', Arunabh Ghosh, *The Journal of Asian Studies,* Vol. 76, no. 3 (August 2017) pp. 697–727.

3. A. Ghosh, 'Before 1962', p. 706.

4. https://histecon.fas.harvard.edu/chinaindia1950/timeline/index.html (Accessed 22 January 2021).

5. It took thirty-one years before the next Indian Film Week would be held in China, in March 1986.

6. Two lines in Act III of Shakuntala, 'You will not leave my heart no matter how you are away/ the shadow of a tree will not leave the root no matter how long it is before dark' are known to many Chinese who quote them often. (Encylopedia of India-China Cultural Contacts), https://www.mea.gov.in/in-focus-article.htm?23520/Encyclopedia+of+IndiaChina+Cultural+Contacts (Accessed 8 May 2019).

7. Marwah, Reena: 'Interview of Mira Sinha Bhattacharjea', Pts. 1 & 2, April 2008:
   http://politics.ntu.edu.tw › RAEC › act › india04
   DOC.

8. Subimal Dutt, *With Nehru In The Foreign Office,* Minerva Associates, Calcutta, 1977, p. 106.

9. A. Ghosh, 'Before 1962', pp. 715-717.

10. Ibid.

11. Ibid.

12. Quoted in Indira Chowdhury: 'Travelling across cultures: reflections on a visit to Beijing', *Inter-Asia Cultural Studies,* Vol. 7, no. 3, 2006, p. 519–26. [p. 520.]

13. Ibid.

14. K. Natwar Singh, *My China Diary, 1956-88* (Rupa & Co. 2009) p. 73.

15. K. Natwar Singh, 'Pat on the cheek for Chairman Mao', *Mail Today*, New Delhi, 4 December 2011.

16. Letter from the British Embassy, Beijing, September 28, 1957, FO 371/127296, TNA.

17. Sanjib Baruah, 'India and China: Debating Modernity', *World Policy Journal*, Vol. 23, no. 2 (Summer, 2006), pp. 62–70.

18. Although, Baruah (ibid. p. 68-9) also draws reference to the linkages rather than the contrast between Gandhi and Mao in citing Prasenjit Duara who says that Mao shared with Gandhi the preference for 'economic and politically autarkic communes, the loathing of urban domination, the mistrust of technological expertise, and the superiority of spontaneously self-governing communities over systems of representation, whether this was the Party or Parliament.'

19. Jagat Singh Mehta, *The Tryst Betrayed: Reflections on Diplomacy and Development* (Penguin Viking, 2010) p. 114.

20. Despatch from British Embassy Peking, September 28, 1957, FO 371/127296, TNA.

21. Tan Chung, 'Fond Memory of Sino-Indian Camaraderie: The Beloved and Respected Ji Xianlin I Knew', *China Report* 48, 1&2 (2012), pp. 199–205.

22. Prabodh Chandra Bagchi, *India and China: A Thousand Years of Cultural Relations,* 2nd ed., Hind Kitabs Limited, Bombay, 1950.

23. Ibid., preface.

24. Mathew Mosca, *From Frontier Policy to Foreign Policy: The Question of India and the Transformation of Geopolitics in Qing China*, Stanford University Press. 2013, Chapter 1 'A Wealth of Indias: India in Qing Geographic Practice, 1644-1755'.

25. Chapter 1, Ibid.

26. Chapter 2, 'The Conquest of Xinjiang and the Emergence of 'Hindustan', 1756-1790', ibid.

27. Chapter 2, ibid.

28. Panikkar, *In Two Chinas,* p. 78.

29. Panikkar, *In Two Chinas,* p. 137.

30. Ibid., p. 156.

31. Telegram from the U.K. High Commission in India, 26 February, 1951, FO 371/92248, TNA.

32. Letter dated 25 May 1954 from the British Embassy, Beijing to the Far Eastern Department, FO 371/110226, TNA.

33. Letter from the British Embassy, Beijing, 5 July 1956, FO 371/120902, TNA.

34. Letter from the British Embassy, Beijing, 18 November 1955 to the CRO, FO 371/115018, TNA.

35. Frank Moraes, 'India and China', *The American Scholar*, Vol. 32, no. 3 (Summer 1963) pp. 445–50.

36. Tan Chung, 'Sino-Indian Cultural Synergy: Twenty Centuries of Civilisational Dialogue', *China Report* (2006) 2:121 (Accessed 27 February 2014).

37. Krishna Prakash Gupta, 'The Making of China's Image of India', *China Report* (1979) 15:39 (Accessed 1 May 2014).

38. Ibid.

39. Jin, Kemu. *A Short History of Sino-Indian Friendship*, Translated by Yang Hsien-Yi and Gladys Yang, Foreign Languages Press, Beijing, 1958.

40. Ibid, p.96.

41. Ibid, p. 102.

42. K.R. Narayanan, Speech, on the occasion of the Birth Centenary celebrations of Professor Tan Yun-shan at Santiniketan, 7 November 1998, *China Report* (1999) 35:205, published by Sage Publications (Accessed on 27 February 2014).

43. Vinay Lal, 'Framing a Discourse: China and India in the Modern World', *Economic and Political Weekly,* 10 January 2009, pp. 41-45.

44. "Kimayagar', Mr. Vasantrao Desai (1912–1975)', *The Record News*, Volume: Annual-TRN 2012.

45. Lal, 'China and India in the Modern World', p. 41.

46. Parvathi Thampi, 'Memories of China: 1943 to 1946': *China Report* (2000) 36:89, published by Sage Publications, pp. 89–92 (Accessed 27 February 2014).

47. Herbert Passin; 'Sino-Indian Cultural Relations', *The China Quarterly,* No. 7, (Jul–Sep 1961), pp. 85–100.

48. Ibid. p. 88.

49. *A Short History of Sino-Indian Friendship,* ibid.

50. Ibid., p. 92.

51. See Tan Chung & Geng Yinzeng, *India and China: Twenty Centuries of Civilization, Interaction and Vibrations*, Munshiram Manoharlal Publishers, 2010, p. 284.

52. Jiang Jingkui & Yan Jia, 'The history of the production of India-related knowledge in post-1950 China', *History Compass*, 2018;16:e12448. https://doi.org/10.1111/hic3.12448

53. Jiang and Yan, 'Production of India-related knowledge' p. 5.

54. Tan Chung, *Himalaya Calling: The Origins of China and India*, World Scientific Publishing Company, 2015 p. 221.

55. Tansen Sen, *India, China and the World: A Connected History* (London: Rowman & Littlefield, 2017) pp. 396–97.

56. Adhira Mangalagiri, 2019. 'Ellipses of Cultural Diplomacy: The 1957 Chinese Literary Sphere in Hindi.' *Journal of World Literature* 4 (4): 508-529.

57. Ibid.

58. Ibid.

59. V.V. Paranjpe; 'How to Understand China', in *Across the Himalayan Gap,* ed. Tan Chung, 1998, www.ignca.gov.in

Chapter 9: The Other Neighbour

1. Anwar H. Syed, *China and Pakistan: Diplomacy of an Entente Cordiale* (The University of Massachusetts Press, Amherst, 1974) p. 54.

2. Press Conference by Sir Zafrulla Khan, 12 June 1951, FO 371/92872, T.N.A.

3. Letter from the British Embassy in Beijing, 30 November 1951, FO 371/92384, T.N.A.

4. Ibid.

5. Inward Telegram to the Commonwealth Relations Office, dated 30 August 1950, FO/371/83326, TNA.

6. Syed, *China and Pakistan,* p. 55.

7. Cheng Xiaohe, 'From Ally to Partner: The Evolution of Sino-Pakistan Relations', *Journal of Renmin University of China*, Vol. 2, no. 1 (Spring 2007) pp. 61–81.

8. Letter from the British Embassy in Beijing, dated 26 September 1951, FO 371/92249, TNA. These Pakistani writers were the left-leaning

elements among the Pakistani literati who were agitated about the situation in Korea and US policy on the question. This naturally pleased the Chinese who publicized it prominently in *World Culture*.

9. Letter to the Map Office, classified 'Top Secret' dated 30 January 1952, FO 371/101199, TNA.
10. Letter from the U.K. High Commission, Karachi to the CRO, dated 26 November 1954, FO 371/110229, TNA.
11. Ibid., article in *Times of Karachi*, dated 21 November 1954.
12. Letter from the U.K. High Commissioner in Karachi, dated 10 February 1956, F.O. 371/120909, TNA.
13. Letter from the U.K. High Commission, Karachi, 5 May 1956, ibid.
14. Letter from the U.K. High Commission, Karachi to the CRO dated 20 September 1956, FO/371/120986, TNA.
15. *New China News Agency*, 7 December 1956, 'Premier Answers Pressmen's Questions', ibid.
16. 'Mr. Chou En-lai's Mission', comment in *The Times* dated 16 November 1956, ibid.
17. Letter from the British Embassy in Beijing, 8 November 1956, ibid.
18. Ibid.
19. Letter from the U.K. High Commission, Karachi, 8 November 1956, ibid.
20. Ibid.
21. Ibid.
22. Letter dated 8 November 1956 from Karachi, ibid.
23. Letter from the British Embassy in Beijing, 22 November 1956, ibid.
24. 'Note of discussion with the Prime Minister of Pakistan on 2 February 1957' by the U.K. High Commissioner, FO 371/129785, TNA.
25. Inward telegram to the CRO from the U.K. High Commissioner in Pakistan, 25 December 1956, F.O. 371/120909, ibid.
26. Gopal, *Jawaharlal Nehru*, Vol. 2, p. 252.
27. Ibid.
28. Ibid., p. 235.
29. Steve Tsang, 'Target Zhou Enlai: The 'Kashmir Princess' Incident of 1955', *The China Quarterly*, No, 139 (Sep 1994), pp. 766–82.
30. Sally Percival Wood, 'Retrieving the Bandung Conference…moment by moment', *Journal of Southeast Asia Studies,* Vol. 43, no. 3 (October 2012), pp. 523–30.

31. Naoku Shimazu, 'Staging the Bandung Conference of 1955', *Modern Asian Studies,* Vol. 48, no. 1 (January 2014), pp. 225–52.
32. Sally Percival Wood, 'Zhou Gags Critics in Bandoeng' or How the Media Framed Premier Zhou Enlai at the Bandung Conference', *Modern Asian Studies* Vol. 44, no. 5 (Sep 2010), pp. 1001–27.
33. Ibid. p. 1005.
34. Ibid. p. 1007.
35. Ibid. p.1007.
36. Quoted in Pang Yang Huei, 'Four Faces of Bandung: Detainees, Soldiers, Revolutionaries and Statesman', *Journal of Contemporary Asia* (Jan 2009), Vol. 39, no.1, pp. 63–86.
37. Ibid.
38. T.N. Kaul cited in Manorama Kohli, 'Nehru's World View and China Policy', *China Report* (1 November 1985), Vol. 21, no. 06, pp. 497–502.
39. Memo from Zhou Enlai to Zhang Jingwu, 28 September 1951 and 8 June 1952, quoted in Xiaoyuan Liu, 'Friend or Foe: India as Perceived by Beijing's Foreign Policy Analysts in the 1950's', *China Review,* Vol. 15, no. 1 (Spring 2015), pp. 117–43.
40. Ibid.
41. Ibid.
42. Ibid.
43. Nehru himself was to note that the Five Principles had 'somehow become a bone of contention' during the Conference and that India for her part, 'was not anxious for the particular phraseology or the principle.' ('Note on the Asian-African Conference at Bandung', dated 28 April 1955, J.N. (S.G.) – File 341, Pt. 1 pp. 71–76, NMML) Ultimately, the Conference agreed on a declaration of Ten Principles which Zhou called 'an extension and development of the Five Principles of Peaceful Coexistence' ('Report on Asian-African Conference' by Zhou Enlai to the Standing Committee of the National People's Congress, 13 May 1955).
44. Shi Guang Zhang, 'Constructing 'Peaceful Coexistence': China's Diplomacy toward the Geneva and Bandung Conferences, 1954–55', *Cold War History* (October 2007) Vol. 7, no. 4, pp 509–28.
45. Ibid.
46. 'Speech by Premier Chou En-Lai, Head of the Delegation of the People's Republic of China at the Plenary Session of the Asian-

African Conference', 19 April 1955, V.K. Krishna Menon Papers, Subject File 869, NMML.

47. 'Note on the Asian-African Conference at Bandung', dated 28 April 1955, J.N. (S.G.) – File 341, Pt. 1 pp. 71–76, NMML.

48. Telegram from the US Ambassador in India (Cooper) to the Department of State, 1 May 1955, Foreign Relations of the United States, 1955–1957, China, vol. 11.

49. As quoted in Jairam Ramesh, *A Chequered Brilliance: The Many Lives of V.K. Krishna Menon,* (Penguin Viking, 2019) p. 437.

50. Ibid., pp. 443–45.

51. Nancy Jetley, *India-China Relations, 1947–1977: A Study of Parliament's Role in the Making of Foreign Policy,* Humanities Press, N.J., 1979, p. 26.

52. Anton Harder, 'Not at the Cost of China: New Evidence Regarding US Proposals to Nehru for Joining the United Nations Security Council', Cold War History Project Working Paper Series, #76, Woodrow Wilson International Center for Scholars, March 2015.

53. Vijaya Lakshmi Pandit to Jawaharlal Nehru, 21 August 1950. V.L. Pandit (II Instalment) Subject File -19, NMML.

54. The offer was made by Soviet Premier Nikolai Bulganin to Nehru in 1955: 'we propose suggesting at a later stage India's inclusion as the sixth member of the Security Council' although he added that the proposal was being made to get Nehru's views and that he agreed with Nehru 'this is not the time for it and it will have to wait for the right moment later on. We also agree that things should be taken one by one'. (See Anton Harder, 'Nehru Refused American Bait on a Permanent Seat for India at the UN' in The Wire, 14 March 2019).

55. Ibid., p. 13, quoting Nehru to Pandit, 24 August 1950. Harder, 'Not at the Cost of China', p. 13 . . .

56. Ibid., p. 14.

Chapter 10: Buddha Jayanti: An Anniversary Remembered

1. Dhi Lhaden: 'Do You Know the Tales of Our Forefathers?' (Poem in *Burning the Sun's Braids: New Poetry from Tibet,* Blackneck Books, Dharamshala, 2017)

2. Speech to the Congress Parliamentary Party, 27 November 1956, quoted in S. Gopal, *Jawaharlal Nehru*, Vol. 3 , p. 32.

3. Telegram to Krishna Menon, 23 November 1956, quoted in S. Gopal, *Jawaharlal Nehru*, Vol. 3 (1956–1964), p. 32.

4. S. Gopal, *Jawaharlal Nehru*, Vol. 3 (1956–1964), p. 32.

5. Ibid., p. 34.

6. Nehru to Katju, 28 July 1956, as quoted in Ibid.

7. Nehru to Zhou, 12 September 1956, quoted in ibid., p. 35.

8. Thondup and Thurston, *Noodle Maker of Kalimpong*, p. 153.

9. Report by Chris Buckley in Reuters; https://www.reuters.com/article/us-china-tibet-dalai/china-recalls-days-of-poems-and-promise-with-dalai-lama-idUSPEK28409120080422 (Accessed on 1 May 2020). The same report quotes Wang Lixiong, the Beijing-based author as saying: 'The Dalai thought he could find a way to bring Buddhism and communism into harmony for Tibet'. Tsering Shakya, the historian of Tibet, is also quoted in the same report as saying: 'Today, the Tibetan side spins that the Dalai Lama was playing Mao. But I think he thought it was very possible to work with Mao.'

10. Author's Interview with His Holiness the Dalai Lama, Dharamshala, 3 April 2014.

11. Alexander Norman, *The Dalai Lama: An Extraordinary Life*, Kindle ed., Harper Collins India, 2020, ch. 11.

12. 'Talk with Tibetan Delegates', *People's Daily*, November 22 1952, *Selected Works of Mao Tse-tung* https://www.marxists.org/reference/archive/mao/selected-works/volume-7/mswv7_267.htm (Accessed 28 July 2021).

13. Ibid., Inner-Party directive drafted for the Central Committee of the Chinese Communist Party, April 6 1952.

14. Thondup and Thurston, *Noodle Maker of Kalimpong*, p. 155.

15. Norman, *The Dalai Lama*, ch. 11.

16. Author's Interview with the Dalai Lama, Dharamshala, 2014.

17. What we may call ethnographic Tibet or ethnic Tibet, areas inhabited by Tibetans, outside the borders of what is now the Tibetan Autonomous Region.

18. Halper and Halper, *Tibet*, p. 180.

19. Jianglin Li, *Tibet in Agony: Lhasa 1959*, Harvard University Press, 2017, p. 11.

20. Ibid., p. 181.

21. Jianglin Li also notes how in early 1956, the PLA rolled out Tupolev TU-4 bombers—presented to Mao by Stalin three years earlier— to bomb three historic monasteries in restive areas of Sichuan: Jamchen Chokhor Ling (in Lithang), Saphel Ling (in Chathreng), and Gaden Phendeling (in Bathang), Ibid., p. 13.

22. Extracts from the speech of the Dalai Lama translated from the News Summary No. 124 of 2 August 1955 in J.N. (S.G.) F. no. 392, Pt. II, pp. 245–47, NMML.

23. Li, *Tibet in Agony,* p. 15.

24. 'Report of the Foreign Secretary on his visit to Yatung on the way to Bhutan', 5 July 1955, in J.N. (S.G.), F. No. 359, pp.159–63, NMML.

25. Note by the Prime Minister after his meeting with the Maharajkumar of Sikkim, 25 July 1955 in J.N. (S.G.), F. no. 364, pp. 228–29, NMML.

26. Apa Balasaheb Pant (1912–1992), born into the princely family of the state of Aundh, later merged into Maharashtra, served in various international capitals as an Indian diplomat, including Nairobi, Djakarta and London (from where he retired as India's High Commissioner in 1972).

27. Nari Rustomji, *Enchanted Frontier: Sikkim, Bhutan and India's North-Eastern Borderlands* (Oxford University Press, 1971) p. 208.

28. Telegram, Foreign (Ministry of External Affairs) New Delhi to Indian Embassy Peking, 21 August 1956, Ambassador from T.N.Kaul. J.N. (S.G.) F. no. 486, Pt.-II, p. 215, NMML.

29. Apa Pant, *A Moment in Time,* (e-edition) Orient Blackman Pvt. Ltd, 2014, ch. 5.

30. 'The Visit of His Holiness the Dalai Lama and His Holiness the Panchen Lama to India – A Joint Report by Apa B. Pant, Col. P.N. Luthra and Shri P.N. Menon', Apa B. Pant (Ist Inst.) Subject File No. 4, 195–657, NMML.

31. The Panchen Lama is the incarnation of the Buddha of Boundless Light, Amitabha or Amita Deva, while the Dalai Lama is the incarnation of the Bodhisatva Avalokiteshwara.

32. Subimal Dutt Papers, Sub. File no. 6, NMML.

33. Quoted in Chen Jian, 'The Tibetan Rebellion of 1959 and China's Changing Relations with India and the Soviet Union', *Journal of Cold War Studies,* Vol. 8, no. 3 (Summer 2006) pp. 54–101.

34. J.N. (S.G.) F. no. 486, Pt. I, p. 90, NMML.

35. Rustomji, *Enchanted Frontier,* p. 214.

36. Ibid., p. 216.

37. Apa Pant, 'The Visit of His Holiness the Dalai Lama', NMML.

38. Oral History Transcript, Apa Pant, NMML, p. 24.

39. Ibid.

40. Documentary in Tibetan, *H.H. the Dalai Lama: Visit to India 1956–57,* https://youtu.be/fTO4WWI0ucs (Accessed 4 May 2020).

41. Notes jotted down by the Prime Minister during his talk with the Dalai Lama on 26 and 28 November 1956. Subimal Dutt Papers, Sub. File S. no. 7, NMML.

42. Ibid.

43. Dutt, ibid.

44. Li, *Tibet in Agony*, p. 35.

45. Memcon of Zhou Enlai's talks with the Dalai and Panchen Lamas as conveyed in a memorandum from Zhou to the Chairman and the Central Authorities, cited in Sulmaan Wasif Khan, 'Muslim, Trader, Nomad, Spy: China's Cold War and the People of the Tibetan Borderlands', in *The New Cold War History,* ed. Odd Arne Westad (The University of North Carolina Press, Chapel Hill, 2015) p. 25.

46. Halper and Halper (*Tibet,* p. 185) citing the Dalai Lama's first autobiography, *My Land and My People.*

47. Grandfather of Ashi Kesang Choden Wangchuck, the Royal Grandmother of Bhutan.

48. Thondup and Thurston, *Noodle Maker of Kalimpong,* pp. 165–66.

49. Ibid., p. 166.

50. Note by Prime Minister Nehru to the Secretary General, Foreign Secretary and the Joint Secretary, Ministry of External Affairs, 18 June 1954, Subimal Dutt Papers, NMML.

51. Letter of 3 January 1957 to Prime Minister Nehru from Apa Pant, Apa B. Pant Papers (1st Inst.), Subject File no. 6, NMML (includes P.N. Menon's report). Pant notes in his papers that the Tibetans told Nehru in a meeting during the Dalai Lama's 1956 visit that Zhou Enlai had told the Kashag officially that in matters of religion and culture, 'Tibet should deal directly with India.' (Pant (1st Inst.) Subject File No. 4, 1956–57, NMML)

52. He flew back to Lhasa. Claude Arpi notes in his book (*Tibet: When the Gods Spoke: India Tibet Relations (1947–1962)*, Pt. 3, Vij Books India Pvt Ltd, 2019), quoting from Reports sent by Consul-General P.N. Menon from Lhasa, that aviation came to Tibet in April 1956. The aerodrome at Umathang near Lhasa was constructed under the supervision of Soviet experts. The first Chinese planes landed there on 26 May 1956. Indian planes also flew into Tibet with an Indian Air Force Ilyushin flying from Jorhat to Tangshung on 24 October. According to Menon, the Chinese appeared keen to establish an Indo-Tibetan air link. The flight time from Tangshung to Bagdogra in Assam was a little over an hour.
53. Pran Nath Luthra, Padma Bhushan, Indian Frontier Administrative Service (1917–2000).
54. P. N. Luthra, 'Discussions with His Holiness the Panchen Lama', 9 January 1957, J.N. (S.G.), F. no. 500 – Pt. I, NMML.
55. Luthra noted that at the interpersonal level, there was friendly accord between the Dalai and Panchen Lamas, and that he had seen them joking with each other, 'thumping on each other's backs and exchanging warm greetings.' (ibid.)
56. Note by P.N. Menon attached to letter of 3 January 1957 from Apa Pant to Prime Minister Nehru, Apa B. Pant Papers (1st Instl.), Subject File no. 6, NMML.
57. Apa B. Pant (1st Instalment) Subject File No. 4, 1956-57, NMML.
58. P.N. Menon, ibid. Apa B. Pant, 'A Himalayan Tournament', p. 3, NMML.
59. Letter No. 3/NGO/57/1 61—PO dated 28 November1957 from Apa Pant to B.K. Acharya, Joint Secretary, Ministry of External Affairs; Apa B. Pant Papers, Subject File No. 5, NMML.
60. Pant, 'Himalayan Tournament', ibid, p. 9.
61. Ibid.
62. Ibid.
63. Ibid.
64. Ibid., p. 5.
65. For a detailed account of these activities, see Halper & Halper, *Tibet*, pp.187–93. The Halpers particularly cite File no. 793B. 11/9-1852, (U.S.)National Archives Record Administration (NARA).
66. The inclusion is understandable given Pakistan's closeness to the United States as a Treaty ally in the politics of the Cold War.

67. Halper & Halper, *Tibet,* p. 192.
68. Pant, 'Himalayan Tournament', p. 193.
69. Pant, 'Himalayan Tournament', p. 9.
70. Ibid, pp. 6, 12.
71. K.C. Johorey: Transcript, Pt.-II, NMML.
72. Ibid.
73. Nehru made his first visit to Bhutan transiting the Chumbi Valley in Tibet in the autumn of 1958, spending five days in the Himalayan kingdom. The extracts are from his Report, 'PM's Notes on Visit to Bhutan', J.N. (S.G.) Papers, File no. 652 (Pt.-I), NMML.
74. As cited in Steven A. Hoffmann: 'Rethinking the Linkage between Tibet and the China–India Border Conflict', *Journal of Cold War Studies,* Vol. 8, no. 3 (Summer 2006) pp. 165–94.
75. The term is used by Hoffmann in his article, Ibid.

Chapter 11: Borderlines

1. 'Chinese Troops in Tibet: Frontier Defences Strengthened', Reuters report in *The Scotsman,* 23 February 1953.
2. Letter of 1 May 1953 from the British Embassy in Nepal to China and Korea Department, British Foreign Office in FO 371/105628, TNA.
3. 'Our China Policy: A Personal Assessment': R. K. Nehru, Note of 30 July 1968 in R.K. Nehru Papers, NMML.
4. Disputed territory between India and China in the northeastern section of the Union Territory of Ladakh.
5. R.K. Nehru, 'Our China Policy'.
6. Note by PMJN dated 18 June 1954 to Secretary-General, Foreign Secretary and Joint Secretary, MEA, in Subimal Dutt Papers, Sub File no. -6, NMML.
7. Letter from PMJN to Ambassador G.L. Mehta in Washington, 29 June 1954. J.N. (S.G.) File 264, Pt.-II, NMML.
8. J.N (S.G) File 252, Pt.-II, p. 358–65 NMML.
9. The Indian response to this was that all pending questions had been intimated to the Chinese government, the inference being that the boundary question was not a pending question.
10. Ibid.

11. See 'On Issues of Relations between China and India in Tibet', Cable from Zhang Jingwu, 21 October 1953 1953, PRC FMA 105-00032-23, 76–81, Wilson Center Digital Archive.

12. 'China's India policy and the frontier dispute, 1950–62', in *The Sino-Indian War of 1962: New Perspectives*, ed. Amit R. Das Gupta and Lorenz M. Luthi, Routledge, 2017, pp. 68-85.

13. Zhang Jingwu cable.

14. The CCP's Instruction about Work in Tibet, 4 April 1952, from Selected Documents about the Work in Tibet, 1949–2005, Beijing, 2005 as quoted in Dai Chaowu, 'From 'Hindi-Chini Bhai-Bhai''.

15. PRC FMA, 105-00119-02 (1), 'Summary of the conversation between Director Chen Jiakang and Counsellor Kaul', 26 March 1951, quoted in Dai Chaowu, 'From 'Hindi-Chini Bhai-Bhai.''

16. Dai Chaowu, 'From 'Hindi-Chini Bhai-Bhai'', p. 71.

17. Ibid.

18. 'The Indo-Tibet Frontier Issue: Reply to a Debate in the Council of States', 24 December 1953, *SWJN* 2, Vol. 24, p. 583.

19. Speech in Parliament, 30 September 1954 by Nehru quoted in Subimal Dutt, *With Nehru in the Foreign Office*, Minerva Associates (Publications), 1977, p. 90.

20. See Ministry of External Affairs, Government of India: White Paper 1, Notes, Memoranda and Letters Exchanged and Agreements signed between The Governments of India and China 1954–1959.

21. *SWJN* 2, Vol. 36, p. 594–601.

22. Dutt, *With Nehru in the Foreign Office*, p. 117.

23. Ibid.

24. Steven A. Hoffmann, *India and the China Crisis*, University of California Press, 1990, p. 35.

25. Subimal Dutt Diary, entry 1.5.1956 about a conversation with Nehru as quoted by Amit R. Das Gupta in his paper 'Subimal Dutt and the Prehistory of the Sino-Indian Border War'. A version of this paper was subsequently published in *The Sino-Indian War of 1962: New Perspectives*, ed. Amit R. Das Gupta and Lorenz M. Luthi, 2017, pp. 48-67.

26. Das Gupta & Luthi, *New Perspectives*, p. 55.

27. Jagat Singh Mehta, *Negotiating for India* (Manohar, 2007) p. 59.

28. *The Times* report on the opening of various highways in Tibet is carried in FO 371/99338, TNA.

29. John W. Garver, *Protracted Contest: Sino Indian Rivalry in the Twentieth Century* (Oxford University Press, 2001) pp. 81–83.

30. See Mullik, *Chinese Betrayal*, p. 196. Mullik claims that Chinese troops did not enter western Tibet in 1951 through the Aksai Chin and says that Zhou Enlai was making an unverified claim when he said in 1960 that Chinese troops had entered western Tibet through this route in 1950. This of course does not contradict reports that the Indians did indeed have stray intelligence about the construction by the Chinese of roads in Ladakh.

31. P.N. Haksar papers, Instls. I-II, Subject File no. 114, NMML.

32. Mehta, *Negotiating for India*, p. 59.

33. Ibid., p. 60.

34. Mullik, *Chinese Betrayal*, p. 197.

35. Sidney Wignall, *Spy on the Roof of the World: A True Story of Espionage & Survival in the Himalayas*, Edinburgh: Canongate Books, 1996.

36. Francine R. Frankel, *When Nehru Looked East: Origins of India–US Suspicion and India–China Rivalry* (Oxford University Press, 2020) p. 252.

37. Neville Maxwell (1926–2019) was the journalist who authored *India's China War* (published 1970), what many in India regard as biased analysis of the 1962 conflict heavily weighted in favour of China.

38. R.K. Nehru, Oral History Transcript, Acc. no. 324, NMML.

39. Ranjit Singh Kalha, *India–China Boundary Issues: Quest for Settlement* (Indian Council for World Affairs, Pentagon Press, 2014) p. 82.

40. J.N. (S.G.) F. 593, Pt.-II, p. 254.

41. Note Verbale, Ministry of External Affairs, 2 July 1958, Notes, Memoranda and Letters Exchanged and Agreements signed between the Governments of India and China 1954-1959, White Paper 1.

42. Letter to Krishna Menon, 14 October 1958, in S. Gopal, *Jawaharlal Nehru*, Vol. 3, p. 83.

43. Kalha, *India–China Boundary Issues*, p. 84.

44. Ibid.

45. Mullik, *Chinese Betrayal*, p. 202.

46. Ibid., p. 204.

47. Ibid.
48. White Paper 1, p. 26–27.
49. Ibid., p. 28.
50. Ibid., p. 29.
51. Dutt, *With Nehru in the Foreign Office*, p.119.
52. C.S. Jha, *From Bandung to Tashkent: Glimpses of India's Foreign Policy* (Delhi: Sangam Books, 1983), p. 83.
53. Amit R. Das Gupta, 'Prehistory of the Sino-Indian border war' in the *Sino-Indian War of 1962: New Perspectives,* ed. By Amit R. Das Gupta and Lorenz M. Luthi (Routledge, 2017), p. 55.
54. Kalha, *India–China Boundary Issues*, p. 76.
55. Garver, *Protracted Contest,* p. 80.
56. The Chinese had been unwilling to respond to the British moves, well aware of their country's intrinsic weakness at the time. 'Protecting China's position with a policy of evasion and procrastination – to which succeeding governments in China, down to the present, have adhered with considerable success—the Chinese and Tibetans thwarted British objectives'. Margaret W. Fisher, Leo E. Rose, Robert A. Huttenback, *Himalayan Battleground: Sino-Indian Rivalry in Ladakh* (Pall Mall Press, 1963), p. 62.
57. Garver, *Protracted Contest,* p. 89.
58. Hoffmann, *India and the China Crisis*, p. 23.
59. Ibid.
60. Margaret Fisher et al., *Himalayan Battleground*, p. 10.
61. Ibid., p. 10.
62. Yaacov Y.I. Vertzberger, *Misperceptions in Foreign Policy Making: The Sino-Indian Conflict, 1959–1962* (Westview Press, 1984) p. 104.
63. Ibid., p. 105.
64. Ibid., p. 105.
65. 'Secret note for Prime Minister Nehru', 8 October 1958: Subimal Dutt Papers, Special File 33, NMML.
66. Letter to Provincial Premiers, 20 July 1949, J.N. (S.G.) – 1st Instl. post 1947, F.no. 26 (II), NMML.
67. White Paper: Notes, Memoranda and Letters Exchanged And Agreements Signed Between The Governments of India and China, 1954–1959, p. 46.
68. Ibid., p. 47.

69. Ibid., p. 48.
70. Ibid., p. 52.
71. Ibid., p. 54.
72. Amit Das Gupta, 'Prehistory of the Sino-Indian border war', p. 55.
73. Dai Chaowu, 'From 'Hindi-Chini Bhai-Bhai' to 'international class struggle' against Nehru: China's India policy and the frontier dispute, 1950–62' in Das Gupta and Luthi, eds., *Sino-Indian War of 1962*, p. 74.

Chapter 12: The Unravelling

1. 'Draft Report, 'On the Trip of the Soviet Party-Governmental Delegation to the PRC,' by M. Suslov to CC CPSU Presidium for Presentation to a Forthcoming CC CPSU Plenum (excerpt),' December 18, 1959, History and Public Policy Program Digital Archive, Center for the Storage of Contemporary Documentation (TsKhSD), Moscow, fond 2, opis 1, delo 415, II. 56–91. Translated by Vladislav M. Zubok. http://digitalarchive.wilsoncenter.org/document/112989
2. Kalha, *India–China Boundary Issues*, p. 86.
3. Ibid., p. 89.
4. Ibid., p. 90.
5. Telegram from Charge d'Affaires Embassy of India in Beijing to the Foreign Secretary, Ministry of External Affairs, 4 March 1959 J.N. (S.G.) File 672 Pt.-1, NMML.
6. Kalimpong had long acquired a notoriety of being a 'nest' of foreign spies.
7. Thondup and Thurston, *Noodle Maker of Kalimpong*, p. 168.
8. Ibid., p. 171.
9. Ibid., p. 177.
10. Ibid.
11. Li, *Tibet in Agony*, p. 70.
12. Ibid., p. 81.
13. Ibid., p. 165.
14. The Dalai Lama, *My Land and My People: Memoirs of The Dalai Lama of Tibet* (Potala Corporation, 1962) p. 162.
15. Ibid., p. 194.

16. Ibid., p. 198.
17. Ibid., p. 216.
18. Li, *Tibet in Agony*, p. 218, quoting the memoir of Ji Youquan, resident writer in the Propaganda Department of the PLA Tibet Military Command.
19. Ibid., p. 224.
20. Ibid., p. 167.
21. Ibid., p. 222.
22. Ibid., p. 192.
23. Ibid., p. 221.
24. Telegram from Apa Pant to the Foreign Secretary, 31 March 1959, J.N. (S.G.), File 678, Pt.-I, pp. 295–96, NMML.
25. Telegram from the Political Officer in Gangtok to the Ministry of External Affairs (MEA), 14 March 1959: J.N. (S.G.) File 676, Pt.-II, pp. 374–75, NMML.
26. Telegram from the MEA to the Political Officer in Gangtok, 15 March 1959, J.N. (S.G.) File 677, Pt.-I, p. 14, NMML.
27. Speech of Prime Minister Nehru in the Lok Sabha, replying to the debate on the Demands for Grants for the Ministry of External Affairs, 17 March 1959.
28. Proclamation of the Tibet Military Area Command of the Chinese People's Liberation Army on The Revolt in Tibet, 20 March 1959.
29. The Dalai Lama's Message to the Prime Minister, 26 March 1959, in Bhasin, *India–China Relations*, Vol. 3, p. 2080.
30. 'Communique on the Rebellion in Tibet', *Renmin ribao* (Beijing), 28 March 1959.
31. Bhasin, *India–China Relations*, pp. 2120–24.
32. Rani Singh, *An Officer and His Holiness, How the Dalai Lama Crossed into India*, Penguin, 2020.
33. Ibid.
34. Message from the Prime Minister to the Dalai Lama, 3 April 1959 in Bhasin, *India–China Relations*, p. 2147.
35. Instructions issued by the Foreign Secretary Subimal Dutt to K.L. Mehta, Advisor to the Governor of Assam, 3 April 1959 in Bhasin, *India–China Relations*, p. 2147.

36. Press Information Bureau, Government of India, Prime Minister's Press Conference, 5 April 1959, in Bhasin, *India–China Relations*, p. 2159.
37. Bhasin, *India–China Relations*, p. 2161.
38. Ibid., p. 2163.
39. Ibid., p. 2164.
40. Ibid., p. 2170.
41. Letter from Har Mander Singh, Political Officer, Kameng Frontier Division, Camp: Tawang to K.L Mehta, Adviser to the Government of Assam, Shillong, 5 April 1959, Subimal Dutt Papers, Sub File no. 6, NMML.
42. Ibid.
43. Ibid.
44. Ibid.
45. Letter from Prime Minister Nehru to C. Rajagopalachari, 8 April 1959, J.N. (S.G.) File 679, Pt.-I, NMML.
46. Ibid.
47. Telegram from Ambassador Parthasarathy to Foreign Secretary Dutt, 8 April, 1959: J.N. (S.G.) Pt.-I, p. 327–28.
48. Ibid.
49. Statement of the Dalai Lama on arrival in Tezpur, 18 April 1959, in Bhasin, *India–China Relations*, p. 2258–60.
50. Ibid.
51. Letter from the Political Officer, Kameng Division, to Advisor to the Governor of Assam, 16 April 1959, in Bhasin, *India–China Relations*, p. 2245.
52. Telegram from Ambassador Parthasarathy to Foreign Secretary Dutt, 20 April 1959, J.N. (S.G.) Pt.-II, p. 320–22, NMML.
53. Ibid.
54. Record of Prime Minister's Meeting with the Dalai Lama, 24 April 1959, Subimal Dutt Papers, Subject File no. 9, NMML.
55. Ibid.
56. Telegram from Ambassador Parthasarathy to Foreign Secretary Dutt, 24 April 1959, J.N. (S.G.) F. 681, Pt.-I, p. 74, NMML.
57. Telegram from Ambassador Parthasarathy to Foreign Secretary Dutt, 26 April 1959, J.N. (S.G.) File 681, Pt.-II, pp. 183–84, NMML.

58. The Dalai Lama's Statement of 20 June 1959, Mussoorie, in Bhasin, *India–China Relations*, pp. 2352–55.
59. Thondup and Thurston, *Noodle Maker of Kalimpong*, p. 196.
60. Clarification by the Government of India regarding the status of the Dalai Lama in India, 30 June 1959, in Bhasin, *India–China Relations*, p. 2356.
61. Thondup and Thurston, *Noodle Maker of Kalimpong*, p. 196.
62. Ibid. p. 197.
63. 'Letters Exchanged between the Dalai Lama and Secretary-General Dag Hammarskjold,' 9 September 1959, History and Public Policy Program Digital Archive, S-0442-0367-03, United Nations Archives and Records Management Section. https//digitalarchive.wilsoncenter.org/document/19330
64. Telegram from Krishna Menon to the Prime Minister, 10 October 1959, J.N. (S.G.) File 692 Pt.-I, pp.166–68, NMML.
65. Note by the Foreign Secretary on the telegram from Krishna Menon of 10 October, ibid.
66. Telegram from Krishna Menon to the Prime Minister 13 October 1959, J.N. (S.G.) File 692 Pt.-I, p.185, NMML.
67. Statement by the Indian Representative V.K. Krishna Menon at the U.N. General Assembly on the Question of Tibet, New York, 21 October 1959, in Bhasin, *India–China Relations*, pp. 2744–46.
68. Ibid.
69. Ibid.
70. Letter from the Prime Minister to the Dalai Lama, 7 August 1960, J.N. (S.G.) File 706, Pt.-II, p. 188–191, NMML.
71. Ibid.
72. Ibid.
73. Note of the Government of China given to the Ministry of External Affairs, New Delhi: Notes, Memoranda and Letters Exchanged and Agreements Signed Between the Governments of India and China 1954–1959, White Paper I, Ministry of External Affairs, p. 70.
74. Telegram to the Foreign Secretary, 28 April 1959, J.N. (S.G.) File 681 Pt.-II, pp. 256–57, NMML.
75. Text of Resolution of First Session of Second National People's Congress of the People's Republic of China on the question

of Tibet, 28 April 1959, J.N. (S.G.) File 681 Pt II., pp. 283–85, NMML.

76. Telegram to Ambassador Parthasarathy from the Foreign Secretary, 29 April 1959, J.N. S.G. File 681 Pt.-II, p. 296, NMML.

77. Telegram to the Foreign Secretary from Ambassador Parthasarathy, 30 April 1959, J.N. S.G. File 681 Pt-II, p. 313, NMML.

78. Telegram to the Prime Minister from Ambassador Parthasarathy, 29 April 1959, J.N. S.G. File 681 Pt-II, p. 300, NMML.

79. Telegram from Parthasarathy to the Prime Minister, 3 May 1959, J.N. S.G. File 682 Pt.-I, pp. 68–69, NMML.

80. Ibid.

81. Chen Jian, 'The Tibetan Rebellion of 1959 and China's Changing Relations with India and the Soviet Union,' *Journal of Cold War Studies*, Vol. 8, no. 3 (Summer 2006) pp. 54–101.

82. Statement by the Prime Minister in the Rajya Sabha on the Motion Re: Situation Arising out of the Recent Events in Tibet, 4 May 1959, Bhasin, *India–China Relations*, pp. 2449–59.

83. Ibid.

84. Excerpts from the Editorial in the People's Daily ('Renmin Ribao'): 'The Revolution in Tibet and Nehru's Philosophy', Beijing, 6 May 1959, Bhasin, *India–China Relations*, pp. 2459–70.

85. Chen Jian, 'The Tibetan Rebellion of 1959', p. 86.

86. Ibid., p.88

87. Ibid., p. 88

88. Statement made by the Chinese Ambassador to the Foreign Secretary in New Delhi, 15 May 1959. Bhasin, *India–China Relations*, pp. 2496–2500.

89. Ibid.

90. Telegram to the Foreign Secretary from Ambassador Parthasarathy, 23 July 1959. J.N. (S.G.) File 687 Pt.-I, pp.138–40, NMML.

91. Ibid.

92. From the Diary of P.F. Yudin, Report of Conversation with the General Secretary of the CC CCP, Deng Xiaoping, 03 June 1959. History and Public Policy Program Digital Archive, TsKhSD, f.5, op.49, d.235, II. 40–44. Obtained by Paul Wingrove and translated by Aldrich-Moodiehttp://digitalarchive.wilsoncenter.org/document/111506

93. 'From the Journal of Ambassador S.F. Antonov. Summary of a Conversation with the Chairman of the CC CPC Mao Zedong', 14 October 1959. History and Public Policy Program Digital Archive, SCCD, Fond 5, Opis 49, Delo 235, Listy 89–96. Translated by Mark H, Doctoroff. http://digitalarchive.wilsoncenter.org/document/114788
94. Chen Jian, 'The Tibetan Rebellion of 1959', p. 91.
95. Ibid.
96. Ibid.
97. Ibid.
98. 'Record of Conversation of N.S. Khrushchev with CC CCP Chairman Mao Zedong, Deputy Chairman Liu Shaoqi, Zhou Enlai, Zhu De, Lin Biao, Politburo Members Peng Zhen and Chen Yi, and Secretariat Member Wang Jiaxiang,' 02 October 1959. History and Public Policy Program Digital Archive, APRF, copy on Reel 17, Volkgonov Collection, Library of Congress, Washington, DC. Translated by David Wolff. http://digitalarchive.wilsoncenter.org/document/18883
99. Chen Jian, 'The Tibetan Rebellion of 1959', p. 80
100.   Draft Report, 'On the Trip of the Soviet Party-Governmental Delegation to the PRC,' by M. Suslov to CC CPSU Presidium for Presentation to a Forthcoming CC CPSU Plenum (excerpt),' 18 December 1959, History and Public Policy Program Digital Archive, Center for the Storage of Contemporary Documentation (TsKhSD), Moscow, fond 2, opis 1, delo 415, II. 56-91. Translated by Vladislav M. Zubok. http://digitalarchive.wilsoncenter.org/document/112989
101.   Annual Reports from Lhasa, Gyantse, Yatung: Annual Report of the Indian Trade Agent, Gyantse, for the year 1959, File No.3(19) R&I/60, NAI.

Chapter 13: Disputed Frontier, Divided Histories

1. Olaf Caroe, 'The Indian-Chinese Boundary Dispute: Review of the Report of the Officials', *The Geographical Journal,* Vol. 127, no. 3 (Sep 1961) pp. 343–46.
2. Thomas Holdich, *Political Frontiers & Boundary Making* (1916, Macmillan, (reprint)1956, p. 280) describing the Himalayas.

3. White Papers, Vol. 1, pp. 48–51.
4. Question in the Lok Sabha: 'Chinese Occupation of Ladakhi Territory', 28 August 1959, Bhasin, *India–China Relations*, pp. 2589–95.
5. Telegram from the Foreign Secretary to Indian Missions abroad, 29 August 1959. J.N.(S.G.) File 689, Pt-II, pp. 286–88, NMML.
6. Telegram from the Prime Minister to the Ambassador in Washington, 29 August 1959, J.N. (S.G.), File 689, Pt.-II, p. 338, NMML.
7. Letter from the Prime Minister of China to the Prime Minister of India, 8 September 1959, Bhasin, *India–China Relations*, p. 2611.
8. The Prime Minister in the Lok Sabha, 28 August 1959, 'Chinese Occupation of Ladakhi Territory', Bhasin, *India–China Relations*, pp. 2589–95.
9. Telegram from Ambassador Parthasarathy to the Foreign Secretary, 9 September 1959; J.N. (S.G.), File 690 Pt.-II, pp. 374–81, NMML.
10. (Commenting on this last revelation, Ambassador Parthasarathy writing to the Foreign Secretary said that such an event would only go to prove that Tibet exercised fully sovereign status in 1947 and was discussing matters of territory directly with the Government of India.) Telegram from Ambassador Parthasarathy to the Foreign Secretary, 22 September 1959, J.N. (S.G.), File 691 Pt.-II, pp. 308–16.
11. Ambassador Parthasarathy message to the Prime Minister, September 9, op.cit.
12. Telegram from Ambassador Menon to the Foreign Secretary, 12 September 1959. J.N. (S.G.), Pt.-II, pp. 204–06, NMML.
13. 'Record of Conversation of N.S. Khrushchev with CC CCP Chairman Mao Zedong, Deputy Chairman Liu Shaoqi, Zhou Enlai, Zhu De, Lin Biao, Politburo Members Peng Zhen and Chen Yi, and Secretariat Member Wang Jiaxiang,' 02 October 1959, History and Public Policy Program Digital Archive, APRF, copy on Reel 17, Volkogonov Collection, Library of Congress, Washington, DC. Translated by David Wolff. http://digitalarchive.wilsoncenter.org/document/11883 (Accessed on 6 October 2020).
14. Editorial published by the *Peking Daily*, 'Truth about Sino-Indian boundary question', 12 September 1959, Bhasin, *India–China Relations,* pp. 2651–59.

15. Telegram from Ambassador Parthasarathy to the Foreign Secretary, 16 September 1959, J.N. (S.G.), File 691 Pt.-II, p. 263, NMML.
16. Note on the Border Dispute with China, 13 September 1959, Bhasin, *India–China Relations*, pp. 2661–63.
17. Letter from the Prime Minister of India to the Prime Minister of China, 26 September 1959, Bhasin, *India–China Relations*, pp. 2694–710.
18. Foreign Secretary S. Dutt's Speech at the Governor's Conference on 26 October 1959, Bhasin, *India–China Relations*, pp. 2782–89.
19. Telegram from Prime Minister to Krishna Menon, 5 November 1959, J.N. (S.G.) File 694 Pt.-II, pp. 169–70, NMML.
20. https://www.theweek.in/news/india/2020/05/27/when-nehru-rejected-pakistan-offer-of-joint-defence-pact-against-china.html (Accessed on 6 October 2020).
21. Kalha, *India–China Boundary Issues*, p. 101.
22. Ibid.
23. Ibid., p. 104.
24. Kingsley Martin and Dorothy Woodman, recorded by Mr B.R. Nanda on 8 August 1967 in London for the NMML Oral History Project, NMML.
25. Minutes of Meeting held in Foreign Secretary's room on 8 January 1959, Subimal Dutt Papers, Subject File No. 79, 1953, 54, 56 & 59, NMML.
26. Letter from the Prime Minister of China to the Prime Minister of India, 7 November 1959. Bhasin, *India–China Relations*, pp. 2806–09.
27. Telegram to Krishna Menon, November 10, 1959. J.N. (S.G.), File 694, Pt.-II, p. 311, NMML.
28. Telegram to Moscow, Washington, Cairo, and London, 10 November 1959, Bhasin, *India–China Relations*, pp. 2810–12.
29. Bhasin, *India–China Relations*, pp. 2828–33.
30. Telegram to the Foreign Secretary, 10 November 1959, J.N. (S.G.), File 694, Pt.-II, pp. 315–18, NMML.
31. Telegram from C d'A Chatterjee at the Indian Embassy in Washington DC to the Foreign Secretary, 13 November 1959, J.N. (S.G.) File 694 Pt.-II, p. 354, NMML.
32. Statement made by V.K. Krishna Menon in the plenary meeting of the General Assembly, on the 'Question of the representation of

China in the United Nations', on 29 September 1959, V.K. Krishna Menon Papers, Subject File no. 928, NMML.

33. Bhasin, *India–China Relations*, pp. 2850–5.7
34. Dutt from Parthasarathy, 18 December 1959. Bhasin, *India–China Relations*, pp. 2857–59.
35. Bhasin, *India–China Relations*, pp. 2863–64.
36. Nancy Jetly, *India China Relations, 1947–1977* (Humanities Press, Atlantic Highlands, N.J.,1979) p. 79.
37. Ibid., p. 81.
38. Ibid.
39. Ibid., p. 97.
40. Ibid., p. 98.
41. Ibid., p. 100.
42. Ibid., p. 109.
43. Ibid., p. 119.
44. 'The Road to the Border Conflict' in *India and China: The Way Ahead after 'Mao's India War*, by C.V. Ranganathan and Vinod C. Khanna (Har-Anand Publications, 2000) p. 29.
45. In fact, the British had a distinct preference for China exerting its influence and interests here as opposed to Russia, even against protests from the Kashmir government—as for instance, tacitly acquiescing when the Chinese erected boundary pillars at the Karakoram Pass in 1892.
46. Including the section that is today under Pakistani occupation, the total length of the India–China boundary (as claimed by India) is approximately 3,488 kms. This includes the sector west of the Karakoram Pass under Pakistani occupation since 1947–48, the sector east/southeast of the Karakoram Pass in Ladakh, the middle sector (i.e., the Himachal Pradesh and Uttarakhand-Tibet Autonomous Region border), the Sikkim sector and the eastern sector (Arunachal Pradesh-Tibet).

Chapter 14: The River of No Return

1. A.G. Noorani, *India–China Boundary Problem, 1846–1947: History and Diplomacy* (Oxford University Press, 2011) p. xiv.

2. Jagat S. Mehta, *The Tryst Betrayed: Reflections on Diplomacy and Development* (Penguin Viking, 2010) in a parody of Heinrich Heine's *Watch on the Rhine,* p. 119.

3. Kalha, *India–China Boundary Issues*, p. 131.

4. Jagat S. Mehta, *Negotiating for India: Resolving problems through diplomacy* (Manohar, 2007) p. 68.

5. Ibid. (Mehta, a member of the Indian Foreign Service, worked at the eastern division in the Ministry of External Affairs at the time as deputy to K.L. Mehta. By the time of the Zhou visit, he was in charge entirely of work concerning China and Tibet.)

6. Ibid., p. 69.

7. Tanvi Madan, *Fateful Triangle: How China Shaped US–India Relations During the Cold War* (Penguin Viking, 2020) p. 125.

8. Kalha, *India–China Boundary Issues,* p. 132.

9. Maung Maung: 'The Burma-China Boundary Settlement', *Asian Survey*, Vol. 1, No. 1 (Mar., 1961), pp. 38-43.

10. Press report in The Nation, Rangoon, 7 January 1961, quoted in Daphne E. Whittam: 'The Sino-Burmese Boundary Treaty', *Pacific Affairs*, Vol. 34, No. 2 (Summer, 1961).

11. Anuj Dhar, *CIA's Eye on South Asia* (Manas Publications, 2009) pp. 121–22.

12. Dai Chaowu, 'from 'Hindi-Chini Bhai-Bhai'' , p. 76.

13. Ibid.

14. Dai Chaowu, 'From 'Hindi-Chini Bhai-Bhai' to the 'International Class Struggle' against Nehru: China's India Policy and the Frontier Dispute, 1950-1962' *Unpublished draft version of chapter in* Das Gupta and Luthi, ed. *Sino-Indian War.*

15. Telegram to Dutt, 21 March 1960, Haksar Papers, NMML.

16. M. Taylor Fravel, 'Regime Insecurity and International Cooperation: Explaining China's Compromises in Territorial Disputes', *International Security*, Vol. 30, no. 2 (Fall 2005), pp. 46–83.

17. Dhar, *CIA's Eye,* p. 123.

18. Francine Frankel, *When Nehru Looked East: Origins of India–US Suspicion and India-China Rivalry* (Oxford University Press, 2020) p. 252.

19. Ibid., p. 253.

20. Ibid., p. 255.

21. Ibid., p. 257.

22. Dhar, *CIA's Eye*, p. 123.
23. Ibid., p. 124.
24. Mehta, *Negotiating for India*, p. 78.
25. Ibid., p. 80.
26. Note on a Talk between Mr. Morarji Desai and Mr. Malcolm MacDonald on 5 April 1960. FO 371/52543, TNA.
27. Dai Chaowu, ibid. p. 77.
28. Dorothy Woodman, *Himalayan Frontiers: A Political Review of British, Chinese, Indian and Russian Rivalries* (The Cresset Press, 1969) p. 256.
29. Inward Telegram to CRO from UK High Commission, Delhi, 22 April 1960, FO 371/152543, TNA.
30. Mehta, *Negotiating for India*, p. 78.
31. Ibid., p. 252.
32. Telegram from Subimal Dutt to Dayal in Kathmandu, 25 April 1960. P.N. Haksar Papers, Instls. I-II, Subject File No. 114, NMML.
33. Circular Telegram to Heads of Mission from the Foreign Secretary, 27 April 1960, P.N. Haksar Papers, NMML.
34. Gopal, *Jawaharlal Nehru*, Vol. 3, *1956–1964*, p. 134.
35. Dutt, Telegram of 25 April 1960, P. N. Haksar Papers, p. 127.
36. Ibid.
37. 'Record of Talks between P.M. of India and Mr. Zhou Enlai, Premier of China, 20,21,22,23,24 and 25 April 1960', Haksar Papers, Instls. I-II, Subject File no. 114, NMML.
38. Ibid.
39. Record of Talks, P.M. of India and . . . Haksar Papers.
40. Ibid.
41. Ibid.
42. Ibid.
43. Ibid.
44. Ibid.
45. 'Meeting of the Chinese Premier Zhou Enlai with the Finance Minister Morarji Desai on 22 April 1960', Bhasin, *India–China Relations*, p. 3241.
46. K. Natwar Singh, *My China Diary, 1956–88* (Rupa & Co., 2009) pp. 106–07.
47. Ramesh, *Chequered Brilliance*, pp. 516–20. The 'so-called Krishna Menon formula—that India would accept China's claims in

Ladakh, and in return China would accept India's claims on the strategically vital Chumbi Valley' was believed to be Menon's idea of a package deal. It is interesting how the idea of gaining control of the Chumbi Valley was a subliminal thought in the Indian psyche. Harishwar Dayal, the Political Officer in Sikkim had raised the issue in 1950, when the Chinese were marching into Tibet and he spoke of 'retaining' a foothold in the Chumbi Valley 'even against a direct Communist attack' since in his view, the 'lack of such foothold would greatly complicate the task of guarding India's north-east frontier.' (See A.S. Bhasin: *Nehru Tibet and China*, Penguin 2021, pp. 51-52)

48. Note recorded by Krishna Menon on his conversation with Premier Zhou and his dinner talk with the Chinese Premier, 20 April 1960; V.K. Krishna Menon Papers, Subject File 969, NMML

49. Krishna Menon Note, ibid.

50. K.P.S. Menon interviewed by B.R. Nanda, Oral History Transcript, 8 November 1976, Oral History Project, NMML.

51. Hoffmann, *India and the China Crisis* p. 86.

52. Ibid., p. 88.

53. Srinath Raghavan, *War and Peace in Modern India* (Permanent Black, 2010) p. 263, quoting Report on conversation with Morarji Desai, 5 April 1960, UKHC India to CRO, Do35/8822, TNA.

54. Ibid., p. 264.

55. Ramesh, *Chequered Brilliance,* p. 521.

56. Ibid.

57. Srinath Raghavan, 'A Missed Opportunity? The Nehru–Zhou Enlai Summit of 1960', NMML Occasional Paper, History and Society, New Series 74, NMML, 2015.

58. To these five points, Zhou Enlai added a sixth during his press conference in New Delhi on the 25–26 April (starting at 2245 hours, the conference ended at 0100 hours in the early morning): 'In order to ensure tranquility on the border so as to facilitate the discussions, both sides should continue to refrain from patrolling along all sectors of the boundary.' See Bhasin, *India–China Relations,* p. 3328.

59. See Mehta (*Negotiating for India*, p. 81) where he recounts his advice to Prime Minister Nehru that India 'could not accept that 'there is

a dispute" on the boundary to which Nehru impatiently told him: 'It is obviously a dispute, otherwise why am I talking to Zhou Enlai and wasting his time and mine?' Mehta's view was that if India were to accept that there existed a dispute (not just a problem), then 'we cannot charge the violation of our frontier.'

60. The distinction between a Joint Statement or a Joint Communique is blurred—both are statements that reflect formal understandings reached between two governments that are binding and expected to be adhered to in letter and spirit. For example, the three China–US Joint Communiques of 1972, 1979 and 1982.

61. 'Verbatim proceedings of the meeting of the Indian and Chinese officials held at Rashtrapati Bhavan, New Delhi, on 25 April 1960 at 4.30 pm', Bhasin, *India–China Relations*, pp. 3309–19.

62. Ibid.

63. Ibid., pp. 3324–25.

64. Natwar Singh, *China Diary*, p. 108.

65. 'Press Conference of the Chinese Premier Zhou Enlai, New Delhi', Bhasin, *India–China Relations*, pp. 3326–40. This is the text of the Indian version of the proceedings of the Press Conference. In the Chinese version of the proceedings of the press conference, Zhou is quoted as saying: 'Since we have adopted such an attitude of understanding and conciliation, it seems that comparatively less time has been spent on discussions of the eastern sector of the boundary.' The Chinese version refers to the western sector as 'a relatively bigger dispute'. Bhasin, *India–China Relations*, pp. 3341 and 3343.

66. In 1985, China was to reverse this stand, calling the eastern sector the sector of 'the largest dispute'. This remains the current Chinese position.

67. Bhasin, *India–China Relations*, p. 3332.

68. Garver, *Protracted Contest*, p. 101.

69. S. Gopal, *Jawaharlal Nehru*, Vol. 3., p. 136.

70. Statement of Prime Minister Jawaharlal Nehru in The Lok Sabha on the visit of the Chinese Premier (Extracts) in Bhasin, *India–China Relations*, pp. 3351–59.

71. 'Comments by Premier Zhou Enlai on the statement of the Prime Minister in Lok Sabha on 26 April 1960 on talks with the Chinese

Premier, Kathmandu, 26 April 1960' in Bhasin, *India–China Relations,* p. 3360.

72. Jetley, *India–China Relations,* p. 130.

73. Ibid., p. 134.

74. Letter from Jawaharlal Nehru to Vijaya Lakshmi Pandit, 3 August 1948. Vijaya Lakshmi Pandit Papers. Subject Files 1947-49, Pg. 3, NMML.

75. 'Krishna Menon-A Clue to Nehru': A.M. Rosenthal, The New York Times, 7 April 1957.

76. 'Note of A Talk with General Thimayya', 1 July 1960, FO 371/152544, TNA.

77. W. Kirk, 'The Inner Asian Frontier of India', *Transactions and Papers (Institute of British Geographers),* No. 31 (Dec. 1962), pp. 131–68, http://www.jstor.org/stable/621091. (Accessed 1 March 2014).

78. Ibid.

79. Raghavan, 'Nehru-Zhou Enlai Summit', p. 31.

80. Samuel Taylor Coleridge 1772-1834, *Table Talk* (1835) 18 December 1831 in Susan Ratcliffe, ed. *Oxford Essential Quotations (6 ed.)* (Online) 2018. https://www.oxfordreference.com/view/10.1093/acref/9780191866692.001.0001/q-oro-ed6-00003129

81. Declassified Chinese Foreign Ministry Note, quoted in Ananth Krishnan, 'Crossing the Point of No Return', *The Hindu,* 25 October 2012.

Chapter 15: The Decline

1. Appendices to Notes, Memoranda and letters Exchanged and Agreements signed between the Governments of India and China, White Paper II, September–November 1959, Ministry of External Affairs, Government of India.

2. Mehta, *Negotiating for India,* p. 84.

3. Callahan, 'Cartography of National Humiliation', p. 141.

4. Hoffmann, *India and the China Crisis,* p. 25.

5. Miller, *Wronger by Empire, Post-Imperial Ideology and Foreign Policy in India and China,* 2013.

6. Shankar, *The Reputational Imperative: Nehru's India in Territorial Conflict,* 2018.

7. S. Gopal, *Jawaharlal Nehru,* Vol. 3, p. 139.
8. Ibid., p. 140.
9. Mehta, *Negotiating for India,* p. 84.
10. Ibid.
11. Ibid., p. 86.
12. Mehta, *Negotiating for India,* p. 91.
13. Srinath Raghavan, ed., *Sarvepalli Gopal Imperialists, Nationalists, Democrats, The Collected Essays,* Permanent Black, 2013, p. 21.
14. Jagat S. Mehta, 'S. Gopal and the Sino-Indian Boundary Question', *China Report,* Vol. 39, Issue 1 (2003), pp. 71-75.
15. Mehta, *Negotiating for India,* p. 92.
16. Woodman, *Himalayan Frontiers,* p. 273.
17. Mehta, *Negotiating for India,* p. 95.
18. Ibid., p. 102.
19. Ibid., p.100.
20. Editorial, *The Hindu,* 15 February 1961.
21. Woodman, *Himalayan Frontiers,* p. 273.
22. Ibid.
23. *Asian Recorder* (New Delhi), VI, No. 19, p. 3302.
24. Woodman, *Himalayan Frontiers,* p. 272.
25. Ibid., p. 272.
26. The 1960 Border talks between India and China: Notes on the five sessions of border talks between India and China in 1960, p. 63. (http://www.archieve.claudearpi.net/maintenance/uploaded_pics/1960BorderTalksbetweenIndiaChina.pdf)
27. Fisher et al., *Himalayan Battleground* p. 99.
28. Ibid., p. 127.
29. Ibid.
30. Despatch from the UK High Commissioner in New Delhi to the Secretary of State for Commonwealth Relations, 30 May 1960, FO 371/150441, TNA.
31. In Greek mythology, the twins Otus and Ephialtes piled Mount Pelion on Mount Ossa and both on Mount Olympus in an attempt to reach heaven and attack the gods. The idiom 'to pile Pelion on Ossa' is to make a challenging task even more difficult and complicated by piling something on top of it. https://wordsmith.org/words/pelion.html

(Accessed 4 March 2021).

32. Caroe, 'Indian-Chinese Boundary Dispute' p.346.

33. Dhar, *CIA's Eye*, p. 127.

34. Ibid., p. 128.

35. Ibid.

36. Purnendu Kumar Banerjee, *My Peking Memoirs of The Chinese Invasion of India* (Clarion Books, 1990) pp. 13–14.

37. 'Memorandum of Three Conversations Between Director Zhang Wenji(n) and the Indian Ambassador Regarding Sino-Indian Border Issues and the Two Countries' Relations,' 17 July 1961, History and Public Policy Program Digital Archive, PRC FMA 105-01056-03, 47–50. Obtained by Sulmaan Khan and translated by Anna Beth Keim. http://digitalarchive.wilsoncenter.org/document/111724 (Accessed on 29 November 2020).

38. Banerjee, *My Peking Memoirs*, p. 23.

39. Transcripts of R.K. Nehru (Oral History), Acc. no-324, NMML.

40. 'Our China Policy: a personal assessment': R.K. Nehru Papers, Note dated 30 July 1968, 'Confidential', NMML.

41. Chen Yi to Zhou Enlai, July 1962, Quoted in Ananth Krishnan, 'A Last Opportunity Missed', *The Hindu*, 26 October 2012.

42. Neville Maxwell and A.G. Noorani, 'India's Forward Policy', *The China Quarterly*, No. 45 (Jan–Mar 1971) pp. 157–63.

43. Email correspondence (2009) with Ajit Gupte, the son of Major (retd.) V.D. Gupte who raised a battalion of Ladakh Scouts and fought in the 1962 war.

44. Hoffmann, *India and the China Crisis*, p. 97.

45. Ibid.

46. Ibid., p. 98.

47. Dhar, *CIA's Eye*, p. 131.

48. Michael Brecher, *India and World Politics: Krishna Menon's View of the World* (New York: Frederick Praeger, 1968) p. 148.

49. Quoted in Shiv Kunal Verma, *1962: The War That Wasn't* (Aleph, 2016) p. 45. The term 'forward policy' is a misnomer and Indian moves had no similarity with the British colonial policy known by the same name pursued earlier in relation to India's northern frontier. But the nomenclature being convenient has

now slipped into the lexicon of terms used in regard to the India–China conflict.

50. Hoffmann, *India and the China Crisis,* p. 100.

51. R.D. Pradhan, *Debacle to Resurgence: Y.B. Chavan, Defence Minister (1962-66)* (Atlantic Publishers & Distributors, 2013), Kindle edition, ch. 16.

52. Kalha, *India–China Boundary Issues,* p. 138.

53. Ibid.

54. Ibid., pp.140–41.

55. Hoffmann, *India and the China Crisis,* p. 121.

56. Dhar, *CIA's Eye,* p. 132.

57. Woodman, *Himalayan Frontiers,* p. 277.

58. Ibid.

59. Kalha, *India–China Boundary Issues,* p. 139.

60. The only consulate of a foreign government in Lhasa today is that of Nepal.

61. Note given by the Ministry of External Affairs, New Delhi to the Embassy of China in India, 17 July 1962, in Bhasin, *India–China Relations,* pp. 3760–63.

62. Sulmaan Wasif Khan: *Muslim, Trader, Nomad,Spy: China's Cold War And The People of The Tibetan Borderlands,* (Kindle Edition) New Cold War History Series, Odd Arne Westad, ed., University of North Carolina Press, 2015.

63. Wasif Khan, ibid. ch. 4,p.108, quoting FMPRC 105-01131-01, Telegram to Foreign Ministry from Chinese Embassy in India, 6 June 1962.

64. Ibid., p. 107.

65. See John W. Garver, 'China's decision for War with India in 1962', in *New Directions in the Study of China's Foreign Policy,* Ed. Alastair Iain Johnston and Robert S. Ross (Stanford University Press, 2006) pp. 86–130.

66. Roderick MacFarquhar, *The Origins of the Cultural Revolution: The Coming of the Cataclysm 1961-1966* (Vol. 3), (The Royal Institute of International Affairs, Studies of the East Asian Institute; Oxford University Press and Columbia University Press, 1997) p. 304.

67. D.R. Mankekar, *The Guilty Men of 1962,* (The Tulsi Shah Enterprises, 1968) p. 43.
68. Verma, *1962,* pp. 39–41.
69. Larry M. Wortzel, 'Concentrating Forces and Audacious Action: PLA Lessons from the Sino-Indian War in Larry M. Wortzel et al., *The Lessons of History: The Chinese People's Liberation Army at 75* (Defense Technical Information Center, July 2003), p. 334.
70. MacFarquhar, *Origins of the Cultural Revolution,* Vol. 3, pp. 300–01.
71. 'Compilation of Papers on China-India Boundary Problem (new situation)', 1 Jan–29 Dec 1962. PRC MFA Archives File no. 105-01638-01.
72. 'The statements made and Action taken by India on the boundary problem and information on our contact with Indians', PRC MFA Archives, File No. 105-01131-01.
73. PRC MFA Archives, 'Compilation of Papers', ibid.
74. 'The statements made and Action taken by India . . . with Indians', PRC MFA Archives, File No. 105-01131-01, which contains the details of the meeting/s between Krishna Menon and Chen Yi described in the preceding paragraphs.
75. Ramesh, *Chequered Brilliance,* p. 570.
76. 'Cable from the Chinese Embassy in India, 'Overview of India's Foreign Relations in 1961', 01 January 1962. History and Public Policy Program Digital Archive, PRC FMA 105-01519-01, 1–14. Translated by Anna Beth Keim. http://digitalarchive.wilsoncenter.org/document/116482

Chapter 16: The Fall

1. 'The Destruction of Sennacherib': George Gordon (Lord) Byron, 1815.
2. Eric Hyer, 'China's Policy of Conciliation and Reduction and its Impact on Boundary Negotiations and Settlements in the Early 1960's', Cold War International History Project Working Paper # 85, 2017.
3. Wang Jiaxiang xuanji bianjizu, ed., *Huiyi Wang Jiaxiang* (Beijing: Renmin chubanshe, 1985), 189, Xu Zehao, *Wang Jiaxiang zhuan*

(Beijing: Dangdai Zhongguo chubanshe, 1996), 555–63 quoted in Hyer, 'China's Policy of Conciliation'.

4. Dong Wang, 'From Enmity of Rapprochement: Grand Strategy, Power Politics, and US–China Relations, 1961–1974' (Ph,D dissertation, UCLA, 2007), p. 209 quoted in Hyer, 'China's Policy of Conciliation'.

5. MacFarquhar, *Origins of the Cultural Revolution*, Vol. 3, p. 273.

6. Hyer, 'China's Policy of Conciliation', p. 24.

7. 'Note given by the Ministry of External Affairs, New Delhi, to the Embassy of China in India, 26 July 1962', in Notes, Memoranda and Letters Exchanged Between the Governments of India and China, July 1962–October 1962, White Paper No. VII, Ministry of External Affairs, Government of India, 1962.

8. Jetley, *India–China Relations*, p. 163.

9. Ibid., p. 170.

10. Hoffmann, *India and the China Crisis*, p. 113.

11. Conversation with Jianglin Li (Chinese writer, and author of *Tibet in Agony*) in Philadelphia, December 2014.

12. 'Reports (other than annual) from LHASA (Tibet)', Government of India, Ministry of External Affairs (Research & Intelligence Section), Reports for 1961, Monthly Political Report for the month of April 1961, File no. 6 (35-R&I/61), NAI, Para 22.

13. Monthly Political Report for the month of May 1961, ibid., Para 26.

14. Monthly Political Report for the month of July 1961, ibid., Para 18.

15. 'Blaming Nehru: a superficial way of looking at India-China War' (Interview with Bertil Lintner). The Deccan Herald, 27 March 2014.

16. S. Gopal, 'India, China and the Soviet Union', *The Australian Journal of Politics and History*, Vol. 12 (1966) pp. 241–57.

17. Andreas Hilger, 'The Soviet Union and the Sino-Indian border war, 1962' in *The Sino-Indian War of 1962: New Perspectives*, Ed. Amit R. Das Gupta and Lorenz M. Luthi (Routledge, 2017) p. 148.

18. Kalha, *India–China Boundary Issues*, p. 143.

19. Report from the Chinese Foreign Ministry, 'The Soviet Union's Stance on the Sino-Indian Boundary Question and Soviet-Indian Relations', April, 1963, History and Public Policy Program Digital

Archive, PRC FMA 105-01272-01, 1–119. Obtained by Dai Chaowu and translated by 7Brands.
http://digitalarchive.wilsoncenter.org/document/116949

20. Ibid.
21. MacFarquhar, *Origins of the Cultural Revolution*, Vol. 3, p. 303.
22. Ibid., p. 304.
23. Gopal, 'India, China and the Soviet Union', p. 218.
24. MacFarquhar, *Origins of the Cultural Revolution*, Vol. 3, p. 305.
25. *People's Daily Online,* 3 June 2011.
26. William H. Mott IV and Jae Chang Kim: *The Philosophy of Chinese Military Culture Shih vs. Li,* Palgrave Macmillan, 2006; Chapter 6, The Sino-Indian War pp. 131-160.
27. Brigadier J.P. Dalvi, *Himalayan Blunder* (Thacker and Company, 1969) p. 184.
28. Steven Hoffmann: 'Anticipation, Disaster, and Victory: India 1962–71', *Asian Survey,* Vol. 12, no. 11 (Nov 1972), pp. 960–79.
29. Hoffmann, 'Anticipation, Disaster', p. 970.
30. Bhasin, *India–China Relations,* Vol. 4, p. 3869.
31. Ibid., p. 3864.
32. Ibid., p. 3891.
33. Dalvi, *Himalayan Blunder,* p. 254.
34. MacFarquhar, *Origins of the Cultural Revolution*, Vol. 3, p. 308.
35. Ibid.
36. Gopal, *Jawaharlal Nehru,* (Vol. 3) *1956–1964,* p. 224.
37. 'A Chronology of the Sino-Indian Border Dispute and Related Developments', Department of State, Bureau of Intelligence and Research, December 19, 1962. National Sec Files, Papers of President John F. Kennedy, Robert W Komer Files, The Kennedy Library, Boston.
38. JN SG File no. 738 Pt, III, pp. 328–33, NMML.
39. Chronology, ibid. p. 6.
40. Letter from the Prime Minister to the Chief Ministers of the States, 21 October 1962. JN SG File no. 738 Pt.-II, p. 309–13, NMML.
41. Ramachandra Guha 'Jawaharlal Nehru and China: A Study in Failure?', Harvard-Yenching Institute Working Paper Series, 2011, p. 20.
42. *The Economist,* 13 January 1962.

43. Paul McGarr, 'India's Rasputin?: V.K. Krishna Menon and Anglo-American Misperceptions of Indian Foreign Policymaking, 1947–1964', *Diplomacy & Statecraft* 22 (2011) pp. 239–60.

44. Brecher, *India and World Politics*, p. 289.

45. Bruce Riedel, *JFK's Forgotten Crisis* (Brookings Institution Press, 2015) p. 120.

46. Riedel, *JFK*, p. 120.

47. Riedel, *JFK*, p. 119.

48. 'Telegram from the U.S. Secretary of State Dean Rusk to the U.S. Ambassador in India, 27 October 1962', in Bhasin, *India–China Relations*, pp. 3984–85.

49. Frankel, *When Nehru Looked East*, p. 274.

50. Madan, *Fateful Triangle*, p. 145.

51. Nehru, 5 December 1962, as quoted in A.G. Noorani, 'India's Quest for a Nuclear Guarantee', *Asian Survey*, Vol. 7, No. 7 (July 1967), p. 490.

52. Bhasin, *India–China Relations*, pp. 4043–44.

53. Telegram from the U.S. Secretary of State Dean Rusk to the American Ambassador in India, 20 November 1962, in Bhasin, *India–China Relations*, pp. 4049–51.

54. Bhasin, *India–China Relations*, pp. 3954–83.

55. 'Conversation between Soviet Ambassador in New Delhi, Ivana Benediktov and R.K. Nehru at a reception, 2 November 1962', Bhasin, *India–China Relations*, pp. 3990–92.

56. 'Letter from Ambassador T.N. Kaul to Prime Minister, Moscow, 16 November 1962', Bhasin, *India–China Relations*, pp. 4034–37.

57. 'Entry from the journal of Soviet Ambassador to India Benediktov, conversation with the Indian Prime Minister J. Nehru', Bhasin, *India–China Relations*, pp. 4123–24.

58. Mohan Guruswamy, 'Don't forget the heroes of Rezang La', *The Hindu*, 20 November 2012. https://www.thehindu.com/opinion/lead/Don't-forget-the-heroes-of-Rezang-La/article12513562.ece

59. Inder Malhotra: 'The Courage of 13 Kumaon', *The Indian Express*, 20 February 2012. (https://indianexpress.com/article/opinion/columns/the-courage-of-13-kumaon/)

60. Riedel, *JFK's Forgotten Crisis*, p. 141.

61. 'Telegram no. 531 from British Embassy in Beijing to Foreign Office, 9 November 1962', FO371/164929, TNA.

62. Bertil Lintner, *China's India War: Collision Course on the Roof of the World* (Oxford University Press, 2018) p. 114.

63. Mott and Kim, ibid, p. 151.

64. Ibid, p. 156.

65. Air Vice Marshal AK Tiwary, 'No Use of Combat Air Power in 1962', *Indian Defence Review*, Vol. 21, no. 3 (Jul–Sep 2006) http://www.indiandefencereview.com/spotlights/no-use-of-combat-air-power-in-1962/ (Accessed 14 January 2021).

66. George K Tanham, *The Indian Air Force—Trends & Prospects*, Vision Books, New Delhi, 1995, pp. 44-5, quoted in Tiwary, ibid.

67. 'Resolution adopted by the Lok Sabha on the Chinese Aggression, 14 November 1962', Bhasin, *India–China Relations*, p. 4062.

68. *Prime Minister on Chinese Aggression*, External Publicity Division, Ministry of External Affairs, New Delhi, 1963.

69. Speaking in Parliament, 24 January, 1963.

70. Statement in the Lok Sabha, 19 March 1963.

71. Statement in the Rajya Sabha, 3 September 1963.

72. 'Statement by the Defence Minister regarding NEFA Enquiry', 2 September 1963; Appendix II in Mankekar, *Guilty Men,* pp.174–80. The text of the statement can also be accessed at http://www.indiandefencereview.com/spotlights/statement-by-the-defence-minister-regarding-nefa-enquiry-new-delhi-sep-2-1963/

73. Pradhan, *Debacle to Resurgence*, ch. 16.

74. Ibid.

75. Statement by Defence Minister Chavan, in Mankekar, *Guilty Men,* p.178

76. Chavan, in Mankekar, *Guilty Men,* p. 179.

77. Pradhan, *Debacle to Resurgence,* ch. 17.

78. Ibid.

79. Ibid.

80. *A History of the Counter Attack War in Self Defence Along Sino-Indian Border*, Academy of Military Science Publications, 1994.

81. Kang Yongsheng, 'The 1962 Sino-Indian Border Conflict: A War that casts its shadow till date,' *China Youth Daily* 26 October 2012; translated by Jera Huang.

82. 'Mao Zedong in order to ease domestic conflict, launched a surprise attack on India' by Yang Zhifang; Phoenix TV, 1 November 2012, translated by Jera Huang.

83. Liu Zongyi, Shanghai Institutes For International Studies, 'India still conserves frontier mentality over 1962 border war with China', translated by Jera Huang.

84. Shan Zhiqiang, 'Himalayas Quiet for 50 Years: Why India and China Cannot really be Neighbours' *National Geography*, December 2012 (translated by Jera Huang).

85. 'Suppressing Rebellion in Tibet and the China-India Border War', War on Tibet. Chinese and Tibetan documents in the history of the Communist Occupation in English translation: Jianglin Li, 5 December 2017. http://historicaldocs.blogspot.com/p/chinese.html

86. Cheng Xiaohe, 'From Ally to Partner: The Evolution of Sino-Pakistan Relations', *Journal of Renmin University of China*, Vol. 2, no. 1 (Spring 2007) pp. 61–81.

87. *From the Memoirs of Geng Biao: 1949–1992*, quoted in Cheng Xiaohe, 'From Ally to Partner'. Geng Biao, later to be Defence Minister, had served as China's Ambassador to Pakistan in the 1950s.

88. Geng Biao, *From the Memoirs of Geng Biao*, quoted in Cheng Xiaohe, p. 63.

89. Cheng Xiaohe, 'From Ally to Partner', p. 64.

90. Syed, *China and Pakistan*, p. 83.

91. Ibid.

92. Ibid., p. 84.

93. 'Summary of Conversation between Premier Zhou Enlai and Pakistan's Ambassador to the PRC, Rashidi (Excerpt),' March 08, 1962, History and Public Policy Program Digital Archive, PRC FMA
105-01799-02, 9-16. Obtained and translated by Christopher Tang. http://digitalarchive.wilsoncenter.org/document/121570

94. 'Record of Conversation following Pakistani Ambassador to the PRC Raza's Presentation of Credentials to Liu Shaoqi', September 01, 1962, History and Public Policy Program Digital Archive,
PRC FMA 105-01801-02, 28-34. Obtained and translated by Christopher Tang http://digitalarchive.wilsoncenter.org/document/121571.

Raza was returning to China to serve his second term as Pakistan's Ambassador; he had earlier served in Beijing in the early 1950s and claimed to have a close personal relationship with Zhou Enlai.

'Cable from the Chinese Embassy in Pakistan, 'Minutes of the Conversation Between the Chinese

Ambassador Ding Guoyu and Pakistan's Foreign Affairs Secretary on the Sino-Indian Border Clash',

20 October 1962, History and Public Policy Program Digital Archive, PRC FMA 105-01111-01, 1-4.

Obtained by Dai Chaowu and translated by 7Brands.

http://digitalarchive.wilsoncenter.org/document/114763

95. Andrew Small, *The China-Pakistan Axis: Asia's New Geopoliitcs*, Oxford University Press, 2016, p. 23.

96. Syed, *China and Pakistan*, p. 87.

97. Inward Telegram to CRO from UK High Commission, Karachi, 22 February 1963 in File F.O. 371/170676, TNA.

98. Enclosure to telegram 23 February 1963 from UK High Commission, Karachi to Foreign Office, London in F.O. 371/176076, ibid.

99. Letter from UK High Commission, New Delhi, 7 March 1963 to Foreign Office, ibid.

100. 1042/63 Letter from the Charge d' Affaires, British Embassy, Beijing, 11 March 1963, ibid.

101. Kalha, *India–China Boundary Issues*. Kalha notes that the 'old princely state of Jammu and Kashmir had an area of 222,236 square kilometres of which 106,567 square kilometres was with India, 78,114 square kilometres with Pakistan (POK) and 38,000 square kilometres under Chinese occupation. An additional 5,180 square kilometres was ceded by Pakistan to China.' (p. 172).

102. 'Nehru's statement regarding Pakistan-China boundary negotiations, 7 May 1962', in Bhasin, *India–China Relations*, pp. 3666–68.

103. Note: 'Meaning of Chinese involvement in the Indo-Pak conflict', V.L. Pandit Papers, IInd Instalment, Sub. File 44, NMML.

104. Ibid.

105. Jagat S. Mehta: 'Note on Sino-Pak relations' October 1965, enclosure to Director (China), K.R. Narayanan's letter to Ambassadors and Heads of Mission of 28 October 1965 in V. L. Pandit, ibid.

106. Mehta, ibid.

107. Jagat Singh Mehta 'Nehru's Failure with China: Intellectual Naivete or the Wages of a Prophetic Vision?', Paper prepared for a conference at the University of Toronto, October 1989, p. 41.

108. Guha, 'Jawaharlal Nehru and China', p. 12.

109. Mehta, 'Nehru's Failure', p. 27-28.

110. K.P.S. Menon, 'The Sixties in Retrospect', Address at the Fourth Convocation of The Indian School of International Studies, 13 December 1969, pp.1-15.

111. Berlin, 'Russian Thinkers', Penguin, 1979, p. 81.

112. Guha, 'Jawaharlal Nehru and China', p. 29.

113. Purnendu Kumar Banerjee: 'My Peking Memoirs of The Chinese Invasion of India', Clarion Books, 1990.

114. Banerjee, ibid. p. 101.

115. Menon, 'Sixties in Retrospect', p. 11.

116. http://ignca.gov.in/diary-of-an-old-china-hand-a-k-damodaran/ (Accessed on 17 January 2021).

117. Memorandum of Conversation, Beijing, 23 February 1972. Foreign Relations of the United States, 1969-1976, Volume XVII, China, 1969–1972. (https://history.state.gov/historicaldocuments/frus1969-76v17/d197)

118. Sunil Khilnani, 'Making Asia: India, China & The Struggle for An Idea', 33rd Jawaharlal Nehru Memorial Lecture, 2012, Sponsored by India Advisory Partners & Jawaharlal Nehru Memorial Trust.

119. The phrase is part of a passage from Nehru's Autobiography quoted by Daw Aung San Suu Kyi in her Jawaharlal Nehru Memorial Lecture, 2012 'Discovery of Nehru', 14 November 2012.

Coda

1. Robert Kaplan, 'Geopolitics and the New World Order'. *Time* magazine, 31 March 2014: https://time.com/31911/geopolitics-and-the-new-world-order/ (Accessed 31 January 2021).

2. Frankel, *When Nehru Looked East*, p. 283.

3. Lord Curzon, Romanes Lecture, 1907: 'Frontiers are indeed the razor's edge on which hang suspended the modern issues of war and peace, the life and death of nations.'

4. Archibald Rose, 'The Chinese Frontiers of India', *The Geographical Journal*, March 1912 No. 3, Vol. XXXIX.

5. Nimmi Kurian, *India-China Borderlands, Conversations beyond the Centre,* Sage Publications, 2014, p. 5.

6. Kunal Mukherjee, 'Comparing China and India's Disputed Borderland Regions: Xinjiang, Tibet, Kashmir, and the Indian Northeast', *East Asia*, an International Quarterly, 2015, pp. 173-205

7. Kurian, ibid. p. 8.

8. Kurian, ibid, p. 151.

9. Mahasagara – Ocean; Shambhala – from the Sanskrit- a mythical and utopian mountain heaven.

10. Agehananda Bharati, 'References to Tibet in Medieval Indian Literary Documents', *Tibet Society Bulletin*, vol. 3 (Bloomington, 1969), pp. 46-70, quoted in Dawa Norbu below.

11. Norbu, Dawa: 'Tibet in Sino-Indian Relations: The Centrality of Marginality', *Asian Survey*, Vol. 37, No. 11 (Nov., 1997), pp. 1078-1095.

12. Jabin Jacob, Institute of Chinese Studies, Delhi in Conference: 'Focusing the Frontiers: The Borderland, Identity, Perceptions and Imaginings of Monpas of Tawang in India-China Border'. Ed. M. Mayilvaganan, Nasima Khatoon, Sournina Bej. International Strategic and Security Studies Programme, National Institute of Advanced Studies (NIAS), Bengaluru (NIAS ISSSP Report: RT02-2017), December 2017.

13. Matthew Akester, Independent Scholar, Dharamshala, at same conference, Ibid.

14. Jigme Yeshi Lama, Calcutta University, at same conference, ibid.

15. Dr. Swargajyoti Gohain, Ashoka University, at same Conference, ibid.

16. Mirza Zulfiqur Rahman, I.I.T. Guwahati, at same Conference, ibid.

17. Murty, T.S., 'The Eastern Himalayas in Sino-Indian Relations' (https:// idsa.in/system/files/TheEasternHimalayasinSinoIndianRelations_ TSMurthy.pdf)

Acknowledgements

This book has been some years in the making. The idea for it grew out of the S. Gopal Memorial Lecture that I was invited to deliver at King's College, London, by Sunil Khilnani in early 2014. In preparing for that lecture, I was encouraged by the fact that the canvas of available archival sources for the study of the subject of India's relations with China had grown phenomenally since the early nineties when I had worked on the subject while in the Foreign Service. The Jawaharlal Nehru Fellowship awarded to me in 2015 to undertake my research and begin the writing of this book, spurred my efforts further. The Meera and Vikram Gandhi Fellowship at the India Initiative of the Watson Institute in Brown University during 2014, and the steadfast encouragement and support of Professor Ashutosh Varshney were immeasurably useful in the conduct of my research work in the United States, the United Kingdom, and China. I would like to place on record my deep appreciation of my research assistants at Brown University—Jera Zhe Huang, Yang Guo, Zhou Shengjie, Supriya Das, Divya Mehta, and Viveka Hulyalkar.

While the records of the Ministry of External Affairs in New Delhi on the period covered in this book remain largely closed, the personal papers of officials like P.N. Haksar, K.P.S. Menon, R.K. Nehru, Subimal Dutt and the oral history transcripts at the Nehru Memorial Museum and Library, of a number of senior officials associated with our relations with Tibet and with China, for instance, were invaluable sources. The decision taken recently to open the papers of V.K. Krishna Menon at the Nehru Memorial Museum and Library to scholars has also been of great help. A published anthology of documents on India–China Relations from 1947 to 2000 by Avtar Singh Bhasin proved extremely useful. All these have provided scholars who wish to dive deeper into the evolution of independent India's relations with China with a wealth of information to study and analyse. Access to Chinese-language and archival sources of this period has been limited because of the Chinese government's decision to close/restrict access to the archives of the Ministry of Foreign Affairs in Beijing after a brief period of opening these resources for scholars from 2007 to 2012 (well before the commencement of my research for this book). However, the digital archive of the Cold War History Project at the Wilson Center in Washington D.C. has been enormously useful for consulting translations of Chinese official documents from the period of this study as also of Soviet archival material of relevance. I am also grateful to Professors Shen Zhihua and Dai Chaowu for their valuable insights and perspectives. I benefitted from my discussions with Ziad Haider in Washington (and now Singapore) on Pakistan–China relations.

Tempa Tsering, the then Representative of His Holiness the Dalai Lama in New Delhi, was immensely helpful to me in arranging the interview at Dharamshala with His Holiness in the summer of 2014.

It was a joy and privilege to work with the exceptional Ranjana Sengupta as my editor, as also with Rea Mukherjee whose patience and professionalism as we put the final touches to this book I am very grateful for. P.S. Chopra, a valued friend for close to four decades, was most generous with his time and his wise and outstanding counsel on the cartography of the India-China boundary. Nitendra Srivastava of Spatial Technologies, New Delhi worked dedicatedly with me in the preparation of the maps for this book. All the maps included in the book are for illustrative purposes only, they are sketch maps and not to scale.

I am thankful to Srinath Raghavan, Ashutosh Varshney, Sugata Bose, Padma Desai, Robbie Barnett, Orville Schell, David Shambaugh, James Mann, Susan Shirk, Liaquat Ahamed, Kanti Bajpai, Chandrasekhar Dasgupta, Vijay Nambiar, Shivshankar Menon, and T.C.A. Raghavan for their valuable insights and comments.

Dr S. Jaishankar, the External Affairs Minister of India, was very supportive of my research for this book during his tenure as Foreign Secretary. His encouragement was important to me.

This book would not have been possible without the affection, care and support of my family—my husband Sudhakar, my sons Nikhilesh and Kartikeya, my daughter-in-law, Suhasini Ranganathan and Ananya, our granddaughter—who have been the embodiment of unwavering constancy, through this and so many other journeys—keeping the vigil to ensure that I did not stray from my writing and that the book was completed. For them, there can be no sufficient measure of my gratitude.

My extraordinary parents, Narayani and Narayana Menon, were responsible for inculcating my love of literature, language, history, and diplomacy. To them, and their love, their nurture, and their belief in me, I dedicate this work.

Bibliography

Primary Sources

Declassified Files, Ministry of External Affairs, National Archives of India, New Delhi

Official Papers, Nehru Memorial Museum and Library (NMML), New Delhi

The Nehru Papers (post-1947)

P.N. Haksar Papers

T.N. Kaul Papers

Vijaya Lakshmi Pandit Papers

V.K. Krishna Menon Papers

Subimal Dutt Papers

Apa B. Pant Papers

R.K. Nehru Papers

K.P.S. Menon Papers

Declassified Foreign Office Files (India and Pakistan) of the U.K., The National Archives, Kew

Hugh Richardson Papers, Bodleian Library, Oxford University

Frank Moraes Papers, School of Oriental and African Studies, London

Foreign Relations of the United States, Office of the Historian. https://history.state.gov/historicaldocuments

J.F.K. Papers, John F. Kennedy Presidential Library, Boston

Cold War International History Project, Wilson Center, Washington D.C. (Translations of Chinese Foreign Ministry Archives and Soviet Archives covering the period of this study)

Archives of the Ministry of Foreign Affairs of The People's Republic of China

Notes, Memoranda and Letters Exchanged and Agreements Signed between the Governments of India and China, White Papers I-VIII, New Delhi: Ministry of External Affairs, 1954–1963.

Maoist Documentation Project by Marxists.org

Selected Works of Mao Tse-tung

1950s China–India Chronology: A Resource for Research and Teaching by Arunabh Ghosh, Harvard University

Oral Histories, Nehru Memorial Museum and Library, New Delhi
R. K. Nehru
K.P.S. Menon
His Holiness the Dalai Lama
A.K. Damodaran
T.N. Kaul
K.C Johorey
S.M. Krishnatry
Apa B. Pant
Kingsley Martin and Dorothy Woodman

Recordings/Podcasts/Videos
Author's interview of The Dalai Lama, Dharamsala, India, April 2014

Melvyn Bragg: In our Time, BBC Sounds, 3 December 1998 on the Relevance of the Study of History in the 20th Century with Simon Schama and Antonia https://www.bbc.co.uk?sounds/playp00548g

Dasgupta, Chandrashekhar. 'Nehru, Patel and China', Audio file, 19 April 2014. NMML

Documentary in Tibetan, 'H.H. the Dalai Lama Visit to India, 1956–57'. https://youtu.be/fTO4WWI0ucs

Books
Aris, Michael and Aung San Suu Kyi, eds. *Tibetan Studies: In Honour of Hugh Richardson*. New Delhi: Vikas Publishing House, 1980.

Arpi, Claude. *Tibet: When the Gods Spoke: India Tibet Relations (1947–1962)*, Pt. 3, Vij Books India, 2019.

Atlas of the Northern Frontier of India, Ministry of External Affairs, New Delhi, 1960.

Atwill, David G. *Islamic Shangri-La: Inter-Asian Relations and Lhasa's Muslim Communities, 1600 to 1960*. Oakland: University of California Press, 2018.

Bagchi, Prabodh Chandra. *India and China: A Thousand Years of Sino-Indian Cultural Contact*. Calcutta: China Press Limited, 1944.

Bajpai, G.S. *China's Shadow Over Sikkim: The Politics of Intimidation*. New Delhi: Lancer Publishers, 1999.

Bajpai, Kanti, et al., eds. *Routledge Handbook of China-India Relations*. Abingdon: Routledge, 2020.

Bajpai, K.S. "Weightlifting" https://www.outlookindia.com/magazine/story/weightlifting/262753

Banerjee, Purnendu K. *My Peking Memories of the Chinese Invasion of India*. New Delhi: Clarion Books, 1990.

Barpujari, H.K. *An Account of Assam and Her Administration (1603–1822 A.D.)*. Guwahati: Spectrum Publications, 1988.

------. *Inner Line to McMahon Line*. Guwahati: Spectrum Publications, 1981.

Barnett, Robert, et al., eds. *Conflicting Memories: Tibetan History Under Mao Retold*. Leiden: Brill, 2020.

Berlin, Isaiah. *Russian Thinkers*. London: Penguin Books, 1978.

Bhagavan, Manu, ed. *India and the Cold War*. Chapel Hill: The University of North Carolina Press, 2019.

Bhasin, Avtar Singh. *India–China Relations, 1947–2000: A Documentary Study*. 4 Vols. New Delhi: Geetika Publishers, 2018.

Bhutani, Sudarshan. *A Clash of Political Cultures: Sino-Indian Relations (1957–1962)*. New Delhi: Roli Books, 2004.

Brecher, Michael. *Nehru: A Political Biography*. London: Oxford University Press, 1959.

------. *India and World Politics: Krishna Menon's View of the World*. London: Oxford University Press, 1968.

Burkitt, Laurie, et al., eds. *The Lessons of History: The Chinese People's Liberation Army at 75*. Carlisle, PA: Strategic Studies Institute, 2016.

Byron, Lord George Gordon. *Hebrew Melodies*. John Murray, 1815.

Central Tibetan Administration, Department of Information and International Relations. *Facts About The 17-Point "Agreement" Between Tibet and China.* Ganchen Kyishong, Dharamsala, 2001.

Chakravarti, Shyamalkanti. *Prabodhachandrodaya: Prabodh Chandra Bagchi: A Centenary Tribute.* Kolkata: P.C. Bagchi Centenary Celebration Committee, 1997.

Chen, Jian. *Mao's China and the Cold War: The New Cold War History.* Chapel Hill: University of North Carolina Press, 2001.

Chung, Tan. *Himalaya Calling: The Origins of India and China.* Hackensack, NJ: World Century Publishing Corporation, 2015.

------, ed. *Across the Himalayan Gap: An Indian Quest for Understanding China.* New Delhi: IGNCA, 1998.

Chung, Tan, and Geng Yinzeng. *India and China.* Centre for Studies in Civilisations, 2005.

Coleridge, Samuel Taylor. *Specimens of the Table Talk of the Late Samuel Taylor Coleridge.* Vol. 2, London, 1835.

Crocker, Walter R. *Nehru: A Contemporary's Estimate.* New York: Oxford University Press, 1966.

The Dalai Lama. *Beyond Religion: Ethics for a Whole World.* Noida: HarperCollins Publishers India, 2012.

------. *My Land and My People: Memoirs of the Dalai Lama of Tibet.* New York: Potala Corporation, 1985.

------. *Freedom in Exile.* Harper Collins, 1990.

Dalvi, J.P. *Himalayan Blunder: The Curtain-raiser to the Sino-Indian War of 1962.* Mumbai: Thacker, 1969.

DasGupta, Probal. *Watershed 1967: India's Forgotten Victory Over China.* New Delhi: Juggernaut Books, 2020.

Dhar, Anuj. *CIA's Eye on South Asia.* New Delhi: Manas Publications, 2009.

Dutt, Subimal. *With Nehru in the Foreign Office.* Kolkata: Minerva Publications, 1977.

Encyclopedia of India–China Cultural Contacts http://www.mea.gov.in/images/pdf/India-ChinaEncyclopedia_Vol-1.pdf

http://www.mea.gov.in/images/pdf/India-ChinaEncyclopedia_Vol-2.pdf

Fisher, Margaret W., Leo Rose, and Robert A. Huttenback. *Himalayan Battleground: Sino-Indian Rivalry in Ladakh.* London: Pall Mall Press, 1963.

Frankel, Francine. *When Nehru Looked East: Origins of India-US Suspicion and India-China Rivalry.* New York: Oxford University Press, 2020.

Galbraith, John Kenneth. *A Life in Our Times: Memoirs.* Boston: Houghton Mifflin Company, 1981.

Mahatma Gandhi. *Collected Works,* https://gandhi.gov.in/gandhian-literature.html

Gandhi, Rajmohan. *Patel: A Life.* New Delhi: Navjivan Trust, 2011.

Gao, Wenqian. *Zhou Enlai Zhuan/ Zhou Enlai: The Last Perfect Revolutionary* (Biography of Zhou Enlai), Public Affairs, 2007.

Garver, John W. *Protracted Contest: Sino-Indian Rivalry in the Twentieth Century.* New Delhi: Oxford University Press, 2001.

Goldstein, Melvyn. *A History of Modern Tibet,* Vol. 2: *The Calm Before the Storm, 1951–1955.* University of California Press, 2007.

Gopal, Sarvepelli. *Jawaharlal Nehru: A Biography.* 3 Vols. New Delhi: Oxford University Press, 1975–1984.

Gopal, Sarvepelli, et al., eds. *Selected Works of Jawaharlal Nehru,* 2nd Series, Vols. 10–82. New Delhi: Nehru Memorial Fund, 1989–2015.

Guha, Ramachandra. *India After Gandhi: The History of the World's Largest Democracy.* London: Macmillan, 2007.

------, ed. *Makers of Modern Asia.* Cambridge, MA: The Belknap Press of Harvard University Press, 2014.

Gundevia, Y.D. *Outside the Archives.* 2008 ed. New Delhi: Orient Blackswan, 2008.

Gupta, Amit R. Das, and Lorenz M. Lüthi, eds. *The Sino-Indian War of 1962: New Perspectives.* South Asia ed. Abingdon: Routledge, 2017.

Guruswamy, Mohan, and Zorawar Daulet Singh. *India China Relations: The Border Issue and Beyond.* New Delhi: Viva Books, 2009.

Guyot-Réchard, Bérénice. *Shadow States: India, China and the Himalayas, 1910–1962.* New Delhi: Cambridge University Press, 2017.

Halper, Lezlee Brown, and Stefan Halper. *Tibet: An Unfinished Story.* New York: Oxford University Press, 2014.

Harris, Clare, and Tsering Shakya. *Seeing Lhasa: British Depictions of the Tibetan Capital, 1936–1947.* London: Serindia Publications, 2003.

Hoffmann, Steven A. *India and the China Crisis.* Berkeley: University of California Press, 1990.

Holdich, Thomas. *Political Frontiers and Boundary Making*. Reprint. London: Macmillan, 1956.

India, Ministry of External Affairs. *Notes, Memoranda and Letters Exchanged and Agreements Signed Between the Governments of India and China, 1954–1959*. White Paper. New Delhi: Government of India Press, 1959.

India, *Ministry* of External Affairs. *Report of the Officials of the Governments of India and the People's Republic of China on the Boundary Question*. New Delhi: Government of India Press, 1962.

India Publications Division. *For a United India: Speeches of Sardar Patel, 1947–1950*. New Delhi: Government of India Press, 1967.

Jetly, Nancy. *India–China Relations, 1947–1977: A Study of Parliament's Role in the Making of Foreign Policy*. Atlantic Highlands, NJ: Humanities Press, 1979.

Jin, Kemu. *A Short History of Sino-Indian Friendship*. Trans. Yang Hsien-Yi and Gladys Yang. Foreign Languages Press, Beijing, 1958.

Jha, C.S. *From Bandung to Tashkent: Glimpses of India's Foreign Policy*. Delhi, Sangam Books, 1983.

Johnston, Alastair Iain, and Robert S. Ross, eds. *New Directions in the Study of China's Foreign Policy*. Stanford: Stanford University Press, 2006.

Kalha, Ranjit Singh. *India–China Boundary Issues: Quest for Settlement*. New Delhi: Pentagon Press, 2014.

Kaplan, Robert D. Monsoon: *The Indian Ocean and the Future of American Power*. New York: Random House, 2010.

Karaka, D.F. *Chungking Diary*. Mumbai: Thacker, 1942.

Karnik, V.B., ed. *Chinese Invasio: Background & Sequel*. Mumbai: Bharatiya Vidya Bhavan, 1966.

Kaul, B.M. *The Untold Story*. New Delhi: Allied Publishers, 1967.

Kennedy, Andrew Bingham. *The International Ambitions of Mao and Nehru*. Cambridge University Press, 2012.

Khan, Sulmaan Wasif. *Muslim, Trader, Nomad, Spy: China's Cold War and the People of the Tibetan Borderlands*. Chapel Hill: The University of North Carolina Press, 2015.

Kissinger, Henry. *On China*. New York: Penguin, 2011.

Krishnan, Ananth. *India's China Challenge: A Journey Through China's Rise and What It Means for India*. Noida: HarperCollins Publishers India, 2020.

Kudaisya, Gyanesh. *A Republic in the Making: India in the 1950s*. New Delhi: Oxford University Press, 2017.

Kurian, Nimmi. *India–China Borderlands: Conversations Beyond the Centre*. New Delhi: SAGE India, 2014.

Laird, Thomas. *The Story of Tibet: Conversations with the Dalai Lama*. London: Atlantic Books, 2006.

Lall, John. *Aksai Chin and Sino-Indian Conflict*. New Delhi: Allied Publishers, 1989.

Lamb, Alastair. *Tibet, China & India, 1914–1950: A History of Imperial Diplomacy*. Hertingfordbury: Roxford Books, 1989.

Lattimore, Owen. *Inner Asian Frontiers of China*. 2nd ed. Irvington-on-Hudson, N.Y.: Capital Publishing Co., 1951.

Li, Jianglin. *Tibet in Agony: Lhasa 1959*. Trans. Susan Wilf. Harvard University Press, 2016.

Lintner, Bertil. *China's India War: Collision Course on the Roof of the World*. New Delhi: Oxford University Press, 2018.

Macaulay, Thomas Babington Macaulay, Baron. *The lays of ancient Rome: and other poems* / illustrated by C.G. Bush, and others. 1871.

Madan, Tanvi. *Fateful Triangle: How China Shaped US–India Relations During the Cold War*. Gurugram: Penguin Random House India, 2020.

Mankekar, D.R. *The Guilty Men of 1962*. New Delhi: Tulsi Shah Enterprises, 1968.

Mao Tse-tung. *Selected Works*. Online at www.marxists.org

Maxwell, Neville. *India's China War*. Garden City, NY: Anchor Books, 1972.

MacFarquhar, Roderick. *The Origins of the Cultural Revolution*. Vol. 3: *The Coming of the Cataclysm 1961–1966*. New York: Oxford University Press, 1997.

Martin, Peter. *China's Civilian Army: The Making of Wolf Warrior Diplomacy*. New York: Oxford University Press, 2021.

Mehra, Parshotam. *An 'Agreed' Frontier: Ladakh and India's Northern-most Borders, 1846–1947*. New Delhi: Oxford University Press, 1992.

------. *Negotiating with the Chinese, 1846–1987: Problems and Perspectives*. New Delhi: Reliance Publishing House, 1989.

------. *The McMahon Line and After: A Study of the Triangular Contest on India's North-eastern Frontier between Britain, China and Tibet, 1904–1947*. New Delhi: Macmillan, 1974.

Mehrotra, L.L. *India's Tibet Policy: An Appraisal and Options*. Tibetan Parliamentary and Research Centre, New Delhi, 1997.

Mehta, Jagat S. *Negotiating for India: Resolving Problems Through Diplomacy (Seven Case Studies 1958–1978)*. New Delhi: Manohar, 2007.

------. *The Tryst Betrayed: Reflections on Diplomacy and Development*. New Delhi: Penguin Books India, 2010.

Menon, K.P.S. *Delhi-Chungking: A Travel Diary*. Oxford: Oxford University Press, 1947.

Menon, K.P.S. *The Sixties in Retrospect*: Address at the Fourth Convocation of The Indian School of International Studies, 13 December, 1969.

Menon, Shivshankar. *Choices: Inside the Making of India's Foreign Policy*. Gurugram: Penguin Random House India, 2016.

Meyer, Karl E., and Shareen Blair Brysac. *Tournament of Shadows: The Great Game and the Race for Empire in Central Asia*. Washington, D.C.: Counterpoint, 1999.

Miller, Manjari Chatterjee. *Wronged by Empire: Post-Imperial Ideology and Foreign Policy in India and China*. Stanford University Press, 2013

Mosca, Matthew. *From Frontier Policy to Foreign Policy: The Question of India and the Transformation of Geopolitics in Qing China*. Stanford University Press, 2013.

Ministry of External Affairs, External Publicity Division. Prime Minister on Chinese Aggression, 1963

Mott, William H., and Jae Change Kim. *The Philosophy of Chinese Military Culture: Shih vs. Li*. New York: Palgrave Macmillan, 2006.

Mullick, B.N. *My Years with Nehru: The Chinese Betrayal*. Mumbai: Allied Publishers, 1971.

Mulmi, Amish Raj. *All Roads Lead North: Nepal's Turn to China*. Chennai: Context, 2021.

Murty, T.S. *India–China Boundary: India's Options*. New Delhi: ABC Publishing House, 1987.

Nanda, Neeru. *Tawang: The Land of Mon*. New Delhi: Vikas Publishing House, 1982.

Narayanan, K.R. *Nehru and His Vision*. New Delhi: D.C. Books, 1999.

Nehru, Jawaharlal. *Selected Works, Series 1 and 2*. https://nehruselectedworks.com

------. *China, Spain and the War": Essays and Writings*. Kitabastan, 1940 https://archive.org/stream/in.ernet.dli.2015.174465/2015.174465. China-Spain-And-The-War_djvu.txt

------. *Independence and After: A Collection of Speeches, 1946–1949*. N.Y.: The John Day Company, 1950.

------. *Letters for a Nation: From Jawaharlal Nehru to His Chief Ministers, 1947–1963*. Ed. Madhav Khosla. Penguin, 2014.

Noorani, A.G. *India–China Boundary Problem: 1846–1947*. History and Diplomacy. New Delhi: Oxford University Press, 2011.

Norman, Alexander. *Dalai Lama: An Extraordinary Life*. New Delhi: Harper Collins India, 2020.

Okamoto Takashi, ed. 岡本隆司 編. *Sōshuken no sekaishi: Tōzai Ajia no kindai to hon'yaku gainen* 宗主権の世界史：東西アジアの近代と翻訳概念 [A world history of suzerainty: A modern history of East and West Asia and translated concepts]. Nagoya: Nagoya daigaku shuppankai, 2014. 399 pp. ISBN: 9784815807870.

Palit, D.K. *War in High Himalaya: The Indian Army in Crisis, 1962*. London: Hurst & Company, 1991.

Panikkar, K.M. *In Two Chinas: Memoirs of a Diplomat*. London: George Allen and Unwin, 1955.

------. *India and China: A Study of Cultural Relations*. Mumbai: Asia Publishing House, 1957.

Pant, Apa. *A Moment in Time*. E-book ed. New Delhi: Orient Blackswan, 2018.

Paranjpe, V.V. *How to Understand China: Across the Himalayan Gap: An Indian Quest for Understanding China*. Ed. Tan Chung. Gyan Publishing House, 1998.

Party Documentation Research Office of the Communist Party of China Central Committee, CPC Tibet Autonomous Region Committee and China Tibetology Research Center, eds. *Selected Works on Tibet of Mao Zedong*. Beijing: Central Party Literature Press and China Tibetology Publishing House, 2001.

Ping, Li, and Ma, Zhisun. *Zhou Enlai Nian pu 1949–1976* (A Chronological Biography of Zhou Enlai). Beijing: Zhongyang Wenxian Chubanshhe, 1997.

Pradhan, R.D. *Debacle to Resurgence: Y.B. Chavan: Defence Minister (1962–1966)*. New Delhi: Atlantic Publishers, 2017.

Radhakrishnan, Sarvepalli. *India and China: Lectures Delivered in China in May 1944*. Mumbai: Hind Kitab, 1944.

Raghavan, Srinath, ed. *Imperialists, Nationalists, Democrats: The Collected Essays of Sarvepalli Gopal*. Ranikhet: Permanent Black, 2013.

------. *War and Peace in Modern India: A Strategic History of the Nehru Years*. Ranikhet: Permanent Black, 2010.

Rahul, Ram. *The Himalaya Borderland*. New Delhi: Vikas Publications, 1970.

Ramesh, Jairam. *A Chequered Brilliance: The Many Lives of V.K. Krishna Menon*. Gurugram: Penguin Random House India, 2019.

Ranganathan, C.V., and Vinod C. Khanna. *India and China: The Way Ahead After "Mao's India War"*. New Delhi: Har-Anand Publications, 2000.

Rao, D.V.L.N. Ramakrishna, and R.C. Sharma, eds. *India's Borders: Ecology and Security Perspectives*. New Delhi: Scholars' Publishing Forum, 1991.

Rasgotra, Maharajakrishna. *A Life in Diplomacy*. New Delhi: Penguin Random House India, 2016.

Richardson, Hugh E. *Tibet and its History*. 2nd ed. Boulder, CO: Shambala, 1984.

------. *Tibetan Precis*. New Delhi: Government of India Press, 1948. http://pahar.in/wpfb-file/1945-tibetan-precis-by-richardson-from-high-peaks-pure-earth-maps-added-pdf/

Riedel, Bruce. *JFK's Forgotten Crisis: Tibet, The CIA, and Sino-Indian War*. Washington D.C.: Brookings Institution Press, 2015.

Rustomji, Nari. *Enchanted Frontiers: Sikkim, Bhutan and India's North-Eastern Borderlands*. 2nd ed. New Delhi: Oxford University Press, 2008.

Ryavec, Karl E. *A Historical Atlas of Tibet*. Chicago: The University of Chicago Press, 2015.

Sahgal, Nayantara, ed. *Nehru's India: Essays on the Maker of a Nation*. New Delhi: Speaking Tiger Books, 2015.

Sandhu, P.J.S., ed. *1962: A View from the Other Side of the Hill*. New Delhi: Viji Books, 2015.

Saran, Samir, and Akhil Deo. *Pax Sinica: Implications for the Indian Dawn*. New Delhi: Rupa Publications, 2019.

Saran, Shyam. *How India Sees the World: Kautilya to the 21st Century*. New Delhi: Juggernaut Books, 2017.

Sen, Tansen, and Bangwei Wang, eds. *India and China: Interactions Through Buddhism and Diplomacy, A Collection of Essays by Professor Prabodh Chandra Bagchi*. New Delhi: Anthem Press, 2009.

Sen, Tansen. *Buddhism, Diplomacy, and Trade: The Realignment of Sino-Indian Relations, 600–1400*. New Delhi: Manohar, 2004.

------. *India, China and the World: A Connected History*. Lanham, MD: Rowman and Littlefield, 2017.

Shakya, Tsering. *Dragon in the Land of Snows*. Pimlico Books, 1999.

------. *The Thirteenth Dalai Lama, Tubten Gyatso* https://treasuryoflives. org/biographies/view/Thirteenth-Dalai-Lama-Tubten Gyatso/3307

Shambaugh, David. *China's Future*. Cambridge, UK: Polity Press, 2016.

Shankar, Mahesh. *The Reputational Imperative: Nehru's India in Territorial Conflict*. Stanford, California: Stanford University Press, 2018.

Shipton, Eric. *That Untravelled World: An Autobiography*. Reprint. Seattle: Mountaineers Books, 2015.

Singh, J.J. *The McMahon Line: A Century of Discord*. Noida: HarperCollins Publishers India, 2019.

Singh, K. Natwar. *My China Diary, 1956–88*. New Delhi: Rupa & Co., 2009.

------, ed. *The Legacy of Nehru*. New Delhi: Vikas Publishing House, 1984.

Singh, Rani. *An Officer and His Holiness: How the Dalai Lama Crossed into India*. Penguin, 2020.

Small, Andrew. *The China–Pakistan Axis: Asia's New Geopolitics*. New York: Oxford University Press, 2015.

Snellgrove, David. *Asian Commitment: Travels and Studies in the Indian Sub-Continent and South-East Asia*. Bangkok: Orchid Press, 2000.

Sonam, Bhuchung D., trans. *Burning the Sun's Braids: New Poetry from Tibet*. Blackneck Books, 2017.

Sreenivasan, T.P., and James M. Peck, eds. *Venkat Forever: A Tribute to Ambassador A.P. Venkateswaran*. New Delhi: Konark Publishers, 2015.

Syed, Anwar H. *China and Pakistan: Diplomacy of an Entente Cordiale.* Amherst: The University of Massachusetts Press, 1974.

Tagore, Rabindranath. *Nationalism.* London: Penguin Classics, 2010.

Thampi, Madhavi. *Indians in China: 1800–1949.* New Delhi: Manohar, 2005.

Thondup, Gyalo, and Anne F. Thurston. *The Noodle Maker of Kalimpong: The Untold Story of My Struggle for Tibet.* London: Rider, 2015.

United Nations, International Commission of Jurists. *Tibet and the Chinese People's Republic.* Geneva: Impr. H Studer S.A., 1960.

Van Eekelen, Willelm. *Indian Foreign Policy and the Dispute with China: A New Look at Asian Relationships.* Nijhoff Classics in International Law, Vol. 5. Brill/Nijhoff, 2015.

Verma, Shiv Kunal. *1962: The War that Wasn't.* New Delhi: Aleph Book Company, 2016.

Vertzberger, Yaacov Y.I. *Misperceptions in Foreign Policymaking: The Sino-Indian Conflict, 1959–1962.* Boulder, CO: Westview Press, 1984.

Viehbeck, Markus, ed. *Transcultural Encounters in the Himalayan Borderlands: Kalimpong as a "Contact Zone".* Heidelberg: Heidelberg University Publishing, 2017.

Wenqian, Gao. *Zhou Enlai: The Last Perfect Revolutionary.* Trans. Peter Rand and Lawrence R. Sullivan. Public Affairs, 2007.

Whiting, Allen S. *The Chinese Calculus of Deterrence: India and Indochina.* Ann Arbor: The University of Michigan Press, 1975.

Whitson, William W., and Chen-hsia Huang, *The Chinese High Command A History of Communist Military Politics 1927–71.* Praeger Publishers, 1973.

Wignall, Sidney. *Spy on the Roof of the World: A True Story of Espionage & Survival in the Himalayas.* Edinburgh, Canongate Books, 1996.

Woeser, Tsering. *Forbidden Memory: Tibet During the Cultural Revolution.* Trans. Susan Chen. Potomac Books, 2006.

Woodman, Dorothy. *Himalayan Frontiers: A Political Review of British, Chinese, Indian and Russian Rivalries.* London: Barrie and Rockliff/ The Cresset Press, 1969.

Wortzel, Larry M. *The Lessons of History: The Chinese People's Liberation Army at 75.* Defense Technical Information Center, July 2003.

Yang, Gongsu: *Nine Decades of Vicissitudes: The Memoir of Ambassador Yang Gongsu*, Cangsang jiushinian: yige waijiao teshi de huiyi, Hainan: Hainan Publishing, 1999.

Zelikow, Philip. "The Nature of History's Lessons" in *The Power of the Past: History and Statecraft*, ed. Hal Brands and Jeremi Suri. Brookings Institution Press, 2015.

Journals

Chung, Tan, ed. *India and China* [Special issue]. *Indian Horizons*. Vol. 43, nos. 1–2, 1994.

Kumar, B.B., ed. *India's North-East* [Special issue]. *Dialogue Quarterly: A Journal of Astha Bharati*, New Delhi. Vol. 10, no. 3 (Jan–Mar 2009).

Pande, Ira, ed. *India 60* [Special issue]. *IIC Quarterly*. Vol. 33, nos. 3&4, (Winter 2006–Spring 2007).

Sen, Tansen, ed. *Kolkata (India) and China* [Special issue]. *China Report: A Journal of East Asian Studies*. Vol. 43, no. 4 (Oct–Dec 2007).

------. *Studies on India-China Interactions Dedicated to Professor Ji Xianlin (1911-2009)* [Special issue]. *China Report: A Journal of East Asian Studies*. Vol. 48, Nos. 1 & 2, Feb–May 2012.

Mayilvaganan, M., et al. "Focusing the Frontiers: The Borderland, Identity, Perceptions and Imaginings of Monpas of Tawang in India–China Border." NIAS-ISSSP (Bengaluru), 2017.

Visva-Bharati Quarterly, 1929 https://www.loc.gov/newspapers/ Articles

Acharya, Amitav. "Studying the Bandung conference from a Global IR perspective." *Australian Journal of International Affairs*, Vol. 70, no. 4, (2016) pp. 342–57.

Aiyadurai, Ambika, and Claire Seungeun Lee. "Living on the Sino-Indian Border: The Story of the Mishmis in Arunachal Pradesh, Northeast India." *Asian Ethnology*, Vol. 76, no. 2 (2017) pp. 367–95.

Alexandrowicz-Alexander, Charles Henry. "The Legal Position of Tibet". *The American Journal of International Law*, Vol. 48, no. 2, April 1954.

Alexandrowicz, C.H. "India and The Tibetan Tragedy". *Foreign Affairs*, April 1953.

Anand, Dibyesh. "Revisiting the China-India Border Dispute: An Introduction." *China Report.* Vol. 47, no. 2, 2011, pp. 65–69. DOI: 10.1177/000944551104700201

Anand, Dibyesh. "The British Imperial Scripting of Tibet's Geopolitical Identity", *The Journal of Asian Studies*, Vol. 68, no. 1 (2009) pp. 227-252.

Arora, S.K. "Indian Attitudes Towards China." *International Journal*, Vol. 14, no. 1, Winter 1958/1959, pp. 50–59.

Arpi, Claude. The Closure of the Consulate in Kashgar and the Aksai Chin Road www.claudearpi.blogspot.com

Athale, Col. Anil. The Untold Story: How Kennedy came to India's aid in 1962; https://www.rediff.com/news/special/the-untold-story-how-the-us-came-to-indias-aid-in-1962/20121204.htm

Bajpai, K. Shankar. "The unlearned lesson of 1962." *The Hindu*, 16 April 2014, https://www.thehindu.com/opinion/lead/the-unlearned-lesson-of-1962/article4055276.ece.

Bajpai, Kanti. "Pakistan and China in Indian Strategic Thought." *International Journal*, Vol. 62, no. 4, (Autumn 2007) pp. 805–22.

Banerjee, Avijit. "Tagore's Visit to China" *Muse India* (The Literary E-Journal), Issue 33, Sep–Oct 2010, https://museindia.com/Home/ViewContentData?arttype=focus&issid=33&menuid=2131.

Banerjee, Payal. "Chinese Indians in Fire: Refractions of Ethnicity, Gender, Sexuality and Citizenship in Post-Colonial India's Memories of the Sino-Indian War." *China Report*, Vol. 43, no. 4 (2007) pp. 437–63.

Barnes, Robert. "Between the Blocs: India, the United Nations, and Ending the Korean War." *Journal of Korean Studies*, Vol. 18, no. 2 (Fall 2013) pp. 263–86.

------. "Younghusband Redux: Chinese Dramatisations of the British Invasion of Tibet." *Inner Asia*, Vol. 14, Issue 1, 2012, pp. 195–233.

Baruah, Sanjib. "India and China: Debating Modernity." *World Policy Journal*, Vol. 23, no. 2 (Summer 2006) pp. 62–70.

Bork, Ellen. "Caught in the Middle India, China, and Tibet." *World Affairs*, Vol. 178, no. 1, (May–June 2015) pp. 52–58.

Brecher, Michael. "Towards the Close of the Nehru Era." *International Journal*, Vol. 18, no. 3 (Summer 1963) pp. 291–309.

Buckley, Chris: "China recalls days of poems and promise with Dalai Lama". 22 April 2008 https://www.reuters.com/article/us-china-tibet-dalai/china-recalls-days-of-poems-and-promise-with-dalai-lama-idUSPEK28409120080422

Callahan, William A.: The Cartography of National Humiliation and the Emergence of China's Geobody", *Public Culture* 21:1 (2009) pp. 141-173.

Caroe, Olaf. "The Geography and Ethnics of India's Northern Frontiers." *The Geographical Journal*, Vol. 126, no. 3 (Sep. 1960) pp. 298–308.

------. "India and the Mongolian Fringe": Note by the Foreign Secretary, 18 January 1940, India Office Records, L/P and 5/12/36/23, Part I. In Parshotam Mehra, *The North-Eastern Frontier: A Documentary Study of the Internecine Rivalry between India, Tibet and China.* Oxford University Press, 1979, 1980.

------. "The Indian-Chinese Boundary Dispute: Review of the Report of the Officials". *The Geographical Journal*, Vol. 127, no. 3 (Sep 1961) pp. 343-346.

Chakrabarty, Dipesh. "Legacies of Bandung: Decolonisation and the Politics of Culture." *Economic and Political Weekly*, Vol. 40, no. 46, (Nov. 12–18, 2005) pp. 4812–18.

Chandvankar, Suresh. "'Kimayagar' Mr. Vasantrao Desai (1912–1975)" *The Record News* (The Journal of the 'Society of Indian Record Collectors'), Vol. 23 (2012) pp. 5–27.

Chatterjee, Sourabh. "Tagore: A Case Study of His Visit to China in 1924." *IOSR Journal of Humanities and Social Science*, Vol. 19, Issue 3, Ver. V (Mar 2014) pp. 28–35.

Chaudhuri, Rudra. "The Making of an 'All Weather Friendship' Pakistan, China and the History of a Border Agreement: 1949–1963." *The International History Review*, Vol. 40, no. 1 (2018) pp. 41–64.

Cheema, Pervaiz Iqbal. "Significance of Pakistan–China Border Agreement of 1963." *Pakistan Horizon*, Vol. 39, no. 4 (Fourth Quarter 1986) pp. 41–52.

Chen, Jian. "The Tibetan Rebellion of 1959 and China's Changing Relations with India and the Soviet Union." *Journal of Cold War Studies*, Vol. 8, no. 3 (Summer 2006) pp. 54–101.

Cheng, Xiaohe. "From Ally to Partner: The Evolution of Sino-Pakistan Relations", *Journal of Renmin University of China*, Vol. 2, no. 1 (Spring 2007) pp. 61-81.

Cheng, Zaoxia. "The Historical Changes of the U.S. Policy toward Tibet in the 1940s and 1950s." *Frontiers of History in China*, Vol. 5, Issue 4 (2010) pp. 616–630. DOI: 10.1007/s11462-010-0113-9.

Cheney, Amanda J. (2017) "Tibet Lost in Translation: Sovereignty, Suzerainty and International Order Transformation, 1904–1906", *Journal of Contemporary China*, 26:107, pp. 769–83, DOI: 10.1080/10670564.2017.1305490

Chowdhury, Indira. "Travelling Across Cultures: Reflections on a Visit to Beijing." *Inter-Asia Cultural Studies,* Vol. 7, no. 3, (2006) pp. 519–26. DOI: 10.1080/14649370600849447.

Chung, Tan, and Huang I-Shu. "Farewell to Vasant Paranjpe." *China Report*, Vol. 46, no. 2 (May 2010 pp. 183–86.

Chung, Tan. "Chinese Civilisation: Resilience and Challenges." *China Report*, Vol. 41, no. 113 (2005) DOI: 10.1177/000944550504100201.

------. "Fond Memory of Sino-Indian Camaraderie: The Beloved and Respected Ji Xianlin I Knew." *China Report*, Vol. 48, Nos. 1 & 2 (2012) pp. 199–205. https://doi.org/10.1177/000944551104800211.

------. "Sino-Indian Cultural Synergy: Twenty Centuries of Civilisational Dialogue". *China Report* 42 :121 (2006) pp. 121-128.

Cowan, Sam. "All Change at Rasuwa Garhi." *Himalaya: The Journal of the Association for Nepal and Himalayan Studies*, Vol. 33, no. 1 (Fall 2013) pp. 97–102.

D'Souza, Dilip. "Fear and Forgetting: The 1962 Internment of Indian–Chinese." *The Caravan*, 1 November 2012, www.caravanmagazine. in/reportage/fear-and-forgetting.

Dabi, Tajen. "Medicine in British Frontier Policy: Disease, Epidemics and Dispensaries in Arunachal Pradesh c. 1912–47." *Indian Historical Review*, Vol. 45, no. 1 (2018) pp. 124–50.

Dalai Lama. "Exclusive interview: 'Reincarnation' isn't important, says the Dalai Lama." *The Week*, 6 July 2020, https://www.theweek.in/theweek/cover/2019/07/05/exclusive-interview-reincarnation-isnt-important-says-the-dalai-lama.html.

------. "Statement of His Holiness the Dalai Lama on the 47th Anniversary of the Tibetan National Uprising Day." International Campaign for Tibet, 10 March 2006, https://savetibet.org/statement-of-his-holiness-the-dalai-lama-on-the-47th-anniversary-of-the-tibetan-national-uprising-day/.

Danhui, Li, ed. "China's Settlement to Indian Prisoners of War and Sino-Indian Negotiation (1962-1963)." *Cold War International History Studies*, no. 15 (Summer 2013) pp. 43–91.

Deshingkar, Giri. "The Nehru Years Revisited", in *Across the Himalayan Gap*, http://ignca.nic.in/ks_41046.htm

Devereux, David R. "The Sino-Indian War of 1962 in Anglo-American Relations." Journal of Contemporary History, Vol. 44. No. 1, Jan. 2009, pp. 71-87.

Dobell, W.M. "Ramifications of the China-Pakistan Border Treaty." Pacific Affairs, Vol. 37, No. 3, Autumn 1964, pp. 283-295.

Egreteau, Renaud. "'Are We (Really) Brothers?': Contemporary India as Observed by Chinese Diplomats." Journal of Asian and African Studies, Vol. 47, No. 6, December 2012, pp. 695-709.

Fang, Tien-Sze. "An Assessment of Ambassador Luo Jialun's Mission to India: 1947-9". China Report, Vol. 50, no. 3, pp. 189-201.

Fettweis, Christopher. "On Heartlands and Chessboards: Classical Geopolitics, Then and Now." Orbis, Vol. 59, Issue 2, 2015, pp. 233-248.

Fravel, M. Taylor. "Power Shifts and Escalation: Explaining China's Use of Force in Territorial Disputes." International Security, Vol. 32, No. 3, Winter 2007/2008, pp. 44-83.

Fravel, M. Taylor. "Regime Insecurity and International Cooperation: Explaining China's Compromises in Territorial Disputes." International Security, Vol. 30, No. 2, Fall 2005, pp. 46-83.

Frayel, M. Taylor. "International Relations Theory and China's Rise: Assessing China's Potential for Territorial Expansion." International Studies Review, No. 12, 2010, pp. 505-532.

Frost, Mark R. "That Great Ocean of Idealism: Calcutta, the Tagore Circle and the Idea of Asia, 1900-1920." NSC Working Paper Series, No. 3, June 2011.

Gagné, Karine. "Building a Mountain Fortress for India: Sympathy, Imagination and the Reconfiguration of Ladakh into a Border Area." South Asia: Journal of South Asian Studies, Vol. 40, No. 2, 2017, pp. 222-238. DOI: 10.1080/00856401.2017.1292599.

Garver, John. "China's Decision for War with India in 1962" in "New Directions in the Study of China's Foreign Policy", Johnston, Alastair Iain and Ross, Robert S. (Ed), Stanford University Press, 2006.

Garver, John. "India, China, The United States, Tibet, and The Origins of the 1962 War." India Review, Vol. 3, No. 2, pp. 9-20. DOI: 10.1080/14736480490465054.

Ghosh, Arunabh. Before 1962: The Case for 1950s China-India History; The Journal of Asian Studies, Vol. 76, No.3 (August) 2017, pp. 697-727.

Gohain, Swargajyoti. "Producing Monyul as Buffer: Spatial Politics in a Colonial Frontier." *Modern Asian Studies*, Vol. 54, no. 2 (2020) pp. 432–70. DOI: 10.1017/S0026749X17000592.

Gopal, S. "The Formative Ideology of Jawaharlal Nehru." *Economic and Political Weekly*, Vol. 11, no. 21, (May 22, 1976) pp. 787–89, 791–92.

Gopal, S. "India, China and the Soviet Union": *Australian Journal of Politics and History*, Vol. 12, Issue 2 (August 1966) pp. 241-257.

Gupta, Karunakar. "Distortions in the History of Sino-Indian Frontiers." *Economic and Political Weekly*, Vol. 15, no. 30 (Jul 26, 1980) pp. 1265, 1267–70.

------. "Hidden History of the Sino-Indian Frontier I-1947–1954." *Economic and Political Weekly*, Vol. 9, no. 18 (May 4, 1974) pp. 721-726.

------. "Hidden History of the Sino-Indian Frontier-II: 1954–1959." *Economic and Political Weekly,* Vol. 9, No. 19, (May 11, 1974) pp. 765, 767, 769–72.

------. "How Did the Korean War Begin?" *The China Quarterly*, No. 52, Oct.-Dec., 1972, pp. 699-716.

------. "The McMahon Line 1911–45: The British Legacy." *The China Quarterly*, No. 47, (Jul-Sep 1971) pp. 521–45.

------. "Sino-Indian Agreement on Tibetan Trade and Intercourse: Its Origin and Significance." *Economic and Political Weekly*, Vol. 13, no. 16 (Apr 22, 1978) pp. 696–702.

Gupta, Krishna Prakash. "The Making of China's Image of India." *China Report*, Vol. 15, no. 39, 1979, pp. 39–50. DOI: 10.1177/000944557901500202.

Guruswamy, Mohan. "Don't forget the heroes of Rezang La", *The Hindu*, 20 November 2012. https://www.thehindu.com/opinion/lead/Don't-forget-the-heroes-of-Rezang-La/article12513562.ece

Guyot-Réchard, Bérénice. "When Legions Thunder Past: The Second World War and India's Northeastern Frontier." *War in History*, Vol. 25, no. 3, 2018 pp. 328–60.

Hao, Yufan, and Zhai Zhihai. "China's Decision to Enter the Korean War: History Revisited." *The China Quarterly*, No. 121 (March 1990) pp. 94–115.

Harder, Anton. "Not at the Cost of China: New Evidence Regarding US Proposals to Nehru for Joining the United Nations Security Council": Cold War History Project Working Paper Series, #76, Woodrow Wilson International Center for Scholars, March 2015.

------. "When Nehru Refused American Bait on a Permanent Seat for India at the UN." The Wire, 14 March 2019, https://thewire.in/diplomacy/when-nehru-refused-american-bait-on-a-permanent-seat-for-india-at-the-un.

Hoffmann, Steven A. "Anticipation, Disaster, and Victory: India, 1962-71", *Asian Survey*, Vol. 12, no. 11 (Nov. 1972), pp. 960-979.

------. "Rethinking the Linkage between Tibet and the China–India Border Conflict: A Realist Approach." *Journal of Cold War Studies*, Vol. 8, no. 3 (Summer 2006) pp. 165–94.

Holdich, Thomas H. "The North-Eastern Frontier of India." *Journal of the Royal Society of Arts*, Vol. 60, no. 3092 (Feb 23, 1912) pp. 379–92.

Holsag, Jonathan. "The Persistent Military Security Dilemma between China and India." *Journal of Strategic Studies*, Vol. 32, no. 6 (2009) pp. 811–40.

Hongwei, Wang. "Initial Period of Establishing Diplomatic Relations (1949–1954)." *Cold War International History Studies*, No. 15 (Summer 2013) pp. 137–61.

https://doi.org/10.1111/hic3.12448

https://doi.org/10.1177/0021909611429923

Hopkinson, Arthur J. C.I.E. (1950) "The position of Tibet", *Journal of The Royal Central Asian Society*, 37:3-4, pp. 228–39, DOI: 10.1080/03068375008731376

Huang, I-shu. "Tan Yun-shan Centenary and Track II in Beijing." *China Report*, Vol. 35, no. 2, 1999, pp. 179–82. https://doi.org/10.1177/000944559903500205

Huber, Toni. "A Tibetan Map of IHo-kha in the South-Eastern Himalayan Borderlands of Tibet." *Imago Mundi*, Vol. 44, Issue 1 (1992) pp. 9–23.

Hudson, G.F. "The Frontier of China and Assam: Background to the Fighting." *The China Quarterly*, No. 12, (Oct–Dec 1962) pp. 203–06.

Huttenback, R.A. "A Historical Note on the Sino-Indian Dispute over the Aksai Chin." *The China Quarterly*, No. 18 (Apr–Jun 1964) pp. 201–07.

Indurthy, Rathnam. "India and China: Conflict, Competition, Cooperation, and Prospects for Peace." *International Journal on World Peace,* Vol. 33, no. 1 (March 2016) pp. 43–108.

Jiang, Jingkui, and Yan Jia. "The History of the Production of India-Related Knowledge in Post-1950 China." *History Compass*, Vol. 16, no. 4 (2018), pp. 1-12.

Kalha, Ranjit S. "Tibet as a Factor in Sino-Indian Relations Past and Present". *Journal of Defence Studies*, Vol. 6, Issue 4 (Oct 2012) *pp. ??*

Kang, Yongsheng. "The 1962 Sino-Indian Border Conflict – A War that casts its shadow till date". *China Youth Daily*, 26 October 2012.

Kaplan, Robert. "Geopolitics and the New World Order". *Time* magazine, 31 March 2014: https://time.com/31911/geopolitics-and-the-new-world-order/

Kapoor, Ria. "Nehru's Non-Alignment Dilemma: Tibetan Refugees in India." *South Asia: Journal of South Asian Studies*, Vol. 42, no. 4 (2019) pp. 675–93.

Khan, Sulmaan Wasif. "Cold War cooperation: New Chinese evidence on Jawaharlal Nehru's 1954 visit to Beijing", *Cold War History*, Vol. 11, no. 2 (May 2011) pp. 197-222.

Kingdon Ward, F. and Malcom Smith. "The Himalaya East of the Tsangpo." *The Geographical Journal*, Vol. 84, no. 5 (Nov 1934) pp. 369–94.

Kirk, W. "The Inner Asian Frontier of India". *Transactions and Papers* (Institute of British Geographers), No. 31 (Dec. 1962).

Kohli, Manorama. "Nehru's World View and China Policy". *China Report*, Vol. 21, Issue 06 (Nov 1, 1985) pp. 497-502.

Krishnan, Ananth. "A Last Opportunity, Missed." *The Hindu*, 26 October 2012, https://www.thehindu.com/opinion/op-ed/a-last-opportunity-missed/article4031762.ece.

------. "Behind the War, a Genesis in Tibet." *The Hindu*, 20 October 2012, https://www.thehindu.com/opinion/op-ed/behind-the-war-a-genesis-in-tibet/article4013766.ece.

------. "A Last Opportunity Missed." *The Hindu*, 26 October 2012, https://www.thehindu.com/opinion/op-ed/a-last-opportunity-missed/article4031762.ece.

------. "Behind the War: A Genesis in Tibet." *The Hindu*, 20 October 2012, https://www.thehindu.com/opinion/op-ed/behind-the-war-a-genesis-in-tibet/article4013766.ece.

------. "Crossing the Point of No Return." *The Hindu*, 25 October 2012, https://www.thehindu.com/opinion/op-ed/crossing-the-point-of-no-return/article4028362.ece.

------. "From Tibet to Tawang: A Legacy of Suspicions." *The Hindu*, 22 October 2012, https://www.thehindu.com/opinion/op-ed/from-tibet-to-tawang-a-legacy-of-suspicions/article4019717.ece.

Lal, Vinay. "Framing a Discourse: China and India in the Modern World." *Economic and Political Weekly*, Vol. 44, no. 2, (Jan 10, 2009) pp. 41–45.

Lamb, Alastair, and S. Gopal. "A Historical Note on the Sino-Indian Dispute over the Aksai Chin." *The China Quarterly*, No. 21 (Jan-Mar 1965) pp. 182–83.

Lattimore, Owen. "The New Political Geography of Inner Asia." *The Geographical Journal*, Vol. 119, No. 1 (Mar 1953) pp. 17–30.

Laud, Rajnath P. "The Perception Gap: U.S.-Indian Relations and the Chinese Invasion of 1962." *Archive: A Journal of Undergraduate History*, Vol. 6 (May 2003) pp. 32-53.

Lee, Yu-ting. "Tagore and Orientalism: Tagore Studies as a Focus for East-West Debate." *Taiwan Journal of East Asian Studies*, Vol. 10, no. 1 (Issue 19) (June 2013) pp. 219–59.

Lei, Guang. "From National Identity to National Security: China's Changing Responses toward India in 1962 and 1998." *The Pacific Review*, Vol. 17, no. 3 (2004) pp. 399–422.

Leys, Simon. "The Path of an Empty Boat". *The Times Literary Supplement*, 26 October 1984.

Li, Jianglin. "Suppressing Rebellion in Tibet and the China–India Border War.", War on Tibet. Chinese and Tibetan documents in the history of the Communist Occupation in English translation. 5 December 2017. http://historicaldocs.blogspot.com/p/chinese.html

Liao, Kuang-sheng, and Allen Whiting. "Chinese Press Perceptions of Threat: The U.S. and India, 1962." *The China Quarterly*, No. 53, (Jan–Mar) 1973 pp. 80-97.

Liu, Zongyi. "India still conserves frontier mentality over 1962 border war with China.", Shanghai Institute for International Studies, 2012.

Macmillan, Margaret. "The Uses of History", *International Affairs* 95:1 (2019) pp. 181–200, The Royal Institute of International Affairs.

Majumdar, Neepa. "Immortal Tale or Nightmare? Dr Kotnis between Art and Exploitation." *South Asian Popular Culture*, Vol. 6, no. 2 (Oct 2008) pp. 141–59.

Malenbaum, Wilfred. "India and China: Development Contrasts." *Journal of Political Economy*, Vol. 64, no, 1, (Feb 1956) pp. 1–24.

Malhotra, Inder. "The Courage of 13 Kumaon", *The Indian Express*, 20 February 2012 (https://indianexpress.com/article/opinion/columns/the-courage-of-13-kumaon/

Mangalagiri, Adhira. "Ellipses of Cultural Diplomacy. The 1957 Chinese Literary Sphere in Hindi". *Journal of World Literature*, 4(4), (December 2019) pp. 508-529.

Mansergh, Nicholas. "The Asian Conference." *International Affairs* (Royal Institute of International Affairs), Vol. 23, no. 3 (July 1947) pp. 295–306.

Marshall-Cornwall, James and Lord Birdwood. "The Geography and Ethnics of India's Northern Frontiers: Discussion." *The Geographical Journal*, Vol. 126, no. 3 (Sep 1960) p. 309.

Marwah, Reena: "Interview of Mira Sinha Bhattacharjea", Pts. I & II, April 2008: http://politics.ntu.edu.tw

Mastro, Oriana Skylar. "The Great Divide: Chinese and Indian Views on Negotiations, 1959–62". *Journal of Defence Studies* (IDSA), Vol. 6, no. 4 (Oct 2012) pp. 71–108.

Mathou, Thierry. "Moving toward a New Chinese Strategy in the Himalayan Region." *Asian Survey*, Vol. 45, Issue 4, (July–August 2005) pp. 503–21.

Maung Maung. "The Burma-China Boundary Settlement." *Asian Survey*, Vol. 1, no. 1 (Mar 1961) pp. 38–43.

Maxwell, Neville and A.G. Noorani. "India's Forward Policy." *The China Quarterly*, No. 45 (Jan–Mar 1971) pp. 157–63.

Maxwell, Neville. "China and India: The Un-Negotiated Dispute." *The China Quarterly*, No. 43 (July–Sep 1970) pp. 47–80.

Maxwell, Neville. "Jawaharlal Nehru: Of Pride and Principle." *Foreign Affairs*, Vol. 52, no. 3 (April 1974) pp. 633–43.

McGarr, Paul. "India's Rasputin? V.K. Krishna Menon and Anglo-American Misperceptions of Indian Foreign Policymaking, 1947–1964". *Diplomacy & Statecraft*, 22 (2011) pp. 239–60.

McKay, A.C. "The Establishment of the British Trade Agencies in Tibet: A Survey." *Journal of the Royal Asiatic Society* (Third Series), Vol. 2, no. 3 (Nov 1992) pp. 399–421.

Medeiros, Evan S. and Fravel, M. Taylor. "China's New Diplomacy." *Foreign Affairs*, Vol. 82, no. 6, (Nov–Dec 2003).

Mehra, Parshotam. "India–China Border: A Review and Critique." *Economic and Political Weekly*, Vol. 17, no. 20 (May 15, 1982) pp. 834–38.

Mehra, Parshotam. "India's Border Dispute with China: Revisiting Nehru's Approach." *International Studies*, Vol. 42, nos. 3–4 (Oct 2005) pp. 357–65, DOI: 10.1177/002088170504200311

Mehta, Jagat S. "S. Gopal and the Sino-Indian Boundary Question". *China Report*, Vol. 39, Issue 1 (2003) pp. 71–75.

Military Science Publishing Group, Beijing, "The Sino-Indian Border War of Self Defense and Counter Attack" August 1994.

Miller, Manjari Chatterjee. "Re-collecting Empire: "Victimhood" and the 1962 Sino-Indian War." *Asian Security*, Vol. 5, no. 3 (Sep 2009) pp. 216–41.

Mirsky, Jonathan. "Message from Shangri-La: Review of *High Peaks, Pure Earth: Collected Works on Tibetan History and Culture* by Hugh Richardson", *The New York Review of Books*, 8 April 1999.

Mookerjee, Girija K. "Tagore's View of Asia." *East and West*, Vol. 12, nos. 2/3 (Jun–Sep 1961) pp. 122–24.

Moraes, Frank. "India and China." *The American Scholar*, Vol. 32, no. 3 (Summer 1963) pp. 445–50.

Mukherjee, Kunal. "Comparing China and India's Disputed Borderland Regions: Xinjiang, Tibet, Kashmir, and the Indian Northeast" in

East Asia: An International Quarterly Vol./Issue no. ?? (2015) pp. 173-205.

Murty, T.S. and Neville Maxwell. "Tawang and "The Un-Negotiated Dispute"." The China Quarterly, No. 46, April-June 1971, pp. 357-362.

Murty, T.S. The Eastern Himalayas in Sino-Indian Relations. Institute of Defence Studies and Analyses, https://idsa.in/system/files/TheEasternHimalayasinSinoIndianRelations_TSMurthy.pdf

Nair, Kusum. "Where India, China and Russia Meet." Foreign Affairs, Vol. 36, No. 2, January 1958, pp. 330-339.

Narayan, Raviprasad. "Tibet within India – China relations: An interlude or ad finum ultimum . . .?" The Tibet Journal, Vol. 42, No. 2, Autumn/Winter 2017, pp. 59-70.

Narayanan, K.R. "Speech by Indian President K R Narayanan at the Birth Centenary Celebrations of Professor Tan Yun-shan at Santiniketan on 7 November 1998." China Report, Vol. 35, No. 2, May 1999, pp. 205-208. https://doi.org/10.1177/000944559903500211

Narayanan, K.R. "The 50th Anniversary of Panchsheel. Speech at International Seminar on the occasion of the 50th Anniversary of Panchsheel." *Chinese Journal of International Law*, Vol. 3, no. 2 (2004) pp. 369–72.

Nehru, Jawaharlal. "Changing India." *Foreign Affairs*, Vol. 41, no. 3 (April 1963) pp. 453-465.

Noorani, A.G. "Nehru's Contradictions." *Frontline*, 24 July 2015, https://frontline.thehindu.com/books/nehrus-contradictions/article7391772.ece.

------. "The Truth About 1962." *Frontline*, 30 November 2012, https://frontline.thehindu.com/cover-story/article30168362.ece.

------. "Our Secrets in others' Trunks", *Frontline*, 15 July 2005, https://frontline.thehindu.com/books/article30205364.ece

------. "Nehru's China Policy", *Frontline*, Vol. 17. Issue 15, 22 July–4 August 2000.

------. "India's Quest for a Nuclear Guarantee", *Asian Survey*, Vol. 7, no. 7 (July 1967) pp. 490-502.

Norbu, Dawa. "Tibet in Sino-Indian Relations. The Centrality of Marginality", *Asian Survey*, Vol. 37, No. 11 (Nov 1997) pp. 1078-1095.

Nyman, Lars-Erik. "Tawang—A Case Study of British Frontier Policy in the Himalayas." *Journal of Asian History*, Vol. 10, no. 2 (1976) pp. 151–71.

Oksenberg, Michel. "The Strategies of Peking." *Foreign Affairs*, Vol. 50, no. 1, (Oct 1971) pp. 15–29.

Otte, T.G. "The Inner Circle: What is Diplomatic History? (And Why We Should Study It): An Inaugural Lecture" *History*, Vol. 105, Issue 364 (Jan 2020).

Pang, Yang Huei. "Four Faces of Bandung: Detainees, Soldiers, Revolutionaries and Statesman". *Journal of Contemporary Asia*, 39:1 (January 2009), pp. 63-86.

Passin, Herbert. "Sino-Indian Cultural Relations." *The China Quarterly*, No. 7 (Jul – Sep1961) pp. 85–100.

Pauker, Guy J. "Panikkarism, the Highest Stage of Opportunism." *World Politics*, Vol. 7, no. 1 (Oct 1954) pp. 157–77.

Phillips, Andrew. "Beyond Bandung: The 1955 Asian-African Conference and its Legacies for International Order." *Australian Journal of International Affairs*, Vol. 70, no. 4 (August 2016) pp. 329–41.

Power, Paul F. "Indian Foreign Policy: The Age of Nehru." *The Review of Politics*, Vol. 26, no. 2 (April 1964) pp. 257–86.

Publications Division, Ministry of Information and Broadcasting, 1967: *For a United India: Speeches of Sardar Patel, 1947–1950.*

Qiang, Zhai. "China and the Geneva Conference of 1954." *The China Quarterly*, No. 129 (March 1992) pp. 103–22.

Qureshi, Khalida. "Pakistan and the Sino-Indian Dispute – 1." *Pakistan Horizon*, Vol. 15, no. 4 (Fourth Quarter 1962) pp. 310–22.

Rao, Nirupama. "Lost Horizons: The Tangled History of Tibet." The Wire, 11 July 2015, https://thewire.in/books/lost-horizons-the-tangled-history-of-tibet.

------. "Once More, With Feeling." The Wire, 16 May 2015, https://thewire.in/diplomacy/once-more-with-feeling.

Raghavan, Srinath. "Beyond Victimology"; https://forums.bharat-rakshak.com/viewtopic.php?t=6171&start=160

Raghavan, Srinath. "Sino-Indian Boundary Dispute, 1948-60: A Reappraisal", *Economic and Political Weekly*, (09 September 2006) pp. 3882-3892.

Ramaswamy, Sumathi. "Visualizing India's geo-body: Globes, maps, bodyscapes", *Contributions to Indian Sociology* (n.s,) Vol. 36, nos.1&2 (2002) pp. 151-189.

Rongjen, Syu. "Another Perspective of Modernization – Gupta's Analysis on China from the 1960's to the 1990's." *China Papers,*

New Zealand Contemporary China Research Centre, No. 33 (2010).

Rose, Archibald. "Chinese Frontiers of India." *The Geographical Journal*, Vol. 39, no. 3 (March 1912) pp. 193–218.

Rosenthal, A.M. "Krishna Menon—A Clue to Nehru." *The New York Times*, 7 April 1957, https://www.nytimes.com/1957/04/07/archives/krishna-menona-clue-to-nehru-westerners-and-indian-politicians.html.

Roy Chowdhury, Debasish. "Neville Maxwell Interview: The Full Transcript." *The South China Morning Post*, 31 March 2014, https://www.scmp.com/news/china/article/1461102/neville-maxwell-interview-full-transcript.

Roy, Nabarun. "Why Did Nehru Want the People's Republic of China in the United Nations?", *The Diplomat* (Tokyo) 6 April 2018.

Samphel Thubten. "The Dalai Lama's China Experience and its Impact." The Huffington Post, 15 April 2015, https://www.huffpost.com/entry/the-dalai-lamas-china-experience-and-its-impact_b_7068928

Scott, David. "The Great Power 'Great Game' between India and China: 'The Logic of Geography'." *Geopolitics*, Vol. 13, no. 1 (2008) pp. 1–26.

Sen, Chanakya. "Chou En-Lai's African Journey as Viewed by the Indian Press." *Asian Survey*, Vol. 4, no. 6 (June 1964) pp. 880–89.

Sen, Narayan. "Remembering My Meetings with Ji Xianlin." *China Report*, Vol. 48, nos. 1 & 2 (2012) pp. 207–10.

Sen, Tansen. "Introduction: Ji Xianlin and Sino-Indology." *China Report*, Vol. 48, nos. 1 & 2 (2012) pp. 1–10.

Sen, Tansen. "The Formation of Chinese Maritime Networks to Southern Asia, 1200–1450." *Journal of the Economic and Social History of the Orient*, Vol. 49, No. 4 (2006) pp. 421–53.

Sethi, Chitleen K. "General Zorawar Chand Bakshi, the greatest wartime hero who 'just faded away", The Print, 28 May 2018 (https://theprint.in/theprint-profile/lt-gen-zorawar-chand-bakshi-the-greatest-wartime-hero-who-just-faded-away/63532/

Shao, Kuo-kang. "Zhou Enlai's Diplomacy and the Neutralization of Indo-China, 1954–55." *The China Quarterly*, No. 107 (Sep 1986) pp. 483–504.

Shelvankar, K.S. "China's Himalayan Frontiers. India's Attitude." *International Affairs*, Vol. 38, no. 4, (Oct 1962) pp. 472–84.

Shen, Quanyu. "Sino-Indian Friendship in the Nehru Era: a Chinese Perspective", *China Report* 41:3 (2005) pp. 237-252.

Shenchi, Liu. "China's Relations With Tibet". *The China Weekly Review*, 12 June 1948; ProQuest Historical Newspapers: Chinese Newspapers Collection (1852–1853).

Sheng, Michael M. "Mao and China's Relations with the Superpowers in the 1950s: A New Look at the Taiwan Strait Crises and the Sino-Soviet Split." *Modern China*, Vol. 34, no. 4 (Oct 2008) pp. 477–507.

Shi Guang Zhang. "Constructing 'Peaceful Coexistence': China's Diplomacy toward the Geneva and Bandung Conferences, 1954-55". *Cold War History*, 7:4 (Oct 2007) pp. 509-528.

Shimazu Naoku. "Diplomacy as Theatre: Staging the Bandung Conference of 1955." *Modern Asian Studies*, Vol. 48, no. 1 (Jan 2014) pp. 22552.

Shukla, Sonia. "Forging New Frontiers: Integrating Tawang with India, 1951." *China Report*, Vol. 48, no. 4 (2012) pp. 407–26. DOI: 10.1177/0009445512471174.

Sikri, Rajiv. "The Tibet Factor in India–China Relations." *Journal of International Affairs*. Vol. 64, no. 2 (Spring/Summer 2011) pp. 55–71.

Singh, Biswanath. "Legality of the McMahon Line." *The Indian Journal of Political Science*, Vol. 28, no. 3 (July–September 1967) pp. 163–77.

Singh, Sinderpal. "From Delhi to Bandung: Nehru, 'Indian-ness' and 'Pan-Asian-ness'." *South Asia: Journal of South Asian Studies*, Vol. 34, no. 1 (April 2011) pp. 51–64.

Singh, Zorawar Daulet. "Himalayan Stalemate: Revisiting the Sino-Indian Conflict of 1962" Pts. 1 & 2 *Fair Observer*, 27 November 2012, https://www.fairobserver.com/region/central_south_asia/himalayan-stalemate-revisiting-sino-indian-conflict-1962-part-1/. https://www.fairobserver.com/region/central_south_asia/himalayan-stalemate-revisiting-sino-indian-conflict-1962-part-2/.

------. "Reading Henderson in historical context", Op-Ed in *The Tribune*, 21 March 2014. https://www.tribuneindia.com/2014/20140321/edit.htm#7

Spence, Jonathan. "The Mystery of Zhou Enlai". *The New York Review of Books*, 28 May 2009.

Stolte, Carolien. "The People's Bandung": Local Anti-imperialists on an Afro-Asian Stage." *Journal of World History*, Vol. 30, nos. 1–2 (June 2019) pp. 125–56.

Subrahmanyam, K. "Neville Maxwell's War." *Hindustan Times*, 18 and 25 October 1970, https://www.idsa.in/system/files/K.Subrahmayam%27sBook%20Review.pdf.

Subrahmanyam, Sanjay. "One Asia, or Many? Reflections from Connected History." *Modern Asian Studies*, Vol. 50, no. 1 (2016) pp. 5–43.

Tempa, Lobsang. "The Centenary of the McMahon Line (1914–2014) and the Status of Monyul until 1951–2." *The Tibet Journal*, Vol. 39, no. 2 (Autumn/Winter 2014) pp. 57–102.

Thampi, Parvathi. "Memories of China: 1943 to 1946." *China Report* Vol. 36, no. 1 (February 2000) pp. 89–92. DOI: 10.1177/000944550003600106.

The Deccan Herald, 27 March 2014. "Blaming Nehru: A superficial way of looking at India-China War" (Interview with Bertil Lintner)

Tiwary, A.K. "No Use of Combat Air Power in 1962." *Indian Defence Review*, Vol. 21, no. 3 (July–Sep 2006) http://www.indiandefencereview.com/spotlights/no-use-of-combat-air-power-in-1962/.

Tsang, Steve. "Target Zhou Enlai: The "Kashmir Princess" Incident of 1955." *The China Quarterly*, No. 139 (Sep 1994) pp. 766–82.

Tsui, Brian. "Chinese Views of Tagore and Gandhi: Then and Now." *The China Story Journal*, 29 (July 2013) pp. 1-6.

------. "The Plea for Asia, Tan Yunshan, Pan-Asianism and Sino-Indian Relations". *China Report* 46:4 (2010) pp 353-370.

Uberoi, Patricia. "China in Bollywood." *Contributions to Indian Sociology*, Vol. 45, no. 3 (Oct 2011) pp. 315–42.

Utami, Nila Ayu. "Revisiting the Bandung Conference: berbeda sejak dalam pikiran." *Inter-Asia Cultural Studies*, Vol. 17, no. 1 (2016) pp. 140–47.

Vajpeyi, Ananya. "Asian Intellectuals and the Roads Not Taken." *World Policy*, 19 September 2012, http://worldpolicy.org/2020/09/19/asian-intellectuals-and-the-roads-not-taken/.

------. "The Problem." *Seminar Magazine*, 23 June 2011, http://www. india-seminar.com/2011/623/623_the_problem.htm.

Verghese, B.G. "The War We Lost—1962 Sino-Indian Conflict." *Tibet Sun*, 5 October 2012, https://www.tibetsun.com/ opinions/2012/10/05/the-war-we-lost-1962-sino-indian-conflict.

Vertzberger, Yaacov. "India's Border Conflict with China: A Perceptual Analysis." *Journal of Contemporary History*, Vol. 17, no. 4 (Oct 1982) pp. 607–31.

Westaway, Jonathan. "That Undisclosed World: Eric Shipton's Mountains of Tartary (1950)", *Studies in Travel Writing* (2014) 18:4, pp. 357-373.

Whiting, Allen S. "China's Use of Force, 1950–96, and Taiwan." *International Security*, Vol. 26, no. 2, (Fall 2001) pp. 103–31.

------. "The Use of Force in Foreign Policy by the People's Republic of China." *The Annals of the American Academy of Political and Social Science*, Vol. 402, no. 1 (July 1972) pp. 55–66.

Whittam, Daphne E. "The Sino-Burmese Boundary Treaty." *Pacific Affairs*, Vol. 34, no. 2 (Summer 1961) pp. 174–83.

Wolf, Albert B., and M. Taylor Fravel. "Structural Sources of China's Territorial Compromises." *International Security*, Vol. 31, no. 2 (Fall 2006) pp. 199–205.

Wood, Sally Percival. "'Chou Gags Critics in Bandoeng' or How the Media Framed Premier Zhou Enlai at the Bandung Conference, 1955." *Modern Asian Studies*, Vol. 44, no. (5 Sep 2010) pp. 1001–27.

------. "Retrieving the Bandung Conference . . . moment by moment." *Journal of Southeast Asian Studies,* Vol. 43, no. 3 (Oct 2012) pp. 523–30.

Xiaoyuan, Liu. "Friend or Foe: India as Perceived by Beijing's Foreign Policy Analysts in the 1950s." *China Review*, Vol. 15, no.1 (Spring 2015) pp. 117–43.

Yang, Zhifang. "Mao Zedong in order to ease domestic conflict, launched a surprise attack on India." Phoenix TV report, 1 November 2012.

Yun-yuan Yang, "Controversies over Tibet", *The China Quarterly*, No. 111 (Sep 1987).

Zhiqiang, Shan. "Himalayas quiet for 50 years: Why India and China cannot really be neighbours". *National Geography* (Chinese Journal), December 2012.

Published Papers

Goldstein Melvyn C. "Tibet, China and the United States: Reflections on the Tibet Question." The Atlantic Council of The United States, 1995, Occasional Paper.

Guha, Ramachandra. "Jawaharlal Nehru and China: A Study in Failure?" Harvard-Yenching Institute Working Paper Series, 2011, Working Paper.

Hyer, Eric. "China's Policy of Conciliation and Reduction (Sanhe Yishao) and its Impact on Boundary Negotiations and Settlements in the Early 1960s." Cold War International History Project, December 2017, Working Paper.

Rao, Nirupama. "Telling it on the Mountain: India and China and the Politics of History, 1949–1962." NMML Occasional Paper, History and Society, New Series. 73. NMML.

Raghavan, Srinath. "A Missed Opportunity? The Nehru–Zhou Enlai Summit of 1960", NMML Occasional Paper, History and Society, New Series 74, NMML.

Samarani, Guido. "Shaping the Future of Asia; Chiang Kai-shek, Nehru and China-India Relations During the Second World War Period." Working Papers in Contemporary Asian Studies (Centre for East and South-East Asian Studies, Lund University, Sweden), 2005, Working Paper.

Unpublished Papers

Khathing, Major Ralengnao 'Bob'. "The Assam Rifles and the McMahon Line" (1987).

Mehta, Jagat Singh. "Nehru's Failure with China: Intellectual Naivete or the Wages of a Prophetic Vision", Paper for a Conference at the University of Toronto, October 1989.

Lectures

Curzon, Lord George Nathaniel. "Frontiers", The Romanes Lecture, 1907. https://ia800203.us.archive.org/27/items/frontiers00curz/frontiers00curz.pdf

Dasgupta, Chandrashekhar. "Nehru, Patel and China." 19 April 2014, Nehru Memorial Museum and Library, New Delhi.

Kabir, Humayun. "Rabindranath Tagore". Lecture at the School of Oriental and African Studies, 1962. Record held at The British Library, Asian and African Studies, London.

Khilnani, Sunil. "Making Asia: India, China & The Struggle for An Idea." 33rd Jawaharlal Nehru Memorial Lecture, 2012, Nehru Memorial Museum and Library, New Delhi.

King, Dr. Martin Luther, Jr. "On The Vietnam War". (Speech delivered on 25 February 1967) https://www.theatlantic.com/magazine/archive/2018/02/martin-luther-king-jr-vietnam/552521/

Mountbatten, Louis. "Reflections on the Transfer of Power and Jawaharlal Nehru." Nehru Memorial Lecture, 14 November 1968, Trinity College, University of Cambridge.

Rao, Nirupama. "A Tale of Two Countries: India and China in Our Times." Jawaharlal Nehru Memorial IFFCO Lecture, 20 November 2015, New Delhi.

------. "Geo-civilizations: India and China in Tagore's Century", King's College London, 2014.

Index